THE SACRED CALLING

· THE ·
SACRED
CALLING

Four Decades of Women in the Rabbinate

Edited by
RABBI REBECCA EINSTEIN SCHORR
AND RABBI ALYSA MENDELSON GRAF
WITH RABBI RENEE EDELMAN
Foreword by Rabbi Sally J. Priesand
Preface by Rabbi Jacqueline Koch Ellenson

CCAR Challenge and Change Series

Every effort has been made to ascertain the owners of copyrights for the selections used in this volume and to obtain permission to reprint copyrighted passages. The Central Conference of American Rabbis expresses gratitude for permissions it has received. The Conference will be pleased, in subsequent editions, to correct any inadvertent errors or omissions that may be pointed out.

Library of Congress Cataloging-in-Publication Data
Names: Schorr, Rebecca Einstein, 1971- editor. | Graf, Alysa Mendelson, 1972- editor. | Edelman, Renee, editor.
Title: The sacred calling : four decades of women in the rabbinate / edited by Rabbi Rebecca Einstein Schorr and Rabbi Alysa Mendelson Graf, with Rabbi Renee Edelman ; foreword by Rabbi Sally Priesand.
Description: New York, NY : Central Conferene of American Rabbis CCAR Press, [2016] | ?2016 | Series: CCAR challenge and change series
Identifiers: LCCN 2016004336 (print) | LCCN 2016005303 (ebook) | ISBN 9780881232172 (pbk. : alk. paper) | ISBN 9780881232806 ()
Subjects: LCSH: Women rabbis--History. | Women in Judaism--History. | Feminism--Religious aspects--Judaism. | Reform Judaism.
Classification: LCC BM652 .S225 2016 (print) | LCC BM652 (ebook) | DDC 296.6/1082--dc23
LC record available at http://lccn.loc.gov/2016004336

10 9 8 7 6 5 4 3 2 1

CCAR Press, 355 Lexington Avenue, New York, NY 10017
(212) 972-3636
www.ccarpress.org

Contents

Acknowledgments

There were an immense number of people involved in the journey of this book from conception to publication. First and foremost, a tremendous debt of gratitude to Rabbi Hara Person and the CCAR Press for bringing us onto this project and providing us with unending support. Hara's critical eye and editorial discernment have been a godsend. Boundless appreciation to the incomparable Debra Corman, whose copyediting skills surpass all others, as well as proofreaders Michelle Kwitkin-Close and Leslie Rubin. Thanks also to Rabbi Steven A. Fox and CCAR Press staff members, Debbie Smilow, Ortal Bensky, Sasha Smith, Rabbi Dan Medwin, and Carly Linden, as well as publishing interns Andy Kahn, Hilly Haber, and Rabbi April Peters. And most of all, our deepest thanks to the writers, for they are the ones who truly gave voice to this project.

In many ways this book was a group process. It began in the summer of 2011 as an idea expressed in the Women's Rabbinic Network group on Facebook by Rabbi Renee Goldberg Edelman. Renee had been inspired by reading our female colleagues' blogs and called for an anthology that would "share with the world who we are." She hoped such a book would also be a resource for women entering the rabbinate and a teaching tool to raise awareness in our congregations. This project owes its genesis to Renee's vision and enthusiasm, as well as to the support of Rabbi Marci Bellows Lindenman. The members of the advisory group were very helpful, especially in getting this project launched. Throughout the process, WRN colleagues were supportive of this idea from its inception and helpful at every stage of putting this book together. We thank them all deeply.

Rabbi Rebecca Einstein Schorr
and Rabbi Alysa Mendelson Graf

Because I can never thank him enough for all that I've learned about Codes (especially *Choshen Mishpat*), maritime law, grammar, and so much more, my gratitude to my thesis advisor and mentor, Rabbi Stephen M. Passamaneck, PhD. No writer worth her mettle exists in a literary vacuum. Neverending thanks to Jennifer M. Einstein (the one I always call first and who is my hugest support), Nina Badzin, Helen Chernikoff, Rabbi Pamela J. Gottfried, Elisa Heisman, Jane Herman (aka JanetheWriter), Jordana Horn, Esther Kustanowitz, Rabbi Rebecca W. Sirbu, Rabbi Phyllis Sommer (aka *Ima on the Bima*), and Molly Tolsky. And also to my wise writing teachers: Abigail Green, Christina Katz, and Jena Schwartz. Finally, I remain the recipient of unending love, which inspires me daily. The source of this love comes from my parents, Robin and Rabbi Stephen J. Einstein; my siblings, Jennifer M. Einstein, Diana and Heath Einstein, and Jen and Zachary Einstein; my children, Ben, Lilly, and Jacob; and the one in whom my soul delights, Warren.

RES

Rabbi Jackie Koch Ellenson and Rabbi Liza Stern, my rebbes on speed dial, I am blessed to call you mentors and beloved friends. I am forever grateful to my soulmates in the rabbinate, Rabbi Julie-Saxe Taller, Rabbi Rebecca Gutterman, Rabbi Sarah Reines and Rabbi Laurie Katz Braun, to Rabbi Sally J. Priesand for being the "first," and to Rabbi Debbie Zecher for being my first rabbi. Fern Grayer, you are not only my coach, but also my teacher and my guide in finding genuine balance and renewed beauty in my work. Amy Berkin, Emily Glasberg and Deb Greenberg, you were the truest and best on-the-ground teachers I could have had in my rabbinate and you have helped me grow immeasurably as a rabbi and a human being; thank you for ever and always. And from the depths of my soul, thanks and love to my parents, Sherry and Barry Mendelson; my sister, Ali Mendelson Winaker and brother-in-law, Rabbi Jeremy Winaker; the sweet loves of my life, Gideon, Rafi, and Solomon; and my true love, Adam Graf.

AMG

Foreword

Rabbi Sally J. Priesand

This is a book of history, created to present and preserve the details of something our children and grandchildren take for granted: the ordination of women as rabbis. Someone once said that feeling gratitude and not expressing it is like wrapping a present and not giving it; therefore, I feel compelled to begin with words of gratitude for some of those leaders of the Reform Movement—there are many more—who played a role in making it possible for me and all the women who followed me to become rabbis, serving God and the Jewish people.

When I entered Hebrew Union College–Jewish Institute of Religion, I did not think very much about being a pioneer, nor was it my intention to champion women's rights. I just wanted to be a rabbi. I had no female mentors; no women on the faculty; no women rabbis to whom I could turn for advice. I was the only woman in a class of thirty-six, but there were four men, none of them alive today, to whom we all owe a debt of gratitude. The first was Dr. Nelson Glueck *z"l*, at that time president of HUC-JIR. While others were hoping that I would marry a rabbi rather than be one, he gave me his unqualified support and took care of a lot of little problems in the background that I probably never even knew about.

Unfortunately, he died the year before I was ordained, but his wife Helen, a distinguished physician in Cincinnati, told me that prior to his death he said there were three things he wanted to live to do and one of them was to ordain me. His vision and his commitment laid the foundation for the ordination of women.

Fortunately for me, and for all of us, his successor, Dr. Alfred Gottschalk *z"l*, shared that vision, and when he became president of HUC-JIR, he ordained me. Only in recent years have I come to understand how bold and daring that action was. Apparently, certain members of the faculty tried to convince him that I should not be ordained. Forty years ago, I did not really realize the amount of pressure he was under, nor did I understand the courage it took for him to step into someone else's shoes and fulfill a mission someone else had begun. How grateful I am that he was willing to do that and thereby affirm the equality of women in the Reform Jewish community.

On June 3, 1972, he and I stood together before the ark at the historic Isaac M. Wise Temple on Plum Street in Cincinnati, and he declared publicly that he was ordaining me with "pride, dignity, and pleasure." My thirty-five male classmates spontaneously stood up to honor this extraordinary moment in Jewish history. It is a memory I will never forget.

The third person who played an important role in the success of my rabbinate was Rabbi Edward E. Klein *z"l*. As ordination approached, I discovered that finding a job was not all that easy, but Rabbi Klein welcomed me as assistant rabbi of Stephen Wise Free Synagogue in New York City. It always seemed particularly appropriate to me that I would come to a synagogue with a reputation for commitment to equality and social justice, and Rabbi Klein took great pride in being introduced as the first equal opportunity employer in the American rabbinate. He shared his pulpit with me and encouraged me to be involved in every aspect of the synagogue and the community. If a family balked at having me officiate at a funeral (i.e., "My father was traditional, how can I have a woman rabbi at his funeral?"), he would say, "Rabbi Priesand will officiate; otherwise, you will not have a rabbi from this synagogue." In many ways, Ed Klein taught me how to be a rabbi, and I shall always be grateful.

The fourth person to whom we owe a debt of gratitude is Rabbi Joseph B. Glaser *z"l*, executive director of the Central Conference of American Rabbis. For me and so many others, Joe was mentor, teacher, counselor, friend. I admired his prophetic nature, and when I say prophetic, what I mean is that always there was reflected in his life and in his work a sense of vision and a deep and abiding commitment to the concept of justice for all people. Many benefited from that commitment, but none more so than women in the rabbinate. He was among the first in the Reform Jewish community to champion equality, and although progress was sometimes slower than we would have liked, he never faltered in his devotion to the cause, striving always to provide new opportunities for women in the leadership of the CCAR and in the congregations of our Movement. His death came too soon, and I often wonder what could have been accomplished on behalf of women in the Jewish community had he lived longer. Nonetheless, I was honored when his family asked me to speak at his funeral. There was a message in that too.

As America's first female rabbi, I always assumed it was my obligation to become the rabbi of a large congregation in a major American city, but the members of Monmouth Reform Temple, where I served for twenty-five years, taught me that success does not mean bigger. It simply means we are doing better today than we did yesterday. I am grateful that MRT always allowed me to be myself, to experiment and be creative and have ideas, treating me always as their rabbi and not as the first woman rabbi.

Finally, I want to express my gratitude to the Women's Rabbinic Network for the affection and honor with which its members always treat me and for the visiting professorship in Jewish Women's Studies that they established at Hebrew Union College–Jewish Institute of Religion in my name. By a quirk of history, I was first, and since that time, many others have followed in my footsteps. Their creativity, passion, and insight continue to energize and inspire me. I admire and respect them all and am grateful for the many contributions they have made in their own communities and in the larger Jewish world of which we are a part.

Last summer, I was privileged to participate in a study mission to Berlin, learning about Regina Jonas, the world's first woman rabbi, and dedicating a plaque in her memory at Terezin, guaranteeing that her story will never again be hidden away. Before being deported to Terezin, Rabbi Jonas gave her documents to the Berlin Jewish community for safekeeping. Had she not done so, we would know even less than we do now about her life and the significant contributions she made to the Jewish community.

When I retired from the active rabbinate, I announced that I would be donating my documents and papers to the American Jewish Archives in Cincinnati, and I encouraged all female rabbis of whatever denomination to do the same so that those doing research on the history of women in the rabbinate can come to one place to find what they need. This book makes an enormous contribution to that effort, gathering together in one volume much of what we have accomplished in the first forty years and preserving for future generations the firsthand knowledge of those who lived through it all. How grateful we are to Hara Person, Alysa Mendelson Graf, and Rebecca Einstein Schorr for their foresight and attention to detail and to all the writers for sharing their experiences with us. I am confident that readers will be enriched by what they find here and inspired by the realization that each and every person can indeed make a difference.

Preface

Rabbi Jacqueline Koch Ellenson

I entered Hebrew Union College–Jewish Institute of Religion in 1977, as a new and proud graduate of Barnard College. I had studied Hebrew, had been a leader in my temple youth group, and had always been a teacher. I was so eager to learn more about Judaism, to live a full Jewish life, to become a Jewish leader. I knew very little, but as a twenty-one-year-old, I entered this stage of my life with enthusiasm and excitement. I had been taught that women could do anything and be anything, and I believed it.

When I arrived in Jerusalem for my first year at HUC-JIR, women constituted one-third of our entering rabbinic class. We felt strong and empowered, buying our first tallitot, leading *t'filah* on Shabbat morning, speaking Hebrew fluently. We were part of the first wave of women accepted to rabbinic school and knew that the rabbinate was the perfect path for us. We dreamed of large pulpits, having egalitarian relationships, finding time for and balancing work and family.

Our generation of women were the happy recipients of a new reality of women entering the workplace. We were grateful for the breaking down of barriers. The world was changing, and women becoming rabbis was a sign that anything was possible. For so many of us in the early years of our rabbinates, we were making history. I was excited to be one of the first women rabbis. I knew I was doing something new and different, like so many women across the professions. Early on in my rabbinic career, I imagined my future contribution to the evolving and emerging world of women in the rabbinate. However, I could not have predicted our impact on the rabbinate and the Jewish world in the years and decades to come.

Our entrance into the world of Jewish leadership led to new conversations. We knew we were breaking convention, and we needed to ask the important gendered questions of our lives. How could we, as women and as rabbis, live, work, and keep focused on our desire for leadership and our drive for success? As women rabbis, how could we find new answers to our pressing questions about God and our holy texts when the traditional answers did not apply? What parts of the lives of girls and women had been ignored but now would be celebrated because we were there? How could we, as women rabbis, bring our newfound power to social issues that mattered to us? Our efforts to answer these questions pushed all of us to reframe synagogue life, to change the rabbinate for men as well as for women, and to expand our understanding of Jewish life and identity.

Reading the articles and hearing the voices in this volume affirms the immense transformation that has taken place in the Reform rabbinate and in the Jewish organizational world. As I read through them all, I felt as though I was watching a home movie, reading my story, our story, reflecting back on all that has happened in the past four decades. So much creativity, so much work, so much change! I felt that that I was sitting at a long table with everyone I know, listening to their stories (many of which I have heard before), laughing and crying, grieving and celebrating.

Hearing the voices in this volume reminded me of everything I love about being a member and then, until recently, the director of the Women's Rabbinic Network. The WRN is the only rabbinic organization whose sole mission is the support of and advocacy for women in the Reform rabbinate. As a member of the WRN, I have always cherished our commitment to each other and rejoiced over the ever-increasing number of women rabbis.

Our early conventions consisted of fifteen or twenty of us sitting together in a classroom or, as at one memorable convention in the hills above Palm Springs, sitting in a circle while the young children played in the middle. Over the years, our gatherings became more and more important. In the WRN, we supported and pushed each other. We challenged our communities, congregations, and organizations, most of which had never seen a woman rabbi before. We fought for equality and justice in our rabbinic organization. And sometimes, we talked about hair and clothes and pregnancy and the ways that they played a role in how people saw us and how we saw ourselves. In the WRN, we were well aware that we were participants in the story of women in the rabbinate and that we were creating the story at the same time. And so, we have worked together to help each other become the rabbis we wanted to be.

For the past twelve years, as the WRN's first executive director, I have been privileged to work alongside so many remarkable women ordained over the last four decades. Together, we had a shared goal of strengthening our organization so that the WRN would continue to be the central address for women in the Reform rabbinate. Indeed, our organization has played a significant role in raising people's awareness about the realities of women in the rabbinate in the Reform Movement and in the larger Jewish community.

This volume fulfills that purpose and reflects the very motto adopted by the Women's Rabbinic Network: We are better when we are together. Only by hearing each other's experiences can we acknowledge what is and envision what should be. In those early years, we lived with many challenges, including the reality of gender discrimination, sexual harassment, and sexism in the Jewish workplace. Some women could not find jobs, and others were not paid an equitable salary. Many became parents and did not receive a reasonable maternity leave or any leave at all. And, there were women who were fired for their sexual orientation. In this environment, the WRN became a haven, a space in which we could be honest about our challenges and feel safe sharing them. The WRN became the strong public voice in helping our community address these iniquities. Our work has often been focused on bringing issues of personal significance into the public square. This helps not only women rabbis but our male colleagues, too. In this way, the WRN has been an agent for social change.

Over thirty years after my ordination, I celebrate each and every woman rabbi, for her professional choices and expression of her rabbinate. I celebrate our colleagues' integration into the rabbinic workforce, as senior rabbis of large congregations, as leaders in social justice, as entrepreneurs forging new understandings of what community means.

There is a Yiddish greeting among women, "Skotsl kumt," which means "You're here!" or "I'm here." There is no definitive explanation for this practice, but there is a story that attempts to answer the question of why this is said:

> Because it seemed like everything important in the world belonged to men, the women decided to make their unhappiness known to the Ribono shel olam, the Master of the universe, by building a tower of women, one on top of the other, until they reached heaven. Because Skotsl was clever, wise, and good with words, the women chose her to be at the top of the pile in order to voice the women's complaint to God. Just before Skotsl reached the top of the tower, it collapsed. In all the confusion, the women tried to locate each of their friends. To their surprise, Skotsl was nowhere to be found. Thus their situation remained as it had been, and no change was made in their status. Women still hope that Skotsl will return in order to talk to God, and that is why they welcome each other with the greeting "Skotsl kumt."[1]

In this gendered version of the Tower of Babel, the women work together to approach God, to make their claim on Jewish life and learning. They reject the way the world is. They desire to make the system change. They assent to sharing the burden of this request, and the appointed leader finds her way to the top, to be lost in the dust as the women fall to the earth. But instead of being perceived as a punishment, the disappearance, and prayed for reappearance, of Skotsl is understood as the harbinger of a messianic time, when women's requests and women's interpretations and women's leadership will be a part of the norm.

Maybe Skotsl didn't truly disappear. Perhaps, at that moment, feeling so close to God, she knew what she had to do. She went out into the land, and everywhere she went, she initiated a new tower of women, pushing them to reach for the heavens, to feel close to God. And each time the women saw how close Skotsl could get, they also went out, found more groups of women, and made their own towers, taking the possibility of change everywhere. Our teacher and colleague Rabbi Rachel Adler points out, "The tower, like its protagonist, tumbles in confusion, but the builders remain optimistic. The story is left open-ended, awaiting Skotsl's return."[2] This hope for her return becomes empowering and pushes women to work together, to work harder, to create a better world for women, with status and knowledge.

When I entered HUC-JIR, I could not have anticipated that in addition to reaping the benefits of struggles overcome by the women who came before me and the gifts of the social change that marked the 1970s, we would also be the initiators of this continued move toward equal access in Jewish institutional life. None of us has done it alone. We have shared our lives and our struggles, our growth and our ambition with each other.

Looking back, and then looking forward to the work we have before us, questions still remain. Have we arrived? Is the struggle over? Every conversation with a colleague about salary, benefits, and advancement inequities, every struggle to include a maternity or family leave clause, has strengthened my commitment to continuing the original vision of the WRN, to support each other and to advocate for change. We are all still awaiting that potentially messianic time when women and men receive equal pay for equal work, when women ascending to the senior rabbinic position in a synagogue will not be a surprise, when women's choices in their career track are affirmed and acknowledged and accommodated by their organizations and congregations, when women rabbis' voices are heard. Until then, we are all making sure that we have a voice and that it goes all the way to heaven, to God's ears. I'd prefer to think of Skotsl's disappearance as an acknowledgment that we all stand on the backs of those who came before us. We all must work together to create change; we have to work together pleading our case before the Holy One. Talking truth to power has its place, but nothing is as strong or as empowering as our efforts to work together. Skotsl was the leader in the efforts in our folktale. Where would we be without Sally? But in our lives, we are all the leaders, climbing up, moving forward, creating justice, and making change. We find that power together as we climb to the top, however we may define it.

Skotsl kumt…Skotsl may be here…Welcome!

NOTES

1. Adapted from "Skotsl Kumt," trans. Lisa Anchin, http://www.yiddishbook-center.org/files/pt-articles/PT58_skotsl_anchin_sm.pdf.
2. Rachel Adler, *Engendering Judaism: An Inclusive Theology and Ethics* (Boston: Beacon Press, 1999), 23.

Introduction: What Kind of Job Is That for a Nice Jewish Girl?

It's been more than four decades since Sally J. Priesand ascended the steps of the bimah at Plum Street Synagogue in Cincinnati, Ohio, and descended as HaRav Sarah bat Yisrael v'Shoshana. It was a transcendental moment—for her, of course, as well as for contemporary Judaism. For although there had been others, long before, who had sought the right to have access to ordination and/or a rabbinic education, she was the first to be ordained rabbi by a seminary. The impact of this decision could not have been imagined by Rabbi Dr. Nelson Glueck, z"l, who had permitted the ordination of the first woman, or by Sally Priesand herself. That is what this book sets out to examine, taking a long view of what it has meant to the Jewish community in the forty-plus years since Rabbi Priesand was ordained.

In a November 1973 interview with Frank Reynolds,[1] Rabbi Priesand remarked that people would stare at her the first few weeks at a synagogue before becoming accustomed to a woman on the pulpit. She also admitted to the feeling that she had "to be better…to work a little bit harder…that when you are the first, people are waiting for you to make a mistake."

For those of us who are a generation or two removed from Rabbi Priesand and her contemporaries, it is difficult to imagine what it must have felt like to be the only woman on campus. Not just the only student, but the only woman period, as there was no woman on the faculty of the Hebrew Union College–Jewish Institute of Religion (HUC-JIR) until 1985.

It is only natural to ask why this book needed to be written at this point in history. After all, at this point women have been ordained as rabbis across the spectrum of the Jewish community, with more than 650 women rabbis ordained by HUC-JIR alone. It is fair to say that women rabbis are no longer an anomaly. In fact, 2012 saw the first all-women ordination class at the Los Angeles campus, and women rabbis serve in every capacity where male rabbis are found. However, many of the questions that were asked in those first few years remain unanswered.

Rabbi Dr. Judith Abrams, *z"l*, gives us one answer in the opening essay, "Who Controls the Narrative: A 'Stop Action' Analysis of the Story of Beruriah and the Implications for Women Rabbis":

> Women's stories are particularly vulnerable since, until recently, we were not the keepers of these stories. What will happen to our stories, the stories of women breaking through the barriers at the admissions office of HUC-JIR, coping with an institution built only for male students, professors who were not used to women students, and barriers of congregations who didn't want women rabbis as their leaders, once we, who experienced these things, pass from this world? Our sources actually give us a hint of what might happen.

We must gather these stories and experiences while we still can so that future generations can understand the journey.

However, this book is about more than just history. It is also about how our congregations, our Jewish world, and indeed even our collective identity as Jews have changed because of the reality of women in the rabbinate. Many of the essays in this collection explore those changes and the implications of those changes on how the Jewish community sees itself. In looking at the past forty-plus years, the writers included in this volume ask important and challenging questions about how we move forward into a Jewish future of possibilities.

When I was a rabbinical student, there was nothing that I loved more than being asked to visit a synagogue and speak. And there was nothing that I hated more than being asked to speak about being a female rabbinical student. For me, modifying my status as a rabbinical student made me feel diminished, as though being a female rabbinical student was somehow different from, or less than, being a male rabbinical student. I never really knew what to say. I came of age "after Sally." Though my own childhood rabbi was a man, it simply never occurred to me that women couldn't be rabbis. I'd heard of them; I'd even met a few as a child. But I don't recall taking special notice of them simply because of their gender. I was reared in an egalitarian home and synagogue. No ritual had ever been denied me because I was female. My ordination class was 50 percent women, and I have never, even to this day, served a congregation that had not already had a woman on the bimah in some official capacity. I had never broken any barriers. So it felt disingenuous to speak about my experience as a female rabbinical student when my experience didn't feel any different from that of my male classmates.

With hindsight, I can acknowledge my discomfort and understand that it was coming from my own truth. But what I failed to recognize, in my immaturity, was the yearning by those who had invited me to speak to learn about the struggles of that first generation of women rabbis who had enabled my own path to the rabbinate to be a smooth one. People, especially but not only women, wanted to hear about this because they had *not* come of age "after Sally." The story of Rabbi Sally Priesand was part of their Jewish narrative, and they wanted to hear it contextualized. They wanted to hear it reflected upon and to learn about what it meant in terms of Jewish life. They had known only a male-dominated Judaism, one that had suppressed the female experience for far too long. They wanted to know, vicariously, what it was like to experience a rabbinate that wove male and female voices into a rich tapestry, because that was the Judaism they wanted to claim as theirs.

This book is for them.

The newness of women rabbis has dimmed, but only somewhat. Even with the ever-growing number of women rabbis, there remains disparity in salaries between men and women, differing expectations based on gender, and a plethora of other inequalities.

With the great distance we have traveled, there is still far to go and much to change. We cannot forget where we've been as we consider the obstacles still to overcome. The current generation of young Jews and the generations to come need to remember upon whose shoulders they stand. They must know what battles have been fought and won, so that they learn how outdated modes of operation take time to dislodge from the status quo.

This book is also for them.

It is not just our history that matters but also our future. The Jewish world that the next generation inherits will be a radically different one than it would have been if HUC-JIR had not opened its doors to women, followed by the Reconstructionist Rabbinical College, then the Jewish Theological Seminary, and now Yeshivat Maharat. It is hard to imagine what twenty-first-century Judaism would look like without the contributions and challenges of women rabbis. How the fact of women rabbis will continue to impact on all areas of Jewish life in important and transformative ways remains to be seen, but the possibilities are endless, and future generations will only benefit from a rabbinate that recognizes and encourages the gifts of all genders.

This book then is also for them.

No matter where you find yourself on the Jewish spectrum, your life has been touched, whether you know it or not, by a rabbi who just happens to be a woman.

And so this book is for you.

NOTE

1 "Interview with First Female Rabbi," *ABC News*, ABC, November 25, 1973, http://abcnews.go.com/Archives/video/sally-priesand-first-female-rabbi-10124653.

Short Takes

*How have women rabbis made an impact on your life
or on the life of the Jewish people?*

Aseih l'cha rav, u'kneih l'cha chaverah. Women rabbis are my dearest
friends and greatest teachers. They inspire me in my love affair with
Torah—and in both the sweetness and the struggle, they have helped
me find myself within its words. These pioneering women have taught
me to be a refuge for the exiled; to be inclusive, to celebrate and mark
life-cycle events in new ways, and to rise up with confidence against
injustice and complacency. Women rabbis made me who I am today,
and I sing with their voices wherever I go.

Julie Silver, singer/songwriter

*   *   *

As a student in my early years at HUC-JIR in New York, I had convinced myself—for a variety of reasons—that the congregational rabbinate just wasn't for me. But then I had the brilliant fortune to spend
a summer interning with Rabbi Deborah Zecher, whose fierce love of
Torah and compassion for all things Jewish and congregational turned
my world upside down. At the time, Rabbi Zecher was a full-time rabbi,

a mom of three young children, a spouse, and the leading Jewish moral voice of conscience in the Berkshires. She inspired me with her teaching, her creativity, her willingness to let me take risks and fall, and, ultimately, to grow into the rabbi and father and husband and man I am today. It is surely possible I could have become a congregational rabbi without Rabbi Deborah Zecher's mentoring, but my life would be far less dynamic and interesting. She saw the spark of Torah in me and, with determined resolved, called me forth to let it shine. I am forever grateful.

Rabbi Michael Adam Latz
Shir Tikvah Congregation, Minneapolis, MN

*   *   *

How have women rabbis made a difference in my life? Not at all.

That is to say, I am of the generation that has never known anything different. Women have been in the rabbinate longer than I've been alive. Their presence throughout my childhood and into my adult life has been, well, normal. Despite the fact that I did not choose to pursue ordination myself, I never steered away from the idea because of my gender. So how have women rabbis made a difference in my life? Not at all. And, in every way imaginable.

Carrie Bornstein
Executive Director, Mayyim Hayyim Living Waters
Community Mikveh and Paula Brody & Family Education Center
Newton, MA

*   *   *

As one of the first Orthodox women to enter the clergy, it was often my non-Orthodox rabbinic colleagues who gave me the support that I needed to move forward. These women knew firsthand the challenges that female religious leaders face, and they welcomed me as part of their sisterhood. Who stands out are two women rabbis, one Conservative and one Reform, who were both ordained in the early years of women's ordination. When I met them, they said, "We've been waiting for you for twenty-five years, and we are so glad that you've arrived." At that moment, I knew I was not alone.

Maharat Rachel Kohl Finegold
Congregation Shaar Hashomayim, Montreal, Canada

* * *

When I was young, the rare sight of a woman in a *kippah* amused me. God and rabbis were indisputably male. Then, as a teen, I encountered a female rabbinical student and I was baffled, but also nervously excited. Today I wear a *kippah* so my students may perceive this as normal. I ensure that God is God, neither he nor she, and I am fortunate to have worked with two outstanding rabbis who happen to be female. This is the Judaism our sons have inherited. They will never laugh at a woman because she chooses to wear a *kippah*.

Pia Kutten, Livingston, NJ

* * *

We walked into the JCC in the town we had just moved to and were greeted warmly by a woman wearing a *kippah*. She didn't know it, couldn't possibly, that the first impression she gave us was our first impression of the entire community. She couldn't have known that her genuine smile made us feel instantly comfortable. After all those years of avoiding women rabbis, I had to ask myself why it all seemed to vanish into a non-issue so quickly. In the end, it wasn't about male versus female rabbi. It was about finding the right rabbi, period.

Cara Paiuk, West Hartford, CT

* * *

In my freshman year of college, I thought about becoming a rabbi for the very first time. However, I was unaware that women could become rabbis. Over five years later, I accepted a position as youth director at a synagogue with a woman rabbi. The doors to my world blew wide open. Women in the rabbinate bring an important voice to our collective narrative as a Jewish people. There is an important balance that is set, one that goes beyond egalitarianism. This provides a more complete reflection of the vibrant spectrum that makes up our Jewish community.

Rabbi Aderet Drucker
Congregation B'nai Shalom, Walnut Creek, CA

*   *   *

In grade school, I asked a more observant friend why we sat apart from men; she replied that women's voices distracted men from their prayer. Later, in college, I met a young woman who said that she was majoring in Judaic Studies and training for the rabbinate. I'd never heard of a woman rabbi—the phrase itself is still strangely gendered—and asked her why. She said that she wanted to weave her voice and intellect within the rich tapestry of women in Judaism. It was the first time I'd considered that Jewish women could—and should—be heard.

Monica Gebell, Rochester, NY

*   *   *

When I was eleven years old, girls at my Conservative synagogue were not permitted to read from the Torah. Girls were "bat mitzvah'ed" at a Friday night service without ever having read or studied a word of Torah. In the fifty years since then, American non-Orthodox Jewry has undergone a veritable revolution. The most exquisite symbol of that revolution is the decision, first by the Reform and then by the Conservative Movements, to ordain women rabbis. But, the rabbinic ordination of women is far more than just a symbol. Bringing women into the rabbinate has fundamentally changed the narrative of American Jewry. Women's distinctive voices, analysis, sensitivities, and perspectives, previously virtually absent for thousands of years, have been unleashed and have produced radical results. The most profound impact of a feminine rabbinate is the empowerment of Jewish women to fully engage in all aspects of Jewish life. Women are no longer relegated to distancing themselves physically or spiritually from Torah;

the feminine embrace of Torah, thanks to the bold creativity of the female rabbinate, is not the same. The feminization of the rabbinate has enabled the growth and development of a panoply of new rituals that reflect fundamental changes in what it means to be a Jew in America.

Janice Kamenir-Reznik
Co-Founder and President, Jewish World Watch

*   *   *

Women rabbis have certainly impacted my life! Upon seeing my first woman rabbi in 1980—Rabbi Lynn Gottlieb— I had an instant emotional, psychological click. If she could be a rabbi, then so could I! My path began then—to claim my spot in the ongoing dynamic of the evolving history and destiny of the Jewish people.

The creativity of the last forty years added to Torah and midrash; poetry and song; ritual, study, and teaching will be remembered as the golden age of Jewish women's contributions—fusing Judaism and feminism—new waters springing forth from Miriam's Well.

Rabbi Geela Rayzel Raphael, Philadelphia, PA

*   *   *

When my son was three years old, someone asked him if he wanted to be a doctor (like his mother) when he grew up. He looked up wide-eyed and incredulous and said, "I cannot! Only women can be doctors!" Today, if someone were to ask my three children whether they might be a rabbi, I am sure that their first impulse would be to think of their own rabbi: a smart, exuberant, passionate, engaging rabbi, who is also a woman. As a strong feminist and a convert to Judaism, I am forever grateful for the rabbi in our family's and community's lives. Not only does she model the kind of Judaism that we bring into our home, but she is a symbol for the hope of possibilities for my children's future—a future that is about engagement, passion, and service to something bigger no matter what your background. Today, my ten-year-old son knows that both men and women can be doctors, and my daughters know that both men and women can be rabbis. There are no limits to hope.

Katherine Gergen Barnett, MD
Boston University Medical Center

*   *   *

At our wedding, there was a moment of silence after we and the rabbi arrived under the chuppah. Into the silence, Eliza's three-year-old cousin was heard clearly asking, "Mommy, why is their rabbi a boy?"

This happened in 1991. Seth attended preschool at the Reconstructionist synagogue. The only rabbi he knew was a woman.

As far as how women rabbis have made an impact on my life, since my sister is a rabbi, and I have had many women rabbis as teachers and colleagues, the answer is "greatly."

Simcha Daniel, Rabbi Daniel Burstyn,
Kibbutz Lotan, Israel

*   *   *

As I contemplated conversion nearly ten years ago, I believe the presence of a female rabbi was extremely powerful, both in motivating my decision and allowing me to see Judaism as something for me as a person, not only my family. Having a female rabbi as the head of our congregation allowed me to see that Conservative Judaism values a woman's role in prayer and the spiritual aspect of Judaism. By choosing to become Jewish, I would not be relegated to a subservient role while men pursued the intellectual and spiritual aspects of our faith.

Karen Beckman, Fayetteville, NY

*   *   *

She spoke from a place inside that I had never heard on a rabbi's lips—her words came from her heart; at the same time, she used her knowledge of Jewish texts and stood as firmly in the flow of Jewish tradition as any male rabbi.

Female rabbis have recaptured the *Shechinah* (feminine aspect of God) from exile and brought her back to the Jewish people. Most female rabbis bring a depth of compassion, keen sensitivity, and a lack of hierarchical orientation to their work.

Each morning, we lay *t'fillin* on our heads and near our hearts in order to "know" God. Through their leadership, female rabbis bring an alignment with both head and heart energy, and inspire and empower others in the community to do the same.

Rav Shoshana Mitrani Knapp, Chappaqua, NY

*   *   *

Only male voices dominated my childhood synagogue, but a pregnant rabbi officiated at my wedding in 1990, a lesbian rabbi led my study of Spanish Jewish history, and several women rabbis regularly inspire me spiritually. Whether primarily as chaplains, teachers, charismatic religious leaders, or many of the other roles that rabbis fulfill, women rabbis have changed the face and practice of Judaism. Dramatic is the insertion of women's perspective in Jewish study and texts. Language has changed in liturgy. Because of these developments, I am both hopeful for the future of our people and proud to have a daughter in rabbinical school.

B. P. Laster, EdD
Professor, Towson University

*   *   *

As a first-year rabbinic intern in 2010, I officiated at a Passover seder at Temple Beth-El of City Island (New York, NY). Among the forty guests assembled to relive Passover's ancient story of liberation from bondage, a young girl raised her hand to ask a question. "Reb David," she asked, "I didn't know that boys can be rabbis. Every rabbi I've known is a girl."

I smiled. My own rabbinical school dean, teachers, and spiritual director are women who crossed the desert so this young girl would know a world of women rabbis.

We relive Passover's ancient story of liberation for what God still does for us as we come forth from Egypt.

Rabbi David Markus
Temple Beth-El of City Island, New York, NY

*   *   *

Women rabbis offered me wisdom, taught me new ways to find wisdom, and had a faith in me that I didn't have in myself. In the shelter of their compassionate loving-kindness, I was finally able to understand that God's Infinite Love had been hidden inside me all along. For now, I study, pray, and write, learning to walk my own path, humbly and with faith in God. But one day, God willing, I will honor the amazing women rabbis who helped me by sharing with others the same compassionate loving-kindness that my rabbis continue to share with me.

Jennifer Warriner, Indianapolis, Indiana

*   *   *

I remember the moment it happened. The woman on the bimah sang out in full voice, breaking an age-old silence. In her voice, I heard a great power and beauty set free. It felt as if the Jewish people had been playing on just one-half of a piano, and suddenly the other half was available, and finally the full range of melody, harmony, tone, pitch, and cadence was ours! I knew in that moment that I would add my voice to the song of the Jewish people. In the reverberation of that voice, I heard the permission to join the chorus, and co-create the complexity, harmony, dissonance, and beauty of a Living Tradition.

Rabbi Shefa Gold, Jemez Springs, New Mexico

*   *   *

September 2000: a female Reform rabbi co-officiated at my wedding in Toronto, Canada, a first, groundbreaking same-sex wedding. She honors us, blesses each *simchah*. She inspires healing; holds our hands, shares joy and tears, through *simchah*s and funerals, through yoga, through acts of *tikkun olam*. Celebrator of all the good in this world, my sister-in-law Rabbi Faith Joy Dantowitz rejoices in change. A same-sex marriage champion, a "Woman of the Wall," a role model to my children and to the Jewish community, she compels her village forward. To me she is a sister, a religious inspiration. Most important, she is a spiritual mentor to all.

Faith Michelle Dantowitz, Brookline, MA

*   *   *

My most dynamic and interesting friends are women rabbis. I'm amazed at the new frontiers they have charted for all Jews, of all genders. Some work with the elderly, others as educators, some are activists, and others work in organizations and congregations—where they get to do all of the above. New avenues to explore and express one's Judaism have been opened as women rabbis apply their own lenses to the Jewish community and to the world at large.

Rabbi Susie Heneson Moskowitz
Temple Beth Torah, Melville, NY

*   *   *

Sally Priesand was my rabbi for twenty-five years, period, not my woman rabbi. While learning and worshiping with her, the only consideration about gender was how amazing it was that the first woman rabbi was at our Monmouth Reform Temple. My nickname for her, starting when I was Social Action chair, was Boom Boom, because she would say, "We could do this and then do that and boom boom boom we'd be done." Captivating sermons, caring concern, nonstop creativity, and a fascination for wordplay and numbers with a sense of humor inform this rabbi's life. There when needed!

Lila Singer, Tinton Falls, NJ

*   *   *

Women rabbis shaped me into the man I am today. It was a woman rabbi who inspired my mother to become a rabbi as a second career. It was my mother's rabbinic studies and her classmates, many of whom were women, that inspired me to go to rabbinical school. During my rabbinic studies I met my wife, and the future mother of my children, who is now a rabbi. And now, a woman rabbi is my supervisor and mentor. Without women rabbis, my life would have less meaning and less happiness. Thank you, women rabbis.

Rabbi Dan Medwin, MAJE
Central Conference of American Rabbis

*   *   *

Nine years old when the newly ordained Sally Priesand appeared on the cover of *People*, I purchased the celebrity weekly and hung the photo in my bedroom. There it stayed—reinforcing my budding pride in Reform Judaism and women's equality—until I removed it, frayed and yellowed, before heading to college. Fast-forward twenty-five years. As I waited to board a flight, my childhood "heartthrob," by chance, sat beside me. Seizing the moment, I relayed my story of the magazine's cover photo, once again awash in the pride and potential her ordination had sparked in me so many years ago.

Jane E. Herman, New York, NY

*   *   *

When I was first ordained (1984), many rabbis out in the field who were, perhaps, a decade older seemed to resent us, sensing that the rules of the game had changed without their being consulted: they entered the rabbinate thinking it was an exclusive club for men, and now that secure footing was being pulled out from under them. Fifteen years later, many of these same men volunteered that women were the greatest thing to happen to the American rabbinate: they could now attend their children's school performances, chaperone field trips, stay home with a sick child, and reserve time with their spouses. They could finally have a fulfilling family life.

Rabbi Amy R. Scheinerman, Columbia, MD

*   *   *

Female rabbis have impacted my life both professionally and personally. I have been a designer of tallitot for the past twenty-seven years. The influx of female rabbis has allowed me to expand my creativity. I think that male counterparts have seen the females broadening the styles of what sacred garments can be, and that, in turn, has allowed the males to stretch their boundaries as well. They are role models for congregants to incorporate *hidur mitzvah* in their sacred garments.

I think females are, in general, more compassionate and freer with their emotions than males. As a member of a congregation with a female rabbi, I found that the sermons resonated more with me, as they often seemed to contain more of the emotional side of a particular subject.

Of course, it goes without even mentioning that it is wonderful that our daughters have a strong role model in female rabbis.

Reeva Shaffer
REEVA'S 'ritings with ruach, Oakton, VA

* * *

At a time when there were few female rabbis, I am proud to have been instrumental in bringing the first women to Columbia, Maryland, and Nashville, Tennessee, to work with me as rabbinical colleagues. Some years later, I was proud to bring the first lesbian rabbi to work with me in the same capacity in West Hartford, Connecticut. Each was a pioneer at the time of her appointment. Although they made some congregants uncomfortable, each one enriched the congregation we served together, and each made the path of the women who followed them an easier one.

Rabbi Stephen Fuchs, Rabbi Emeritus
Congregation Beth Israel, West Hartford, CT

* * *

There were no role models for girls on the bimah in my childhood Conservative synagogue in the 1950s and '60s. In fact, there were no women on the bimah at all, for they were prohibited from going up there. They were not even counted in the minyan. The message to girls was very clear: you are a spectator, not a participant. I felt no connection to the synagogue because the synagogue itself was telling me I had no place in it. With the ordination of women, how blessedly different was my daughters' experience growing up in the Reform Movement!

Debra Hirsch Corman, Sharon, MA

*   *   *

Women rabbis are my friends, my *tantes*, and, perhaps most importantly, my mother. I am used to and completely comfortable with rabbis talking about learning, food, holidays, clothing, kids, work, and everything else. My own Jewish identity bleeds into all other aspects of my life as a result. I experienced from an early age that spirituality, community, and faith set a road map of how to live a meaningful and full life. I feel immeasurably lucky to have been raised by women who showed me that one does not need to keep parts of herself separate in order to be successful.

Hannah Ellenson, Oakland, CA

*   *   *

The decision to ordain women by Hebrew Union College–Jewish Institute of Religion changed my life as a woman and a Jew. Becoming a rabbi was a fulfillment of a lifelong dream held by me before there were women rabbis. Ordination has given me the privilege of working in the Jewish community and enabling me to be a role model for generations of Jewish youth. I believe that women rabbis have had a profoundly positive effect on helping more people engage with Judaism. We have changed ritual and worship and created a new body of literature that includes women's voices.

Rabbi Dr. Janet B. Liss
North Country Reform Temple, Glen Cove, NY

*   *   *

My synagogue, during my seventeen-year life, has had five female rabbis. At five years old, at ten, at thirteen, I wasn't thinking of what an anomaly this was. To me, it was normal. I think this represents progress, that in a world where there is so much opposition to women in powerful positions, my synagogue has had women leading our religious lives for not only the seventeen years of my life, but the last three decades. I, and many others, have grown up witnessing this supposedly "unnatural" occurrence as being nothing but natural.

Sarah Silverstein, Port Washington, New York

An Offering Made in Honor of Those
Who Have No Time to Make an Offering

Rabbi Karen Bender

Upon celebrating 25 years of women in the Rabbinate, the CCAR solicited writings from colleagues for the CCAR Journal. I asked my colleague with whom I worked at the time, Rabbi Renni Altman, if she wanted to co-author a piece. "Who has time? Call me in 10 years when you have three kids and a full-time pulpit." I wrote this piece in her honor, attempting to echo and respond to Merle Feld's point in her poem, "We All Stood Together," that women had no time to keep a record of what we experienced at Sinai. Incidentally, Renni surprised me and did write a beautiful gender-neutral sheva brachot. I surprised her with this. I received many calls from overwhelmed mom-rabbis to say thanks.

> For the women
> the rabbis
> who haven't the time
> to contribute to this
> tapestry

because just
as they sit down
to write
the phone rings
and just as they
wake up with an idea
the baby cries
and just as they
finally find the hour,
the kid needs
help with the homework,
and just as they
squeeze the ten minutes
into a Shabbat afternoon
to make this offering,
exhaustion sets in
and they fall asleep.

For the women
The heroic rabbis
The friends
And role models
Who haven't the time
To contribute to this
Tapestry

I, we
say thank you
we say you are
not forgotten
this time.

Women Rabbis' List of Firsts

Women rabbis are still a new enough phenomenon that most of us have been firsts at something—the first woman rabbi in our town, at our congregation, on a local board of rabbis, to address a state legislature. We have all been trailblazers in different and remarkable ways. Such a list could have been a whole book in and of itself. In order to keep it to a manageable size, the following list focuses on the first firsts on a national and international stage, as well firsts in the personal lives of women rabbis. We recognize that in addition to the firsts listed here, there are numerous other accomplishments to celebrate among our trailblazing and talented colleagues.

1935: **First woman to be called "rabbi":** Regina Jonas (private ordination). She was ordained by Rabbi Max Dienemann in Munich, Germany, and killed in Auschwitz in 1944.

1972: **First woman officially ordained as a rabbi:** Sally Priesand (HUC-JIR '72), at age twenty-six

1973: **First woman to enter rabbinical school, HUC-JIR, married to an HUC-JIR entering rabbinical student:** Deborah Prinz (HUC-JIR '78)

1974: **First woman ordained by Reconstructionist Rabbinical College:** Sandy Eisenberg Sasso (RRC '74).

1975: **First woman to be ordained at Leo Baeck College after WWII:** Jackie Tabick (LBC '75)

1975: **First woman rabbi to marry a rabbi:** Jackie Tabick (LBC '75), to Larry Tabick (LBC '76)

1976: **First presiding female rabbi in a North American congregation:** Michal Mendelsohn (HUC-JIR '75), at Temple Beth El Shalom in San Jose, California

1976: **First woman rabbi to have a child:** Jackie Tabick (LBC '75)

1976: **First woman rabbi to head a Hillel:** Laura Geller (HUC-JIR '76)

1977: **First to serve with her spouse:** Sandy Eisenberg Sasso (RRC '74), with Dennis Sasso (RRC '74)

1978: **First woman rabbi to serve as UAHC (now URJ) regional director:** Karen Fox (HUC-JIR '78)

1979: **First WRN co-chairs:** Karen Fox (HUC-JIR '78) and Deborah Prinz (HUC-JIR '78)

1979: **First woman to be ordained while pregnant:** Ellen Weinberg Dreyfus (HUC-JIR '79)

1980: **First daughter of a rabbi (David Hachen, HUC-JIR '52) to become a rabbi, and also first great-granddaughter of a rabbi (Solomon Kory, HUC-JIR 1903) to become a rabbi:** Debra Hachen (HUC-JIR '80)

1980: **First two sister-brother rabbinic pairs:** Karen Fox (HUC-JIR '78) and Steven Fox (HUC-JIR '80); Ellen Weinberg Dreyfus (HUC-JIR '79) and Michael Weinberg (HUC-JIR '80)

1981: **First woman rabbi to serve in the U.S. military (U.S. Army):** Col. (Ret.) Bonnie Koppell (RRC '81), who first entered the military as a student in 1979 and took a position full-time upon ordination in 1981

1981: **First second-career woman rabbi:** Helene Ferris (HUC-JIR '81)

1981: **First woman rabbi to serve in Australia:** Karen Soria (HUC-JIR '81)

1981: **First woman rabbi to serve in Canada:** Joan Friedman (HUC-JIR '80)

1983: First woman rabbi to serve in Israel: Kinneret Shiryon (HUC-JIR '81)

1985: First woman rabbi/male cantor couple to be ordained from HUC-JIR: Barbara Goldman-Wartell (HUC-JIR '85) and Cantor Kevin Wartell (HUC-JIR '85).

1985: First woman ordained from Jewish Theological Seminary: Amy Eilberg (JTS '85)

1985: First openly gay rabbi ordained from RRC: Deborah Brin (RRC '85)

1985: First woman rabbi to serve on the faculty of HUC-JIR, New York: Margaret Moers Wenig (HUC-JIR '84), who is also the longest-serving woman faculty member (1985–present) and the only woman to serve on the CCAR Ad Hoc Committee on Homosexuality in the Rabbinate (1985–1990)

1986: First women rabbi/cantor congregational team: Sally Priesand (HUC-JIR '72) and Cantor Ellen Sussman, at Monmouth Reform Temple, Tinton Falls, NJ

1986: First woman rabbi to serve in the U.S. Navy: Julie Schwartz (HUC-JIR '86)

1986: First woman rabbi to serve on the Committee of Jewish Law and Standards: Amy Eilberg (JTS '85)

1986: First woman rabbi to serve on the (then) Rabbinical Pension Board (now Reform Pension Board): Stacy Offner (HUC-JIR '84)

1987: First woman to serve as president of the RRA: Joy Levitt (RRC '81)

1988: First openly lesbian rabbi hired by a mainstream congregation: Stacy Offner (HUC-JIR '84), at Shir Tikvah in Minnesota

1988: First woman to win the Canadian National Jewish Book Award: Elyse Goldstein (HUC-JIR, '83), for *ReVisions: Seeing Torah through a Feminist Lens* (published by Jewish Lights)

1988: First pair of ordained sisters: Elaine Zecher (HUC-JIR '88) and Deborah Zecher (HUC-JIR '82)

1989: First native Israeli woman to be ordained: Einat Ramon (JTS '89)

1990: First French woman to be ordained: Pauline Bebe (LBC '91)

1991: First Australian-born woman to be ordained: Aviva Kipen (LBC '91)

1992: First American woman ordained in Israel: Naamah Kelman (HUC '92)

1992: First woman rabbi to serve in the U.S. Marines: Karen Soria (HUC-JIR '81)

1993: First Israeli-born woman to be ordained in Israel: Maya Leibovich (HUC-JIR '93)

1993: First ordained deaf rabbi: Rebecca Dubowe (HUC-JIR '93)

1994: First woman to be ordained by an Orthodox rabbi in Israel: Mimi Feigelson

1994: First woman senior rabbi: Laura Geller (HUC-JIR '76), at Temple Emanuel in Beverly Hills

1995: First Australian-born woman to serve in Australia: Linda Joseph (HUC-JIR '94)

1995: First Syrian-American woman ordained: Dianne Cohler-Esses (JTS '95)

1996: First Persian-American woman ordained: Michelle Missaghieh (HUC-JIR '96)

1996: First South African woman ordained: Glynis Conyer (HUC-JIR '96)

1996: First pulpit rabbi to announce being diagnosed with AIDS while serving as rabbi: Cynthia Ann Culpeper (JTS, '95)

1997: First woman rabbi to serve as a *mashgichah*: Mary Zamore (HUC-JIR '97)

1998: First ordained woman serving in Hungary: Katalin Kelemen (LBC '98)

1999: First father/daughter rabbinic team to lead a congregation: Stephen Einstein (HUC-JIR '71) and Rebecca Einstein Schorr (HUC-JIR '99), at Congregation B'nai Tzedek in Fountain Valley, California

2000: First Holocaust survivor to be ordained: Helga Newmark, *z"l* (HUC-JIR '00)

2000: First ordained woman serving in Brazil: Sandra Kochman (Rabbi Marshall Meyer Seminario Rabínico Latinoamericano, '00)

2001: First lesbian rabbinic couple to be ordained: Tamar Malino and Elizabeth Goldstein (HUC-JIR '01)

2001: First Asian-American rabbi: Angela Warnick Buchdahl (HUC-JIR '01), who was also ordained as a cantor in 1999

2001: First woman rabbi to throw out the first pitch: Mindy Portnoy (HUC-JIR '80)

2001: First woman rabbi to be the mother of a woman cantor: Susan Laemmle (HUC-JIR '87), mother of Rebecca Joy Fletcher (HUC-JIR '01)

2002: First Chinese-American rabbi: Jacqueline Mates-Muchin (HUC-JIR '02)

2003: First woman rabbi to serve in Scotland: Nancy Morris (LBC '02)

2003: First ordained woman serving in Berlin: Gesa Ederberg (Schechter Institute of Jewish Studies '03)

2003: First woman rabbi to serve in the U.S. Air Force: Chaplain (Major) Sarah Schechter (HUC-JIR '03)

2003: First woman to serve as president of the CCAR: Janet Marder (HUC-JIR '79)

2003: First woman rabbi to serve as editor-in-chief of URJ Press: Hara Person (HUC '98)

2003: First woman rabbi ordained who was also a Rhodes Scholar: Lisa Grushcow (HUC-JIR '03)

2004: **First woman rabbi to serve a congregation with her father-in-law:** Roxanne J. S. Shapiro (HUC-JIR '99), with Ronald Shapiro (HUC-JIR '74)

2005: **First lesbian rabbi/cantor couple to be ordained from HUC-JIR:** Robin Nafshi (HUC-JIR '05) and Cantor Shira Nafshi (HUC-JIR '05)

2006: **First woman to serve as dean of Hebrew College:** Sharon Cohen Anisfeld (RRC '90)

2007: **First woman to serve as dean of HUC-JIR (New York campus):** Shirley Idelson, PhD (HUC-JIR '91)

2007: **First full-time woman rabbi on CCAR staff, and thereby the first woman rabbi to serve as a senior staff member of a major Reform Movement organization:** Deborah Prinz (HUC-JIR '78)

2007: **First woman rabbi to serve in Poland:** Tanya Segal (HUC-JIR '07)

2007: **First woman to be editor of a CCAR siddur:** *Mishkan T'filah*, Elyse Frishman (HUC-JIR '81)

2007: **First lesbian to serve as president of the RRA:** Toba Spitzer (RRC '97)

2008: **First woman vice president of the URJ:** Stacy Offner (HUC-JIR '84)

2008: **First woman to serve as COO of Rabbinical Assembly:** Julie Schonfeld (JTS '97)

2008: **First woman to serve as publisher of CCAR Press:** Hara Person (HUC-JIR '98)

2008: **First women rabbis to win the National Jewish Book Award:** Andrea Weiss (HUC-JIR '93) and Tamara Eskenazi (HUC-JIR '13), for *The Torah: A Women's Commentary* (published by Women of Reform Judaism and URJ Press)

2008: **First rabbi to be the daughter of two rabbis:** Carmit Harari (HUC-JIR '08), the daughter of Laura Schwartz Harari (HUC-JIR '08) and Ze'ev Harari HUC-JIR '81). Carmit and

Laura are also the first mother-daughter pair to be ordained the same year.

2008: **First woman rabbi to become the mother of a rabbi**: Margaret Meyer (HUC-JIR '86), of Daniel Meyer (HUC-JIR '08)

2009: **First woman to be ordained by an Orthodox movement:** Rabba Sara Hurwitz ('09), ordained by Rabbi Avi Weiss, originally with the title "maharat ."

2009: **First ordained mother-in-law and daughter-in-law pair:** Suri Friedman (HUC-JIR '96) and Kate Speizer (HUC-JIR '08).

2009: **First African-American Reform rabbi:** Alysa Stanton (HUC-JIR '09)

2010: **First woman to be ordained from Abraham Geiger College:** Alina Traiger (AGC '10).

2011: **First openly gay rabbi to be ordained from JTS:** Rachel Isaacs (JTS '11)

2012: **First trio of sisters to be ordained:** Mari Chernow (HUC-JIR '03), Jordana Chernow Reader (HUC-JIR '10), and Ilana Chernow-Mills (HUC-JIR '12)

2012: **First time an all-female class is ordained from any of the HUC-JIR campuses**: All eight ordination students in the Los Angeles class

2013: **First woman rabbi to serve as executive director of Women of Reform Judaism:** Marla Feldman (HUC-JIR '85)

2013: **First woman to earn ordination and a PhD from HUC-JIR:** Kari Hofmaister Tuling (HUC-JIR '04, '13)

2013: **First women rabbis to offer blessings at the Presidential Inaugural Prayer Service at the National Cathedral in Washington, DC:** Sharon Brous of IKAR (JTS '01) and Toba Spitzer (RRC '97)

2014: **First lesbian to serve as president of the CCAR:** Denise Eger (HUC-JIR '88)

2014: **First woman HUC-JIR rabbinical student to give birth during the year-in-Israel:** Rachel Gross-Prinz (HUC-JIR 2019)

2015: **First woman rabbi to serve as president of the Academy of Homiletics:** Margaret Moers Wenig (HUC-JIR '84). Previously, she was also the first woman rabbi to be accepted as a member of the Academy, in 1991.

Editors' note: We have made every attempt to verify the above information. We apologize, in advance, for any historical omissions or inaccuracies.

CCAR = Central Conference of American Rabbis; HUC-JIR = Hebrew Union College–Jewish Institute of Religion; JTS = Jewish Theological Seminary of America; LBC = Leo Baeck College; RRA = Reconstructionist Rabbinical Association; RRC = Reconstructionist Rabbinical College; UAHC = Union of American Hebrew Congregations (now Union for Reform Judaism); URJ = Union for Reform Judaism.

Part One

Those Who Came Before Us:
The Pre-history of Women Rabbis

Though this volume reflects on the impact of women rabbis over the past forty years, it would be remiss to think that the ordination of women emerged as a concept solely in the post-feminist era.

Part 1 opens with a critical examination of the historic figure Beruriah and how her narrative shifted in the generations after her life. Rabbi Judith Abrams, *z"l* ("Who Controls the Narrative? A 'Stop Action' Analysis of the Story of Beruriah and the Implications for Women Rabbis") questions how future generations will regard the advent of the rabbinic ordination of women and what might be done to protect that narrative.

An essay by Rabbi Renee Edelman ("Chasidic Women Rebbes from 1749 to 1900") introduces previously unknown Chasidic women whose learning and wisdom and, in some cases, family connections positioned them as religious leaders in their communities.

The annals of history typically name Rabbis Sally Priesand, Sandy Eisenberg Sasso, and Amy Eilberg as the first Reform, Reconstructionist, and Conservative women rabbis, and Rabba Sara Hurwitz as the first Orthodox one. However, a number of women preceded them as being regarded as rabbinic foremothers. Their desire to be counted among those who received *s'michah* is shared by Dr. Pamela S. Nadell ("'The Long and Winding Road' to Women Rabbis") and Rabbi Laura Geller ("Rediscovering Regina Jonas: The First Woman Rabbi").

The support for the ordination of women rabbis as well as women on the pulpit was cultivated from within the synagogues. Rabbi Marla J. Feldman ("The Women Who Set the Stage: Celebrating One Hundred Years of Women of Reform Judaism") takes a critical look at how the Women of Reform Judaism (formerly the National Federation of Temple Sisterhoods) helped pave the way for women to become rabbis.

Part One concludes with personal reflections from Rabbi Naamah Kelman-Ezrachi ("A First Rabbi, from a Long Line of Rabbis") and Rabbi Sue Shankman ("Going into the Family Business"), two women rabbis who followed in the rabbinic footsteps of their forefathers.

1

WHO CONTROLS THE NARRATIVE?

A "Stop Action" Analysis of the Story of Beruriah and the Implications for Women Rabbis

RABBI JUDITH ABRAMS, PHD *z"l*

The history of women in the rabbinate is a young one, indeed. Almost all of the pioneers are still alive and can write their own histories. We can document this history with eyewitness accounts of what took place and store them in a safe repository (e.g., the American Jewish Archives or the Jewish Women's Archive). But we should probably accept that what will truly last are the memories of us, rather than the history of us.

Memory versus History

Judaism venerates memory over history. For example, the Passover seder is a recital of our communal memory of the liberation from Egypt, not a yearly examination of the archeological proof of the Exodus and conquest of the land.[1] Yosef Yerushalmi puts it clearly:

> Not history, as is commonly supposed, but only mythic time repeats itself. If history is real, then the Red Sea can be crossed only once, and Israel cannot stand twice at Sinai....Yet the covenant is to endure forever....Memory flowed, above all, through two channels: ritual and recital.[2]

Only recently has history even come close to being valued in the way that memory is. And the messy reality of how women broke through the gender barrier is what must now be captured if it has any chance of being equally valued with the memory of us that will be crafted from our disparate kinds of rabbinates.

What will happen to our narratives once they become memory? In other words, what will happen once we lose control over our own narratives? We, the first generation of women rabbis, share this dilemma with another population: Holocaust survivors. Soon, anyone with a living memory of these events will have died. Then it will truly be the triumph of memory over history. For example, the Holocaust is already being reduced in communal *memory* to a shorthand of the swastika and Auschwitz, whereas a recently released study from the U.S. Holocaust Memorial Museum documents some 42,500 Nazi ghettos and camps throughout Europe, from 1933 to 1945.[3] Or to put it cinematically, memory is *Schindler's List*. History is all the people who did not make it onto Schindler's List and a chronicle of their fates as well. Memory records story. History records reality. Memory can be shaped. History records facts. If not for this chapter, would anyone soon recall the "hostile takeover" of the men's locker room at the gym and pool of HUC-JIR in Cincinnati?[4]

Women rabbis are hardly the first Jews to face such a generational shift. Our greatest sages faced it when mourning the Temple's destruction:

> Rabbi would derive by exegesis twenty-four tragic events from the verse "The Lord has destroyed without mercy all the habitations of Jacob; in wrath God has broken down the strongholds of the daughter of Judah; God has brought down to the ground in dishonor the kingdom and its rulers" (Lam. 2:2).
> Rabbi Yochanan derived sixty tragic events from the same verse.
> Did Rabbi Yochanan then find more than Rabbi did in the same verse? Surely not.
> But because Rabbi lived nearer to the time of the Temple's destruction, there were old men in the congregation who remembered

what had happened, and when he gave his exegesis, they would weep and fall silent and get up and leave.

(Jerusalem Talmud, *Taanit* 4:5, PM 24a)

Here is a snapshot of memory versus history. Rabbi Y'hudah Hanasi speaks to an audience among whom are witnesses who lived through the event, who did not need to have traumatic images painted before them with words. They had their own personal memories of the event. But once the Temple's destruction had passed beyond the realm of living memory, then the event could be embroidered and molded to fit the exegetical needs of a given sage and his audience.

Women's stories are particularly vulnerable since, until recently, we were not the keepers of these stories. What will happen to our stories, the stories of women breaking through the barriers at the admissions office of HUC-JIR, coping with an institution built for only male students, professors who were not used to women students, and the barriers of congregations who didn't want women rabbis as their leaders, once we, who experienced these things, pass from the world? Our sources actually give us a hint of what might happen.

Beruriah is the closest equivalent to a woman rabbi in the world of the Sages (ca. 150 CE). In the sources recorded closest in time to her lifetime, she is simply a very smart and learned woman. However, as the centuries go by, she is portrayed as a tragic figure. This chapter will examine the different layers of the Beruriah stories and draw lessons from it for women rabbis and how our narratives may be told in future generations.

Beruriah's Stories Layer by Layer

Beruriah is portrayed as both the daughter and the wife of a sage. Her father was said to be Chanina ben Teradyon (also known as Chananiah), a teacher in the second century CE in the Galilee (Babylonian Talmud, *Sanhedrin* 32b).[5] Beruriah is also said to have been the wife of Rabbi Meir, an extremely important sage whose teachings shaped the Mishnah as we have it today.[6]

From those materials that are preserved in Beruriah's, or Rabbi Chanina ben Teradyon's daughter's, name, we can discern a clever intellectual who was able to find solutions to intricate problems as well as a woman able to develop ingenious explanations, and uses, of biblical verses. In addition, she may have suffered her share of hardships, but there is nothing to suggest that she did anything immoral until some one thousand years after the period during which she lived.

Beruriah in the *Tosefta*

Our earliest teachings from Beruriah are found in the *Tosefta* (ca. 220 CE). (No teachings are attributed to her in the Mishnah.) The first pertains to a specific item's ability to become ritually impure. Whether something can become impure relates, in part, to its fitting into a cultural category. Generally, the item must be a whole, recognizable item in order to have ritual impurity adhere to it.

Beruriah's ruling helps to identify the exact moment when an item moves from the category of "complete item," in which it can receive uncleanness, to the category of "incomplete item," in which it cannot become ritually impure:

> When does it [a certain kind of oven] become clean?…Rabbi Chalafta of K'far Chananya said, "I asked Shimon ben Chananya who asked the son of Rabbi Chanina ben Teradyon, and he said, 'When one will have moved it from its place.' And his daughter says, 'When he will have removed its garment.' When these things were reported before Rabbi Y'hudah ben Bava, he said, 'Better did his daughter rule than his son.'"
>
> (*Tosefta Keilim, Bava Kama* 4:17)

The item under discussion here is a small oven that is covered with plaster. Something impure, such as a lizard, has entered the oven and died there, making the oven impure. The question is, "What is the minimum amount of disassembling the oven must undergo until it no longer fits the cultural category 'oven'?" One doesn't want to disassemble it more than one must. The best solution will be the one that requires the least damage to the oven so that we may put it back in working order as quickly, and with as little expense, as possible. The suggestions in the Mishnah (*Mishnah Keilim* 5:7) range from cutting it into pieces to moving the pieces about. The latter is the opinion that Chanina ben Teradyon's son appears to be echoing.

Beruriah suggests a less disruptive solution: one need only remove the mud coating on the oven to render it no longer culturally recognizable as an oven. When Rabbi Y'hudah ben Bava hears of Beruriah's decision, he lauds it: hers is the least disruptive decision that still achieves its goal of rendering the oven a "non-oven."

Rabbi Chanina ben Teradyon's daughter's other ruling is similar. At issue is the status of a part of a door bolt. The Sages had difficulty in placing it in a category. The passage discusses the part of the door bolt that is used to slide the bolt across the door. It is a large peg with a rounded top, which is used as a handle to move the bolt. Apparently people could take this peg out of the door bolt. So is it an item unto itself (in which case it can always become unclean)? Or is it simply a part of the door bolt, that is, not a whole item unto itself (in which case it is not susceptible to uncleanness)? There is great puzzlement on this issue (e.g., in *Mishnah Eiruvin* 10:10 and *Mishnah Keilim* 11:4). The issue is resolved in *Tosefta*:

> A door bolt—Rabbi Tarfon declares it unclean, and the Sages declare clean. And Beruriah says, "One removes it from this door and hangs it on another on the Sabbath." When [these] rulings were reported before Rabbi Y'hudah, he said, "Better did Beruriah rule."
>
> (*Tosefta Keilim, Bava M'tzia* 1:6)

The majority of sages suggest that the door bolt, even if it might be used for something else (e.g., as a pestle), is clean, that is, it is not an item unto itself. However, there is some conflict about this. So what does Beruriah suggest? She suggests that we take it from one door and hang it on another door on Shabbat. This way it is surely clean, since it does not work except in the door for which it was made.

Why? A modern analogy may help. A key may always be a cultural item, recognizable on the face of it. But it is only "real" when it is in the lock it is designed to open. If you put a car key in your front door lock, it is clear that the key is not accomplishing anything. Beruriah's solution makes the logic of the Sages' decision clear: the door bolt (the "key") is only a whole item when it is used in the bolt for which it was designed. And just as one may use a key to accomplish tasks besides opening doors (e.g., one can use a key as an awl), it is not the real purpose for which it was created and so may be considered culturally insignificant.

And why does Beruriah suggest that the bolt be transferred on the Sabbath? To indicate decisively that it is not a whole item and may be moved on the Sabbath—something that is ordinarily prohibited for whole items (e.g., a lock and a key or the door bolt and the door together). Rabbi Y'hudah comments once more on Beruriah's cleverness.

Beruriah in *Sifrei D'varim*

The early midrash on the Book of Deuteronomy, *Sifrei D'varim* (ca. 350 CE) contains an account of Rabbi Chanina ben Teradyon's martyrdom and Beruriah's denigration. This may be unremarkable. Jewish life was filled with misfortune in the years after the Bar Kochba Revolt. It would actually be amazing if her story did *not* reflect the turbulence of that time and place.

> When they apprehended Rabbi Chanina ben Teradyon, he was condemned to be burned together with his Torah scroll. When he was told of it, he recited the verse "The Rock!—whose deeds are perfect" (Deut. 32:4). When his wife was told, "Your husband has been condemned to be burned and you to be executed," she recited the verse "A faithful God, never false" (Deut. 32:4). And when his daughter was told, "Your father has been condemned to be burned,

your mother to be executed, and you are to be assigned to work," she recited the verse "Great in counsel and mighty in work, whose eyes are open (upon all the ways of the sons of men, to give every one according to his ways)" (Jer. 32:19).

(*Sifrei D'varim* 307)

Rabbi Chanina ben Teradyon accepts his own death sentence by reciting the first half of Deuteronomy 32:4, and his wife recites the second half. The story is placed in *Sifrei D'varim*'s commentary on that verse.[7]

Here we see the first move to shape Beruriah's story into something other than what it is in *Tosefta*. In *Tosefta*, she is simply a very clever woman. Here, her whole family comes to naught (except her ever-unnamed brother; see below). Both of her parents are executed, and she is made to work, *but the sort of work to which she is consigned is not specified.* It is possible she is sent to a brothel.[8] But it could just as likely mean that she became a menial worker or was forced to cook nonkosher food. The text simply does not specify what kind of work she must do; there is no reason beyond sexist assumptions to assume that this meant she worked in a brothel.

Beruriah in Later Midrash Collections

Was Beruriah's family more unfortunate than most? Obviously, the parents were martyred, but their son turned toward sin and predeceased his parents. Lamentations states, "God has also broken my teeth with gravel stones, God has made me to wallow in ashes" (Lam. 3:16). What specific series of events could cause someone to have his mouth filled with gravel and then to be covered in ashes? We learn his story from Beruriah's reaction to it. *Eichah Rabbah* (ca. first half of the fifth century CE) provides the answer:

It is related of the son of Rabbi Chanina ben Teradyon that he became friends with robbers whose secret he disclosed, so they killed him and filled his mouth with dust and pebbles. After three days, they placed him in a coffin and wished to praise [i.e., pronounce a eulogy] over him out of respect for his father, but he [Rabbi Chanina ben Teradyon] would not permit them to do so. He said to them, "Allow me and I will speak concerning my son." He opened [his discourse] and said, "Neither have I hearkened to the voice of my teachers, nor inclined my ear to them that instructed me! I was well nigh in all evil in the midst of the congregation and assembly" (Prov. 5:13–14). And his mother recited over him, "A foolish son is the vexation to his father, and bitterness to her that bore him" (Prov. 17:25). His sister recited over him, "Bread of falsehood is sweet to a man; but afterwards his mouth shall be filled with gravel" (Prov. 20:17).

(Eichah Rabbah 3:16/S'machot 12:13)

This is an echo of the way Rabbi Chanina, his wife, and his daughter accept misfortune in *Sifrei D'varim*. Here, Rabbi Chanina ben Teradyon, his wife, and his daughter use verses from Proverbs to express their acceptance of their loss and their confidence in God's judgment of their kin. He did not live up to the family's standards of morality and scholarship, which was hinted at even in *Tosefta*.

Perhaps one of the best known stories of Beruriah comes in a late document indeed, *Midrash Mishlei* (Midrash on Proverbs; late eighth to late tenth centuries).[9] In other words, this is a story first attested at least six hundred years after Beruriah lived.

> Another interpretation: "What a rare find is a capable wife" (Prov. 31:10). A tale is told of Rabbi Meir that while he was sitting and expounding in the academy on a Sabbath afternoon, his two sons died. What did their mother do? She left them both lying on their couch and spread a sheet over them.
>
> At the close of the Sabbath, Rabbi Meir came home from the academy and asked her, "Where are my two sons?"
>
> She replied, "They went to the academy."
>
> He said, "I looked for them at the academy but did not see them."
>
> She handed him the cup [of wine] for the *Havdalah* benediction, and he pronounced the blessing over it. Then he asked her again, "Where are my two sons?"

She replied, "Sometimes they go someplace [*makom*] [first]; they will be back presently." She served him [his meal] and he ate. After he recited the Blessing after Meals, she said to him, "Master, I have a question to ask you."

He replied, "Ask your question."

She said, "Master, some time ago a certain man came by and left something on deposit with me. Now he has come to reclaim this deposit. Shall I return it to him or not?"

He replied, "My daughter, is not one who holds a deposit obligated to return it to its owner?"

She said, "Without your opinion [on the matter] I would not give it back to him."

What did she do [then]? She took him by the hand, led him up to the children's room, brought him to the bed, and removed the sheet, so that Rabbi Meir saw them both lying on the bed dead. He burst into tears, saying, "My sons, my sons! My masters, my masters! My natural born sons, and my masters who enlightened me with their [learning in] Torah."

At this point Rabbi Meir's wife said to him. "Master, did you not just now tell me that we must return a pledge to its owner?"

To which he replied, "The Eternal has given, and the Eternal has taken away; blessed be the name of the Eternal" (Job 1:21). Rabbi Chanina said, "In this manner she comforted him and brought him solace, hence it is said, 'What a rare find is a capable wife!' (Prov. 31:10)."

(*Midrash Mishlei* 31 on Prov. 31:10)

David Goodblatt suggests that "the identification of Beruriah as the wife of Meir is a Babylonian invention."[10] He argues that this story about Rabbi Meir's wife, without the name Beruriah, could suggest that this midrash originated in the Land of Israel and that the authors were unaware that the *Bavli* (Babylonian Talmud [BT]) equates Rabbi Meir's wife with the woman named Beruriah and Rabbi Chanina ben Teradyon's daughter.

What is relevant here is that her story becomes more tragic over time. Here, she faces a mother's ultimate loss, and she confronts it with the wisdom and fortitude that is consistent with descriptions of her in the earlier texts. Nonetheless, we can see a tendency to portray her as having suffered great misfortune, beginning with the story of her father's martyrdom, her brother's shame, and now her sons' deaths.

Did this tragic development of her story arise in order to provide a cautionary tale for women who might want to follow in Beruriah's footsteps? The experiences of the early modern women rabbis suggest this might be so. Certainly the early generations of women rabbis were warned that we would end up alone, since no man would want to marry an authority figure such as a rabbi. That sounds laughable today, but in the 1980s, this was a common warning directed at women rabbinical students. And, of course, openly gay students could not be ordained in the 1980s. Women also endured their share of "tests" by professors, senior rabbis, and congregants, looking to see of what mettle we were made. How many times have women rabbis answered the question "What do you call a rabbi's husband?" And, of course, women in all professions are *still* being told that we can't "have it all."

Of course, all major sages' biographies have been shaped by subsequent generations over time. As Jacob Neusner has pointed out in too many books to name, there is little, if any, historicity in these tales. But we simply do not have many women's stories in Rabbinic literature. Perhaps most women's stories are shaped to highlight tragedy or infamy. A woman remembered as happy, fulfilled, and important to her family and the world is a true rarity in Rabbinic literature. Queen Helena of the Adiebene may be one of those few such persons.

Beruriah in the *Y'rushalmi*

The *Y'rushalmi* (Jerusalem Talmud [JT]; ca. 425 CE) does not identify Rabbi Meir's wife with Rabbi Chanina ben Teradyon's daughter, nor is the name Beruriah used. In JT *D'mai* 2:1, 22c (and BT *Chulin* 6b), Rabbi Meir's father-in-law is identified as Rabbi Zeruz. Of course, Rabbi Meir may have had more than one wife or may have married another woman either before or after his marriage to Beruriah.

Beruriah in the *Bavli*

The Babylonian Talmud's final redaction is generally dated from 500 to 800 CE. In this text, Beruriah is portrayed in ways that amplify earlier depictions of her. She is brilliant but plagued by family misfortune.

Beruriah's Brilliance and Her *Obligation* to Learn

In the passage below, we find some evidence of discrimination against Jews from Lod, in the south of Israel, and those from Nehardea, in Babylonia. A passage in JT *P'sachim* 5:3, 39b explains that the discrimination is based on the notion that those from these locations are too full of pride and do not study Torah enough. A scholar from these ancient locations is compared unfavorably with Beruriah:

> Rabbi Simlai came before Rabbi Yochanan [and] said to him, "Let the Master teach me the Book of Genealogies [a commentary on Chronicles]." Said he to him, "From where are you?" He replied, "From Lod." "And where is your dwelling?" "In Nehardea." Said he to him, "We do not discuss it, either with the Lodians or with the Nehardeans, and how much more so with you, who are from Lod and live in Nehardea!" But he urged him, and he consented. "Let us learn it in three months," he proposed. [Thereupon] he took a clod and threw it at him, saying, "Beruriah, wife of Rabbi Meir [and] daughter of Rabbi Chanina ben Teradyon, who studied three hundred laws from three hundred teachers in [one] day could nevertheless not do her duty in three years, yet you propose [to do it] in three months!"
>
> (BT *P'sachim* 62b)

Here, it would seem, is an elaborate put-down of Rabbi Simlai. He comes from places that make it inappropriate for him to learn this commentary on the Books of Chronicles, and he proposes to do it in an inappropriately quick way, reinforcing the stereotype about sages from Nehardea and Lod being too proud and not studying Torah appropriately. As part of this denigration, Rabbi Simlai is compared unfavorably with Beruriah, who apparently ordinarily learned intensely and quickly, yet could not complete studying this commentary in three years.

Perhaps the most interesting thing about this passage is that the phrase "do her duty" (*yatzah y'dei chovatah*) is a technical phrase usually applied to those who are obligated to perform a mitzvah. Here, it is applied to Beruriah. This seems to imply that whoever composed this story felt that Beruriah was *obligated* to study this commentary to Chronicles, just as a man would be. Usually, women are not considered obligated to study Torah. Yet, here we find that Beruriah *is* considered to be obligated for at least one specific act of Torah study. This means that not only *may* a woman study Torah; she is *obligated* to study it. One of the principle objections to women as *sh'lichot tzibur* is that they are not obligated to recite the *Sh'ma*. This passage suggests that such hard and fast categories may not have applied universally or to all women during the Sages' era.

Beruriah and Rabbi Meir

In the following passage, Beruriah demonstrates her moral authority over her husband, Rabbi Meir. She also shows how cleverly she can interpret biblical verses, as well.

> There were once some highwaymen in the neighborhood of Rabbi Meir who caused him a great deal of trouble. Rabbi Meir would pray that they should die. His wife Beruriah said to him, "How do you make out [that such a prayer should be permitted]? Because it is written, 'Let *chata'im* (sins) cease' (Ps. 104:35)? Is it written [let] *chot'im* (sinners) [cease]? It is written *chata'im* (sins)! [No!] Then look at the end of the verse, 'and let the wicked be no more' (Ps. 104:35). Since the sins will cease, there will be no more wicked men! Rather pray for them that they should repent, and [then] 'the wicked will be no more.'" He did pray for them and they repented.
>
> (BT *B'rachot* 10a)

Rabbi Meir was using as his prayer the verse from Psalm 104:35, mentioned in the text above. Beruriah then rebuked him and reinterpreted the verse using the literal meaning of the word *chata'im* as it should be pronounced. Beruriah is able to correct Rabbi Meir's quotation of a biblical text, delve into the text's proper meaning, and successfully rebuke her learned husband. In this story, she is literally and morally correct and is able to lead her husband to a correct prayer that solves his problem. Her *chidush*, or new interpretation, is remembered here in the standard way that any sage's would be.

Rabbi Chanina ben Teradyon's Martyrdom and Beruriah's Denigration in the *Bavli*

When her father is martyred, Beruriah is able to cope with the great loss by using Torah knowledge to help her deal with her grief.

> They then brought up Rabbi Chanina ben Teradyon and said to him, "Why have you occupied yourself with Torah [forbidden by Hadrian under penalty of death]?" He said to them, "Thus the Eternal my God commanded me." At once they sentenced him to be burnt, his wife to be slain, and his daughter to be consigned to a brothel....[As the three of them went out from the tribunal] they declared their submission to [the divine] righteous judgment. He said, "The Rock!—whose deeds are perfect. Yea, all God's ways are just" (Deut. 32:4). His wife said, "A faithful God, never false, true and upright indeed" (Deut. 32:4). And his daughter said, "Great in counsel and mighty in work, whose eyes are open upon all the ways of the sons of men, to give everyone according to his ways, and according to the fruit of his doing (Jer. 32:19)."...They found Rabbi Chanina ben Teradyon sitting and occupying himself with the Torah, publicly gathering assemblies, and keeping a Scroll of the Law in his bosom. Straight away they took hold of him, wrapped him in the Scroll of the Law, placed bundles of branches round him, and set them on fire. They then brought tufts of wool, which they had soaked in water, and placed them over his heart, so that his soul should not depart quickly. His daughter said to him, "Father, that I should see you in this state!" He said to her, "If it were I alone being burnt it would have been a thing hard to bear; but now that I am burning together with the Scroll of the Law, God, who will have regard for the plight of the Torah, will also have regard for my plight."
>
> (BT *Avodah Zarah* 17b–18a)

This is an embellished version of the story we first encountered in *Sifrei D'varim*.[11] One of those additions is the specification that Beruriah is to work in the tent of prostitutes (*kubah zonot*) rather than the simple work (*m'lachah*) we found originally. (Note she is *sent* there, but she may have escaped this fate. The text is unclear.) Whether the daughter of Rabbi Chanina ben Teradyon in this story was Beruriah or a different daughter is a matter of dispute. Both Beruriah and her mother are once more portrayed as dealing with suffering through devotion to Torah, just as their father and husband do. In other words, the skills and attitudes needed to deal with adversity are not bound by gender roles.

Beruriah and Scandal

In the *Bavli*, it is Beruriah's *sister* who is rescued from a brothel. An elaborate story is told (BT *Avodah Zarah* 18a–b) of Rabbi Meir's daring rescue of his sister-in-law, who has remained a virgin even while dwelling in a house of prostitution. This is followed by a story about Rabbi Meir, who, on the run from Roman authorities himself, dodges into a house of prostitution, or into a "house of *t'reif*." Even in this relatively late document, *Beruriah* is not located in a brothel. Beruriah is surrounded by nuclear-family misery; her brother and her sister are said to have led troubled lives. But never, in all these sources, does she betray her love of learning or morality.

So how do we come to the "traditional" understanding that Beruriah's story ends up in immorality? Up to this point, we only have texts that attest to her cleverness, wisdom, creativity, and faithfulness in the face of terrible circumstances. We would have no reason to consider hers as anything but an unfortunate, but righteous, life. This interpretation is hinted at in a comment by Rashi on the story above, BT *Avodah Zarah* 18b.[12] The Talmud text here is not well edited, and a "story about Beruriah" is mentioned but never explained. It is to fill in this void that Rashi provides the story about Beruriah being lured into a dalliance with another sage, after which she hangs herself. It seems that it is the conjunction of the story about Beruriah's sister and Rashi's comment that taints Beruriah's legacy today.

Rashi was born in 1040, some nine hundred years after Beruriah walked the earth. The Beruriah we first encounter in *Tosefta*, and whom we continue to encounter in all the Rabbinic documents of the classical Rabbinic era (i.e., to the close of the *Bavli*), may have lived a tragic life. But it is likely that most Jews in this era encountered their fair share of tragedy. It is only many centuries after the close of the *Bavli* that Beruriah's life is portrayed as not only tragic but ignominious.

Lessons for Women Rabbis

What can women rabbis learn from the ways Beruriah's narrative has been shaped (some might say twisted) over the course of many centuries? We can learn that according to contemporary sources, she was a learned and clever woman whose learning was taken seriously by the men around her. It is only very much later that her story goes from having a life filled with tragedy to a life in which she undermines the very learning all the early texts testify that she treasured. It is only on the edges of the page, quite literally, that her story is truly distorted. I can easily imagine that there are those, on the edges of the Jewish world (though they might not think of themselves as being on the edges), who might distort our stories as Beruriah's story was twisted.

Why is this so important for women rabbis and their histories? Something like this may happen as later generations look back on us. For example, they may say that our struggle was heroic. Or, if women someday stop becoming rabbis, that we represented a fruitless attempt by women to grab power. It could start innocently enough, as it does in *Sifrei D'varim*. The story of Rabbi Chanina's martyrdom is embroidered by bringing down disaster on almost his entire family, not just himself.

To even have a chance that history will triumph over memory, we have to stubbornly stick up for history, messy though it may be. Our stories, once they are memories, may be shaped by those who come afer us—as Beruriah's were. We may be remembered as clever, brilliant sages. We may be seen as replacements for sons who should have been learned but weren't. We may be seen as brave in the face of adversity or simply as rabbis who make other rabbis look bad by comparison. Or our stories may be utterly distorted and become cautionary tales about the dangers of straying into a man's domain of expertise. Beruriah's story grows from the simple versions found in *Tosefta* onward in all these ways. We should accept that ours may undergo a similar fate. We may have to accept that future generations will understand our stories in their own ways and for their own ends. We may be remembered as trailblazers who revived Jewish communal life or as the harbingers of assimilation and low birth rates. Or we may be seen as competent professionals whose families suffered because of our work.

What we *can* do is to make sure that *our* versions of our stories are stored in a safe place that is easily accessible to all, such as the American Jewish Archives or the Jewish Women's Archive. And we can warn future generations about the ways our stories may be distorted. By being alert to this possibility, future generations may avoid having their stories distorted, making them more tragic or ignominious than they actually were.

NOTES

1. Yosef Hayim Yerushalmi, *Zakhor: Jewish History and Jewish Memory* (Seattle: University of Washington Press, 1982). Also see *Mishnah Pesachim* 10:5.

2. Yerushalmi, *Zakhor*, 10 and 11. There are six things that we are commanded to remember every day: (1) the Exodus from Egypt, (2) the receiving of Torah on Mount Sinai, (3) Amalek, (4) the Golden Calf, (5) Miriam's leprosy, (6) Shabbat.

3. Eric Lichtblau, "The Holocaust Just Got More Shocking," *New York Times*, March 1, 2013.

4. The men had a beautiful, roomy locker room. The women's locker room was fashioned out of a very small room and had only one shower. Frequently, several women would swim together and then had to wait as each swimmer took a quick shower while no one would be in the men's locker room at all. So one day, a group

of women just decided to appropriate the men's locker room. Thereafter, women and men traded off days using the nice locker room. Sadly, I don't remember the names of the women who made the audacious move.

5. Only a few of his teachings have been preserved: *Pirkei Avot* 3:2; *Mishnah Mikvaot* 6:3; BT *M'nachot* 54a.

6. According to David Goodblatt, "The Beruria Traditions," in *Persons and Institutions in Early Rabbinic Judaism*, ed. William S. Green (Missoula, MT: Scholars Press, 1977), 207–35, the equivalence of Rabbi Meir's wife, Rabbi Chanina ben Teradyon's daughter, and the woman named Beruriah is tentative at best. He suggests that her identity as the wife and daughter of sages is a Babylonian literary invention. For our purposes, we will agree with the traditional convention that all three of these women are actually the same woman, i.e., Beruriah. There is one more data point that Goodblatt did not have in 1977: many rabbis, we now know, marry other rabbis or cantors and are the daughters of rabbis.

7. A study of Rabbi Chanina's wife might also be profitable. After all, people do not come into the world as pre-manufactured rabbis, and it stands to reason that their mothers may play some role in determining who becomes a rabbi.

8. *Sifre on Deuteronomy*, ed. Louis Finkelstein (New York: Jewish Theological Seminary of America, 1969), 346. Even Reuven Hammer's usually excellent translation of *Sifre: A Tannaitic Commentary on the Book of Deuteronomy* (New Haven, CT: Yale University Press, 1986), 312, falls into the trap of specifying that the work is "disgraceful" when, in fact, no adjective at all is found describing Beruriah's work in any of the texts here.

9. *The Midrash on Proverbs*, trans. Burton L. Visotzky (New Haven, CT: Yale University Press, 1992), 9–10.

10. Goodblatt, "The Beruria Traditions," 218.

11. *Sifrei D'varim* was redacted earlier than the *Bavli*, and stories of the Sages are often embroidered over the centuries in the *Bavli*. This is a general literary tendency one can see over time in the *Bavli* and the later midrash collections, among which we could include the Minor Tractates.

12. See Rachel Adler, "The Virgin in the Brothel and Other Anomalies: Character and Context in the Legend of Beruria," *Tikkun* 3, no. 6 (1988): 28–32, 102–5. Also see Tal Ilan, "The Quest for the Historical Beruriah, Rachel, and Imma Shalom," *AJS Review* 22, no. 1 (1997): 1–17.

2

CHASIDIC WOMEN REBBES

From 1749 to 1900

RABBI RENEE EDELMAN

When we celebrate forty years of women in the rabbinate, we remember that moment in 1972 when Rabbi Alfred Gottschalk, president of the Hebrew Union College–Jewish Institute of Religion, stood before Sally Priesand, hands on her head, and granted her *s'michah*. With one simple gesture, Rabbi Gottschalk declared to the world that a woman could be called "rabbi." Yet there had in fact been women in earlier periods in Jewish history who had achieved a rabbinic-like status in their communities, even if they were not called "rabbi." Even before Regina Jonas and some of the other proto-rabbis of the modern period, a number of Chasidic women in Eastern Europe were acknowledged as learned sages.

These women and the roles they played in their communities have largely been erased from history. One of them, the Maid of Ludmir, was buried in anonymity on the Mount of Olives until a group of women provided a tombstone for her in 2004. To avoid controversy, her new tombstone does not call her rabbi, but at least her name has finally been restored.[1] There are other female *tzaddikot*, some we know about and others whose names and contributions remain forgotten. As we celebrate forty years of women in the modern rabbinate, we should also remember these foremothers, women who challenged the limits of the scholarship and leadership roles available to women, and not allow them to be buried anonymously by history.

Early Chasidism

In the early eighteenth century, Chasidism, a populist religious movement, was started by the folk healer and charismatic traveling preacher Rabbi Israel ben Eliezer, known as the Baal Shem Tov, or the Besht. The Chasidic community believed that the Besht possessed certain mystical powers that grew out of his relationship with God. He had the ability to look deep within the human soul and heal using amulets and herbs.[2] Most importantly, the Besht was seen as the cosmos of the universe, who could intervene to reverse even the decree of heaven.[3] In Chasidism, he was the Tzaddik, the Rebbe, the heart, soul, and lifeblood of the community.

Eidel, Daughter of the Besht

During the entirety of his ministry, the Baal Shem Tov relied heavily on his sole daughter, Eidel.[4] Her father was reported to have said about her, "She was taken from the treasury of the most holy souls," and her name is an acronym of the words *eish dat lamo*, "A fiery law unto them," from Deuteronomy 33:2.[5] She was learned in Torah and all other texts and disseminated Chasidic thought and philosophy when her father was away or ill. As a teacher, Eidel surpassed the popularity of her only brother and gained fame in Poland for her counsel and wisdom. She served as her father's proxy agent and had complete access to his book of healing powers.

A surviving letter from the Baal Shem Tov, written as he left for an extended trip, shows the scope of her power:

> To my daughter Eidel,
>
> The righteous one who fears the Lord, may she live in peace. Since I must remain a bit longer on my journey, I permit you to

issue *s'gulot* [advice and prescriptions]....However, do not send these through any third party, but through your own mouth tell the *s'gulah* to the one who needs it. This is the word of your father who blesses you with all good forever.[6]

She was truly his trusted partner and exercised the duties of a rebbe.

Even after her father's death, Eidel continued to perform works in his name. She, unlike her brother, had the ability to see deeply[7] and to work with people. She was also thought to have the ability to communicate with her dead father and fulfilled her rabbinic duties in conjunction with him, especially marriages, where she would wait for her father's spirit to arrive before entering the ceremony.

> Once it happened that she waited for five hours. The people were ashamed. People came from the world over for this wedding and they were sitting and waiting, doing nothing. After many hours she saw her father. He yelled at her that she should never arrange a wedding between such a bride and groom again. "When I come to a wedding with you, I take all the dead relatives from the Bride's side and the Groom's side. I went to heaven and easily found the Bride's relatives and looked and looked for the Groom's relatives as well. I could not find them in Paradise and had to pull them out of *Gehenna* [Hell]. That is why it took me so long. Please cancel this wedding."[8]

Eidel's significant work as a female rebbe relied on collaboration with her father's spirit to guide her work. In addition to making marriages, Eidel preached, counseled, led prayer for both men and women, and healed souls.

Eidel was able to serve as a rebbe due to her abilities and her *yichus*, the familial connection to her renowned father, as well as her ability to maintain social norms. Like the paradigmatic Jewish woman of that time and place, she was married, had children, and maintained her own grocery store so that her husband could study Jewish law. She took on the rabbinic mantle, but she did not challenge her community's conception of a woman's role.

The Rebel Rebbe

Another remarkable, but more radical Jewish woman, Hannah Rachel Werbermacher, also known as the Maid of Ludmir, had no familial connection to any Chasidic dynasty, yet she went on to develop the qualities of a rebbe. A myth surrounds Hannah's birth. Seemingly unable to have any children, the Werbermachers were told by the Seer of Lublin that in many months they would give birth to a child who would dominate the world of Chasidism. Hannah's father inferred from his audience with the Seer that he would soon be father to a baby boy who would become a Chasidic master. He planned a tremendous *b'rit milah* for his "son," inviting all the Chasidic rebbes to come and pay homage to this little child.

He was more than surprised to see that their supposed master was a girl child, whom they named Hannah. As she grew, Hannah listened to her father read and analyze Talmud and Torah. He taught her midrash, aggadah, and the books of *musar*. When Hannah turned fourteen, it was time for her to marry, just as did the other women who acted as rebbes.

But as Hannah was preparing to become a bride, her mother fell gravely ill and died. Hannah became withdrawn, spending solitary days in her room. Once, during a fit of depression, she fell asleep on her mother's grave. Upon awakening, she grew frightened, seeing that night had fallen, and tried to run quickly home. As she ran around the stones, she tripped and landed headfirst on another gravestone. She was found in the morning and was brought quickly to her father's home. Her condition was very grave; she had an injury to her head, as well as a high fever, and the doctors declared the likelihood of her imminent death. On the third day after falling, Hannah awoke, speaking of an odd vision that she had been in the *Beit Din Shel Malah* (the court of justice on high) and had been given a new and sublime soul.

From that moment on, Hannah Werbermacher conducted herself as a man, praying with ecstasy, wrapping herself in tallit and *t'fillin*, and publicly studying Torah. When her father died, she recited *Kaddish* for him, breaking Jewish law, which prohibited this act for a woman. She broke off her engagement with her fiancé, saying that a man could not marry another man.

With her inheritance, she built the Green Shul and lived in an attached apartment. During the week, she meditated and studied there. Come Shabbat, the doors to her shul were open to both men and women, and she gave discourses from behind a screen, out of a concern for modesty. Her fame spread near and far, and both the learned and the unlearned Chasidim came to hear her teach. Her congregants called themselves *Chasidei Ludmir* (the Ludmir Chasidim).

Although the Maid of Ludmir was admired by many for her quick mind and gifted soul, she was seen as a radical by her opponents, who threatened to bring a *cheirem* (expulsion) upon her head unless she married. Finally, at the request of Rebbe Mordechai of Chernobyl, she wed a scholar from among her followers. After less than a week, the marriage ended, as did the popularity of the Maid. Hannah made *aliyah* and finally married, at the age of fifty, a man who treasured her scholarship. There are conflicting reports about whether this second marriage lasted. Hannah continued her studies until 1892, the year of her death, when legend says she was found in a cave waiting for the Messiah.[9]

Relevance of These Stories to Modernity

Eidel and the Maid of Ludmir both serve as examples of how women acted as rebbes in Chasidic Europe. While we know their names, they were not the only ones. Within collections of Chasidic tales, stories of women who performed the functions of a rebbe abound. Most of these women shared a common bond; they, like Eidel, were wives or daughters of tzaddikim whose own personal merit guaranteed public acclaim. Some of these women were said to have "divine inspiration" and achieved fame for their knowledge of Rabbinic literature. They were sought by members of the Chasidic movement for a blessing or a teaching.[10] Significantly, these women were married with children and could therefore work within the public religious realm. Others, like the Maid of Ludmir, challenged their society's conception of women and encountered resistance.

Several other Chasidic dynasties that arose in the late 1800s through the 1930s had a woman considered a rebbe. This usually occurred when a rebbe died and his wife or daughter assumed his position. Many of these dynasties, including those of the Twerskys, the Shapiras, the Belzers, and the Lubliners, still exist today, but with no female leadership. The remarkable women of their past, like Eidel Baal Tov, Hannah Werbermacher, Malka Shapira, Fruma Twersky, and Rachel Belzer, are considered mere teachers. These courageous, talented women now exist primarily in the minds of their biographers and from the names on their diaries and the sermons that they preached.

The incomplete accounts of their existence raise so many questions for us. In their time, were they truly seen as equal to their male counterparts? Did they possess legitimacy in the eyes of their communities? How were they able to maintain the life of a rebbe while balancing other duties of home, marriage, raising children, and running businesses? Did these women see themselves as boundary breakers? And how did their actions set the stage for the ordinations of Regina Jonas in 1935 and Sally Priesand in 1972?

We will never know the full stories of these women or the answers to these questions. We will never know the names of all the women who took on rabbinic roles during the Chasidic era. But we can remember them and their struggles and not let them be buried by history. As we celebrate forty years of women in the rabbinate—women who make their own way, have greater social freedom, and possess their own legitimacy—we can honor the struggles and achievements of Eidel, the Maid of Ludmir, and other women from the past who served in the rabbinic role and thus restore them to their proper place in our chain of tradition.

NOTES

1. Renee Levine Melammed, "His Story/Her Story: Hannah Rochel Veberm-acher," *Jerusalem Post*, April 11, 2012, http://www.jpost.com/Jewish-World/Judaism/His-StoryHer-Story-Hannah-Rochel-Vebermacher.

2. Samuel Abba Horodezky, *HaChasidut V'HaChasidim* (Tel Aviv: Dvir, 1923).

3. Ibid.

4. Zalman Meshullam Schachter-Shalomi, *Spiritual Intimacy: A Study of Counseling in Hasidism* (Northvale, NJ: Jason Aronson, 1991), 250–51.

5. Ibid.

6. Jerome R. Mintz, *Legends of the Hasidim: An Introduction to Hasidic Culture and Oral Tradition in the New World* (Northvale, NJ: Jason Aronson, 1995), 380–81.

7. Ibid.

8. Ibid.

9. Horodezky, "Hannah Rachel Werbermacher," in *HaChasidut V'HaChasidim*.

10. Ada Rappaport-Albert, "On Women in Hasidism," in *Jewish History: Essays in Honor of Chimen Abramsky*, ed. Ada Rappaport-Albert and Steven Zipperstein (London: Peter Halban, 1988), 495.

3

"THE LONG AND WINDING ROAD"
TO WOMEN RABBIS

Pamela S. Nadell, PhD

In 1889, on the front page of Philadelphia's *Jewish Exponent*, the writer Mary M. Cohen asked, "Could not—our *women*—be ministers?"[1] That question propelled forward a century-long debate over women's right to rabbinic ordination. Not until 1972 did the first woman in America shatter the historic tradition of an exclusively male rabbinate, and then only for Reform Judaism. But the road to women's ordination continued as the first women wound their way to their destinations in Reconstructionist and Conservative Judaism. In the twenty-first century, another, traveling along one of the byways of Orthodox Judaism, saw her journey come to a fruitful end.

Laying the Path for Women's Ordination: 1890s–1930s

The notion of women rabbis sits against the backdrop of the nineteenth-century woman's rights movement. Although best known for demanding female suffrage, a right won only in 1920, the woman's rights movement also railed against men for excluding women from the learned professions—from medicine, law, and the ministry. In the nineteenth century, a few women managed to break into these professions, becoming the first female doctors, lawyers, and even clergy.

The promise of ordaining women struck a particular chord among Reform Jews, whose leaders, proclaiming their intentions of emancipating women in the synagogue, pointed proudly to the seating of men and women together during worship as evidence of Reform's progressive stance on women's issues. Contemplating women in the rabbinate was consistent with Reform's championing of women's equality.[2] But, while some girls and women found their way into classes at Hebrew Union College (HUC) after the seminary was established in Cincinnati in 1875, none seems to have ever been considered a serious candidate for ordination. This includes Ray Frank (Litman), dubbed by the press "the girl rabbi of the golden west" for her lay preaching, teaching, and leading of religious services.[3]

In the late 1890s Hannah Solomon, the founding president of the National Council of Jewish Women and a Reform Jew, boasted, "We are receiving every possible encouragement from our rabbis, and should women desire to enter the ministry, there will be no obstacles thrown in their way."[4] Nevertheless, not until the 1920s, when the United States was in the midst of an era of rising expectations for women's new opportunities following the ratification of the Nineteenth Amendment granting women suffrage, did women seeking ordination begin carving out a trail others could follow. They drove the debate about women rabbis from the realm of the abstract to the actual.

The first, Martha Neumark (Montor), left her imprint on the path to women rabbis when, in 1921, she asked Hebrew Union College for a High Holy Day pulpit. Every fall, small Jewish communities scattered across North America invite rabbinical students to lead them in prayer on the holiest days of the year. Seventeen-year-old Neumark, who had started course work at HUC when she was just fourteen, asked for the same opportunity her male classmates would soon have—to lead and to preach to Jews in the hinterlands. She thus raised the very real question of what would happen if she completed the nine-year rabbinical course. Would Hebrew Union College ordain her?

For the next two years, HUC faculty, alumni, and trustees debated women's ordination. Delving into the classical texts of Jewish tradition, scholars lined up on opposite sides, shaping the lines of the debate that would, in decades to come, echo throughout American Jewish life. Some believed Jewish law unequivocally prohibited women from becoming rabbis. Others argued that nothing in Judaism forbade this, in large measure because the sages of old had simply never considered the question. In the end, the HUC Board of Governors voted, six laymen to two rabbis, to exclude women from the rabbinate.

Even as Neumark's hopes to become a rabbi were quashed, elsewhere, this time at New York's Jewish Institute of Religion (JIR), a non-denominational but decidedly liberal seminary founded by Rabbi Stephen S. Wise, Irma Levy Lindheim was raising the same challenge. By the time Lindheim joined JIR's inaugural class in the fall of 1922, this mother of five was a deeply committed Zionist who wanted higher education to fill in the gaping holes in her knowledge of Jews and Judaism. But in the spring of 1923, she asked the faculty to change her status from that of a special student to that of rabbinical student. The faculty yielded, and JIR announced that it trained men *and women* for the Jewish ministry. Nevertheless Lindheim, failing to complete the rabbinical course, eventually settled in Palestine and dedicated the remainder of her life to Zionism and the State of Israel.

However, she was not the only female special student at the Jewish Institute of Religion. Dr. Dora Askowith was also in her class. Askowith, who had earned a doctorate from Columbia University for a dissertation on Jews in the ancient Roman Empire, taught at New York City's Hunter College. Intensely interested in Jewish life and scholarship, Askowith, like Lindheim, sought ordination. As she explained, "I took the work at the Institute because of my deep interest in Judaica and Hebraica rather than because I sought to enter the ministry, though I hoped to open the road for women who might be desirous of being ordained."[5] But Askowith too left JIR without paving that road.

But in the 1930s, another woman stayed the course at JIR. Helen Levinthal (Lyons), the daughter of the prominent Brooklyn

Conservative rabbi Israel Levinthal, had the intensive Jewish education typical of rabbis' children. After college and graduate school, she joined a number of Jewish women's organizations and, perhaps to occupy her time, enrolled first as an auditor at JIR and then as a rabbinical student. As she approached her final year in school, the faculty debated what to do. In the end, they concluded that despite their earlier decision to train both women and men for the ministry, the time was not ripe for women's ordination.

In 1939, as her classmates became rabbis, Helen Levinthal graduated with a master's degree in Hebrew literature and a special certificate recognizing her accomplishments. *Time* magazine ordained her "as near to being a rabbi as a female might be." She told the press, "It is all a process of evolution....Some day there will be women rabbis."[6] Apparently, neither she nor the press knew then that already one woman had indeed completed the path to ordination.

In 1935 in Germany, Regina Jonas became the first woman rabbi. As a student at Berlin's Hochschule für die Wissenschaft des Judentums (College of Jewish Studies), Jonas had wanted to be a rabbi, but when she graduated in 1930, she received the only diploma women could earn, that of academic teacher of religion. Jonas, however, remained determined and, in 1935, took an oral exam in Jewish law with Rabbi Max Dienemann, one of the leaders of German Liberal Judaism, and he signed her rabbinic diploma. Although he cautioned her against using the title "rabbi" until she consulted with other authorities, from then until her death some called her Rabbiner Doktor Regina Jonas.

What joins the pioneers of women's ordination of the 1920s and 1930s to those who followed them and to those who argued their cause before them is that all believed Jewish tradition permitted women to be rabbis. Each on her own, and largely unaware that others had already made similar arguments, turned to the Jewish past, especially to the history of women in Judaism, to find support in Jewish tradition for her aims—even though, as a woman who wanted to be a rabbi, she seemed destined to overturn that very tradition. Martha Neumark, Irma Levy Lindheim, Dora Askowith, Helen Levinthal, and Regina Jonas, and those who championed their cause, all pointed to the prophetesses Miriam, Deborah, and Hulda, claiming that their religious leadership proved unequivocally that Judaism permitted women rabbis. They brought forth—in articles and speeches, in student sermons, and for Levinthal and Jonas, in their theses—remarkable medieval and modern Jewish women, those who taught, who founded schools, and who knew Jewish law, including several "accepted by their contemporaries as '*rabbinim.*'" In the end, they argued, as Regina Jonas did in her thesis "Can a Woman Hold Rabbinical Office?," that "other than prejudice and unfamiliarity, almost nothing opposes a woman holding the rabbinical office *halakhically,*" that is in terms of Jewish law.[7]

Finally, what binds the pioneers of the 1920s and 1930s is that each—with the tragic exception of Jonas, who was murdered by the Nazis at Auschwitz in December 1944—would again take up the cause of women's ordination. In decades to come, these women wrote seminary faculty and presidents, and even the press, trying to "complete the circle" of the path they had laid out for the women who followed them and who wanted to be rabbis.[8]

Closing the Circle in Reform

In 1947 another woman applied to the Jewish Institute of Religion bent on becoming a rabbi. This time the seminary, which once boasted it trained women for the ministry, responded that it was impossible to admit female students. That seemed to close the door on women rabbis. Yet, during the 1950s, the debate about women's ordination continued.

The decade opened with the extraordinary case of a woman succeeding her husband as rabbi. In 1924, when Temple Beth Israel in Meridian, Mississippi, called Rabbi William Ackerman to its pulpit, his wife, Paula Herskovitz Ackerman, was by his side. The *rebbetzin*, the rabbi's wife, was traditionally a full partner in her husband's rabbinate and was crucial to his success.[9] Ackerman was no exception. She taught Sabbath school and was active in the National Federation of Temple

Sisterhoods. When her husband was ill or away, she often substituted for him in the pulpit.

In November 1950, her husband of thirty-one years died. Temple Beth Israel's president asked the widow to lead them until they could find a new rabbi. Ackerman well understood what this meant: "I also know how revolutionary the idea is…if perhaps it will open a way for women students to train for congregational leadership—then my life would have some meaning."[10] Leading Reform rabbis opposed her. She was not ordained. She did not have the right education. She set a dangerous precedent. Would other rabbis' wives dare to follow in her footsteps? But despite the opposition, from December 1950 until the fall of 1953, Paula Ackerman was Temple Beth Israel's "rabbi."

However, disapproval of Ackerman did not mean that Reform rabbis opposed women's ordination in principle. In the mid-1950s, these rabbis returned again to the matter many had supported back in the 1920s. This time they were propelled by the news that the Presbyterian Church, one of the largest and most important of the mainline Protestant denominations, had decided, in 1955, to ordain female clergy and that Harvard Divinity School would begin accepting female students.

Now Reform's Central Conference of American Rabbis created a commission to study the question. Its 1956 report favored women's ordination provided, of course, that women completed the requisite rabbinical education. Yet the rabbis were convinced that the matter was purely hypothetical—there were no female candidates for the rabbinate, or so they presumed. But they were wrong. Other young women were poised to set out on the path plowed by the women who would have been rabbis, if they could have been rabbis, in the 1920s and 1930s.

This time their journey started at the University of Cincinnati. In 1957, Hebrew Union College–Jewish Institute of Religion (HUC-JIR)—the two colleges had merged in 1950—offered to University of Cincinnati students the chance to complete the first-year rabbinical curriculum as undergraduates. HUC-JIR hoped to speed young men on the road into the rabbinate in an era when American Judaism was exploding and in need of new rabbis. Scores of students took advantage of this opportunity. Among them were a dozen women. Some of the coeds saw Jewish education as the path to religious school teaching or scholarship. But a few wanted to be rabbis.

Among them was Sally Priesand. As a teenager at Cleveland's Beth Israel–The West Temple and at Reform's Goldman Union Camp Institute at Zionsville, Indiana, Priesand had found herself deeply attached to Judaism. Already her friends knew she hoped one day to become "Rabbi Sally."

In her junior year of high school Priesand wrote HUC-JIR to find out what she needed to do to get in. College officials responded cautiously. The school had never ordained a woman. Most women preferred the field of Jewish education. Nevertheless, in 1964, when Priesand entered her freshman year at the University of Cincinnati, she enrolled at HUC-JIR as an undergraduate. Already, the *Cleveland Plain Dealer* announced, "Girl Sets Her Goal to Be First Woman Rabbi."[11]

By 1968, when Priesand graduated with her BA and entered the regular rabbinical program, the question of women's ordination had become inextricably tied to the new wave of American feminism. Just as in the nineteenth century, the notion of women's ordination was set against the backdrop of the women's rights movement; now, in the 1960s, the second wave of American feminism drove forward the question of women rabbis.

The signs of feminism's second wave bursting forth were everywhere. In 1961, President John F. Kennedy convened a Commission on the Status of Women. Two years later Betty Friedan published *The Feminine Mystique*. Title VII of the 1964 Civil Rights Act prohibited discrimination in employment on the basis of race and sex. These events propelled American women to push anew on multiple frontiers, and all at once, for political, social, and economic equality. In the annals of American Judaism, Priesand appeared unique. But in the annals of the new wave of feminism, her ambition to become the first woman rabbi appeared simply as part of a larger story of tremendous changes under way for American women. As headlines blazoned "Women's 'Lib' on the March in the Churches" and reported more Protestant denominations ordaining women, *Time* and *Newsweek* covered "Rabbi Sally" in her student pulpits.

The publicity was crucial to Priesand's ultimate success. The attention of the press not only helped to sustain her but also to convince others to champion her cause. It guaranteed that in the end, if she finished rabbinical school, whatever HUC-JIR did would make national headlines.

The publicity led synagogues and Jewish groups to invite rabbinical student Priesand to come and speak. In these settings, she carefully distanced herself from radical "women's libbers"—inaccurately, but persistently, dubbed "bra burners" by the press. Instead, she presented herself as a champion of the movement that called for the right of men—and of women—to fulfill their potential. Having spoken her piece on feminism, she turned instead to what was really important to her, to Judaism—to God, Torah, and the Jewish people—and of how she hoped to become a rabbi, desiring to serve her people and to preserve Jewish tradition, not to overthrow it.

As Priesand entered her last year of rabbinical school, one major hurdle remained—her thesis. Deciding to write on the historic and changing role of the Jewish woman, she was unaware that all before her who had championed women rabbis had done the same thing. Now she found herself turning over a few pages in the history of the women who would have been rabbis, if they could have been rabbis. She found that in 1963, the members of the National Federation of Temple Sisterhoods, the women of Reform Judaism, had resolved in favor of women's ordination. Discovering Regina Jonas's story let her claim that she "was not truly the first woman rabbi," only the first ordained by a seminary.[12]

On June 3, 1972, the high school junior of a decade before who had written, "Although I am a girl, I would like very much to study for a rabbinical degree," was ordained rabbi, teacher, and preacher.[13] The first American woman had become a rabbi. She would not be the last.

A Winding Road Becomes a Highway:
Reconstructionist and Conservative Judaism

The debate over women's ordination was never confined exclusively to Reform Judaism. Mary M. Cohen, who first raised it, was not a Reform Jew. Each time the controversy about women's ordination had swelled in Reform circles, it had spilled over to other sectors of American Jewish religious life. As Cyrus Adler, president of the Conservative Movement's Jewish Theological Seminary of America (JTS), declared in the 1920s, "So far as the Jewish Theological Seminary is concerned, it would not entertain the idea for a moment."[14]

A half century later with Rabbi Priesand's ordination approaching and with the women's movement urging it forward, the question, which had periodically surfaced in Conservative Judaism in the past, emerged anew and for far longer than a moment. By now, those raising the issue also knew that the Reconstructionists would soon also ordain their first female rabbi.

Reconstructionist Judaism, for many decades the liberal wing of the Conservative Movement, had split off when, in 1968, its leaders opened a new rabbinical school, Philadelphia's Reconstructionist Rabbinical College (RRC). From the first the RRC admitted both women and men. In the fall of 1969, Sandy Eisenberg Sasso, who, although raised a Reform Jew, had become intrigued with the ideology of Reconstructionism's founder, Mordecai M. Kaplan, enrolled. In 1974, she was ordained.

In the spring of 1972, committed Conservative Jewish—and passionately feminist—women began vociferously demanding religious equality in their movement. Three months before Sally Priesand was ordained, a group of these women, calling themselves Ezrat Nashim (referring both to "the help of women" and also to the women's court in the ancient Jerusalem Temple) announced that they had tired of apologetics and of the parades of the great Jewish women of the past. Decrying women's "separate but equal," second-class status in

Conservative Judaism, they demanded full religious equality, including admission to rabbinical school.

At the same time, other young women were already applying to JTS's rabbinical school. Over the course of the next decade, as more and more such women kept writing for applications, they compelled the seminary's leaders to keep confronting the question. Some entered other JTS graduate programs, pursuing as master's and doctoral candidates as much of the rabbinical curriculum as they could on their own, hoping that when, in the near future, the faculty would accept them into the rabbinical school, they would already be well on their way to becoming rabbis.

Meanwhile Conservative leaders struggled with the question. For a long decade between 1972 and 1983, the issue both drained and electrified Conservative rabbis, JTS faculty and students, the women who would be rabbis if they could be rabbis, and their supporters and opponents out in Conservative congregations across America. Some young women reluctantly abandoned their movement and were ordained at other seminaries. Meanwhile, Conservative leaders engaged in an intricate political dance of shifting alliances, studies undertaken, commissions formed, hearings held, motions tabled, and votes counted. At last, in October 1983, the JTS faculty voted to admit women to the rabbinical school. A year later, Amy Eilberg, one of the women waiting in the wings who had been biding her time by taking the curriculum necessary for ordination, entered rabbinical school with the first class of women accepted. In May 1985, JTS chancellor Gerson Cohen, who had personally shifted his view on women's ordination over the course of the heated debate, ordained her a rabbi.

A Byway off the Highway: Orthodoxy

Even as those within Conservative Judaism concluded their debate on women rabbis, Orthodox Jews launched theirs, as some voices, among them leading Orthodox feminist activist Blu Greenberg, began asking

"Will there be Orthodox women rabbis?"[15] In 1993, Haviva Ner-David, then known as Haviva Krasner-Davidson, applied to Yeshiva University's rabbinical school. Her application was ignored.[16]

Orthodox Judaism, however, encompasses an extraordinarily wide spectrum of voices and views, from those who one historian has styled as "accommodators"—Orthodox Jews who observe halachah but whose dress, education, and employment integrate them fairly well into American life—to the "resisters"—whose distinctive dress, educational patterns, and rigid gender roles limit, to a great extent, interactions with modern American culture.[17]

Only some sectors of the "accommodationist" Orthodox have been open to experimenting with innovative strategies for pushing women along the byway toward Orthodox ordination. They have permitted women who have the requisite training to become legal advisors, to answer questions women pose about observing the laws of family purity, and to deal with issues related to fertility and sexuality. Some Orthodox rabbis have appointed female congregational interns, whose responsibilities for teaching and preaching are analogous to those of rabbis.[18] In 2006, in Israel, Rabbi Aryeh Strikovsky granted Haviva Ner-David what she calls private *s'michah*, that is, Orthodox ordination, but which he characterizes as "more an official recognition of her studies and not intended to be construed as an ordination." Because Strikovsky also affirmed that she had "covered exactly the tractates and the issues that men have to master in order to get ordination," Ner-David took this as a signal that she could "act in the role of a rabbi" if her community recognized her as one.[19]

A few other Orthodox women have also received private ordination.[20] In the United States, the best known is Rabba Sara Hurwitz. Originally "ordained" by Rabbi Avi Weiss in 2009 with the invented title of "maharat," an acronym from the Hebrew for a leader in legal, spiritual, and Torah matters, Weiss changed Hurwitz's title to "rabba" in 2010 when he made her a full member of the rabbinic staff at his Hebrew Institute of Riverdale in New York. The new title sparked a firestorm of condemnation from the resisters in the Orthodox world.[21]

Nevertheless, Rabba Hurwitz's participation in several public programs featuring the first female rabbis finds her standing alongside Rabbis Priesand, Sasso, and Eilberg.[22] This suggests to many that she is indeed the first Orthodox female rabbi. Yet, movement on women's ordination in the Orthodox world, even in the quarters open to feminist change, remains slow and tentative.

The Road Taken

Rabbi Sally Priesand, Rabbi Sandy Sasso, Rabbi Amy Eilberg, and Rabba Sara Hurwitz set out on trails laid by others, but they completed the course. As they reached the end of the journey to women's ordination, they looked behind to see the long and winding road they had forged expand into a highway. Hundreds of women have followed Rabbis Priesand, Sasso, and Eilberg into the Reform, Reconstructionist, and Conservative rabbinates. Others have now begun to follow Rabba Hurwitz into Orthodox congregations.[23]

At the end of their journey to ordination, these rabbis halted before a new and unmapped pathway, one that they and those behind them would pave. How women rabbis would be received; the questions and issues they would raise for their seminaries, congregants, and male colleagues; and the challenges they would pose to Jewish tradition by bringing women's voices and perspectives to bear would line the surface of the road taken into the future by the women who had become rabbis.

NOTES

1. Mary M. Cohen, quoted in Pamela S. Nadell, *Women Who Would Be Rabbis: A History of Women's Ordination, 1889–1985* (Boston: Beacon Press, 1998), 1. This chapter is based on my book *Women Who Would Be Rabbis: A History of Women's Ordination, 1889–1985*. Unless otherwise noted, all material appears there. I have cited

pages in the book for all direct quotations. Original sources for all quotations can be found in the notes to those pages.

2. Reform's stance on women's equality was largely rhetorical; see Karla Goldman, "Women in Reform Judaism: Between Rhetoric and Reality," in *Women Remaking American Judaism*, ed. Riv-Ellen Prell (Detroit: Wayne State University Press, 2007), 109–34.

3. Nadell, *Women Who Would Be Rabbis*, 39.

4. Ibid., 45.

5. Ibid., 79.

6. Ibid., 85.

7. Ibid., 79, 85. On Jonas, see Elisa Klapheck, *Fräulein Rabbiner Jonas: The Story of the First Woman Rabbi* (San Francisco: Jossey-Bass, 2004).

8. Nadell, *Women Who Would Be Rabbis*, 104.

9. Shuly Rubin Schwartz, *The Rabbi's Wife: The Rebbetzin in American Jewish Life* (New York: New York University Press, 2006).

10. Nadell, *Women Who Would Be Rabbis*, 121–22.

11. Ibid., 148.

12. Ibid., 168.

13. Ibid.

14. Ibid., 174.

15. Ibid., 215.

16. Haviva Ner-David, *Life on the Fringes: A Feminist Journey Toward Traditional Rabbinic Ordination* (Needham, MA: JFL Books, 2000).

17. Jeffrey S. Gurock, "Resisters and Accommodators: Varieties of Orthodox Rabbis in America, 1886–1983," in *American Rabbinate: A Century of Continuity and Change, 1883–1983*, ed. Jacob Rader Marcus and Abraham J. Peck (Cincinnati: American Jewish Archives, 1985), 10–97.

18. For an excellent discussion of Orthodoxy and feminism, see the chapter "Open and Closed to Feminism," in Jeffrey S. Gurock, *Orthodox Jews in America* (Bloomington: Indiana University Press, 2009), 273–311.

19. Strikovsky, quoted in ibid., 281–82. For Ner-David's claim that she has *s'michah*, see Haviva Ner-David, "Orthodox Women Rabbis: It's About Time," *Jerusalem Post*, December 3, 2010.

20. Ner-David, "Orthodox Women Rabbis: It's About Time."

21. For the statement, see Ben Harris, "Maharat Becomes Rabbah," *Jewish Telegraphic Agency*, January 10, 2010; Debra Nussbaum Cohen, "Woman 'Rabba' Roils Orthodox World," *Forward*, March 3 2010.

22. Listen, for example, to "Leading the Way: America's First Women Rabbis," National Museum of American Jewish History, June 4, 2012, parts 1 and 2, available from http://www.nmajh.org/publicprograms/.

23. Rabba Hurwitz is dean of Yeshivat Maharat, which is "the first institution to train Orthodox women as spiritual leaders and halakhic authorities" (http://yeshivatmaharat.org/).

4

REDISCOVERING REGINA JONAS
THE FIRST WOMAN RABBI

RABBI LAURA GELLER

We[1] gathered inside a huge mausoleum-like cave where the cremated ashes of those who died at the Terezin concentration camp had once been stored. We gathered to dedicate a plaque that reads: "To be blessed by God means to give wherever one steps in every life situation blessing, kindness, faithfulness."

The text continues: "Regina Jonas (1902–44), the first woman rabbi in history, spoke these words in a sermon at Terezin. Born in Berlin, Jonas was ordained in 1935. She served the Jewish community of Berlin in a rabbinical capacity from 1937 through November 1942, when she was deported to Terezin. With extraordinary spiritual strength, she continued to preach uplifting sermons, give lectures and provide pastoral care to her fellow prisoners. In October 1944, she was deported to Auschwitz, where she was murdered."

We chanted the *El Malei Rachamim* in her memory, asking that the soul of HaRav Malka Reyna bat Ze'ev Wolf v'Sarah find perfect peace.

At that moment, I could feel her soul soar.

It was the first time that prayer was sung for her. She left no survivors, and her legacy was nearly forgotten.

What we know of Regina Jonas is that she was born in Berlin in 1902 into a poor, Orthodox Jewish family. As a young girl, she attended the Rykestrasse Synagogue, where the rabbi, Dr. Max Weil (1873–1942), tried to connect Orthodox practice with a liberal approach to Judaism, including allowing girls to have bat mitzvah ceremonies. At his urging, Jonas continued her Jewish studies at the liberal Hochschule für die Wissenschaft des Judentums (Higher Institute for Jewish Studies) in Berlin from 1924 to 1930. All the other women in her classes were there to become Jewish teachers; Jonas, like the men with whom she studied, wanted to become a rabbi. In her quest, she had little support, except from Rabbi Eduard Baneth, who was determined to ordain her. Just before she finished her training, Rabbi Baneth died. Her thesis on the topic "Can a Woman Be a Rabbi according to Halachic Sources?" received praise from the rabbis at the Hochschule; however, none of them, not even the influential Rabbi Dr. Leo Baeck, who admired her scholarship, piety, and commitment, agreed to ordain her. As head of the National Representation of Jews in Germany, he apparently was unwilling to risk the unity of the Jewish community in the face of the Nazi threat. So upon graduation, Jonas received a certificate qualifying her as an "Academic Teacher of Religion."

When Hitler came to power in 1933, all Jewish children were forced out of the German schools, so even nonreligious families turned to Jewish schools, where Jonas taught. Students who survived the war remembered her as an inspiring teacher who encouraged them to celebrate being Jewish in spite of the anti-Semitic persecution they endured.

On December 27, 1935, Regina Jonas was ordained in a private ceremony by Rabbi Max Dienemann, the president of the General Association of Rabbis in Germany and a well-known scholar. Still, Fraulein Rabbinerin Jonas (Miss Rabbi Jonas) struggled to be accepted. An 1936 article in *Der Israelit*, an Orthodox newspaper, cites a remark by Rabbi Joseph Carlebach (1883–1942) describing Jonas's ordination as a form of "treason and a caricature of Judaism" and as "the introduction of hysteria to the sacred halls of our temple."

At first, Rabbi Jonas performed her rabbinical duties in hospitals, in homes for the elderly, and in schools. As more rabbis chose to leave Germany, she began to receive invitations to preach in synagogues in Berlin and elsewhere in the country, even as the Nazis forced her to work in a factory. In November 1942, she and her mother were deported to Terezin, where she continued teaching and worked with Victor Frankl, the famous psychoanalyst (who would later write *Man's Search for Meaning*), to counsel and comfort the newly arrived prisoners.

In October 1944, Rabbi Jonas and her mother were transported to Auschwitz, where they were murdered.

Though some survivors of Terezin, including Leo Baeck and Victor Frankl, certainly knew Jonas, they didn't refer to her by name in their writings. The reason, in part, may be found in the forward to Frankl's classic *Man's Search for Meaning*, in which he wrote that he erased from his memory everything that happened before he entered Auschwitz. Part of what he erased was the legacy of Regina Jonas.

How, then, do we know her story?

Her name began to appear in the early 1970s. Rabbi Sally Priesand, the first woman ordained by the Hebrew Union College–Jewish Institute of Religion (1972), mentions Rabbi Jonas in her book *Judaism and the New Woman* (1975). Jonas is cited in a 1972 article by Rabbi Jacob R. Marcus, founding director of the American Jewish Archives, and by Rabbi Alexander Guttmann, in an article celebrating the hundredth anniversary of the Hochschule für die Wissenschaft des Judentums. She is also mentioned in *The Jewish Almanac* by Richard Siegel and Carl Rheins (1980). Despite these passing references, Jonas remained an obscure figure in the history of the Reform Movement. In my five years as a rabbinical student at HUC-JIR (1971–76), not once did I hear her name.

Rabbi Jonas's story didn't really come to light until 1991, when Dr. Katerina von Kellenbach, the German-born scholar and professor of religious studies at St. Mary's College of Maryland, discovered a small archive in East Berlin containing Regina Jonas's papers. It was housed in the Centrum Judaica in the Neue Synagogue, in East Berlin. This had been the spiritual home of the famous composer Louis Lewandowski.

Among her papers is a note dated November 6, 1942, written by an acquaintance of Jonas, explaining that these documents were given to him on the day that Jonas and her mother were deported to Terezin. It's believed that this acquaintance was deported a few days later. Jonas's biographer, Rabbi Elisa Klapheck, wrote that Rabbi Jonas "designed her legacy. She was very aware of what she wanted to leave for the...world. She took into consideration that one day someone would come and find it and write about her."[2]

Her papers, contained in a small box, included a photo of her wearing rabbinical robes and holding a book in her hand, a copy of her thesis, and the ordination certificate written by Rabbi Max Dienemann, which includes the following words: "Since I saw that her heart is with God and Israel, and that she dedicates her soul to her goal, and that she fears God, and that she passed the examination in matters of religious law, I herewith certify that she is qualified to answer questions of religious law and entitled to hold the rabbinic office. And may God protect her and guide her on all her ways." Rabbi Dienemann's signature was attested to by Rabbi Leo Baeck.

Jonas had also kept some newspaper clippings from Germany and Switzerland that referred to the challenges she faced in her struggle for acceptance as a rabbi, letters from Jewish refugees abroad thanking her for taking care of their parents who had remained in Germany, and thank-you notes from German congregations where she had preached. This archival collection inspired Klapheck, who was born in Germany and would became the first woman rabbi in the Netherlands, to write her 2004 biography of Jonas. Most recently, Diane Groo's documentary film *Regina* fills out the Jonas story. It reveals that shortly before Rabbi Jonas was deported to Terezin, she fell in love with the much-older Rabbi Joseph Norden. In a letter dated July 13, 1942, just as he was about to be deported from Hamburg to Terezin, he wrote, "The time has come to say goodbye...maybe Berliners will be sent, too. In that case perhaps there will be a chance for us to see each other again." They never did see each other again.

A few of Jonas's papers remain at Terezin, including a handwritten list of more than twenty lecture topics delivered at the camp, including the role of women in Judaism, women in the Bible, women in the Talmud, and Jewish holidays and beliefs. An excerpt from one of these sermons survives:

> Our Jewish people was planted by God into history as a blessed nation. "Blessed by God" means to offer blessings, loving-kindness, and loyalty, regardless of place and situation. Humility before God, selfless love for His creatures, sustain the world. It is Israel's task to build these pillars of the world—man and woman, woman and man alike have taken this upon themselves in Jewish loyalty. Our work in Theresienstadt [Terezin], serious and full of trials though it is, also serves this end: to be God's servants and as such to move from earthly spheres to eternal ones. May all our work be a blessing for Israel's future (and the future of humanity)....Upright "Jewish men" and "brave, noble women" were always the sustainers of our people. May we be found worthy by God to be numbered in the circle of these women and men....The reward of a mitzvah is the recognition of the great deed by God.

It is signed: "Rabbi Regina Jonas, formerly of Berlin."

All women rabbis stand on the shoulders of Rabbi Regina Jonas. She had been totally alone, independently ordained, unsupported by most of the Jews around her. I wondered if Rabbi Jonas had imagined us when she left her papers to be discovered. Could she have imagined the rebirth of Jewish life in Europe and the role of so many young women rabbis and activists in nurturing that renewal? Could she have imagined the flowering of Jewish scholarship from gifted women academics or the number of Reform, Conservative, Reconstructionist, and, even Orthodox woman rabbis? Could she have imagined the way feminism has totally transformed Jewish life so that women's experience is no longer marginal and that women's stories are fully part of the larger Jewish story?

We don't know the exact date of Rabbi Jonas's death, but we will say Kaddish for her. The memory of Regina Jonas is a blessing.

NOTES

1. In July 2014, a delegation of rabbis, scholars, and lay leaders traveled to Berlin and Terezin to memorialize and celebrate the life of Regina Jonas. The trip was organized as part of the U.S. Commission for the Preservation of America's Heritage Abroad, the Hebrew Union College–Jewish Institute of Religion, and the Jewish Women's Archive. Participants included pioneering American women: Rabbi Sally Priesand, ordained in 1972 by HUC-JIR; Rabbi Sandy Sasso, ordained in 1974 by the Reconstructionist Rabbinical College; Rabbi Amy Eilberg, ordained in 1985 by the Jewish Theological Seminary; and Rabba Sara Hurwitz, ordained by Rabbi Avi Weiss in 2009.

2. Elisa Klapheck and Toby Axelrod. *Fraulein Rabbiner Jonas: The Story of the First Woman Rabbi* (New York: Jossey-Bass, 2004)

5

THE WOMEN WHO SET THE STAGE

Celebrating Over One Hundred Years of Women of Reform Judaism

Rabbi Marla J. Feldman

I was blessed to have had the opportunity to become a rabbi and serve the Jewish community in a time when the doors to the rabbinate were open to women. As we approach the forty-fifth anniversary of Sally Priesand's ordination, I am acutely aware that this was not always the case. Rabbi Priesand and the generation of pioneering women who came before me pushed through closed doors and laid out a welcome mat for women like me. We owe them a debt of gratitude for their perseverance.

But even before Rabbi Priesand's ordination there were women chipping away at the barriers to women's spiritual leadership. Generations of Reform women as far back as the late 1800s advocated for the ordination of women; they brought women out of the kitchen and into the center of Reform Jewish life. They set the stage for women to take their place on the bimah and in the boardroom. They, too, deserve our gratitude, not only for their role in the past, but also for what they continue to bring to our congregations, our communities, and the Jewish world at large. These are the women of our sisterhoods, auxiliaries, and women's groups; they were, and are, Women of Reform Judaism.

While Pamela S. Nadell brought to life the "women who would be rabbis" in her seminal book of the same name,[1] much remains to be written of the women who stood by their side as lay leaders. These unnamed women supported them, trained them, and raised up generations of Reform Jews who would eventually bring to fruition the dream and the promise of equality for women in the Reform Movement. As Nadell wisely cautions in her introductory remarks, "As the story of the women who asked to become rabbis unfolds, this book echoes what so many others have already affirmed, that uncovering women's history remains a political enterprise. Women need to know that others preceding them have wrestled with the same questions and ideas. Without this knowledge, they remain disadvantaged, unable to build upon the creativity of those who came before."[2]

Reform Women's History

Women of Reform Judaism (WRJ), formerly the National Federation of Temple Sisterhoods (NFTS), celebrated its milestone one-hundredth anniversary in 2013. Formed before women even had the right to vote or serve on the board of the Union of American Hebrew Congregations (UAHC, now the Union for Reform Judaism, or URJ), this historic organization was initially convened by the men of the Movement then gathering for the 1913 Biennial held in Cincinnati, Ohio. Many of the early leaders were the wives of UAHC board members and congregational rabbis. The first meeting of the NFTS brought together 156 delegates from 49 sisterhoods. Their mandate was to support the growth of congregations and to bring their unique skills as wives and mothers from their homes into congregational life.

The opening address of their first gathering was given by Rabbi David Philipson, who provided a brief overview of the role of women in Jewish life and the expanded opportunities available to them within the Reform Movement. His perception of equality was inspiring and aspirational, if not yet complete:

The last word in woman's relation to the congregation will not be spoken until she be received into full membership, if she so desires, on the same footing as man. This is the case in some of our congregations, but not in all. If a woman is willing and desires to bear the full burden of membership and to incur all the responsibilities involved, why shall she not be permitted to do so? There is no valid reason against this and all reasons for it.[3]

Further, he clarified in his address the anticipated role that these women's auxiliaries would have in their newly constituted federation and with their combined strength:

I should like to see in every congregation women enlisted in the high service of bringing the homes and the congregations into close relation. I should like to see every mother in our congregation a committee of one to work for our schools by sending her children, for our confirmation classes by having her children confirmed, for our post confirmation and other young people's classes by inducing her sons and daughters to attend. It is for mothers to reach mothers, and possibly a woman's organization with a committee of mothers to persuade mothers to interest themselves along these lines is the best way of reaching such a consummation so devoutly to be wished. All this fine and necessary work and other work of a similar kind can be and in all likelihood largely is, accomplished through the women's congregational organizations.[4]

The opening addresses offered by the leading rabbis of the Movement at the time reinforced the message that the women were needed to support the work of the men by furthering the education of their children. With some ambivalence about their role as leaders, the women were charged to inspire and enrich their congregations and to bring culture and morality to the growing, modern Reform Movement in North America:

Women organize not to change institutions, but to maintain them. It is the function of women to uphold what is necessary and valuable, and, when women come together with a common aim and for concerted action, you may be sure some large social interest is at stake. Woman is [*sic*] conservative, and saves for us the goods of culture and religion men so often jeopardize. There is good reason, even though it be unconscious, for every large movement on the part of women, and this effort of the Jewish women of this country to organize for the specific purpose of doing what they can for American Judaism is demanded by the times and the conditions. The Jewish men of this country built up the congregation, the lodge, the temples, the asylums, the colleges and seminaries and the schools. And they have made them efficient. Now the opportunity and the need of the Jewish woman has arrived. These institutions must have her pervasive influence, her moralizing presence, her motherly thoughtfulness and her piety.[5]

To be sure, the women took up this challenge, establishing and running religious schools, raising funds for scholarships for rabbinical students at the Hebrew Union College (HUC), and forming "Young Folks Temple League" chapters, which would eventually become the National Federation of Temple Youth (NFTY). They took quite seriously the need to deepen public religious experience within congregations. Among their earliest resolutions during their first biennial convention in 1915 was a call for sisterhoods to enhance the Passover seder and Shabbat *Kiddush*. Their place in the congregational kitchen was thus established early on. They called upon member sisterhoods to provide free religious school education for children who could not otherwise afford to attend (1917) and to fund the congregational libraries (1919). They called for congregations to provide children's services for the holidays and pledged to help run them (1921), and committed themselves to funding education and training for religious school teachers (1923). Other early resolutions called for NFTS to support resources for home observance (1923) as well as the broad range of holiday observances within congregations, setting the stage for many publications about Jewish holidays, rituals, and observance that would be produced by NFTS/WRJ over the years. Sisterhoods have been doing this work ever since.

But the founding leaders of NFTS/WRJ also took seriously the need for Jewish education and leadership development among their own members. One of their initial programs launched in 1913 was the creation of women's study circles for their own self-edification. Resolutions in 1919 urged women to subscribe to Jewish periodicals and called on sisterhood leaders to attend religious services on a regular basis.

Among the first committees established by NFTS was the National Committee on Religion. Through its work, the organization encouraged new roles for women and girls in congregational life, including the establishment of congregational choirs, where both boys and girls could raise their voices in worship. Initially providing support for vacationing clergy, the women took responsibility for leading summer worship services and for the first time carved out space for themselves on the bimah. In her 1919 report of the activities of the NFTS National Committee on Religion, Mrs. Leon Goodman reported on this new phenomenon:

> The members of the Sisterhoods are also expressing for themselves their religion [*sic*] attitude. Many Sisterhoods open all meetings with prayer and a scripture reading. Several Sisterhoods have even taken complete charge of summer services. One Sisterhood reports the reading of the Sabbath prayers and congregational singing as a notable feature.[6]

Within a few years, the summer services led by women transitioned into a new trend to hold an annual Sisterhood Sabbath service for the congregation. The institution of these Sisterhood Sabbaths expanded opportunities for women to lead worship, read Torah, and preach from the bimah and exposed increasing numbers of Reform Jews to women as spiritual and ritual leaders. Such efforts would lay the foundation and help generate the cultural shift that was necessary to alter attitudes and eventually change the policies of Reform institutions regarding women's spiritual leadership.

In 1948, NFTS produced its first *Book of Prayers*, written specifically for women to use during their meetings and worship services. Today this practice continues with the publication of WRJ's Covenant Book Series[7] and, most notably, the landmark publication of *The Torah: A*

Women's Commentary.[8] It was through the work of NFTS and its National Committee on Religion that Reform women first found, and raised, their spiritual voice.

Although they embraced the role in congregational life that had been assigned to them, the women of NFTS were not satisfied by its limitations. At its third biennial convention, founding president Carrie O. Simon, wife of Rabbi Abram Simon of Washington Hebrew Congregation, noted the advancing role of women in Reform institutional life:

> There is a fair unanimity of opinion that the congregations should be more democratic and that ways should be devised whereby the personal responsibility of every man and woman should be given full scope. I note that many congregations have gone so far as to elect women on their official Board; the future of this experiment will be watched with intense interest all over the country.[9]

It would not be long before the women of NFTS challenged the institutions of Reform Judaism to give them a voice, even if not an equal role, among its leadership. Did the men who convened this women's association in 1913 foresee that by 1923 they would demand a seat on congregational boards and on the UAHC Board itself?[10]

Advocates for Women's Ordination

The prospect of women as rabbis was also a topic of conversation early on in the history of NFTS. Mention of "women in ministry" pops up periodically in the earliest reported minutes of the organization. By way of example, in her welcome address to the delegates of the 1923 Assembly, Mrs. Daniel P. Hays noted:

> The position of woman has undergone a great change in the past twenty-five years by reason of economic and social conditions, and the enlightenment of man. Now with her enfranchisement she has shown her capability in many fields, education, medicine, Law,

civics, in official positions in city, state and nation. We want to add the ministry. Surely there is a place for her in religion.[11]

Carrie Simon was a passionate advocate for expanding the role of women in Reform leadership as both lay leaders and clergy. As the founding president of NFTS (1913–1919), she traveled around the country speaking in congregations and establishing sisterhoods, and her travels continued after her term as she endeavored to raise funds to build the dormitory at the Hebrew Union College in Cincinnati. During her travels, she not only raised funds for HUC but also spoke out to change its policy in regard to the ordination of women. On the occasion of the NFTS Silver Jubilee in 1938, she reflected on the emerging role of women over the course of the organization's first twenty-five years:

> We find that Temple duties and religious schools, Jewish litera-
> ture and the larger realm of Jewish and adult education are within
> their mature and ample sphere. Who knows but that before many
> decades, theirs will also be the Ministry of Preaching! This is a
> Trend toward the Golden Jubilee of the National Federation of
> Temple Sisterhoods.[12]

Simon's prediction proved prophetic—it was indeed during the golden anniversary of NFTS in 1963 that the issue would emerge in earnest. Simon had found a kindred spirit in Jane Evans, the first executive director of NFTS (1933–1976), who continued Simon's campaign to seek the ordination of women for the next twenty-five years. The issue attained national attention in the 1950s when Paula Ackerman, a board member of NFTS, was tasked with serving Temple Beth Israel in Meridian, Mississippi, after her husband, the congregation's rabbi, passed away. Evans secured the support of the president of the Central Conference of American Rabbis (CCAR), Rabbi Barnett Brickner, who initiated a reconsideration of the CCAR policy regarding women's ordination. The CCAR reaffirmed an earlier position in support of the ordination of women. Yet, in the absence of any female students at the Hebrew Union College (which had recently merged with the

New York–based Jewish Institute of Religion), their deliberations were only theoretical.

Evans then brought her quest to the leadership of the UAHC, calling for the ordination of women in an address at the 1957 Biennial in Toronto. "Women are uniquely suited by temperament, intuition and spiritual sensitivity to be rabbis," she said.[13] To the women in attendance at their NFTS Assembly that year, she noted in her director's report that of all the funds contributed by NFTS to HUC-JIR over the years, except for one graduate fellowship in Jewish music, none of the funds raised had supported a women.[14] Surely her dissatisfaction would have been shared by the women in the room who collectively had raised hundreds of thousands of dollars (today's equivalent of many millions of dollars) to support HUC-JIR.

Her advocacy up to that point was to no avail. Frustrated by the lack of response from the male-dominated bodies of the Reform Movement, Evans placed the issue on the agenda of the NFTS Fiftieth Anniversary Biennial Assembly in 1963. Following two years of planning, study, and outreach, a resolution calling for the ordination of women was overwhelmingly adopted, with a demand that the major institutions of the Reform Movement be convened to resolve the matter expeditiously.

No such gathering of Reform leaders took place. Yet, less than ten years later, Sally Priesand was ordained by HUC-JIR. No doubt, the years of cajoling, organizing, challenging, and demanding change had a role in making that moment possible.

Finding Common Cause

The relentless determination of Carrie O. Simon, Jane Evans, and the thousands of sisterhood women they inspired helped unlock the doors for Sally, for me, and for all our women colleagues. The laywomen of Reform Judaism, from the inception of NFTS until today, set the stage for women in congregational leadership. They placed women around the Movement's institutional tables, carved out new roles for women in the sanctuary, and helped women discover their spiritual voice in prayer. They tirelessly nurtured the attitudinal changes taking place in American Jewish life and brought those changes into our synagogues.

All of this history begs the question: why do most of us (women rabbis) see as our spiritual matriarchs, women who served pulpits, like Ray Frank, Martha Neumark, Paula Ackerman, Regina Jonas, and Sally Priesand, rather than the laywomen who laid the groundwork for us to succeed? The women of NFTS were not trailblazers like these other historical figures; but they were the ones who cleared the trail. They did not seek a revolution but painstakingly led the Movement to evolve—and to do so at a more rapid pace than might have been the case otherwise.

Admittedly, I and many of my colleagues did not consider sisterhood women to be our inspiration as we claimed our place on the bimah. I have spoken often about being the first woman rabbi in each community I served in the early years of my rabbinate and have discussed the dilemma of doing so without prior role models. Despite having warm and loving relationships with the sisterhood women of my congregations, I failed to acknowledge the many ways in which they made it possible for me to thrive in my rabbinate.

Again, as Nadell asserts, "uncovering women's history remains a political enterprise."[15] It is no surprise that as the first generation of women rabbis and cantors we sought to distinguish ourselves, as professional clergy, from the laywomen of our congregations. Like so many others, we may have dismissed their value by relegating them to the kitchen or the rummage sale. We may have viewed them more as mothers than as mentors, dismissing the insight and wisdom that comes from their many decades of experience.

The publication of *The Torah: A Women's Commentary* once and for all established WRJ as a leading force in serious women's scholarship. It marked yet another seminal moment in Reform Jewish history. Leveraging the resources of women clergy, scholars, philanthropists, and lay leaders, WRJ's historic contribution to Jewish learning and knowledge would not have been possible by any one of those cohorts alone. That publication marked a new role for Women of Reform Judaism as a "connector" for Jewish women beyond the ranks of sisterhoods and women's groups.

Now that we are in the second, or even the third, generation of women serving as rabbis and cantors, perhaps we are secure enough in our respective roles to find common cause with our lay partners. Just as the women of WRJ have accepted a rabbi at the helm for the first time (me!), it is time for women clergy to finally let down our guard to see the women who are lay leaders in our congregations as true allies. Whether as female religious professionals or lay leaders in our congregations, we are all working to enhance the religious life of Reform Jews, educate and inspire our youth, enrich women's spiritual growth, advance the role of women in society, and anticipate the needs of the next generation of women. We may use different tools and experiences to accomplish this work, but both professional and volunteer women play roles that are equally vibrant and necessary to advance Reform Jewish life.

What might be possible if the professional women and lay women of Reform Judaism worked collaboratively? There is tremendous power in sisterhood, yet so much of that power has yet to be tapped. It is difficult to believe, but the Women's Rabbinic Network (WRN) and WRJ have never engaged in a joint enterprise. What might such a venture make possible? What if WRJ and WRN worked together, along with the CCAR, URJ, and other arms of the Movement, to secure equal pay for professional Jewish women, or to enhance the bat mitzvah experience for girls, or to advocate in the public arena for women's health? Separately we may make an impact on some of these issues, but working together, there is no limit to what we can accomplish.

There is much we can learn from the women—lay and professional—who set the stage for us. After forty years of women in the rabbinate and one hundred years of laywomen organized to advance Reform Judaism, the show has just begun.

NOTES

1. Pamela S. Nadell, *Women Who Would Be Rabbis: A History of Women's Ordination, 1889–1985* (Boston: Beacon Press, 1998).

2. Ibid., xiii.

3. "Woman and the Congregation," address given by Rabbi David Philipson, DD, as reported in the minutes of the inaugural meeting of National Federation of Temple Sisterhoods, Cincinnati, January 21, 1913.

4. Ibid.

5. "The American Jewess," address by Rabbi Louis Grossmann, DD, as reported in the minutes of the inaugural meeting of National Federation of Temple Sisterhoods, Cincinnati, January 21, 1913. Emphasis is author's.

6. "Report of the National Committee on Religion," Mrs. Leon Goodman, chairman, as recorded in the minutes of the executive board, 1919, Louisville, p. 21.

7. *Covenant of the Heart* (1993), *Covenant of the Soul*, (2000), *Covenant of the Spirit* (2005), and *Covenant of the Generations* (2013), published by Women of Reform Judaism, New York.

8. *The Torah: A Woman's Commentary*, ed. Dr. Tamara Cohn Eskenazi and Rabbi Andrea L. Weiss (New York: WRJ and URJ Press, 2008).

9. Carrie O. Simon, "President's Message," as reported in the minutes of the NFTS Biennial Assembly, 1919, Boston.

10. Resolution on Representation on Union Boards and Committees (1923):

Whereas, women by their loyalty, cooperation and devotion to the best interests of the synagogues have been elected to the Board of Trustees of numerous congregations throughout the country, and

Whereas, the National Federation of Temple Sisterhoods has shown the same devotion, loyalty and cooperation to the interests of the Union of American Hebrew Congregations,

Be it resolved, that the Pennsylvania Federation of Temple Sisterhoods recommends that the Executive Board of the Union of American Hebrew Congregations grant the same privilege and consideration to representatives of the National Federation of Temple Sisterhoods, as shown by other organizations.

11. Welcome address of Mrs. Daniel P. Hays, as reported in the minutes of the 1923 Assembly, New York, p. 90.

12. "Four Presidents on the N.F.T.S. Silver Jubilee," *Topics and Trends*, January–February, 1938. Box K-3, folder 2, MS-73, Women of Reform Judaism Records, American Jewish Archives, Cincinnati, OH.

13. Cited by Pamela S. Nadell, *Women Who Would Be Rabbis*, 133.

14. "Report of the Executive Director," April 25, 1957. Box B-4, folder 4, MS-73, Women of Reform Judaism Records, American Jewish Archives, Cincinnati, OH.

15. See note 2, above.

PERSONAL REFLECTION

A First Rabbi, from a Long Line of Rabbis

RABBI NAAMAH KELMAN-EZRACHI

I was raised to marry a rabbi; that's what women in my family did. Both grandmothers, my mother, and many of my aunts married rabbis. On my father's side—that is, the Chasidic and Orthodox side—we go back more than ten generations. My mother, meanwhile, was born to a prominent Reform rabbi. In short, this was the family business—if you were a man, that is.

In 1968, just two years before the first feminists marched down Fifth Avenue and ignited a revolution, my father, Conservative rabbi Wolfe Kelman, designed my bat mitzvah ceremony. Though I had never attended one myself, synagogue attendance was not strange to me. So I went ahead and learned the haftarah and bought a pretty dress to wear when I chanted it on a Friday night. One prominent rabbi congratulated me but sternly informed me that this would be the first and last time I would be chanting haftarah in my life.

What a ride it has been since then. When I was ordained in 1992 as the first woman to become a rabbi in the State of Israel, I was not aiming to be the first. It was a triumph, however, after years of feeling that I was not entitled to the title. No longer was I preparing the podium or bimah for someone else to speak, preach, daven, read Torah; now, the bimah was welcoming me.

How fortunate I have been to have a father who understood the tidal wave of Jewish feminism coming his direction in the 1970s. Long before, as head of the Rabbinical Assembly, he was the "rabbi's rabbi." As "union chief," he helped rabbis in their placement and advancement, often smoothing their transitions. He was one of the Conservative Movement leaders who helped to shepherd the fantastic growth of Conservative Judaism. He marched in Selma with Abraham Joshua Heschel and Martin Luther King Jr. and was involved with the first steps of interfaith dialogue. The rise of Jewish feminism was the next "natural" step for him. He regarded feminism as a new source for energizing Judaism.

My father's "congregation" was our home, our Shabbat table, and there I had both a front seat and the typical dutiful daughter's seat. I helped my mother in the kitchen but was privy to incredible conversations on every aspect of Jewish life, the Jewish people, Jewish history and current events, communal institutions, and new ideas. There was one rule: no one was to gossip or speak ill of rabbis. My father's life mission was to protect and promote rabbis, even ones he didn't like. To his last day, he never shared names or identifiable stories; just moral tales. "This is how rabbis should conduct themselves," he observed, "this is how synagogue presidents should behave." And it was always with warmth and humor and incredible clarity regarding the rabbinic mission. Simply put, the rabbi's mission is to love the Jewish people and serve God—in that order—with Torah study, acts of *chesed* for all humans, joyful worship, and building the State of Israel as the means. Always looking for and cultivating the sparks of renewal and rebirth, my father intuitively understood that in the last quarter of the twentieth century, women held one of the most important keys to Judaism's revival and renewal. My father praised the characteristics of the rabbis he admired from all denominations, and he agonized over certain behaviors he could not tolerate. He did not mythologize rabbis either. Rabbis were imperfect humans, yet their sacred mission needed protection and guidance.

One might say that from the earliest age, I was being "trained" to follow in his rabbinic footsteps. For my brother, it was totally explicit:

you will not break the rabbinic chain. He did not, of course, nor did nearly any of my male first cousins. Our generation of women took the implied road or, to quote Gloria Steinem, became "the man you were destined to marry!" My brother founded a thriving Reform synagogue in Jerusalem over twenty-five years ago and remains my rabbi and my rabbinic *chevruta*, every day, while our sister became a lawyer who represents clergy.

We never knew our Chasidic grandfather, and my Reform grandfather died when I was eight years old, but they both have loomed large in our rabbinic DNA. Rabbi Zvi Yehuda Kelman was a Chasidic *rav* whose learning and kindness were revered. He demanded the strictest observance of himself, but not of others. He modeled; he did not preach. He loved every Jew who came his way. His three sons and two sons-in-law became outstanding rabbis representing different branches of Judaism.

Rabbi Felix Levy was, in his day, the new paradigm of American Reform. Ordained in 1907, born and bred in New York, he served just one congregation for fifty years and was president of the CCAR when he needed to break the tie to vote for acceptance of the Columbus Platform in 1937. He was an early Zionist, a Bible and Near East scholar, and classically Reform in his ritual and worship practices. In 1925, he traveled to Palestine to attend the inauguration of Hebrew University, an institution I would attend years later.

Their wives were no less remarkable and in many ways served as shadow "rabbis" for them. My widowed grandmother maintained her home with great piety and generosity, taking in refugees and strangers, while demanding of her children total loyalty to their father's traditions. My Chicago grandmother gave up her law career to support my grandfather as an unpaid "assistant," working with youth, organizing the Sisterhood, and serving as a great public speaker.

When I arrived in Israel in 1976, words like "feminism," "Reform," "Conservative," and "woman rabbi" had no Hebrew equivalent. I was a foreign implant in my "native" land. It would be another ten years until I found the courage to embark on my rabbinic studies and be completely embraced by HUC's Israeli Rabbinical Program.

There were no women rabbinic models for me, only great male rabbinic models. And still, rabbis like Kinneret Shiryon, who got here first, held up a beacon. My classmate Maya Leibovic and I tried to stumble our way forward together in our first years as students. Luckily for me, I was able to spend two formative years in New York at HUC-JIR, where faculty, classmates, and my students were supportive and inspiring. Rabbi Rachel Cowan held my hand and guided and mentored me in matters of the soul then and now. So too do two other remarkable rabbis, Shira Milgrom and Joy Levitt, who have transformed synagogue and community centers in revolutionary ways. These are just three examples of women who have transformed Judaism in the twentieth century.

From my position as dean of HUC's Jerusalem campus, I now oversee the training of rabbis in two programs: the Year-in-Israel and the Israeli Rabbinical Programs. My family background, walking the footsteps of *chalutzim* in Israel, and the blessings of my biography shape and inspire my rabbinate. Thankfully, I now have over thirty Israeli women colleagues, and we challenge and stretch ourselves toward the next generation. And my daughter has begun her steps to the rabbinate. Like my father, I look for the sparks of holiness and vitality everywhere; my grandfathers bequeathed me their respective Torah: tradition and Reform. Luckily, my husband and children keep me laughing at myself and remind me that feminists must have a sense of humor.

PERSONAL REFLECTION

Going into the Family Business

Rabbi Sue Shankman

I don't know how many times people have asked me when I first knew I wanted to be a rabbi. I often say that I really knew when I was in high school, but my parents believe my epiphany came much earlier—Yom Kippur afternoon 5732 (1972) in the middle of the children's service, to be precise. The Webster Avenue Sanctuary of Temple Israel of New Rochelle was packed. I needed a bathroom and couldn't wait any longer. As soon as we reached the aisle, my mother, then seven months pregnant, began to lead me toward the exit in the rear of the sanctuary. Knowing full well that there was a bathroom in the rabbi's study located behind the bimah, I pulled on her arm impatiently, in an effort to change directions. My mother gently pulled me back, hoping that I would willingly follow her. I stopped dead in my tracks, oblivious to the fact that the rabbi was in the middle of his sermon. In a booming voice, according to my mother, I broke the hush as I pointed to the bimah: "No! I want to go where Papa is!" My mother was mortified, but the rabbi, Rabbi Jacob K. Shankman, more familiarly known to me as Papa Jake, calmly peered down from the pulpit and reassured the congregation thus: "It's perfectly okay, don't worry, this happens all the time. This time it just happens to be my own granddaughter."

I didn't fully realize the significance my words would hold in eventually leading to my decision to pursue a professional career in the rabbinate. To me, it always seemed as though becoming a rabbi was not a career I had chosen. It ran much deeper than that—I felt called to serve God and the Jewish people. My grandfather was, in many ways, the vehicle through whom I first heard that call. Papa Jake's choice to enter the rabbinate came as no surprise to his family either. "Rabbi" had been a main occupation on both sides of his family for generations, going back to the thirteenth century. He would, however, be the first rabbi in the family born and trained in America. That Yom Kippur afternoon in 1972 was merely months after Sally Priesand was ordained as the first woman rabbi. I would not have recognized any difference as a child—despite the fact that I did not know any female rabbis until I was in high school. In the synagogue environment, and in our familial synagogue, women and men were treated equally.

In my rabbinic thesis, I reflected on the example my grandfather set for me and for the many colleagues who shared the rabbinate with him. Candidates for the rabbinate search for mentors and models, rabbis who will be teachers not just through what they teach, but through how they live their lives. There are standards and expectations toward which we each strive, while attempting to balance our own needs for honesty to self and the needs of our families with the needs and demands of congregations, communities, and those with whom we work. How is it possible to live up to one's own personal ideals and stand up for one's beliefs while keeping the best interest or even the desires of an entire community in mind? At times, a rabbi must stand up as a role model for his or her community. At times, one's personal ideals may be in conflict with the congregation by whom the rabbi is employed. Is a rabbi merely an employee of a congregation? In today's culture, this may often seem to be the perception.

Papa Jake lived through incredible moments and trends that transformed the Reform Movement and greatly affected his own congregation over the duration of his lengthy rabbinate (1930–86). He was a teacher of and preacher to children, a role model and pastor to adults, and a statesman known throughout the Reform Movement and the greater Jewish community. Throughout his endeavors on behalf of Reform Judaism, he kept intact his values regarding the centrality of the synagogue. Papa Jake taught me about the essence of a rabbinic soul. He was a truly humble man. He accomplished so very much, in his building up of a vibrant congregation and in his work as president of the World Union for Progressive Judaism. He was truly one of the *g'dolei hador*, one of the greats of his generation, yet he always carried himself as a simple man with simple tastes, always concerned for the well-being of those around him.

Upon receiving his honorary doctorate from the Hebrew Union College—Jewish Institute of Religion in 1955, Dr. Nelson Glueck described him as

> consecrated Rabbi in Israel who has served his faith and people with ardor and distinction; champion of the rights of men, whatever their condition, color or creed; valiant servant of his country, who in time of national emergency responded with alacrity to the call of patriotic duty; lover of mankind, who ministers also to the distraught, the defeated, the friendless with sympathetic understanding; teacher and exemplar of the true religious spirit, by whose guidance and personal influence many are led into the ways of righteousness.

Almost thirty years later, when Rabbi Jacob Shankman reflected on his own rabbinate to me and his other grandchildren, not much had changed. "One of the things I learned to do was to be able to occupy the pulpit with dignity, to write with clarity, understanding, to speak frankly, to love people, to work hard....My deepest values are truth and goodness and beauty; to have an appreciation for everything that's beautiful. To know that when I plant a tulip bulb in November, there will be a flower in April or May and that I have a partner and that partner is God in nature."

I am grateful to have had his unparalleled wisdom, his inspirational words, and his gentle spirit set me on a path toward loving and living Judaism. May my personal and professional efforts continue to honor his memory.

· Part Two ·

Reform Ordination of Women

Before looking at the ordination of Rabbi Sally Priesand or discussing the process that Hebrew Union College–Jewish Institute of Religion (HUC-JIR) undertook in normalizing women in the rabbinate, part 2 presents copies of the responses that Sally Priesand received from the HUC-JIR regarding her application to rabbinical school. The originals are currently housed in the American Jewish Archives in Cincinnati, Ohio, and provide important documentation of what led to a watershed moment in Jewish history.

There is no better way to understand the journey undertaken by Rabbi Priesand than to view it from her own perspective. In 2007, at the biennial gathering of the Women's Rabbinic Network, an historic interview with Priesand was conducted by Rabbi B. Elka Abrahamson ("The Ordination of Sally Priesand: A Historic Interview"). It chronicles not only her days as the only woman student on campus, but how being the first woman, and the pressure of being the first, shaped her own rabbinate.

The path of the first woman rabbi was not made in a vacuum. She was accompanied by a group of male classmates, from the classroom to ordination at Plum Street Temple in 1972. Rabbi Richard F. Address ("Looking Back to See Ahead") shares experiences of both those who were there alongside Priesand as well as some of the women who followed in her footsteps.

Though the act of ordaining women has been in place now for more than four decades, there remains a disparity when it comes to the language on the ordination documents issued by HUC-JIR. Rabbi Mary Zamore ("What's In a Word? Inequality in the Reform *S'michah*") looks at the differences between the certificates, the history behind the first one issued to a woman, and where the issue stands today.

Though the first woman was officially ordained in 1972, it wasn't until a few years later that any policies concerning the hiring of women rabbis, and any issues pertaining thereof, were discussed in any formal way. Rabbi Neil Kominsky ("A Brief History of the Task Force on Women in the Rabbinate") chronicles the advent of the Task Force on Women in the Rabbinate and its necessary advocacy work within the CCAR and the Reform Movement at large, while Rabbi Carole B. Balin, PhD ("From Periphery to Center: A History of the Women's Rabbinic Network") tracks the growth of the Women's Rabbinic Network from its infancy until now.

Rabbi Sally Priesand was the first. But what about the rest of that first generation of women rabbis? Rabbi Sue Levi Elwell, PhD ("O Pioneers: Reflections from Five Women Rabbis of the First Generation") looks at the particular challenges faced by those who were writing the rules for the generations to follow and how their rabbinic trajectories differed from their original plans. To truly understand the advances made in the field by women rabbis, it is imperative to hear firsthand accounts. "From Generation to Generation: A Roundtable Discussion with Rabbi Ellen Weinberg Dreyfus" documents a conversation with women rabbis representing the past four decades.

There are, among women rabbis, a small, but significant number who came to the rabbinate after first choosing to become Jewish. These fascinating passages to the rabbinate are covered by Julie Wiener ("Women Who Chose: First a Jew, Then a Rabbi").

Two personal reflections, by Rabbi Debbie Zecher ("The Pregnant Rabbi") and Rachel Marder ("Ima and Abba on the Bimah: Being an RK Squared"), conclude this section with compelling experiences.

6

LETTERS FROM HEBREW UNION COLLEGE
TO SALLY J. PRIESAND

When I was in high school, I participated in a NFTY pilgrimage to the Cincinnati campus of Hebrew Union College–Jewish Institute of Religion (HUC-JIR). I had already decided I wanted to be a rabbi, so during that weekend I looked for an appropriate opportunity to bring up the topic. That moment came when we were gathered together in the Scheuer Chapel, listening to Dr. Samuel Sandmel (*z"l*), at that time provost HUC-JIR. He finished his presentation and opened the floor for questions. I raised my hand and asked if a woman could become a rabbi. He did not say yes, nor did he say no, simply that a woman had not yet been ordained a rabbi. In the optimistic world of a teenager, that was good enough for me. I returned home committed to applying for the undergraduate program, a joint effort between HUC-JIR and the University of Cincinnati.

The letters that follow are the responses I received after beginning the application process. Unfortunately, I do not have the letters I wrote that engendered these replies. Nonetheless, what was on my mind is easily deduced. I wanted to be a rabbi, but there seemed to be a veiled attempt on HUC-JIR's part to guide me toward the field of religious education. When I look back now, I am grateful that I was in the undergraduate program. It enabled me to acclimate myself to the school, and it gave students and faculty the opportunity to get to know me before I was accepted officially as a rabbinical student.

Hebrew Union College-Jewish Institute of Religion

UNDER THE PATRONAGE OF THE UNION OF AMERICAN HEBREW CONGREGATIONS

CINCINNATI
NEW YORK
LOS ANGELES

CLIFTON AVENUE · CINCINNATI 20, OHIO

Administrative Office

June 17, 1963

Miss Sally Priesand
21981 Robinhood Drive
Parkview 26, Ohio

Dear Miss Priesand:

We are pleased to learn of your interest in our College.
Mrs. Weiss, our Secretary for Admissions, will be in
touch with you soon with the information you desire.

Women are welcome in any of our courses, and we would
be glad to discuss with you the various programs in
which you might be interested. Since you state in
your letter that your interests lean specifically to
the rabbinate, we would have to inform you candidly
that we do not know what opportunities are available for
women in the active rabbinate, since we have, as yet,
not ordained any women. Most women prefer to enter the
field of Jewish religious education.

We would appreciate learning the name of your rabbi
so that we may ask him to guide and advise you.

Sincerely yours,

Joseph Karasick

Joseph Karasick, Rabbi
Assistant to the Provost

Hebrew Union College-Jewish Institute of Religion
UNDER THE PATRONAGE OF THE UNION OF AMERICAN HEBREW CONGREGATIONS

CINCINNATI
NEW YORK
LOS ANGELES

CLIFTON AVENUE · CINCINNATI 20, OHIO

Administrative Office

June 20, 1963

Miss Sally Priesand
21981 Robinhood Drive
Parkview 26, Ohio

Dear Miss Priesand:

Rabbi Karasick has told me of your interest in the
rabbinate and of the possibility that you may wish to
apply to our College.

I am sending to you, under separate cover, a copy of our
catalogue and other literature which will be of interest
to you. Perhaps you will want to consult with Rabbi
Litt after you have had the opportunity to study the
materials we are sending you. You might also ascertain
from Rabbi Litt, and he in turn from other rabbis, just
what would be the disposition of the rabbinate respecting
someone like you who is interested in being ordained by
the College-Institute. While we have had women students,
none, so far, has taken the full course of study which
would lead to graduation and ordination as a rabbi. Therefore, some clear knowledge on your part of what it will
mean to you to have graduated from our School is essential
for you prior to your thinking about entering. The question
of a woman as a rabbi is a question for the rabbis rather
than for the School. There is no attempt on our part to
discourage you but to direct your thinking.

Do keep in touch with us. If there are any further questions,
please do not hesitate to write.

Cordially,

Mrs. Miriam O. Weiss
Secretary for Admissions

Hebrew Union College-Jewish Institute of Religion

UNDER THE PATRONAGE OF THE UNION OF AMERICAN HEBREW CONGREGATIONS

CINCINNATI
NEW YORK
LOS ANGELES
JERUSALEM

CLIFTON AVENUE · CINCINNATI 20, OHIO

Administrative Office

February 5, 1964

Miss Sally Jane Priesand
21981 Robinhood Drive
Parkview, Ohio 44126

Dear Miss Priesand:

I am pleased to inform you that we are prepared to
admit you as a special student in the Undergraduate
Department of the Hebrew Union College-Jewish
Institute of Religion, enrolled for credit but not
enrolled as a Pre-Rabbinic student. Your acceptance
will become formal as soon as we receive from you
written confirmation of this letter and a transcript
of your final grades for the current academic year.

Our President, Dr. Nelson Glueck, and the Faculty
join me in welcoming you to our College. We trust
that your stay with us will bring you inspiration and
spiritual growth.

Cordially,

Samuel Sandmel
Provost

SS/mw

Hebrew Union College-Jewish Institute of Religion

UNDER THE PATRONAGE OF THE UNION OF AMERICAN HEBREW CONGREGATIONS

CINCINNATI
NEW YORK
LOS ANGELES
JERUSALEM

CLIFTON AVENUE · CINCINNATI 20, OHIO

Administrative Office

February 18, 1964

Miss Sally J. Priesand
21981 Robinhood Drive
Parkview, Ohio 44126

Dear Sally:

In reply to your letter of February 9th to Dr. Sandmel, let me assure you that the word "Special Student" has no adverse connotation. Since we require all unmarried Undergraduate students to live on the campus and we do not have housing for women, we must use this term to grant permission for your living elsewhere.

I look forward to seeing you in the Fall.

Sincerely yours,

Joseph Karasick
Rabbi
Assistant to the Provost

JK:rmn

7

THE ORDINATION OF RABBI SALLY J. PRIESAND

An Historic Interview

In honor of Rabbi Sally Priesand's retirement from her position of rabbi at Monmouth Reform Temple, where she served from 1981 to 2006, the Women's Rabbinic Network feted her at its biennial conference in the spring of 2007, in Chicago, Illinois. The theme of the conference was leadership, and participants spent several days exploring different leadership styles, including their own. The highlight of the conference was Rabbi Elka Abrahamson's interview of Rabbi Priesand. All participants in the conference, over one hundred women rabbis, attended the interview, and the room where it took place was completely full. The room was silent while Rabbi Priesand talked, except for occasional bursts of laughter and a few tears. All who were there felt they had shared in something incredibly special, and most were sure that their two hours listening to Sally would never be forgotten. It is with this in mind that we share the transcript of the interview here.

Rabbi Elka Abrahamson (interviewer): Good evening. This interview represents a special opportunity for all of us, and it is my special privilege to be able to interview Sally Priesand this evening. Before launching into questions, allow me to provide just a bit of background about how I ended up in this chair next to our beloved colleague. In trying to determine the way to best honor Sally at this occasion in her life and at this historic moment in the life of the Reform Movement, of the College [Hebrew Union College–Jewish Institute of Religion], and indeed the Jewish people, it was clear we wanted to dedicate an evening to Sally and determined an interview would be the right spirit. To that end, we considered a list of some high-profile professionals outside of our rabbinic community, perhaps a journalist and television personality to do the interview. And then Jackie [Ellenson] said, "I don't think we should bring in an outside person. That is how we have conducted our interviews over the years, and we are often disappointed and always want time to ask our own questions. Really, who would be more qualified than any of the women in this precious network to ask questions of the first woman to be ordained as a rabbi?" The answer was obvious. Nobody. Jackie asked if I would accept this honor, and in agreeing to sit next to our honored guest, Rabbi Sally Priesand, please know that I am speaking with and for everyone seated here tonight. These are our questions, both literally and emotionally. I have the rare honor of asking them out loud to Sally. And yes, I also possess the chutzpah, also in no short supply among this crowd, to go off the page...with your permission. Or not!

So let me start with this. Recently, as I was watching the anniversary of Jackie Robinson's first game, I was quite moved by the ceremony. I was taken by the brilliant decision, the rare tribute, to have all the players wear his number, forty-two. It occurred to me that tonight, recalling your ordination, we are all ordained with you in 1972. We all want to be in that moment with you. We all, if you will, want to wear your number. In some ways we all feel like we were there with you on that bimah, and perhaps it is for this reason that we never tire of honoring you, even if you've had enough. Like all of you, I have listened to Sally over the years. Over and over again you repeat the same powerful and selfless sentiment. When asked about being the first woman rabbi, you answer with some version of this: "It is not about me, it is about all of you. It's about all of you." Well tonight, damn it, it's about you.

Let us begin with your story. We want to hear the story of how this woman, this girl, how you turned into someone who had the chutzpah, the vision, to write to the College seeking ordination beginning when you were a teenager in 1963. Please tell us the story of how you began to imagine yourself as a rabbi. What contributed to such an amazing dream, even when nobody knew such a thing was possible? What made you the person you are, even stretching back to when you were barely out of childhood?

Rabbi Sally Priesand: Well, I decided I wanted to be a rabbi when I was sixteen years old. Unfortunately, I don't remember why.

I: Let's bring on the next guest [*laughter*].

S: I always wanted to be a teacher, so whatever my favorite subject was, that was what I was going to teach. So one year I was going to be an English teacher and one year a math teacher and one year a French teacher, and in the end I decided to be a teacher of Judaism. Fortunately, for me, my parents gave me what I think is one of the greatest gifts a parent can give a child and that is the courage to dare and to dream, and when I said I wanted to be a rabbi, my parents didn't throw up their hands and say, "What kind of a job is that for a nice Jewish girl?" They said, "If that's what you want to be, then do it." So they gave me a tremendous amount of support. They never implanted in my mind any doubt as to whether or not I could do it. And I think that in terms of the letters that you saw outside, the first letter was written to me when I was a junior in high school and I think I had gone on a NFTY pilgrimage to the Hebrew Union College in Cincinnati. I was from Cleveland. And we went down and I remember asking the question—there were all these different kids there—and I asked the question about whether or not a woman could be a rabbi, and the answer was that so far we haven't had any. They didn't say no. What were they going to say in front of all these kids? They didn't say no, so I just proceeded with the different steps, and I was in the undergraduate program, which allowed me to attend the University of Cincinnati, take classes at HUC at the same time, and then skip the first year of the rabbinic program—the Jerusalem program came afterwards. So one day I was an undergraduate, and the next day I was in the second year of the rabbinic program and everybody said, "Uh, she's still here."

I: Do you think the wheels were turning somewhere? Like…

S: The man who deserves the credit, really, for ordaining women was Nelson Glueck. He was the president of Hebrew Union College; he very much wanted to ordain women. And it was really his decision in terms of convincing the Board of Governors that this should be done, and he took care of a lot of little problems in the background that I never heard about. I remember being invited to give an opening prayer at a meeting for the governors. I led services and read Torah in the College chapel, and again, what you need to think about is that I was the only woman in the school. I think it is sometimes difficult for you to understand that because, fortunately, most of you have had a very different kind of experience, where you had other women to be with. And so…sometimes I will admit to being a little envious of all of you because, when you come to a gathering like this, you immediately go to see all your friends. And—

I: But now we're all your buddies.

S: Absolutely. And so unfortunately, Nelson Glueck died before I was ordained. It was, to be honest, a great blow to me because all those years I was thinking of that moment when he was going to put his hands on my shoulders. And I do have a picture and a letter from his wife that hangs in my office, which reminds me that one of the things he wanted to do before he died—he said there were three things—and one of those things was to ordain me. And fortunately for all of us, Fred Gottschalk carried on that tradition and was in favor of ordaining women as well.

I: Talk about how the other students treated you. You were in this world of all men. How did the teachers treat you? There's some fascination out there with what's the weirdest thing that happened to you. Can you remember just the most outrageous thing that was said to you? What was it like to be the only woman and the first woman? Was there resentment? Was there acceptance? Was there alienation? What did it feel like?

S: Well, there probably was a little bit of all of that, but I think mostly I remember acceptance. Maybe that's because I just want to look at it that way. I think the faculty was used to having only men in class, and so they would begin by saying "Gentlemen, and lady." They would suddenly remember that I was sitting there. I did feel that I had to be better than everyone else. There were some classes—in Talmud, for example, my classmates never prepared because they knew the professor would always call on me.

I: Wow.

S: So I always felt I had to be better than anyone else, work harder than anyone else, and my classmates often invited me to study with them, but I just didn't do it because I knew at the day of the test I was going to be by myself and I better learn it myself. I do also want to mention one thing because it was very moving to me. When I was ordained, on that day when I was called to the bimah, my classmates spontaneously stood up. And that was very, very special for me.

I: We've all, I bet, in this room, probably without exception, heard at some point along our journey, you're the first "fill in the blank"— "woman rabbi I've ever kissed," "woman rabbi I've ever seen on the bimah," "woman in the *whatever* who served as a rabbi"—I mean just on and on and on. But you really were the first. How did you manage it with such grace?—at least from the outside, as we've all experienced you over the years. Just ceaseless grace and dignity. Did you ever just go home and break dishes, I mean, what... How did you manage that, like, constant firstness?

S: Well, it's sort of the paradox of my personality because I'm a very private person and somehow I chose a public career and, you know, I just was the one who got to be the first. I didn't go into the rabbinate to do that. I only wanted to be a rabbi. I didn't think about what it means to be the first of something. That just kind of unfolded along the way. I always tried to maintain my sense of humor, and I made a rule right at the beginning never to argue with anyone. I did not think that you score points by trying to argue with somebody who wants to tell you why women shouldn't be rabbis.

I: So I read that in a few places about this rule. I didn't get that gene. I'm just wondering. Did you really maintain that? Did you ever just... I want you to tell me you got really mad at some point. What is it about you that allows that rule to continue?

S: Well there are a couple, there are a couple of times...

I: Oh, I wish I could have been there.

S: Mostly, I would just listen to what a person said and then walk away. Say, "Thank you for your opinion," and walk away. I do remember once early on when I was already ordained, I think, sitting in a meeting with some of the leaders of the Reform Movement talking about some important issue or something, and they called me "honey."

I: And you said, "Thank you for your opinion," and walked away.

S: And they said, "Honey, you have to be patient." And I do remember saying, "My name is not 'honey.'" I did do that, and also I once walked into a meeting with the Placement Commission and there were sixteen men sitting around a table, and I walked in and I said, "I hope you all realize you're part of the problem." And, I remember one other one. I spoke to the faculty of HUC-Cincinnati. Ever since I was ordained, I really fought for having women on the faculty. I have always spoken about it, and when I was in rabbinical school, of course there were no women on the faculty. Many of the men who were on the faculty were students, who then moved up. So I was speaking to the faculty and explaining the need for women faculty members, and I said, "You know there's something I don't understand. If I remember correctly most of you got here because someone took an interest in you and groomed you to move up. So why don't you do that with some of our female scholars who are students here at the College–Institute?" So they were probably a little surprised that I said that, but I always had a reputation for saying what I thought. I have the same experiences that you have of people coming up to you in your synagogue where guests of the bar mitzvah say, "I never saw a woman rabbi before." I usually try to say, "I hope I won't be the last." But, my organist told me to say, "Don't get around much, do you?"

I: Are there more angry times? Do you want to keep going?

S: No, that's about it.

I: Okay. I know that your own placement experience was very unsettling and disappointing in your early career. Right? And, I don't know if you were angry or just profoundly sad, but I think you were kind of angry. So talk about that, because it was a real disappointment for you.

S: I was about to be ordained. I was the last person in my class to get a job. In the end, I always thought I got the best job because I went to the Stephen Wise Free Synagogue in New York. The only real reason I got that job was that everybody else had a job, and of course the Free Synagogue always likes to pride itself on being in the forefront of social justice, following in the footsteps of Stephen Wise. So I thought it was appropriate for me to be there.

Rabbi Ed Klein, the senior rabbi, *alav shalom*, always enjoyed being introduced as the first equal opportunity employer of the Reform rabbinate. He taught me how to be a rabbi. I learned many things from him. I also learned some things I realized I wouldn't do, because he came from a different model than what I thought I wanted to be. He was Stephen Wise's assistant and handpicked successor, and he always decided what was to happen in the temple. So I remember going to board meetings, we would go to the executive board, five o'clock or something, and Rabbi Klein would say "This is what we're going to do," and everybody would say, "Yes, Rabbi Klein." Then we would go, walk down the street to have dinner at Café des Artistes, then we would come back for the board meeting, and the same thing would happen again. And I kind of decided then and there that I wanted to have a partnership with my congregation. And I said that when I was interviewed, that I thought we would make decisions together. And so empowerment was always very important to me, and that is the kind of rabbinate I have had. As for the [Stephen Wise] Free Synagogue, I stayed there for seven years. As I look back now, I probably stayed because basically I was happy and I was afraid of what was going to be the next step. Every year I probably said, "Well, everything's okay here, so I will stay." That was probably a mistake.

I: The length of time?

S: The length of time and, unfortunately, Rabbi Klein had a stroke at a board meeting. He was able to come back, but really he was paralyzed. I used to assist him, push him in the wheelchair to the bimah, have his book ready, and all of these kinds of things. It was okay. I didn't mind doing any of that. But then I suggested that maybe when he was ready to retire they ought to give me a chance to be senior rabbi.

I: Who are you talking about, the leadership?

S: Yes. And that was unacceptable, and so yes, I was hurt actually. I wasn't as much angry as I was hurt. And it has, I think, taken a long time to get over that; there are still scars to this day. It was a disappointment to me that after seven years at a major synagogue I wouldn't be given that opportunity. And so, as is my wont, I took matters into my own hands. In November I resigned but stayed until June and ran the synagogue. And as I look back now, I remember, they wanted to have a special *Oneg Shabbat* [in my honor]. I said, "Let's not be hypocrites," and I also did not attend the last board meeting, when they gave me a gift. They had to deliver the gift to me. I have mostly positive memories of the Free Synagogue but disappointment that a congregation that is so committed to social justice has never, to this day, been able to take the step of having a senior rabbi who is a woman. And, so then I had to face the placement process. It was very discouraging.

There were many congregations that wouldn't talk to me at all. Out of my experience came the pledge that congregations must now sign the application saying they will not discriminate, and part of the way that came about is that I wrote a very to-the-point article for *Reform Judaism*, which I took to Malcolm Stern, *alav ha-shalom*, and he said to me, "You cannot publish this; it will destroy your whole career." I was angry, very angry. I was angry because I felt that the Reform Movement was not helping me in any way to get a job. And I did not get a job for two years. And I wrote this article, and he looked at it and said, "You can't, so I will write it for you." He sat right down, in front of me, and redid the article. That should be in the archives somewhere. Redid the article to bring up many of the issues.

I remember once having a telephone interview. The people forgot to hang up.

I: Divine intervention.

S: So I listened.

I: Isn't this great! I didn't know about it.

S: They said, "She was so terrific! She would be so wonderful, but we can't have a woman." So I went to Temple Beth El in Elizabeth, New Jersey, for the weekends, and during the week I was chaplain at Lenox Hill Hospital in New York and then found Monmouth Reform Temple in Tinton Falls, New Jersey, which I almost didn't apply to because of the name Tinton Falls. I said, where is that? And I had a wonderful twenty-five-year career there and learned a lot of lessons. But I'll let you continue.

I: Well, I want to hear about those lessons. But just whom did you go to during these times of remarkable frustration? We have this incredible circle of women whom we know. We can pick up the phone and kvetch and moan, and they're going to understand. Who understood you?

S: Not a lot of people. I had one or two very close friends that I could discuss things with and vent.

I: And you did?

S: And I did.

I: Good. Talk about the lessons that you learned in those twenty-five years, and if you feel like it, how far have we come when we hear the story of seven years as a successful associate and then you weren't named senior. Do you feel like that story is repeating itself?

S: Yes, actually, I do. I think that's too bad.

I: What's that about?

S: It saddens me when senior rabbis who are men don't stand up for their female assistants and associates and say, "Give her a chance." I think they have an obligation to do that. In my case, Rabbi Klein couldn't do that. I mean, he just...

I: Do you think he would have?

S: He would, but I don't know. He did, he always said that, that he... See I'm nervous because this is being taped. I am just saying that he always would say, publicly, that I was the best assistant that he ever had. And he allowed me to do everything. And if a family would say, "How could I have a woman rabbi at my father's funeral? He was traditional," Rabbi Klein would say, "Well, this is who you've got." He would stand by me and, as I said, I learned a lot from him. Going to Monmouth Reform Temple I think that most people in my congregation felt that I was just coming for a few years. That it was a transition. I maybe thought that too. I'll be honest.

The early years of my career, most decisions that I made, I made for what was best for women in the rabbinate. I did not make the decision as to what was best for me. And I felt that obligation, and there are many times when I made those choices. I'm not sorry about making those choices. I did have an understanding that people were looking at me, and by looking at me were judging the whole concept of women in the rabbinate. So for many years I did make those kinds of decisions, and I thought that my obligation as the first was to be the rabbi of a major congregation in our country. Probably because in rabbinical school, I don't know about now, but when I was there it was always "move on up." Though I think that we as women have changed that in many ways. My congregation taught me that success is not being bigger. Success means are you doing better today than you did yesterday. And that's my definition of success. And so I stayed in my congregation because I was happy, I was fulfilled, I continued to be challenged, and my congregation accepted my ideas, some of which were a little crazy.

But as a matter of fact, when I retired they said the words they were going to miss the most would be "I have an idea."

I: Well, let's hear some of those crazy ideas.

S: No, it's just that I think it's really important for a rabbi to have a vision and to be able to move people forward, and you don't have to take credit for the idea, you can let other people run with the idea. But you have to inspire people to know there are things they can do—things that otherwise they may not even think that that they could do. For example, I gave a High Holy Day sermon when the war in Kosovo was going on, and I said I think we could do something to help the people of Kosovo and I got all these volunteers. We had this community-wide concert where all the artists volunteered their time, and we raised $17,000 that went to some of the relief groups. And there are lots of examples of things we did. Being involved in the community is very, very important for me. When I came to Monmouth Reform Temple, the congregation was not really involved in the community, in the Reform Movement. They just were into themselves. They weren't involved in the local Federation, and I have to say when I left they were involved in all of those things and in a meaningful way. So that's part of what our job is, to have some vision and to help move people along.

I: Is that the most rewarding thing about your rabbinate? Giving the people that journey?

S: I think that's a rewarding thing. I think it's very rewarding and I'm sure you all have the same feeling of being able to touch people's lives in ways that you don't even know about. And sometimes years and years later, somebody will come up to you and say, "Rabbi, twenty-five years ago you officiated at my wedding. I haven't seen you since then, but this is what you said to me under the chuppah." So there are just so many wonderful opportunities to be there for people in their time of need and also to teach people to become responsible for their own Jewishness. When I interviewed at Monmouth Reform Temple, I said very clearly, "I'm not here to be Jewish for all of you. I'm here to suggest ways in which we can all be Jewish together." And so for many years during my vacation or my sabbatical…by the way, I highly recommend this model of a sabbatical, which we all deserve. I used to get six weeks' vacation in the summer and the month of January as a sabbatical. It's a very good thing that you break the middle of the year when you need it. The idea is that you don't necessarily have to go study but relax, do the things you haven't had time to do. You know, whatever. But during those times I always sat in the pews. I always came to Shabbat services. I come now every Friday night and every Saturday morning and I sit in the last pew, and I just sort of watch and see how things are going.

I: You talked about when you were sixteen, just knowing this is what you wanted to do, you just knew. So many years later after a magnificent career, what do you just know about life?

S: What do I know about life? Well recently, I was asked to contribute to a book called *If I Only Had Five Things to Pass On*, and so these are the five things. I think, if I can remember. I'm getting older.

I: We're not going to know. You can say anything you want.

S: Know yourself and be yourself. When I was ordained a lot of people thought they knew what the role of the first woman rabbi should be. I try, I've tried all these years just to be me, and if that upsets people, then it upsets people. You know, when I was ordained my skirts were up to here and my hair was down to here, and people didn't think that was very good, but that was the style then. If you read some of the interviews that I did many, many, many years ago, I am not always so proud of all those things that are in those interviews. For example, marriage was always part of my plan. One time I was interviewed and I said that if I married a rabbi, I would only be his assistant. Well, that was a stupid thing to say. But I did say that, and I had this whole plan that I was going to marry and have kids, and I would have a nursery in my synagogue next to my study and I was going to have the kids with me and all of those things. Somewhere along the way I decided, knowing myself, that I could not do both—have a career and have a family. So I consciously chose my career. I admire those of you who can do both. And I admire all the new models that you have brought to the rabbinate. But I know that I would not have been able to do both and so—know yourself, be yourself.

Do they still have that private little ceremony before ordination when everybody gets the Torah and everything? That was very meaningful for me, and I said that my verse was "Say little and do much," and that has served me very well throughout my career. I don't talk a lot about things. I listen and I try to encourage people to move forward.

Don't worry. Okay. I have a worry rule. The worry rule is just sit down ten minutes every day and worry as much as you want.

I: I didn't get that gene either.

S: And then get up and get on with it. The next day you can have ten more minutes.

One time I happened to say that to somebody in my congregation, and apparently to somebody else I said, take fifteen minutes. And when I was telling someone ten, the person to whom I said "fifteen" was standing there and said, "Wait a minute, you said fifteen."

I: I'm so worried. I have five extra minutes to worry about.

S: Don't be afraid to fail. The greatest failure is never daring to fail. Every day the world moves forward because somebody is willing to take the risk.

And finally, always maintain your sense of humor. Laughter's a great thing in life, and it takes care of a lot of situations.

I: Those are great. The things you know. So if you were to be ordained this year, do you think your life would be incredibly different?

S: My life or my rabbinate?

I: You choose. I'll take your rabbinate.

S: I think it would be. I think it would be because of being ordained with other women, having female faculty members, having many more congregations open to the idea of welcoming female rabbis. You know, one of the differences between the Reform and the Conservative Movements is that in the Conservative Movement they studied and talked about having women rabbis. So when they ordained women, congregations were ready. In the Reform Movement, the College just ordained me, and there was no discussion yet in the Union (UAHC) and nobody was really ready. So I think today my life would be different because more congregations would be ready. That is not to say that we've made it. We haven't. But we've made a lot of progress, and we still have to be pushing for the kinds of things for women in leadership roles in all the different areas of the Jewish community. In the top roles.

I: There's a couple of things that you would never know about Sally Priesand. She loves Bette Midler and does a mean imitation of Bette Midler.

S: I just want to say I volunteer for the next time that we have our "Rabbis Gone Wild." I'll be the opening act.

I: "Rabbis Gone Wild" starring Sally Priesand. You know what, we'll have 100 percent attendance. And men clamoring at the door to get in. She told us at dinner that she had a birthday party for her dog at the synagogue. She rented out the social hall and had a doggy party for Shadow, the dog's name is Shadow, because—

S: He is my Shadow.

I: And she made doggy bags for everybody.

S: There were twenty-five dogs that came. The kids loved it. They got to bring their dogs. It was great fun.

I: So those are a couple of things you haven't talked about. So you told us about what you know. Tells us what we don't know.

S: About?

I: You.

S: I don't know. My life's been pretty much of an open book.
    Okay, I've got one. This will really... I've decided that my next challenge should be to win the World Series of Poker.

I: Wait. Wait. Do you play poker?

S: Well . . .

I: It's never stopped you before, right?

S: That's right. I'm brushing up on it. Last year, the winner of the World Series of Poker won $12 million and I was thinking to myself what we could do for *tzedakah* with $12 million, but the thing that was kind of holding me back was...

I: Besides not playing.

S: You know, I was, I was afraid that it might not be appropriate. I was trying to imagine what it would be like if I was the one on TV...

I: Well, take sunglasses.

S: So that has held me back.

I: And the ticker running across the bottom: "Rabbi Sally..." So are you in training?

S: Yes, certainly.

I: Anyone here play poker? Okay, well another first, another first. What other challenges are left for you?

S: What are the challenges? Well, I have to say that I'm enjoying retirement very much. I highly recommend it. And I think things are going pretty well. Some of you may or may not know that several years ago I started painting. I work in abstract watercolor, and it's something I want to pay a little bit more attention to. I do recommend that as you begin to think about retirement, you should plan for it and have a general idea of things that you might want to do. I immediately volunteered for about four or five boards in my community, so I'm very involved in a wide variety of organizations. Most of this past year has been spent building a house. I've always lived in apartments. Most people my age are downsizing. But I do things backwards. And so I have recently moved into a house in an adult community, but they're single-family detached homes. Shadow and I are having an open house for our whole temple in a few weeks. I've kind of staggered them, you know, twelve to two, two to four, four to six. I figure come in the front door, look around, get a little something to eat, go out the back. But I know everybody really wants to see my house. I may be doing some, well, I have a few other projects. I would like to create a Kollel in my community, and maybe some writing and maybe some speaking. I'm keeping things open. But there is one thing I did want to tell everyone about rainbows.

I: I've got it. When you look back, what personal rewards and blessings have you absorbed that you just never have imagined?

S: I don't think that I ever imagined what a difference you can make in people's lives. And you really can. And in ways that we don't know. It's like when you throw a stone into a river, you see the splash, but you don't know about all the things that are underneath. And all of you are so very gracious always in honoring me, but you are—to quote Bette Midler—the wind beneath my wings.

I: Will you sing it? Will you sing the line please?

S: No, and really I was the first; it's recorded in history. I've said that before. I believe it's true. I was in the right place at the right time. It happened to be me, but all of us are part of the story. I do hope that you'll take very seriously the challenge we presented at this conference to begin to collect all of the things that relate to [women in the] rabbinate that are so important so that we can give them to the archives. Don't decide what you think is important or unimportant. Everything is important, and things you might even think are, you know, nothing, they have stories to tell and they are all part of a larger story. As I said earlier at the workshop, think of what it would have been like if we had all the records of Regina Jonas. So we have an obligation to do that. Keep that in mind and start putting things away. Having just moved, I can't tell you how much stuff I found. So I would encourage you to start, just take a file box, whatever, and start putting things in it, and at some point it will be time to give it to the archives. I'm always very touched by your graciousness. But all of you inspire me with your energy and your enthusiasm and your creativity. That's a gift that you've given to me, and I'm grateful for it.

I: You're remarkable. Every time I hear you talk about being the first rabbi who's a woman, you inevitably give it back to all of us, and I have been part of many conversations where, with many of you, we reflect upon how right you were to be the first woman rabbi. And it wasn't just the right time and the right place, it was the right person.

S: Thank you.

I: Sally loves rainbows, and I know she wants to talk about it. Tells us why you love rainbows.

S: Yes. True story about rainbows. Rainbows are very important to me. When I came to my synagogue Monmouth Reform Temple to sign my contract, I was having dinner with some people. We looked outside and there was a rainbow. So I've always considered that rainbow to be God's sign that our partnership was going to work. And, over the years, there have been many other times when rainbows have occurred in my life. Times that, I even remember one day sort of sitting there saying I could use a rainbow today. And I didn't want to write my sermon and I didn't want to do anything, and sure enough I looked out the window and there was a rainbow. During the [High] Holy Day services there is a line that says, "And we remember a rainbow." It's Noah's rainbow, but I always think of it as my rainbow, and I always look at the people at whose home we had dinner when I saw that rainbow.

When I retired I wanted to give my congregation a gift. And I commissioned Benji Ellen Schiller to write a song for my congregation. And I said I wanted it to be a song that could be sung by the cantor and the choir and the congregation and that it had to include a rainbow, and the verse should be "Wherever you go God goes with you." She wrote a beautiful song called "B'chol Makom—I Am with You." And we had her come to our synagogue for a Shabbat *Kallah*, and the choir learned the song and they sang it. It was a wonderful, wonderful experience. And as I said, I just moved to my new house, and my cantor Gabrielle Clissold and her family were visiting me. We were standing at the patio looking out, and there was a rainbow. Her little boy, Asher, about six years old, said, "It's a miracle." Well, it is a miracle. Rainbows are miracles and every day is a miracle, and we should live it to the fullest and understand that it's not repeatable, so make the most of it when it's here.

I: So do you ever get up in the morning, look in the mirror and go: Look what I did. You know like…

S: Nope.

I: Well, I think you should. Just once. I want you to look out at this group, these questions were validation of all of your questions. There's a sort of a hunger in the room for you to bless us, to offer up a prayer not only for the women in the room but for all of our daughters and our daughters' daughters and all those little girls who are going to grow up and look at that letter up there dated 1963 and say, "Wow, that's a long, long time ago." That they can't even remember when there weren't women who were also rabbis. So take a minute, look at the faces of [this group], look in this mirror, if you would, and there's a little bit of a hunger for a blessing from you.

S: Eternal God, Source of all goodness, the One who is Creator of us all, the One who creates through us and so makes us all creators too, help us to accept the many challenges that lie ahead, to move people forward, to know that no one ever really gets to go into the Promised Land but that we have an opportunity to move things forward for the benefit of all, and to know that our people have survived from generation to generation, to teach them, to inspire them, to guide them, to help them dream, to help them become all that they are capable of becoming so that one day our daughters, our granddaughters, our great-granddaughters, and all of our children will live in a better world than we live in now. Amen.

I: Thank you.

I can't thank you enough. I know that the taping was not something that came easily, and I am so grateful to you and to God that we have you on tape. And I'm going to invite our double-aught representative to conclude our evening with one more teaching and we have one last moment.

Jennifer Clayman: *Thanks to Sally from the '00s:*

It's a profound honor for me to represent the women of the new millennium.

I don't usually speak about my age in this way, but I hope that you'll indulge me given the circumstances. I was born in June of 1972, fifteen days *after* Sally was ordained—and so, obviously, I've never known a world without women rabbis—and I'm sure that's true for many of us ordained since 2000.

Because of you, Sally, and those who came after you, I was never told that a woman can't be a rabbi. Because of you and those who came after you, my rabbi was able to stand up on the bimah at my bat mitzvah and tell me that he thought I should be a rabbi. And because of you and those who came after you, my years at HUC and the first years of my rabbinate have been blessed by the presence of rabbinic mentors both male and female.

I wouldn't say that I take women rabbis for granted, because I don't. And I won't say that we're accepted everywhere, because we're not. But we're not so unusual, either. I was the fourth woman rabbi hired by my congregation, and we've since been joined by the fifth. By the time I got there, the battle of pants on the bimah (and other struggles) had already been fought—and won. The congregation is accustomed to women's voices from the pulpit, women's ideas about God, Torah, and Israel, and women's authority in difficult times.

We owe you a great deal. In many ways, what you've done for us could be called *chesed*, an act of loving-kindness.

Shavuot is only a short time away, and I'm sure many of us have been thinking about the Book of Ruth, which is seen by many as the archetypal tale of *chesed*. Ruth demonstrates *chesed* when she pledges herself to Naomi and again when she gleans in the fields and brings home grain to feed them both. She puts herself "out there"—she risks her safety and her dignity—to help not only herself, but to help Naomi as well. And Ruth is not the only one who engages in *chesed.* Boaz does as well, when Ruth comes to him on the threshing floor. He becomes a *go-eil,* a redeemer, for both Ruth and Naomi.

Perhaps it's not too much of a stretch to say that Sally has embraced both of these types of *chesed.* Like Ruth, she put herself "out there"—she took the first steps—not knowing how the world would respond; like Boaz, she became a redeemer for us all.

Rachel Adler says that the Book of Ruth "is strung upon a chain of *chesed* and blessings."[1] In the final scene of the book, the women of the community gather together to offer blessings in response to the *chesed* they have witnessed—a *chesed* so profound that it will alter the course of the world. They give Ruth's newborn son his name—the only time in the *Tanach* when a child is named in this way—and they make their *b'rachah,* speaking to Naomi:

"Blessed is Adonai, who has not caused you to lack for a redeemer today."

The women call Ruth's son Oved a *meishiv nefesh,* a soul restorer—a child, born of *chesed,* who will save Naomi from destitution and become the grandfather of David.

Thank you, Sally, for being a soul restorer for all of us. And even more so, for our world, which missed out on women rabbis for far too long. Your *chesed* has changed our lives and changed our world—and it is only fitting that this community of women should respond to your *chesed* with a *b'rachah.*

Please join with me:

בָּרוּךְ אַתָּה יְיָ אֱלֹהֵינוּ מֶלֶךְ הָעוֹלָם,
אֲשֶׁר לֹא הִשְׁבִּית לָנוּ גֹּאֶלֶת הַיּוֹם
שֶׁהָיְתָה לָנוּ לְמֵשִׁיב נָפֶשׁ.
בָּרוּךְ אַתָּה יְיָ, מַרְבָּה חֶסֶד בָּעוֹלָם.

Blessed are You, Adonai, our God, Ruler of the universe,
who has not caused us to lack for a redeemer in our day;
she has been for us a soul restorer.
Blessed are You, Adonai, who increases *chesed* in the world.

NOTE

1. Rachel Adler, *Engendering Judaism: An Inclusive Theology and Ethics* (Philadelphia: Jewish Publication Society, 1998), 150.

8

LOOKING BACK TO SEE AHEAD

Rabbi Richard F. Address, DMin

We all stood. That is the memory; we all stood on that Shabbat morning, June 2, 1972, at Plum Street Temple in Cincinnati, Ohio. Realizing that something historic was taking place, the ordination class of 1972 stood as one to salute our classmate, Sally Priesand. The rest, as the saying goes, is history.

Looking back over the four-plus decades since that sun-splashed day, we can only wonder at the changes that time has wrought on us, on Judaism, and on the no-longer strange phenomenon of women in the rabbinate. That ordination day in 1972 was reported in the *New York Times*. History was made; American Judaism took notice, and the Reform Movement basked in the glow of another frontier crossed. Fast-forward to the current day, and the pioneering path taken by Rabbi Priesand and those who immediately followed her is acknowledged as a legacy that has become part of history.

Reaching back into time can be a challenge. So much has changed in the more than forty years, including each of us. As we reflect on the years that have passed since that ordination day, I reached out to some of our 1972 classmates to get their recollections of being with Sally in school.[1] I pulled out a somewhat faded picture of our class as we were preparing to march into Plum Street Temple. Looking at us just a few moments before the service brought forth several emotions—from the hope that was present in our faces, to a sadness that some of my closest friends in that class have since died. Nostalgia and memory are interesting filters. It was not uncommon, in the days before the mandatory Year-in-Israel program, for students to take a year off from rabbinical school in order to study in Jerusalem. I, however, opted to spend a year in London, serving a congregation as an interim rabbi. I returned to Hebrew Union College–Jewish Institute of Religion (HUC-JIR) in the fall of 1970 and was grafted onto Sally's class. As Sally was already traveling a lot, speaking on behalf of the school and the Reform Movement, we were fully aware that as her classmates we were going to be a part of history. To be honest, though, we were mostly focused on doing our work, writing our theses, serving our student pulpits, and counting the months until ordination. My memory of that time is that Sally was a classmate—a classmate with a unique burden, but one united with us in a shared cause of doing what we had to do to complete those last two years.

Fred Natkin (HUC-JIR, '72) recalled those years at HUC fondly:

> There was a struggle to make sure that Sally was one of us. Our joking…always was inclusive. We did not watch our language around Sally; instead, she helped us formulate our words to be inclusive. Reflected glory, shared preeminence, uniqueness. Of all the firsts and lasts of our class, that Sally was with us made it special. Of all the degrees, honors, and achievements, that Sally was one of our thirty-six made it unique. Of all the years, congregants, students, and families—the most poignant for me was speaking at someone's congregation about my military experience and a college-age student approached me and said, "You mean boys can be rabbis too!"

Rabbi James (Jim) Kessler (HUC-JIR, '72) summed up some of this feeling of being part of rabbinic history. Reflecting on a moment at a recent CCAR convention that honored our 1972 class, Jim wrote of a conversation he had with Sally at the post-service lunch where he said that it now seemed that we are "old." "Sally pointed out that we are and that now *we* are the 'older' rabbis. I felt so honored to be in

Sally's presence, for she devoted her life to honoring the special place she had in Jewish history."

There can be no doubt, looking back through the clouds of memory, that a major shift in the reality of American Jewry took place that June morning. The baby boom generation, now solidly encamped in their sixties, are the parents of young women who have followed in Sally's footsteps and along the path of those early pioneers. It was this generation that gave birth to the third wave of the Jewish feminist movement, and while there may still be hurdles and speed bumps, the expectation of this generation, which has been handed down to their children, is that the world is open to them. I think that is one of the reasons that the rabbinic students and recent graduates of today see themselves as post-feminist. They take this choice of becoming a rabbi as a natural one, perhaps as part of their Jewish birthright.

When Rabbi Jennifer Frenkel (HUC-JIR, '09) decided to apply to rabbinical school, she told me that she never had any hesitation about it. Rabbi Frenkel, who assumed the position of senior rabbi at her seven-hundred-plus-family congregation in July 2014, sees herself "as a rabbi, not a female rabbi" and as part of what she described as a "post-feminist rabbinate." The "revolution" has been won, so to speak. Perhaps the greatest triumph in these past forty years is the fact that there seems to be so little difference in the way rabbis are treated, be they male or female. Indeed, another one of our 1972 classmates, Rabbi Larry Kotok, summed it up as follows: "Over the years…it has been my experience that women rabbis have displayed the same wide range of personality [traits] and commitment as male rabbis."

"The journey has been an interesting one," remarked Rabbi Amy Schwartzman (HUC-JIR, '90), who has been at the same congregation since ordination, succeeding her then-longtime senior rabbi, Rabbi Laszlo Berkowits. I spoke with Amy about her perception of the decades since Sally's ordination, and she recalled, as a young rabbi, getting some comments on her hair or dress. She also mentioned the fact that there still remains some economic disparity between male and female colleagues and noted a feeling that despite great progress, the rabbinate is still "not as ready to embrace non-traditional women."

Forty-plus years of female rabbis has produced major changes. Yet, despite the fact that at least fifty percent of students at our non-Orthodox seminaries are female, some concerns remain. Rabbi Sue Levi Elwell (HUC-JIR, '86) has served both in congregations and on the staff of the Union for Reform Judaism. She also served as co-chair of the Women's Rabbinic Network. I asked her why a rabbinic network specifically for women was necessary. Rabbi Elwell answered, "We need an advocacy group for women in the rabbinate. The total concerns of women are not yet integrated into the totality of the CCAR." Elwell went on to equate some of this ongoing struggle with cultural struggles within American society for equality. "We are still figuring out the work-family issue. We Reform Jews need to continue to be countercultural, as the culture has not fully embraced women, gays, and people of differences."

There is no doubt that in these past forty years, American Judaism has been reshaped and restructured in many ways by the presence and impact of rabbis who are female. The feminist movement in Judaism is largely responsible for the surge in the awakening of so many to a spiritual quest or hunger that has found root in new forms of liturgy, rituals, and experiences. Outward acceptance of female rabbis is now the norm for the overwhelming non-Orthodox population. Yet the experiences of Rabbis Elwell, Schwartzman, and others illuminate some of the gender-specific complications in today's rabbinate.

Rabbi Denise Eger (HUC-JIR, '88), currently president of the CCAR, offers one example in a 2012 blog post for Reform Judaism's celebration of the fortieth anniversary of Rabbi Priesand's ordination. Rabbi Eger made the following observation, commenting on the striking absence of women in major leadership positions in the Reform Movement:

> That is why it is so troubling when, in our own denominational settings, women are still falling behind. Women rabbis earn less

and proportionally, women rabbis are not being chosen to serve as senior rabbis of large congregations. After forty years and after the numbers of women ordained, statistically, women are not on equal footing despite our progress.[2]

A few weeks after Rabbi Eger's blog post, Rabbi Mary Zamore (HUC-JIR, '97) added her take on the issue of where women stood after forty years. Rabbi Zamore acknowledged the progress that has been made in achieving numerous "firsts" but recognized that additional change needed to be forthcoming:

> Over the course of my rabbinate, discrimination has greatly diminished. With rare exceptions, today, the discrimination is not blatant as in "women cannot be rabbis," rather it exists in a more subtle form. I still observe discrimination in the guise of assumed limitations and roles. While many know a woman is capable of being any type of rabbi which her interests and talents support, there are plenty of people in our Jewish community, even Reform Jewish community, who still consciously or unconsciously limit women rabbis by assuming that gender defines her rabbinate. They are the ones who may praise our sweet, nurturing manner, yet fail to see strong leaders in the same rabbis. Of course, this is equally unfair to men. Both men and women deserve to be defined by their aptitudes and affinities. Personally, I simply want to be a rabbi, not a woman rabbi—that is why I embrace the term *rav*.[3]

Rabbi Zamore discussed the need for people to be seen as individuals, regardless of gender. That does not, however, detract from the fundamental issue that one cannot totally ignore: the fact that differences between the genders exist.

In a May 2012 blog post, Dr. Arnold Eisen, the chancellor of the Jewish Theological Seminary, asked two soon-to-be-ordained women about their views of their role. In answer to the response of one of the students, Dr. Eisen writes of the need to celebrate the individuality of colleagues:

> Clearly we have a long way to go when it comes to acceptance of women rabbis in the Conservative Movement (and beyond)

and appreciation of the distinctive skill set that women bring to the rabbinate. I, myself, believe that gender matters enormously when it comes to that skill set. Without "essential zing" on gender grounds—that is, assuming that "all men" share attributes A, B, and C, and "all women" share attributes X, Y, and Z—I'd say from observation that women rabbis as a group do bring different experiences, sensibilities and concerns to their rabbinates. This is as it should be. One question is how our communities can best take advantage of the opportunities that female leadership brings.[4]

Not quite ready to take advantage of those leadership qualities is the contemporary Orthodox Movement. Rabbi Darren Kleinberg notes some interesting parallels between the struggles of some women such as Regina Jonas to become ordained in 1930s Germany and some modern Orthodox women. Rabbi Kleinberg summarized some of the current concerns in his essay entitled "Orthodox Women (Non-)Rabbis" (see pp. 317–38). He noted that at the same time that the Jewish Theological Seminary was considering the ordination of women, a similar discussion was taking place among some Orthodox leadership. Kleinberg's article reviews the story of one woman who received private ordination in Israel but who has since moved away from the Orthodox world. The issue of the title "rabbi" was also noted in the current discussions within the Orthodox community. Much like Regina Jonas, whose use of the title brought concern, a recent situation discussed by Kleinberg seems to tell us that some things are very difficult to change.

On March 22, 2009, after completing an eight-year course of intensive study that included three years at the Drisha Institute for Jewish Education, a pioneering institution for advanced women's Torah study in New York, and five years under the private guidance of Rabbi Avi Weiss, the founder of the Yeshivat Chovevei Torah rabbinic school in New York, with a curriculum modeled after that of the male rabbinical students at Yeshivat Chovevei Torah, Sara Hurwitz faced a challenge to her desire to be called "Rabbi" when Rabbi Weiss held a "conferral" ceremony (see Neiss, pp. 305–16).

As Darren Kleinberg notes, "At this ceremony, and in similar fashion to the experience of Regina Jonas, despite studying and being examined on the self-same curriculum and materials as men studying for the rabbinate...Hurwitz was *not* ordained—in fact the word 'ordination' was never used to describe the ceremony—as a *rabbi*. For her conferral ceremony, the neologism 'MaHaRa"T,' was coined."[5] The term 'MaHaRa"T,' as explained in a footnote, is an "acronym made up from the sounds of the first letters of four Hebrew words: *Manhigah Halachtit, Ruchanit, Toranit*, which translates as Legal, Spiritual, and Torah Guide."[6]

Clearly, then, there is still no level playing field forty years after Rabbi Priesand's ordination at Plum Street Temple. What does seem to be true is that American Jewry in the early twenty-first century is experiencing an evolution in the role of what it means to be a rabbi, regardless of the rabbi's gender. The impact of women in the rabbinate is part of that evolution. In reality, this should not surprise anyone. The rapidity of change in the last forty years in American culture has impacted our Jewish community. The growing presence and power of women in all aspects of society is one of the great changes to which we are all witnesses. We would not have it any other way—just ask our own daughters! Adaptation has been a key to Jewish evolution and survival, no less today in this "age of transition." As we evolve, it is not about the gender of the rabbi. It is, as it should be, about the person who is the rabbi.

The importance of the individual person and not the person's gender was reinforced by Rabbi Peter Grumbacher (HUC-JIR, '72):

> It was a moving moment for us when Sally stood before Dr. Gottschalk. Our classmates had not spoken about it, but we all rose to our feet at that moment. She deserved the *kavod* [honor] for many reasons. Looking back these forty years, I cannot imagine anyone other than Sally Priesand being the first. Rabbi Priesand and those who followed in her footsteps have added something special to the rabbinate. Greater sensitivity? More compassion? No, male and female colleagues have their own share of sensitivity

and compassion; they are not only in the realm of one gender over another. Rather, what Sally and the other women in the rabbinate have gifted Jewry with is every characteristic we hope will be in the professional and personal lives of every colleague.

NOTES

1. In preparation for this piece I reached out to several classmates of our 1972 class as well as other female colleagues ordained in the generations that followed our class. Their responses were collected by e-mail or telephone conversations.

2. Denise L. Eger, "Thoughts on Celebrating Rabbi Priesand's Ordination," *RJ Blog*, May 4, 2012, http://blogs.rj.org/blog/2012/05/04/17717/.

3. Mary L. Zamore, "Women in the Rabbinate: Equal Leaders in Our Community," *RJ Blog*, May 21, 2012, http://blogs.rj.org/blog/2012/05/21/women-in-the-rabbinate-equal-leaders-in-our-community/.

4. Arnold Eisen, "Let's Talk about Women Rabbis," *On My Mind: Arnie Eisen* (blog), May 22, 2012, http://blog.jtsa.edu/chancellor-eisen/2012/05/22/lets-talk-about-women-rabbis/.

5. Darren Kleinberg, "Orthodox Women (Non-)Rabbis," p. 320, this volume.

6. Ibid., p. 334 n.19.

9

WHAT'S IN A WORD?

Inequality in the Reform *S'michah*

RABBI MARY ZAMORE

I was recently asked if the day of my ordination was a transformative experience or just another graduation. The answer: both, neither, a little bit of both. The multiple-hour ceremony flew by in the manner that truly moving events do; the speeches were so inspiring that I still remember snippets. I watched in curiosity as my classmates ascended the grand bimah of Temple Emanu-El of the City of New York. Blessed with the last name "Zamore," I waited and waited. Finally, it was my turn. I went up to the bimah; words were whispered in my ear, hands were laid on my head, *mazal tov* was said. I continued walking across the bimah to shake hands and collect the coveted *s'michah* for which I had labored five years. I remember none of the blessing I received; I recall being grateful that I did not trip or stray from the tight choreography. I do remember thinking about the gender-based inequalities that were evident to me but few would address openly. Foremost was my consternation that my *s'michah*, ordination certificate, would not say the same words as those bestowed to my male classmates.

This issue came to my attention the year before my ordination when my super-sharp husband, Terje, was reading a promotional brochure from Hebrew Union College–Jewish Institute of Religion that featured the picture of two brand-new rabbis standing outside of Temple

Emanu-El, fresh from their ordination. Their grins are huge as they pose with their *s'michah* documents unfurled in their hands. In the photograph, one man and one woman stand side by side, liberal Judaism's gender equality at its best. However, Terje saw something different: he saw that the wording, albeit tiny in the photo, was different on the two documents.[1]

I should have said something, but I did not feel empowered to make waves at that time as I faced job placement. And so, I said nothing. After ordination, I was swept into my new career. The language on my *s'michah* was secondary to trying to be a rabbi. I would periodically forget about the disparity until something would remind me, but I still said nothing.

In 2012 I was asked to contribute to the Union for Reform Judaism (URJ) blog celebrating women rabbis on the fortieth anniversary of Rabbi Sally Priesand's ordination. My article focused on the achievements I have witnessed over the course of my unfolding rabbinate (then, fifteen years) and on the types of gender discrimination that still need to be addressed. I wrote most of my article, including the story of the gender disparity in the *s'michah* and of how the document used to be unequal. I confidently wrote how fifteen years later, thank God, everything is good and equal in the language used to document that one is a rabbi. In order to finish the article, I needed to confirm the new language on the degree. Expectantly, I picked up the phone and called a younger colleague, told her my mission, and waited eagerly to learn the new wording. Sitting at her desk, she clearly read from the *s'michah* hanging on her office wall the same outdated language on my *s'michah*. Together we mused that perhaps it was the male document that had been changed. Neither of us could fathom that no change had taken place in fifteen years. Therefore, she quickly offered to call her husband, another recently ordained HUC-JIR rabbi, who could be found at that hour working at his desk, sitting near his *s'michah*. She assured me that she would call back in less than five minutes to set the record straight. She called back thirty minutes later, truly upset. The disparity was still the same. I had mistakenly made the assumption that in this day of improved gender equality, the *s'michah* had been changed. It had not.

My discovery has sent me on a journey of asking questions and seeking answers to better understand the inequality in the Reform *s'michah*, its origin, the history of the written documentation of ordination, and how the Reform Movement compares to the other movements that ordain women. As I gathered enough background information, I finally did what I should have done so many years ago: I asked the administration of HUC-JIR to change the *s'michah* documentation.

Finding the Roots of the Problem

My first step was contacting Rabbi Sally Priesand, who graciously returned my call in the middle of the festivities celebrating her fortieth year in the rabbinate.[2] When I asked her about the origin of the disparity, it turned out that she did not know about it either. Rabbi Priesand recalled that on the day of her controversial ordination, the tube handed to her was empty! In 1972, the faculty could not come to agreement as to what to write on her *s'michah*. At that time the documents were hand-calligraphed on rich vellum, requiring a great deal of lead time to produce. The deadline came and went without a decision, so Rabbi Priesand received nothing but an empty tube. This explains why, despite the presence of a corps of international photographers, there is no photograph of Rabbi Priesand holding her history-making *s'michah* in full view. During our May 2012 conversation and several times since, Rabbi Priesand indicated that she was unsure of the full story behind her ordination document. However, she always believed that her male colleagues had received documents that contained the same language as the one she finally received. In fact, she thought, although with a good dose of equivocation, that perhaps the male version may have been changed to prefigure her sole female version. We agreed that I should call one of her classmates to confirm this story. A few minutes later, Rabbi Richard F. Address was reading his *s'michah* to me over the phone. It was not the same as Rabbi Priesand's, mine, or that of any Reform woman rabbi.

Different Degrees

Since 1972, Reform woman rabbis have received *s'machot*, ordination certificates, that document their acceptance as rabbis, declaring in English (here I preserve the original text and format):

The Faculty and
Board of Governors of the
Hebrew Union College–
Jewish Institute of Religion
hereby certify that whereas

Sally Jane Priesand

has fulfilled all requirements for
Graduation she is herewith
ordained as

Rabbi

and is authorized and licensed to
perform all Rabbinical functions
in the name of God and Israel

In Hebrew, the degree declares:

אנחנו החתומים מטה
הראש וחבר המורים של
בית המדרש לרבנים
מעידים כי תלמידתנו החברה
שרה בת ישראל
למדה בבית מדרשנו תורה וחכמת ישראל
וגמרה את חק הלמודים הדרוש

לכך נמנינו וגמרנו בהסכמת מועצת הנאמנים
לסמכה ולהכתירה בתואר
רב ומורה
תורה תורה תדין תדין
תדרש תורת ה' ברבים, חפץ ה' בידה יצלח,
ויהי ה' עמה להגדיל תורה ולהאדירה

Here is my translation of the Hebrew, as it differs significantly from the English (I mimic the format of the Hebrew):

We, the undersigned
Head and faculty of the teachers of
the Rabbinical School,
Attest that our student and colleague
Sarah Bat Yisrael
Studied at our school Torah and Jewish scholarship
And she completed all of the required studies.
Therefore, we have decided, with the agreement of the Board of
Overseers
to ordain her and to bestow upon her the title
Rabbi and Teacher
She is authorized to teach; she is authorized to judge.[3]
May she interpret God's Torah among the people;[4]
May God's will find fulfillment through her hand;[5]
May God be with her to extol and glorify the Torah.[6]

Here is the male version:

The Faculty and
Board of Governors of the
Hebrew Union College–
Jewish Institute of Religion
hereby certify that whereas

Richard Fred Address
has fulfilled all requirements for
Graduation he is herewith
ordained as

Rabbi

and is authorized and licensed to
perform all Rabbinical functions
in the name of God and Israel

In Hebrew, the degree declares:

אנחנו החתומים מטה
הראש וחבר המורים של
בית המדרש לרבנים
מעידים כי תלמידנו החבר
ראובן בן מרדכי
למד בבית מדרשנו תורה וחכמת ישראל
וגמר את חק הלמודים הדרוש
לכך נמנינו וגמרנו בהסכמת מועצת הנאמנים
לסמכו ולהכתירו בתואר
מורנו הרב
יורה יורה ידין ידין ויהי ה׳ אלהיו עמו
יצלח וירכב על דבר אמת
וענוה-צדק

Here is my translation of the Hebrew, as it too differs significantly
from the English:

We, the undersigned
head and faculty of the teachers of
The Rabbinical School,
Attest that our student and colleague
Reuven ben Mordechai

Studied at our school Torah and Jewish scholarship
And he completed all of the required studies.
Therefore, we have decided with the agreement of the Board of
Overseers
to ordain him and bestow upon him the title
Our Teacher the Rabbi.
He is authorized to teach; he is authorized to judge.
May Adonai his God be with him
Causing him to succeed, directing him to the path of
truth, humility, and justice.[7]

There are two notable differences between the male and female
Hebrew versions of these documents. The first is small, but very significant; the second is more glaring, but less noteworthy. The more
sizable, but innocuous, difference is in the last three line of the *s'machot*.
The male degree declares in Hebrew, "He is authorized to teach; he
is authorized to judge. May Adonai his God be with him causing him
to succeed, directing him to the path of truth, humility and justice"; in
contrast, the female version pronounces, "She is authorized to teach;
she is authorized to judge. May she interpret God's Torah among the
people; may God's will find fulfillment through her hand; may God be
with her to extol and glorify the Torah."

Creating a conclusion to the degrees, both these sections begin with
the ancient and auspicious declaration "יורה יורה ידין ידין," presented
here with a translation more true to its original context: "May he teach?
He will teach. May he judge? He will judge." This line is taken from a
story in the Babylonian Talmud, *Sanhedrin* 5a, which is confirming
and defining the bounds of rabbinic authority for the second-century
CE leader Rabbah bar Chanah. Reflecting a time period in which the
rabbinate and its authority is in formation, this Talmudic story uses
the declaration " יורה יורה ידין ידין," "May he teach? He will teach.
May he judge? He will judge," to proclaim that Rabbah had rabbinic
authority even though he was about to lead the Jewish community in
the Diaspora of Babylonia, far from the Land of Israel. Today these

phrases have frequent usage in Orthodox *s'machot*.[8] A liberal seminary that often struggles for recognition in the greater Jewish world, Hebrew Union College–Jewish Institute of Religion surely chose this ancient declaration of authority because of its providence, contextual message, and parity in the Orthodox world. The message is clear and unequivocal: HUC-JIR is asserting that its rabbis can take their proper place in the ongoing chain of tradition alongside all rabbis, ancient and modern. Therefore, the Talmudic phrase used, although switched into the feminine form in the women's *s'michah*, creates a strong statement concerning the authority of women rabbis.

Strangely enough the rest of the three-line conclusion differs greatly in content, but not apparently in intent. The differences neither communicate varying levels of authority nor reflect gender discrimination. The two versions simply seem to be an unneeded divergence.

The most troublesome difference between the male and female *s'machot* is that although the English declares a man or a woman to be a rabbi, the Hebrew uses the phrase מורנו הרב, *moreinu harav* (our teacher the rabbi), for men, but רב ומורה, *rav u'morah* (rabbi and teacher), for women. Subtle, yet quite troubling, the disparate appellations reflect varying authority and historical authenticity. Found in both *s'machot*, the term רב, *rav*, is the ancient term for a male rabbi used from the first century CE on. Found as a straightforward noun in the female *s'michah*, the term *rav* is linked to *morah*, the feminine form of "teacher." Of course, מורה does not have vowels, and it is the reader who chooses to put (or not to put) the word into the feminine form. The word רב is clearly in the masculine form, even though the rabbi is a woman. In 1972, there was no feminine version of *rav* (rabbi) in Hebrew, a gendered language. It was only in recent years that the Academy of the Hebrew Language officially documented the word רַבָּה, *rabbah*, meaning "female rabbi," although they have not yet considered it for formal acceptance into their dictionary.[9] Therefore, the 1972 use of the masculine language is understandable. However, the use of a much different phrase for men—the phrase מורנו הרב, *moreinu harav* (our teacher the rabbi)—smacks of gender inequality.

The *moreinu harav* phrase is ancient, rooted in the fourteenth century, when the French Jewish community was reinstituting the ordination ceremony after a long hiatus.[10] Born out of an effort to link a 1386 ordination to the so-called unbroken chain of Jewish tradition, the phrase continues to communicate authenticity, authority, and stature. For these reasons, it is still used today in the Orthodox community as an additional honor to a learned and revered rabbi. The term *rav* is currently used as a formal form of address when referring to any man in some Jewish circles; such usage reaches back to medieval times. In contrast, *harav* gives the recognition of being a rabbi, one who has studied and been ordained. *Moreinu harav*, therefore, gives even more honor and authority to its bearer.

A Request

On May 21, 2012, after fifteen years of silence, I e-mailed Rabbi David Ellenson, then president of Hebrew Union College–Jewish Institute of Religion, writing:

> From: Mary L. Zamore
> Sent: Monday, May 21, 2012, 12:03 PM
> To: Pres Off Website Email
> Subject: request
>
> Dear David,
>
> I hope this e-mail finds you well. This past week I wrote a posting for the URJ blog; they had invited me to reflect on being a woman rabbi: http://blogs.rj.org/blog/2012/05/21/women-in-the-rabbinate-equal-leaders-in-our-community/. My first draft actually read differently. Here is the missing paragraph:
> "When I received my *s'michah* (certificate of rabbinic ordination) from HUC-JIR, it was one of the proudest days of my life. However, I have to admit, when I discovered that the Hebrew on my *s'michah*, and that of all the new women rabbis, was different from my male classmates, I was disappointed. The document declaring me a rabbi referred to me as '*rav u'morah*—rabbi

and teacher,' while the men's version said '*moreinu harav*—our teacher the rabbi.' The difference is subtle, but the men's version is a classic Jewish appellation for an honored rabbi. Now both men and women rabbis are referred to as 'xxx' on these important documents."

I was going to use the *s'michah* as an example of the great progress we have achieved in terms of equality in the rabbinate. So, I called a few new colleagues to ask what the new version said in order to fill in the placeholder "xxx" in my article. I had assumed this many years later things had changed. I was shocked to find there was no change. I know that is what I get for assuming and not voicing my opinion. Please know that the women and men I contacted were dismayed to learn of the difference between the men's and women's degrees.

After fifteen years of not saying anything, I would like HUC-JIR know that it was hurtful and disappointing to learn in 1997 that there were two versions of the *s'michah*. It is more hurtful to learn that it is still different. Of course, I understand the challenges of Hebrew and gender, and I would love to know the history of the present situation, as well as what language the Jerusalem campus uses.

I hope my words can open a dialogue in order to revisit the present approach to all the Hebrew throughout these documents.

In friendship and respect,

Mary L. Zamore

In less than three hours, I received a response in which Rabbi Ellenson wrote, "Assuming that most colleagues feel as you do, I am happy to initiate a process to change this distinction in the wording of our male and female colleagues' *s'michah*." Rabbi Michael Marmur, provost of HUC-JIR, was copied on this e-mail and promptly replied, "Since this issue was raised with me I have convened a group comprising faculty colleagues." He hoped to have a new text determined by the 2013 ordination season.

While the faculty committee appointed did meet, conducted research, and discussed the issue, a proposal for a new *s'michah* was not approved for the 2013 ordinations. In March 2013 Rabbi Michael

Marmur shared with me the research culled together by Kevin Prof-fitt,[11] senior archivist for Research and Collections, American Jew-ish Archives, by request of Rabbi Laura Baum.[12] At that time, Rabbi Marmur expected to have this issue settled by the 2014 ordinations. Proffitt's research documented part of the behind-the-scenes discus-sions before Rabbi Priesand's 1972 ordination. Unfortunately, the vital part of the history that would document the exact roots of the gender disparity is missing. However, the few pages that exist show the initial intent to create a female version of the *s'michah* that is very equal to the existing male one.

Behind the Scenes 1971–72

In a letter dated November 9, 1971, from Professor Alexander Gutt-man to Dr. Alfred Gottschalk, the president of HUC-JIR, Professor Guttman indicates that then senior student Sally Priesand has made repeated inquiry if the school has prepared the necessary changes for her unique *s'michah* degree. Professor Guttman further explains that he always studies the language of the *s'michah* document with the seniors as part of their Codes class before their ordination. In his letter, Gutt-man explores the options and challenges that he sees for the female version of the degree. He refers to two attached proposals for Rabbi Priesand's degree and even reports that Professor Uri Tal, a visiting professor from Israel, has "scrutinized both texts, is pleased with both, but considers version (2) superior."[13] While this letter is missing its attachments, a later correspondence between dean Rabbi Kenneth D. Roseman and the HUC-JIR faculty[14] refers to the two Guttman pro-posals and has them attached with another proposed text (see below). Therefore, we will assume that these proposals went unchanged and were the same as the attachments in this original letter.

In his first version, Professor Guttman uses the now familiar phrase *rav u'morah*, but in his second version he offers י"נ מרותנו, *morateinu*, being the female form of "our teacher" followed by two Hebrew letters, an abbreviation that can mean נרו יאיר, *nero ya-ir*, meaning "May his light shine." Although he modifies the Hebrew of "our teacher," Guttman does not change the gender of this classic phrase of praise. It is not clear why the key word "rabbi" is missing. Earlier in version two, the document does bestow the title *rav*, "rabbi," but it does not appear in the large central spot on the *s'michah*. On November 16, 1971, Dr. Gottschalk acknowledges receipt of Professor Guttman's letter and indicates that he too prefers the version above.

On January 6, 1972, dean Rabbi Kenneth D. Roseman sent a memo to the faculty announcing a meeting on January 11, 1972, to vote on the wording of Rabbi Priesand's *s'michah*. He enclosed three possible versions—two by Professor Guttman and a third by Professor Werner Weinberg. Rabbi Roseman also warned that discussion on the issue will be limited, because the faculty has "other issues of significance… which will require substantial discussion." Attached to Professor Weinberg's proposal is a letter dated January 10, 1972, explaining that he and "Dr. Wacholder acted as a sub-committee of the Committee of Academic Procedures and Evaluation." He explains that "we did not change *Moreinu HaRav* to the feminine, because we felt that it is a title comparable to 'doctor,' the gender of which is ambiguous." The Weinberg/Wacholder version closely follows the original male version, creating a virtual parallel document. Guttman's two proposals suggest many changes. However, it is important to note that in his letter of November 9, 1971, Professor Guttman says, "The wording of our *s'michah* (as well as the question of the signatures) has been a controversial issue for many years." He even recalls that "the class of 1970 petitioned the Faculty to omit the words יורה יורה ידין ידין. Dr. Glueck and the Faculty rejected the petition. Omitting these words would make our *s'michah* appear inferior to the *Semichot* issued by Yeshivot and Jewish Theological Seminaries[15] (though the latter give יורה יורה ידין ידין only exceptionally while most students receive יורה יורה only." It is possible that Professor Guttman saw the challenge of creating a female *s'michah* as an opportunity to revisit *in toto* the ordination certificates.

Therefore, some of the new language he suggested may have had nothing to do with gender.

On January 31, 1972, Dr. Ben Zion Wacholder, now identified as chairman of the Academic Council, sent an in-house memo to Professors Alexander Guttman and Eugene Mihaly, with copies to Dr. Alfred Gottschalk and Rabbi Kenneth D. Roseman. In the memo he simply announces, "The committee to determine the wording of the diploma for Sally Priesand will meet at 12:30 p.m., Monday, February 7, 1972 in the Sisterhood Dormitory." In Weinberg's January 10, 1972, letter to the faculty, which accompanied the Weinberg/ Wacholder version, they propose that "the Faculty should authorize a committee of rabbis to write a text." It seems that Wacholder is referring to such a committee. Unfortunately, the document trail ends there, and we know only of the final product, not of the discussions that produced it. Perhaps, in the future, others will uncover more of this history.

Looking Forward

In November 2015, Rabbi Michael Marmur convened a faculty task force to discuss changing the HUC-JIR *s'michah*. Faculty representatives from all four campuses were invited to weigh in on the new document which will correct the gender inequality. Rabbi Marmur invited me to serve *ex-officio* on this task force in order to share my research and to represent the voice of the Women's Rabbinic Network, the international organization of Reform Women Rabbis, which I now serve as Executive Director. In under an hour the faculty quickly came to a consensus after debating some of the options. The conversation especially centered on the problematic grammar which may be created in order to offer gender equal language. The benefits and drawbacks of using רַבָּה, *rabbah*, vs. רב, *rav*, when referring to a female rabbi were argued. In the end, the group decided to give the female ordinees the choice of which Hebrew title they want. This mirrors the approach of

HUC-JIR's Israeli rabbinical program. However, this decision led to another choice to be made, whether to follow the appropriate Hebrew grammar of the female version of the phrase "מורנו הרב *Moreinu Ha-Rav*" or to disregard Hebrew grammar and create the phrase "מורתנו הרב *Moriteinu HaRav*" which is blatantly wrong grammatically speaking, but uses the phrase "הרב *HaRav*" in an innovatively gender-neutral case which does not exist in present day Hebrew. Ironically, this solution brings the entire argument of the female *s'michah* full circle to some of the discussions of 1972 in which the Professor Weinberg and Dr. Wacholder argue that "הרב *HaRav*" is "comparable to 'doctor,' the gender of which is ambiguous." The final decision, sealed with a follow up email shortly after the phone meeting, calls for women ordinees to be offered the choice of "מורתנו הרב *Moriteinu HaRav*" or "מורתנו הַרַבָּה *Moriteinu HaRabba*." It should be mentioned that using the phrase "רב ומורה *rav u'moreh/morah*" was briefly entertained for the convenience of being able to use it interchangeably for men and women, depending on how the reader fills in the vowels. This option was quickly dismissed as it does not have the historical weight of "מורנו הרב *Moreinu HaRav*." After this most important decision was made during the conference call, attention was brought to the ending lines of the document. The faculty quickly agreed that the present female ending is superior to the traditional male version since these two lines "better described the rabbinate," as one faculty member remarked. With this decision, Professor Guttman *z"l* will have a lasting impact on the *s'michah* document.

I look forward to the new *s'michah* text making its public debut at the spring 2016 ordinations, allowing HUC-JIR to join all the liberal movements of Judaism in conferring a fully equalitarian rabbinical degree. At the time of the writing of this article, the graduating female rabbinical students are excitedly engaged in discussions deciding which title they each want to choose. While the changed text was the most important goal, I also implore the administration and faculty of HUC-JIR to recognize publicly the new text to start the process of healing concerning the former gender disparity. It would be easy to merely switch out the offending text quietly without recognizing the past. That would be unfortunate.

Do the Words Matter?

One could claim that the words on the women's *s'michah* do not matter, especially since few have vocalized objections. It is even possible that few have noticed the disparity at all. Following this train of thought, one could further argue that the piece of paper is merely a part of the pomp and circumstance and that what really matters is the acceptance and authority of women rabbis. However, I see it a different way: The disparity on the degree reflects the gender differences that exist every day for women rabbis. While we no longer, thank God, live with the constant question if we can be rabbis or with the blatant discrimination that held back women in all expressions of the rabbinate, there are still challenges. These inequalities are further compounded by the fact that many do not want to recognize them. The Jewish community wants to proudly shout that everything is equal and problem free. However, it is like that ordination photo in the HUC-JIR brochure from so many years ago. Things look equal until you carefully examine the fine print. Unless we are willing to address the challenges faced by women rabbis as loudly as we are celebrating the successes, these inequalities will remain. Women rabbis continue to face pay inequality, as well as glass ceilings. A legacy of unequal pay and job advancement leaves many women rabbis at a disadvantage during retirement. Young women rabbis face terrible struggles to secure maternity leave and career advancement, as congregations and Jewish institutions often see childbearing as a liability. Women rabbis are not equally represented in the leadership of our Reform Movement. And finally, what I consider the most insidious of all, our community uses different language when referring to women rabbis. We are frequently referred to as teachers and nurturers, not as strong leaders. We are praised for being great with the kids and the elderly, not for being inspiring role models and learned teachers.

This type of stereotyping undermines the individuality of every rabbi and does not honor the varied expressions of the rabbinate. In addition, as the liberal rabbinate becomes an increasingly feminized profession, we must ensure that it does not lose stature or pay scale. This is clearly not fair to the women or men who are devoted, hardworking rabbis who strive to be kind, compassionate leaders, helping to create a vision for the future of the Jewish community while expressing themselves as individuals with personal lives. As Judy Chicago wrote, "And then all that has divided us will merge / And then compassion will be wedded to power / And then softness will come to a world that is harsh and unkind / And then both men and women will be gentle / And then both women and men will be strong."[17] I hope true equality will be reflected in our s'machot and will live in every rabbi's career path.[18]

NOTES

1. The gender disparity only applies to the degrees conferred at the three U.S. campuses of HUC-JIR, not their Jerusalem campus.

2. Personal phone interview with Rabbi Sally Priesand, May 2012.

3. This declaration comes from the Babylonian Talmud, *Sanhedrin* 5a. An exact translation renders it, "She will teach; she will teach. She will judge; she will judge." Taking the context of this text in account, it is better translated, "Is she authorized to teach? Yes, she is authorized to teach. Is she authorized to judge? Yes, she is authorized to judge." I have removed the question from the translation because the new context does not call for it.

4. The first half of this line is based on Ezra 7:10.

5. The second half of this line is based on Isaiah 53:10.

6. This last line is based on Isaiah 42:21.

7. This last line is based on Psalm 45:5.

8. *Yoreh yoreh, yadin yadin* (he shall teach, he shall judge). These two phrases represent two different levels of *s'michah* in the modern Orthodox community. The former is the designation for the most general form of *s'michah*, while the latter is awarded for more advanced study.

9. http://hebrew-academy.huji.ac.il/sheelot_teshuvot/MivharTeshuvot/Pages/25031003.aspx.

10. *Encyclopaedia Judaica*, corrected ed., s.v. "Semikhah" (Jerusalem: Keter Publishing House, no date).

11. I thank Kevin Proffitt, senior archivist, as well as Elisa Ho, associate archivist, at the Jacob Rader Marcus Center of the American Jewish Archives, for their efforts to fulfill my many research requests for this chapter.

12. Rabbi Baum had recognized the difference between the male and female versions in 2009 when sitting in a male colleague's office. She then raised the question of the disparity's origin with HUC-JIR.

13. Alexander Guttmann, letter to Alfred Gottschalk, November 9, 1971.

14. Kenneth D. Roseman, letter to the members of the faculty, HUC-JIR, January 6, 1972.

15. It should be noted that modern JTS ordination certificates do not use this phrase nor does the seminary refer to the ordination process or certificate as *s'michah*.

16. Personal conversation with Rabbi Aaron Panken, March 2014.

17. Judy Chicago, *The Dinner Party*, 1996.

18. My thanks to Rabbi Robert Scheinberg and Raziel Haimi-Cohen for being early readers of this chapter.

10

A BRIEF HISTORY OF THE TASK FORCE ON WOMEN IN THE RABBINATE

RABBI NEIL KOMINSKY

The Task Force on Women in the Rabbinate was established by a 1976 vote of the Executive Board of the Central Conference of American Rabbis. This vote followed by one year the 1975 Resolution on Women in Reform Judaism adopted by the CCAR Convention, which, in addition to urging egalitarian inclusion of women in temple worship and leadership as well as in educational materials produced by the Reform Movement, resolved

> that we express once again our total support of the ordination of women. We call upon the Hebrew Union College–Jewish Institute of Religion to continue to seek qualified female candidates for the rabbinate and cantorate, and we urge our congregations and all others who employ rabbis and cantors to choose their spiritual leadership not on the basis of sex but in terms of individual ability and competence.[1]

Both the resolution and the creation of the task force reflected a growing awareness that a proactive approach was the best way to smooth the path for a coming generation of women who would serve as rabbis.

The task force, convened for the first time on March 9, 1977, was chaired by Rabbi Sally Priesand, whose landmark ordination almost five years before had moved the question of women as rabbis from the theoretical realm to the practical one. There had been few women in the HUC-JIR "pipeline" when Priesand was ordained. By 1977, there were only three ordained women, but already enrolled rabbinical students promised thirty-four more in the following four years.

The initial meeting included Rabbi Joseph Glaser representing CCAR leadership, Rabbi Malcolm Stern as director of the Joint Placement Commission, Al Vorspan on behalf of the UAHC (as it was then named), Rosalind Gold and Steven Mason as rabbinical student representatives, and, as appointed members of the task force, Rabbi Edward Klein and me. This set the pattern for future meetings, involving representation of CCAR staff and elected leadership, placement directors, UAHC liaisons, and regular task force members. Although he was not present at the initial meeting, Dr. Eugene Mihaly was a frequent presence as liaison from HUC-JIR.

Members of the task force understood from the onset that it was much easier for people to harbor objections to women as rabbis in theory than to do so in the presence of an actual rabbi who happened to be a woman. Thus, a primary goal of the task force over its first few years was to encourage positive publicity about women in the rabbinate and to expose as broad a population of Reform Jews as possible to firsthand contact with women who were rabbis or rabbinical students. Special attention was paid to providing Reform rabbis with the opportunity to interact with female colleagues and colleagues-in-training; many rabbis, as well as laypeople, needed to become accustomed to the new reality. Arrangements were made, when possible, for women who served student pulpits and other HUC-JIR women nearing ordination to attend and participate in regional CCAR *Kallot*, which offered numerous informal opportunities for rabbis to become acquainted with the coming generation of female colleagues. Opportunities were also sought for women rabbis to appear in public roles at UAHC events in order to accustom lay leaders as well to their presence. I was one of a number of Reform rabbis who shared responsibility for a Sunday morning religious program on Hartford television, and I used my slot early in this period to host a discussion with two women who were nearing the end of the their studies at the New York school. The task force also hoped to arrange summer internships for female rabbinical students in congregations around the country as a way of increasing visibility, but such opportunities proved difficult to fund.

As it became clear that public advocacy of the cause of women in the rabbinate would be a prime responsibility of the chair of the task force, Sally Priesand became convinced that such advocacy would be more effectively delivered in a male voice and stepped down as chair in the fall of 1978, although she remained an active and important member of the task force. I succeeded her and served as chair until 1984, when David Hachen took over. By 1986, the situation of women in the rabbinate had become normalized enough that it was felt that a female colleague could successfully lead the work of the task force, and Rosalind Gold became chair. All subsequent chairs of the task force were women.

Advocacy for women in the rabbinate also entailed, on a few occasions, writing rejoinders to published pieces that inaccurately portrayed the situation and prospects of female Reform rabbis. Two memorable instances occurred in 1979. In March, Rabbi Pinchas Stolper, executive vice president of the Union of Orthodox Jewish Congregations, published an article in *Sh'ma* entitled "Women Rabbis as a Death Sign."[2]

While primarily intended as an attack on the Jewish Theological Seminary's decision to begin ordaining women to the Conservative rabbinate, Stolper's article also took aim at the experience of women as Reform rabbis, describing it as unsuccessful and producing dissatisfied rabbis who could not fulfill the role to which they had been ordained. A letter to the editor was promptly dispatched to correct the disparaging misinformation.

Not all opposition, though, came from outside the Reform Movement. In the fall of 1979, Rabbi Norman M. Goldburg, a retired Reform rabbi, wrote in the *National Jewish Post & Opinion* that the

Reform Movement should discontinue the ordination of women, as they "should not expect to function as rabbis." In response, I pointed out that with eight Reform women serving in congregational positions and four in Hillel, besides two in England and three ordained by the Reconstructionist Movement, women were, in fact, already functioning very successfully as Reform rabbis. I granted that some additional "consciousness-raising" would be in order as women matured in their careers and became eligible for larger pulpits of their own, but I pointed out that being quite young in their careers, most of our women were in fully appropriate positions, in which they were succeeding admirably.

By 1981, with seven women established in full-time pulpits of their own, I was able to write an article for *Reform Judaism* highlighting the experiences of these colleagues and the positive responses of lay leaders in their congregations. Both rabbis and congregational leaders made it clear that once the rabbi had entered into her position, she was perceived primarily as a rabbi, not as a "woman rabbi." A number of the rabbis noted specifically that while the wider community called on them for reflections on being a female rabbi, their role in the congregation was teaching Judaism.

The task force's next major challenge was maternity leave. While none of our rabbis had had a baby when the topic was taken up for the first time in 1979, it was self-evident that this was only a matter of time. Reaching a consensus on an appropriate approach to maternity leave was a complex task. Among CCAR and Placement Commission leadership, there were concerns that a formal maternity leave policy would impede the placement of women and should not yet be pursued. Congregations being served by women, it was argued, would deal with the question when it arose in practical terms and would, in all likelihood, be more forthcoming in the specific instance of their own rabbi, with whom they already had a relationship, than they would when negotiating a contract. This was a good-faith argument, and the task force considered it seriously. What we found, however, was that the women who had been or were shortly about to be ordained almost universally believed that a concrete guideline for maternity leave was desirable, even allowing for the possible repercussions in placement. This was the goal we chose to pursue.

There was also a strong feeling on the task force that the desirable language would be "parenting leave," acknowledging the need of fathers as well as mothers to free up time to be with the newborn. Here, we reluctantly made a practical judgment that maternity leave was a concept that would make sense to the Placement Commission and its constituent groups, while parenting leave would be less widely accepted and had the potential to sink the whole proposal. We went with the incremental approach.

In 1981, the task force formally recommended to the Joint Placement Commission that a policy of three months' maternity leave be added to the *Guidelines for Rabbinical-Congregational Relationships*, which, depending on the edition, was popularly known as the Blue Book or the Gold Book. Discussions continued over the following years and, in 1983, the task force agreed to a proposal of two months' maternity leave plus the right of the rabbi to append the coming year's one-month vacation to the leave. This policy was added to the *Guidelines* in 1984. A 1987 survey of twelve women who had given birth while serving as rabbis reported that the congregations and organizations for which they worked had been helpful and generous in their handling of maternity leave.

As the number of women in the Reform rabbinate increased year by year, there was a growing sense that rabbis in this historically unprecedented position needed better opportunities to communicate with each other as well as share wisdom and experience.[3] In the fall of 1979, the CCAR Executive Board authorized and funded a meeting of all ordained women within the CCAR as well as female junior and senior rabbinical students. The meeting was called under the auspices of the task force, which requested Rabbi Laura Geller to act as convener on its behalf. The meeting took place in New York on February 5–7, 1980, and was felt by participants to be a great success. Indeed, the sense that such support and communication ought to continue regularly led to the creation of the Women's Rabbinic Network (WRN) during the meeting. The WRN, at its inception, was anticipated to be an autonomous organization rather than a formal constituent of the CCAR, as was the task force. At the same time, the agendas and membership of the task force and the WRN were inherently intertwined, and the task force enthusiastically welcomed the WRN as a partner in serving a common interest.

There was some concern among CCAR leadership that an autonomous "women's caucus" might be unnecessary and potentially problematic. It fell to me, as chair of the task force, to serve as a diplomatic liaison, assuring CCAR leadership of the important role that the WRN had to play and of the task force's close communication with and support of the WRN. Ultimately, in the interests of clarity, I drafted a paper in 1981 on "The Roles and Interrelationship of the CCAR Taskforce on Women in the Rabbinate and the Women's Rabbinic Network."[4] The role of the task force was defined as "the oversight and facilitation of the complete professional and collegial integration of women as rabbis." Implicit in the term "taskforce," I pointed out, was the idea that the work could be completed, and if so, the role of the task force would be ended. The WRN, I suggested, grew out of "the legitimate need of women serving in the rabbinate for the kind of support, [and] sharing of experience and concerns that only those in their unique position are able to offer each other." It provided not only mutual support, but also an opportunity for the women in the Reform rabbinate to reach and voice consensus as to their needs and concerns. The paper concluded that close cooperation and communication between the task force and the WRN, as was already the case, best served the goals of both groups. The paper was adopted as a policy statement by both the task force and the WRN, and in my experience, conflicts between the two groups were nonexistent.

A major responsibility of the task force was monitoring women's experience of the rabbinic placement process. Each year, the director of placement (Rabbi A. Stanley Dreyfus, z"l, during most of this period) reported to us on the placement status of our female colleagues, and additionally, the task force members were in touch with recently ordained women to obtain their view of their placement experience. As women matured in the rabbinate and became eligible for second placements, concerns began to arise. In general, women and men did equally well in seeking immediate post-ordination positions as assistant rabbis, although there were reports of some inappropriate questions during interviews, and a few senior colleagues were clearly unwilling to have women as assistants. Getting fair consideration of women for positions as sole rabbi of a congregation, however, was proving more difficult. When Sally Priesand shared with the task force her experience seeking a pulpit in 1979, when she left her position as associate rabbi at the Stephen Wise Free Synagogue in New York, she noted that nine of the twelve congregations in which she had expressed an interest declined even to interview her, a number of them explicitly indicating that this was due to the fact that she was a woman.[5] Ultimately, Priesand was offered only a part-time pulpit in Elizabeth, New Jersey, where she served for three years before moving on to a full-time position at the Monmouth Reform Temple in Tinton Falls, New Jersey, the congregation to which she devoted the rest of her career in the active rabbinate.

It seemed clear that many congregations regarded a female rabbi as a controversial choice that it was prudent to avoid. The task force responded by requesting that the Placement Commission build a non-discrimination pledge into its congregational application form, which was done in 1980, and establish Placement Assistance Teams—lay/rabbinic teams that would meet with each congregation seeking a rabbi and help them to understand the process, including the fact that female candidates for their pulpits were to be evaluated on an equal footing with their male colleagues. As the process developed, UAHC regional directors took on much of this responsibility, and the message started to spread. As I noted above, in 1982 seven women began serving in full-time congregational positions of their own.

Beginning in the mid-1980s, Rabbi Mark Winer conducted a national survey of rabbinic salaries, broken out by congregation size, on behalf of the CCAR. Winer's findings were of great interest to the task force, and he met with us regularly to explore the meaning of his survey for gender equality. As with placement, Winer found that financial arrangements for men and women were essentially equal in assistantships and small congregations. As women began to move into larger congregations, however, women's compensation tended to cluster toward the lower end for each size category. Whether this was a problem of congregations believing that women were worth less, or of women being less effective than men in negotiating on their own behalf, or some combination of these was impossible to determine from the data. It did, though, flag the problem for the task force as something to be addressed. Pay equity became a permanent part of the task force's portfolio.

Another concern arising around 1984 was the ability of women rabbis to serve as chaplains in the United States Armed Forces. The problem was not with the Pentagon, which was open to the idea, but with the fact that Jewish chaplains needed to be certified by the Commission on Jewish Chaplaincy of the Jewish Welfare Board. The commission included representation from Reform, Conservative, and Orthodox rabbis, and the Orthodox members could in no way agree to endorse rabbis who were women. CCAR representatives, at the same time, were committed to opening opportunities for those women who wished to serve in chaplaincy. With the assistance of the CCAR commission members, the task force monitored the situation as it developed toward a successful conclusion. In 1986, the process was reorganized so that each Jewish denomination independently certified its own candidates to the Department of Defense. While the Jewish Welfare Board continued to supervise and support the work of Jewish chaplains, Reform rabbis, male and female, could now enter the service without requiring the approval of Orthodox rabbis.

The Task Force on Women in the Rabbinate continued to meet annually, usually at CCAR conventions through 1991, monitoring concerns about pay equity and placement opportunities for women.

In 1992, there was no report from the task force in the *CCAR Yearbook*, and the task force was no longer listed among CCAR committees.

In 1993, the Committee for Women in the Rabbinate became a standing committee of the CCAR and became responsible for areas previously overseen by the task force.

In the fourteen years of its existence, the Task Force on Women in the Rabbinate saw the female population of the Reform rabbinate increase from 3 to over 150, serving in congregations of increasing size and geographic diversity and in a wide variety of organizational positions. By 1991, women were serving on the Executive Board of the CCAR and would soon after be officers. All problems on the task force agenda had not been resolved, but clear and measurable progress had been achieved in multiple areas, and women were visible and valued colleagues among their male counterparts. In these terms, I believe one can justly conclude that the Task Force on Women in the Rabbinate succeeded in its mission.[6]

NOTES

1. *Yearbook of the Central Conference of American Rabbis*, vol. 86 (Cincinnati: CCAR, 1975), 78.

2. Pinchas Stolper, "Women Rabbis as a Death Sign" *Sh'ma* 9, no. 170 (1979): 73.

3. Looking back from the age of social media, one must work hard to remember how much more cumbersome and expensive long-distance contact was in 1980!

4. Task Force on Women in the Rabbinate Collection, MS-677, Box 1, Folder 3, American Jewish Archives, Cincinnati, Ohio.

5. Minutes of Meeting of the CCAR Task Force on Women in the Rabbinate, October 17 and 18, 1979, Task Force on Women in the Rabbinate Collection, MS-677, Box 1, Folder 1, American Jewish Archives, Cincinnati, Ohio.

6. The author wants to express his gratitude to Dr. Gary Zola, director of the American Jewish Archives, and Dr. Kevin Proffitt, senior archivist for Research and Collections, for their generous assistance in accessing minutes and papers contained in the Women in the Rabbinate Collection, which were no longer in my possession.

11

FROM PERIPHERY TO CENTER

A History of the Women's Rabbinic Network

RABBI CAROLE B. BALIN, PHD

When I first wrote this essay for publication in the CCAR *Jour-nal in 1997, I set out to document the founding narrative of the Women's Rabbinic Network (WRN). By that time—twenty-five years since the first woman had been ordained—the WRN had already gained prominence and relevancy among Jewish profes-sionals for its ability to connect and advocate on behalf of female rabbis. Over the past two decades, the WRN has not only contin-ued its proud legacy of advocating on behalf of its members for equal pay and family leave, but has also put itself at the forefront of broader human rights initiatives within the Reform Movement. For example, the WRN has championed the rights of LGBTQ clergy and congregants, serving as a beacon of progressive values for the world Jewish community, in partnership with the CCAR.*

The organization remains a powerful voice within the rabbini-cal context. Boasting a membership of over 650 female rabbis as of this writing,[1] the WRN represents women serving in all venues of Jewish life, including congregations, Hillels, hospitals, schools, seminaries, universities, organizations, and senior communities. The WRN offers its members a yearly retreat for meeting and engaging in professional, spiritual, and intellectual enrichment, as well as programming throughout the year. Most important, the WRN has challenged Jews to consider feminist approaches to religious leadership, which de-emphasize hierarchical relationships between rabbis and laity and make all aspects of Judaism accessible to all. The WRN has not only humanized the rabbinate but brought male colleagues along in its pursuit of work-life balance.

Though some of the facts and context have changed since this essay was first published in 1997, it remains an important piece of the historical record and as such is presented here in its original form.

Prologue

One measure of an organization's success is its members' attention to its past. Initially, there is concern with the present, with the day-to-day business of infrastructure and participation. Only after its survival is assured does the membership begin to act toward creating a future forged of shared expectations and objectives. Finally, it turns backward to record its history, to chronicle how it got from there to here, crystallizing into the thriving organization that it has become. In 1987, a mere seven years after its founding and fifteen years after the first woman had been ordained, the Women's Rabbinic Network (WRN)—the organization founded to give professional and personal support to women in or about to enter the Reform rabbinate—developed a historical consciousness. For in that year, the leadership of the WRN had the prescience to establish an Archive Committee with the mandate to collect and preserve documents for posterity. This crucial step illustrates that female Reform rabbis and their professional organization had come of age. As the proposal for the Archive Committee put it in 1987: "We are an historical phenomenon of no small significance, and our organization, therefore, is an important subject of historical inquiry."

So be it.[2]

Early Attempts at Organizing: WRA and ROW

"We used to joke," reminisced Rabbi Mindy Portnoy, "that meetings of the Women's Rabbinic Network [WRN] could be held in the women's restroom during conventions of the Central Conference of American Rabbis."[3] Indeed, at its inception in 1980, the Women's Rabbinic Network could necessarily yield only a short roster, given the fact that those eligible for membership included the fifteen female Reform rabbis and the nearly sixty female rabbinical students of the day. But the early numbers are in no way indicative of the immense impact that the WRN has come to have on the Reform rabbinate. The WRN has led the CCAR membership to reconsider such crucial topics as measuring success in the rabbinate and the nature of the rabbi-congregant relationship. Many issues raised in the earliest deliberations of the WRN have found their way onto the agenda of the CCAR. According to its [then] placement director, Rabbi Arnold Sher, recognizing "pulpit-free" rabbis, hierarchy in the rabbinate, and the development of a mentoring program are the chief concerns presently facing the CCAR's Placement Commission.[4] And members of the WRN may justifiably take credit for bringing these three important issues to bear. In fact, as its history shows, chronicling the WRN's movement through time is tantamount to charting its progress from the periphery to the center of the Reform rabbinate.

The story of the WRN's birth, growth, and influence is not unique in the annals of women's history. It is only one expression of a major upheaval in popular attitudes about both gender and family to emerge in the United States in the second half of the twentieth century. In 1978, one-half of all adult women were enrolled in the labor force, and as the center of gravity for womanhood shifted from the family toward outside employment, the gender cast of the rabbinate underwent a transformation as well: fewer than one in fifteen rabbinical students at Hebrew Union College–Jewish Institute of Religion (HUC-JIR) were female in 1975; almost one in three were female in 1980. At the same time, as an estimated 300,000 women enrolled in formal feminist organizations, female rabbis and rabbinical students, too, banded together to share their common concerns.[5]

The first such recorded meeting took place on February 8, 1976, when fifteen female rabbis and rabbinical students of Hebrew Union

College–Jewish Institute of Religion's New York campus, Philadelphia's Reconstructionist Rabbinical College, and independent ordaining organizations gathered to "investigate topics of general concern."[6] Although acknowledging and welcoming the press's powerful role in educating the public about the new phenomenon of female rabbis but at the same time conflicted about becoming the focus of a media circus, those gathered expressed their fear of and pain over the possibility of distortion or misrepresentation in the press. Ever conscious of the novelty of their situation, the pioneering female rabbis and rabbinical students of 1976 sought to encourage more young women to follow in their footsteps, but did so without the benefit of having female models of their own to trail behind. Thus the first formal meeting of women rabbis and rabbinical students was regarded as a welcome opportunity to share concerns and apprehensions among a population of Women's Rabbinical Alliance (WRA) to offer "mutual support and encouragement, maintain communication…[and] work together on problems facing [them]." While two chapters of this "national" organization were to function in New York City and Philadelphia—where, it was explained, "the largest concentration of female rabbis and [rabbinical] students was and remains"[7]—the East Coast originators encouraged their sisters on HUC-JIR's Cincinnati and Los Angeles campuses, along with women in the field, to join their cause.

This friendly action nearly backfired when the Cincinnati students announced that they had established the Rabbinical Students' Organization for Women (ROW—a deliberate nod to the colloquialism "raise a row," according to a founder) as a local answer to the "so-called national WRA."[8] Inclusive of students of both sexes, ROW directed itself to the "development of more open and mutually constructive relations between men and women on [the Cincinnati] campus."[9] Though secondarily interested in issues like the Equal Rights Amendment, legalized abortion, and participation of female laity in the synagogue, ROW sponsored (and continued to sponsor the far less revolutionary GROW—Graduate and Rabbinical Students' Organization for Women) inter-campus programs designed to foster communication between women and men. The WRA immediately responded with apologies for its audacity, and the rapprochement led to the continued presence of Cincinnati women among the ranks of the WRA and the joint founding two years later of the Women's Rabbinic Network.[10]

Over the course of its three-year life span, the WRA continued to wrangle over issues of self-identity, geographic and otherwise. From time to time, the question of maintaining an exclusively female membership arose, but it was perpetually tabled for later discussion. As reported in the minutes of May 7, 1977, when (then Cincinnati student rabbi) Deborah Prinz—who later became the WRN's first official coordinator—sent her dues for membership to the WRA along with those of her husband (then student rabbi) Mark Hurvitz, the treasurer promptly returned his check. The general consensus was and remained that a single-sex organization guaranteed the trail-blazing female rabbis a haven in which to discuss openly issues of interest primarily, though admittedly not restricted, to them. The range of topics considered was as diverse as it was volatile and as theoretical as it was practical: relations with male colleagues and congregants, dressing for success on the bimah and off, changes in liturgical and theological language, and disappointment over the convening of the 1979 CCAR Convention in Arizona, one of the non-ratifying ERA states.

That female rabbis and rabbinical students needed a refuge while navigating the rough waters of their journeys appears indisputable in light of a report presented in 1978.[11] Upon returning from a Northeast Regional Conference of the CCAR, (then student rabbi) Laurie Rutenberg relayed to members of the WRA that future colleagues met her discussion on "Problems Women Face in the Rabbinate" with the following three questions:[12] (1) How would a woman officiate at the ritual of *hatafat dam b'rit*? (2) What are the women of the WRA discussing among themselves without males present? (3) Is Judaism becoming "emasculated" in that most of the active participants in congregations are women whose ranks will surely swell with the advent and subsequent encouragement of female rabbis? Additionally, some rabbis' wives expressed jealousy over their husbands' working so intimately with female rabbinical assistants. Given claims such as these, the members of the WRA rapidly expanded their focus on professional support, in the form of combating workforce discrimination, to encompass the goal of personal support for women in the rabbinate.

To that end, the WRA convened a *kallah* for its membership in Princeton, New Jersey, over Presidents' Day weekend in 1978. The charter conference was wildly successful in that the participants, for the first time, found "comfort in knowing that their problems as rabbis [were] shared by others."[13] Besides raising mutual concerns, they worshiped together using *Siddur Nashim* (the feminist liturgy generated by then–Brown University students [Rabbi] Margaret Moers Wenig and Naomi Janowitz), studied halachic texts on *nidah*, devoted an afternoon to the subject of mothering and being mothered, and collected topics to be discussed at future WRA meetings including "the problem of congregants propositioning us, using sexist language, and making sexual innuendoes."[14]

The euphoria generated by the first *kallah* not only spawned a second, but led to the adoption of the conference format as a staple of WRA/WRN programming to this day. Female rabbis and rabbinical students have on an almost biannual basis retreated from the workaday world to out-of-the-way places across North America in order to convene with like-minded individuals at settings ideal for contemplation and relaxation.[15] Exactly one year after the initial *kallah*, a second was held on "Images of the Jewish Woman" with a keynote address by Dr. Arthur Green. This *kallah*, unlike the first, managed to kindle more sparks than heat and resulted, ultimately, in splitting asunder the membership of the WRA. As reported only months later, "New York (Reform women) and Philadelphia (Reconstructionist women) are now virtually separate groups, except for the upcoming [third] *kallah*."[16] The latter apparently never took place. Rather, a final blow to movement-wide unity among female rabbis and rabbinical students was struck when the CCAR's Task Force on Women in the Rabbinate usurped the role of *kallah* organizer from the WRA by planning a separate conference for Reform women only at Manhattan's Central Synagogue.[17] Although the WRA continued to function for at least two additional years with a focus on feminist spirituality and women's prayer, interested Reform female rabbis and rabbinical students began to channel their energies into the workings of the Women's Rabbinic Network, which sprang to life at the 1980 New York City Conference.[18]

The CCAR's Task Force on Women in the Rabbinate

With travel subsidies provided by the CCAR, thirteen female Reform rabbis joined twenty-three fourth- and fifth-year rabbinical students in New York for a three-day conference in February 1980 under the auspices of the Task Force on Women in the Rabbinate.[19] Recognizing the tug-of-war between professional obligations and family responsibilities being played out in the lives of these women, the conference centered on the question: "What Gives— Home, Career, or Sanity?" While sessions were led by an outside facilitator trained in psychology, participants were urged to move beyond "personal sharing" to joint action that could result in policy shifts within the larger Reform Movement. Thus, after discussing issues of concern and formulating those issues into concrete proposals, the women met with representatives of the National Federation of Temple Sisterhoods (NFTS), the Union of American Hebrew Congregations (UAHC), the CCAR, and HUC-JIR to discuss ways of working together toward common goals. The three main pertinent areas to emerge were job placement, inclusion of women in leadership positions in the Reform Movement, and parenting. "We, female rabbis, are not a fluke or a passing fad," declared one participant at conference's end, "but a growing presence in the American rabbinate."[20]

The need to blend this "growing presence" with the existing rabbinical organization weighed heavily upon the minds of the CCAR leadership. In the mid-1970s, the Executive Board established the Task Force on Women in the Rabbinate to "overs[ee] and facilitat[e]…the complete professional and collegial integration of women as Rabbis."[21] By 1977, Rabbi Sally Priesand—HUC-JIR's first female rabbinical alumna—was chairing the task force, to which all female rabbis were automatically admitted.[22] Implicit in the creation of a task force rather than a standing committee was the optimistic expectation that integration could be achieved in a circumscribed period of time. Some twenty years after its inauguration, however, in recognition of the fact that its agenda is ongoing, the task force became a committee.

In its infancy, the task force functioned mainly as an advisory council of men and women who suggested ways for female rabbis to gain wider acceptance among colleagues and congregants. It was no small matter that a group of men and women set about thinking concertedly about questions of gender and their implications for liberal Judaism. Most agreed that exposure to a woman functioning in her role as rabbi was the key factor in boosting her approval rating. So, for example, in 1977 the task force proposed that female rabbinical students be invited to participate in CCAR conventions, UAHC biennials, and the like.[23] As the entity that stood watch over female rabbis and defended them against job discrimination, the task force additionally implemented a system of "Placement Assistance Teams" (PATs) to prepare and familiarize congregations with the placement process prior to its interviewing for a new spiritual leader. It was hoped that the PATs, which were fully functioning by 1981, would help to alleviate some of the prejudice encountered by female rabbis searching for employment.

At the behest of the committee planning the training for the PATs, leaders of the WRN collected data in the fall of 1980 summarizing the accumulated fears of congregants, boards, and senior rabbis with regard to hiring women as rabbis. The resulting list points out the very novelty involved in being a female professional in the early 1980s, along with the pervasive attachment to stereotypes about women's nature and capabilities. Among the apprehensions cited were the following:[24]

I. A basic fear that women cannot do the job because

    a. the rigors of the rabbinate are too great and women too weak for the demanding routine;

    b. the *Torah* is too heavy;

    c. women are too soft-spoken;

    d. women do not know how to, nor care to, wield power or authority;

    e. women will need to be protected by the board or senior rabbi in confrontational situations;

    f. women will cry at meetings when pressured or criticized;

    g. women will create more work for the senior rabbi because congregants won't want to employ the services of women for certain events, plus the senior rabbi won't want to call her late at night, in dread of pulling her away from family responsibilities.

II. A fear that women in the rabbinate will not be able to balance a career and personal life because

    a. the first priority will be to family and therefore either when female rabbis become pregnant or husbands are transferred, they will leave the congregation;

    b. their work will lead to dissension within their families.

III. A fear that female rabbis are too political, too new, too "in," too faddy so female rabbis may alienate the more traditional-religious and social-segments of the congregation because

    1. female rabbis are feminists only;

    2. female rabbis wish to attract public attention to themselves;

    3. female rabbis will give the same sermon on feminism;

    4. in towns where the ordination of women in Christianity is at issue, it may not bode well for the Jews to have a female rabbi.

IV. A fear of the unfamiliar: the untoward aesthetic of seeing a woman carrying a Torah or wearing a tallit and *kippah*.

V. A fear of women succeeding. Women who succeed will reflect poorly on their colleagues. If women can read from the Torah, preach, and teach, the rabbis' duties become accessible to everyone. The mystique is lost. This possibly leads to the breakdown of the hierarchy of the rabbi-congregant relationship.

Indeed, the PATs had their work cut out for them. Through the years the task force has worked closely with the Placement Commission of the CCAR in an effort to eliminate by education and regulation discrimination against rabbinical candidates on the basis of sex. At the same time, it has given several issues involving women—such as parenting leave, salary differentials between male and female rabbis, and sexual harassment—a prominent place on the CCAR's agenda.

The Women's Rabbinic Network Is Born

While the CCAR's Task Force on Women in the Rabbinate was turning the legitimate concerns of female rabbis into policy issues of the CCAR at large, a need was emerging for a separate organization for the CCAR's female membership, apart from male colleagues. Many women serving in the rabbinate yearned for the kind of sharing of experience that only those in their unique position were able to offer one another. As stated in the report on the task-force-sponsored conference of February 1980, "all the [female participants] agreed that there should be some kind of communications network to facilitate support and contact."[25] Thus the Women's Rabbinic Network was born, with Rabbi Deborah Prinz chosen as the overall coordinator and Rabbi Myra Soifer as editor of the newsletter.

Though exclusively female, from the outset the WRN maintained and acknowledged its association with the Central Conference of American Rabbis. Its very constitution—in both senses of the word—demonstrates that fact. First, in terms of its population, it was and is a body of Reform rabbis and rabbinical students, defined by ordination from or current attendance at HUC-JIR, or membership in the CCAR.[26] Secondly, the preamble to its Constitution explicitly reinforces its connection to the CCAR, stating: "The Women's Rabbinic Network was created in cooperation with the CCAR Task Force on Women in the Rabbinate." In effect, the WRN could not be primarily separatist, for the professional goals of its membership could and can be met only within and with the cooperation and support of the CCAR. Therefore, while organizationally independent in its pursuit of specific programs and concerns of primary relevance to its membership, it was and is interlocked with the CCAR.[27]

Of course, not all agreed that a Women's Rabbinic Network was necessary. Some among the CCAR leadership feared that female rabbis and rabbinical students were driving a permanent wedge between themselves and their male colleagues by "forming their own corporation." Others expressed concern that women were not being adequately grateful for the good work being done by the task force in their behalf and preferred instead to "carry the ball themselves."[28] This, they argued, would surely doom prospects for women's entree to the Reform rabbinate. Yet the opposite became true as integration continued apace. Only one month after the founding of the WRN, five female rabbis served on CCAR committees; three years later, a woman sat on the Executive Board.[29]

True to its name, the Women's Rabbinic Network functioned early on as a communal bulletin board of sorts for its close-knit membership. As evidenced by the oldest editions of its newsletter, serious discussion competed with information of a personal nature (that is, marriages and births and rabbinical appointments) as women of the WRN attempted to find their pitch among the mostly male chorus of the CCAR. In the interim between the biannual conferences, the newsletter became the bread and butter of the organization. Published three or four times yearly, its pages reveal the poignant struggles waged by WRN members attempting to negotiate the novelty of their situation: "When signing an official document in Hebrew, should one sign *ravnit* or *rav*?" queried Rabbi Ellen Lewis in the second newsletter. And, in anticipation of conversations that reverberate at CCAR conferences today, Rabbi Karen Fox asked: "What status, salary, and benefits ought to accrue to part-time rabbis?"[30]

Through the years, the WRN has stayed faithful to its goal of offering women a safe environment for discussing issues of importance to its membership. The biannual conference remains the principal vehicle for such dialogue. Whether in formal sessions with noted lecturers like Drs. Judith Plaskow and Rachel Adler or in casual conversation over meals, participants in the conferences vouch for their effectiveness. An opportunity for worship, study, and camaraderie, they are for many the antidote to a rabbinate spent for long stretches in solitary contemplation of the unique challenges facing women rabbis.

In general, considerations of gender have had important consequences for the WRN. Internally, this is most noticeable in the model of leadership it has developed and maintained since the early years of its existence. In particular, the WRN has repeatedly elected to its helm a pair of coordinators who share, with a board of regional representatives, responsibility for daily management and an ongoing agenda.[31] Though not codified as such within the WRN's bylaws, co-coordination has been the rule since the early 1980s. Besides allowing for a fair division of labor, the cooperative arrangement underscores the feminist appreciation for relationship. Externally, the WRN has contributed immeasurably to raising the feminist consciousness of the Reform Movement. When the reality of female rabbis outpaced the system's preparation for it, the WRN burst onto the scene to fill the gap, first on a grassroots level and then as an official arm of the CCAR. By the early 1990s, in fact, the CCAR granted the WRN the right to send a representative to Executive Board meetings, on a nonvoting basis. This means that, in addition to the several women who regularly sit on the Executive Board, one of the co-coordinators is present specifically to represent the concerns of the WRN.[32] Throughout the 1980s and 1990s, along with the Task Force on Women in the Rabbinate, the WRN has served up for the entire CCAR membership the far-reaching implications of ordaining women as rabbis. Significantly, for instance, the 1993 CCAR Conference featured a WRN-sponsored panel entitled "Changing Models in the Rabbinate," which drew an audience of men and women interested in finding new ways of defining professional fulfillment and success. Indeed, the establishment of a separate women's organization has not engendered further segregation but rather has inspired the CCAR membership to reconsider, and in some cases transform, long-standing attitudes and prejudices.

Paradoxically, as the WRN nears its twentieth anniversary, it faces challenges that are a direct result of its success. As the membership of the WRN has expanded geometrically, numbering now over two hundred, differences in factors like geography and generation preclude the assumption of an easy acquaintance among all women. To take but one example, identifying oneself merely on a first-name basis (as in the early newsletters) is no longer viable. (In many ways, perhaps, the biannual conferences are an attempt to recapture the cherished intimacy of a bygone era.) Although older generations of WRN members may rightfully bemoan such a loss of intimacy, they must admit that it signals an expansion of power and influence on the part of the WRN. At the same time, it is altogether conceivable that the increased diversity of age, experience, viewpoint, and personality has rendered the WRN membership fully as varied as the CCAR, leading to an escalation in the number of subjects vying for a place on the WRN's agenda.[33] Thus, in an ironic twist of fate, as the WRN's goal of integrating women into the CCAR becomes less elusive, the WRN's ability to define itself becomes more elusive. Determining the changed nature of the organization remains a desideratum of the next generation.

Conclusion

During the early stirrings of the feminist movement, women rediscovered the bonding between members of their own sex that had been the special resource and strength of many generations before them. Capitalizing on that knowledge, female rabbis and rabbinical students joined together like professional women of all stripes to offer a preliminary blueprint for building a web of social relations within a man's world. Over its seventeen-year history, the WRN has created opportunities for what its members call "womanspace"—moments in time wholly devoted to female rabbis and their concerns.[34] Simultaneously, the WRN has reached beyond its immediate membership to its parent organization to offer sensible models of leadership that challenge notions of success in the rabbinate. While raising and scrutinizing issues related to economic inequality and cultural stereotyping in the Reform rabbinate, the WRN has become an advocate not only for women but for men as well.

NOTES

1. The Reform rabbinate is presently one-third female (725 out of a total of 2,195 CCAR members). Approximately half of American HUC-JIR students identify as women, while over 80 percent of Israeli rabbinical students are female.

2. *WRN Newsletter*, June 1987.

3. With regard to Mindy Portnoy's joke, in fact, the meeting of the WRN at the CCAR Conference in Jerusalem in 1981 took place in the Turkish bath. In attendance were four members: Rosalind Gold, Deborah Prinz, Karen Fox, and Bonnie Steinberg. See *WRN Newsletter* (August 31, 1981).

4. Presentation by Arnold Sher at the CCAR Regional Conference of NER, April 7, 1997. Arnold gave credit to the WRN for coining the phrase "pulpit-free" to designate rabbis in non-congregational positions.

5. Statistics relating to the general American populace are from Mary P. Ryan, *Womanhood in America* (New York: Franklin Watts, 1983), pp. 314 and 318.

6. Letter to all Women Rabbis/Rabbinical Students (February 8, 1976).

7. Letter to prospective members of the WRA (September 19, 1978).

8. Minutes of WRA (November 13 1977). It was reported as well that two of the twelve female rabbinical students at the Cincinnati campus had paid dues to the WRA.

9. "Notes from ROW" by Sue Berman in the *WRN Newsletter* #1 (May 30, 1980).

10. See "Notes from Meeting between 3 ROW Members" regarding the status and future of the WRN (January 12, 1980). Note that the ROW Constitution

(March 1980) appears to have been the prototype for Laura Geller's initial draft of the WRN Constitution, which appears in the *WRN Newsletter* #2 (November 2, 1980). Note as well that the four female rabbinical students in Los Angeles in 1976 met to discuss the formation of the WRA. See letter of Deborah Prinz to Cathy Felix (March 12, 1976).

11. Report by Laurie Rutenberg included in minutes of the WRA (April 2, 1978).

12. Of course, the irony is that these questions bolster the very need for Rutenberg's presentation on "Problems Women Face in the Rabbinate" in the first place.

13. *Summary of the Proceedings of the First Annual Kallah of the WRA* (February 18–20, 1978, Princeton, NJ), p. 3.

14. Ibid.

15. The most recent WRN conference was held in March 1997 in San Diego, California.

16. Minutes of WRA Meeting (December 16, 1979).

17. A subsequent and recent attempt to reunite female rabbis and rabbinical students of all movements began over the Internet two years ago.

18. Report on WRA in Business Minutes of WRN (March 3, 1982).

19. *WRN Newsletter* #1 (May 30, 1980). The Report on the Gathering of Women Rabbis and Rabbinical Students of the CCAR's Task Force on Women in the Rabbinate puts the number at forty-one.

20. Temple Bulletin message of Melanie Aron included in *WRN Newsletter* #1 (May 30, 1980).

21. Neil Kaminsky, "The Role and Interrelationship of the CCAR TaskForce on Women in the Rabbinate and the Women's Rabbinic Network," American Jewish Archives (AJA), Cincinnati.

22. Report by Ellen Dreyfus, Letter of WRA (November 11, 1979).

23. Report of Task Force on Women in the Rabbinate, *CCAR Yearbook*, 1977.

24. Paraphrased from the report by Deborah Prinz in the *WRN Newsletter* #2 (November 2, 1980).

25. Report on Gathering of Women Rabbis and Rabbinical Students of the CCAR's Task Force on Women in the Rabbinate.

26. Of course, not all female rabbis and rabbinical students join the WRN. In the mid-1980s, there was a major membership drive, which succeeded in enrolling nearly 100 percent of all eligible members. See *WRN Newsletter* (Winter 1993).

27. See Neil Kaminsky, "The Role and Interrelationship."

28. See letter of Joe Glaser to Neil Kaminsky (October 27, 1980), American Jewish Archives, Cincinnati.

29. As reported in *WRN Newsletter* #2 (November 2, 1980): Rabbi Joan Friedman to Reform Practice Committee, Rabbi Judith Lewis to Sexuality Committee, Rabbi Rosalind Gold to Joint Committee on Social Action, Rabbi Bonnie Steinberg to Task Force on Synagogue Structure, and Rabbi Karen Fox to Nominations. By 1983, Rabbi Bonnie Steinberg served on the Executive Board of the CCAR.

30. See *WRN Newsletter* #5.

31. See Bylaws of the Women's Rabbinic Network, Article ill, Section 3 (August 10, 1995).

32. Note that this arrangement is only temporary. At the end of five years, an assessment will be made as to the viability of continuing observer status for the WRN.

In contrast to the WRN, the NAORRR has been granted an ex-officio position on the Executive Board. That is, the NAORRR has a vote.

33. This was raised as early as 1985. See Susan Einbinder's letter in the *WRN Newsletter* (Fall 1985).

34. WRN Minutes (June 21, 1995).

This essay originally appeared in *Wisdom You Are My Sister: Twenty-five Years of Women in the Rabbinate*, a special issue of *CCAR Journal* (Summer 1997). The author wishes to thank the following for their documents and/ or assistance: Rabbis Joan Friedman, Rosalind Gold, Deborah Hachen, Neil Kominsky, Ellen Lewis, Judith Lewis, Janet Liss, Mindy Portnoy, and Elliot Stevens, and Dr. Kevin Proffitt of the American Jewish Archives. Thanks also to Hilly Haber for the updated introduction.

12

WOMEN WHO CHOSE

First a Jew, Then a Rabbi

JULIE WIENER

Rabbi Ruth Adar (HUC-JIR '08) still laughs about the time when she was a student rabbi serving in Los Angeles' San Fernando Valley and a woman congregant took her aside, saying, "Rabbi, I need to talk to you." Once they were alone together, the woman implored, "I just had to ask you, who did your nose?"

"I was standing there with my mouth hanging open, and all of a sudden I realized I'd 'passed,'" as a Jew by birth, Adar recalls. "I laughed and said, 'God did it.'"

Like many other converts to Judaism, Adar, who is of Irish ancestry and was raised Catholic in central Tennessee, doesn't "look" Jewish, in that she doesn't have the East European Ashkenazi physical traits many Americans define as signature Jewish. Had she not changed her name while in rabbinical school, she would not have a "Jewish-sounding" name. And she can't reminisce about Hebrew school or the Yiddish-accented *bubbe* and *zayde* who served up matzah ball soup.

But that hasn't stopped Adar, or a cadre of other Jews-by-choice—among them Rachel Cowan (HUC-JIR '89), who has spearheaded several major initiatives in Jewish life, and Alysa Stanton (HUC-JIR '09), the first African-American woman ordained—from becoming a Reform rabbi.

Despite, or perhaps because of, their atypical backgrounds, Jew-by-choice rabbis have made significant contributions to Jewish life as teachers, counselors, role models, spiritual leaders, and, in Cowan's case, at the helm of a major Jewish foundation. While being a Jew-by-choice can pose challenges in the rabbinate, making it difficult at times to feel truly accepted or self-confident in one's Jewishness, it also offers advantages: a fresh perspective, an ability to empathize with people just starting out in their Jewish journeys, and a unique life story that often inspires appreciation for Judaism in born Jews.

Little data is available on how many rabbis—Reform or other—are Jews-by-choice. Indeed, very little demographic information is available about conversion in general, whether among rabbis or laypeople, although the Pew Research Center Portrait of Jewish Americans released in October 2013 reports that 2 percent of American Jews became Jewish through a formal conversion and another 1 percent identify as Jewish without having formally converted.

While Judaism discourages proselytizing, in recent years communal leaders have increasingly embraced conversion as a means of stemming American Jewry's demographic decline. Since Jews-by-choice tend to be among the most enthusiastic and knowledgeable American Jews, more research about their experiences and greater publicizing of their often inspiring stories might well be beneficial.

Anecdotal reports suggest that there are at least twenty Reform rabbis in the United States who are converts, the overwhelming majority of them female. Rabbi Dvora Weisberg, director of the School of Rabbinic Studies at Hebrew Union College–Jewish Institute of Religion's Los Angeles campus, said that out of a cohort of forty, she knows of two rabbinical students on her campus who are Jews-by-choice. Since starting her job five years ago, she has consistently had "about two or three" Jews-by-choice at any given time. Rabbi Ken Kanter, associate dean and director of the Rabbinical School at the Cincinnati campus, said he sees one or two per year, "and certainly more women than men." Rabbi Renni Altman, associate dean and director of the Rabbinical Program on the New

York campus, said that at any given time, three of all the rabbinical students on campus are Jews-by-choice.

An informal search conducted for this chapter turned up names of fourteen Jew-by-choice rabbis who were willing to be interviewed; not all Jew-by-choice rabbis wish to publicize the fact that they were not born Jewish. Interestingly, the phenomenon of converts going on to become rabbis indeed seems to be an overwhelmingly female trend; no one interviewed for this essay could identify any male Reform rabbis who are Jews-by-choice, although several knew of current rabbinical students who are male converts, and one person knew of a male convert who dropped out of rabbinical school. Another commonality: all the rabbis identified, whether given a religious upbringing or not, came from Christian backgrounds—perhaps not surprising, since the vast majority of Americans are Christian.

Adar, who teaches Introduction to Judaism classes at Lehrhaus Judaica and elsewhere in the Bay Area, came to Judaism after a long period of spiritual searching, which included studies at the University of Chicago Divinity School and involvement first in Episcopal and then Unitarian churches.

"I had a good Catholic education, but there was something I was looking for; I didn't know what it was, but I kept coming back to it," she said. "I kept thinking I'd be able to believe if I learned more. I didn't know at the time that was a very Jewish solution—to say I just needed to study more." For ten years she gave up on religion altogether, after realizing "I simply could not believe the things I was supposed to believe as a Christian." But she missed being part of a congregation, and in the mid-1990s, when a Jewish friend new to Berkeley, where Adar had settled with her partner and two sons from a dissolved marriage, asked for help finding a place to spend the High Holy Days, Adar was inspired to explore Judaism.

"After the High Holy Days, I beat a path to the first rabbi I could find, and I was home," she said. "I liked the cyclical nature of the High Holy Days and the emphasis on self-improvement, the framework of mitzvot within to become a better person. I also like to have a lot of tradition mashing down at all times—it makes me feel more secure. Even when I'm struggling with things, the fact that there's a long tradition of people struggling with these questions and coming up with many different thoughts about them is very helpful."

After converting, Adar, then working as a writer and investor, volunteered on her synagogue's outreach committee. In 2000, she took a job as regional outreach director for the Reform Movement in San Francisco, but she soon realized she wanted to learn more. With the encouragement of her rabbi, Adar began studying Hebrew, and when her younger son entered college, she headed to Jerusalem for her first year of rabbinical school at HUC-JIR.

While there, Adar—who declined to share her birth name—began using her Hebrew name, Ruth, because it was easier for Israelis to pronounce. Soon after, she adopted Adar as her surname. "I had gone to Israel with the idea that I would come back with a new last name," she explained. "I had been going by my ex-husband's last name, and I wanted my name to be something that connects to my life now. I was born in the month of Adar, and what clinched it was a classmate saying the Jewish calendar came from Babylon, that it was not originally Jewish—and I thought, 'I didn't start out Jewish either.' Then I found out Adar in the Babylonian calendar was a sad time. It went from being a sad-sack month in the Babylonian calendar to becoming the luckiest, happiest month in the Jewish calendar. And I went, 'This is the story of my life.'"

Adar is not the only Jew-by-choice rabbi to have changed her name. Ahuva Zaches (HUC-JIR '14), who was raised with no religion by a single, teenage mom (raised Catholic), switched her name from Amanda in high school. (While Zaches sounds like an Ashkenazi pronunciation of z'chut, the Hebrew word for "right" or "credit," it is actually the surname of Zaches's gentile father.) Zaches, who converted as an adolescent, began using her Hebrew name, Ahuva, while at American Hebrew Academy, a Jewish boarding school in Greensboro, North Carolina. Originally a day student there, she moved into the dorms midway through her first year, rooming with her best friend and another girl named Amanda. To avoid confusion, Zaches decided to go by her Hebrew name, and by the time she was registering for the SAT college entrance exam, she decided it was time to change her name legally.

Her mother initially was upset "because she'd chosen my name, and I'd already gone on this different religious path," but eventually all the relatives, except for Zaches's younger sister, accepted the new name.

Adar's name change also went relatively smoothly, despite her fear that her sons, then grown, would find it "traumatic." "I talked with them at some length about it, and their response was, 'Your name is Mom.' My family of origin had some trouble with it, but they had trouble with my becoming Jewish," she said, adding that "it was a little bit of a puzzle to the people back in Tennessee, but I'm already the crazy one who moved out West and came out as a lesbian."

Of course, not every Jew-by-choice rabbi changes her name. Some, like Rabbi Heidi Hoover (Academy for Jewish Religion, '11), who, though not a member of the CCAR, serves Temple Beth Emeth v'Ohr Progressive Shaari Zedek in Brooklyn, and Rabbi Jean Eglinton (HUC-JIR '10), of B'nai Sholom Congregation in Huntington, West Virginia, have insisted on holding onto their birth names, even though each could easily have taken the name of her Jewish-by-birth husband. (Hoover's husband is named Michael Rose, and Eglinton's is Steven Snyder.)

Ironically, Rabbi Rachel Cowan—who was ordained in 1989 and is believed to be the first Jew-by-choice to become a Reform rabbi—took the last name of her Jewish late husband, Paul Cowan, when they wed in the 1960s, long before she converted. But Paul Cowan's ancestors had chosen the name generations earlier, changing it from the more common and distinctly Jewish "Cohen."

Eglinton was raised in a wholly secular Christian household (although her brothers subsequently became fundamentalist Christians) and doesn't mind having a Scottish last name, even though her husband teases her that "Rabbi Snyder" would sound better.

Meanwhile, Hoover—the daughter of a Lutheran bishop—has not only kept her name but her and Rose's daughters, while raised Jewish, go by Hoover as well. Hoover converted in 1999, after years of discomfort with Christianity and learning about Judaism through her lengthy courtship with Rose, whom she met while in college at Carnegie Mellon University. "I guess I never internalized why Christianity is better," she said. "There are a lot of paths up the mountain; everyone has to find his or her own path. I like the intellectual nature of Judaism, the rituals, especially the home-based rituals. It helps me connect with the Divine. Paramount to me is Torah study."

Hoover knew she wanted to become a rabbi even before she completed her conversion, drawn to the way the job combined her interests in public speaking, counseling, and teaching both children and adults. "Whenever I was at services or in class, part of my brain was thinking, How do I do that?" she said. "It felt like I had a call."

The name Hoover—and a face that reflects her German and British heritage—can attract unwanted attention and scrutiny, however. At times, Hoover has been frustrated by questions about her background, especially because "as a rabbi, you're not always in a situation where you can set people straight—like when you're in the middle of a counseling session. Every convert learns you're not supposed to be asked about your conversion, but few born Jews know about that," she added. "It sets up converts for a lot of hurt feelings. In the liberal world, there's little stigma against converts, but people still say stupid stuff sometimes," such as referring to her as a "shiksa" or saying, "You don't look Jewish."

There are also the assumptions—that she's an expert on interfaith dialogue or that she can offer both Judaism and Christianity to interfaith families. Of course, she admits, her Christian background—and the fact that she and her husband were an interfaith couple for many years—can be helpful in interfaith situations or in counseling intermarried families.

"One benefit of having converted is I understand the questions Christians ask, the underlying concerns behind them, what's important to them," she said, adding that she loves being a rabbi. "I'm very fortunate to have a congregation full of people I really like—it's a very menschy group," she said of the members in her small, historic synagogue, in a neighborhood that for many years had few Jews but, with gentrification, is now seeing its Jewish population grow.

One thorn in Hoover's side, however, is Israel—specifically the chief rabbinate's unwillingness to recognize Reform, or even many Orthodox, conversions. In March 2013 she published an op-ed in the *New York Jewish Week* titled "Israel Doesn't Want Me," noting that while she feels connected to Israel and supports its "right to exist safely," it is "difficult for me to think of the State of Israel as my homeland, and that hurts."

Asked about Israel, Cowan said that despite the government's failure to recognize her conversion, she cares "tremendously" about the country, feels "at home there" and feels "engaged in the struggle for social justice, environmental sustainability, women's equality, religious pluralism, minority rights, and peace in the same way I am engaged at home." She added, "I love being there and go as often as I can, but am never blind to its complexity."

Other Jew-by-choice rabbis interviewed were less interested in discussing Israel, however, noting that they have no plans to make *aliyah*. Asked about it, Adar noted that her odd status vis-à-vis Israel was "brought home to me" while in rabbinical school, "every time I had a conversation with security at El Al [Israel's national airline], because I made no sense to them." However, she said, she still could obtain Israeli citizenship if she wanted—which she doesn't, particularly because her children, who are not Jewish, live in the United States.

"The difficulty comes with the Orthodox rabbinate, who wouldn't officiate at a wedding for me or bury me. I don't need them to marry me, and I don't want 'em to bury me, so it's kind of a non-problem." And she is cautiously optimistic that the rabbinate's grip on Israeli policies may be loosening.

"Israel seems to be in the process of some interesting movement, what with the new political situation around the *Haredim* [ultra-Orthodox]," she said. "Also, I'm very much aware that Israel is a very new state and they're still figuring things out. They're not even one hundred years old. This is something I think they'll get straightened out eventually. I'm here for Torah. So I have a difference of agreement with the Orthodox rabbinate. That makes me really Jewish. That there's a *machloket*, a difference of opinion, that's a very Jewish thing. Would I like to be universally loved, adored, and accepted? Of course, everyone would, but that's not the way the world is."

Eglinton, who converted to Judaism after years of marriage to a Jew and then was ordained in 2010, said she is more concerned about many of the gender issues in Israel. "We were just back there in November for a congregational trip, and I talked to one of my former HUC professors there and asked about all the things that feel anti-woman there," she said. "His idea was that because ultra-Orthodox women are more educated secularly, the whole male-oriented culture feel threatened and this is a reaction against that.... They're working through a really hard time right now. It will be interesting to see which way it goes. I try not to feel animosity, even though it's frustrating sometimes....My way of supporting Israel is to support organizations supporting the pluralistic development of Israeli culture, like the Israel Movement for Progressive Judaism and the Israel Religious Action Center."

Zaches, who originally had a Reform conversion and then underwent a Conservative one in high school, going to the mikveh with friends who were Jewish by patrilineal descent and who wanted to ensure their Jewishness would be recognized beyond the Reform and Reconstructionist Movements, said Israel's lack of recognition for liberal conversions "used to bother me....But now I know I'm not going to make *aliyah*, so it doesn't affect me as directly," she said. "I think I might feel more passionate about it if one of my conversion students wanted to make *aliyah*."

Zaches, who entered rabbinical school just a month after graduating Occidental College, may well be the youngest Jew-by-choice to be ordained. Zaches's Catholic-raised mother, who got pregnant with her at age seventeen, was not at all religious. "We were secular Americans who had a Christmas tree, and Easter was about eggs and chocolate bunnies; I didn't realize there was religious significance to any of it," Zaches recalled. Meanwhile, Zaches's father was "out of the picture" for most of her childhood, and her mother quickly married and divorced several other men.

At age eleven, Zaches, who didn't get along with her third stepfather, moved in with her grandmother for the summer and refused to call her mother. Because mother and grandmother had a "stormy relationship," her mother ended up reporting Zaches as kidnapped, setting off a custody battle that temporarily landed the girl in foster care. Zaches's first exposure to religion was with one of the foster families; they happened to be strict Christians. "That whole experience of losing what was familiar to me kind of left me searching spiritually," she said. In seventh grade, having moved back in with her mother, she began researching Judaism for a school project, mostly because she and her mother loved the TV comedy *The Nanny* and were curious about the show's Jewish references.

At that point, she was living in Sacramento, Califonia, and her grandmother called several synagogues for her to ask if they could attend worship services, as part of the research. "Most said yes, but one, which was Reform, was substantially more friendly," she recalled. Zaches and her grandmother, who had some Jewish ancestors but was not raised Jewish, visited the synagogue around Simchat Torah. "I was like, 'This is awesome,'" Zaches recalled. "I liked the music, the people were really nice. When I first saw the prayer book I was like, 'What's this squiggly gibberish? I need to learn to read it!'" Granddaughter and grandmother enrolled in a Hebrew class together, and both soon realized they wanted to convert. The two ended up going to the *beit din* and mikveh on the same day.

"My mom said, 'It's your life, I'll let the rabbi know it's OK with me,'" she explained. While studying for her conversion, she found it increasingly difficult socially at her public school, which served a largely low-income, non-Jewish population. She tried homeschooling, but during the days when her mother was at work and she was supposed to be doing her academic work, she'd study Torah instead.

Her rabbi connected her to a Jewish day school, which she loved, but it only went through eighth grade. As they began researching Jewish high schools, they discovered American Hebrew Academy, which was just launching and was offering free tuition. "That experience at AHA was truly amazing—even better than day school in California," she said.

Forging friendships with teachers and the parents of friends provided her with surrogate Jewish parents. Even before going to AHA, she'd found a Jewish father figure in her rabbi, who let her shadow him and see what his job was like. "I got to see how he was able to help so many people, and I wanted to be like that," she recalled. At 13½ she celebrated becoming a bat mitzvah, "and by the time I was really preparing for it and writing a mini-sermon, I was like, 'I like this a lot, I want to do it.'"

Zaches believes that because she converted at such a young age, her experience has been easier in many ways than that of those who convert later in life. "I got in by the last-minute deadline for a semi-normal time for a bat mitzvah; I got to attend Jewish schools and have a Jewish teenage experience," she said. More challenging for her has been grappling with the economic class gap between her and her mostly middle-class and upper-middle-class Jewish peers. Though attending a private school may have given Zaches the appearance of an upper-middle-class life, it was challenging socially to come from a background where college was not an expectation and her mother was on welfare and getting food stamps.

While Zaches went to Jewish high school and was active in her college Hillel, other Jew-by-choice rabbis say they at times feel the absence of a Jewish upbringing and a personal Jewish history. But the lack of personal Jewish history can be an advantage as well, bringing with it confidence and a fresh perspective.

"I don't know what it is to be discriminated against," said Cowan, who grew up in a non-practicing Congregationalist family which, upon moving to Wellesley, Massachusetts, in the 1950s, joined a Unitarian church primarily because everyone in town belonged to some church and the Unitarian one seemed the most palatable. "The Unitarian church was where the Democrats and the Jews in disguise were," she recalled. She attended a Quaker summer camp "full of New York City Jewish kids" and was drawn to their "energy." At Bryn Mawr College and while volunteering in the civil rights movement, she made many Jewish friends, meeting her husband Paul while doing civil rights work in Maryland.

As the two courted, then married and headed off to Ecuador to serve in the Peace Corps, Cowan was continually struck by her husband's visceral ties to Judaism, even though he had no Jewish education and had grown up in an assimilated home more likely to celebrate Christmas than Chanukah. He wanted to fast on Yom Kippur without knowing anything about the holiday. During the Six-Day War, he thought about volunteering for the Israeli army because "my people are under attack."

Returning from Ecuador, the two settled into an apartment on the Upper West Side and welcomed their first child. Cowan, who had a social work degree, helped organize a cooperative nursery school that met in Congregation Ansche Chesed, a Conservative synagogue that was on the brink of death. Most of the other parents were Jewish, and she and Paul, a journalist, gradually became more immersed in Jewish life, eventually helping to revive Ansche Chesed.

In 1980, when her children were ten and twelve, Cowan underwent a Conservative conversion; a few years later, she began thinking about rabbinical school. "I'm a community organizer—my heroine is Jane Addams," she said, referring to the early-twentieth-century advocate for immigrants and the poor. "I wanted to change society, create a home for people—I thought being a congregational rabbi was way of doing that." She enrolled at HUC-JIR and "was all set to become a congregational rabbi." But in Cowan's fourth year of the program, her husband Paul was diagnosed with leukemia.

She spent most of the year in the hospital with him, and when he died the following year in 1988, "I wasn't in a place to be a pulpit rabbi." Instead, she helped establish Derekh Torah, the yearlong conversion course that is now housed at the 92nd Street Y. In 1990, she became program director for the newly formed Jewish Life department at the Nathan Cummings Foundation. Working with the Cummings family, she sought out progressive, innovative Jewish projects, helping to create the Jewish Healing Center and supporting initiatives like Jewish meditation and Jewish chaplaincy programs.

"Because of being a convert, I had a beginner's mind," she said. "I'd think, what do you mean there's no places for people to study to convert? What do you mean there's no spirituality? No Jewish environmental voice? No distinctly Jewish social justice projects? My being an outsider, I couldn't take for granted what was there."

Later, Cowan helped found the Institute for Jewish Spirituality, which she led as executive director until 2011. Now, in her mid-seventies, she is involved in various projects, focusing particularly on developing more spiritual resources for aging Jews. "As a convert rabbi, I think I've been less focused on Jewish identity and peoplehood, and more on meaning," she said.

Others also identify ways in which being a Jew-by-choice has affected their rabbinic work. "I think being a Jew-by-choice forces you to study harder than other people," Ahuva Zaches said. "A lot of my classmates have been blown away by how much I know. That's partly because I've devoted myself to Torah and Jewish knowledge for a while. I put more time into it than people who took it for granted."

Ruth Adar, whose work is mostly with "people at the beginning of their Jewish journey," notes that "I know from the inside out many of the experiences, questions, and emotions people bring to beginner-hood." When her conversion students are ready for the final step, Adar takes them to the same mikveh where she completed her own conversion, adding to the emotional intensity. "I can't possibly get through the mikveh with a new Jew without just crying my eyes out," she said. "I let people know about that beforehand because otherwise their reaction is, 'Oh, rabbi, what did I do wrong?'"

13

O PIONEERS

Reflections from Five Women Rabbis
of the First Generation

RABBI SUE LEVI ELWELL, PhD

"None of us has the rabbinate we think we're going to have."

These are the words of Ellen Lewis, who was ordained in 1980. She was one of five pioneering rabbis I interviewed who were ordained between 1978 and 1981. The others are Karen Fox (1978), Rosalind Gold (1978), Deborah Prinz (1978), and Helene Ferris (1981). Each one of these women is exceptional: in their courage to enter a seminary that was not ready for them, in their audacity to imagine a career in a world that had could not conceive of linking the images of "rabbi" and "woman," in their perseverance to make their way through five years of school where they were taught by too many unsympathetic and sometimes hostile professors, in their willingness to sit in classrooms with male classmates who, too often, could not figure out how to be allies and supporters.

Speaking with these pioneers underscored that we are now engaged in the process of compiling "The Chapters of the Mothers." As heirs of a tradition that has studied and taught and cherished *Pirkei Avot*, "The Chapters of the Fathers," we have the challenge in the twenty-first century to continue to explore and compile the Chapters of the Mothers. These five representatives of the first generation of women rabbis have much to teach us. They entered a profession that was in the process of change even as they came into their first positions. That transformation has accelerated in the past decade. In many ways, these pioneers' career trajectories and personal choices anticipated some of the challenges that are defining and redefining Jewish communities and Jewish communal careers as we make our way through the second decade of this twenty-first century. These women are pioneers not only because they were the first women to enter Hebrew Union College–Jewish Institute of Religion, but because each of them has crafted and shaped a rabbinate that enables her to bring together her passion for service to the Jewish people with her unique gifts and abilities.

Four of these women graduated from college in the 1970s; one of them, the first "second-career" rabbi to enter HUC-JIR, graduated in 1959. Let's take a quick look back at that time. In 1970, the percentage of women in the labor force was 11.2 percent.[1] *Ms.* magazine's inaugural issue was published in 1972, the same year that Sally Priesand was ordained by HUC-JIR. It took another four years for women to be admitted to U.S. military academies. Women were not able to apply for credit in their own names until the Equal Credit Opportunity Act was passed in 1974. Until the Pregnancy Discrimination Act in 1978, women could be fired from their workplace for being pregnant. In 1980, the Equal Employment Opportunity Commission issued the first guidelines to prohibit sexual harassment in the workplace, and the next year, Sandra Day O'Connor was named the first woman justice of the Supreme Court.[2] These were the years before the advent of programs and departments of women's studies, gender studies, or Jewish studies. When each of these women embarked on her rabbinic career—although women had always been in the workplace, although women had always worked in the home—women were just becoming visible, to ourselves and to others.

Ms. magazine was one tangible symbol of that visibility. *Ms.* welcomed thousands of women across the English-speaking world into what today we recognize as a virtual community. The publication invited women to "hear one another into speech," the theologian Nelle

Morton's beloved phrase. In 1987, Mary Thom collected and published *Letters to Ms. 1972–1987*, sharing selections from the thousands of letters to the editors received over the first fifteen years of the magazine's existence. Here is one example to remind us of the workplace that our colleagues faced:

> I resigned from my job yesterday as a matter of principle. I was given a letter to type by a senior secretary to the auditing firm that had recently been in our books. A woman headed up the team of accountants at our company for several weeks.
>
> The letter was opened to "Gentlemen." I changed it to "Greetings." I was told that the letter must be redone because it was the policy of the company to use the salutation "Gentlemen." I was told that management determined company policy, not uppity secretaries who didn't know their place. I decided to resign and didn't redo the letter.
>
> I'm looking for another job, but I did raise quite a few eyebrows and, hopefully, someone's consciousness.
>
> *Name Withheld*
> *September 12, 1982*[3]

These pioneers entered the workplace when women were beginning to recognize that such experiences were "click" moments, described as "that tangible sensation of the tumblers falling into place in our heads, the 'Click' that signals a permanent recognition that the women's movement is…me."[4] Ellen Lewis entered the job market "with a baby on my resume. I encountered enormous sexism." Her first job was as a rabbi educator in a large congregation. Roz Gold entered the job market as a single woman, which seemed to be a disability when considered by a congregation populated by families with young children. She traveled to one congregation for an interview and was told when she arrived that "the job had changed." Rabbi Ferris was forty-four when she was ordained, yet that maturity was not considered an advantage.

Rabbis Gold, Prinz, and Ferris began their careers as assistant rabbis in large synagogues. Not only were they, as well as Ellen Lewis, the first women to serve as clergy in each of these institutions, but they were working with male colleagues who were disadvantaged by attending school only with men. Debbie Prinz said, "As the first women, we felt an additional burden: be the best rabbi you possibly can be because if you fail, you're going to ruin it for everyone else." So these women turned to one another. They created what became the Women's Rabbinic Network (WRN), and the connections between them, personal and political, social and spiritual, were essential to their very survival for those first challenging years.[5]

And they turned to others, as well. Both Debbie Prinz and Helene Ferris were mentored by Jerome Malino, a past president of the CCAR. Helene said, "I would have quit my first job without him." While in school, Ellen Lewis met and was befriended by Dr. Millie (Mira) Brichto, a dynamic and accomplished teacher with two doctorates whose husband, Chanan (Herb) Brichto, was an HUC-JIR professor. Millie's children's books, *The God Around Us*, volumes 1 and 2, became important resources for Ellen as a parent and teacher. Ellen was also mentored by Dr. Sophia Ralson, a clinical psychologist who worked with HUC-JIR students to integrate mental health concepts into their rabbinates. "Dr. Ralson once famously looked at us and said, 'The problem with you rabbinic students is you think when someone asks you for a book, they really want a book!'" Ellen was later mentored by Dr. Estelle Borowitz, an esteemed psychoanalyst, the longtime partner of Rabbi Eugene B. Borowitz, HUC-JIR professor. Karen Fox named Harvey Fields, the longtime and beloved rabbi of Wilshire Boulevard Temple, as her mentor.

Their connection with one another was a source of continuing support, both through and beyond the WRN. Roz Gold told me, "For me, a primary challenge was understanding how to claim, use, and manage power and authority." Together and one by one, these pioneers came to own their power. The 1979 convention of the CCAR was held in Phoenix, Arizona. However, Arizona had not passed the Equal Rights Amendment. Newly ordained Karen Fox and Debbie Prinz, along with a small but determined group of rabbinical students and rabbis, challenged holding the CCAR's convention in Arizona. The rabbis reached a compromise: the convention went ahead and included a day of lobbying the members of the Arizona legislature[6] (see Balin, chapter 11 for more on this).

Rabbi Karen Fox was the first woman rabbi to work for the Union of American Hebrew Congregations (UAHC; later Union for Reform Judaism). Early in her tenure, she invited three colleagues to join her, together with Rabbi Sally Priesand and Rabbi Deborah Prinz, for lunch. These colleagues were Rabbi Joe Glaser, who headed the CCAR; Ted Broido, who oversaw the UAHC's finances and what would become the Department of Synagogue Management; and Rabbi Alexander Schindler, the president of the UAHC. They met at a posh Upper East Side restaurant. The men were stunned when they learned that the bill had been paid; Karen had picked up the check. Karen was what we would today call "leaning in" and owning her power.

Sometime later, Karen, a planner, had repeatedly attempted to arrange an appointment with Alex Schindler to discuss maternity leave. (Debbie Prinz described herself as a planner as well; clearly this is a trait of many pioneers). However, Karen was not able to secure a meeting until the issue of maternity leave was no longer theoretical. In the early weeks of her first pregnancy ("My pants were getting too tight!"), Karen finally sat down with Alex. Rabbi Schindler's response: "None of our other rabbis have ever asked for this." They worked out a plan and he said, "Don't tell anyone about this. This is not a Union policy." Karen immediately copied it and sent it out to her female colleagues. Word spread: women deserve maternity leave. And it must begin at what may be considered to be "the top."

Karen Fox subsequently returned to her native Los Angeles and became the director of Camp Hess Kramer, one of the Wilshire Boulevard Temple camps, joining the rabbinic staff of the temple. Each of the pioneers who had begun their careers at large synagogues eventually moved on to solo pulpits. As Roz Gold said, "In a solo, you can make your own rabbinate." Helene Ferris spoke about the increased ability to connect with congregants in a smaller pulpit: "You can preach in front of more, but you can't touch more."

Over the years, these women asked for and won maternity coverage, for themselves and for all the women who followed them. In the synagogues they served, these rabbis established nursery schools where none had existed, started homeless shelters, raised awareness about the need for women's shelters, and created and extended programs for women in the congregation to connect to one another and to Judaism. They created support groups and opportunities to explore the spiritual aspects of bereavement, miscarriage and pregnancy loss, menopause, and divorce. They developed and trained *bikkur cholim* groups that transformed congregations. They shared their passion for Judaism and for justice, initiating programs that others were too timid to present; Helene Ferris was the moving force behind the first synagogue-sponsored gathering of gay and lesbian Jews and their families in the country, in 1986. Others began programs for addicts and their families. A prominent feminist once told Helene, "You hide your light." How often have women felt that we burn too brightly, take up too much space, speak too loudly, or draw unnecessary attention to ourselves? Leaders shine: they take risks, speak out, and place themselves in the public eye to bring attention to the issues and the people they serve. The first generation of women rabbis were profoundly challenged to serve as leaders in a cultural context that saw them as women, not as leaders. Too often, the gifts and achievements of these pioneers were neither noticed nor celebrated, and sometimes, others took the credit.

These rabbis also served the communities in which they lived, the Movement, the rabbinate, and the Jewish people. Several of them served as WRN president; others have held or hold significant positions in local and regional clergy organizations. Karen Fox is the immediate past president of the Pacific Association of Reform Rabbis, and Roz Gold served with distinction as the chair of the CCAR Ethics Committee. Helene Ferris was one of the organizers of the 1988 *Shacharit* service at the Kotel that launched Women of the Wall. All of these rabbis have published essays, sermons, and a range of articles; Karen Fox has written *Seasons for Celebration* (Putnam, 1992), and Debbie Prinz is the author of *On the Chocolate Trail: A Delicious Adventure*

Connecting Jews, Religions, History, Travel, Rituals and Recipes to the Magic of Cacao (Jewish Lights, 2012).

In addition to serving their congregations, all of these rabbis continue to study, locally, in national programs, and in Israel. Three of them pursued graduate studies toward additional degrees: in psychotherapy and psychoanalysis, in marriage and family counseling, and a doctorate in ministry degree. Two have developed and pursue private practices in psychotherapy. One called this additional training "extremely nurturing; I loved the opportunity to study with really smart people, and to translate this learning into my Jewish world." Several of them took one course at a time, on days off from congregational responsibilities.

At this writing, four of the five have retired from full-time positions; Roz Gold is rabbi emerita of the Northern Virginia Hebrew Congregation she served for twenty-three years, and Helene Ferris is rabbi emerita of Temple Israel of Northern Westchester. Both of them are engaged in a wide range of activities, including active participation in a Jewish chorus, a regimen of daily walks and regular tennis, service to the community as a prison chaplain and as rabbi in a senior center, and for Roz Gold, coordination of the Brickner Rabbinic Studies Program at the Religious Action Center.

As Debbie Prinz approached her twentieth anniversary as the rabbi of Temple Adat Shalom in Poway, California, she decided to retire. She was about to leave for a congregational trip to Eygpt, with a personal add-on to Israel and Spain, when she saw a listing for a two-year interim position at the CCAR which she then applied for and was hired. Debbie's work as Director of Program and Member Services dramatically increased the reach and the depth of the CCAR's service to colleagues engaged in many streams of rabbinic work. She brought a clear and strong feminist voice to and from the CCAR, reminding us that "much remains to be done to diminish the incongruities among expectations, values, and realities. The disconnect between articulated Reform positions related to pay equity, fairness in hiring practices, and granting of family leave policies in our congregations and organizations remains.[7] Prinz left the CCAR in 2014 and now serves as a Senior Fellow at the HUC-JIR Center for the Study of Ethics and Contemporary Moral Problems."

Karen Fox served Wilshire Boulevard Temple in Los Angeles for twenty-three years. At the time of her retirement, her very full rabbinic portfolio included pastoral counseling and program development, as well as supervision of the educational directors of the congregation's nursery school, elementary day school, religious school, and summer camp. Fox's retirement includes teaching at HUC-JIR as an Adjunct faculty in Pastoral Counseling and a private counseling practice for clergy of all faiths. Ellen Lewis, now rabbi emerita of Jewish Center of Northwest Jersey, is a therapist in private practice. She works with a wide range of individuals, couples, families, and groups and has developed models of clinical supervision for rabbis, cantors, and other members of the clergy. She teaches psychoanalysis and provides clinical supervision to students in analytic training. Her greatest love is working with rabbis, who she says, suffer needlessly. "When they talk with others about their rabbinates, they reclaim the passion that led them to this work. It is possible," she says, "to have a joyous rabbinate."

Each of these five women, in her own way, has created a unique and joyous rabbinate. Each of these women is a committed Jew and a hardworking rabbi. Each of these pioneers serves as a model for all who wish to live a rich and full Jewish life, a life of integrity, study, and service. In 2012, in celebration of forty years of women in the rabbinate, four women who had served Stephen Wise Free Synagogue in New York gathered for a historic presentation in the synagogue sanctuary.[8] Helene Ferris concluded her presentation with these words:

> I have a dream: that the next generation of women rabbis will be judged not by the color of their attire, but by the strength of their character. Not by the length of their hair, but by the length and breadth of their wisdom. Not by their speaking voice, but by the voice of their soul. Not by their age, but by their knowledge of our ageless teachings. Not by their physical appearance, but by their spiritual power.

Rabbi Ferris's words were greeted with a standing ovation. May the light of these pioneers illumine the path of all who are privileged to follow them.

NOTES

1. Mark Brenner and Stephanie Luce, "Women and Class: What Has Happened in Forty Years, *Monthly Review* 58, no. 3 (July–August 2006), http://monthlyreview.org/2006/07/01/women-and-class-what-has-happened-in-forty-years.

2. Natasha Turner, "10 Things That American Women Could Not Do before the 1970s," *Ms. Magazine Blog*, May 28, 2013, http://msmagazine.com/blog/2013/05/28/10-things-that-american-women-could-not-do-before-the-1970s/.

3. Maria Popova, *"Letters to Ms.*: How Mary Thom Built 'Social Media' for Women's Rights in the 1970s," *Brain Pickings*, http://www.brainpickings.org/index.php/2013/05/07/letters-to-ms-mary-thom/.

4. Jane O'Reilly, quoted by Debra Ornstein in *Lifecycles: Jewish Women on Life Passages and Personal Milestones* (Woodstock, VT: Jewish Lights, 1994), 377. Debra was the first to collect what she called Jewish feminist "click stories."

5. Carole B. Balin's essay on the history of the WRN provides essential background: "From Periphery to Center: History of the Women's Rabbinic Network," pp. 137–52 of this volume.

6. It is hard to believe that the ERA is still not the law of the land and that the CCAR has, since 2000, held conventions in at least two states, Louisiana and Illinois, that have not yet ratified the ERA.

7. *CCAR Newsletter*, July/August 2013.

8. "4 Decades of Women Rabbis in the Rabbinate and SWF," Stephen Wise Free Synagogue, http://www.swfs.org/4-decades-women-rabbis/.

14

FROM GENERATION TO GENERATION

A Roundtable Discussion with
Rabbi Ellen Weinberg Dreyfus

Part 1

At the CCAR Convention in Chicago, in 2014, we convened a round-table discussion between women rabbis of different eras. Rabbi Ellen Weinberg Dreyfus led the conversation.

Alysa Mendelson Graf: We wanted to have a conversation be-tween generations of women rabbis, so we asked Ellen Dreyfus to moderate this discussion with people from all of the different genera-tions. Hopefully many of you know Ellen. She is the second woman to be president of the Central Conference of American Rabbis [CCAR] and is one of our esteemed *vatikot*.

Ellen Weinberg Dreyfus: I was ordained in New York in 1979. Back then there were very few women at HUC [Hebrew Union College-Jewish Institute of Religion], and my historical distinction is, as far as I can tell, that I was the first rabbi in Jewish history to be ordained pregnant. We'll have a chance to talk about different experi-ences in our rabbinates as we go around. If you have one little nugget that you want to share while you're identifying yourself, please do so; otherwise just give us your name, rank, serial number, whatever.

Amy Memis-Foler: I was ordained on the New York campus in 1993. I spent twenty-one years of my rabbinate in Chicago, in three different congregations, going from assistant and associate to solo. I was the first woman rabbi in my first pulpit, which was Congregation BJBE. The irony is that when I moved to Temple Sholom in Chicago in 2002, there were two associates who came in [at the same time] and both of us were women. They had a female cantor for many years prior, so, thank goodness, in some ways it was less of an anomaly to have these two women rabbis because of having had a female cantor.

Debby Hachen: I was ordained at HUC in New York in 1980, and I was the first, of the many since then, daughter of a Reform rabbi and great-granddaughter of a Reform rabbi to be ordained. We all have lots of firsts; I was the first woman rabbi in all of New England, in those early years. You've got to have a lot of things on your list. Now it's more of an adventure for the other women to find that something that's a first. There are still a few things out there.

Julia Weisz: I was ordained on the Los Angeles campus in 2011, and I just finished my third year, going onto my fourth year, at Congregation Or Ami in Calabasas, California.

Roxanne Shapiro: I was Roxanne Schneider when I was ordained in 1999 on the Cincinnati campus. I then worked at the College-Institute [Hebrew Union College–Jewish Institute of Religion] as National Director of Admissions and Recruitment. I was the first female to fill the national role in admissions and recruitment, and since then I have worked in Milwaukee and in St. Louis, where I am currently a rabbi and director of lifelong learning.

Ilene Haigh: I'm in the class of 2012 in New York. It's kind of a funny story because I was there for ten years. I started in 2002, having worked for twenty years before I went to rabbinical school. So, I'm a new rabbi but not so young. The question of generations is very interesting for me. I am a solo rabbi in Woodstock, Vermont, and it's a fabulous, amazing place. So, ten years in rabbinical school because I raised two children through rabbinical school, and that informs a lot. What am I going to do as my first? I keep thinking that because I was so old when I was ordained, I am going to be one of the first people whose grandchildren can say, "My grandmother was a rabbi." You know we don't hear that: My grandmother's a rabbi.

Andrea London: My name is Andrea London. I was ordained in New York in 1996, and I think the only first that I have is being the first rabbi in my family. It was a kind of a shock that I would go into the rabbinate. My father thought that my becoming religious was the great sign of my being a heretic from the family. He didn't know what he had done wrong. My father is one of these people who have four kids all married to born Jews, when he had told all of us not to marry Jewish. He said, "We live in an open society, and you should marry whoever you want to marry!" So the big surprise was, "How did you all end up marrying Jews and becoming involved in congregational life?"

Lisa Greene: I'm Lisa Greene. I was ordained in New York in 1995. I don't think I have any firsts, but it's nice to know that Debby Hachen was the first rabbi's daughter. I am a second-generation Rabbi Greene, and there are five rabbi's kids in my house, like it happened in your house too, so I'm not a first on anything. And that's okay.

Rebekah Stern: I'm Rebekah Stern, and I was also ordained in Los Angeles in 2011. I have been the assistant rabbi at Peninsula Temple Sholom in Burlingame, which is just south of San Francisco, since ordination. I'm about to move across the Bay to Congregation Beth El in Berkeley. Actually, in contrast to what you say about there being lots of firsts still available, I'm glad not to be a first. I actually think that's where we are with our generation, that being a female rabbi is normative. I don't want to speak for the previous generations or what you all worked so hard to accomplish. At this point, though, I don't think that being a female rabbi is a question anymore and that there is no issue that I am a woman in this next pulpit.

Alysa: I was ordained in 2004, and I've been working with a congregation for the last nine years. I took this year off, and I'm starting a new position in July. I have spent a lot of my rabbinate really involved in the Women's Rabbinic Network [WRN]. I have found that community of rabbis to be an incredible support and resource to me over the last decade, and I have spent a lot of time serving that community, as well as being involved at the CCAR.

Ellen: So we have a number of questions that we are going to use as jumping-off points to have a conversation that we want to have. Let's just kind of go at it, and remember to identify yourself when you begin to speak.

The first question is, how much do you feel that being a woman plays a role in your rabbinate and in what ways? So Rebekah already shared with us that it's kind of a non-issue to some extent, but I wonder if there are ways in which, for you, it's not an issue in placement or in the perception of your congregation, but in other aspects of your rabbinate?

Rebekah: I think that for me the next stage of feminism in the rabbinate is congregants having equal access to rabbis of both genders. It is a natural human thing for people to be able to relate to someone differently, both men and women, and sometimes simply because the rabbi is either male or female. There are just different approaches to everything that we bring as women—to text, to liturgy, to pastoral moments, to particular kinds of issues around life cycle that are really important. These make a huge difference to the people we work with, and I think the fact that I am a woman informs the way that I am as a rabbi. I cannot separate those things, and that is appreciated. As they're looking for the person who is going to fill the position that I am in the process of leaving, there are a large number of people who say, "So, are they going to get another woman?"

This is not a first in the Reform world, and I'm glad for that, and it's not an issue in a negative way, but they are looking for balance. My senior is a man, and our cantor, who has been there for a very long time, is a man, and other members of the senior staff are male. There is another woman on the senior staff, but they are seeking out greater gender balance.

Andrea: I think the issue of gender is really complicated. I'm also speaking as a mother of a nineteen-year-old who is a sophomore in college where they begin all their meetings asking which pronouns you'd like to be referred to as. To see that the next generation is he, she, or hir makes me wonder: What does it mean to be a person of a particular gender or to not identify with a gender or to be transgender? The last three people who walked into my office to look for conversion are all transgender. They were men transitioning to women.

So, I think that the whole idea of gender is one that I feel that I'm confronting every day. I used to feel like I knew and understood what it meant for me to be a woman in the rabbinate. Now I have to say I'm not so sure exactly what it means that I'm a woman. Besides my physical characteristics, I don't know necessarily what is female about me. Early on in my rabbinate there were ways that people responded to me based on my gender, but I don't think that it was necessarily about how I felt about myself. For example, when I was in my student congregation and was pregnant, people made a lot of comments about my body, the public nature of what it meant to be in front of people, and should I be holding the Torah or not. Who was going to tell me what to do and what not do was certainly something that I felt that I had to deal with. In my student congregation, where I was the first woman to serve, I felt at that point like I was trying to represent my whole gender, because whatever I did was understood as representing all women.

I remember going to a conference at HUC when I was a student and there was a lay woman who was there. This was in the '90s, when there still weren't that many woman rabbis out there. She was talking about how the congregation she was a part of had hired a woman rabbi and they were really excited about it. The new rabbi came and she worked there a few years, but things didn't work out and she left. Now they're in placement again, and they're hiring a male rabbi. So I looked at her and I said, "Would you tell that story again and just change the pronouns? As in, 'We hired a male rabbi, it didn't work out, he stayed for a few years, and now we're going to hire a female rabbi.'"

All of a sudden she realized how absurd what she had just said was. She had to retract her words, but I wonder where we are today, since this is a story from twenty years ago.

Amy: In 2002 I came to Temple Sholom, and I was one of the two female assistant associates who were joining the clergy team. Someone came up to me in the hall and said, "Oh, I hear you're the feminist rabbi."

I didn't know how to take it. I wondered, "Is this a good thing or bad thing?" and I just kind of smiled. Somewhere along the way in the conversation the person assured me that it was a positive.

While I was at Temple Sholom, one of my portfolios was working with the Women of Reform Judaism, which I really enjoyed. I think that in my years at Temple Sholom I was able to migrate toward some of these women's issues because that was in my portfolio. I have enjoyed my interactions and work with the WRN. Now that I'm in a solo pulpit, I almost want to be careful that I'm not too feminist. I remember for that one woman who approached me and said, "Oh, I hear you're the feminist rabbi," that it was good for her, or something she was seeking. Because I'm a solo rabbi now in a congregation, with all different kinds of people, I want to make sure that I don't only migrate toward women's issues.

Ilene: I'm in a similar situation with a very small congregation, but it's just me. They're selling this book *Teen Boys*, about how to access teen boys and how to be a role model. I think about that all the time. I would love for the men to study together, for themselves to be role models for the kids. We don't have that many boys that we are retaining, and I don't know how to affect that. I don't know that for sure it matters, but I'd love the men to study together in some lay led, or they don't have to be lay led, group about who's going to lead for the boys. All of the staff in our religious school is female and I'm female, and we're all part-time anyway. So it's an interesting question: Does my gender, in fact, limit my rabbinate?

Lisa: I think it mattered more to people when I got out. That's almost twenty years ago. My senior has announced his retirement in the year, and it has been really interesting. I'm very clear that I don't want that job, but it is going to be interesting because we've had two female associates for thirteen years. I'm fifteen years. Someone else is thirteen. The congregation has only had, you'll excuse me, a guy wearing a tie. I mean good guys wearing ties. People say, "What do you think is going to happen?"

I respond, "I don't know," because there are people who say, "Oh, you both should go for the job," when I'm very clear that I'm not applying for that job. It's interesting to me to see if people can go to someone they like and trust and respect who is already there, or if they will default to what they know, not to minimize any male's credentials. So there's that piece.

I have struggled for a long time with the women's stuff. That's stuff I really like, and I do it well. I've been doing women's seders for a long time. I've written two women's Haggadot, studying with a group of women and studying the Haggadah. We do a women's retreat every year. I worked with our Sisterhood's Shabbat participants to study and create the service. We do meaningful learning, and I don't want to let go of that. If I were solo, I don't know if I would do it differently. People will periodically still say, "Well, why don't we have a men's seder?" You know, for all of history we had men doing the seders.

There is something powerful to having women in the room. I'm sure people relate to me differently, but I don't see myself any differently. I mean, I just see myself as who I am. I no longer feel like people are coming up to me saying, "Oh, you're the first female rabbi I've met."

So, I have to unpack that, right? When I was a student rabbi at Rodeph Sholom in Manhattan, the guys would come give me a kiss on the receiving line and not the senior rabbi. For a while I was conscious of not over-preaching on women's topics. I do women's programming, and it is good. It is really important for women of our congregation. I don't think, for all of the talents of my male colleagues, that it would go over the same way. So I think that's an advantage.

Roxanne: It's interesting as I hear this because I think I'm on the opposite side. When I think about people's perception that I would be a champion to the female issues, I don't necessarily want to be looked at as a female in this role. "Why of course I'm doing the women's Torah study," or "of course I'm doing the women's seder," I want to connect in different ways. What I realized through my time is that people are going to perceive me as they perceive me, and I have to respond that way. But I'm also in St. Louis, Missouri, where out of five Reform congregations, four them over eight hundred members, four of them have women as their senior rabbis. I mean this is St. Louis, where we can't talk about politics, but out of all five there's one congregation with a male senior, and he has a female associate. I'm at a congregation where my senior rabbi is female as well. I don't want to say that it's not an issue. We do hear people say, "Oh, with all of the females here," but it's really interesting to be in the Midwest, where no one would expect it, and it's just part of how it is.

I do notice issues. I do see congregants who respond to our cantor more as the male voice on high, but my experience in the rabbinate has been open. I'm appreciative for all of the struggles people have gone through with it, but I haven't struggled in that way because of those who have come before me. I actually see many of my male colleagues struggle more with family issues and it being turned on them, that they're not supposed to do things with their family and be a parent as a rabbi. The expectation of me when I don't go to something of my child's because I have a work event, people say, "Oh, why aren't you going?" but male colleagues were expected not to go.

Lisa: I thought of something as you were talking about this. Part of this is that these are issues and topics that matter to me. One of the best and most eye-opening papers I wrote while I was at HUC was on feminist theology. Glynis Conyer and I wrote the paper for Dr. [Eugene] Borowitz. It opened up my world about God and my own theology.

I also feel responsible to raise it. I mean, I don't spend all of my sermons on it, but raising things that relate to gender and creating ritual, which is not exclusively female, but tends to go that way. Last Rosh HaShanah I gave one High Holy Day sermon and I spoke about

Women of the Wall. Somewhere in that sermon I felt like I also had to say, "Don't dismiss this as only a women's issue. I'm a woman standing up here, but don't write this off because of that."

I think that if my senior rabbi, who is a male, got up there and gave that sermon, it might have been heard differently. By which I mean that people listening understood that I gave my sermon from a very personal vantage and that I was at the Wall in July. So, I still feel like I have to give the caveat of "don't write this off because I'm a female" standing up there. It's an interesting thing that I'm responsible to take on these issues, but people probably do hear me a little bit differently.

Julia: It's interesting because I grew up not knowing anything but female because I was raised by a single mom and I had a sister. I didn't really have a male presence in my life to even know any gender issues. I didn't know that it would be to my advantage to be a female rabbi. When Rebekah and I were in school, there were so many females that it was an advantage to be a married male who could play guitar. I was pretty sure that a lot of my friends were going to get really good jobs if they were male, they played guitar, and they were married. It was an advantage. I was like, "Oh my goodness, what's it going to be like for me?"

It's interesting that my advantage at first was not that I am female, but my age. It was three years ago, so it wasn't that long ago, but I was younger. I was working with teens and I was working with kids. I had parents approaching me for parent issues because I could relate. I was closer in age to their teens than they were. Now I have a nine-month-old, and people are coming to me wanting women's things. I don't know if it's now that I'm a mom or that I've been there for a couple of years, but there's this request for a women's spiritual group, and a this, and a that, which is really cool. What ended up happening was that I have a very progressive, liberal, male senior who is actually taking the women's night out and he's doing them. He does the men's night out and the women's night out, so we will see how that ends up working. I'm doing the women's spirituality groups, which fits well in my schedule, and he's doing the women's night out, which just doesn't fit in my schedule. So it will be a very interesting thing to see what is happening and the reaction that the women have. I've found the movement from my age initially being a benefit because I was closer in age to the kids, and now being a mom with people approaching me in a different way, and wanting different things in the community, to be a really interesting transition. It could just have to do with the amount of time that I've been there.

Debby: I've been in three congregations and I've always thought this way. I come out of a sociology and anthropology background. I like what people were saying, that sometimes it's how people perceive us and sometimes it's how we think about ourselves. It varies a lot from congregation to congregation, which many of you have experienced in the different places in which you've grown up or worked. I found going straight to a solo in 1980 that there were all of those "first" issues. People had all of those questions about what I should wear, and how they look at me as a woman, and pregnant, or this or that—all that people were projecting on me about how a woman should behave. You would all know better from your own places, but I later had other experiences where congregational leadership or members of congregations still had a certain vision of what a woman is, what a woman should be, how we should behave, especially when it comes to leadership, conversational style, warmth. On Myers-Briggs, I'm more Thinking than Feeling. Luckily, I'm married to a Feeling type, and that saves me. It's not that I don't love everybody, but I don't start out naturally with the hugs and all of that. I think that there are some projections, and when I don't match them, it's an issue.

I was in a congregation for so long that the woman issues were not there anymore for the regular members of the congregation, but the new people coming in had to adjust over time. That worked fine because they had a whole community sending them the message about what it was like to have a woman rabbi. Then I moved to a very different congregation following a solo male rabbi. A lot of the people didn't have a very developed, non-gender or post-gender kind of view. It was very difficult to go back to the old stuff that I thought didn't exist anymore. I thought that with all of you out there now, isn't everybody past this?

I think a lot of it is, somebody said it the other day, "place-ism." There's a lot of place-ism, and now I'm back in an urban place, as Andrea and some of you are, and we are really very post-gender. I don't have any issues about this anymore. We don't even notice what color people's skins are or what gender they are unless they bring it up. It's a different experience.

In my rabbinate, I've had some different experiences with my desire to do women's things. I felt like some of you at the beginning, like I have to do these things because there isn't a Rosh Chodesh group, and there are men out there in congregations doing Rosh Chodesh groups, so how can I not do it? In my early tenure in the rabbinate, I would often take a look at what my male peers were doing. If the men were giving sermons about Women of the Wall, for example, or about abortion rights, or about something like that, I felt I had more permission to do it without it sticking out as a women's issue.

This isn't just in congregational life, though. When you asked the question, Ellen, about how we feel being a woman plays into our rabbinates, I don't think it's only in congregations. I was involved with CCAR's structure throughout the early years, from the beginning when we had a task force on women in the rabbinate, to when we became a committee, and then the WRN. There was a lot of stuff about how women fit into the structures here. There was life before the first woman was head of CCAR, and it was a very tumultuous time. In some ways even a little bit more tumultuous than in a synagogue, because we had male colleagues who really understood this stuff and we had male colleagues who really didn't. You didn't have the time to make long-term relationships with them except for those who were in your own class. I think there is some women's stuff that's connected with our institutions still from the old days.

Alysa: I've been ordained for ten years, and at the same time I was getting ordained, I was getting married. I got ordained and married a week apart. I was thirty-two, so when I was interviewing for a position, a temple president said to me, "Well, if you take the job here, we hope that you'll wait at least a year before you start to try to have children."

Unidentified voice: That was when they were offering you no maternity leave.

Alysa: Right. I should have gone running in the other direction as soon as I heard that. I think that in congregations it depends, in many ways, upon who your partners are. I don't mean your marriage partners; I mean your professional partners and the kind of environment you're working in. I found that amongst my congregants my gender was not really an issue, but having a strong woman to deal with was a little bit more challenging amongst the leadership. It was challenging with my colleagues, as well. I was in a really male place, and if I behaved in a way that was perceived as being male, I was sucking the air out of the room. I was once told that. I have a real presence on the bimah, and I was told that was it was perceived by some of my colleagues as sucking air out of the room. It was hard for them to have a dynamic woman on the team. I know that it was specifically related to my gender, and I think that's still very much out there. You may work in a congregation, Andrea, where three transgender people walk into the room, but in the suburbs where I'm from, that doesn't happen very often. There's a more traditional setting there, if you want to call it that, where women are in more traditional roles. Most families who moved out there had the mom and the dad, and the dad commuted into the city and the mom stayed home and was raising the children because it was just too far to commute. To have me as a strong woman in that context and a working parent around all of these women who had given up great careers was also a difficult dynamic to navigate. I'm really proud of the way I did navigate it, but it was certainly challenging and something that required real sensitivity on my part.

Ilene: What Debby said really struck a chord with me because having been around the College, you know, we have lots of woman professors, so we don't think about it, right? More women, right? When we get here to the CCAR Convention, and this is actually my first conference, the math of the gender difference is so clear. Here you see how many men there are versus how many women there are. We don't see the generations that came before us except for in this room when we're here, and I think what you're saying is absolutely the institutional presence—the generations of men in that room behind us. I don't know when women really started to become half of the class.

Roxanne: 1999 was the first year that it was fifty-fifty.

Ellen: I have to bring these historical experiences here. First of all, when we were at the College, there were no women on the faculty. There was one woman who was brought in as a speech teacher, but she wasn't really faculty, and there were no female professors. During my year, we were the first class in which there were more than two women, and they didn't know what to do with us. We were still on West Sixty-Eighth Street, in the JIR [Jewish Institute of Religion] building. The only female toilets were on the floor with the secretaries, so there were two stalls in the entire building for women. That tells you something, just structurally, about how ready the College was to welcome us.

The other thing that I experienced was being pregnant my senior year at the College, and I chose not to take a full-time position, which was really unprecedented. The notion of a part-time rabbi was simply unheard of, but I couldn't do it all. I turned in my cape, I was not superwoman, I couldn't do everything. I wanted to nurse my babies. I didn't want somebody else to raise them, and there wasn't the kind of wonderful full-time day care that is available to my kids now for their kids. It just didn't exist, and in those days if you put your kid in day care, you were almost an abusive parent. It was a very different world thirty-five years ago.

The responses I got from the men were very condescending and paternalistic, saying, "Of course you'll stay home with your baby, darling. How sweet; isn't that nice."

The women, unfortunately, were not supportive either. The women were saying, "You're going to brand all of us as unreliable."

In those days, every congregation wanted a female rabbinic student or the few female rabbis who were out there to come and speak about women in Judaism. We had all of these speaking gigs all over the place.

Unidentified voice: We didn't get paid for them, but we did them.

Ellen: No, I got paid, I got paid.

Unidentified voice: [*Laughter.*] This is Ellen you're talking about!

Ellen: Our male classmates were really pissed, actually, because we were getting paid for these speaking gigs and they didn't have that opportunity, but that's another story. One of the other women at the College actually said to me at some point, when I was heavy with child, "Well, when you go and speak to these places, you will tell them what you are doing is not typical."

I mean it was almost like, "Be sure to mention your leprosy." It was very hurtful, very difficult, and very lonely. I had lots of male rabbinic role models who were wonderful men and wonderful people and all of that. I had female role models like my mom and other women in careers, but there were no women who were rabbis and moms out there. Well, Sandy Sasso, but she was far away and she was in a different movement and all that. It wasn't smooth sailing in those days, and we weren't terribly supportive of each other. During the first WRN conference in 1980, I had a two- or three-month-old, and Leah Kroll had a toddler. There was no child care provided, and any time either of these kids made a peep, everybody turned and glared. It was just a different world.

Unidentified voice: And now none of us want to bring our kids to WRN conference because…

Ellen: Because you want to be liberated from them. Right. Right. I know, I understand that. The other thing is about the CCAR. I remember the conference when we were celebrating Sally's twenty-fifth anniversary in the rabbinate, and they invited all of the women to come up for an *aliyah*. There were very few wives at that conference for some reason or whatever, but all of the women rabbis were invited to come up for the *aliyah*, so we sang out the first line of the *b'rachah* and all of these male voices responded. I thought, "Oh my God, that's what the conference used to sound like!"

Because when I came in to the conference it was all male voices. I was the eleventh woman ordained out of HUC; we were so few and we were so young and conspicuous, and many of us didn't have funds to go to conferences either. They thought we were the wives. Anyway, I'll stop for a moment.

Debby: What Ellen is saying is absolutely true. Ellen and some of us from the same time have had a debriefing on the issue of how Ellen was treated during that time, and she's had a chance to share that with many of us. There was definitely all of this pressure that the first ones were going to model for everybody, and you know what? That was true. It's not Ellen's fault or her responsibility or our fault. We just bought into feeling like we had to do things a certain way. It was a really, really difficult time, and there were those of us who needed to work full-time anyway. We didn't have a choice about it. Not all of us could financially manage to not be full-time, but there was a lot of pressure to be a full-time pulpit rabbi in those early years. It did ease up eventually.

About seven, eight years after that, I think that it started to change. There were enough people, feminism was in a different place, but there were times when we women were at each other's throats in lots of ways. "Are you a woman first or a rabbi first?"—you know, all these old conversations judging people. I can remember the first time there started to be some women in the rabbinate who wore fancy nail polish. It was like, "What kind of women are those? Are those like us or not?"

I mean, there were so many little things because we were also women judging other women in a time when things were so in transition. The men used to judge each other on how big their congregations were, and we judge each other on all kinds of things, too. The WRN has been more helpful with that stuff.

Roxanne: I feel we still are expected to be the model. For example, I am not a member of the WRN. I consciously choose not to be, never have. I get a lot of comments and a lot of flack for not doing it; I'm accused of not being supportive of my female colleagues. I'm also a mother of two children, who was fortunate to have maternity leave, but I went back to work within days. I set up my schedule so that I could work part-time, because I wanted to have a longer period of time rather than the full-time at the beginning. I was fortunate to be able to have my child at work with me and have a babysitter to take care of the child. I was fortunate with my first child to be able to plan when I was pregnant, and I made those choices. I honestly have to say that I received a lot of flack from other females because I made these personal choices. They said that I wasn't being supportive of what other women were choosing to do because I was not representing the female cause. Now, from my perspective, we're all humans, we're all very different. I've often been accused of being more male-like than female-like, so I resonate with what you were saying with that, but I do see some areas that we, as women, still need to work on being careful about respecting the choices that others have made.

Amy: I want to make one comment to Ilene. It's been a long time since I've been at a CCAR convention. I'm here because it's Chicago and it's in my backyard, whereas with my limited convention line I've been committed to going to the WRN. To go to both the WRN and CCAR is beyond my budget. When I walked into the big ballroom here, I said, "Wow, I don't feel like a minority as a woman, as I did so many years ago."

Ilene: I feel indebted. It's all perspective. It's completely about perspective, but how indebted are we? It's so much easier for us. I will say that as a part-time rabbi, I made a conscious choice when I was ordained to look for a part-time position, and there's still that, you know, "Really?"

At CCAR there's like three lines of part-time positions. I think it has changed, and I'm not sure it's entirely gender-based, but there's the assumption that if it's part-time, it's because you aren't good enough to get a real job, or that you're not creative enough to want a real job, whatever it is. Of course it's easier today than it was, but a choice to say I'm going to work part-time is still…it's not really accepted and still definitely not the norm.

Lisa: It's easy for me to say. I'm working full-time. I wrestle with it; I have three young children. But if we're really honest, society hasn't come around on this. The CCAR has come light-years on it. I don't think that we can just look at our little insular world. The WRN is important. Part of it is because of the advocacy and issues we're able to take up. For example, maternity leave. I've spent a lot of time encouraging people to stand up for themselves on this front. Alysa and I first met because she had a congregation that wanted to give her zero leave. I was able to give her a list of people who had leave and good leave at that. I was and am angry that other people weren't getting leave. I started collecting a list through my role. I am present as the only female rabbi on the RPB [Reform Pension Board]. I'm conscious when we have conversations in the RPB about pension. I think a lot about rabbinic contracts. I think a lot about the part-time/full-time stuff, and I think about the WRN in terms of advocacy. While in some ways some of the issues have gone away, and I hope people aren't still judging, I think societally we still have to stand up for each other in terms of the opportunities. To say, "You're part-time, but you should have a convention allowance, or you should be getting pension, and you should get health insurance," and all those things.

Julia: Lisa, thank you. I used that chart and I got three months maternity leave, and there was no question in my synagogue, so thank you for that. Sara Mason-Barkin gave it to me. I was telling one of my friends who is graduating right now, "Let me show you others that are getting this."

Rebekah: Picking up on what she said, I've also been frustrated that the conversations we're having as women are just with women. I think that the future of women's issues is actually in conversation with our male partners. Moving our issues forward at this stage of the game can no longer take place only in conversation with one another. We have many caring, eager, supportive male colleagues, arguably most of them are at this point, who see the way that the rabbinate has changed for the better for everyone as a result of women being part of it. I want to continue to improve the rabbinate and its livability for all of us. That really matters to me. My definition of feminism is equality across the gender spectrum. It's not about women's issues; it's about equality. It's really important to me that we have these conversations with our male colleagues and that they also have some kind of equivalent family leave, for example. It's not maternity leave; it's family leave. It is different because we're doing the delivering, the carrying, and sometimes the nursing, so there's a physical recovery piece to that. Maybe we need more or different or spread-out leave, but it's a benefit to the families of male rabbis, too, in order for them to be cared for in the ways that they need to be cared for.

I have some frustration at what I sometimes feel is us only looking backwards. We need to take what we've learned from looking backwards, especially hearing about the kind of backbiting, infighting, and nasty women judging each other about clothes, and body, and image in general, and whatever else that's been going on. We need to deal with this as women in larger society, too, beyond the rabbinate. That, maybe, is a women's thing, and maybe those are the conversations that we need to be having in exclusively women's circles, but I think that the sort of conversations that we have been having in women's circles need to be expanded out in order to start making a difference for all of us.

Alysa: I left my job a year ago, and I wasn't sure what I was going to do. My first plan was just to take some time off. When I was at the biennial conference three or four months ago, I didn't know. I was in placement, but not really. I was one foot in and one foot out—definitely not committed to getting a job. It was so interesting that there was a sense of, "What are you doing? Why not? What's wrong with you?"

There was almost a sense of pity. Ellen, in some ways I experienced in 2013 the same thing you did so many years ago. It's obviously not the same, but this idea that there was something wrong with me in that I wasn't committed to going back to work. That being said, when I told my congregants that I was going to stop and take time off, their consistent response was, "Oh, good for you, now you can spend time with your kids," as if, as a working mother, I wasn't spending time with my children. You know, I work myself ragged so that I can spend a lot of time with my kids. The self-care part is a little bit more difficult, but my kids get plenty of time with me.

At the end of the day, I decided to go back to work after just one year because I realized that I actually needed to be working. Yet, the kind of job I took was not the one I thought I would be taking. I thought I'd be going for a larger congregation. I can't think of a nice way of saying this, but I thought that bigger is better and that should be my goal.

Ultimately, when I started looking at things, it was through a gendered lens. In part, I had to consider what would work for my family, and in part I had to think, "Well, what do I really want for my life right now?" For the first time, I began to feel that maybe bigger isn't better and that instead this sweeter, smaller, more supportive place might just be a better fit for where I was in my life.

I do think that my most recent career decisions have been connected to this sense of "You can't have it all." And I've realized that I am not settling; I'm just accepting that you just can't have it all.

Amy: I just want to jump in with this as an observation. It seems that everyone around the room today has children. I think there are other issues for women who are rabbis who are single and women who don't have children. Those voices aren't around this room, so I want to make note of that. I was dealing with different issues when I was a single rabbi. One of the male congregants "volunteered" me to this young man who walked in my temple. I responded harshly to the guy, and there was a lot of tension in the relationship that I had with this man because nobody ever talked back to him. He was "the sexist guy" and everybody knew that, and I didn't know him well enough because I had just got there. I said, "Don't ever do that again."

There are different issues for our colleagues who are single and our colleagues who don't have children.

Ellen: The questions we have here are: First, how much do you feel being a woman plays a role in your rabbinate and in what ways? Second, how did being a woman play in to your experience as a rabbinic student? We talked a little bit about some of that. In your first years in the rabbinate, where or how did you find role models for yourself as a woman rabbi? How has being a woman created obstacles for you in your career? How has it created opportunities for you? So I think each of us could probably write an entire chapter on each of those questions. I have a feeling that we all have so much that we can share on this, so I would love to continue the conversation.

Part 2

The conversation that was begun in Chicago was continued by phone a month later. Not all the original participants were able to join the call, and some new people were added.

Alysa Mendelson Graf: Welcome back, everybody. This is the continuation of the intergenerational conversation that Ellen Dreyfus is so graciously moderating for us, which began when we were meeting at the CCAR in Chicago just a few months ago. We have a few new people joining us today: Betsy [Torop], Melanie [Aron], and Darah

[Lerner] are new to the conversation. I'm going to turn it over to Ellen to take us forward.

Ellen Dreyfus: Of course, we didn't finish everything that we wanted to talk about in Chicago. Maybe it would be helpful for those who weren't there to share some thoughts with us, or if there's somebody who was there in Chicago and walked out saying, "Oh, I have the perfect thing I really wanted to say," we could also hear that. Maybe we should begin with the people who haven't had a chance to reflect yet.

Melanie Aron: I wasn't in Chicago. Maybe just a little bit of a flavor of that conversation could be shared with those of us who weren't there.

Ellen: Well, it was definitely intergenerational in terms of how long we've been rabbis, the differences that we see, and some of the same old same old. I found that, as one of the *vatikot* in the crowd, it was sort of amazing that some of the stuff we thought would have been done with thirty or forty years ago is still happening. It was mainly about how you feel about things, what your experience is, and maybe it would be helpful to say when you were ordained and what kind of situation you're working in, or were working in, when you are reflecting on particular memories or experiences.

Darah Lerner: I'm usually one of the first off the dime to the question, so I'll continue that practice here. I was not part of the earlier conversation. I fit a couple of different check marks because I'm older in age, I'm fifty-three, but younger in the rabbinate, as I'm now in my ninth year, so I'm sort of in a twofer category. I've been in the same pulpit the entire time, which may or may not be an interesting additional piece to the storyline. One of the questions I noticed that you sent out was reflecting on our experience in school. I remember having a couple of conversations about what would it mean to be ordained as a forty-five-year-old and then having additional specifics. Not only was I older, but a woman and an out lesbian. I was feeling like there was a reality that I experienced in the business world that people didn't think about in the rabbinic world. I was getting the impression at school that there really wasn't recognition that there might be issues, or a question of what kind of job I might get, or what kind of jobs I might look at and how congregations might look at hiring me. There was a wonderful sense that "no, all of our students are great, and you'll get picked on your merits, unrelated to the demographics."

Something like that was not a realistic assessment of what the world would look like.

Ellen: What were your experiences? How do you want to reflect on them, either as a student or in placement or once you got into your congregation? You're in a congregation, right?

Darah: Yeah, I'm in a small congregation in Bangor, Maine. Reflecting back on getting the first job, I don't remember gender specifically being a defining issue in the interviews or conversations for pulpits. I sometimes felt like age was more of an issue when I looked at some assistant positions, being the same age as the senior rabbi. I felt like the tone and the vocabulary were looking for somebody who would connect with younger demographics, and therefore somebody who was forty-five wasn't necessarily going to do that. When I got to the callbacks, I had two congregations. Again, in both of them gender did not seem to be the issue in hiring. In one case, I wish I had the right vocabulary for what they said or did. It felt like they wanted to be a congregation that would hire a lesbian, but they weren't ready yet. There was something in the tone of things that they saw themselves as a place that should or wanted to do that, but couldn't. As a side note, they did go on to hire a woman.

At my current congregation, it felt like none of my demographics, if you will, were considered. They had already had a woman rabbi for many years, so that was old news to them. They had active women's participation, so in the process of the place that hired me it felt like it was just not an issue. I don't know how to express it any clearer than that. It never felt like an issue. None of my demographic particulars felt like an issue. I felt them more, I think, later in my rabbinate, and actually in the past couple of years, than I did earlier in my rabbinate. I'll be happy to pause and let somebody else chime in with their stories for a while.

Betsy Torop: My name is Betsy. I was ordained twenty-four years ago on Shabbat B'midbar, and I have been in a number of different pulpits. I've worked part-time since my eldest was born, and he's nineteen. I'm also a part of a rabbinic couple, which is a little hard to separate from some of the gender things. I spent the first eight years of my rabbinate in Melbourne, Australia, and gender was an enormous part of my rabbinate. I can talk more about that, but I don't know how relevant it is. I mean, it's a different situation completely, but it really, in a lot of ways, defined my rabbinate. I then came back and spent two years at a JCC in Roslyn, New York, and we've been in Florida since then.

I was ordained in Cincinnati at a time when there were no women faculty members at all. I was actually trying to think about women on campus and having trouble coming up with any female colleagues. It now seems bizarre that that's how it was. You know, it's interesting, gender. I think gender's always been an issue. It always is. So in that respect it continues to be part of my rabbinate, but it plays in a lot of different ways. For example, my congregation, if I say I need to leave or I can't do X or such because I have to do something with one of my kids, it's not that it counts to my credit, but there's a "Yes, we understand, you're a mom."

Part of that is because I work part-time, but my husband doesn't always have that same experience when he has to leave to be a dad. Yeah. Are there specific questions? I can explore any one of those aspects more, but that's kind of an overview.

Melanie: I was ordained back in 1981. At the College, I was certainly very aware of being a woman. The class ahead of me was the first class that had a group of women rather than just a woman here or a woman there. There were no women on faculty. We never read anything written by a woman. I remember at some point there was something written by somebody named Leslie and I got all excited, and then I found out that Leslie was a guy. There were no women's bathrooms in the library except up on the secretarial floor, and there were lots of ways of letting us know that having women there was something weird. I'd say that in my first two job searches and probably in the job search coming here, being a woman was certainly a factor.

The first job I got was an assistantship where I was the head of the religious school as well. I had no education background. I had never taken an education class or shown any interest in religious education. The assumption was that I was a woman, so of course I would be good at religious education, and I got the job, which was handy because it was a job that I needed at a time when I didn't have a job. There was a certain amount of irony to that. The second job I got was a solo in Brooklyn. They had called me and told me that they enjoyed meeting me, but it wasn't going to be a match. Then they had trouble finding someone, and I think Rabbi Stanley Dreyfus said to them pretty strongly, "You had perfectly good candidates. You need to go back to your candidates. We're not sending you anybody else."

Then they came back to me. So you know…

Ellen: You think that gender was the key factor that caused them to reject you initially?

Melanie: Yes, they were a congregation in dire straits. They had lost their building to a girl's yeshivah, and they were meeting in this church in a neighborhood that was mostly Orthodox. A lot of them felt a woman rabbi would be the final nail in the coffin. They just couldn't take risks. Other congregations could take risks, but they couldn't. I think Rabbi Stanley Dreyfus, you know, spoke *musar* [ethical teachings] to them, and I think it made a difference. They gave me a chance, and I had a very positive experience once I got there. On the whole, being a woman within the congregation was not a big issue. It was a bigger issue in the broader community, but that was such a weird broader community anyway. It was a little like being a rabbi in Jerusalem or something.

I have three children, and I had a child while working at each congregation. In Jersey, I could have a family, and that was great as long as it didn't bother anybody or create more work for my senior. In Brooklyn, it was more that they wanted to make things nice for me, but we were very low on staff and so on.

When I came out here to California, being a woman within the congregation has not been a big issue, at least not in the first years. Once we hired a woman cantor, it became more of an issue. As in, one woman is fine, but now all of a sudden we had a woman cantor and a woman educator, now all of a sudden we have all women and that makes us uncomfortable. So, there was a lot of stress on finding male speakers and male leaders. Finding a male co-confirmation teacher as a role model for confirmands was a good thing, but then when we interviewed for an assistant rabbi, there was tremendous pressure to come back with a man, sometimes to the detriment of the process.

In the broader community there are still issues. When I go outside my community in the Jewish world I sometimes feel like, "Have I talked? Did anyone actually hear that I spoke, or do we just go on to the next thing no matter what I say?"

If you stay in the same context, congregation, or organization for a while, it gets easier, but sometimes that doesn't carry over to the broader community. In one local organization, there is concern about not having enough male leadership. They feel that there's a women's division for the women, and they want to have cigar smoking and car racing. They need to reach out for that broader world in some kind of way, but they seem to be thinking that going back to more traditional things is where they're going to have progress, which I find weird.

The other thing I've noticed in my congregation is that when I came here as a working parent I was not exceptional. There were a lot of families of two mid-level engineers working for HP or one of the other big corporations. Now a lot of the younger women are not working, and I think part of it is that salaries in the upper middle class became very uneven, so some of the guys shot off into the stratosphere, and then their job became so all-consuming that somebody needed to keep the home front going. A lot of women fell by the wayside when their income was no longer half of the family's income, but just a small percentage. The need for somebody who wasn't traveling to Asia every two days and was going to be home sometimes was great. I feel that's kind of a backward movement in society. Not that there aren't some exceptions, but I just know a lot of younger women who were engineers and lawyers and doctors who are not engaged in their profession right now. Maybe that's a luxury of a certain group in our society or it's the pressure of the 1 percent versus the rest of the 10 percent. Anyway, I'll stop. That's a bunch of things.

Ellen: Yes. Okay. Let's try something positive for a change. How about the last question? How has being a woman created opportunities for you? I think I said something in Chicago about my being recruited to be the chaplain for the mastectomy floor at Sloan Kettering when I was just out of college. I also found in my congregational roles there were times when women would come and talk to me and even said sometimes, "I could never talk about this to a male rabbi."

Sometimes even women from other congregations would come and talk to me because they felt that they couldn't talk in that way to their own rabbi if he was a man. Also, the mom stuff has been a positive. I recall in one congregation many years ago that I was sending home little things from my religious school, and I would say to parents leaving, "Take this home and stick it up on the refrigerator," for instance, whenever we used a new vocabulary word during the week, and one of the parents came up to me later and said, "You know what, we knew that our new rabbi was a woman, but when you said, 'Stick it up on your refrigerator,' then we knew you were a mom."

They liked that. But what other kinds of things can you think where being a woman has created opportunities for you?

Ilene Haigh: I have a similar experience from the first time I was serving. I had a child with special needs, and there was a tremendous feeling, particularly among women in the congregation, that they had a partner they could talk to—that they had someone who had lived through those things, being married and experiencing a lot of the things that they had been through. They hadn't had that kind of support and empathy and understanding. I was ordained at fifty, so I'm actually a new rabbi but old. I think that there is something in our pastoral quality that is unique. I don't mean that it's impossible for men to have it too, but I think, quite often, women carry a sensibility that people find very comforting.

Debby Hachen: I think that one of the positive things, again connected to what Ellen was saying, was in the early years of my rabbinate. When I was in my first place for twenty-three years, in the '80s and '90s and right up to the early 2000s, I was raising my kids and doing a lot of things with other moms. I ran a "Mom and Me" kind of group when my kids were little, so I had a baby on the rug with the congregants having their babies there, and I was able to do spiritual things and get to know people on a very intimate level as the rabbi. It's not like there were "Dad and Me" groups going on in those days for male rabbis. It was all women in those days in the "Mom and Me" support group. It's something that a male rabbi couldn't easily have done, even had they brought their child along. I just think it was some sort of women-to-women thing.

The flip side of that is that there were certain men's things that I'm sure were going on. When the men would go out to do stuff together, or go out for a beer or whatever it is that men were doing in the congregation, a male rabbi would have been present in some of those circles. So there was extra work that had to be done in certain kinds of relationship building with men who would have their needs heard elsewhere, or their opportunities for informal conversation with the rabbi would have come up in other situations if there had been a male rabbi. I didn't have any issues in that first congregation because I was their very first rabbi ever.

Also, in both my first and second congregations there were opportunities in terms of running Rosh Chodesh groups. I know that there are men who have run those as well, and I think that some of those women kinds of things were available to me if I wanted to do them, but I wasn't pressured in some way to do them. So I think that helped. I also think that in the kind of small-town area of Massachusetts that I was in, in established suburbs but not right in the center of the city, there was a certain amount of having my voice heard more because I was a woman and stood out among the men. I wasn't just one of many clergy. People were interested and curious from the early years of women in the rabbinate. I think that helped quite a few of us.

Melanie: I am of the same vintage as Debby. There were times that there was attention focused on me just because I was a woman when it was new or when there weren't so many women. Another place I found being a woman helpful was in some of the interfaith dialogues, particularly in the Muslim community. I have found it easier to build bridges with groups of Muslim women than in some of the co-ed efforts that we've had for those kinds of dialogues. Female leaders in the Muslim community have been more open to dialogue than the male leaders, and therefore it has been a real advantage to be a woman who can do these women-to-women kinds of things.

Betsy: I want to add some ambivalence, because when I looked at the question, my first instinct was to answer sort of as Ellen did. There is no question that people have come and talked to me and said they talk about things with me they wouldn't talk about with a man—mostly other women, occasionally men as well. On one hand, that's an opportunity, but on the other hand, I have some ambivalence about that. Partly for the reasons that Melanie articulated, and partly because I assume that there are people who aren't coming and talking to me because I'm not a man and they don't feel comfortable talking to me. I don't believe that the rabbinic or pastoral relationship is dependent upon gender. I want people to talk to me about a whole range of experiences that are not mine. I recognize that when you have kids, other people with kids feel that connection, and that's something to be utilized and does provide an opportunity, but I don't feel quite so clear-cut about that. I don't know if that makes any sense. I've wrestled with that.

Ellen: I just wanted to interject one thing. I'm thinking about Betsy, who's also married to a rabbi, and I'm thinking: you know, I have a brother who's a rabbi who is a very sensitive person, too. Some of my ambivalence about the question which I share with you is that we know sensitive men who people would talk to, and we know some brusque and insensitive women, so to some extent it's not a fair question. On the other hand, it still happens and it's something that we recognize, so I just wanted to put that out there.

Darah: I've had a really interesting mixed kind of experience in terms of the gender question. I came into a town with two other rabbis, and part of their identifying features was in the wearing of a yarmulke. My predecessor didn't wear one and didn't exercise his title a lot. I was trying to do communal work, and so my other two models in town were *kippah*-wearing men who used their titles. I made some changes to the choices that I had made to try to become a public figure, etc. So there were some choices that were affected by gender being a substantial component of trying to be in a community with multiple rabbis. I had this experience, not in my own congregation, but when I did things in the Conservative community, of getting sort of these cheerleader-ish, wonderful older women who were so delighted that I was in town. They were so happy I was here, and clearly one of the things that was exciting about it was that I was a woman, but that didn't play directly into what they said. They would pull me aside and say they'd come to my congregation except their families had been a part of their community for 120 years or whatever. So there were some really interesting dynamics that really, in some sense, weren't about me. They didn't necessarily know me well enough to say what they did based on something that I had done, but instead it was based upon my status as a woman.

I also know from my Conservative colleagues that they had people who were not really Conservative contact their congregation to join because they wouldn't join with a woman rabbi. So, I'm aware of a lot of these behind-the-scenes things that are partially to do with gender, partially to do with who I am specifically. The additional component of also very publicly being a lesbian in the community adds another layer to how people think about it. I've been the only rabbi in town for awhile so I've been doing a lot of fill-in work over the years for the Conservative and even occasionally the Orthodox congregations. I feel like there's respect stuff. They know my title. They want or need me to do the function, mostly funerals, some hospital stuff, and some community stuff, yet I'm not sure that the level of appreciation would be the same if I were a man stepping in. Somehow there is sort of a feeling that they're glad I'm here but simultaneously can't wait for them to hire a real rabbi. It's usually not clearly articulated, though. There have been some actual events. Like, I'm told regularly I'm the only rabbi they've ever kissed, or one who insists on grabbing my hand and placing a kiss on my hand. So there are some things that are clearly public gender stuff and some that seems much more subtle. There is sort of a tone that I'm great to call when I'm the only rabbi in town, which has been a lot, and yet not follow through the second I'm not "needed" any more.

Melanie: You just reminded me of something I'd totally forgotten. Every now and then I get a call from someone who's a member of the local Conservative congregation. It always starts out with "Well, Rabbi Pressman (the rabbi at the local Conservative congregation) is much too busy, and so I'm calling you to ask this or that."

I don't know whether the perception is that mom's always available, so don't bother dad, or whether it's that they want to talk to me because I'm a woman and that's the excuse. What Darah was saying was so present, because it's as if I'm sitting here twiddling my thumbs while Rabbi Pressman is off doing important and busy things.

Roxanne Shapiro: I don't know if being a female specifically created opportunities for me, since I have mostly been working in terms of education in the congregational world. I think it's an area where people are used to having women as the director of lifelong learning, even though it has been different having a rabbi be in the position. Actually, when I was the director of admissions for HUC, I got a lot of comments from the leadership about being a female in the position. It was partially related to my having been younger at the time, so I got a lot of comments about how many more males would be coming to rabbinical school. Interestingly enough, I also got comments from leadership about how we couldn't have women featured in some of the pictures because it might change our ratio of men to women if there were too many women in the pictures. That actually came from a female working for HUC. I was little surprised by that but, you know, just people making assumptions either way, along with stereotypes. I don't know if it necessarily helped, but in some people's eyes some of that may have been an advantage.

Ellen: Let me make sure I understood this. Do you mean that they were saying because you were young and cute that men would apply to the College?

Roxanne: Yeah.

Ellen: Oh my God. I thought that's what you were saying, but I hoped that I was wrong. Unbelievable.

Roxanne: On the other side was that one thought that just by featuring women in pictures that it would cause other women to come, too.

Ellen: Was that a group thing or was that something that she was...

Roxanne: No, she was saying they were going to have too many women.

Ellen: Yeah.

Roxanne: Yeah, it was a negative. She told another colleague of mine who was working in admissions that she could not use a certain picture for recruitment purposes because the women in it were too young and cute.

Ilene: There was a whole conversation a few years back about whether or not they should restrict the number of women that they admitted to the College because of the imbalance in the classes. It was a matter of public discussion. I think Rabbi Ellenson said, "I'm not prepared to do that." The repercussions of that were phenomenal, really, that they would even raise the question.

Debby: I think that I mentioned last time that I'd been on the admissions committee for New York twice, and that issue never arose in our preparatory discussions or our discussions on candidates. The age of a candidate, or their gender, or their gender orientation was never brought up. So, I assume that most of the admissions committees were the same. We were never given any pre-instructions, anything about the balance, or given information about what the gender balance, or any other kind of balance, already was.

Roxanne: I can at least speak on '99 through 2003. The representatives of admissions who were hearing about the imbalance knew that it was inappropriate to pass it on to those on the committees. We stopped it going that far.

Betsy: One thing that's interesting to me is the use of "woman" as a modifier. We're not just talking about admitting rabbis. We're talking admitting "woman" rabbis. I think that it's the truth that we're referred to as the "woman rabbis" or a "woman rabbi."

Alysa: Especially with the younger families and with their kids, I was the girl rabbi. I wasn't necessarily called that, but I think that I was at different points known as the woman rabbi. We had one full-time cantor and we had a High Holy Day cantor, and my senior rabbi would lead one service and I would lead the other. They were in two different locations, and we would switch locations the next day. My senior said that the congregation wasn't ready to see two women together on the bimah, so I would never work with the woman cantor whom they had hired as their High Holy Day cantor. It was always me and the male cantor, and the senior and the woman cantor. And that was true until last year.

Debby: In my second congregation, the fact that there was a woman cantor already there when I came and that I came after a male rabbi was a big detriment to my being able to be successful there. There were just people who did not want to see two women together on the bimah, and it wasn't always rational and it wasn't always that they were always conscious of it. As we all know, that happens to both men and women who are looking up at the pulpit. They just weren't prepared for that. This is unlike my first congregation, where I was a solo rabbi with no cantorial help for so long; they were really more gender blind. It was a very different time and there wasn't a full-time cantor, but when they did hire the first full-time cantor at my first pulpit, where I was for those couple of decades, they did what someone else said earlier in this conversation. They looked specifically for a male, meaning: all things being equal, they would hire a male, but all things not being equal, they would have hired a woman. They did it not because of people complaining, but because they understood that children needed to see different kinds of male and female role models.

Ellen: How about if we switch to the question about finding role models. Now, for the younger women or the women who were ordained later than the old folks who were already out there, there were a variety of models that we created, but in any case we all find our own roles models. I know that I certainly had as role models women who worked outside the home as professionals, and I had role models as rabbis, but they weren't the same because there weren't too many female rabbis out there at the time. So, I certainly used my mother as a role model of how to have a career and have a family. There were lots of rabbis that I knew, mostly men, who were both positive and negative role models of how I wanted to be a rabbi. I knew early on that I kind of didn't want to be a "rabbi in drag." I didn't want to become a "man" in my mannerisms, as it were. Regardless, there were teaching models and there were leadership models, and some of them were terrific and some of them were absolutely awful. How did the rest of you find role models? What was that process like, and what kinds of qualities were you looking for?

Alysa: I found role models in a few places. I found role models in the WRN, which has been a tremendous resource to me of amazing women who kind of led the way. Because of it, I met women who I wouldn't have known, women in different stages of their rabbinate, and as I've been going through different things in my own rabbinate, it has really been important to be able to connect with women who, even beyond knowing what it was like to be a pregnant rabbi or to be a rabbi and a mom, are just other women, some of whom are moms, who have become my friends. Also, with respect to personal challenges and dealing with difficulties with my leadership or with my senior rabbi, there have been some really amazing women who've gone through some similar things in their own congregation or who found incredible success, and they have been a great resource.

I also found some amazing role models from within my congregation—successful women in their own fields who sought me out and said, "Hey, I'd love to mentor you a little bit. I know that you're a new rabbi."

That was an extraordinary resource for me in my last congregation. There were women I also sought out. I actually found my phenomenal professional coach through my congregation. She is this amazing woman who had seen me on the bimah, and who had seen me at work, and who really believed in me and sought me out. She has been a really incredible source of learning and mentorship and strength. I don't know if men get that in the same way that women do. Maybe people seek out our male colleagues in the same way. I don't know. It felt a little bit like a club, and that has been really great, in that I often feel like it's still a man's world and it's nice to feel like I have my club. That's really been a gift for me in my rabbinate.

Melanie: Although I was early on [in the history of women in the rabbinate], the fact that there were some women before me was really important to me. Ellen Weinberg Dreyfus, Debbie Prinz, and the women who I bumped into at WRN meetings or who were before me at the College, or who ended up in the regions where I ended up being a rabbi, were really important. Also, Christian colleagues were very important, especially in the very beginning. It was easier to find more female Christian colleagues. For a little while we had this clergy group in Brooklyn that was diverse. It gave us other ways of being clergy in the community, and I found that very helpful.

Darah: My first role model was actually not a Reform rabbi but Rabbi Deborah Brin, a Reconstructionist rabbi who moved to New Mexico, where I was living at the time. She was my first teacher on what would be the road to becoming a rabbi, when I was working with Rabbi Joe Black. I often found a lot of my mentors, actually, were women cantors. I didn't have a lot of exposure to women rabbis. Cantors Jackie Shuchat-Marx and Barbara Finn, both out of New Mexico, who, though I don't have the privilege of having a clergy team, really taught me a lot about not just being a woman in clergy, but working in relationships with others in a congregational team.

Rabbi Deborah Brin also was the first entrepreneurial rabbi. She was one before we knew what it was. She gave me other ideas about what a rabbinate could look like. She was working pastorally, both for the Reform and the Conservative congregations in the town, and was available to people outside the synagogue framework. Those were some of the early models that I had and people that I'm still in touch with. I found that, along the way, attending WRN functions and building not just role models but peers was really important. Developing those relationships and staying in touch and calling when a particular person went to a particular event, or to ask a question of a person who seemed like they might have been through a similar thing and might have a particular insight was invaluable, especially with someone like Robin Nafshi, who has also been on the board of WRN, or with other classmates and people I've met through the WRN. It is so important to have a variety of people to look at where they stand and say, "Hmm, I think that one is the one who might know," and then taking that advice or a recommendation to contact someone else.

Debby: I think we talked about this a little bit at the first session as well, and I just wanted to repeat it so that it will all be in the same section. I had wonderful male colleagues in my region in Massachusetts and New England, who were my main mentors. I really agree with what Darah said. Even though we're in slightly different generations in the rabbinate, it was really that as peers we sort of mentored each other. I remember driving back and forth to regional CCAR meetings in New England with a woman colleague. She and I would make sure we met up somewhere and drove together so that we would have that hour. We did informal mentoring of each other. It was formal in the sense that we said that was what we were going to be doing as we drove back and forth, but it was really helpful even though she was a few years younger than me. Enough can't be said about Ellen Dreyfus's influence on so many of us and her willingness to really be a mentor even for those who are just a few years after her. I want to just put in that plug.

Ellen: Someone mentioning colleagues from other movements reminds me of an extraordinary story. A friend of mine who was an assistant or an associate in her congregation, came back from maternity leave from her second child. Literally the day after she came back from maternity leave, the senior rabbi called her into his office and said, "I want to give you some advice. I don't think you should have any more children."

She called and told me this, and I just gasped! You know, as I heard someone else gasp on the phone just now. We talked for a while, and she said, "Yeah, I'm gonna figure this out; I just really needed to hear somebody go '*gasp*.'" She needed that reality check that this was completely outrageous. P.S., and she succeeded as the senior rabbi of that congregation and had a third child. She is extremely successful. I guess we can be there for each other in the good times but also for those horror stories, just to be the ear and the one who gasps.

How about other role models? Did anyone find sort of unconventional role models or not have any role models, or any thoughts on it?

Ilene: I had a lot of male role models. I think one of the things that my female colleagues have been is my support structure. I've had female rabbis who were not in congregational life who have been quite helpful to me. There is one female rabbi in my community who has been amazing. I've mostly had male, older, and non-congregational mentors—mostly people at the College. I'm sure that's due to my particular circumstances. My congregation isn't near very many rabbis, so I'm definitely in an isolated place where I haven't had a lot of congregational women role models. So I think it's just time to sign up for WRN, right? Isn't that the advertisement?

There's a lot of isolation when people go out into the field. I was with a bunch of colleagues this past week, and it was exactly what you're saying. We had that moment where somebody else said, "That's not okay."

One of our colleagues broke out in tears because no one had said, "That's not okay," and that's now. You know, that's someone just out of school. I think this is really important.

Darah: I want to say in support that a lot of my mentors have been men, and interestingly enough, I was blessed with two wonderful colleagues in Conservative and Orthodox rabbis when I came to Bangor. This is just one plug for the sometimes amazing possibilities. It really quite blew the mind of many people in the community here that the Orthodox rabbi and I were so friendly and did a lot together. On a personal level, he had been in the rabbinate considerably longer than I. We were almost exactly the same age, but he had gone straight into being a rabbi and I took a circuitous route. He was an incredible mentor in a lot of ways—for instance, in dealing with congregational life, and working with your board, and how to make change, and all sorts of things that were really impressive, in particular, because people mistook him for a liberal, which he was far from being. He had a very clear vision of what it meant to be a Jew in a community, of how you interact with others, etc. So there are still many mentors, as well as rabbis that I was fortunate to work with, who I can still call when something really unusual happens and ask, "And what would you do in this circumstance?"

Debby: This may be a little bit of a side issue here, and I don't know if it's interesting or not, but now that I am sixty years old and have been in the rabbinate since my mid- to late twenties, it's also the issue of who we mentor and who naturally comes to talk to us. I certainly have had newer male colleagues who I have conversations with at regional events and I don't feel at all rejected or pushed away, but I do feel that it's more the women who are newer in the field who are turning to other women to ask them for things. Maybe they're also turning to men, but I don't see as many of the men who are just out of school coming up.

I spoke to a mixed group of men and women a few years ago for one of the Tisch programs, and when I've run into the people who attended it at CCAR conventions, it is the women who will come up to comment to me. Maybe it's just a different kind of relationship thinking, between women and women. They want to catch me up on what they're doing in their lives now, but I don't feel the same way for most of the men. I don't overgeneralize, but when I'm at regional things where there's a group of more established colleagues and newer colleagues, the men are tending to talk to the men. I don't find them naturally coming to women the way that some women do. Just something I'm starting to think about in this conversation. Also, in the CCAR mentoring program, there's always some tension around whether women who are established in the field should be working with men who are coming into the field or working with women. Often the women are requesting, from what I hear, to work with women because they feel that those people better understand the issues that they are going through, which is probably true. Sometimes we want to be gender blind, and sometimes gender is useful and we want to use in ways that are most helpful to the younger colleagues.

Ellen: So any of the other questions, anybody have thoughts? You know, nobody ever says to men, "How do you feel that being a man plays a role in your rabbinate?" or "In what way does being male make a difference in your rabbinate?" Nobody asks that question, but we're always asked that question. I recall that I was at an interview with a congregation, and they actually said, "We notice that you're a woman. How do you think that affects the way you are as a rabbi?" I mean it was just, "Yeah?"

I'm proud that they recognized that. You've got to give them credit for grasping the obvious. Well, I said that I wasn't going to be in drag. That was the same interview where somebody asked me, "Are you going to have any more children?"

I couldn't say, "You idiot, that's an illegal question!" So I just smiled and said I don't have any plans, which is a non-answer, but it was awkward to say the least. Anyway they certainly would not have said that to a man, and so what do we do with this question?

Roxanne: I'd actually say, because I work with NATE [now ARJE, Association of Reform Jewish Educators] and I am involved with working with very few men, that I actually hear the men say that when they go on interviews to be educators at a congregation, they are asked how being a male affects doing education. So, while we may not see it in the rabbinate, because it was traditionally a male role, we, as Jewish congregations, are doing the same thing to the men when they are entering what, for our history, have been traditionally female roles. So it's interesting that we see it in the rabbinate, but we are doing the same thing to the men in roles that they want to fill that are not typically or not stereotypically male, and we ask how being a male plays into that.

Ellen: We the Jewish people, or who's the "we" who are doing this?

Roxanne: We the Jewish people, we in congregations. A male friend who has been interviewing has received those questions about why he, as a male, would want to be in this role. I mean, he has been asked by people you would be surprised about. Women in leadership positions and in clergy positions are asking this question about how, as a male, he would enter that role. I just think that it's interesting that it's asked and that gender issues are not just for women. It's the people going into roles that may not have always been seen as normative for their gender. They joke in NATE about the men starting some group for just the men because there is only a handful of them. So, it's actually on both sides with the Jewish professional organizations that I'm in.

Ilene: I have to say that where I am now my congregation I have absolutely no issue around my gender. I mean, occasionally an older man will say something to me that's, I don't know, vaguely endearing toward a younger woman or whatever. Other than that, the bulk of my congregation is incredibly neutral around my gender. If anything, they have been embracing. I am interested to know if people read the recent article about the relationship between confidence and women and women's pay grades and things like that. I think it was in the *Atlantic*. What they were saying was that there's a relationship between women's confidence in themselves and how that translates into our willingness to take on and do different things.

I also came out of rabbinical school in New York, where there were so many women professors and so many women colleagues. You know, I was told on Wall Street twenty-five years ago, "You don't need a raise—you don't have a family. What do you need more money for?"

In terms of the rabbinate, that hasn't been my experience, so I don't know if it is improving. The colleagues I was with last week still feel like there's a tremendous amount of pressure. It was a fellowship meeting, a reunion for Tisch fellows. In the last four or five years, the Tisch family has made a scholarship available like the Wexner, you know, a fellowship program and a couple of students per year. That's where Debby was speaking a few years ago. She was amazing, and I can say that as a woman. I think everyone thought so, though. So we had a meeting the last few days—just a bunch of colleagues, people four years, three years, two years, and one year out. There were conversations about gender even in this population just coming out now. At this meeting, there were men saying things like "No matter what, you should still try and be here for the meetings."

We raised our hands and said, "That woman just had twins. How could she be here?"

Betsy: I know this is a non sequitur, but you know the Jill Abramson article in the *New York Times*? This has made me think about qualities that are lauded in a man that are often not lauded in a woman. You know, the man is aggressive and assertive. When you talk about confidence, a woman is bitchy and argumentative and doesn't get along. Let alone the pay issues that obviously underlie it all. I live in the South. It's Florida, but it's the South, and there's the whole "darling, honey, sweetie" thing, and I think that I'm more forthright by nature, but I have a sense of how it will be received because of my gender in a way that I'm not sure men with those characteristics are received.

Debby: It's interesting to think about what the ideal is. It's kind of like we've come back to where I was when I started rabbinic school. Would we like a world in which gender really was irrelevant, or would we like a world in which gender was considered part of who we are? Can gender be a piece of what we bring to each thing that we do, whether male or female, even though there's a variety within maleness and femaleness in gender in general? I'm not sure exactly where I come down on that. In an ideal society, what does gender-blind mean? It isn't even possible because of the way we are as human beings, the natural ways people react based on gender. Is that what we would want? Would we want a neutral world, and would that neutral mean having to deny who we are? I think those questions will remain for many decades yet to come, not just in the rabbinate, but in many other areas. The more we realize that it is natural for people to at least be thinking, "Are you going to have another baby?"—because what they are really thinking is, "Will we have to pay for another maternity leave? Will you be away from us for three months?"

There are times when we want people to give us the respect of being neutral to our gender, and there are other times when we don't want them to. We want them to see that we have something special to offer the congregants. I've carried both of those around and I don't come down all the way on one or the other, on what kind of vision I would like to see happen when I'm long gone, not just in the rabbinate but in the world. When I think about my own daughters, I don't want them to suffer from gender discrimination, but I do want them to be able to use certain qualities that come from how they use their gender in positive ways.

Betsy: That sums it up. That's beautiful. I agree with that.

Rebekah: I have definitely found some women rabbis who have been role models for me in the way that they are what I would describe as a full self and also a rabbi. I have had really helpful conversations with them about the ways that they have found balance or are striving to find balance. They never seem to actually find it, between their personal aspirations, the people that they want to be outside of the rabbinate, and the people that they want to be inside of the rabbinate. So that's been very helpful to me in talking with them for sure.

Ellen: How did you meet them? Were these colleagues in the area or people you met while you were in rabbinical school? How long ago were you ordained? I forget.

Rebekah: I was ordained in 2011, so three years ago. I met the two that I'm thinking of when I was a song leader before even applying for rabbinical school. So, I met them just working in the Jewish community. I got to know them in the work that we were doing together and by talking to them as rabbis while I was thinking about the rabbinate for myself.

It was helpful to be in school with a number of classmates who were women, too. If I think about the ways that the rabbinate has changed since the first women were ordained, my rabbinical school class was probably 65 to 75 percent women. We were the vast majority, and so we spent a lot of time talking about the issues in terms of differential treatment between men and women and also in terms of issues that seem to focus on women in the rabbinate that are not necessarily only women's issues, like the balance of family life and professional life. It was nice to have the voices of both male and female colleagues in those conversations, for sure. I do wonder if a lot of that was because of the number of women who were in the room and who have been in the room for decades now.

Ellen: Do others have thoughts? Rebekah, how has being a woman created obstacles for you in your career, and how has it created opportunities for you? You can go either way or both. How does that sound?

Rebekah: Right. I don't feel like it has created obstacles for me. It has probably created opportunities for me. I'm thinking especially of an unfortunate experience that I had just last week where we found out that a fifth-grade girl had reported that she was being abused to her religious school *madrichah* [assistant teacher]. Her poor *madrichah* is only an eighth-grade girl herself. So Child Protective Services were called, and I was not involved in the call. It was a male educator who called the report into CPS. The social worker that he spoke with suggested that an adult speak with this fifth-grade girl. When the educator and my senior rabbi, who is also a man, talked about which adult would be best in terms of the girl feeling comfortable sharing her story again, they agreed that it would be best that I try to have that conversation, in spite of the fact that I had no relationship with this girl. To be honest, I didn't know her name. Obviously I had seen her, but I didn't know her name. Ultimately, I was successful. She did share with me, and we were able to make a report and the family is getting help. I don't know if the educator and my senior thought that I would be successful because I am a woman. I don't know if I was successful because I am a woman. It certainly could have hurt my chances as well, because it was her mother who was abusing her.

I do think that we, as women, are trained in our culture to be good listeners, to be sympathetic, to have highly attuned emotional awareness, at least stereotypically, but I do think that it's more than just stereotypically. I think that it is possible that my senior and the educator suggested that I be the one to speak to this girl because I am a woman and I'm a rabbi, so I am a woman who has that social training and a rabbi who has the pastoral training that we all benefited from at school. I don't know if I was successful as a result of that. I don't know if that's why they suggested that I be the one to speak to her, but I think it's quite possible.

So that's one anecdote, when I think about the benefits of being a woman rabbi and having women as rabbis. I think there are people who connect to women rabbis more easily than they do to male rabbis because of whatever they project about authority in general and the lack of approachability of male figures of authority. It gets easier, somehow, for a lot of people when those figures in authority positions are women. So that's my reflection. That's what I would say on that.

Ellen: Thank you. Is someone else willing to say something? I recall many years ago Laura Geller wrote an article about the fact that when people in general see a man up there doing all that stuff, they say, "Wow, that rabbi is doing all that stuff. I could never do that," but when they see a woman doing exactly the same thing, the thing they say is, "Wow, if she could do that, I could probably do that." Somehow we make it all more accessible to *am'cha* [the people]. She was ambivalent about this because it's not necessarily a compliment to say, "If she could, anybody could." On the other hand, it may be an advantage—a mixed blessing. Have you experienced that?

Betsy: I'm not aware of having experienced it. I don't know what people are thinking. I think that more often I hear from people, "I don't know how you juggle all of that, and how you are there for us and serve as a rabbi along with the demands of your own life."

Ellen: I guess I was thinking less about the juggling acts but more about the things like reading Torah or giving the *d'var Torah* or leading services. Maybe when Laura wrote this thirty-five years ago it was unusual for women to be doing any of that; it was something novel. By now it is ancient history, so maybe that's no longer a relevant question.

Betsy: I haven't heard it so much in that way.

Darah: Yeah, I haven't either. One of the things in this issue of the difference of approachability is that some of it is both a gender thing and a personality thing. I came on the heels of somebody who was famous for being really, really smart, but very particular about how things were done. Things had to be in exactly the right place and done in exactly the right way, and I have a much more relaxed, less detail-oriented kind of approach to some of it. I think it is the kind of thinking that gets caught up in whether it is a question of gender or other personality issues at play, as well, that leads to some of the differences in how we're perceived. I haven't encountered the statement that if a woman can do it, well, then anyone can do it.

Alysa: One thing that I've noticed is that a lot of people have come up to me over the ten years that I've been a rabbi and have said that it has been so important for them and for their daughters to have me as a role model—to have a strong woman as a role model on the bimah. They didn't have that growing up, and it has made a difference in the Jewish lives of both men and women for their daughters to see a woman on the bimah, and to see Judaism done differently than they saw growing up, and to see a new generation of rabbis. I think some of that is generational and some of that is very gender driven. It has been a big part of the way women have been given different access to Judaism. I think about all the girls especially, and also the boys, who have seen a strong woman as a leader in front of them. It does affect the way they see women and the way that they treat each other. It has made Judaism more accessible to them. This is reflected in a lot of the articles in the book that this conversation is going to be published in: the issues of accessibility and theology—all of these things.

Betsy: I wanted to say something about the WRN. I served the first eight years of my rabbinate in Australia, and although there were woman rabbis both in my city and in the country by the time I left, in the beginning there weren't any. Gender played a huge part of my rabbinate, being *the* woman rabbi. So when I came back to the States the very first year, I was at my first WRN conference and I found it overwhelming. I remember that feeling so powerfully, of just being in this room with so many amazing women, and I can still feel it. It was tremendously supportive in every way. To think about it now, I'm in a city where there is now another woman rabbi just as of year ago, but for the first ten years that I was here, there wasn't another female in my rabbinic community. There has been a Conservative colleague who I study with, but it's not my rabbinic community directly. I have felt conscious of being the only woman there—the sense of numbers, community, and *chevruta* that's present whether you are the only one or not. I think those things make a difference in how we feel about what it is to be a woman in the rabbinate.

Rebekah: Responding to the statement that Laura made those years ago, I don't know that, at this point, seeing women on the bimah or in all areas of the rabbinate makes Judaism more accessible, but it sort of makes rabbis more accessible. Again, people relate to men and women differently, and we are societally trained into gender roles to some degree. This is still true even as our openness to different permutations of gender roles is getting better. There is still a significant trend that women are more empathetic than men, so I don't know if it makes Judaism more accessible, but perhaps it makes rabbis feel more accessible.

To Alysa's point about the role-model piece, I'm just about to leave my current congregation and move to a new congregation, and I have been receiving all these wonderful notes from people. One of them was from a middle-school girl who said that she's always wanted to be a rabbi, that her father is a rabbi and for most of her life her mother has not worked outside the home. This young girl wrote that she's always wanted to be a rabbi, but she has also always wanted to be a full-time mom, and she didn't ever think she could do both. Somehow she sees what I do as having helped her to feel like she can do both. Of course, that's sort of laughable because I'm not quote-unquote a full-time mom in the sense that I work outside the home. I spend quite a bit of time away from my children, but I guess I am a role model for her in that I could be an engaged mom and also a full-time engaged rabbi.

The last thing I wanted to say was triggered by what you said, Betsy. One of my favorite things is to talk to Israelis, men and women, about the fact that I'm a rabbi. My Hebrew's pretty good, so I am usually speaking to them in Hebrew, and I explain that I'm a rabbi and the word in Hebrew is *rav*. There is no gender conversion. There's no female version of "rabbi" in Hebrew, because any feminization of the word in Hebrew means, actually, the rabbi's wife, not the rabbi. It's always wonderful to have that conversation with them. They sort of think about it for a second, because at first they want to correct me and then realize that it's true. I can watch the wheels turning, and that's always exciting. That's an area of progress too.

Ellen: Actually, there is now officially the word *rabbah* meaning "female rabbi," and it was accepted by the Academy of the Hebrew Language probably ten to fifteen years ago. So I guess we can say *todah rabbah* [thank you]. It is confusing because, you know, you write *harav* [rabbi, masc.] and everybody knows what that is, but if you write *harabbah* [rabbi, fem.], it looks like you're writing *harbeh* [many; spelled the same way as *harabbah* when written without vowels], so it doesn't make any sense. Anyway, it is interesting to think about that.

Ellen: I have some thoughts that I just want to share as we wrap up. One is that I kept hearing over and over about how important it is that we mentor each other, and that we listen to each other, and that we are there for each other even to give the gasps, or to be encouraging, or to encourage those young women we meet at camp or in our congregations. That's hugely important, and I don't think we should at all discount the role that we can play for other younger men and women. I think, particularly, that it ends up that women need to see somebody who looks like them, and the possibility that we can continue to do that for each other and for women in the future is tremendously important. I think we should take it very seriously and have fun with it as well. Other thoughts?

Ellen: Alysa, thank you for convening us, and Hara, for working on this book. It will be interesting to see what gets in and what gets edited out.

Editors Note: These conversations were transcribed and then edited for both confidentiality and style.

PERSONAL REFLECTION

The Pregnant Rabbi

R ABBI D EBORAH Z ECHER

Emblazoned on the front page of the *New York Jewish Week* was the headline "New Role for the Rabbi: Mother," with a picture of six-week-old Joshua, my husband Dennis, and me, proof positive that we were transcending the boundaries of what rabbis look like and what rabbis do. Yep, the pregnant rabbi had given birth and was now a rabbi *and* a mom. That very public feature story was simply a continuation of my very public pregnancy.

Having children, if we could be so blessed, was never a question for either my husband or me; we could not imagine a life without children of our own. By the time I was ordained in 1982, there were only forty-nine women rabbis, and only a few had already had children; being pregnant and giving birth still felt very cutting edge. No policies and few guidelines existed beyond the life experience of those who had come before me. Relatively few of my colleagues who had given birth were working full-time as congregational rabbis, so I truly felt as though I was making it up as I went along. By 1985, when I first became pregnant, no one was yet talking about the work/family life balance, and we didn't wonder whether we could "have it all" because we had every intention of doing it all. Give birth in the morning and lead services that very evening; that seemed like a reasonable expectation for a generation of women who expected to transform the world. I not only worked up to the day that I gave birth; I actually stopped by the synagogue with the "hot-off-the press" religious school weekly newsletter on my way to the hospital while I was already in labor, and I thought nothing of it.

Not once in my wildest dreams, however, did I actually think about what it might really mean to be pregnant. I guess I had skipped that particular chapter in *Our Bodies, Ourselves*. I simply assumed that when we decided to have children, I would get pregnant. That was the first assumption to go. Like so many of my peers, in my life thus far, I had set goals, I had studied and prepared, and then I accomplished those goals. The first life lesson of pregnancy was learning to relinquish control over that particular timetable. I remember thinking that it would be so convenient to give birth right after Shavuot so that I would be back in my office well before the High Holy Days. Was it naivete or arrogance? Either way, it didn't happen on that particular schedule. The best laid plans...

One thing I never doubted was that our decision to have children would become part of my congregational life, but nothing could have prepared me for the way that my congregation both embraced and commented on my pregnancy. Amid exuberant joy and well wishes were the unbelievable comments. "Oh my God, you look big enough to give birth to an entire congregation" was my own personal favorite. I will never forget the loud murmuring of more than twelve hundred people as I walked down the center aisle of my congregation on Erev Rosh HaShanah 5746. When most people left for the summer, as was the case in my suburban New York congregation, I was hardly showing. Three months later, I was at the beginning of my eighth month and, to put it plainly, hugely pregnant. I can still recall the deep flush that permeated my face when I realized that all that murmuring was about me! Leaving the bimah during the service because my contact lens got dislodged caused the service to come to a standstill; everyone assumed I had gone into labor right then and there. Three ob-gyns rushed to the bimah, certain that their services were needed at that moment. When I told the teens in my confirmation class that I was pregnant, one of them looked scandalized and later admitted to her friends that she had never thought of the rabbi "doing it." Here was proof that the rabbi had indeed "done it." And of course, I lost any semblance of personal space, as my burgeoning belly was fair game for anyone who wanted to touch me.

Maternity leave was still a novelty when I was ordained. But I was the one who was shocked when a distinguished congregant raised his hand at a board meeting during my first year as assistant rabbi at Westchester Reform Temple in Scarsdale. The topic was my next contract. "Well," he said, "if we are going to have a female rabbi, then we must include a maternity leave in her next contract." In that first year after ordination, becoming pregnant was the furthest thing from my mind. I even looked around the room to see whom he was talking about. In those early years, there was no such thing as a standard maternity leave policy in the Reform Movement. As I began to contemplate becoming pregnant, I learned of the challenges faced by many of my female colleagues and felt blessed by that congregant's prescient concern for me. I learned of colleagues who were given unpaid maternity leaves or told that their leave began on their due date, no matter when they actually gave birth. I also discovered colleagues who were fortunate, as I was, to have congregational leaders who understood the importance of real time off following the birth of a newborn. And of course, no one thought about parenting leave in those days; my husband was lucky to get a day or two off after our kids were born. And in the same way I endeavored to work as long and hard and put in as many hours as I did before becoming pregnant, so did I never think twice about working thirteen hours on the first day back after my maternity leave. I was so determined to show the world that I could handle it all.

As someone who treasures liturgy, I had all kinds of ideas about how to make my birth experience a meaningful spiritual moment. Special blessings with an opportunity to acknowledge the sacred journey that birth represents—this was my intention in advance of giving birth. Twenty hours of labor, an emergency caesarean, and all thoughts of meaningful ritual flew out of my head. Once again, I learned that my life was not necessarily in my control. I felt grateful that I simply remembered the words of *Shehecheyanu*.

Three beautiful children—Joshua, Adam, and Miriam—are now all adults on their own, but memories of those three pregnancies are still vivid to my husband and to me. One memory that stands out happened soon after Joshua's birth. Even after his *b'rit milah* with family and friends, we wanted to share the joy of this wonderful *simchah* with our congregants. So Joshua was named and blessed twice, once in my husband's congregation and again in mine. And it was on the bimah of my synagogue, where I served as rabbi, as I stood beside my husband, holding our child in my arms, listening to Rabbi Jack Stern, my senior rabbi, pronounce words of blessing upon us all, that I felt all parts of myself and my world converge and become totally, entirely, and simply whole.

PERSONAL REFLECTION

Ima and *Abba* on the Bimah: Being an RK Squared

RACHEL MARDER

Ima on the Bima was one of my favorite picture books during my childhood. Rabbi Mindy Avra Portnoy's 1986 story about what a rabbi's job entails imbued me with the fierce pride only a child can feel at a show-and-tell explaining what her parents do for a living. My mother, ordained in 1979 by HUC-JIR, was one of the first ten women to be called "rabbi" in the Reform Movement. My father had received ordination in 1978, and together they became the first married rabbinic couple since Rabbi Meir and Beruriah.

From the outside, strangers would ask, "So, what's it like with both of your parents as rabbis?" I think they assumed I would complain about how busy they were or describe how much pressure I felt. But none of that was true. Sure, they were busy, but I never felt left out. I participated in their classes and davened beside them. I was moved to tears by their words of Torah. Then and also now, in every *d'rash* and sermon they offer, I hear their unique voices, their *chidushim* (insights), and a loyalty to tradition. Since moving to the Bay Area when I was thirteen, I have loved attending my parents' classes and noticing how they are able to teach people of any age and background. My *ima*'s Shabbat morning Torah study class is packed with congregants, their friends and family, and interested folks in the area. She prepares diligently; in addition to her own insights, she offers medieval and contemporary commentaries, creating openings for personal connection. She makes the words of Torah sweet on their lips.

I attended a Conservative day school and realized my family wasn't the norm, though I had several close friends who were also RKs (rabbi's kids), even a couple who were also "RK-squared." Our family modeled an egalitarian approach to Judaism filled with joyful community, active participation, and question asking. No question was off-limits, and no ritual felt coercive. They offered answers to my questions with humility, always asking me what I thought as well. It is this model that I take with me now on my path to the rabbinate, and one I intend to emulate in my own family.

I am most inspired by my *ima* for her trailblazing work with Beth Chayim Chadashim of Los Angeles, the first gay and lesbian synagogue. Making it her first rabbinic position, she was not afraid to take an unconventional career path to embrace the entire Jewish people and support those wrongly marginalized from our communities. She stood at the forefront of the Jewish world in the 1980s in leading efforts for inclusivity and opening up the conversation about HIV and AIDS, dispelling myths and raising awareness. Though I was very young, I was aware that not every *ima* stood up for justice and compassion.

I am in awe when I attend my father's classes on Jewish poetry, art, Torah, the psalms, and Israeli current events at the Jewish Home of San Francisco, where he serves as the rabbi. Through the material and approachable discussion he offers, the elderly residents are able to show creativity and wisdom. He also teaches a deeply personal and innovative course on end-of-life spiritual counseling for volunteers. I hope to model his patience and compassion as well as my *ima*'s diligence. They have shown me that Torah belongs to every person, and every person has Torah to offer. I witness my parents providing comfort to those in need, encouragement to those who struggle, and enthusiasm to those rejoicing over *simchah*s. They share in all of these moments, and in a small way, I feel I do as well by observing them. I believe they are doing the most important job in the world—God's work: counseling the vulnerable, teaching words of moral inspiration, and bringing people closer to Jewish tradition.

Growing up, I knew that seeing my *ima* and *abba* on the bimah was a privilege. I admired, and still admire, the courageous way they lead— with brilliance, honesty, kindness, and humor. My *ima*'s sermons are penetrating and uplifting, sometimes leaving us in stitches and usually in tears. She preaches about caring for those who are invisible in our communities, the gifts of raising our children as Jews, a strong and ethical Israel, and nurturing our spiritual life. Her *divrei Torah* are precious, a pearl of wisdom in each of them. They are words we need to hear as Jews and as human beings searching for meaning and a relationship with the Divine. She is my model for how to write and deliver a sermon that will say something significant to a person of any age.

My *abba* brings comfort, song, and understanding to the weak. He makes our tradition approachable and encouraging, value-rich and welcoming to residents from diverse Jewish and cultural backgrounds. He ensures the synagogue at the Home actually feels like home to each of them. He puts out Jewish books, art, drums, and tambourines to play during the service, ritual objects, and plays Jewish music as the residents enter Friday afternoons so they can feel and hear their tradition. He invites residents to ask questions during the service—about the *parashah* or any Jewish topic on their minds, and they always do. My *abba* brings a poem, painting, or another text to share during the service so the residents can find words and images with which they resonate. Residents respond eagerly with their memories, feelings the text invokes, and thoughts. I love seeing the desire to learn and grow that he inspires in them.

In recent years, my parents have enjoyed collaborating on their sermons and Purim-spiels, adapting each to fit their community. They are a model for teamwork and support. I love watching their minds work as they discuss philosophy, *Tanach*, rhymes, and jokes. Whether sitting in their study reading or around their computers writing, they are surrounded by stacks of books. There are bookshelves in every room; they are truly parents of the book.

They appreciate insights from each other, and offer encouragement and critiques. Each year, in preparation for her Yom Kippur sermon, my father gives my *ima* his collection of *New York Times* obituaries from that year. This annual ritual has become legendary in my *ima*'s synagogue, and I always look forward to hearing about those who died in the last Jewish year, from the remarkable to the bizarre. My parents are true intellectual and spiritual partners who support and love each other.

They completed an incredible project last year: The Reform Movement's new *machzor, Mishkan HaNefesh.* They put their hearts into translating, writing, and selecting commentaries, crafting an introspective High Holy Day experience for twenty-first-century Jews. I am amazed by the incredible thought and energy, persistence and sensitivity they are putting into this prayer book. I have learned much about the art of translation, watching my father analyze each Hebrew word with care and for context. I have grown up watching them give to the Reform Movement with all of their strength, taking on leadership roles and writing for the publications. I know they are excited for this opportunity and for the meaningful *t'filah* (prayer) it will inspire. I feel great pride in this gift of their talents and wisdom that they are giving, and I know it will be cherished by Jews for generations to come.

There was another question I often heard: "So, do you want to be a rabbi when you grow up—like your parents?" A smile and "I don't know, I'm ten" or "No, I don't think so" were my typical responses. But eventually I came around and realized the rabbinate was where I could have the greatest impact. I, too, want to be engaged in the sacred work of teaching and caring for the Jewish people. I chose a rabbinical school that embraces tradition and innovation, encourages both pluralism and a relational approach to our communities. I chose the Ziegler School of Rabbinic Studies because of the values and examples my parents set for me.

Lately, the Conservative Movement, where I am finding a home, has been grappling with how to be more inclusive of interfaith couples and families. My mother's example at Congregation Beth Am in Los

Altos Hills, California, is serving as tremendous inspiration and as a model for what can be: a robust synagogue life that is welcoming and loving to all and, at the same time, strongly encourages Jewish practice and commitment. Her 2004 Yom Kippur blessing—expressing gratitude to non-Jewish spouses for their commitment to rearing Jewish children—gave recognition to those whose efforts are often overlooked and made those parents feel valued by the entire community. Its power rippled across the Reform Movement and the Jewish world. She spoke from the heart and offered a message of hope for upholding *Yiddishkeit* in the face of our changing demographics. I hope to build a community where everyone who enters feels noticed, accepted, and valued for her gifts. My *ima*'s example is inspiring all of us to think creatively about ensuring our Jewish future; she inspires me to think about our generation's challenges with optimism and diligence.

God willing, I, too, will find my way to the bimah. I won't be the first *ima* on the bimah, but I intend to carve a path like my parents— one filled with Torah learning, commitment to God, and Israel. I am thrilled and thankful that my journey to the rabbinate is greatly inspired by their pioneering and loving service.

Part Three

Ripple Effects:
The Impact of Ordaining Women

Though not an intended outcome, the effects of ordination of women at Hebrew Union College–Jewish Institute of Religion (HUC-JIR) reached far beyond the Reform Movement. Other subgroups within the wider Jewish community, faced with similar biases and restraints, looked to the advances in the Reform Movement and were strengthened in their efforts to move beyond that which historically held them back.

Rabbi Gary Phillip Zola, PhD ("JTS, HUC, and Women Rabbis—Redux") examines the influence that the ordination of women at HUC-JIR had on the decision for the Jewish Theological Seminary of America to ordain women and the differences in the approach of the Conservative Movement toward full acceptance of women. Outside of the liberal movements, the role of the rabbi encompasses not only pastoral and ritual responsibilities, but legal ones as well. Maharat Rori Picker Neiss ("A New Reality: Female Religious Leadership in the Modern Orthodox Community") and Rabbi Darren Kleinberg ("Orthodox Women (Non-)Rabbis") look at the complicated path Orthodox women have taken on the road toward recognition as communal leaders.

The acceptance of women rabbis moved far beyond just one movement. The fight for gender equality influenced the acceptance of gays and lesbians at HUC-JIR and, eventually, on the pulpit. Rabbi Denise L. Eger ("Creating Opportunities for the 'Other': The Ordination of Women as a Turning Point for LGBT Jews") explores the history of LGBT Jews and the move toward full inclusion of all Jews regardless of gender and sexual identity.

Every one of these aspirations and successes helped make the way for women in Israel to articulate and realize their desire to become rabbis. Both Rabbi Dalia Marx, PhD ("Women Rabbis in Israel") and Rabbi Kinneret Shiryon ("The First Thirty Years in Israel—Avnei Derech") reveal the very particular challenges facing women rabbis in Israel.

Finally, four male rabbis, Rabbi Charles A. Kroloff ("The Impact of Women Rabbis on Male Rabbis"), Rabbi Sam Gordon ("The Presence of Women Rabbis: A Transformation of the Rabbinate and of Jewish Life"), Rabbi Michael S. Friedman ("Growing Up with Women Rabbis as Role Models"), and Rabbi Jeffrey Kurtz-Lendner ("A Man's Experience of Women in the Rabbinate"), reflect on how the inclusion of women positively impacts the rabbinate, the Jewish community, and future generations of Jews.

15

JTS, HUC, AND WOMEN RABBIS—REDUX

Rabbi Gary Phillip Zola, PhD

It is worth noting that the widespread acceptance that women rabbis, cantors, and religious leaders enjoy today in many parts of the world was hardly a pervasive expectation in 1983 when I first wrote "JTS, HUC, and Women Rabbis."[1] One who reads this short article today, more than thirty years after it was written, might understandably wonder what prompted me to compose it in the first place. The purpose of this reappraisal is to offer an answer to this query and, simultaneously, to reflect once again on how the determination by Hebrew Union College–Jewish Institute of Religion (HUC-JIR) to begin ordaining women rabbis in 1972 compares with the decision taken by the Jewish Theological Seminary of America (JTS) to follow suit ten years later. These two schools are at the center of the story of how women entered the rabbinate. By resolving to ordain women rabbis, HUC-JIR and JTS contributed mightily to a revolutionary transformation in the world of Jewish religious leadership. The original version of this essay took note of this phenomenon as it was occurring.

When my article first appeared, Sally Priesand had been a rabbi for only twelve years, and Sandy Eisenberg Sasso, who completed her rabbinical studies at the Reconstructionist Rabbinical College (RRC) in 1974, had just marked the tenth anniversary of her ordination. It is important to bear in mind that less than two dozen women received rabbinical ordination from HUC-JIR between 1972 and 1980,[2] and many observers vigorously insisted that the vast majority of the Jewish people would *never* accept women as religious leaders on their pulpits. Throughout the Jewish world—even in the Reform Movement—critics of HUC-JIR's decision to ordain women rabbis insisted that women in the rabbinate would ultimately be viewed as a schismatic phenomenon acceptable only among Judaism's most radical religionists.[3]

Throughout the 1970s, there was plenty of second-guessing concerning HUC-JIR's decision to begin ordaining women rabbis. Jakob J. Petuchowski (1925–1991), a much beloved and widely respected professor of theology and liturgy at HUC-JIR in Cincinnati, believed the decision to ordain women rabbis was nothing more than a passing fancy that was primarily motivated by Reform Judaism's inclination to adopt popular social causes. "As for Reform Judaism," he wrote in 1975, "it tries to be all things to all people, and must, therefore, take up every fad which comes along."[4]

In 1976, the Central Conference of American Rabbis (CCAR) established a "Task Force on Women in the Rabbinate." Initially, the task force focused most of its attention on the issue of "acceptance and integration of women into the Reform rabbinate." The records of the task force testify to the fact that between the years 1972 and 1981, many Reform Jews were ambivalent about HUC-JIR's decision to ordain women rabbis. The daunting struggles for acceptance that the first women in the rabbinate faced are unmistakably evident in the reports of the task force.[5]

The members of the task force strove intensely to address this ambivalence. In order to expose "colleagues and congregations...to women functioning as rabbis," the task force endeavored "to establish a number of summer internships which would enable women rabbinical students to assist rabbis in various congregations throughout the country." In 1978, Sally Priesand, the task force's first chair, confessed in her official report to the CCAR that the overall response to the idea of summer internships for women rabbinical students was "minimal."

The problems these pioneering women rabbis encountered were hardly fleeting. In his 1980 report to the CCAR, Neil Kominsky, chair of the task force, emphasized that many of the women colleagues in the CCAR had encountered "significant instances of bias on the part of particular senior rabbis and congregations"[6] (see also Kominsky, p. 127, this volume).

These problems prompted the task force to convene a national conference of female rabbis and rabbinical students to share concerns and advocate for greater acceptance of women rabbis. This national meeting took place in New York on February 5–7, 1980, and led to the establishment of the Women's Rabbinic Network.[7] A series of proposals was adopted by those in attendance, which were subsequently presented to the Executive Board of the CCAR. These proposals brought the serious challenges that the first women rabbis encountered into bold relief. The conference attendees urged the CCAR to overhaul the process of rabbinical placement so as to "ensure the egalitarian treatment of women candidates for all positions now and in the future." They also wanted the CCAR to provide women rabbis with the tangible support they needed in order to pursue a career while simultaneously raising a Jewish family. They called for the establishment of guidelines and rules so that rabbis—both male and female—could have access to resources that would make these aspirations viable: pregnancy leaves, job sharing, and part-time rabbinical positions. Above all, the conference proposals emphasized that despite the much appreciated support and encouragement they had received from many of their male colleagues in leadership positions, much more had to be done if women were to gain full acceptance as rabbis:

> Many distinct responsibilities, challenges and, therefore, sometimes pressures face rabbis who are women. Male rabbis who do not serve in organizations or congregations with women colleagues often do not see these issues on a daily basis. Therefore, it can be difficult for male rabbis to understand that prejudice is directed at women colleagues and that additional expectations are placed upon women rabbis. Women rabbis are too often viewed as a new item,

a publicity curiosity, a spokeswoman for all women rabbis and/or for all feminists. Women face continual discrimination that is based on memory and upon sociological and psychological expectations. Lack of experience with women professionals, specifically women rabbis, often permits this to continue.[8]

The proposals promulgated by this national conference left no doubt that nearly a decade after Sally Priesand's ordination, women rabbis and rabbinical students were grappling with a considerable level of "prejudice against rabbis who are women." The CCAR and the Reform Movement as a whole would need to take meaningful and deliberative action if they truly aspired "to create a more humane and egalitarian rabbinate."[9]

The non-acceptance that women rabbis faced in the Reform Movement during the late 1970s was amplified by the out-of-hand rejection of women in the rabbinate within the traditional wings of Judaism. Practically no one in the Orthodox Jewish community—not even those who identified with the more centrist wing of Orthodoxy—were willing to suggest in a public forum that women could conceivably occupy an office akin to that of rabbinical leadership. In 1972, a young modern Orthodox rabbi named Haskel Lookstein (b. 1932)—a man who would later become a champion of lenient interpretations of halachah—told the *New York Times* that he was firmly opposed to the prospect of women entering the rabbinate.[10] Even Blu Greenberg (b. 1936), the well-known Orthodox woman who would eventually be one of the first to state publicly that women should be permitted to enter the rabbinate, confessed that in the 1970s the very idea of a woman rabbi repulsed her:

> In 1972, I read an article about the forthcoming ordination of Rabbi Sally Priesand at Hebrew Union College. I was, to put it mildly, horrified. Someone had crossed the line. "It is against halakhah," I argued. "Other things I can understand, but women rabbis—never! There goes Reform Judaism again."[11]

In 1977, the Rabbinical Council of America, the largest Orthodox rabbinical association, hosted a panel discussion on the future role of women in Judaism at its annual convention, held in Fallsburg, New York. Three distinguished rabbis shared their views on women and Judaism. The much respected rabbinical scholar Gedaliah D. Schwartz (b. 1925), then serving Young Israel of Brooklyn, provided his listeners with "an hour of Halachic explanation on why women could take no further role in worship." A second panelist, Rabbi Reuven Bulka (b. 1944), from Ottawa, Canada, provoked at least one female member of the audience to walk out of the program when he opined that everyone knew that Jewish women were already superior to men, and therefore women did not need "all of the trappings of [religious] leadership that chauvinist men had invented for themselves." Rabbi Shlomo Riskin (b. 1940), then of New York, expressed the most liberal views of those on the panel. He told the audience that he "allowed" women in his congregation to make their own prayer shawls and, also, "to hold worship services tailored to their religious needs and professional attainments." Riskin's admission prompted sharp criticism from his fellow panelists, who asserted that he had no authority to "alter the [Jewish worship] services." Although many of the Orthodox women in the audience publicly expressed their bitter dissatisfaction over the vexing problem of recalcitrant husbands "who refused to cooperate with the Orthodox divorce ritual," none in the room "questioned the Halachic rule against women rabbis."[12]

In the early 1980s, however, the number of women rabbis began to burgeon. By June 1984, the combined number of women ordinees from both HUC-JIR *and* the RRC had reached ninety, and many more women rabbinical students would join their ranks by 1988. Since the CCAR's total membership in the early 1980s was just shy of fourteen hundred, it became clear that by the end of the 1980s women would easily constitute more than 10 percent of the American Reform rabbinate. It was at this very time that those who had dedicated themselves to ensuring that the Reform Movement gave women rabbis equal footing in all aspects of rabbinical affairs began to sense that the tide was indeed turning in their favor. The CCAR Task Force on Women in the Rabbinate met twice in 1980 to review "its ongoing monitoring of the placement experience of female colleagues." Neil Kominsky informed the members of the CCAR that his committee had resolved to recommend that a three-month paid maternity leave be considered a "normative" guideline for all rabbinical contracts. In addition, he reported that the women rabbis in the CCAR now planned to initiate a mentoring program for women students at HUC-JIR. They were determined to put their experience to good use in helping to alleviate "questions and concerns" that were on the minds of their future colleagues. Most significantly, Kominsky informed the CCAR that the task force now sensed that a new, more positive spirit concerning women rabbis was taking hold in the Reform Movement:

> From the point of view of the placement of women, the 1981 placement season represented a major breakthrough. During the coming year, seven women will be serving in full-time or nearly full-time pulpits of their own, two of them in B congregations and two of them in AB congregations. The UAHC [Union of American Hebrew Congregations] now has its first woman serving as director of a region as well. The task of "consciousness raising" is far from completed but, clearly, important progress has been made.[13]

It was at this very time—when the idea of women rabbis was shedding its experimental aura in the Reform Movement and when prominent Orthodox leaders were publicly insisting that in "Torah-true" Judaism women simply could not possibly become rabbis—that the Conservative Movement found itself being pulled in two diametrically opposed directions. There were Conservative Jews, among them prominent scholars, who wanted the Movement to endorse traditional halachic practice and refuse to confer the title of rabbi on women. At the same time, a growing number of Conservative Jews believed that the time had come for their movement to adopt a halachic rationale for ordaining women rabbis. Therefore, the vote of JTS's faculty to admit women to its rabbinical school, rendered on October 24, 1983 (thirty-four in favor, eight opposed), not only affected the future direction of the Conservative Movement; it was a decision that appeared to affect all of Judaism's American movements. To many observers, the

1983 vote of the JTS faculty represented a metaphoric Waterloo in the battle for equal religious rights for women in Judaism.[14]

In the aftermath of JTS's historic announcement, questions arose concerning how the advent of Conservative women rabbis would affect Jewish life. Modern Orthodox Jews, most of whom had simply ignored the frenzy of press notices relating to the ordination of Sally Priesand and Sandy Sasso in the 1970s, now spoke out against the trend that the JTS decision represented. The school's vote compelled some in the Orthodox Jewish community to consider the question "from a sober, somber distance." Since many Conservative Jews adhered closely to traditional Jewish practice and belief, JTS's validation of women in the rabbinate moved the issue "one step closer to home" among those who saw themselves as modern Orthodox.[15]

JTS's 1983 announcement sparked a great deal of interest among Reform Jews, too, and many questions began to circulate:

1. How did the decision-making process that culminated in JTS's historic announcement in October 1983 compare with the way HUC decided to ordain Sally Priesand in 1972?
2. Would JTS's decision to ordain women rabbis diminish the number of women seeking admission to HUC-JIR's rabbinical school? Would women applicants now prefer JTS over HUC-JIR?
3. How would the advent of Conservative women rabbis affect Reform Judaism and the Jewish people as a whole?

These were the very questions that "JTS, HUC, and Women Rabbis" attempted to address when it originally appeared in 1984.

Comparing the Two Decisions

The decision-making process that resulted in HUC's decision to ordain Sally Priesand in 1972 was, in many respects, the inverse of that which led the Conservative Movement to the same practice.

The issue of gender equality in Judaism was a concern of the pioneering Reform ideologues that rebelled against Jewish tradition in Europe. Reform Judaism's long-standing and principled commitment to gender equality and the elevation of women's status in the synagogue originally emanated from the Movement's intellectual elite. The case for egalitarianism came from the writings of the early Reformers and not from, to use terminology made famous by social historians, "the bottom up." For example, the Hungarian Reformer Rabbi Aaron Chorin (1766–1844) insisted that "women must not be excluded from the soul-satisfying experiences which come to us through a solemn worship service." The rabbinical Reformers who attended the Breslau Rabbinical Conference of 1846 unequivocally declared that Judaism must acknowledge that the female was rightfully entitled to "complete religious equality."[16]

In America, these liberal pronouncements on gender equality found a hospitable climate in which to flourish. From his earliest days on American soil, Isaac M. Wise (1819–1900), the prominent founder of Hebrew Union College, contributed—as he later put it—"to the demolition of the perverted notions rising from the erroneous prejudice concerning female inferiority." Wise repeatedly bragged about his track record as an advocate and activist for woman's suffrage in the synagogue. Like many of his American contemporaries, "Wise allied himself with the new priorities of the social and economic class he and his congregants had so recently joined." Promoting the religious equality of women was one of his personal causes.[17]

In light of Wise's views on women in the synagogue, it is not surprising that he would invite a twelve-year-old teenager, Julia Ettlinger (1863–1890), to study with the first students to enroll at HUC when the school opened its doors in 1875. Ettlinger did very well academically, but she studied at HUC for only one year. Still, throughout his career Wise continued to insist that if ever a "gifted lady" took interest in pursuing "the theological course," he stood ready "to assist the cause of emancipating women in the synagogue and congregation."[18]

In spite of Wise's rhetoric on the subject, the question of whether or not HUC was actually prepared to ordain a woman was not formally debated until the early 1920s.[19] Martha Neumark (1904–1981), daughter of HUC professor David Neumark (1866–1924), a remarkably intelligent woman who had taken most of the program's course work, asked the school to permit her to complete the practice-based components of the program and receive ordination. HUC's faculty debated Neumark's request and voted to grant her request. The CCAR also voted in Neumark's favor. Yet it was the lay leaders—the members of HUC's Board of Governors—who blocked Neumark's request by voting to uphold the school's long-standing practice of ordaining only men.[20]

Many years later, in the mid-1950s, the Reform Movement once again formally debated whether or not women should be permitted to become rabbis. In fact, it was the National Federation of Temple Sisterhoods (NFTS) that forcefully championed the cause. Practically from its very inception, NFTS leaders advocated for the religious rights of women in the synagogue, and at least one of NFTS's founders, Carrie Obendorfer Simon (1872–1961), insisted that women were qualified to enter the rabbinate.[21]

From the time she served as the first president of NFTS and beyond, Simon unabashedly asserted that women were perfectly capable of ministering "to minds that are unhappy and to people that are seeking the comfort of God." She probably raised many eyebrows when she informed the leadership of the Union of American Hebrew Congregations that "girls view the Jewish ministry as a legitimate field for the operation of their distinctive talents and abilities." Simon never abandoned these convictions. In 1938, when NFTS commemorated the twenty-fifth anniversary of its founding, the organization's founding president unhesitatingly predicted "that before many decades, [women] will also be [in] the Ministry of Preaching!"[22]

Other events encouraged NFTS to raise this topic in the mid-1950s. In the late 1940s, the Presbyterian Church began debating whether or not to ordain women ministers. The church's 1955 decision to ordain women ministers attracted national attention. The controversy surrounding the case of Paula Ackerman (1893–1989) also helped to renew interest in this topic within the Reform Movement. Ackerman, the wife of Rabbi William Ackerman (1886–1950), was asked by her congregation to assume the congregation's pulpit after her husband's sudden death in 1950. These controversies, among others, encouraged some members of NFTS to wonder aloud why Reform Judaism's deeds relating to gender equality seemed so discontinuous with its long-standing creed.[23]

It was Jane Evans (1907–2004), the first woman to serve as full-time executive director of NFTS, who led the charge for the Sisterhood women. Speaking to more than one thousand delegates attending the Biennial General Assembly of the UAHC on April 29, 1957, Evans urged the congregational body to endorse the ordination of women as rabbis. Making what the *New York Times* described as a "strong plea," Evans declared, "Women are uniquely suited by temperament, intuition, and spiritual sensitivity to be rabbis."[24]

For nearly fifty years, the constituent bodies of the Reform Movement professed theoretical support for the idea of women becoming rabbis. Finally, by the late 1960s, support for the idea of women entering the rabbinate was coming from all quarters in Reform Judaism: NFTS, the CCAR, HUC-JIR, and even the leadership of the UAHC. By the late 1960s, in contrast to the circumstances that prevailed in the 1920s when HUC's lay leaders voted not to ordain women rabbis despite the favorable votes taken by HUC's faculty and the CCAR, there seemed to be broad agreement throughout the Reform Jewish community that women could no longer be prohibited from entering the rabbinate. Since the nineteenth century, Reform's ideologues persistently sloughed off the halachic obstacles barring women from entering the rabbinate. It was the early 1960s, however, when Betty Friedan published her famous volume *The Feminine Mystique* (1963), and subsequently founded the National Organization for Women (1966), that the salience of these issues during the 1960s prompted many Reform Jews to view the perpetuation of religious gender barriers as an outmoded, indefensible practice.

In contrast to the long-standing record of pronouncements favoring gender equality in Reform Jewish history, the notion that a woman might become a rabbi "scarcely entered the consciousness of those shaping Conservative Judaism." Conservative Jews did not formally discuss this issue until the early 1970s, although there were some rare exceptions to this generalization. The aforementioned social and cultural barriers came down in the 1960s for Conservative Jews, just as they had for Reform Jews. Yet Conservative Judaism now had to resolve the perceived halachic obstacles to women entering the rabbinate, which Reform Jews had long ago set aside. As one scholar noted at the time, "There would be no way in which we could [justify the ordination of women rabbis] were it halakhically indefensible."[25]

Two years after HUC-JIR ordained its first woman rabbi, Rabbi Judah Nadich (1912–2007), in his 1974 presidential address to the Rabbinical Assembly (RA), asked his colleagues to urge JTS to reconsider its long-standing policy of ordaining only men. The RA adopted Nadich's suggestion and appointed a commission to study the issue. Dr. Gerson D. Cohen (1924–1991), JTS's chancellor, was nominated to serve as head of this commission. Earlier that same year, Cohen had expressed his belief that the Conservative Movement was unready for women rabbis. Perhaps the attitude of the Conservative constituency, properly assessed by Cohen, explains why it took the commission almost four years to complete its task. By 1978, the commission arrived at its recommendation "that qualified women could be ordained as rabbis in the Conservative Movement."[26]

On December 20, 1979, the JTS faculty considered the commission's recommendations but decided not to depart from its standing policy. One factor contributing to the faculty's decision to reject the commission's report was the formidable halachic opposition promulgated by Rabbi Saul Lieberman (1898–1983), a highly venerated professor of Talmud and Rector at JTS. In 1979, at the same time the commission was preparing to issue its recommendations, Lieberman published a responsum dealing with the question of whether or not the halachah would permit the Movement to ordain women as rabbis. Lieberman's erudite responsum culminated in an unyielding conclusion: "A woman is not fit to judge [Jewish legal matters], and [because] she cannot become qualified for this [duty], she cannot be ordained [a rabbi]."[27]

In the four years that followed the faculty's rejection of the commission's recommendations, a number of intervening factors made it possible for the faculty to overcome Lieberman's halachic objections. First, Professor Lieberman's unexpected death in the spring of 1983 left those opposing the ordination of women on halachic grounds bereft of a towering and truly venerated rabbinic authority. Second, the faculty's decision in 1979 to reject the commission's recommendations was received unfavorably by many in the RA, where this discussion first began and where many were convinced that the ordination of women could indeed be halachically justified.[28] Some members of the RA who disagreed with the JTS faculty's 1979 decision to continue prohibiting the ordination of women rabbis were prepared to bring women into the Conservative rabbinate through the ranks of the RA, the Movement's rabbinical organization. This prospect became a viable idea when Beverly Magidson (b. 1952), a woman who received rabbinical ordination from HUC in 1979, immediately applied for membership in the RA. Even if the faculty of JTS refused to admit women to its rabbinical program, it was entirely possible that the RA would accept Magidson as a member, thereby pulling the carpet out from under the seminary altogether. By threatening to admit Magidson to its ranks, the RA was forcing the faculty's hand. If JTS did not act, the RA would! There can be little doubt that Cohen and his colleagues at JTS spent a good deal of time and effort lobbying the leaders of the RA in hopes of dissuading them from bypassing the seminary. The RA's vote on Magidson's application was a cliff-hanger nevertheless. Had three more votes been cast in favor of her admission, Magidson would have become the first woman rabbi in the Conservative Movement.[29] The RA's willingness to give JTS's faculty a chance to revisit its decision and retain its authoritative leadership role in the Movement was, presumably, what Chancellor Gerson Cohen meant when he praised the RA for its commitment:

to resist a variety of pressures and to continue its recognition of the Seminary as the fountainhead of Conservative Judaism. Whether women would or would not be admitted to membership in the Rabbinical Assembly would thus depend in the first instance on the plan for action adopted by the men and women who have traditionally been charged de facto with putting the stamp of authority we call ordination on the overwhelming majority of the members of the Rabbinical Assembly.[30]

Finally, there was increasing recognition that the seminary was not meeting the needs of its congregational constituency. During the 1960s and early 1970s, the United Synagogue of America was the largest congregational association in North America. There were those who insisted that if JTS continued to ordain men only, it would not be able to fulfill the rabbinical needs of its congregational union. In 1977, Rabbi Kassel Abelson (b. 1924) of Minneapolis informed JTS Chancellor Cohen that there were "two very fine young ladies" in his community who wanted to become rabbis. The young women would have preferred to study at JTS, Abelon wrote, but on account of the school's refusal to ordain women rabbis, these promising candidates would "probably apply to the Reconstructionist Seminary or to Hebrew Union College." As far as Abelson was concerned, JTS's refusal to ordain women rabbis constituted "a real loss in (WO)man power for our movement." The commission's report made similar mention of the same demographic reality.[31]

Clearly, then, the subtle interplay of these various factors contributed to Cohen's announcement in the spring of 1983 that he would ask the JTS faculty that fall (1983) to reconsider its 1979 decision to bar women from the rabbinate.

JTS's Decision and Its Effect on HUC-JIR's Applicant Pool

In retrospect, it is clear that for both HUC-JIR and JTS the decision to ordain women rabbis successfully delayed a precipitous decline in the number of rabbinical applicants that was likely to set in during the

1990s. In large part, the expected decline in applications was based on the decrease in birth rate at the end of the post–World War II baby boom.[32] By admitting women to their respective rabbinical schools, HUC-JIR and JTS were able to draw upon a previously untapped pool of prospective rabbinical students. This influx served to compensate, at least to some degree, for the unavoidable decrease (demographically speaking) in male applicants that would have been felt in the 1990s, had doors to the rabbinate remained closed to women.

Similarly, it is important to bear in mind that the United Synagogue of America was the largest congregational union in American Judaism until the beginning of the 1990s. According to the 1971 National Jewish Population Survey, Conservative Judaism was "the predominant ideological identification" for American Jewry, claiming 40.5% of the "heads of household" reporting. The Reform Movement garnered a 30% share in that same survey. Demographers and community planners who were studying these figures in the early 1970s had no inkling that only twenty years later the Reform Movement would become "the largest single [Jewish] denomination" in America, with 38% of the "entire adult core Jewish population" identifying as Reform and 30% as Conservative. Yet the collective dominance of these two large denominations remained virtually unchanged for the last four decades of the twentieth century, and it was manifestly apparent to observers that nearly 70% of American Jewry self-identified with either Reform or Conservative Judaism, and the seminaries serving these two large movements were charged with the responsibility of furnishing their respective communities with a sufficient number of well-educated rabbis.[33] JTS's perceived obligation to supply Conservative Jewish congregations with the number of rabbis it needed was not lost on the school. As early as 1961, the *New York Times* reported that enrollments in the Jewish seminary appeared to be "faltering." Taking note of synagogue efflorescence in post–World War II suburban America, the paper went on to say that the "student shortage" in rabbinical school appeared to be a "continuing fact."[34] If JTS was unable to furnish its congregations with an adequate supply of rabbis, these synagogues would undoubtedly turn elsewhere to fill the gap, and the aforementioned case of Beverly Magidson underscored this concern.

In contrast to JTS in the 1980s, HUC-JIR had its largest rabbinical classes in its entire history during the late 1960s, when Sally Priesand was a student. The end of the baby boom bubble was not yet on the horizon in the early 1970s. By the mid-1980s, however, HUC-JIR was also recognizing that its applicant pool was slowly diminishing. By the early 1990s, the presence of women in the rabbinate provided both JTS and HUC-JIR with an influx of students that would uphold these institutions, enabling them to meet the rabbinical needs of their respective movements.

JTS's 1983 decision caused some Reform observers to wonder whether some of the women who had been planning to apply to HUC might now abandon their plans and matriculate at JTS instead. The highly publicized case of Beverly Magidson suggested that there were women attending HUC-JIR *only* because JTS had barred them from enrolling. With the announcement that JTS would also begin ordaining women rabbis, there were those who predicted a decline in the number of women applying for admission to HUC-JIR's Rabbinical School.

No such flight from HUC-JIR occurred. It is clear today, three decades later, that JTS's 1983 decision had practically no impact on the number of women applicants seeking admission to HUC-JIR. The majority of the women who applied to JTS were, for the most part, Conservative Jews. They were raised in Conservative synagogues, attended Camp Ramah, and were active in United Synagogue Youth (USY). As Conservative Jews, these women saw JTS as the natural and logical place for them to obtain their rabbinic education. This was also the pattern in the Reform Movement. Those who matriculated at HUC were raised in Reform synagogues, attended one of the Reform Movement's camps, and were active in the North American Federation of Temple Youth (NFTY). Over the years there have certainly been many exceptions to this generalization, but all in all, it is clear that for nearly three decades JTS and HUC-JIR have both been admitting denominationally affiliated men and women.

Overall Impact on American Jewry

Only weeks prior to JTS's decision to admit women, Jacob Neusner (b. 1932), a JTS ordinand, predicted that if the Conservative Movement began to admit women, it would inherit, ipso facto, the mantle of American Jewish leadership: "The incipient organization of the Jewish community as we now know it; outreach to the unaffiliated Jews; the building of a whole system of Jewish education...belong (if not exclusively) to Conservative Judaism."[35]

In retrospect, Neusner's contention proved to be much too narrowly conceived. Neither JTS nor HUC-JIR *alone* can claim to have earned the "mantle of American Jewish leadership" as a result of their respective decisions to ordain women as rabbis. Reflecting back over the past three decades, it is self-evident that women rabbis have brought renewed strength and vibrancy to both Conservative *and* Reform Judaism. Moreover, the ordination of women rabbis by JTS and HUC-JIR has arguably contributed to the revivification of modern Orthodoxy as well.

In her oft-cited 1993 essay "Is Now the Time for Orthodox Women Rabbis?" Blu Greenberg pointed out that "the growing reality of women rabbis in liberal denominations [was transforming] the expectations of Orthodox women into a powerful agent for change." There was no denying that the example set by liberal women rabbis stimulated new initiatives within the centrist Orthodox community in America. For more than fifteen hundred years, Greenberg accurately noted, women had been barred from Talmudic study. Yet merely two decades after HUC-JIR ordained Sally Priesand, revolutionary changes had already begun to occur in the world of modern Orthodoxy both in North America and Israel. In Greenberg's opinion, "The existence of women rabbis and the honorable ways they serve [spoke] more powerfully than a thousand debates on the subject."[36]

By 1993, hundreds of Orthodox women were engaged in serious avenues of Talmudic study at dozens of educational institutions established specifically for that purpose. This phenomenon was bolstered by the decision of some Orthodox women to obtain doctorates in Bible and Talmud. Some of the most accomplished Orthodox Jewish women began teaching sacred texts to a new generation of women who were eager to immerse themselves in this field of study.[37] "The ordination of Orthodox women is close at hand," Greenberg prophesied. It was a moral imperative:

> Orthodox women should be ordained because it would constitute a recognition of their intellectual accomplishments and spiritual attainments; because it would encourage great Torah study; because it offers wider female models of religious life; because women's input into *p'sak* [interpretation of Jewish text], absent for 2,000 years, is sorely needed; because it will speed the process of re-evaluating traditional definitions that support hierarchy; because some Jews might find it easier to bring halachic questions concerning family and sexuality to a woman rabbi. And because of the justice of it all.[38]

In the early twenty-first century, a small circle of modern Orthodox rabbis and communal leaders began to contemplate the possibility of women's ordination, and a few breakthroughs began to occur. In 2000, Haviva Ner-David (b. 1969) an Orthodox student engaged in rabbinic study, published an autobiographical volume that documented her desire to become an Orthodox rabbi. Six years later, in 2006, Ner-David received a private rabbinical ordination in Israel.[39]

In 2006, Kehilat Orach Eliezer, a centrist Orthodox congregation based in New York City, invited Dina Najman (b. 1968), a scholar of Jewish law and ancient Jewish texts, to serve as *rosh k'hilah*, "head of the congregation." Najman was not the congregation's rabbi. She did not lead regular worship services nor did she read from the Torah. Najman was, however, the "head of the congregation," and this title gave her the authority to deliver sermons and answer questions on Jewish law.[40]

In 2009, Sara Hurwitz (b. 1977), a South African–born graduate of Columbia University, completed five years of rabbinic training under Rabbi Avi Weiss (b. 1944), the founder of modern Orthodoxy's progressive rabbinical school Yeshivat Chovevei Torah (see Neiss, pp. 305–16). Initially, Weiss authorized Hurwitz to use the title "maharat," a Hebrew acronym for a leader in Torah, spirituality, and Jewish law. Later, he changed her designation to "rabba," the feminine form of "rabbi." After several Orthodox organizations vigorously protested this step, Weiss agreed not to confer the title "rabba" on any other women.[41]

The firestorm of opposition that exploded in the aftermath of Weiss's decision to confer the title "rabba" on Sara Hurwitz serves as a sobering reminder that there yet remains ardent Orthodox opposition to the idea of women in positions of religious leadership. The Rabbinical Council of America (RCA) recently issued a statement avowing that it "cannot accept either the ordination of women or the recognition of women as members of the Orthodox rabbinate, regardless of the title." A number of RCA members have expressed their firm opposition to those who have advocated halachic "leniency" in regard to women's role in religious leadership. The level of opposition in Israel is even more strident. In 2013, the chief rabbi of Ramat Gan bluntly informed his community that "there is no place for a woman to give a *d'var Torah* [a homily] during davening, even if she is dressed modestly....This is a *chilul Hashem* [blasphemy]."[42]

In spite of these ongoing skirmishes, one fact remains unmistakably apparent: there is a growing cadre of Orthodox Jewish women who not only want to engage in serious textual study, but who are concomitantly determined to assume leadership roles in the Jewish community regardless of how the debates concerning titles ultimately resolve themselves. This fact has recently been acknowledged by the RCA. Despite its firm opposition to the idea of Orthodox women rabbis, the RCA adopted a noteworthy resolution on "Women's Communal Roles in Orthodox Jewish Life" in 2010:[43]

> In light of the opportunity created by advanced women's learning, the Rabbinical Council of America encourages a diversity of

halakhically and communally appropriate professional opportunities for learned, committed women, in the service of our collective mission to preserve and transmit our heritage…Young Orthodox women are now being reared, educated, and inspired by mothers, teachers, and mentors who are themselves beneficiaries of advanced women's Torah education. As members of the new generation rise to positions of influence and stature, we pray that they will contribute to an ever-broadening and ever-deepening wellspring of *talmud Torah* (Torah study), *yir'at Shamayim* (fear of Heaven), and *dikduk b'mitzvot* (scrupulous observance of commandments).

This statement validates the opinion of a 26-year-old student at the Graduate Program for Women in Advanced Talmudic Studies at Yeshiva University (GPATS), who recently asserted, "Title or not, rabbi or not, that's not the real issue. The real issue is that Orthodox women are searching [for a meaningful place within the Jewish community] and we need to address that [concern]."[44]

Conclusion

In spite of the fact that HUC-JIR and JTS arrived at their respective decisions to ordain women rabbis in ways that reflect each movement's distinctive character and history, and even though the introduction of women in the rabbinate has largely served the particular interests of each school and movement, it is also true that these two American Jewish institutions have, albeit unintentionally, been collaborative partners in changing the course of Jewish history.

HUC-JIR made history by ordaining the first woman rabbi in 1972, but JTS's decision to follow suit in 1983 was no less significant an event. After JTS announced it would ordain women rabbis, there could be no doubt that in the days ahead both men *and* women would share the mantle of religious leadership.[45] Taking note of the inexorability of this significant change as events were actually transpiring back in 1984 may ultimately prove to be "JTS, HUC, and Women Rabbis" most predictive conclusion:

The appearance of women rabbis in the Conservative Movement portends an inalterable reality: most American Jews will sometime in their lives be served by female spiritual leaders. This undeniable fact will change forever the face of Jewish life in America—and around the world. No amount of halachic maneuvering or protestation can prevent this from occurring.[46]

NOTES

1. Gary Phillip Zola, "JTS, HUC, and Women Rabbis," *Journal of Reform Judaism* 31, no. 4 (Fall 1984): 39–45. In commemoration of the fortieth anniversary of women in the rabbinate and this special volume published by the Central Conference of American Rabbis (CCAR), the author agreed to reassess this essay, which was written in the days following the Jewish Theological Seminary of America's announcement on October 29, 1983, that the school would soon begin ordaining women rabbis.

2. Between June 1972 and June 1980, HUC-JIR ordained twenty-one women rabbis: Sally J. Priesand (1972); Michal S. (Mendelsohn) Seserman (1975); Laura J. Geller (1976); Karen L. Fox, Rosalind A. Gold, Deborah P. Prinz, Myra Soifer (1978); Ellen Weinberg Dreyfus, Vicki L. Hollander, Jan Caryl Kaufman, Beverly M. Magidson, Janet Ross Marder, Sheila C. Russian, Bonnie Ann Steinberg (1979); Aliza S. Berk, Cathy Felix, Joan S. Friedman, Debra R. Hachen, Ellen Jay Lewis, Judith S. Lewis, Mindy Avra Portnoy (1980). Between 1974 and 1984, RRC ordained fourteen women rabbis: Sandy Eisenberg Sasso (1974); Rebecca Alpert (1976); Ilene Schneider (1976); Ruth Sandberg (1978); Linda Holtzman, Gail Shuster-Bouskila (1979); Susan Frank, Bonnie Koppell, Joy Levitt, Hava Pell (1981); Nancy Fuchs-Kreimer, Susan Schnur (1982); Devorah Bartnoff, Cynthia Kravitz (1983).

3. Rabbi Sally Priesand (b. 1946) was ordained on behalf of the faculty by Dr. Alfred Gottschalk, president of HUC, on June 3, 1972. On Priesand, see Pamela S. Nadell, "Sally Jane Priesand" (March 1, 2009), in "Jewish Women: A Comprehensive Historical Encyclopedia," on the website of the Jewish Women's Archive, http://jwa.org/encyclopedia/article/priesand-sally-jane. Rabbi Sandy Eisenberg Sasso (b. 1947) was ordained on May 19, 1974, when Rabbi Ira Eisenstein (1906–2001) was president of RRC. On Sasso, see "Sandy Sasso Ordained as First Female Reconstructionist Rabbi," on the website of the Jewish Women's Archive, "This Week in Jewish History," http://jwa.org/thisweek/may/19/1974/sandy-sasso.

As all of the pioneering women rabbis correctly note, Regina Jonas (1902–1944) of Berlin was the first woman ever to be ordained as a rabbi. Jonas completed her rabbinic studies at the Hochschule für die Wissenschaft des Judentums in 1932. The instructor of Talmud, the ordaining authority of the Hochschule, refused to ordain Jonas, who was later ordained privately by a liberal rabbi in Offenbach, Dr.

Max Dienemann. On Jonas, see Toby Axelrod, "My Year with Regina Jonas," *Bridges: A Jewish Feminist Journal* 14, no. 2 (Autumn 2009): 27–31; Katharina von Kellenbach, "Preaching Hope: Denial and Defiance of Genocidal Reality in Rabbi Regina Jonas' Work," *Shofar* (1998); Katharina von Kellenbach, "God Does Not Oppress Any Human Being: The Life and Thought of Rabbi Regina Jonas," *Leo Baeck Institute Yearbook* 39 (1994): 213–25; Katharina von Kellenbach, "Denial and Defiance in the Work of Rabbiner Jonas," in *In God's Name: Genocide and Religion in the Twentieth Century*, ed. Omer Bartov and Phyllis Mack (New York and Oxford: Berghahn Books, 2001), 243–58; Elisa Klapheck, ed., *Fräulein Rabbiner Jonas—The Story of the First Woman Rabbi* (San Francisco: Jossey-Bass, 2004); Stefanie Sinclair, "Regina Jonas: Forgetting and Remembering the First Female Rabbi," *Religion* 43, no. 4 (2013): 541–63.

4. Jakob J. Petuchowski to Susan Kittner, February 7, 1975, SC-16198, The Jacob Rader Marcus Center of the American Jewish Archives, Cincinnati, OH. The author wishes to express his sincere gratitude to Susan Kittner Huntting for donating this letter to the American Jewish Archives.

5. The papers of the Task Force on Women in the Rabbinate are preserved at The Jacob Rader Marcus Center of the American Jewish Archives, Cincinnati, OH. See http://americanjewisharchives.org/collections/ms0677/.

6. See *CCAR Yearbook*, 1978, 59–60; *CCAR Yearbook*, 1980, 110.

7. See Carole B. Balin, "From Periphery to Center: A History of the Women's Rabbinic Network," pp. 137–52, this volume.

8. *CCAR Yearbook*, 1980, 110–14. For quotation, see 114.

9. Ibid., 114.

10. *New York Times*, June 12, 1972, 43. Today, thirty years later, this same highly regarded modern Orthodox rabbi permits young women attending his renowned Ramaz School in Manhattan to don *t'fillin*—a halachically liberal and controversial decision; see http://www.jta.org/2014/01/22/news-opinion/united-states/a-second-orthodox-high-school-allows-girls-to-don-tefillin#ixzz32bAE88mk. Haskel Lookstein's son, Rabbi Joshua Lookstein, a graduate of Yeshiva University, is a supporter of Yeshivat Chovevei Torah (YCT), a seminary founded by Rabbi Avi Weiss in 1999. YCT has declared itself to be open "to the possibility of expanded roles for women in ritual life"; see Avi Weiss, "Mesorah and Making Room: A Journey to Women's Spiritual Leadership," http://www.yctorah.org/content/view/823/17/.

11. Blu Greenberg, "Will There Be Orthodox Women Rabbis?," *Judaism* 33, no. 1 (Winter 1984): 24.

12. *New York Times*, June 27, 1977, 31.

13. See *CCAR Yearbook*, 1981, 75. The reference to "B" and "AB" congregations is a reference to congregational size, with "A" being a congregation with the smallest membership and "E" being the largest. According to the rules of the CCAR Placement Commission, rabbis must be ordained for a specified number of years before they become eligible to apply for larger congregational positions.

14. For a detailed reconstruction of JTS's debate over the ordination of women rabbis, see Beth S. Wenger, "The Politics of Women's Ordination: Jewish Law, Institutional Power, and the Debate Over Women in the Rabbinate," in *Tradition Renewed: A History of the Jewish Theological Seminary of America*, vol. 2, *Beyond the*

Academy, ed. Jack Wertheimer (New York: Jewish Theological Seminary of America, 1997), 483–523.

15. Greenberg, "Will There Be Orthodox Women Rabbis?," 23.

16. W. Gunther Plaut, *The Rise of Reform Judaism* (New York: World Union for Progressive Judaism, 1963), 252–54.

17. *American Israelite*, November 24, 1892, 4. For an excellent summary of Wise's view on women and the synagogue, see Pamela S. Nadell, *Women Who Would Be Rabbis: A History of Women's Ordination, 1889–1985* (Boston: Beacon Press, 1998), 19–22. For quotations, see 21–22.

18. *American Israelite*, November 24, 1892, 4.

19. Writing in 1892, Wise made this remarkable statement: "In the laws governing the Hebrew Union College the question of sex or race or confession is not touched upon at all." See *American Israelite*, November 24, 1892, 4.

20. Minutes of HUC faculty meetings: December 21, 1921, January 30, 1922, and March 22, 1922; minutes of HUC Board of Governors meeting, January 31, 1922, and February 22, 1922 (American Jewish Archives, Cincinnati, OH), MS-5, box D23.

21. On Carrie Simon and her ideas relating to women in the rabbinate, see Carole Balin, Dana Herman, Jonathan D. Sarna, and Gary Phillip Zola, eds., *Sisterhood: A Centennial History of Women of Reform Judaism* (Cincinnati: Hebrew Union College Press, 2013). See also Nadell, *Women Who Would Be Rabbis*, pp. 70, 121, 132.

22. Marc Lee Raphael, *Towards a "National Shrine": A Centennial History of Washington Hebrew Congregation, 1855–1955* (Williamsburg, VA: William and Mary College, 2005), 46. For 1938 quotation, see "Four Presidents on the NFTS Silver Jubilee," *Topics & Trends*, January–February 1938, 3.

23. For a copy of the Presbyterian Church's 1955 "Report of the Special Committee on the Ordination of Women," see http://www.womenpriests.org/related/presbyt.asp, accessed May 26, 2014. On Paula Ackerman, see Shuly Rubin Schwartz, "From Rebbetzin to Rabbi: The Journey of Paula Ackerman," *American Jewish Archives Journal* 59, nos. 1–2 (2007): 99–106.

24. *New York Times*, April 30, 1957.

25. Nadell, *Women Who Would Be Rabbis*, 173. Anne Lapidus Lerner, "On the Rabbinic Ordination of Women," http://www.jtsa.edu/prebuilt/women/lerner.pdf.

26. "Of Women and Halachah," *Reconstructionist*, June 1974, 5; and Gerson D. Cohen, "On the Ordination of Women," *Conservative Judaism* 32 (Summer 1979): 56–80.

27. Lieberman's 1979 Hebrew responsum on the ordination of women rabbis was subsequently published and translated into English. See Saul Lieberman, "Ordaining Women as Rabbis," in *Tomeikh Kehalakhah: Responsa of the Panel of Halakhic Inquiry*, trans. Wayne R. Allen (Mount Vernon, NY: Union for Traditional Conservative Judaism, 1986), 14–19.

28. A prime example of this hostile reaction to the 1979 JTS faculty decision on the matter of admitting women may be found in Arthur Waskow's angry remarks set down in *Menorah Journal* 3 (February 1980): 1–2. See also Greenberg, "Will There Be Orthodox Women Rabbis?"

29. *New York Times*, April 13, 1983, A23.

30. Cohen, "On the Ordination of Women," 56.

31. Ibid. For Abelson quotation, see Wenger, "Politics of Women's Ordination," 488.

32. Typically, 1963 or 1964 is considered the last year of the post–World War II baby boom. Although there have been what demographers call "mini baby boom years" after 1964, the sustained impact of the baby boom generation is no longer affecting the number of candidates seeking admission to HUC-JIR or JTS.

33. See "Jewish Identity: Facts for Planning," published in 1974 along with all of the results from the 1971 "National Jewish Population Study" conducted by the Council of Jewish Federations and Welfare Funds. Digitized copies of this study are now available on the Berman Jewish DataBank, a project of the Jewish Federations of North America. The figures cited for 1971 are from p. 1 of the report, found on http://www.jewishdatabank.org/studies/downloadFile.cfm?FileID=1449, November 30, 2015. Regarding the figures quoted from the 1990 survey, see Sidney Goldstein, "Profile of American Jewry: Insights from the 1990 National Jewish Population Survey," *American Jewish Year Book* 92 (1992): 129.

34. *New York Times*, April 16, 1961, 1.

35. Jacob Neusner, "Facing the Need for Women Rabbis," *Sh'ma* 13, no. 259 (October 14, 1983): 131.

36. Blu Greenberg, "Is Now the Time for Orthodox Women Rabbis?," *Moment Magazine* 18, no. 6 (December 1993): 50, 52.

37. Greenberg lists many Orthodox women who had established their bona fides as being "totally dedicated to Torah learning within the tradition." She also lists a roster of nearly two dozen seminaries in the United States and Israel where Orthodox women were studying Torah in 1993. See ibid., 52–53.

38. Ibid., 74.

39. See Haviva Ner-David, *Life on the Fringes: A Feminist Journey toward Traditional Rabbinic Ordination* (Needham, MA: JFL Books, 2000).

40. Michael Luo, "An Orthodox Jewish Woman, and Soon, a Spiritual Leader," *New York Times*, August 21, 2006.

41. For an overview of the details pertaining to Sara Hurwitz's ordination, see Batya Ungar-Sargon, "Orthodox Yeshiva Set to Ordain Three Women. Just Don't Call Them 'Rabbi,'" *Tablet Magazine* (June 10, 2013), http://www.tabletmag.com/jewish-life-and-religion/134369/orthodox-women-ordained.

42. See statement of the Rabbinical Council of America on women rabbis, http://www.rabbis.org/news/article.cfm?id=105753. See also Aryeh A. Frimer, "The View of Rav Joseph B. Soloveitchik zt"l on the Ordination of Women," in *Tradition*'s online "Text and Texture" by Aryeh A. Frime, http://text.rcarabbis.org/the-view-of-rav-joseph-b-soloveitchik-zt%E2%80%9Dl-on-the-ordination-of-women-by-aryeh-a-frimer/. See also Avrohom Gordimer, "Orthodox Women Rabbis: A Rejoinder to Rabbi Wolkenfeld," *Cross-Currents*, June 26, 2013, http://www.cross-currents.com/archives/2013/06/26/orthodox-women-rabbis-a-rejoinder-to-rabbi-wolkenfeld/#ixzz33e2uUdTD. See "Rabbi Yaakov Ariel Shlita Opposes Divrei Torah by Women in Shul," *Yeshivah World News*, http://www.theyeshivaworld.com/news/headlines-breaking-stories/203021/rabbi-yaakov-ariel-shlita-opposes-divrei-torah-by-women-in-shul.html#sthash.hkcFAIlV.dpuf.

43. For the text of the RCA's "Resolution on Women's Communal Roles in Orthodox Jewish Life," adopted on April 27, 2010, see the website of the Rabbinical Council of America, http://www.rabbis.org/news/article.cfm?id=105554, accessed on November 30, 2015.

44. Tamar Snyder, *Jewish Week*, March 24, 2010.

45. Readers should not misconstrue my omitting mention of the Reconstructionist Rabbinical College in this paragraph as either a slight or an oversight. RRC's decision to begin ordaining women rabbis in 1974 (only two years after HUC-JIR ordained Sally Priesand) did not spur commentators of the era to predict that a watershed transformation had begun. It was JTS's 1983 decision to ordain women that convinced many Jews to believe that women would have their rightful place in the rabbinate, the cantorate, the Jewish academy, and Jewish religious life in general.

46. Zola, "JTS, HUC, and Women Rabbis," 44–45. A number of noteworthy volumes on women rabbis have been published over the past few decades, including Monique S. Goldberg, Diana Villa, David Golinkin, and Israel Warman, eds., *Ask the Rabbi: Women Rabbis Respond to Modern Halakhic Questions* (Jerusalem: Schechter Institute of Jewish Studies, 2010); Tova Hartman, *Feminism Encounters Traditional Judaism: Resistance and Accommodation* (Waltham, MA: University Press of New England, 2007); Riv-Ellen Prell, *Women Remaking American Judaism* (Detroit: Wayne State University Press, 2007); Blu Greenberg, *On Women and Judaism: A View from Tradition* (Philadelphia: Jewish Publication Society, 1998); Emily Taitz and Sondra Henry, *Remarkable Jewish Women: Rebels, Rabbis, and Other Women from Biblical Times to the Present* (Philadelphia: Jewish Publication Society, 1996); Gary Phillip Zola, ed., *Women Rabbis: Exploration & Celebration: Papers Delivered at an Academic Conference Honoring Twenty Years of Women in the Rabbinate, 1972–1992* (Cincinnati: HUC-JIR Rabbinic Alumni Association Press, 1996).

16

CREATING OPPORTUNITIES
FOR THE "OTHER"

The Ordination of Women
as a Turning Point for LGBT Jews

R A B B I D E N I S E L. E G E R

The 1960s were a time of turmoil in the United States. The awakening feminist movement, along with the powerful civil rights movement of African Americans and the anti–Vietnam War movement, raised numerous challenges to the settled post–World War II suburban American mythos. Each of these justice-seeking movements questioned the then-prevailing wisdom about gender roles, race, and public policy. African Americans asserted racial equality under the law. The civil rights movement fought racism and classism and sought a better life for people of color in this country. The African American civil rights movement, through a variety of tactics and strategies, brought the issue of human dignity to the forefront of the national consciousness.

Young people, including many on college campuses, questioned the wisdom of American military and foreign policy efforts that had been in place throughout the 1950s and early 1960s. These students rejected the military draft and took to the streets in protest. There were sit-ins on campus and demonstrations in every major city against the war in Vietnam. The anti-war movement was instrumental in turning the tide of American opinion against the war.

The women's movement advocated for a different kind of role for women in society beyond wife and mother. It advocated for equality for women in the workplace and in politics, and more than that, it advocated for the equality of women in every aspect of life through efforts like the Equal Rights Amendment (ERA) to the United States Constitution (which failed), women's reproductive health initiatives, and marching for equality. Through these efforts, women demanded to be on the same economic playing field as men and asserted the humanity of women as equals rather than as subservient to men.

Along with these three key social movements, the gay and lesbian community also coalesced during these years, demanding the freedom to associate and be free from police brutality and entrapment. Gay men and lesbians wanted to assert their humanity and dignity and live their lives peacefully.

As each of these groups gave voice to their particular forms of oppression by the larger, white male American majority, their efforts had an important effect on each other, which has continued through many subsequent decades. As the 1960s gave way to the early '70s, Reform Judaism saw a unique convergence of all four of these social justice movements within its ranks. Reform Judaism would come to address each of the larger social justice movements through resolutions and actions. Jews were involved in each of these social movements as leaders. Both the lay arm of the Reform Movement, through the Union of American Hebrew Congregations (UAHC, now Union for Reform Judaism), and the Movement's rabbinic arm, through the Central Conference of American Rabbis (CCAR) would play key roles in all four social movements and in bringing their issues to the Jewish institutional table, as well as contributing greatly to the national discussion and leadership in each of these areas.

Reform Judaism and its leaders, both lay and rabbinic, were instrumental in helping the African American civil rights movement. Jews partnered to help create organizations that would press for the passage of the Voting Rights Act. It was during this time that the Reform Movement's Religious Action Center (RAC) in Washington, DC was formed. In fact, Kivie Kaplan, one of the funders of the NAACP, helped to launch the Religious Action Center. Reform rabbis marched with Dr. Martin Luther King Jr., and Jews rode freedom buses and sat in at lunch counters alongside young African American leaders. It was two Jews, Michael Schwerner and Andrew Goodman, who lost their lives alongside James Chaney in the Mississippi back roads as the three civil rights workers tried to register blacks to vote in 1964. Jews, and in particular Reform Jews, were actively engaged in the struggle for civil rights for African Americans in this country.

The anti-war movement gained strength as the UAHC condemned the bombings in Southeast Asia as early as 1967. Rabbi Maurice Eisendrath, then president of the UAHC, published a letter to President Johnson opposing the war in *American Judaism* magazine,[1] the forerunner of *Reform Judaism* magazine.

Reform Judaism had been founded on the basis of equality of the sexes in religious obligations and education in the 1820s. There were serious discussions about ordaining women as rabbis as early as the 1920s in the United States. The Hebrew Union College and the CCAR had a long discussion including a responsum, written by Professor Rabbi Jacob Lauterbach in 1922, about whether women could be ordained as rabbis. The subsequent vote and discussion are well documented. Professor Rabbi Lauterbach opposed the ordination of women as rabbis, while the committee, headed by Rabbi Henry Cohen, endorsed women as rabbis. The timing of these discussions no doubt came at a time when the role of women in society was changing; women had successfully campaigned for the right to vote in 1920.

Occasionally there were women who served in a rabbinic capacity both in the United States and Europe in Reform Jewish communities. Admitted as a student in a joint program between the University of Cincinnati and the Hebrew Union College–Jewish Institute of Religion (HUC-JIR), Rabbi Sally Priesand was ordained at the completion of her studies in 1972. Rabbi Nelson Glueck, PhD, who was president of the HUC-JIR, had thought it appropriate to ordain Priesand when she finished her studies but died before he could do so. In interviews, both Rabbi Priesand and Rabbi Alfred Gottschalk, PhD, who followed Dr. Glueck as president of HUC-JIR, have said they were not trying to create a radical new imperative but considered ordination a natural outcome of Priesand's learning at HUC-JIR.

As Rabbi Priesand says, "It wasn't until recent years that I realized how much courage it took for him [Gottschalk] to accept someone else's vision and move forward with it."[2] But once again, the Reform Movement, responding to the environment of the times, led the way among Jewish denominational life in North America.

At this same time in the late 1960s and early 1970s, gay and lesbian men and women were beginning to come out of the shadows. In the 1960s in Los Angeles, gay and lesbian social groups began to form, like the Mattachine Society and the Daughters of Bilitis as well as the Metropolitan Community Church (MCC). At MCC, the Reverend Troy Perry, a former Pentecostal preacher, formed a church with a belief that God loves gay people too—a radical notion in 1968.

Just as it had done with the civil rights movement and the ordination of women, the Reform Movement was a place that opened the door. Already in 1964, the National Federation of Temple Sisterhoods (now known as the Women of Reform Judaism) passed one of the first resolutions concerning gays and lesbians,[3] while in 1968, Reform rabbi Steven B. Jacobs, then of Temple Israel of Miami, gave one of the very first sermons calling for the welcoming of gays and lesbians back into the synagogue.[4] Concurrently in Los Angeles, a group of Jews were already beginning to meet together at the newly founded Metropolitan Community Church. Reverend Perry was no stranger to interfaith dialogue and put the group of Jews in touch with Rabbi Erv Herman, the then UAHC regional director. It was Rabbi Herman who helped the group to form a synagogue. Several Los Angeles area rabbis also played a key role, including Rabbi Sandy Ragins of Leo Baeck Temple and lay leader Norm Eichberg, the regional president of the UAHC in Los Angeles. These leaders helped the group that would become Beth Chayim Chadashim seek admittance to the UAHC, which came about in 1972. The convergence of the ordination of the first woman as rabbi and the admittance of the first "gay outreach" congregation of the UAHC happened in the same year.

Clearly the time was ripe for breaking the mold and the vortex of social movements; the shattering of the previously held models of leadership opened the possibility that both women rabbis and gays and lesbians might be welcomed inside the Jewish tent. Reform Judaism became a meeting place of all these social justice movements and responded to them by incorporating their messages of equality into action.

During the following years, more and more gay and lesbian congregations and *chavurot* formed in major metropolitan areas: San Francisco, Miami, New York, Philadelphia, Washington, DC, Houston, Chicago, Cleveland, Atlanta, Seattle, Dallas, and Toronto. Many, though not all, were affiliated with the then UAHC. Like other burgeoning groups, they were served first by student rabbis and later by part- and full-time rabbis as their spiritual leaders. Many of these congregations had women rabbis serve either as students or as ordained rabbis. Today, with just one exception, these congregations that have full- or part-time rabbinic positions have women rabbis as their rabbi or senior rabbi.

As the gay congregations also had strong lay participation, women rabbis brought their unique brand of organizing and teaching to these communities, encouraging a lay-empowered system rather than the traditional hierarchical model that had been so associated with congregations and Jewish communities. Women student rabbis and women rabbis who served in LGBT outreach congregations empowered lay leaders to lead worship and teach alongside them. It would not be unusual to have the rabbi sit in the congregation while a lay leader led the Shabbat service.

The Jewish feminist world of the 1970s also focused much discussion on Jewish rituals and liturgy: How does a very patriarchal religion, with emphasis on the forefathers of Judaism, incorporate the history of the women of Judaism? Further emphasis was placed on creating numerous rituals to celebrate women's lives, including welcoming ceremonies for baby girls (e.g., *b'rit banot*) and celebrations of Rosh

Chodesh, the new Jewish month, traditionally seen as as a women's half-holiday. This experimentation with liturgy and ritual also influenced the gay and lesbian Jewish community, as they sought to create rituals of commitment and affirmation of their families and lives. Many women rabbis contributed toward creating commitment ceremony rituals, including specialized *Sheva B'rachot*, *ketubah* texts, and alternatives to a traditional wedding ceremony that focused on the idea of the groom "acquiring" the bride. These commitment ceremonies and wedding ceremonies for gays and lesbians emphasized the mutuality and equality of the partners, which were similar to the themes and ideas being suggested by Jewish feminists and women rabbis to transform heterosexual marriage ceremonies. Clearly, the experimentation in the area of ritual and liturgy by Jewish feminists opened the door to similar conversations within the gay and lesbian community, and there was often crossover in these two communities as women rabbis wrote and encouraged gay and lesbian communities of the 1970s and 1980s until today to create their own liturgies and life-cycle rituals. A number of women rabbis who serve gay and lesbian communities were instrumental in creating unique prayer books and Haggadot for the gay communities that they served. When Rabbi Janet Marder served Beth Chayim Chadashim of Los Angeles, she, with the help of the ritual committee, wrote numerous special services. Rabbi Camille Angel, of Congregation Shaar Zahav of San Francisco, and Rabbi Sharon Kleinbaum, of Congregation Beth Simchat Torah of New York City, each helped write and publish new prayer books with the help of lay leaders of the congregation.[5] I wrote a new Haggadah during my time at Beth Chayim Chadashim and a new *S'lichot* service and Chanukah service while at Congregation Kol Ami. This experimentation with liturgy focused on the idea of making the text relevant for the community. Women rabbis have been instrumental in helping shape new liturgies wherever they have served and, in particular, in the LGBT community.

The ordination of women as rabbis also opened the possibility that openly gay men and women might be called to a life of service as rabbis. If women could shake up the status quo of the rabbinate, gay men and lesbians would as well. Women rabbis on the scene began to raise many questions about traditional gender roles within Jewish life. Sexuality was no more hidden away. In fact, sexuality of all sorts was brought into daylight, in part because of the visibility of women as rabbis and in part because the larger society was beginning to have questions and discuss homosexuality more openly. In many churches dominated by male clergy or those that exclude women from leadership in the priest or minister roles, homosexuality is always seen as sinful behavior. However, in those churches and religious groups where women are ordained as priests or ministers, gay and lesbian ordination and inclusion are either granted or on the table for discussion. No mere coincidence, it is clearly an outcome of the ordination of women as religious leaders on a par with men. The discussions about acceptance of gay men and lesbians as religious leaders have blossomed not only in Reform Judaism but in Conservative Judaism as well. Increasingly as we see women leaders in modern Orthodoxy, so too have we seen at least a willingness to discuss gay and lesbian issues within the world of modern Orthodoxy in recent years. The more fundamentalist and traditional a religious institution is, the greater the exclusion of women as equal partners, and gays and lesbians as well. The ordination of women as rabbis was a special turning point for LGBT Jews because by breaking the stereotype of who can be a rabbi, it allowed for the possibility of breaking the stereotype even further by allowing the ordination of gay men and lesbians as rabbis. Female rabbis create opportunities for "the other" to enter the mainstream.

Women rabbis have played an important role in giving voice to those who previously haven't had a voice within the Jewish community. This includes gay men and lesbians as well. Both the LGBT civil rights movement and feminism came from the same heady mix of social volatility of the 1960s that empowered society to imagine and ultimately embrace change. Reform Judaism, with its emphasis on equality and ethics, opened the Jewish world to a new way of appreciating the role of women and welcoming gay men and lesbians. The year 1972 was a momentous time that allowed Reform Judaism to take a leadership role and discover the beauty and blessings of bringing women into rabbinic leadership and gay and lesbian Jews back home. Because these blessings happened at the same time, the effects on us and on our Movement are forever entwined.

NOTES

1. *American Judaism*, Winter 1966/1967, p. 25.

2. Michele Alperin, "America's First Female Rabbi Reflects on Four Decades since Ordination," *eJewish Philanthropy*, May 8, 2012, http://ejewishphilanthropy.com/americas-first-female-rabbi-reflects-on-four-decades-since-ordination/#sthash.iB0K7NQF.dpuf.

3. "Resolution of the Women of Reform Judaism National Federation of Temple Sisterhoods 25th Biennial Assembly 1965: Homosexuality," in *Kulanu: All of Us*, rev. ed., ed. Richard F. Address, Joel L. Kushner, and Geoffrey Mitelman (New York: URJ Press, 2007), 247.

4. Al Vorspan, *Jewish Values and Social Crisis* (New York: Union of American Hebrew Congregations, 1968).

5. *Siddur B'chol L'vav'cha: With All Your Heart*, ed. Rabbi Sharon Kleinbaum and Rabbi Ayelet Cohen (New York: Congregation Beth Simchat Torah, 2008); *Siddur Shaar Zahav*, ed. Michael Tyler and Leslie Kane (San Francisco: Congregation Shaar Zahav, 2009).

17

THE IMPACT OF WOMEN RABBIS
ON MALE RABBIS

Rabbi Charles A. Kroloff

Upon ordination in 1960, I was catapulted into an American liberal Judaism whose expectations of its rabbis had remained relatively static for several generations. The sermon was central, decorum was obligatory, leadership was top-down, and success was measured by the size of the congregation. It was, for lack of a better word to describe it, very male.

I studied rabbinics at the Cincinnati campus of Hebrew Union College–Jewish Institute of Religion with other men who looked very much like me. It was not unlike my undergraduate experience at Yale, then a bastion of gender segregation.

One evening in 1964, my wife, Terry, looked up from a volume that had engrossed her for many days and announced, "I think this book is about me!" Shockingly, I would soon discover that it was also about me.

The book was, of course, Betty Friedan's *The Feminine Mystique*[1] and is a significant marker on the journey of liberation of the American woman, an odyssey that subsequently impacted men in general and, more specifically, male rabbis like me.

It is easy to fall into the trap of making sweeping generalizations about women and, in particular, women rabbis. At the risk of doing so, I acknowledge that much of what follows is based on my own experience as well as interviews with other rabbis. From both my own reflections and those of colleagues, these are some of the ways that we male rabbis have been transformed by the impact of our female colleagues.

Theology

Our study of biblical Hebrew at HUC-JIR taught us that there are two Hebrew words that describe fundamentally different aspects of the Divine. One is *Adonai*, which refers to the softer, more compassionate aspect of God; the other is *Elohim*, associated with God's firm, even stern justice. These are understood as the "immanent" and "transcendent" aspects of the Divine. My studies of Martin Buber during undergraduate years nudged me toward the immanent and the more personal. But the available vocabulary for such a relationship was scarce. In our patriarchal world, the term *Shechinah* was rarely noted. Models of spiritual search were almost nonexistent. It was an article by Margaret Moers Wenig (HUC-JIR '84) that began to change the narrative language.[2]

Rex Perlmeter (HUC-JIR '85) remembers that article, in which Wenig describes conversing with God over tea at a kitchen table. Perlmeter recalls, "I was astounded by the thought of such a way of experiencing the Divine, and I wanted it—not *instead* of my previous experience, but *in addition* to it. Theologically, I connected deeply with God, the Father and King. My teaching tended to the intellectual and my positioning to the authoritarian." He points out that these ways of being and thinking were not necessarily a result of the overt examples of his mentors, but were more reflective of the lens through which he interpreted their teaching.[3]

According to Perlmeter, "One of my mentors counseled me that I would only become the rabbi I ultimately had the potential to become if I could learn to bring a gentleness that was absent from my way of 'rabbi-ing.' The problem was that I didn't know where to look for mentors on how to do that. Most of my teachers embodied it fully and gracefully. My own perception of maleness, however, made it very difficult for me to emulate their bearing. I needed a different kind of role model. I needed women who were great rabbis to teach me how to become a man who could aspire to be a better rabbi."

Quality of Life

We men have now found such role models and have come to appreciate women who teach us how to become better men and better rabbis. Our women colleagues have taught us that the "Jewish family" begins with our own families, who deserve the best that we can give them, not what is left over after we have visited every hospital in the region and polished a sermon for the eighteenth time. By integrating their professional and personal needs, they have demonstrated that unless we live what we preach, we are bound to feel less than authentic.

As a generalization, men have placed less emphasis on establishing a healthy balance between personal life and work because when they fell short on the family side, there was usually a wife to carry that load. As women increasingly entered the workforce, the household and child-related tasks overwhelmingly remained their responsibility[4] and came to be known as the "second shift."[5] The never-ending demands placed on a rabbi combined with the "double-duty"[6] women faced at the end of the workday pushed women rabbis to define boundaries that would allow for a healthier, and more desirable, work/life balance. As an example, on accepting a senior position in 2012, Deborah Bravo (HUC-JIR '98) informed her leadership that she would be available just two out of the four weekday evenings (Monday through Thursday). On the other two nights, she had to be with her family.[7] By watching our woman colleagues, we men have learned to develop a new equilibrium as we strive to maintain a healthy home life.

Men sometimes viewed such expectations as unrealistic, even laced with chutzpah. They assumed that there was but one way to do it—sacrifice nuclear family to communal family. But at the same time, men took note of these new kinds of expectations. With some trepidation, women took the initiative to seek family leave. Now men also are granted family leave, an achievement that occurred only because we were emboldened by our female colleagues. Jacqueline Koch Ellenson (HUC-JIR '83) suggests that, for the Jewish community, "women rabbis brought their personal issues into the workplace, and in doing so, they made pregnancy and child-bearing an issue of societal significance requiring a communal response."[8] After years of struggle, my female colleagues are demonstrating that they can be effective leaders while achieving a healthy work/life balance, and this has encouraged men to seek the same. As Amy Schwartzman (HUC-JIR '90) observes, "Women and men can take family leave and the whole place doesn't fall apart."[9]

In recent years, it has become more common for rabbis in congregations both large and small to regularly spend a Shabbat with their families, at home or visiting another synagogue. Once again, this modeling of a healthy work/life balance is the result of initiatives by our female colleagues.

Leadership

For generations, hierarchical, top-down leadership was the *modus operandi* for the North American rabbi, a style reflecting the typical model in the secular business and professional world. This monolithic template for the liberal rabbi was cracked apart in the 1980s and '90s as women gradually entered the rabbinate, and with it came a growing appreciation of diversity and inclusion. On the national scene, the civil rights movement of the 1950s and '60s had already heightened that appreciation in the area of race, while Judaism's historic commitment to the poor had for decades stirred rabbis to address economic inequities.

But those commitments to racial equality and economic fairness rarely translated into advocacy for gender equality. Nor did they spur us to action on behalf of a wide swath of citizens who were excluded from the mainstream, such as gays, lesbians, and the physically challenged. Jokes and innuendos were commonly tolerated; emotional and physical boundaries were disregarded.

But with the arrival of women as co-equal partners, a new dynamic entered the picture. As we adjusted to sharing our titles and roles and consulting professionally on a daily basis with women, male rabbis became more aware of the importance of inclusion. As a result, the "big tent" vision emerged for our congregations, community, and movement.

As men's sensitivities to "the other" were heightened by the inclusion of women, we recognized that we must include other groups that had been excluded either by design or by acquiescence. Advances in gender justice quickened the pace of appreciation of LGBTQ and other social justice issues. Martin Weiner (HUC-JIR '64) notes that "respect for boundaries, verbal and physical, was enhanced as male rabbis began to work alongside of female colleagues."[10]

A 2005 study confirms that women tend to excel at collaborative, team-building competency, are better listeners, and are more sensitive to human needs.[11] The inclusion of women in the rabbinate has introduced new leadership styles[12] and, therefore, impacted our expectations of how rabbis function as part of a staff. As a result, male rabbis have strengthened their team-building skills, heightened their sensitivity to diversity, and moved in the direction of inclusivity rather than exclusivity. Twenty years ago, some of my temple's officers solicited suggestions on how to use proceeds from fundraising. Our then-associate rabbi, Deborah Joselow (HUC-JIR '91), proposed a motorized chair lift for the pulpit to accommodate persons with special needs. Quite frankly, I had paid minimal attention to special needs, but our leadership rapidly embraced her idea. Trained in a top-down mode of leadership, I was less than comfortable with this decision-making process. However, it was clear how effective Deborah's approach was with the lay leaders, and a good example of how our gender differences highlighted our different strengths.[13] I believe that today, faced with a similar situation, I would act differently.

As I experienced moments such as these over and over again, I found myself, as Oshrat Morag (HUC-JIR '08) describes it, "transitioning from seeing women's voices as 'other than something more authentic' to 'other than each other,' i.e., different, but without one being more authentic than the other."[14] Our female colleagues have enhanced our ability to relate to women and men as equally authentic—whether they are members of our leadership team or participants in the larger community. The contributions of all genders to our personal and professional experiences now seem far more significant than they ever did before.

There was a time when the idea of a co-rabbinate was viewed critically and when even retaining associates for the long term was considered unwise. I agreed with this evaluation, pointing to a few examples with unpleasant outcomes. Thanks to our female colleagues who have provided us with new models of leadership, we can now celebrate many successful arrangements of shared rabbinates and long-term associates that provide congregants with more spiritual choices as they seek counsel, learning, and inspiration from their rabbinic leadership.

Nurturing

Twenty-five years ago, a young female rabbi delivered a sermon in which she shared a story from her own life experience. After the service, her male senior rabbi asked, "How did it feel sharing that personal story with the congregation?" Until that time, he had felt forbidden to reveal anything personal about himself from the pulpit. Henceforth, he started to use his own life experience as a teaching tool. With the help of this young assistant, and many other women rabbis, the self-imposed distance between rabbi and congregant has narrowed. Our female colleagues have demonstrated that by not only sharing our intellectual adroitness but also engaging in deep and open relationships, we can more effectively nurture and guide the members of our community.

Male rabbis have become better listeners, better nurturers, better role models—in part because of what we have learned from our women colleagues. As we have become more willing to share our personal side and, yes, to reveal our vulnerabilities, we have become more approachable and more effective.

Janet Marder (HUC-JIR '79) enabled us to gain new perspective on intermarriage when she offered a special blessing on Yom Kippur for non-Jewish mothers and fathers who car-pool their Jewish children to religious school and help to create a Jewish home and family. Certainly a male rabbi could have offered such a blessing; however, since research shows that women have a higher aptitude for seeking inclusive solutions,[15] it is more likely that such a creative approach would come from a woman.

Career Paths

Women rabbis have also opened up new career paths. Consider pastoral care. It is true that our colleague Joshua Loth Liebman (HUC '30) ministered to millions via radio in the 1940s and through his best seller, *Peace of Mind.*[16] Jerome Folkman (HUC '28) pioneered family therapy in the mid-twentieth century. But both did so from their pulpit perches in Boston and Columbus, Ohio, respectively. It remained for our female colleagues to embrace pastoral care, hospital and community chaplaincies, and spiritual wellness as full-time endeavors that now engender a level of respect and appreciation at least comparable to that earned by pulpit rabbis. Those who opened up these new pathways include Rachel Cowan (HUC-JIR '89), Nancy Flam (HUC-JIR '89), Dayle Friedman (HUC-JIR '85), and Shira Stern (HUC-JIR '83), among others. As more male rabbis now choose these fields as their primary career choice, they do so standing on the shoulders of the women who blazed the trail.

Part-time rabbinic positions have also become the path of first choice for a number of colleagues. While this option was initially chosen by some women because it permitted them to attend to responsibilities of home and family, it has blossomed into a constructive arrangement that benefits male and female colleagues alike, as well as the institutions they serve.

Raising the Bar

Paul Menitoff (HUC-JIR '70), executive vice president emeritus of the Central Conference of American Rabbis, suggests that women rabbis have raised the level of intelligence, creativity, and work ethic in the rabbinate. It is his assertion that "the first group of any minority that breaks through significant barriers to achieve success in any field has to be better, brighter, and work harder to be successful. In the process, it tends to raise the standards for everyone in that field."[17]

This theory is not empirically provable. What we do know is that Sally Priesand's ordination in 1972 opened up the option of rabbinic service to more than 50 percent of our Jewish population for whom that opportunity had been foreclosed. As a result, thousands of bright, caring, Jewishly committed women have considered the rabbinate, and hundreds have been ordained. It is probably not coincidental that the academic records of applicants to HUC-JIR's rabbinic school have risen since women have been admitted.

Looking Ahead

"The arrival of women in the rabbinate has been transformational; some would say revolutionary," observes Jacqueline Koch Ellenson (HUC-JIR '83). She adds, "They have broken boundaries, functioned in a transformed world, and managed it with all of its conflict. They have allowed people to say, 'We can break down the old ways and create new modalities for Jewish living.'"[18]

What are some of the future transformations that women can help us achieve in the rabbinate and in Jewish life? Consider the mid-size and large congregation. It is increasingly difficult for individual rabbis to meet the diverse needs of congregants, young and old, Jewishly educated and beginners, intermarried and endogamous. Multi-clergy staffs, with gender diversity, permit rabbis and cantors to specialize in focused areas. This enables individual clergy, female or male, to reach a higher level of expertise and creativity, thereby reducing the stress on any individual rabbi.

In the years ahead, rabbis will need to find more creative ways to enrich people's lives and to reach them in places not yet touched by Jewish experiences. Beyond coffeehouses and clubhouses, these will include the supermarket, the workplace, websites, and social media not yet imagined. New liturgical forms will emerge, based in part on the creative efforts of our female colleagues described in chapter 5 of this volume.

For some time, women have confronted the challenge of "leave taking" in the marketplace. For a variety of reasons, often but not exclusively parenthood, women have taken a number of years of leave from their positions and found it difficult to reenter the workforce. A far smaller number of men have done the same. As the baby boom generation is retiring in increasing numbers, it might very well be that our women colleagues will innovate in unique ways, discovering new possibilities for us to serve the people Israel in our retirements. Perhaps women and men can jointly confront that challenge and together find new ways to hone their skills and sustain their creativity.

In sum, the iconoclasm and creativity of women rabbis should provide us with models for experimentation and radical reconstruction of Jewish life for many years to come.

I owe a profound debt to the women who have accompanied me on this journey, particularly my wife, Terry; our daughter, Sarah; and the female rabbis of the CCAR. I recognize especially my rabbinic associates in Westfield, New Jersey; the many graduates of our congregation now serving as rabbis; and my students over my three decades of teaching at HUC-JIR. We must also acknowledge the pioneering role of women in synagogue lay leadership, especially those who served in past decades as presidents of our synagogues and as officers of what is now Women of Reform Judaism. They were instrumental in illuminating the path for us.

NOTES

1. Betty Friedan, *The Feminine Mystique* (New York: Norton, 1963).

2. Margaret Moers Wenig, "God Is a Woman and She Is Growing Older," *Reform Judaism*, Fall (1992), 26–44.

3. Personal correspondence with Rabbi Rex Perlmeter, November 6, 2012.

4. Alexander Szalai, ed., *The Use of Time: Daily Activities of Urban and Suburban Populations in Twelve Countries* (The Hague: Mouton, 1972).

5. Arlie Russel Hochschild, *The Second Shift* (New York: Avon Books, 1989), 6.

6. Ibid., 3.

7. Personal correspondence with Rabbi Deborah Bravo, September 5, 2012.

8. Elyse Goldstein, ed. *New Jewish Feminism* (Woodstock, VT: Jewish Lights Publishing, 2009), 128.

9. Personal correspondence with Rabbi Amy Schwartzman, January 29, 2013.

10. Personal correspondence with Rabbi Martin Weiner, January 24, 2013.

11. *The Qualities That Distinguish Women Leaders* (Princeton, NJ: Caliper, 2005).

12. Herb Greenberg and Patrick Sweeney, "Female Intuition: Women Leaders Mean Business," *CEO Magazine*, 2008.

13. The Caliper study confirms that women tend to be more comfortable in such collaborative situations.

14. Oshrat Morag, "Theology of Experience: The Heart of a Feminist Theology," *CCAR Journal* 58 no. 3 (Summer 2011): 18–41

15. Corinne Post, "When Is Female Leadership an Advantage? Coordination Requirements, Team Cohesion, and Team Interaction Norms," Journal of Organizational Behavior, 36 no. 8 (June 2015): 1153–1175. http://onlinelibrary.wiley.com/doi/10.1002/job.2031/abstract

16. Joshua Loth Liebman, *Peace of Mind* (New York: Simon and Schuster, 1946).

17. Personal correspondence with Rabbi Paul Menitoff, August 30, 2012.

18. Personal correspondence with Rabbi Jacqueline Koch Ellenson, February 4, 2013.

18

WOMEN RABBIS IN ISRAEL

Rabbi Dalia Marx, PhD

My colleague was startled when a male congregant, a friendly chatty one, told her that she is "ten centimeters short to be a rabbi." Only on her way back home did she realize that he was talking about her skirt length. Needless to say, this realization did not make her feel any better. Indeed, some professional experiences seem to be unique to female clergy. This article is dedicated to a specific topic: the roles, challenges, and horizons of liberal female rabbis in the contemporary State of Israel.

Short History

Until modernity, almost no Jewish women merited being in leadership positions,[1] let alone serving as rabbis. While the question regarding the ordination of women was publicly raised for the first time about 120 years ago,[2] the first woman was ordained (albeit in a private *s'michah*) in 1935 in Nazi Germany. It was Regina Jonas, who served German congregations and perished in 1942 in Auschwitz.[3] It took another thirty-seven years for Sally Priesand to receive rabbinic ordination from Hebrew Union College–Jewish Institute of Religion (HUC-JIR)/Cincinnati in 1972; the other liberal seminaries followed shortly.[4]

Today all the non-Orthodox seminaries ordain women, and eyes are lifted now to modern Orthodoxy, whose leaders fiercely debate this matter.[5]

In Israel, the first woman rabbi to practice was Kinneret Shiryon, born in the United States and ordained at HUC-JIR/New York. In 1981, Shiryon made *aliyah* and later established Yozma congregation in Modi'in. The first woman who was ordained in Israel is Naamah Kelman. Kelman received her ordination at the Jerusalem campus of HUC-JIR in 1992, where she currently serves as the dean. The following year, Valerie Stessin was the first Masorti (Conservative) rabbi ordained in Israel. Maya Leibovich, the founding rabbi of Kamaz congregation in Mevaseret Zion near Jerusalem, is the first Israeli-born woman rabbi. Currently, there are some seventy-five women rabbis in Israel, in various congregational, organizational, and educational positions.

No Longer an "Item"

A sign of normalizations in terms of the female rabbinate in Israel is that it is no longer a news item. Unlike previous years, ordination of women no longer receives attention in the press, and interviewers do not feel the need to make tasteless jokes (such as, What is the title for a rabbi's husband?[6]). Although far from being a normalized situation, in many circles, women rabbis are not an extraordinary sight; in one of our congregations that has a woman as a rabbi, a little girl asked her mother if men too can become rabbis.

As background for our discussion, let us consider first some facts about the women rabbis in Israel. Table 1 shows that women are still a minority, comprising 48 percent of the Reform rabbis. In the American Reform Movement, the gap is much more drastic (Table 2); the women comprise only 32 percent of the Central Conference of American Rabbis (CCAR), but in the current ordination classes they comprise the striking rate of 51 percent. In the Israeli Masorti (Conservative)

Movement (Table 3) the gap is more moderate than it is in the Israel Movement for Progressive Judaism (IMPJ, the Reform Movement), which is at present significantly more egalitarian than the Masorti Movement, with the same number of male and female rabbis serving in congregations, whereas only four out of the twenty-two female Conservative rabbis in Israel are presently functioning as congregational rabbis.

Table 1. Gender Division in MARAM (the Israeli Council of Reform Rabbis)[7]

	Total	Male rabbis	Female rabbis
Members of MARAM	100	52 (52%)	48 (48%)
Rabbis officiating in congregations	31	13 (42%)	18 (58%)
Ordination classes of 2013–2015	13	4 (30%)	9 (70%)

Table 2. Gender Division in the CCAR[8]

	Total	Male rabbis	Female rabbis
Members of the CCAR	2,176	1,477 (68%)	699 (32%)
Ordination classes 2014–15	67	33 (49%)	34 (51%)

Table 3. The Masorti (Conservative) Movement in Israel[9]

	Total	Male rabbis	Female rabbis
Members of the Rabbinical Assembly	160	138 (86%)	22 (14%)
Rabbis officiating in congregations	19	15 (79%)	4 (21%)
Ordination classes of 2013–2015	5	3 (60%)	2 (40%)

Double Exclusion

Many of the challenges that women rabbis in Israel face are not essentially different from those confronting their colleagues in North America.[10] One would also expect that due to the traditionalist and even macho nature of their society, Israeli women rabbis would encounter more discrimination and suspicion. It's been said that the best Israelis can do is allow women to be ordained, but even then they cannot truly accept them as rabbis. However, often this is just part of the larger picture: the immediate problems that non-Orthodox religious Jews encounter in Israel have to do first and foremost with their liberal, modern, and inclusive values and practices, not directly with gender issues.

Non-Orthodox rabbis of both sexes have to close ranks because they are all members of the same *salon des refusés*, laboring under constant challenges to their legitimacy by the Orthodox establishment and denied funding and recognition not only by the Orthodox or ultra-Orthodox chief rabbinate but often also by the Israel Ministry of the Interior and the Ministry of Religion. Israeli Reform and Conservative rabbis are not authorized to officiate at weddings or burials, nor do their synagogues receive government funding as Orthodox synagogues do. The gap between male and female liberal rabbis, especially with regard to officiating in congregations and organizations, is much smaller than the gap between both of them and Orthodox or ultra-Orthodox rabbis. When Rabbi Alona Lisitsa was the Israeli representative to the Women's Rabbinic Network (WRN), she said in her 2009 address to her colleagues in North America, "We are proud to be equally discriminated against with our male colleagues by the Israeli establishment. The de-legitimization campaign against all of us is manifested in the outrageous statement by Rabbi Eliyahu, former Chief Rabbi of Israel, blaming Reform Jews for the Holocaust."[11]

It may be surprising but since both men and women liberal rabbis are marginalized in Israel, there is more equality between them there. In fact, women rabbis in Israel seem to get to be in leadership positions somewhat more easily than do their colleagues in the United States. Women rabbis lead some of the larger congregations in Israel, and many women serve in leadership and executive roles: Rabbi Maya Leibovich heads the Reform Rabbis Council (MaRaM), Rabbi Naamah Kelman is dean of the Jerusalem campus of HUC-JIR, and Rabbi Tamar Elad-Appelbaum served until recently as a dean of the Schechter Rabbinical Seminary in Jerusalem.

Some of my colleagues claim that women's double marginality can be advantageous as well. For some secular Israelis, a woman rabbi is intuitively perceived not only as a nonthreatening and non-authoritative figure, but also positively subversive. The religious coercion in Israel and Orthodoxy's monopoly over Judaism there causes many citizens to shy away from any form of Jewish religiosity and practice, yet some of them find a female rabbi more accessible and accommodating than a male rabbi. Even the new Hebrew word *rabbah*, the title most female rabbis prefer,[12] which sounded at first weird, falls on relatively open ears.[13] A friend of mine who serves as an ultra-Orthodox rabbi has no difficulty calling me *rabbah* since, as he says, it is "a new thing that never existed before."

Working as a Woman Rabbi in Israel

Israeli society is very oriented around family life. Although child care centers are far from optimal, women in Israel can rely on them and on a long day at kindergartens; paid maternity leave is mandatory (albeit relatively short) and is protected by law; short distances, tight relationships, and mutual informal social support facilitate dependence on grandparents and friends for help with young children. For these reasons and due to economic necessity, in most Israeli families both spouses work outside the home. Since juggling work and family is relatively natural for Israeli women, female rabbis are among the beneficiaries.

Liberal congregations in Israel tend to be rather small and therefore, in most cases, present their rabbis with a relatively manageable work load. Moreover, their low budgets enable many congregations to employ only a part-time rabbi (whether male or female).[14] The fact that many synagogues do not have full office and maintenance support does not discourage many women rabbis, who are willing, as one of them said to me, "to get their hands dirty" by sweeping floors, arranging chairs, making phone calls, sending letters, and so forth. It seems that women rabbis often respond more readily to these extra chores than do their male colleagues.

I believe that Israel's relatively informal and nonhierarchical work structure enables women, with what seems to be the readiness of many female clergy to be less hierarchical and authoritative,[15] to fit comfortably into the Israeli rabbinate.

Aside from the cooperation of liberal men and women rabbis in Israel, women rabbis also have projects for women only. The women rabbis of the Masorti Movement formed a group called Yalta,[16] which is famous for its inspiring women's Passover seders. The women Reform rabbis form the Israeli chapter of the Women for Reform Judaism (WRJ). Lately, I was fortunate to be among four Reform rabbis who explored the topic of ritual immersion in a liberal context and eventually edited the book *Parashat Hamayim: Immersion in Water as an Opportunity for Renewal and Spiritual Growth* (Tamar Duvdevani, Maya Leibovich, Alona Lisitsa, and Dalia Marx, eds.; HaKibutz HaMeuchad, Tel Aviv, 2011, in Hebrew). Not all of our colleagues were convinced of the necessity of such an endeavor, but eventually we got much encouragement both from the IMPJ and from MaRaM.

Can Overt Sexism Be an Advantage?

Sexism and machismo can be found in every society, regardless of how progressive it may be; in Israeli society it is overt and explicit and disturbing. Still, it can be argued that a direct and blunt style, which is typical of many Israelis, may sometimes be an advantage: It is easier to detect, less subtle, and therefore easier to respond to. On the other hand, when discrimination is covert and expressed through a veil of political correctness and propriety, it is harder to identify and it is certainly harder to respond to.

My female colleagues and I constantly confront excluding and doubting remarks made by bar mitzvah parents, board members, and school principals, as well as taxi drivers and service providers. We respond to statements like "separation between men and women always existed in the synagogue" by explaining that that isn't necessarily so. We readily tell those who claim that "when a woman is standing on the bimah, congregants will look at her as a woman, not as a rabbi," that our femininity does not contradict our professionalism; on the contrary, it shapes it and enhances it. When young couples tell us that they would really love it if we officiated in their wedding but they "just cannot do it" because their old aunt would freak out to see an officiating female rabbi, and they need a male rabbi, preferably with a beard (to look like a "real rabbi"), we warmly wish them *mazal tov*, and hope that their children will feel otherwise.

Obviously, we do not always have the patience to engage with this kind of conversation, but our everyday experiences provide us with many opportunities to confront sexist attitudes. We believe that responding to these kinds of "petty" questions can affect the whole society, not just the individual. In many cases, prejudice and intolerance vanish when a personal connection exists, and the personal, as we all know, is also the political.

In the last few years, we have experienced a disturbing wave of women's exclusion from the public sphere in Israel. Ultra-Orthodox circles pressure companies and publishers to avoid using pictures of women, not only in commercial advertisements but also in official government publications. Women and even young girls are being harassed for not wearing "modest" cloths, and due to the fear of extreme circles, female singers are not invited to many public events, including military events. These phenomena are not new but they have become more extreme and more frequent in the past few years, and the novelty of the past year or so is that many people openly protest against them. The backlash of these developments is a strong antireligious sentiment as well as the endowment of non-Orthodox expressions of religiosity, and especially of women leaders, whose very being is a bold response to the exclusion of women.

A short anecdote to illustrate this: in my own neighborhood in North Jerusalem, the French Hill, a project among many other local initiatives has recently taken place, as a protest against the exclusion of women in our city. The young leadership of the neighborhood has decided to place large posters of women of different occupations all around the neighborhood. Alongside the teacher, the scientist, and the musician, I was asked to participate as a rabbi. Apparently a rabbi is now one of the feminine "neighborhood professions"!

Ironically, the new awareness of the presence of women in the Israeli public sphere, and the dangers to Israeli democracy caused by those who want to eliminate their participation and their images, has begun to cause larger circles of Israelis to appreciate the missing female voices from the generations-old Jewish choir. We women and men who serve as rabbis in the State of Israel pray that both democracy and pluralism will thrive in the years ahead, so that our voices can be raised more in praise than in protest.

At the end of 2013, Israel's attorney general made a historic announcement that the State of Israel will fund the salaries of Reform and Conservative rabbis who are employed by regional councils. Rabbi Miri Gold, the rabbi of Gezer, provided the case upon which this decision was based. Although the road is still long, it seems that things are indeed changing for Israeli liberal Jews. Of course, the change affects liberal Jews everywhere, and thus it affects Jewish life overall.

What to Call a Woman Rabbi

One of the questions that emerged early on in the history of women's ordination in Israel was what to call a woman rabbi.[17] At first glance it would appear that this is only a technical question, but it is well known that a person's professional title has a great deal to do with how one understands one's professional persona. The question of the appropriate title for a woman rabbi is not separate, really, from other questions about professional titles that were limited at one time to men. For example, there are women who function as academic secretaries who wish to be called by the grammatically masculine form (*mazkir*) instead of the feminine form (*mazkirah*), which implies a more technical and auxiliary nature of the job. Until just a short time ago women who were "ministers" with the government of Israel were called by the male designation *sar*; only lately have they been referred to as *sarah* in the female form, and now we even have a *roshat memshala* (prime minister in feminine form). In this regard, it seems to me that the women's rabbinate takes the question beyond the purely linguistic realm and even beyond common custom.

Dr. Zvia Walden, an Israeli linguist, interviewed twenty-nine Israeli women rabbis for purposes of addressing this issue and has demonstrated that the matter of professional title among women rabbis is quite a live question and arouses quite lively feelings.[18] As noted, nearly twenty years had passed from the time of the first woman's ordination in the United States in 1972 until the time of the first ordination of a woman in Israel; and nearly a full decade passed from that time until 2001, when Mira Raz was ordained with the title *rabbah*.

Kinneret Shiryon, the first woman to fill a rabbinic position as such in Israel, told Walden about the efforts she expended along the way to finding the appropriate title. She asserted,

> "After I arrived in Israel in 1983, I wrote a letter to the Academy of the Hebrew language [the legal Israeli authority in matters of language]. I received the answer that the appropriate term for a woman serving in the rabbinate was *rabbanit* [the Hebrew pronunciation of the term *rebbetzin*], but since that term was used for wives of rabbis, they advised a different term....I was naïve, and decided that I would teach the Israel society to call the rabbi by

an appropriate title, so I took up the title *rabbanit*...and that didn't work. Then I decided to 'go with' *rav*. That way they would understand who I am. It is grammatically awkward but at least I wouldn't have to waste time explaining what I meant."[19] The advantage in using the title *rabbanit* would be that this is an already existing word that is recognizable in Hebrew; yet the disadvantage of the word was that it was already "taken" and therefore Shiryon finally rejected it, as did the other women in the rabbinate.

Walden specifies several proposals for a title for a woman in the rabbinate during the recent decades, and among them has been *rabit*,[20] *rabat*,[21] and more. In the convention of the organization *Kolech* (literally, "your voice"), the Israeli organization of Orthodox women, consideration was given in 2009 to the title that one would associate with a woman who would receive rabbinic ordination. The discussion was interesting especially in light of the fact that Orthodox women had not yet become eligible for the rabbinate and so the question was more cultural and symbolic. Among the names in this instance that were favored were *chachamah* (a title parallel to a title that is used among Sephardim), *maharat*[22] (an acronym for rabbinic teacher of halachah), and again, *rav*. The title that was ultimately preferred was *rabbah*. Unfortunately but not surprisingly, no explicit reference was made to the fact that this title is already in use by many of the women from non-Orthodox streams of Judaism. Rachel Keren, the head of Kolech's executive committee, said, "In the title-choosing contest, we wanted to make the community aware of the need for this need [for women to be religious leaders]. We figured that a public discussion about this subject would encourage women to keep studying."[23] That is to say that the idea was that giving a name to something that is not yet a reality may encourage its being established as something that actually exists.

But, whereas within the world of Orthodoxy the question of what to call women rabbis might be interesting as a matter of "creative midrash," within the non-Orthodox world the midrash becomes more pragmatic and serves to respond to the actual needs of women who are already serving as rabbis. As of today two professional titles have been used by women who are serving in the rabbinate, and lively argument and a plethora of jokes surround them: *rav* and *rabbah*. When a woman is ordained in the Israeli Reform rabbinic program at HUC-JIR, she is asked what should be written on her ordination certificate.

Those who favor the label *rav* point out, as does Kinneret Shiryon, that this term is one that requires no justification or explanation and that using this term serves to emphasize the equality between men and women of the rabbinate. They further contend that the term *rabbah* could wind up being understood as designating an entirely different profession, an innovative position of lesser status. Those who favor the title *rabbah*, on the other hand, stress the importance of normalizing the title, as is the case with so many titles and professions that have a masaculine and feminine form. That is how it should be with the rabbinate, goes this argument, and the feminine form of the title, they argue, emphasizes both their gender and the fact that they have been ordained.[24] In opposition are those who argue that the word *rabbah* is not yet an official word and may even sound strange,[25] and suggests that many words in Hebrew that sound familiar today were once new and may have sounded peculiar, for example, *gerev* (stocking), *iparon* (pencil), *kaletet* (cassette tape). Yet this claim seems not to carry much weight any further, for the title *rabbah* is recognized and no longer requires an explanation. As an example of this, I would recall what I wrote above about the poster in my neighborhood whose title requires no explanation.

Everything that has been said so far deals with the preference of the women themselves—those who are affected by their titles; their religious temperaments and personal style are an important part of their preferences in this regard. But as is well known, it is the Academy for the Hebrew Language that determines matters of linguistic propriety. As I said above, the first efforts in the 1980s and '90s resulted in the response that the word *rabbanit* (parallel to *chazanit*, a woman cantor)[26] would be used, and until the beginning of the new decade the Academy did not really respond to the question regarding the proper title for women in the rabbinate. In a consultation with the Academy's telephone service (customary with some regularity in Israel, where there are community "call-ins"), the response I received was that if the Academy would designate a proper term, it would likely propose a separate term with regard to the rabbinate, probably *rabbah*, but that it would not do so, because that might suggest that the Academy is recognizing the legitimacy of women rabbis.[27] But with the changing reality, and with the fact that there are considerably more women rabbis, the Academy for the Hebrew Language in its effort to pay attention to the zeitgeist has recently published the following response with regard to the appropriate term for a woman rabbi:

> The feminine form these past generations is *rabbanit* (following the fact that the plural is *rabbanim*), but the actual meaning of this term is "the wife of a rabbi," and therefore for contemporary usage, we use the term *ishah-rav*. There are those who believe that just as *malkah* can be the same as *ishah-melech* or *eishet melech*, so the term *rabbanit* could serve (in double service, as it were) as *ishah-rav*. But those who have requested this response were not satisfied with *rabbanit*, and therefore the proposal developed of **rabbah**, which is itself a feminine form of the description *rav* (like the construct *todah rabbah*). Therefore it seems appropriate that the word *rabbah* has some standing within the community as the feminine form of *rav*.[28]

NOTES

This essay is an expansion of a section in the author's article "A Female Rabbi Is Like an Orange on the Passover Plate—Women and the Rabbinate: Challenges and Horizons" (in *Rabbi - Pastor - Priest: Their Roles and Profiles Through the Ages*, Studia Judaica Book 64, ed. by Walter Homolka and Heinz-Gunther Schotler, [Germany: Walter de Gruyter, 2013], 219–40).

1. There are a few salient examples of women who served as leaders in ancient Israel (such as the prophetesses Deborah and Huldah), in the Middle Ages (such as

Asenath Barzani, 1590–1670, in Iraq), and in the Chasidic communities of Eastern Europe from the eighteenth century onwards (such as Edel, daughter of the founder of Chasidism, the Baal Shem Tov); see Renee Goldberg, "Hasidic Women Rebbes from 1749–1933" (rabbinical thesis, HUC-JIR, 1997). See also p. 23, this volume.

2. Pamela Nadell, *Women Who Would Be Rabbis: A History of Women's Ordination 1889–1985* (Boston: Beacon Press, 1998), 1–29. Regarding women in the rabbinate, see Laura Geller, "From Equality to Transformation: The Challenge of Women Rabbinic Leadership," in *Gender and Judaism: The Transformation of Tradition*, ed. T. M. Rudavsky (New York and London: New York University Press, 1995), 234–54; Jacqueline Koch Ellenson, "From the Personal to the Communal," in *New Jewish Feminism*, ed. Elyse Goldstein (Woodstock, VT: Jewish Lights, 2009), 125–32; Janet Marder, "How Women Are Changing the Rabbinate," *Reform Judaism* 19, no. 4 (1991): 4–9; Irit Printz, "Women in the Conservative Synagogue, in *New Jewish Feminism*, 186–94.

3. Until recently, Jonas was almost forgotten, but after the fall of the Berlin Wall and the opening of East Germany's archives, a comprehensive biography on her was written; see Elisa Klapheck, *Fräulein Rabbiner Jonas: The Story of the First Woman Rabbi*, trans. Toby Axelrod (San Francisco: Jossey-Bass, 2004); Elisa Klapheck, ed., *Fräulein Rabbiner Jonas: Kann die Frau das Rabbinische Amt Bekleiden?* (Teetz: Hentrich & Hentrich, 1999).

4. Sandy Eisenberg Sasso was the first woman to be ordained, in 1974, as a rabbi in the Reconstructionist Movement. A year later, in 1975, the first woman rabbi was ordained in Leo Baeck College in London. It took more than a decade and a fierce debate that threatened to split the Conservative Movement before the Jewish Theological Seminary in New York ordained Amy Eilberg, the first Conservative woman rabbi, in 1985.

5. See Sara Hurwitz, "Orthodox Women in Rabbinic Roles," in *New Jewish Feminism*, 133–43; Haviva Ner-David, *Life on the Fringes: A Feminist Journey toward Traditional Rabbinic Ordination* (Needham, MA: JFL Books, 2000).

6. My favorite answer is that of Naamah Kelman, who replied to this question, saying that her husband is *"rav seren"* (a military degree). The Women's Rabbinic Network often quotes a well-known answer as "lucky."

7. The numbers include both part-time and full-time rabbis, as well as some rabbinical students. I thank Rabbi Chen Ben Or-Tsfoni for the information.

8. I thank the Placement Office of the CCAR, for this information (retrieved on January 6, 2015).

9. I thank Rabbi Andrew Sacks and Ms. Rakefet Ginsburg for the information.

10. For information on women rabbis in North America, see note 2.

11. I thank Alona Lisitsa for providing me with her address to the WRN conference.

12. Some of the women prefer to be called *rav*. These two titles (*rav* and *rabbah*) often appear one next to the other, and we need to explain that the different titles are a matter of preference and that there is no difference in terms of its content. With regard to the choice of the title *rabbah*, see Elana Maryles Sztokman, "What's in a Name? Choosing 'Rabba' over 'Rav' and Why," *Forward*, May 2, 2011 (http://forward.com/articles/137448/#ixzz1XLi1OVgp); Zvia Walden, "*Rav, Rabbit, Rabbat, Rabbah* and *Ravrava*," *Panim* 33 (2005): 77–84 [in Hebrew].

13. See http://hebrew-academy.huji.ac.il/sheelot_teshuvot/MivharTeshuvot/Pages/25031003.aspx.

14. It is useful to note the well-known truth that having a half-time job means being paid half of a full salary but does not necessarily mean working half-time.

15. See Jacqueline Koch Ellenson, "From the Personal to the Communal," in *New Jewish Feminism*, 125–33; Janet Marder, "How Women Are Changing the Rabbinate, *Reform Judaism* 19, no.4 (Summer 1991): 5.

16. Yalta was the wise wife of the third- to fourth-century Talmudic sage Rav Nachman; she used to teach the rabbis while sitting behind a veil (BT *Beitzah* 25b).

17. In English-speaking countries, the title "rabbi" is used alike for men and women; therefore the entire question of the appropriate title for a woman rabbi relates primarily to the Israeli situation—and to the title to use on ordination certificates even in America. To this very day it has not yet been decided whether to write *morateinu harav* or *morateinu harabbah*. And in Germany another version of this problem is whether to use the term *Frau Rabbiner* or *Rabbinerin*.

18. Zvia Walden, "*Rav, Rabbit, Rabbat, Rabbah* and *Ravrava*," *Panim* 33 (2005): 77–84.

19. Ibid

20. Yitzhak Tsedaka, "Feminine and Masculine Numbering, a Handsome Man or a Gorgeous Lady, or Male and Female Created He Them," *Leshoneinu Le'am* 45, no. 1 (1994): 31–32.

21. This suggestion was made by Professor Moshe Bar-Asher, and see above, note 2.

22. The title granted to Sara Hurwitz in the United States, and see above.

23. Sophiah Hirshfeld, "What to Call a Woman Rabbi of a Congregation, an Interview with Rachel Keren," *Kolech*, July 23, 2009. Other names that were proposed in that contest were *rabbanit, talmidat chachamim*, and *musmechet* (http://www.kolech.org.il/show.asp?id=33820).

24. Rabbi Mira Raz, who, as noted, was the first ordained rabbi to have *rabbah* written on her *s'michah* certificate, wrote the following: "I believe that just as the world was created with an utterance word—with ten utterances—so it is that words create worlds. A word creates a consciousness and the words create a new world of consciousness. If I say about a woman that she is a *rav*, then the woman becomes an exception. There are many rabbis, and she is different, a woman rabbi" (Walden, above, note 2).

25. One of my colleagues often jokes at her own expense and says that if they call her *HaRabbah* X it will look in Hebrew orthography as if she were saying "Much X," especially out of her tendency to be slightly overweight. This joke brings us back to what we have been discussing above, that is to say, the increasing self-consciousness among professional women, and especially among women rabbis, both intrinsically and in terms of their physical appearance.

26. See "*Rabbanit, Chazanit*" (a response from the scientific secretariat), *Leshoneinu Le'am* 37, no. 1 (1986): 26–27.

27. The spokesperson told me of the angry letters received by the Academy regarding the question of the proper Hebrew pronunciation of "the Palestinian people" (the *shin* versus the *sin*), because it is a subject whose implications involve whether or not to give formal recognition to the Palestinian people.

28. "*Rav* in the Feminine Form" [in Hebrew], the Academy for the Hebrew Language's website (http://hebrew-academy.huji.ac.il/sheelot_teshuvot/MivharTe-shuvot/Pages/25031003.aspx).

Note: The final section of this essay was translated by Rabbi William Cutter, PhD.

19

THE FIRST THIRTY YEARS IN ISRAEL
AVNEI DERECH

Rabbi Kinneret Shiryon, dd

Women have been functioning as rabbis in the State of Israel since 1983. We have not only had an impact on religious life in the country, but our influence has spread beyond the liberal religious movements into the very fabric of Israeli society.

- Women rabbis have sensitized Israelis not only to a more egalitarian approach in prayer settings, but to more inclusive language in liturgy.
- We have brought greater attentiveness to the general gender-based Hebrew language, finding innovative ways of changing the way we communicate our values through language.
- We have raised awareness among adolescent girls to the option of marking their entrance to adulthood through a bat mitzvah ceremony, which is quite foreign to the Israeli mind-set.
- We have brought to the forefront new models of religious leadership.
- We have created new ceremonies for marking life-cycle and pivotal events in women's lives.

- We have influenced educational changes in teaching curriculum toward equality between women and men.
- We have stirred consciousness among women and men in all the various streams of religious and secular life to a more egalitarian society.

As the first woman rabbi of a congregation in the State of Israel, I had to overcome the prejudices of congregants who believed a woman was incapable of community religious leadership, combined with battling what I coined as "the monkey in the cage syndrome," meaning "Let's go see what kinds of tricks that woman rabbi can perform!" Pioneering colleagues paved the way to end both of those responses. Over the years, it has become clear to congregants that women are capable of rabbinic leadership. When the novelty wore off, women were judged by their merits and no longer drew crowds due to their uniqueness. Woman rabbis have also provided opportunities for women to develop themselves spiritually in new ways. We have opened the door to many Israeli women to choose a career in the rabbinate. One of my favorite stories is when I was asked by one of the numerous reporters who interviewed me as the first woman rabbi, "What is your litmus test for success?" I answered, "When the first native-born, Israeli-educated woman is ordained in the State of Israel, I will know that I have succeeded." Rabbi Maya Leibovich was watching the daily news show *Erev Chadash* one late afternoon and saw an interview with me. She was fascinated and said to herself, "I too would like to study to become a rabbi." A decade after I answered the interviewer's question, Maya became the first native-born, Israeli-educated rabbi to be ordained in the State of Israel. Today, the Hebrew Union College–Jewish Institute of Religion (HUC-JIR) rabbinic program in Jerusalem is blessed with numerous indigenous Israeli women studying toward rabbinic ordination.

In the early years, when I was the only woman rabbi in the country, I was interviewed by every form of media available at the time. The first palpable impact of my rabbinate on the greater Israeli scene was when I was interviewed on a popular television talk show in the country that was watched by 80 percent of the Israeli secular public. At the time of the interview, I was pregnant with our second child, and when the interviewer asked me what my "*baal*" (the Hebrew word for "husband") does for a living, I responded, "He is not my *baal*" (which literally means "owner" in Hebrew). There was a collective gasp in the audience (understanding from my remarks that I may not be married), and then I continued: "He is not my *owner*; I am not his property; he is my *ben zug* [my partner]. There is no ownership in our relationship but rather a partnership." There was enormous spontaneous applause by the audience before the interviewer could continue. Even more than my exposure as the first functioning woman rabbi in the country, the impact of my comment about the use of *baal* resonated in the Israeli discourse and permeated the conversation on the street.

Most Israelis use the word *baal* without ever pausing to understand its implications. Language is a conduit of our values; by using sexist expressions that reflect a woman's status as chattel, we maintain that derogatory attitude and pass it down to future generations. In our capacity as rabbis and community leaders, we have the responsibility to sensitize a new generation of young people to egalitarian language that will give us the capacity to relate to women on the same level as men. Most of our colleagues, women and men alike, understand this profound impact on Israeli society.

I moved to Israel just after the weekday and Shabbat siddur *HaAvodah Shebalev* was published. The same year I joined MARAM (the Israeli Council of Progressive Rabbis), in 1983, and became the first woman to become a member of a rabbinic association in the State of Israel, a committee was formed to prepare a new *machzor* for the Israel Movement for Progressive Judaism. My voice on the editorial committee added a new perspective to the issues that were raised regarding the *machzor* by my Israeli male colleagues. After the decision was made to add *Eloheinu Shebashamayim* (*nusach sepharadi*) alongside the *Avinu Malkeinu* prayer, I suggested that we think of a way of relating to God with feminine metaphors as well. I initially suggested that a possible parallel to *Avinu Malkeinu* (Our Father, our King) could be

Imeinu M'kor Chayeinu (Our Mother, Source of our lives). I liked the poetic balance between mother and father, and I particularly was enamored of the rhyme between the words: *imeinu* and *chayeinu*. The other members of the committee felt that my suggestion was too radical for the members of the Movement at the time, and we compromised on the *nusach*: *Shechinah M'kor Chayeinu*. The goal was to open the eyes of our congregants to additional liturgy that would enable them to start speaking about God in female terms. Some of the more senior colleagues objected to the suggestion, for fear of bringing dualism into our liturgy when relating to God. The majority voted on the *Shechinah* language as more suited to the Israeli Hebrew-speaking population, who were familiar with the term and its roots in classical Hebrew literature. The importance of adding a prayer that spoke about God in female language outweighed my original suggestion. Two melodies were composed for the text, and they are chanted alongside of *Avinu Malkeinu* in our congregations across the country. There are generations of Israeli Jews who sing the *Shechinah M'kor Chayeinu* liturgy as naturally and as easily as *Avinu Malkeinu* and *Eloheinu Shebashamayim*.

Hebrew is a gender-based language. Every noun, verb, and adjective is either feminine or masculine; therefore, in order to achieve some form of gender balance in the way we relate to God, we need to be creative. As more and more women rabbis add their outlook and influence to the way we utilize the Hebrew language to be more gender-inclusive in our prayers, we sensitize our male colleagues, as well as both the male and female members of our communities. We have moved well beyond adding the names of the *Imahot* (Matriarchs) alongside the *Avot* (Patriarchs) in the *Amidah* prayer. Congregations have added expressions such as *Ein HaChayim* (Spring of Life) and *Yifat Olam* (Splendor of the World) as feminine descriptions of God into their blessings and prayers. The voices of native Hebrew speakers searching for authentic ways to utilize the poetry of the Hebrew language to bring the feminine aspects of God to the forefront in our liturgy is one of the keys to opening a new era in the growth of spiritual literature of the Jewish people.

All of the Reform congregations in Israel offer bat mitzvah ceremonies for their members and encourage young women from all the outlying areas of their communities to celebrate their passage from childhood into adulthood with a bat mitzvah ceremony. And yet, the vast majority of our congregations still have only a small percentage of young women choosing to become bat mitzvah in our synagogues, compared to the number of young men who embrace the option of marking their entry to adulthood in our congregations.

The average Israeli young woman is not afforded this important ritual. In truth, Israeli culture discourages young adolescent women from exploring this option. The accepted way to celebrate becoming a bat mitzvah in Israel is to throw a big party for the young woman, similar to the sweet sixteen parties that take place in the United States. Young women who choose to celebrate this milestone in their lives with a ceremony at the synagogue are stigmatized by their families and friends regarding their desire to read from the Torah. It makes no difference whether they are from traditional Sephardi or Ashkenazi families, or from secular families who maintain antiquated views of religion. They are told that menstruating women are prohibited from approaching the Torah. They are often mocked by their peers for trying to imitate boys. They need to be very committed and confident to stand up to the various derogatory remarks that are directed at them. As a result, we need programs that will either strengthen their desire to mark their adolescence by going up to the Torah or at least awaken in them the option.

Many of the congregations in the Israel Movement for Progressive Judaism have offered a Mothers and Daughters Bat Mitzvah Experience program, which reaches out to girls and their mothers to remedy this reality. The concept or understanding that girls have the right and obligation to undergo this milestone is often foreign to the girls and their families. Through the Mothers and Daughters Bat Mitzvah Experience, daughters and mothers realize their potential and responsibility as future leaders.

Throughout Israel, girls are intrinsically taught that their coming of age is less important than the coming of age for boys. Until

Israeli society recognizes the obligation and right of an adolescent girl to regard her becoming a bat mitzvah in a manner as important and special as boys, differences will continue to exist. Through the Mothers and Daughters Bat Mitzvah Experience, we strive to change this perception and work against systemic discrimination. The results of the program have been encouraging. The mothers and daughters who participate in the program have a joint Shabbat *b'not mitzvah* ceremony in our congregations as the high point of the program. Initially, the young women feel more secure going up to the Torah in a group setting. Once they have experienced going up to the Torah in this safe environment, they are emboldened to take the next step and opt for celebrating an independent bat mitzvah ceremony for their family and friends as the young men do. The results of this program have been heartwarming. The mothers and daughters cherish this private time together. They learn about each other in a protective environment and are empowered by the experience. Women rabbis are instrumental in leading these workshops; they would not have the same effect if they were run by our male colleagues. One of the positive outgrowths of this program is the desire of some of our male colleagues to create Father and Son Bar Mitzvah Experience programs, allowing the young men to explore issues of adolescent development and changes in their bodies and finding private time for them to study together in a safe setting as the young women have done. Parallel programs for mothers and daughters and fathers and sons augment the general bar and bat mitzvah courses that we offer.

Another important result of women filling the role of rabbi in Israel is the legitimacy they provide for women in general (and not just *b'not mitzvah*–age women) to go up to the Torah and recite the blessings. I cannot begin to count the numerous women who go up to the Torah for the first time in their lives with tears of joy and excitement brimming in their eyes as they recite the blessings. It is an extraordinary event that takes place weekly in our Israeli Reform congregations. Some of the older women tell me that they would not have dared to go up to the Torah if they had not first seen me chanting from the Torah.

My rabbinic title allowed them to trust the authenticity of a woman in that role and gave them the legitimacy to try it themselves.

Women in the rabbinate often convey different models of leadership to their communities, and as a result of those models, Israelis are exposed to new approaches of rabbinic leadership. I built our synagogue community on the principles of empowering others, enabling, involving, and sharing. Success is all the sweeter when shared by others. It is a model that allows for partnerships between lay leaders and the various members of the staff. It is less of a hierarchical model and more of a communal model of leadership. This type of leadership is less familiar and often goes unnoticed by the members of our communities, but it is a very effective form of leadership. Showing concern for the common good and sharing responsibility for decisions engage community members to take active roles and allow everyone to flourish. When women leaders are at the forefront of Jewish communal life, we allow for more women's voices to be heard equally. This is especially important in Israeli society, where the population is less attuned to women's voices in the public sector.

We also become role models for other women and men. The fact that I was a communal leader throughout the entire period we were raising our four children allowed the families of our community to witness and, hopefully, imitate a model of parenting that is still very foreign to Israeli society. My partner, Baruch, was the main caregiver to our children, and our congregants were witness to what they perceived as a role reversal. In reality, it was simply an egalitarian model of raising our children. Of course the ideal is that each family be able to make choices regarding how they choose to raise their children and not just rely on the accepted model of the woman being the main caretaker. When there are options, we enrich the lives of our families and communities.

I am still tickled by the various stories my congregants have shared with me over the years about when their children come in contact with a male rabbi for the first time and their response is that they did not know that men could become rabbis. This is particularly heartwarming in Israel! Just today, I was approached by one of the teachers in our school. Her young daughter explained to her that Rav Nir (my associate, Rabbi Nir Barkin) is confused because only women, like Rav Kinneret, can be rabbis.

Even the Academy of Hebrew Language in Israel has been influenced by women rabbis. When I first arrived in the country, I wrote to the Academy to officially inquire about the proper title for an ordained female rabbi. They wrote that the proper word for female rabbi in Hebrew is *rabbanit*. The problem with *rabbanit* is that it is used as the term for the wife of a rabbi; the equivalent in Yiddish is *rebbetzin*. At first I believed I could re-educate Israelis and teach them that the proper use of the term *rabbanit* is for an ordained female rabbi. I failed in my efforts. I was constantly explaining that I was not married to a rabbi and that *I* was the ordained rabbi. As a result I adopted the title of *rav* in the same way that my male colleagues are addressed. In 2010, the Academy finally added the word *rabbah* to the Hebrew lexicon as the formal title for a woman ordained as a rabbi.

Women rabbis in Israel have also created innovative ceremonies and rituals for women to mark various transitions in their lives. We have helped women cope with the loss of a fetus by creating rituals to carry them through their sorrow. We have fashioned *b'rit labat* ceremonies to welcome newborn girls into the covenant of Israel, in contrast to the *b'ritah* parties devoid of meaning that most Israeli families throw for newborn girls. We have created ceremonies for Rosh Chodesh, for menopausal women, and for widows and have developed coming-out rituals. One of the recent products of some of these innovations is a book published in 2011 by four of our colleagues, Alona Lisitsa, Dalia Marx, Maya Leibovich, and Tamar Duvdevani, called *Parashat Hamayim: Immersion in Water as an Opportunity for Renewal and Spiritual Growth*.

One of my favorite rituals is the *hafrashat challah* (separating the challah) ceremony that I have adopted for marking the entrance of young women soldiers into the army. They invite their closest women friends and family to an evening of baking challot. After my introduction to the evening, explaining the historical and social meaning of *hafrashat challah*, the group decides to which organization they will make a contribution in honor of the soldier. While the challot are baking in the oven, I spread open a tallit and invite four women to hold it like a chuppah, as the soldier stands underneath it while encircled by her family and friends. Each woman is asked to bless the soldier as she begins this new stage in her life. After the personal blessings have been bestowed, we recite the traditional blessing for separating out the portion of the challah. We then toss it to the birds, bless the bread, and partake in eating the freshly baked challah together.

By marking these life passages, we have afforded opportunities for many secular Jews to create sacred time and space. The creative process of bringing these ceremonies into the community has also influenced many of our traditional ceremonies by teaching us to add readings, songs, and original blessings. For example, before our *b'nei* and *b'not mitzvah* put on their tallitot and recite the traditional blessing, we add a poem by Yehudah Amichai that lovingly relates to the experience of wrapping yourself in a tallit. Such innovations enrich Jewish life for all of us.

I am proud to be part of the change that is taking place in Israeli society today. In our educational frameworks, an entire generation of schoolchildren is being taught a different, egalitarian Jewish set of values. Jewish curriculum is being created in the State of Israel today that not only reflects equal opportunities for boys and girls, but is also changing the imbalance of how we study our history. Over the past twenty-five years, I have been developing and teaching a program in our preschools called *Gibburot v'Gibburim Ba-im LaGan* (Heroes and Heroines Come to the Preschool). It is a program about our heroes, both female and male, and about the values they transferred over the years. My emphasis on female heroes such as Sarah, Miriam, Deborah, Judith, Beruriah, Sarah Aaronsohn, and Chana Senesh help to counterbalance the male-dominated stories that have been passed down through the generations. This curriculum helps to raise generations of boys and girls with positive role models from both gender pools.

Women rabbis have been a positive force in bringing about change beyond the liberal religious Jewish frameworks. Witness the Orthodox women's prayer groups across the country, public *m'gilah* readings for Orthodox women, numerous Rosh Chodesh groups, both Orthodox and secular, and most recently on the front pages of the newspapers with the Women of the Wall. All of these trends and changes are a direct result of women rabbis being part of the Israeli reality.

Sheryl Sandberg writes in *Lean In: Women, Work, and the Will to Lead*, "Many studies of diversity tell us that if we tapped the entire pool of human resources and talent, our collective performance would improve."[1] Jewish life is a kaleidoscope of color and sound. By tapping women rabbi's tones, hues, and unique voices, we have enriched the variety of options in the entire Jewish world, enhanced the spectrum of Jewish interpretation, and enlivened the commitment to Jewish living today. In brief, our collective performance has improved.

Women rabbis are the vanguard of innovation of Jewish life in Israel today. Our impact is felt in the religious spectrum and beyond, spreading into the very fabric of Israeli society. Today there are many more paths open to women rabbis in Israel than ever before, which afford greater influence on the future of Israel. It has been a challenging and fulfilling journey thus far, and I have been privileged to have paved one of the paths. May we grow from strength to strength.

NOTE

1. Sheryl Sandberg, *Lean In: Women, Work, and the Will to Lead* (New York: Random House, 2013), 7.

20

A NEW REALITY

Female Religious Leadership in the Modern Orthodox Community

MAHARAT RORI PICKER NEISS

In March 2009, history was made at a ceremony in a synagogue in Riverdale, New York. Sara Hurwitz, a young Orthodox woman who had worked under the tutelage of Rabbi Avi Weiss at the Hebrew Institute of Riverdale (HIR) for nearly six years, had just completed an eight-year course of intensive study—three at the Drisha Institute for Jewish Education, a pioneering institution for advanced women's Torah study in New York, and five under the private guidance of Weiss—with a curriculum modeled after that of the male rabbinical students at Yeshivat Chovevei Torah. Hurwitz had not only completed the coursework, but she had also taken and passed the same rabbinical ordination exams. Weiss planned to bestow a new title upon Hurwitz—who previously served as the *madrichah ruchanit*, or spiritual guide, at HIR—to reflect her accomplishments.

Invitations to the event referred to it as a "conferral ceremony," and there was much speculation in advance of the event as to what the title might be. Congregants, together with the media and the broader Jewish community, were left guessing; conjectures included "rabbi," *morateinu* (meaning "our teacher") and two feminized versions of "rabbi": *rabba* and *rabbanit*.[1]

No one could have predicted the title that was ultimately selected. Standing on the bimah on that Sunday morning, looking over the sanctuary that housed the 850-family congregation that he established, Weiss said, "The authority of Torah will rest upon her shoulders to spread the knowledge of God throughout the land." Looking at Hurwitz, he dotingly said, "We bless you as you rise and come forward to join me in officially becoming part of the religious leadership of Israel and officially becoming a full member of our clergy!"[2] In that moment, Hurwitz was welcomed as the world's very first *maharat*, an acronym for *Manhiga Hilchatit, Ruchanit, Toranit*, a halachic (Jewish legal), spiritual, and Torah guide.

The word *maharat*, while evoking the rabbinic authorities in the Middle Ages who bore similar-sounding monikers, was an entirely new creation, with no root in the Hebrew language. In a sense it served as an apt metaphor for the position itself—in choosing this title Weiss made a clear statement: female clergy are new to the Orthodox community, and they are different from rabbis, but they are no less knowledgeable, no less authoritative, no less members of the clergy, and thus no less deserving of title and recognition.

Only a few months later, on May 14, 2009, a huge announcement came in the form of a very small message. An e-mail was sent to an undisclosed list succinctly stating:

> We are pleased to announce the opening of Yeshivat Mahara"t, an Orthodox Yeshiva of Higher Learning, founded by Rabbi Avi Weiss of The Hebrew Institute of Riverdale.
>
> Yeshivat Mahara"t (*Manhiga Hilchatit Ruchanit Toranit*) will train women to become Orthodox Spiritual Leaders—full members of the Rabbinic Clergy—in Synagogues, Schools, and on University Campuses.
>
> Resumes and letter of interest should be emailed to Mahara"t Sara Hurwitz.[3]

In just two small paragraphs, a revolution began.

One week later, the *Jewish Telegraphic Agency* (*JTA*) reported that the school expected to be up and running by September and would offer women part-time instruction in all areas of Jewish law, pastoral training, and a synagogue internship. "We're training women to be rabbis," Hurwitz told the *Forward*. "What they will be called is something we're working out." However, Hurwitz acknowledged that graduates of the newly formed Yeshivat Maharat may have trouble getting jobs. At the time, only a handful of Orthodox synagogues employed women in positions in which they functioned as recognized spiritual leaders.[4]

However, the debate over whether women should be rabbis was not new to American Jews, nor was it new to the Orthodox Jewish community. In 1984, the non-denominational Drisha Institute in New York launched the Drisha Fellowship Program, the first women's *kollel* with full-time stipended learning focused on Talmud and various other Jewish subjects. Eight years later, in 1992, the Drisha Scholars Circle was founded, a three-year program paralleling rabbinic ordination and the first multi-year, certificate program in Talmud and Jewish law for women in the world.[5] Graduates of the Drisha Scholars Circle (who included Hurwitz) worked in Orthodox synagogues and Orthodox day schools as educators and spiritual advisors. In 2006, the Graduate Program in Advanced Talmudic Studies (GPATS) at Stern College for Women of the Orthodox Yeshiva University expanded to offer an intensive two-year senior fellowship to continue rigorous study of Talmud and halachah, as well as leadership training in areas such as public speaking and facilitation, with the goal of developing women as both Judaic scholars and role models for the Orthodox community.[6] Across the Atlantic, women in Israel had had the ability to serve as *toanot rabaniyot*, rabbinical advocates, in the Jewish court system since the early 1990s. In 1999, Nishmat: The Jeanie Schottenstein Center for Advanced Torah Study for Women—an Israel-based modern Orthodox Jewish institution of higher Torah learning for women—launched the Keren Ariel Yoatzot Halacha program to train women to be *yoatzot halachah*, halachic advisors. *Yoatzot halachah*, as described in their own words, are "women certified by a panel of Orthodox rabbis to be a resource for women with questions regarding *Taharat Hamishpachah* (an area of Jewish Law that relates to marriage, sexuality and women's health)."[7]

Moreover, women had been taking on greater congregational roles in a few of modern Orthodox synagogues across the United States, though primarily in New York City. In 2006, Congregation Kehilat Orach Eliezer on the Upper West Side of Manhattan hired Dina Najman, a scholar of Jewish law with an expertise in bioethics, as its *rosh k'hilah*, or head of community—to date, the only Orthodox woman to have held a senior leadership position at a congregation. In 2007, Shearith Israel–the Spanish and Portuguese Synagogue and the Jewish Center, both also located on the Upper West Side, hired Lynn Kaye and Elana Stein Hain, respectively, graduates of Yeshiva University's GPATS. Kaye served as "assistant congregational leader," while Hain took the role of "community scholar." Outside of New York, Rachel Kohl Finegold, a graduate of the Drisha Scholars Circle, served as the "programming and ritual director" at Anshe Sholom B'nai Israel Congregation in Chicago. These women participated fully in all areas of Jewish communal leadership including delivering sermons,[8] teaching, answering halachic questions, and pastoring to congregants. The only activities they did not do were lead services, count toward the prayer quorum of ten men necessary to recite certain communal prayers, or serve as a judge on a *beit din*, the religious court—activities often absent from the regular job responsibilities of male Orthodox rabbis as well.

Against this backdrop, Yeshivat Maharat sought to innovate women's leadership in the Orthodox community in two ways: first, by standardizing the curriculum and creating a central location through which women would be trained to be leaders in the Orthodox Jewish community; and second, by normalizing a uniform title that would convey the intense learning, deep commitment, and community recognition that each woman held.

"You have to start somewhere," Hurwitz told *JTA*. "We have to put one foot in front of the other and keep moving forward, and I think that the community will follow."[9] The community followed even more than Weiss or Hurwitz had expected. They were overwhelmed by the interest in the program, and they received over thirty applications in less than four months. They accepted six women in the initial application process—four to graduate in 2013 and two more for the class of 2014—and began to craft a curriculum modeled after that of male rabbinical programs and centered on Jewish legal discourse, with an eye toward *p'sak halachah*, Jewish legal rulings—the first Orthodox program aimed at empowering women to be legal decisors.

The very first purchase the yeshivah made was a laptop computer; the most important program on the bulky black machine was ooVoo, the multi-user video chat and instant messaging application. As a new program aiming to train Orthodox women for clergy-level positions in the Jewish community, Yeshivat Maharat recognized that it could not just copy a male rabbinical program and insert female students. The first class of Yeshivat Maharat included two students who learned virtually: Abby Brown Scheier, who participated from Montreal, and Rachel Kohl Finegold, who joined from Chicago. The first year of Yeshivat Maharat offered a half-day of halachah, with students supplementing with their own Gemara learning, seeking opportunities in their local communities. The program became full-time—offering its own curriculum encompassing halachah, Gemara, pastoral counseling, and professional development—in the fall of 2010 under the administration of Rabbi Jeffrey Fox, the first graduate of Weiss's Yeshivat Chovevei Torah and the first *rosh yeshivah* of Yeshivat Maharat.

The program began with surprisingly little fanfare. The students who were based in New York City learned in a small classroom rented from the Drisha Institute. Though there was some media attention around the program, it seemed to peter out as the new denomination that some had portended never actualized.

All of that changed when Weiss amended Hurwitz's title from the newly coined "maharat" to the more rabbinic sounding "rabba." To the surprise of his congregants, his board, and even the students at Yeshivat Maharat, Weiss stood up in January 2010 and announced from the pulpit that the term "maharat" did not seem to fully convey to the Jewish community that Hurwitz served as a full member of the

Orthodox clergy. He clarified that Hurwitz had received *s'michah*, referring to rabbinic ordination, and that she served as an assistant rabbi at the Hebrew Institute. Weiss explained, "This [title] will make it clear to everyone that Sara Hurwitz is a full member of our rabbinic staff, a rabbi with the additional quality of a distinct woman's voice."[10]

In reaction to this event, the Moetzes of Agudath Israel of America—the religious decisors, leadership, and political and policy liaisons of Agudath Israel, consisting primarily of *rosh yeshivot* and Chasidic rebbes—issued the following statement on February 25, 2010:

> These developments represent a radical and dangerous departure from Jewish tradition and the *mesoras haTorah*, and must be condemned in the strongest terms. Any congregation with a woman in a rabbinical position of any sort cannot be considered Orthodox.[11]

The statement, though scathing, came as little surprise. Agudath Israel of America is a *Haredi* Jewish communal organization in the United States, one with which neither Weiss nor the Hebrew Institute of Riverdale is affiliated. The community represented by Agudath Israel is known for strict separation between men and women, both in ritual life and even in secular activities, and so any public role for women would be seen negatively—though they remained remarkably silent when Hurwitz was first conferred with the title "maharat."

Rumors began to spread quickly, though, that the Rabbinical Council of America (RCA)—one of the world's largest organizations of Orthodox rabbis, affiliated with the Union of Orthodox Jewish Congregations of America, with membership primarily affiliating with centrist modern Orthodox Judaism—of which Weiss was a member, was threatening to kick Weiss out of the union unless he retracted the new title.[12]

Weiss, indeed, backed down. In a letter addressed to then-RCA president Rabbi Moshe Kletenik, which was released to the public, Weiss wrote:

> It is not my intention or the intention of Yeshivat Maharat to confer the title of "Rabba" upon its graduates. Yeshivat Maharat prepares women for positions of religious leadership in the Orthodox community. Each student who completes its course of study in Tanakh, Talmud, Halakha and Jewish Thought, and is deemed fit by her faith, knowledge of our Mesoret, ethical integrity and temperament to assume positions of religious leadership in Orthodox institutions will be confirmed as *manhigah hilkhatit, ruhanit, toranit* (Maharat).[13]

On March 5, 2010, the RCA issued the following statement regarding "Orthodoxy and Women's Communal Roles":

> Over the course of the last several weeks, at the request and initiative of Rabbi Avi Weiss, the leadership of Rabbinical Council of America and Rabbi Avi Weiss have engaged in discussions concerning the issue of ordaining women as rabbis. We are gratified that during the course of these conversations Rabbi Weiss concluded that neither he nor Yeshivat Maharat would ordain women as rabbis and that Yeshivat Maharat will not confer the title of "Rabba" on graduates of their program.
>
> We are delighted that we have been able to resolve this matter in adherence with Torah principles and in a spirit of cooperation for the sake of peace and unity within our community. We are confident that continued dialogue of this type will enable us to resolve other important issues facing the Jewish community today.
>
> The RCA reaffirms its commitment to women's Torah education and scholarship at the highest levels, and to the assumption of appropriate leadership roles within the Jewish community. We strongly maintain that any innovations that impact the community as a whole should be done only with the broad support of the Orthodox rabbinate and a firm grounding in the eternal *mesorah* of the Jewish people.[14]

Hurwitz was allowed to keep her title "Rabba," but Weiss had to promise that no future graduates of the program would receive the same title. It seemed a foreboding start for a program that sought to standardize a title for recognized leadership roles for women in the Orthodox community.

On April 27, 2010, the RCA passed a resolution on "Women's Communal Roles in Orthodox Jewish Life." In it, they declared the expansion of Torah study and teaching by "God-fearing Orthodox women" to be a "significant achievement" and affirmed their "sacred and joyful duty" to transmit Judaism "in all its extraordinary, multifaceted depth and richness." Nevertheless, they clarified:

> In light of the opportunity created by advanced women's learning, the Rabbinical Council of America encourages a diversity of halakhically and communally appropriate professional opportunities for learned, committed women, in the service of our collective mission to preserve and transmit our heritage. Due to our aforesaid commitment to sacred continuity, however, we cannot accept either the ordination of women or the recognition of women as members of the Orthodox rabbinate, regardless of the title.[15]

The RCA both affirmed the benefits of advanced Jewish learning for women in the Orthodox community and encouraged professional leadership roles for women in the community, while strongly rejecting any ordination of women and/or recognition of women as members of the rabbinate—even if the title be the ambiguous, though clearly not rabbinic sounding, "maharat."

Amid this controversy and its resolution, two questions continued to overshadow Yeshivat Maharat: would the graduates of Yeshivat Maharat be given jobs, and more specifically, would those jobs be as clergy in the Orthodox community; and what title would graduates of the program be given upon completion? Despite the promises and assurances made to the RCA, the community waited with bated breath knowing that when it came to Avi Weiss, everything was still on the table.

Despite its rocky beginning, the program did not fall into ignominy. While negative-sounding reports would periodically appear in newspapers or on blogs, there was an unofficial policy among students: let the debate stay in the media while the future graduates of Yeshivat Maharat focus their time and energies on doing what they do best—learning Torah and serving the Jewish people.

The program continued to grow and flourish. By 2012, enrollment expanded to include thirteen women. Students held internships at synagogues, college Hillels, and major Jewish organizations; they taught and spoke nationally and internationally. Additionally, the students were recognized as rabbinical students alongside male Orthodox colleagues and colleagues in non-Orthodox institutions, participating in programs such as CLAL's Rabbis Without Borders Rabbinical Student Fellowship Program and the American Jewish World Service Rabbinical Students' Delegation.

In March 2013, a "Save the Date" e-mail was sent out inviting recipients to join in a "truly historic event." The affair was simply labeled: Yeshivat Maharat's Inaugural Graduation Celebration. The names of the graduates were listed, together with a time and location. No language other than "graduation" was used, and there was no indication of what title would be given.

On May 6, 2013, the official invitation was sent out. Citing the verse "*La-eit kazot higaat lamalchut*—For just such a moment you have risen to leadership" (Esther 4:14), the invitation labeled "Yeshivat Maharat's Inaugural Graduation Ceremony" as a "truly historic event," and added a very controversial new line: "Celebrating the Ordination as Clergy of our First Three Graduates." Although once again leaving the title noticeably absent, the fine print at the bottom of the invitation read:

> Yeshivat Maharat, under the leadership of Rabba Sara Hurwitz, is the first institution to ordain Orthodox women as Spiritual leaders and Halakhic authorities. Students are required to complete a four-year rigorous curriculum of Talmud, halakhic decision-making, pastoral counseling, and leadership development. Our first three graduates will be ordained as clergy by Rabbi Daniel Sperber, Rabbi Avi Weiss, and Rabbi Jeffrey Fox.

On May 7, 2013 the RCA issued the following statement:

> In light of the recent announcement that Yeshivat Maharat will celebrate the "ordination as clergy" of its first three graduates, and in response to the institution's claim that it "is changing

the communal landscape by actualizing the potential of Orthodox women as rabbinic leaders," the Rabbinical Council of America reasserts its position as articulated in its resolution of April 27, 2010, that:

"In light of the opportunity created by advanced women's learning, the Rabbinical Council of America encourages a diversity of halachically and communally appropriate professional opportunities for learned, committed women, in the service of our collective mission to preserve and transmit our heritage. Due to our aforesaid commitment to sacred continuity, however, we cannot accept either the ordination of women or the recognition of women as members of the Orthodox rabbinate, regardless of the title."

The RCA views this event as a violation of our mesorah (tradition) and regrets that the leadership of the school has chosen a path that contradicts the norms of our community.[16]

The reiteration of the statement of the RCA, which had caused such anxiety nearly four years earlier, now seemed insubstantial. The ordination of women as clergy in the Orthodox Jewish community would be a violation of tradition and a contradiction of norms, but notably absent were any accusations of a transgression of halachah. In that omission, rather than a condemnation, the statement by the RCA marked a triumph for Yeshivat Maharat.

Moreover, by that point all of the graduates of Yeshivat Maharat, and even one student, had already accepted full-time positions as clergy in the Orthodox community. Abby Brown Scheier, who had established a supplementary education high school of which she served as principal, continued her work as an educator, school administrator, and Jewish community volunteer in Montreal. Rachel Kohl Finegold accepted a position as the director of education and spiritual enrichment at Congregation Shaar Hashomayim in Montreal, a position that situated her as part of the clergy team at one of the largest Orthodox congregations in North America. Ruth Balinsky Friedman was hired as maharat at Ohev Sholom: The National Synagogue in Washington, DC. In addition, after having been accepted as part of the initial cohort to graduate in 2014, I was hired as the director of programming, education, and community engagement at Bais Abraham Congregation in St. Louis, Missouri, serving as clergy in the Orthodox congregation as I completed my last year remotely—a testament that the demand for maharats in the Orthodox community is exceeding the supply.

Approximately five hundred people attended the first graduation ceremony on June 16, 2013, held at Ramaz Upper School in New York City, with hundreds more joining virtually via livestream. Among family, friends, supporters, admirers, congregants, and reporters, three women—Abby Brown Scheier, Rachel Kohl Finegold, and Ruth Balinsky Friedman—were ordained as the first formal graduating class of female spiritual leaders in the Orthodox community. The language on their certificates read והוסמכה בהיתר הוראה לרבים, "Decisor of Jewish Law for the Community," and the title bestowed upon them was *maharat*—leaving Sara Hurwitz as the lone *rabba*, a bittersweet reality four years after beginning her journey to train women to share her role and title.

Later that fall, the Orthodox Jewish community celebrated yet another graduation: the commencement of the first American-trained cohort of *yoatzot halachah*. Five women were certified by rabbinic authorities to serve as halachic advisors in the area of *taharat hamishpachah*, and all were hired to work in Orthodox communities across America. At the same time, another five women joined Yeshivat Maharat, with twenty-six women expressing interest in enrolling the following year.

In the years that followed, Yeshivat Maharat continued to grow, and new programs sprouted in Israel offering Orthodox rabbinic training to women. Each institution chose to focus the emphasis on the training offered and the degree conferred rather than on the title. Female Orthodox clergy now serve in a myriad of positions across the globe and boast an array of titles, including: *maharat, rabba, rabbanit, morateinu,* and, as of 2015, even rabbi.

The history of female religious leadership in the Orthodox Jewish community is still in its infancy, and many questions still remain. What role will these women be asked to play in the Jewish community? In which communities will they gain acceptance? What title will be used to refer to expertise and training they have attained? On one point, though, there is no question: female religious leadership is a new reality in the modern Orthodox community.

NOTES

1. Ben Harris, "Orthodox Female Rabbi? False Alarm," *Jewish Telegraphic Agency*, March 3, 2009, http://www.jta.org/2009/03/03/life-religion/orthodox-female-rabbi-false-alarm.

2. Abigail Pogrebin, "The Rabbi and the Rabba," *New York Magazine*, July 19, 2010, http://nymag.com/news/features/67145/index1.html.

3. "Breaking News: Yeshivat Mahara"t," *Jewschool*, http://jewschool.com/2009/05/14/16291/breaking-news-yeshivat-maharat/.

4. Ben Harris, "Yeshiva to Train Women to Function as Rabbis," *Jewish Telegraphic Agency*, May 21, 2009, http://www.jta.org/2009/05/21/life-religion/yeshiva-to-train-women-to-function-as-rabbis.

5. "Scholars Beit Midrash," Drisha Institute for Jewish Education, http://www.drisha.org/scholarscircle.php.

6. http://blogs.yu.edu/news/tag/advanced-talmudic-studies/.

7. "Yoatzot Halacha," Nishmat, http://www.yoatzot.org/topic.php?id=98.

8. Although it is important to note that Elana Stein Hain was not permitted to speak from the bimah during services at the Jewish Center.

9. Harris, "Yeshiva to Train Women to Function as Rabbis.

10. Mayer Fertig, "Frum & Female but a Rabbi?" *Jewish Star*, Feb. 3, 2010, http://www.thejewishstar.com/stories/Frum-amp-female-but-a-rabbi,1485.

11. Gil Student, "Moetzes Condemns Ordination of Women," *Torah Musings*, Feb. 25, 2010, http://torahmusings.com/2010/02/moetzes-condemns-ordination-of-women/.

12. Jonathan Mark, "Rabbis Set to Rumble over over Rabba," *Jewish Week*, Feb. 23, 2010, http://www.thejewishweek.com/viewArticle/c41_a18006/News/Short_Takes.html, available via web archive http://web.archive.org/web/20100227220514/http://www.thejewishweek.com/viewArticle/c41_a18006/News/Short_Takes.html.

13. Michael Orbach, "RCA, Rabbi Weiss Agree: Todah, No Rabba," *Jewish Star*, March 3, 2010, http://thejewishstar.com/stories/RCA-Rabbi-Weiss-agree-Todah-no-Rabba,1560?page=1&content_source=.

14. "The Rabbinical Council of America Issues a Statement regarding Women's Communal Roles in Orthodox Jewish Life," Rabbinical Council of America, March 5, 2010, http://www.rabbis.org/news/article.cfm?id=105534.

15. "2010 Convention Resolution: Women's Communal Roles in Orthodox Jewish Life," Rabbinical Council of America, April 27, 2010, http://www.rabbis.org/news/article.cfm?id=105554.

16. "RCA Statement Regarding Recent Developments at Yeshivat Maharat," Rabbinical Council of America, May 7, 2013, http://www.rabbis.org/news/article.cfm?id=105753.s

21

ORTHODOX WOMEN (NON-)RABBIS[1]

Rabbi Darren Kleinberg, PhD

"Under no circumstances should you call yourself a rabbi."

—*Max Dienemann's advice to Regina Jonas*

In the decades since Regina Jonas became the first ordained woman in Jewish history (1935), the Reform Movement within which she studied and worked has become accustomed to calling its female clergy by the title "rabbi." Although Jonas was permitted to study at the rabbinical seminary at Der Hochschule für die Wissenschaft des Judentums in Berlin in 1924 and had, by 1930, "passed the general obligatory exams in religious history and education, the philosophy of the Talmud, and Hebrew language and Bible study,"[2] and submitted her "halachic work...and a biblical final paper,"[3] she did not receive formal ordination from the institution. Eduard Baneth, the man in charge of rabbinical ordinations at the time, had passed away unexpectedly and was succeeded by Chanoch Albeck, who "represented a conservative viewpoint."[4]

In addition, it was Leo Baeck's wish to "avoid controversy in the general rabbinical council" and, according to Albeck's son as recorded in Elisa Klapheck's *Fraulein Rabbiner Jonas: The Story of the First Woman*

Rabbi, "the Academy committee was dominated by fear of a scandal and the view that Jewry in Germany, despite being liberal, was not yet ready for a female rabbi."[5] The result was that Jonas received "only a certificate of passing the 'Academic Religion Teacher Exam' with a grade of 'overall good.'"[6]

Finally, Jonas was tested and ordained privately[7] on December 26, 1935, by Rabbi Dr. Max Dienemann. It is recalled that Dienemann's advice to Jonas was that "under no circumstances should you call yourself a rabbi."[8] This, despite the fact that Jonas had studied for the rabbinate, had taken the same courses and examinations as her male peers, and had written a halachic work entitled "Can Women Serve as Rabbis?" Her halachic work considered in depth the question of women rabbis from the perspective of Jewish law and concluded that there was no prohibition against women holding such an office. And yet, despite all of this, the institution she studied in, and even the rabbi that personally ordained her, felt uncomfortable with her taking the title of "rabbi."[9]

Almost forty years later, in 1972, when Sally Priesand became the first Jewish woman to be ordained formally by a rabbinical seminary, the Reform Movement overcame Der Hochschule's and Dienemann's apprehensions and she entered the clergy as *Rabbi* Sally Priesand. Soon enough, following Rabbi Priesand's ordination by the HUC-JIR, the Reconstructionist Rabbinical College ordained its first woman rabbi, Sandy Eisenberg-Sasso, in 1974, and the Conservative Movement's Jewish Theological Seminary of America followed suit in 1985 when it ordained Amy Eilberg as its first woman rabbi.

More recently, the question regarding the title that women who undertake the same course of study as their male counterparts should receive has been revived, this time in the Orthodox community.[10] The question of women's ordination in the Orthodox Jewish community started to become a live issue more generally as a result of the sexual revolution of the 1960s,[11] and has grown in importance in recent decades, specifically due to the decision of the Conservative Movement in the 1980s to ordain women rabbis. Orthodox Jews see halachah as a binding force in their lives and so, because Conservative Judaism has always claimed to be a denomination guided by halachah, its rulings have often been more noteworthy in the Orthodox world than those of the Reform Movement, which does not make any such claim. Precisely at the time that the Conservative Movement's Jewish Theological Seminary of America was confronting the question of women's ordination, Orthodox leaders began to discuss the possibilities for their own community.[12]

Although a number of women have (or claim to have) received *s'michah* from Orthodox rabbis, none have yet been formally ordained as *rabbis* from an existing Orthodox rabbinical school.[13]

In recent years, two women in the Orthodox community have propelled the issue of women rabbis further than ever before. In the 1990s, Haviva Krasner-Davidson (now Haviva Ner-David) applied to the Rabbi Isaac Elchanan Theological Seminary at Yeshiva University, the institutional bastion of modern Orthodoxy in America.[14] She received no response to her application to Yeshiva University, but did receive a great deal of attention from the larger Jewish community and beyond. Eventually, she moved to Israel and studied privately with Rabbi Aryeh Strikovsky,[15] from whom she received private ordination. Interestingly, and in a manner reminiscent of Max Dienemann's advice to Regina Jonas decades earlier in Germany, it was reported that "Aryeh Strikovsky, the Orthodox rabbi who ordained her, doesn't want her to use the title ["rabbi"] in places where it might arouse controversy. 'He told me, "The Orthodox community is not ready for it, and they'll just laugh at you.' "[16] In the end, Ner-David's ordination has become a moot point with respect to the Orthodox community, as she has since disassociated herself from the movement. As her bio on the website of the organization she directs states, "Rabbi Dr. Ner-David...considers herself a post-denominational rabbi."[17]

The most recent case of an Orthodox woman following the same course of study as men training for ordination as rabbis is that of Sara Hurwitz. On March 22, 2009, a conferral ceremony was held for

Hurwitz at the Hebrew Institute of Riverdale, New York, under the auspices of Rabbi Avi Weiss. At this ceremony, and in similar fashion to the experience of Regina Jonas, despite studying and being examined on the self-same curriculum and materials as men studying for the rabbinate (incidentally, Rabbi Weiss is also the founder of Yeshivat Chovevei Torah Rabbinical School),[18] Hurwitz was *not* ordained—in fact, the word "ordination" was never used to describe the ceremony— as a *rabbi*. For her conferral ceremony the neologism "MaHaRa"T"[19] was coined.

At the conferral ceremony of Maharat Hurwitz, copies of a document entitled "Responsa Regarding Women's Roles in Religious Leadership" were distributed.[20] The document includes, among other things, a copy of the relatively brief remarks offered at the ceremony by Rabbi Avraham (Avi) Weiss. It is in the context of Weiss's remarks as the conferring rabbi that the ceremony, the document, and the title "maharat" are so noteworthy. The title and role that is being conferred upon Hurwitz is central to his remarks specifically and to the document in general. In addition to Weiss's remarks, three legal responsa are also included in the document. Crucially, the leadership role(s) for women that the authors of the responsa are considering in their legal arguments are inconsistent with Weiss's characterization of what is being conferred. Furthermore, as we shall see, the very title "maharat" belies Weiss's central claim in his remarks. These documents and the legal arguments therein offer some insight as to how at least these four men (rabbis) appear to understand the place of women in relation to the Orthodox rabbinate. As we will see, withholding the title "rabbi" from women and the invention of a new title, along with curtailing the role of women in positions of religious leadership, is not simply a case of "separate and unequal"; rather, it is an exertion of oppressive power on the part of Orthodox Jewish men over Orthodox Jewish women.

Rabbi Avi Weiss is the senior rabbi of the Hebrew Institute of Riverdale, a modern Orthodox synagogue in the Riverdale area of the Bronx.[21] Weiss has been the senior rabbi of this congregation for over thirty years and has often been an advocate for greater equality between the sexes with respect to religious concerns confronting Orthodox women.[22] As reported in the pages of the *New York Times*, in 1997 Weiss hired Sharona Margolin Halickman as the first female congregational intern at his synagogue. This event came only days after Julie Stern Joseph became the first woman to take on such a role in the Orthodox community, when she was hired by the Lincoln Square Synagogue in Manhattan.[23] Halickman went on to become the synagogue's first *madrichah ruchanit* (spiritual guide), described on the Hebrew Institute of Riverdale website as "a member of the professional religious leadership team of the Congregation."[24] After describing the function and role of the *madrichah ruchanit*, the website makes it clear that she "is not a Poseket Halakha, nor can she perform ritual actions in the Synagogue, or at weddings and other Semachot, which Halakha limits to males."[25] It is unclear exactly how to understand the end of this sentence ("which Halakha limits to males"), that is, whether it is a contravention of halachah for Halickman to act as a "Poseket Halakha" (decisor of Jewish law) *and* to perform ritual actions of various kinds, or whether the breach of Jewish law occurs only in the performance of ritual actions (or maybe even that it occurs only with regard to the rituals occurring at "weddings and other Semachot"). In the last two readings, it would seem that the other roles would be prohibited for nonlegal (extra-halachic) reasons.

Leaving this question aside, what *is* clear however is that, even though the description of her role is never explicitly distinguished from that of a male rabbi,[26] the role of *madrichah ruchanit* is unquestionably being delimited in that way. While it certainly would be unnecessary to state that the *madrichah ruchanit* is not a rabbi—after all, the creation of a new title for a woman taking a leadership role in an Orthodox synagogue makes that quite clear—it was still apparently necessary for the Hebrew Institute to make it explicit that the woman filling this position would not be taking on the *roles and responsibilities* traditionally associated with a (male) rabbi. To be clear, it was precisely the roles of "Poseket Halakha" and performer of "ritual actions in the synagogue, or at weddings or other Semachot"—roles traditionally associated with the (male) rabbi—that were indicated as *not* being within the orbit of a woman's leadership role at Weiss's synagogue. The implicit meaning being thus: a woman serving in the role of *madrichah ruchanit* in Weiss's synagogue was not, and could not be, a rabbi because certain roles central to the office of a rabbi cannot be fulfilled by a woman.

In 2004, Sara Hurwitz became the *madrichah ruchanit* at the Hebrew Institute of Riverdale following "three years of learning at Manhattan's Drisha Institute." During her tenure in that position, she "repeated the course work under Weiss' supervision,"[27] which led to her formal conferral as Maharat Sara Hurwitz on March 22, 2009. Hurwitz's conferral as a maharat communicated that Hurwitz was filling some new office, both distinct from that of her previous role as *madrichah ruchanit* and, crucially, from that of a (male) rabbi.

Presumably with the intention of both celebrating the occasion and, at the same time, defending against the appearance of a radical break from tradition, the program for the morning leading up to the conferral ceremony included study sessions on issues related to women in Jewish communal leadership roles.[28] The actual "Tribute and Conferral Ceremony" included speeches from leaders in the modern Orthodox Jewish community as well as a speech from one of the authors of the legal responsa distributed on the day.[29]

The program reached its crescendo with Weiss's remarks and the formal conferral of Hurwitz as maharat, followed by Hurwitz offering her own prepared remarks in the form of a talk entitled "Women in Ritual Leadership: Past, Present, and Future."

In addition to the study sessions and speeches, the document "Responsa Regarding Women's Roles in Religious Leadership" was also distributed at the ceremony. Halachic responsa play the critical role of demonstrating in traditional Orthodox literary form that a given custom, practice, or interpretation of Jewish law is defensible from the Bible, Talmud, and codes of Jewish law.[30] The document includes three responsa from three different rabbis: two in Hebrew with accompanying English translations from rabbis living in Israel and a third in English from an American rabbi. In addition, the document includes a copy of the (unsigned) "Writ of Authorization and Title" in Hebrew and English and, as noted above, a copy of the text of the conferral speech offered by Weiss[31] at the ceremony.[32]

Weiss's remarks emphasize the new title that Hurwitz will receive and the nature of her role once she has been conferred. The speech begins by declaring that "today, we confer on Sara Hurwitz, the title מנהיגה הלכתית רוחנית תורנית—מהרת,[33] as she becomes a religious leader in Israel.[34] This title reflects everything that religious leadership is about and welcomes Sara as a *full*[35] member of the clergy." Over the course of his short speech, Weiss refers to the scope ("full") of Hurwitz's role as a religious leader four more times: "מנהיגה הלכתית רוחנית תורנית—מהרת[36] a halakhic, spiritual and Torah leader. A *full* communal, congregational, religious leader, a *full* member of the clergy, leading with the unique voice of a woman"; "Sara's step of becoming מהרת שרה [Maharat Sara]—a *full* communal, congregational, and religious leader"; and "Sara, under the tutelage of halakhic experts, has studied the established traditional texts that are required to become a religious leader, and based on her mastery of these texts, is assuming a *full* religious leadership position in a synagogue." Although the word "rabbi" is never used in Weiss's speech, it is clear from the repeated reference to the "full"ness of Hurwitz's position that it is the role of the male rabbi that Hurwitz's new position as maharat is being compared to.

When Weiss refers to the fact that Hurwitz "has studied the established traditional texts that are required to become a religious leader," the "established traditional texts" refer to the curriculum of male rabbinical programs, and the "religious leader[s]" he mentions refer to male rabbis. Put differently, and taking Weiss's own synagogue as an example, what it means to be a person assuming "full religious leadership" is to serve in all of the varied roles assumed by male rabbis. These roles include, but are not limited to (and in no particular order), teaching classes and giving sermons, answering questions related to Jewish law, offering pastoral care, leading synagogue services, presiding over life-cycle rituals from birth to death, acting as a member of a religious court for conversions to Judaism, serving as a witness to various life-cycle rituals (weddings and divorces being the most prominent), and, more generally, being a role model of Jewish living for the congregation.[37] "Full religious leadership" for a (male) rabbi in an Orthodox synagogue undoubtedly includes much more than this, but certainly no less. And, of course, part of assuming a position of "full religious leadership" for a male rabbi includes taking on the title of "rabbi."[38]

At the same time that Weiss presses the point that Hurwitz is "a full member of the clergy," he undermines it by explaining the meaning of Hurwitz's new title and the scope of her role as a "full" member of the religious leadership of Israel. In his speech, Weiss explains that "Sara is a מנהיגה הלכתית [manhigah hilchatit], a halakhic leader with the authority to answer questions of Jewish law asked by her congregants and others" and that "Sara is a מנהיגה רוחנית [manhigah ruchanit], a spiritual leader with the qualifications to offer pastoral care and spiritual guidance, and the right to lead life-cycle ceremonies within the framework of halakha." And, finally, that "Sara is a מנהיגה תורנית [manhigah Toranit], with the knowledge to teach Torah, the written as well as the oral law in every aspect of Jewish learning." In this description we see that the roles that Hurwitz will fill as Maharat Hurwitz are limited to responding to questions of Jewish law, pastoral care and spiritual guidance, limited involvement in life-cycle rites, and teaching. Certainly, this distinguishes the role of maharat from that of madrichah ruchanit, for whom halachic decision making was clearly proscribed.[39]

At the same time, however, the responsibilities outlined in Weiss's speech fall far short of describing a "full member of clergy" when measured up against a male rabbi. Weiss's speech is contradictory in that it claims one thing while describing another. As such, it is an apparent attempt to obfuscate the very real differences between the role of a maharat and that of a (male) rabbi.

The distance between the role of a maharat and that of a male rabbi is further underlined in the responsa from the same document. The rabbis whose responsa are collected in the document are, in the order they are presented, HaRav Yoel Bin-nun,[40] Rabbi Dr. Daniel Sperber,[41] and Rabbi Joshua Maroof.[42] The responsa do not address the question of whether or not Orthodox women can become "rabbis." Interestingly, they each provide their own formulation of the question they are responding to. In addition to the clear distinction between the role being considered in the responsa and that of a male rabbi, it is also important to note how each of the authors diminishes what might otherwise be considered a monumental step forward for the role of women in the Orthodox community. Rather than heralding a new age of female not-yet-rabbis who are advancing the improved place of Orthodox women in religious leadership, the authors each offer one or more reasons why this should not be considered the case. In all, three arguments are presented to "contextualize" the justification of this apparently not so new, or not so special, role for women in Orthodoxy. I refer to these three arguments as (1) the argument from history, (2) the argument from capacity, and (3) the argument from redundancy. Each argument offers, in its own way, an undermining of what might otherwise be considered the importance of the moment. The tension between Weiss's heralding of a new role of "full religious leadership" for women in Orthodoxy (even as he describes a role that is anything but that) and the respondents' diminishing of the importance of the moment is unmistakable. Not only is the role of maharat far less than that of a "full member of the clergy" but, as the respondents further argue, the conferral ceremony offered nothing new to the landscape for women in Orthodox Jewish life. Put differently, while Weiss overstates the nature of the role and responsibilities of the maharat, the authors of the responsa understate, and effectively undermine, the importance of the moment for Hurwitz and other Orthodox women who might wish to follow in her footsteps. What is left is a role for women that is, apparently, neither "full" nor all that noteworthy.

As mentioned above, each of the three authors of the responsa offers their own formulation of the question that they are answering. For Bin-nun, his responsum offers an answer to the question "regarding the

possibility of appointing a woman, who has learned Torah, and espe-
cially the *halakhot* of *Orah Hayyim*[43] and *Yoreh Deah*[44] from outstanding
Torah scholars, and who according to her skills, knowledge, *middot*[45]
and lifestyle is worthy of serving in Rabbinic roles, fulfilling a [*sic*]
Rabbinic responsibilities in the community, and to be called *Morateinu*
[Our Teacher], or *Hakhama* [wise one]."[46]

In this responsum, the question being answered is whether or not
a woman, assuming she has fulfilled all the necessary prerequisites related to her education and character ("*middot* and lifestyle"), can "serve
in Rabbinic roles," fulfill "Rabbinic responsibilities," and take a title
appropriate to those roles and responsibilities. What is clearly implied
by "serving in Rabbinic roles" and fulfilling "Rabbinic responsibilities"
is that the roles and responsibilities are part of, but do not amount to
the sum of, the role of a male rabbi. As such, the title "rabbi" would be
out of place, hence the consideration of alternative titles. Here there are
no claims that a woman in this role will be a "full member of the clergy."
Instead of "rabbi"—and, interestingly, instead even of "maharat"—the
titles "Our Teacher" and "wise one" are offered as possibilities.

Bin-nun goes on to explain the meaning of the specific roles and
responsibilities that this woman would take on in this capacity. He
writes that "this question touches upon the questions of offering Torah instruction and teaching Halakha in the community, giving *psak*,[47]
women in authoritative positions (שררה), and the boundaries of modesty (*tzniut*) in an [*sic*] congregation that consists mainly, or entirely, of
men." This elaboration of the question at hand clarifies why the title
"rabbi" is not under consideration: conspicuously absent from the description of rabbinic roles and responsibilities are the additional and, in
the contemporary Orthodox congregational rabbinate, critical rabbinic
roles of prayer leader, life-cycle officiant, and witness to legal-halachic
transactions such as marriages and divorces, as well as the central role
played by rabbis in conversions to Judaism.

In the responsum of Rabbi Dr. Daniel Sperber, the question at hand
is much narrower: "Can a woman answer halachic questions, that is
to say be a halachic decisor?" Here, in contrast to Bin-nun, there is

no mention of "Torah instruction and teaching Halakha in the community" nor of "women in authoritative positions." For Sperber, the question at hand is that of *p'sak halachah* (ruling on questions of Jewish law). It is therefore clear why there is no mention in Sperber's responsum of the question of whether it is permissible in the Orthodox community for women to become rabbis; according to Sperber, all that is at question is the permissibility of a woman to answer questions of Jewish law. This, of course, falls far short of even approximating the responsibilities that come with being a "full member of the clergy."

In the last of the three responsa, Rabbi Joshua Maroof frames the question in a similar vein to Sperber. As Maroof writes, "I was asked to respond to the question of whether a woman who is knowledgeable in Torah Law may issue rulings on matters of halakha." Here again, as with Sperber, the question is narrowly focused on the ability to decide questions of Jewish law, with other concerns left by the wayside. And here again, the question of whether or not women can become rabbis in the Orthodox community is not raised because the role of a rabbi includes so much more than simply that of halachic decisor.

Not surprisingly, given the fact that these responsa were distributed at the conferral ceremony, each of the three respondents answers their stated question in the affirmative. However, in the course of confirming that Jewish law permits women to serve in the limited roles outlined in their questions, the authors manage to further marginalize and minimize the place of women in leadership roles in the Orthodox community. They achieve this by employing one or more of three arguments to support their ruling. As mentioned above, I refer to these three arguments as (1) the argument from history, (2) the argument from capacity, and (3) the argument from redundancy.

The argument from history is found in both the responsa of Binnun and Sperber. As Bin-nun puts it, "This is not a new question and there is nothing in it that is revolutionary, or 'modern.'" Of course, Bin-nun is only at pains to make this clear at the outset (this quote is from the beginning of the third paragraph of a three-and-a-half-page typed responsum) because something new and revolutionary does, in fact, *appear* to be happening. Bin-nun goes on and writes that "the appointment of an exceptional and unique woman to a *tafkid torani* (religious office), even the premier position in its generation, is an act that has been performed from time immemorial"—after which he lists the names of women who held such positions throughout Jewish history: Sarah, Miriam, Devorah, Hannah, the wife of Manoah, the Shunamite, Queen Shlomtzion, Marat Beila, Marat Osnat, and Marat Hava Bachrach. Sperber offers a similar argument from history, declaring that "from the time of our ancestral mothers, Sarah, Deborah the Prophetess, Beruriah the wife of R. Meir, there were learned women who dealt in halachah, and gave halachic rulings." Both authors appeal to Jewish history to downplay what they see as the possibility that one could mistakenly conclude that the conferral of Maharat Hurwitz is a new development for women.

Here again we encounter the tension of the moment: Bin-nun and Sperber declare that nothing new is happening, in the very responsa written for distribution at the conferral ceremony of a woman taking on a new title and role in the Orthodox community. Furthermore, while they claim that nothing new or revolutionary is taking place, Weiss claims (mistakenly, as I have shown) that Hurwitz is taking on the role of a "full member of the clergy," which is certainly nothing short of a new development. Finally, it is curious that both authors can claim that these roles have "been performed from time immemorial" and "from the time of our ancestral mothers," and yet are able to name most of the women known to us from Jewish history who have taken on such roles. These women have unquestionably been the exception in Jewish history, not indicators for the way things have always been. The very fact that we have the names of these few women (some of whom are themselves fictional) does not suggest that nothing new is happening in the conferral of a maharat, but rather that Hurwitz is another rare exception to the rule. And yet, by employing the argument from history, these authors undermine the possibility of Hurwitz being seen as a groundbreaking force for greater equality for women in religious leadership in the Orthodox community.

Instead, according to this argument, she is just another woman doing something that Jewish women have always done.

The second argument, the argument from capacity, can also be found in the responsum of Yoel Bin-nun. In this responsum, the author states that "a community can accept upon themselves an *Isha Hakhama*[48] as their teacher (*Morah*) in Torah, in all of the regular roles of a community and synagogue rabbi." As quoted above, for Bin-nun the "regular roles of a community and synagogue rabbi" are defined as "offering Torah instruction and teaching Halakha in the community, [and] giving *psak*." In this formulation of the argument from capacity, Bin-nun states that a woman can certainly serve as a rabbi while at the same time limiting the definition of what it means to be a rabbi. Better yet, by implying that the rabbinic roles not available to women are other than the "regular roles" of the rabbi, women are not excluded from being "rabbis" as such, but only from performing "special" additional functions only available to men. By downgrading what it means to be a rabbi, Bin-nun is able to allow women into the role. The tension here between extending and retracting is palpable.

The third argument, the argument from redundancy, can be found in the responsum of Rabbi Joshua Maroof. Maroof's responsum considers the larger question of what it means to be a rabbi. Maroof distinguishes between "the original form of *semikha* [ordination]" and "ruling on matters of halakha." According to Maroof, "the original form of *semikha*...was conferred from Rabbi to student from the days of Moshe Rabbenu until persecution led to its discontinuation during the Talmudic period."[49] In effect, this form of ("real") *s'michah* was replaced by what Maroof calls "ruling on matters of halakha." Referring to the second, lesser, form of *s'michah*, Maroof writes that "the core of any given act of הוראה[50] is the process of Torah study upon which it is based and from which it emerges, and that this process is equally accessible to competent men and to competent women." As opposed to the earlier form of *s'michah*, which was handed down from (male) teacher to (male) student, this latter form is, at least in theory, available to anyone (male or female) who studies the material and is successfully examined on it. Furthermore, the earlier form of *s'michah* is of an entirely different nature from the latter form in that, according to Maroof, "the quality of being a מוסמך[51] or a בעל המסורה[52] inheres in the recipient, endowing his person with unique legal authority (שררה) and his decisions with legitimacy and binding force." While it is hard to know what it is that Maroof means when he refers to certain qualities "inhering" in people who received this earlier form of *s'michah*, what *is* clear is that it is of a higher caliber than the form of *s'michah* that eventually replaced it. Not only was the original form of *s'michah* believed to have been handed down in an unbroken chain from Moses, but that it also reflected or invested some new and different quality in the recipient; whereas the latter form of *s'michah* is simply an indicator of a given person's level of knowledge. It is also noteworthy that Maroof does not suggest that, as in the case of "rulings on matters of Halakha," the recipient of the original form of *s'michah* could just as well be female as male. Apparently, the special quality inherent in (male) recipients of the original form of *s'michah* was not present in, or available to, women.

What Maroof seems to be saying is that, first, what it means to be a rabbi today is to answer questions of Jewish law. We have already seen in the argument from capacity that this is a severe downgrading of the role of the contemporary Orthodox rabbi. Secondly, he states clearly that women can be qualified to rule on questions of Jewish law, that is, to receive our diminished form of *s'michah* because, after all, our form of *s'michah* is not the "real" *s'michah* and so it is available to anyone. Here Maroof makes the role of halachic decisor available to women by devaluing it. Third, and finally, Maroof implies that, *if we did have "real" s'michah*, it would be reserved for men only because it is related to certain inherent qualities that, evidently based on the record, are only found in men. Taking these three arguments together, we can understand the argument from redundancy: in effect it states that women can certainly take on this role because, after all, *anyone* can take it on.[53]

Again, as with the argument from history and the argument from capacity, the argument from redundancy leaves us with the conclusion that the conferral of Maharat Hurwitz is not noteworthy. In fact, according to these responsa, her conferral only highlights the meaninglessness of what she has achieved: according to these authors her conferral is neither new nor revolutionary; it is limited in its scope; and it is available to her only because it is available to all.

The chasm between Weiss's overstatement that Maharat Hurwitz is a full member of the clergy and the understatement of the authors of the responsa that, at least when it comes to women in religious leadership, there is nothing new under the sun, is clear, and no doubt, the reality is somewhere between these two poles. Put simply, the fact is that Maharat Hurwitz has more responsibility than in her previous role as *madrichah ruchanit* but less than that of a male rabbi in the Orthodox community. Both Weiss and the authors of the responsa have misrepresented the meaning of this new role and the title that accompanied it. But what of Hurwitz herself?

In her speech at the conferral ceremony, Hurwitz restates many of the themes already discussed above. Echoing the argument from history, she shares her belief that "in every generation there have been 'nashim chachamot' who have felt a spiritual calling and dedicated themselves to the service of their communities" and goes on to list some of the names of women who, rather than crop up in every generation, stand out as rare exceptions. Hurwitz also embraces the argument from capacity when she, the only person bold enough to explicitly identify her role with that of a male rabbi, states that "a rabbi is an authority on halakha....A rabbi is a pastoral counselor...a rabbi is a public leader." By limiting the role of the rabbi, Hurwitz is able to identify with that role, all the while knowing that a rabbi is so much more in practice. She makes this case most strongly when she declares that "when one begins to focus on the day-to-day practical aspects of the rabbinic job, we find that there is a very short list of rabbinic functions that women cannot halakhically perform." As of now, "Orthodox women do not lead services and women are barred from acting as *edim*—witnesses—for marriage, divorce, and conversion....Beyond these few halakhic constraints, women with the appropriate training can perform the other 95 percent of the tasks performed by Orthodox rabbis."

Hurwitz's claim that leading prayer services—which take place thrice- daily in the Orthodox community, not to mention the Sabbath and holiday services—and officiating at critical moments in the life cycle as well as conversions to Judaism account for only 5 percent of the contemporary rabbinate is impossible to defend.[54] It is especially ironic that Hurwitz would make this claim while working at Weiss's synagogue, which has placed prayer and ritual at the very heart of that community's identity.[55] Here one is hard-pressed to avoid the conclusion that Hurwitz is either knowingly obfuscating reality (presumably for political ends) or that she is subject to a state of false consciousness[56] and is in denial about the reality of her situation.

Of all the teachers, speakers, and documents that were a part of the conferral ceremony on March 22, 2009, the only clear understanding of the meaning of what was taking place was heard in the words of Blu Greenberg.[57] In Greenberg's remarks, following her praise for Hurwitz's achievements, she states that

> "even as our hearts are full of praise and joy today…I would be less than candid were I not to acknowledge that even this joyous day has its moments of qualification, that I and many others, and I suspect Sara [Hurwitz] and Rabbi Weiss as well—had hoped that the new credential this day would have been "rabbi," as Sara has shown herself to be qualified both in her learning and her leadership in that she has met the test for 5 years of dedicated and loving service to this congregation, and has passed the same *bechinot* that entitle men to *semicha* and the title of rabbi. I would be less than honest not to wonder aloud whether this is an interim title or one that will stick and become for all time the full fledged female counterpart title for rabbinic leadership."

Greenberg's sage insight and ability to see the conferral ceremony for what it really was—a step, but not the completion of the journey—was a lone voice.[58] It is her appreciation that titles matter that separated her from the other speakers and writers from that day. The difference in title is a reflection of the difference in role and that, even if Hurwitz were correct that her role amounts to 95 percent of that of a male rabbi, as long as there is even 5 percent of difference between them, women will not be "full" members of the clergy alongside male rabbis.

Even in the modern branches of the Orthodox community, men who claim that women are equal while withholding equality from them (in this case, Weiss) and men who offer women equality, but at a cheaper price (Bin-nun, Sperber, and Maroof) serve only to maintain power over women. While these men may not be self-aware of their role, and the women themselves may be subject to false consciousness (as I am suggesting Hurwitz might be), it is nevertheless the case that men in the Orthodox community maintain a paternal grip over women and get to decide *on behalf of women* what they can and cannot be, what titles they can and cannot claim, and what roles they can and cannot take on. The conferral ceremony of Maharat Hurwitz is a clear example of this imbalance of power at work in the Orthodox community.

If Sara Hurwitz is the Regina Jonas of the American modern Orthodox Jewish community, then there is hope that at some point in the next thirty-seven years (the time between Jonas's private ordination and the public ordination of Rabbi Sally Priesand) there will be women rabbis in the Orthodox community. But it will take an honest appraisal of how far women have *and have not* come before that step can be taken.

NOTES

1. In this essay, I offer an analysis of the documents distributed at the conferral ceremony of Maharat Sara Hurwitz. As has been well documented in general and Jewish media outlets, there have been subsequent developments in this story and much controversy within the Orthodox community. These latter developments will not be considered in this essay.

2. Elisa Klapheck, *Fräulein Rabbiner Jonas: The Story of the First Woman Rabbi* (San Francisco: Jossey-Bass, 2004), 34.

3. Ibid.

4. Ibid.

5. Ibid.

6. Ibid.

7. Private ordination refers to students being tested in areas of Jewish law by rabbis outside of the context of a rabbinical seminary or similar institution. For more on the history of rabbinic ordination, see Julius Newman, *Semikhah [Ordination]: A Study of its Origin, History, and Function in Rabbinic Literature* (Manchester: Manchester University Press, 1950).

8. Klapheck, *Fräulein Rabbiner Jonas*, 443.

9. Ibid., 38–93, for a lengthy discussion of the extent to which Jonas was referred to as "rabbi" (*rabbiner/rabbinerin*) following the completion of her studies and up until her final years at Theresienstadt.

10. It is overly simplistic to refer to the Orthodox Jewish community as a singular entity; in truth, there is a spectrum of affiliations within Orthodoxy. Groups commonly identified as part of the Orthodox community include: modern Orthodoxy, centrist Orthodoxy, *Yeshivish*, *Litvak*, Chasidic, *Chareidi*, etc. For more on Orthodox Judaism in America, see Jeffrey S. Gurock, *Orthodox Jews in America* (Bloomington and Indianapolis: Indiana University Press, 2009).

11. For one of the early influential essays to take a progressive view on the subject of women and Orthodox Judaism, see Saul Berman, "The Status of Women in Halakhic Judaism," *Tradition* 14, no. 2 (1972): 5–28.

12. For the best example of this, see the symposium entitled "Women as Rabbis: A Many-Sided Examination of all Aspects, Halakhic— Ethical—Pragmatic," *Judaism* 33, no.1 (1984): 6–90. Noteworthy contributors to the symposium from the Orthodox community are Blu Greenberg, Emanuel Rackman, and Chaim Seidler-Feller.

13. The two best known examples are Mimi Feigelson and Evelyn Goodman-Thau. For more, see Mimi Feigelson, "The Matmida" (no citation available). Also see http://www.jweekly.com/article/ full/17388/outed-as-a-rabbi-orthodox-woman-to-speak-here/ and http://www.haaretz.com/rabbi-thau-versus-rabbi-thau-1.136206.

14. Haviva Ner-David, *Life on the Fringes: A Feminist Journey toward Traditional Rabbinic Ordination* (Needham, MA: JFL Books, 2000).

15. Aryeh Strikovsky is the most senior teacher at the Pardes Institute of Jewish Studies in Jerusalem.

16. http://www.jwi.org/Page.aspx?pid=841.

17. http://www.reutcenter.org/eng/.

18. For more about Weiss's rabbinical school see www.yctorah.org.

19. "MaHaRa"T" is an acronym made up from the sounds of the first letters of four Hebrew words: *Manhigah Hilchatit, Ruchanit, Toranit*, which means Legal, Spiritual, and Torah Guide.

20. The full document can be accessed at http://www.jofa.org/pdf/ Responsa%20on%20Ordination%20of%20Women.pdf.

21. For a sympathetic description of the synagogue community led by Weiss, see Rabbi Sidney Schwartz, *Finding a Spiritual Home: How a New Generation of Jews Can Transform the American Synagogue* (Woodstock, VT: Jewish Lights, 2003), 95–134.

22. Weiss was one of the early supporters of separate women's prayer groups in Orthodox synagogues. For his case on this subject, see Avraham Weiss, *Women at*

Prayer: A Halakhic Analysis of Women's Prayer Groups—Expanded Edition (Hoboken, NJ: Ktav, 2001/1990). Additional examples of Weiss's progressive views on women and Orthodoxy can be found in Avraham Weiss, "Women and the Reading of the Megilah," *The Torah U-Madda Journal* 8 (1998–1999): 295–317; and Jeffrey S. Gurock, *Orthodox Jews in America* (Bloomington: Indiana University Press, 2009), especially chapters 9 and 10.

23. http://www.nytimes.com/1998/02/06/nyregion/unusual-but-not-unorthodox-causing-stir-2-synagogues-hire-women-assist-rabbis.html?pagewanted=all (accessed July 20, 2011). A defunct page on the HIR website contradicts the order of events and states that Margolin Halickman became the congregational intern in 1997, thereby predating Lincoln Square Synagogue and making her the first female congregational intern. See http://www.hir.org/torah/sharona/sharona.html. Rabbi Adam Mintz was the senior rabbi of Lincoln Square Synagogue at the time.

24. http://www.hir.org/madricha_ruchanit.html (accessed January 6, 2011).

25. Ibid.

26. For the purposes of this paper, I will consider the specific role of the synagogue rabbi. While it is true that there are rabbis who are teachers in day schools, chaplains, and university-based educators, etc., these roles are not being considered per se in this essay.

27. Abigail Pogrebin, "The Rabbi and the Rabba," *New York Magazine*, http://nymag.com/news/features/67145/.

28. The three study sessions were: "Honoring Women Torah Scholars: A Sephardic Perspective" presented by Lynn Kaye; "Maintaining Personal Boundaries as a Leader: Biblical and Talmudic Models" presented by Rachel Kohl Finegold and Dr. Carol Fuchs; and "Women's Leadership Avenues in Orthodoxy: History, Challenges, and Triumphs" presented by Dina Najman.

29. The speakers were: Devorah Zlochower, Rabbi Joshua Maroof (responsa author), Rabbi David Silber, and Blu Greenberg.

30. "Codes of Jewish law" refers to those legal works, beginning with the *Mishneh Torah* of Maimonides (1135–1204), that codify Jewish law systematically based on different categories.

31. The text can be compared to a video recording of Weiss's speech—they are essentially identical, http://www.youtube. com/watch?v=CguoGS9Mc0s.

32. There is also a copy of a letter of congratulations from one of the authors.

33. See note 19, above.

34. Here, "Israel" refers to the Jewish people and not the country.

35. Emphasis added here and on each successive use of the word "full."

36. See note 19, above.

37. While some may make the case that a rabbi, from the perspective of Orthodoxy, is halachically defined as no more than someone who has studied Jewish law and passed exams to demonstrate proficiency, such a definition, while possibly technically accurate, is immaterial when measured up against the myriad responsibilities undertaken by the contemporary congregational rabbi.

38. Or another equivalent title, such as "rav," "rebbe," etc.

39. It is worthwhile to ask what has changed—was it merely the lack of training that prevented the *madrichah ruchanit* from deciding questions of Jewish law, or is this a clear example of the sociological tides shifting within the modern Orthodox camp?

40. Rabbi Yoel Bin-Nun is an Israeli educator and *rosh yeshivah* who has spearheaded the revolution in *Tanach* study in Israel, primarily at Yeshivat Har Etzion and the Herzog Teachers' College in Alon Shevut. He has written numerous articles and books on *Tanach*, Jewish history, Jewish thought, and halachah. Bio taken from http://www.yctorah.org/component/option,com_ docman/task,doc_view/gid,703/ (accessed July 21, 2011).

41. Rabbi Dr. Daniel Sperber is a professor of Talmud at Bar-Ilan University in Israel and an expert in classical philology, history of Jewish customs, Jewish art history, Jewish education, and Talmudic studies. Bio taken from http://www.torahinmotion.org/spkrs_crnr/faculty/bioDanielSperber.htm (accessed July 21, 2011).

42. Rabbi Joshua Maroof was the rabbi of Magen David Sephardic Congregation-Bet Eliahu Synagogue in Rockville, Maryland. He received his baccalaureate degree with honors from the State University of New York at Stony Brook and his master's degree in Educational Psychology from the City University of New York (CUNY). He received *s'michah* (ordination) from Rabbi Yisrael Chait, Rosh Yeshiva of Yeshiva B'nai Torah in Far Rockaway, New York. Bio taken from http://www.mdscbe.org/OurRabbi.html (accessed July 21, 2011).

43. One of the four sections of the *Shulchan Aruch*, dealing with the laws of daily life.

44. Another one of the four sections of the *Shulchan Aruch*, dealing with, among other things, dietary laws.

45. Character traits.

46. An English translation of Bin-nun's responsa is included in the document. The translation is by Mishael Zion.

47. Answering questions of Jewish law.

48. A wise woman.

49. See note 7, above.

50. *Hora-ah* (legal ruling).

51. *Musmach* (ordinee).

52. *Baal HaMesorah* (master of the tradition).

53. This formulation is reminiscent of the statement of Rabbi Herschel Schachter, *rosh yeshivah* of Yeshiva University, who, in reference to the question of whether a woman is permitted to read the marriage document under the wedding canopy at an Orthodox wedding, wrote, "Yes, even if a parrot or a monkey would read the *kesuba*, the marriage would be one hundred percent valid." Interestingly, there is an editor's note at the beginning of the essay that reads in part: "The statement about monkeys or parrots reading the *kesuba* was clearly intended to dramatize the *halachic* insignificance of the reading of the *kesuba* from the standpoint of the *siddur kiddushin* (marriage ceremony). It was not intended to imply or insinuate anything else." http://www.torahweb.org/torah/2004/ parsha/rsch_dvorim2.html (accessed July 21, 2011).

54. It is true that in the Orthodox rabbinate there is no requirement for rabbis to lead prayer services. Many Orthodox synagogues, in fact, employ cantors or can rely on (male) members of the laity to lead services. The extent to which Orthodox rabbis lead prayer services is different from congregation to congregation. There is no doubt, however, that the ability to do so, especially on special occasions, adds to the charismatic authority of the rabbi in his given community.

55. See note 21, above.

56. For an argument against the claims of false consciousness, see Tova Hartman, *Feminism Encounters Traditional Judaism: Resistance and Accommodation* (Waltham, MA: Brandeis University Press, 2007). For another argument against the conclusion of false consciousness in the Muslim world, see Saba Mahmood, *Politics of Piety: The Islamic Revival and the Feminist Subject* (Princeton, NJ: Princeton University Press, 2005).

57. Greenberg is the matriarch of the Orthodox feminist community.

58. Maroof comes close to Greenberg's observation, although does not go so far as to lament the fact that Hurwitz was not given the title of "rabbi" or that she would not fill the role of a (male) rabbi. For Maroof's speech at the conferral ceremony, see http://www.youtube.com/watch?v=wNZLnXdwi2Q.

PERSONAL REFLECTION

The Presence of Women Rabbis
A Transformation of the Rabbinate and of Jewish Life

RABBI SAM GORDON

With women rabbis a reality in many parts of the Jewish world for over forty years, it can be easy to take this fact for granted and overlook the significance of this shift in the Jewish community. The ordination of women rabbis has meant that women now hold positions of authority and power as never before in our history. It means that women's voices are part of Jewish life as never before. And with these changes, we can understand more clearly both the gift that a fuller range of voices and experiences bring and also what happens when these voices are silenced.

Think about the biblical story of the *Akeidah*, the near sacrifice of Isaac by his father Abraham. Sarah, his mother, is not present as this story progresses, and her absence adds to its tragic nature.

The *Akeidah* is a story of action, not emotion. Abraham displays neither introspection nor doubt. He is not a skeptic. *Sarah* is the one who laughed when God announced that at her late age she would bear a child. *She* was the skeptic. *She* doubted the word of God. Sarah questioned God's promise and laughed at the very idea of a miracle. Sarah laughed at the seeming absurdity of this prophecy from God. She showed no intimidation or fear. But Sarah is not around when

God tests Abraham by telling him to take his son, Isaac, and offer him up as a sacrifice on Mount Moriah. Abraham is commanded to do the unthinkable, to sacrifice his son, and Abraham responds without a question. There was no doubt, no skepticism. Abraham did not laugh, and the skeptical voice of Sarah is not heard. If only Sarah *had* been present at that critical time. Perhaps if Sarah had been there, she would have questioned this test. Perhaps the story would have unfolded differently, and less traumatically. The rabbis in the midrash recognize Sarah's absence. They look at the text and ask: Why does it say, "And Abraham rose up early in the morning"? Why early in the morning? Because Abraham said to himself, "It may be that Sarah will not give permission for us to go. So, I will get up early while Sarah is still asleep. It is best that no one sees us."

This biblical story is a cautionary tale, teaching us that Abraham's blind obedience is an example of what happens when the voice of the woman is silenced. Certainly not every woman would doubt the voice of God, or be skeptical or laugh, but Sarah is the paradigm of the one who does. The story of the *Akeidah* reminds us of the danger inherent in not hearing her voice.

Recent events remind me of the need for the voice of Sarah in our world. We are hearing the voice of women on college campuses, demanding that they be heard in cases of sexual harassment and violence. Emma Sulkowicz, a senior at Columbia University, has been recognized for her performance piece "Carry That Weight," as she has carried her mattress around the campus as a protest against sexual assault on campus and the failure of university officials to adequately address those assaults and punish the perpetrators. Similar voices are being heard on other campuses, in the military, and in other fields.

When the NFL domestic abuse scandals occurred, the *New York Times* ran a story on the front page of the Sports section titled "In Coverage of NFL Scandals, Female Voices Puncture the Din." It mentioned ESPN anchor Hannah Storm, Rachel Nichols of CNN, and Katie Nolan of Fox Sports. The *Times* pointed out that the domestic abuse story was seen differently through women's eyes, and their voices helped to define the issue of a culture of violence and misogyny.

The American rabbinate, and indeed Jewish life as a whole, has been transformed by the presence of women rabbis. I consider myself fortunate indeed that I became a rabbinical student and then a rabbi at the very beginning of that movement. I have spent my entire career working with women rabbis as equal colleagues. I still remember my first CCAR Convention in Pittsburgh in 1980, at which Reverend William Sloane Coffin spoke and stated that the most important issue in the women's liberation movement was liberating the female within each male.

The American rabbinate has been profoundly changed for the better by the entrance of women rabbis who have been fully integrated into the leadership of the American Jewish world. That is true for the Reform, Conservative, and Reconstructionist Movements, but it is still not the case within Orthodox Judaism. While some progress is being made in the Open Orthodox group within Orthodoxy, it still does not approach equality in the role of women.

A recent scandal in Washington demonstrates the danger of exclusive male rabbinic authority. Rabbi Barry Freundel, a highly respected modern Orthodox rabbi, was arrested and convicted of setting up cameras in the showers and changing areas of the mikveh, the ritual bath, attached to his synagogue. This was an incredible violation of privacy, trust, and authority. Rabbi Freundel was a leading figure in conversion within the Orthodox community, and it appears that he particularly targeted women studying for conversion, as well as the many Orthodox women who use the mikveh on a monthly basis.

The human impact was enormous. The female victims of his voyeurism were often in their most vulnerable and powerless state. Indeed, the very nature of Orthodox Judaism creates a power imbalance between male rabbis and their female students and congregants. Women studying for traditional conversion are particularly dependent on Orthodox male rabbis, who exercise complete control of the process.

Within Orthodox Judaism, women still cannot be rabbis, judicial witnesses, or members of the court determining conversion status. The voice of the woman is largely silent within Orthodoxy. The Freundel case is a result of an all-male system of religious authority. Male rabbis maintain exclusive control over the laws of Orthodox conversions, and that power can too often be used capriciously and irrationally. While Orthodox rabbinic authority seldom results in sexual abuse, the power imbalance is very real. It might be possible to argue that Rabbi Freundel was a deeply flawed individual whose alleged sexually exploitative acts have no wider implications. But I would disagree. The absence within Orthodoxy of women rabbis of equal stature and authority to the male rabbis creates a culture where abuse of authority is more likely. In contrast, the role of women rabbis in liberal Judaism serves as a counterbalance to an anachronistic patriarchal tradition.

So I return to the story of the *Akeidah*. How might the story have been different had Sarah's voice been heard? What would the mother of Isaac have answered if she had been the one to be tested by God? Where was her laughter, her doubt, her skepticism? We regret not hearing Sarah's voice, but we do know the result of that silence. The very next chapter is *Chayei Sarah*—"Sarah's Life." But the story isn't about Sarah's life. Genesis 23 begins: "The life of Sarah came to 127 years. And Sarah died in Kiryat Arba—Hebron." Sarah died. The lesson is learned. Sarah's voice brought life, laughter, skepticism, and doubt. Without that voice, there was silence; there was death. The more voices we hear, the more we understand each other and the more we can do to care for each other and our communities. With the presence of women rabbis working alongside men rabbis, our communities are healthier, and Jewish life is richer.

PERSONAL REFLECTION

Growing Up with Women Rabbis as Role Models

Rabbi Michael S. Friedman

Perhaps I am the wrong person to ask about being influenced by women rabbis. I was raised to know that there is nothing in the world that a woman cannot do. My mother made sure we understood that. She didn't only preach and teach it, she lived it. She made a point of pursuing a successful career, working throughout my youth at IBM during a period when women were a small minority at that corporation.

Sally Priesand and Sally Ride were unquestionably trailblazers, but for me, female clergy or female astronauts were no big deal. Barbara Ostfeld-Horowitz was the first woman to be invested as a cantor by Hebrew Union College–Jewish Institute of Religion (HUC-JIR). She was hired by my childhood synagogue, Temple Beth-El of Great Neck, New York, immediately after her investiture in 1976. Deborah Hirsch became the synagogue's first female rabbi in 1982. Our senior rabbi, Jerry Davidson, was a pioneer in establishing equality on the bimah. By the time I came of age, a woman on our bimah was far from newsworthy.

When Rabbi Susie Moskowitz arrived at Temple Beth-El in 1991, I was a shy and lost ninth grader. She called and asked me to come to a youth group event. "I want you to try it. I think you'll like it." That one phone call changed my life. The next month she asked me to participate in youth Shabbat. The following month she asked me to run for the youth group board...and all these years later here I am.

Somehow Susie recognized potential in me that I did not see in myself. When I became the ritual chair of my youth group, she taught me the *matbei-a t'filah* step by step. ("There are always two prayers between *Bar'chu* and *Sh'ma.*") She taught me how to be a *sh'liach tzibur*—a service leader. ("Sometimes it's okay just to be quiet.") She enjoyed teaching and was immensely patient with my innumerable questions. She loved seeing teenagers explore their potential and discover the person they are coming to be. I have spent much of my career working with teens, and most of what I do I learned from her example. If I am half as successful in engaging teens as she is, then I will be immensely proud of my rabbinate.

The summer before my senior year of high school, soon after I was elected youth group president, Karen Bender assumed her role as our congregation's new assistant rabbi. Karen was the coolest rabbi I had ever met—heck, she was the coolest *adult* I had ever met. She was fearless and irreverent and self-aware. She modeled honesty and authenticity with a vigor that thrilled my teenage self. I loved her for the respect she showed me and the way she pushed me to new insights about myself, about Judaism, about the world.

If Karen was a trailblazer for me, it is because she was the first openly gay adult to play an important role in my life. It's not that she had to convince us that homosexuality was okay; she didn't, and didn't try. It's that we never actually knew any (openly) gay people before her. I cheered her marriage in 1996, and I cheered Rabbi Davidson when he chose to openly bless Karen and her partner in front of the congregation. To this day, when I sense that I am not living authentically, I hear Karen's voice asking, "Well, why not?"

In the course of my education, I read the works of Rachel Adler, Judith Plaskow, and others who laid the theoretical foundation for the full inclusion of women in liberal Jewish life. I had occasion to hear Sally Priesand speak about breaking barriers as she gained admission to HUC-JIR, studied at the Cincinnati campus, and made her way in the rabbinate. Thanks to them, I was fortunate to grow up in a time when I viewed women rabbis as...utterly commonplace.

To me, Susie Moskowitz and Karen Bender were never women rabbis. They were rabbis who are women. Most importantly, they are *extraordinary* rabbis.

PERSONAL REFLECTION

A Man's Experience of Women in the Rabbinate

RABBI JEFFREY KURTZ-LENDNER

I grew up in a family that was involved in an egalitarian Conservative synagogue in Buffalo, New York. I became active in my youth group during high school in the early 1980s and was proud of the fact that the women and girls in our congregation participated equally. My younger sister had an amazing bat mitzvah. In my congregation, girls and boys participated equally, with the exception of a tallit, and we were all offered the chance to shine. My sister worked very hard and led more of the service than most other students. She read from the Torah, chanted the haftarah, and led both *Shacharit* and *Musaf*. And then at the end of the service I joined her on the bimah, and we sang *Adon Olam* together with harmony. My mother cried during *Adon Olam*. All of this was possible because in my synagogue there were virtually no differences in opportunities for boys and girls.

Yet, when I attended youth group regional conventions, egalitarianism was not yet fully established, and those who remained traditional often projected an aura of greater authenticity. While I was passionate about my egalitarianism, there were times when I experienced a sense of inferiority in my conversations of synagogue practice with some of my more traditional peers.

I was in high school when the Jewish Theological Seminary of America (JTS) decided to allow women to be rabbis in 1983, ordaining Rabbi Amy Eilberg in 1985 as its first woman rabbi. That decision had a profound impact on my own journey into the rabbinate. Having always been passionate about religious equality for women, I was overjoyed that my movement had taken this step that supported my own philosophy. As long as the Conservative Movement had failed to ordain women, my belief in egalitarianism remained secondary. By deciding to ordain women, my philosophy was validated. And, eventually, my view came to be the primary approach of the Conservative Movement, a development I did not anticipate.

By the time I began rabbinical school at JTS in 1990, more than half of my class was made up of women. The presence of women made a very real, tangible impact on the experience of being a rabbinical student, rather than making a political or philosophical statement. As rabbis we need to attend to the needs of *all* of our members, and a mixture of genders in our classes helps each of us to grow professionally in ways that a single-gender profession could never reach. I am a better rabbi when I am more sensitive to the needs of women and men alike. The presence of women in my classes and as colleagues has helped me to strengthen my own ability to better understand the totality of human experience.

In 2004, I became a member of the Central Conference of American Rabbis and joined the Reform Movement. One early difference I experienced with my new movement was that it has had women rabbis since the early 1970s, over a decade sooner than the movement from which I had come. There were also many more women in positions of movement leadership in the CCAR than there were in the Rabbinical Assembly. In fact, Rabbi Janet Marder was the president of the CCAR at the time that I was admitted to membership.

The prominence of women rabbis in the Reform Movement and in its leadership, I believe, has fostered the expansion of other demographics within the Movement. When I was a student at JTS in the mid-1990s, many of my peers and I supported the concept of ordaining gay and lesbian rabbis. The leadership of the Conservative Movement at that time was far from ready to move in that direction. Interestingly, my own peers are now in leadership positions within the Movement. In 2006, JTS approved the admission of gay and lesbian students to its rabbinical school, and its first openly gay rabbi was ordained in 2011.

These developments are now old news within the Reform Movement. As a rabbi in the CCAR, whether my colleagues and friends are male or female, straight or gay is not noteworthy. During my ten years as part of the CCAR I have developed friendships with many of my CCAR colleagues. Together we work to further the impact of Reform Movement values on the Jewish community as well as striving to strengthen that community as a whole. When I discuss issues with colleagues, the conversations are the same whether my colleagues are male or female, straight or gay. The conversations are about synagogue programming, retaining teen members, working with boards of directors as well as career issues, options, and opportunities. We are not distracted by judgmental issues of identity. Instead, *all* of our members are equally invested in the success of our thriving three-thousand-year-old heritage.

The inclusion of Jews who were previously excluded from the conversation—women, gays, lesbians, multicultural Jews, and all of those our movement has embraced as equals and as peers—has enriched the entire Jewish people. And on a very personal level these conversations have equally enriched those rabbis, like myself, who were for far too long blocked from any such dialogue at all.

Women Rabbis and Feminism

It would be an oversimplification to state that women rabbis are, by definition, feminists. On the other hand, as this section will show, the first generation of women rabbis and the feminist movement enjoy a shared history. Rabbi Laura Geller ("Women Rabbis and Feminism: On Our Way to the Promised Land"), the third woman to be ordained, reflects on her experiences and the parallel paths of feminism and Judaism in the 1970s and the intervening years.

Women's contributions to text have gone unheard for far too long. In her piece, Rabbi Oshrat Morag ("'I Find by Experience': Feminist Praxis of Theology and Knowledge") introduces the notion that feminist thought has had a lasting impact on ritual practice, thereby allowing for the emergence of a uniquely feminist religious experience. Rabbi Kari Hofmaister Tuling, PhD ("Shifting the Focus: Women Rabbis and Developments in Feminist Theology") furthers this with her assertion that gender and leadership directly influence, modify, and even change our understanding of theological premises.

Rabbi Rebecca W. Sirbu ("Real Men Marry Rabbis: The History of the Jewish Feminist Movement") examines the social upheaval out of which the feminist movement emerged and how it spurred Jewish women to redefine their role in Jewish communal life, while Rabbi Carole B. Balin, PhD ("Betty Friedan's 'Spiritual Daughters,' the ERA, and the CCAR") considers the role that women rabbis played in the (still unsuccessful) passage of the Equal Rights Amendment.

Finally, this section concludes with two very different personal reflections. With the number of female rabbinical students outnumbering their male counterparts, Rabbi Daniel Kirzane ("Finding a Seat at the Right Table: Gender at HUC-JIR") shares the discovery of his male privilege while being in the minority as a rabbinical student. Rabbi Susan Silverman ("Becoming a Woman of the Wall") expresses her Judaism by forcing past the narrowness established by the male rabbinate in Israel.

22

WOMEN RABBIS AND FEMINISM

On Our Way to the Promised Land

RABBI LAURA GELLER

The history of women wanting to be rabbis didn't begin with Rabbi Sally Priesand. Since the 1890s, the question was raised in the Anglo-Jewish press and in certain Jewish organizations. Beginning in the 1920s, women applied and some even were admitted to rabbinical school, though none were permitted to be ordained.[1]

That changed in 1972, the year Rabbi Priesand was ordained. It was just nine years after *The Feminine Mystique*[2] had been published. The feminist movement was beginning to enable women to discover their own voices and raise questions about equality between men and women. Critical issues of the day focused on equal pay for equal work and the ability of women to enter professional schools that had preciously restricted the number of women who could be admitted.

Questions about equality were emerging in the Jewish world as well. In 1971, a student magazine, *Davka*, published the now classic article by Rachel Adler called "The Jew Who Wasn't There: Halakha and the Jewish Woman."[3] It was the first time that anyone had looked at the question of Jewish law from a feminist perspective. That perspective empowered a group of women who called themselves "Ezrat Nashim" to challenge the Conservative Movement in 1972 to count women in a minyan. Their success eventually led to new kinds of questions, no longer just about the equality of women but also about the experience of women as religiously engaged Jews.

In 1976 I was ordained as the third woman rabbi in the Reform Movement. I had been the only woman in my class; there were as yet no women professors teaching Rabbinics. One day when my Talmud class was studying Tractate *B'rachot*, I discovered the tradition that a Jew is to say one hundred blessings a day. My teacher explained, "God is present at every moment. We make that Presence real through saying blessings. There is no important moment in the lifetime of a Jew for which there is no blessing." Suddenly I realized that it was not true. There had been important moments in my life for which there was no blessing. One such moment was when I first got my period. Suddenly I remembered something I had long forgotten—being a thirteen-year-old girl reporting to my mother that I had just got my period, and hearing my mother say to me, "When I got my period, my mother slapped me!" She didn't know why—just that it was a tradition. I began to wonder in that Talmud class: What if my mother and I had prepared for that moment in a spiritual way? What if we had celebrated it together by saying a blessing: "Thank You, God, for making me a woman," or "Thank You, God, for keeping us in life and bringing us to this sacred moment." What impact would that have had on my sense of myself as a woman and as a Jew? What would Judaism look like if what my teacher taught were true: there should be no important moment in the lifetime of Jew for which there is no blessing? How would Judaism be different if women's experiences were truly celebrated as part of Jewish experience?

Years later, Rachel Adler reflected on that story in her book *Engendering Judaism*. "Geller's story depicts a paradoxical situation. She appears to be a full participant in an egalitarian Judaism. She is even a rabbinical student. But her internal experience is of exclusion: vital components of her personhood have been ignored. What is more, her invisibility is invisible. Her teacher and classmates do not know that they do not see her....Geller's story suggests...that egalitarian Judaism may integrate women as participants by ignoring their distinctive experiences and concerns as women."[4]

Another similar moment occurred when my class studied the Talmudic *sugya* that describes intercourse with a little girl as "nothing... (it is only) as if one puts a finger into the eye" (Babylonian Talmud, *K'tubot* 11b). While I understood that the Rabbis were trying to protect the girl by asserting that she was really still a virgin and therefore the rape wouldn't affect her bride price, to me this was a "text of terror."[5] No one, neither my male classmates nor my male professor, understood how painful this text was for me. How could the rape of a little girl be "nothing"? To me, it was very personal; I was once a little girl.

A year before my ordination, in 1975, the CCAR had published its new prayer book, *Gates of Prayer*. The introduction contained an important statement: "We have been...keenly aware of the changing status of women in our society. Our commitment in the Reform Movement to the equality of the sexes is of long standing. In this book, it takes the form of avoiding the use of masculine terminology exclusively when we are referring to the human race in general."[6] It was a radical idea in those days that women were actually part of the Jewish community. It took years for the consciousness to evolve that we also need to change the way we speak about God, to liberate us from the gendered metaphors of God as exclusively father and king. Until we can imagine a Divinity that transcends gender, it is hard to speak about women and men as truly equal, each created in the image of God.

In 1979, when there were still only a handful of women rabbis in the Reform Movement (and none yet in the Conservative Movement—that didn't happen until 1985), the CCAR Convention was scheduled to take place in Arizona, a state that had not supported the Equal Rights Amendment, the proposed amendment to the United States Constitution designed to guarantee equal rights for women. It felt important that women rabbis be at the convention, but we wanted to honor the boycott of non-ERA states. Not knowing what to do, I called Betty Freidan. Her advice was clear: "Go to the convention and invite me to speak!" We did, and that speech was the first time Betty Friedan made a public connection between her feminism and her Judaism.

Friedan began her remarks to the convention:

> Sometimes history books say that the modern Woman's Movement began with my book *The Feminine Mystique*. Many people have asked me…what made me do it? Probably the simplest answer is that my whole life made me do it, or that I grew up as a Jewish girl in Peoria, Illinois. I grew up isolated and feeling the injustice, the burning injustice of the subtle and not so subtle anti-Semitism that was the experience of my generation. Girls and boys grew up in towns like Peoria, where we were very largely isolated and where there was the injustice, the irrationality of being barred from sororities, fraternities, and all the other things, like country clubs, that you were barred from as Jews. I think that the passion against injustice that I have had all my life must have come from that.…I had this burning feeling, all that I am I will not deny. It's the core of me. I had this feeling as a Jew first. First as a Jew before I had it as a woman. All that I am I will not deny. And if I've had strength and passion, and if that somehow has helped a little bit to change the world or the possibilities of the world, it comes from that core of me as a Jew. My passion, my strength, my creativity, if you will, comes from this kind of affirmation.…
>
> All the visions of the world, all the passions of injustice, all the things that had been a part of me, that I think, therefore I am; that was also true of me. You can see why so many Jewish women particularly gave their souls to feminism, when you think of all these girls brought up by the book, brought up to the book, to the worship of the word, as our brothers were. When you think of all the passion and energy of our immigrant grandmothers, in the sweatshops without knowing the language! When you think of mothers rearing sons to be doctors, and coping with all the realities of life! When you think of all of that passion, all of that strength, all of that energy, suddenly to be concentrated in one small apartment, one small house as happened with Portnoy's mother!…A lot of women realized they were not alone and we broke through the feminine mystique. A lot of women began to say, "All that I am I will not deny."…
>
> And I always thought that the unique aspect of the Woman's Movement, which is what made it change things so rapidly, comes from the unique experience of women. Later, as my children, my

own son and my spiritual daughters (some of whom are in this room), began to educate me on Jewish theology, I discovered that it's also profoundly Jewish. Someone said to me: "The essence of Jewishness [is]…that it's not just holy words and some secret pact with God, or some ritual, but it is actions, deeds in society." I guess I'm very Jewish, because that was my whole legacy to the Woman's Movement: that we take action, not words, to break through the barriers that keep us from participating.[7]

It is hard for us now to remember all those barriers that Betty Freidan spoke of, now that as of 2015 there are 669 women rabbis in the Reform Movement. It is hard to remember those barriers when we know that there are Orthodox women who function as rabbis, though their official title is "maharat." Pioneer Sara Hurwitz, ordained by Rabbi Avi Weiss and Rabbi Daniel Sperber, is the dean of Yeshivat Maharat, whose mission is to confirm Orthodox women as halachic and spiritual leaders. It is hard to remember those barriers when in Los Angeles, in a groundbreaking appointment, the Academy for Jewish Religion, California, selected Tamar Frankiel as its new president, making her the first Orthodox woman to lead an American rabbinical school.

But it is important to remember what it was like in the late 1970s. One memorable moment was on a radio show where a very well known Jewish host demanded of me, "What is more important—your Judaism or your feminism?" I paused, and then asked him, "And what is more important to you, your heart or your liver?" Silence. I was never invited back on the show!

In 1980, leaders of the Women's Rabbinic Network (an organization of Reform Women Rabbis founded in 1980) collected data "summarizing the accumulated fears of congregants, boards, and senior rabbis with regard to hiring women as rabbis." The apprehension ranged from the perception that women couldn't be successful to the fear that women would be too successful. In fact, the final concern was: "Women who succeed will reflect poorly on their colleagues. If women can read from the Torah, preach, and teach, the rabbis' duties become accessible to everyone. The mystique is lost. This possibly leads to the breakdown of the hierarchy of the rabbi-congregant relationship."[8]

Part of that is indeed true. The ordination of women has led to a breakdown of hierarchy between rabbis and congregation. It has re-shaped Jewish institutions, particularly the synagogue. In 1976, at the conclusion of High Holy Day services during my first year as a rabbi, a congregant rushed up to talk with me. "Rabbi, I can't tell you how different I feel about services because you are a woman. I found myself feeling that if you can be a rabbi, then I could be a rabbi, too. Seeing you as rabbi makes me realize that I can take responsibility for my own Jewish life." That congregant was a man. I didn't fully understand his reaction until I shared it with a woman who was an Episcopal priest.[9] She told me that when she consecrates the Eucharist, a highly scripted and central moment in her worship, she wears the same robes and follows the same pattern as any male priest. Still, she reported, people take the Eucharist differently from her. Why? She believes it is because people are used to being fed by women, so the experience is less mysterious, less hierarchical, and more shared.

With women as clergy, the boundary between clergy and laity begins to break down, and shared leadership becomes possible. Laypeople become empowered to take responsibility for their own religious lives. This has led to an explosion of interest in adult learning and to changing models of pedagogy to promote more shared learning and *chevruta* work. It has also changed the model of relationships between professionals, with more collaboration and less hierarchy. Career patterns are changing as we see more clergy teams in congregations rather than the old model of senior rabbis, associates, and assistants.

The breakdown of religious hierarchy has also led to the desire to be a participant instead of a passive observer in prayer. This shift changes the nature of liturgical music; it affects the way we organize prayer experience and even the way we use sacred space. More and more synagogues, like Temple Emanuel of Beverly Hills, have redesigned their sanctuaries so seating is flexible, enabling different kinds of worship experience where people can see the face of God in the faces of other people by praying in the round, with participants facing each other. In this sense the move toward synagogue transformation is an outgrowth of Jewish feminism. It has led to a more inclusive Judaism and to more openness to spirituality.

It has also led to a new understanding of life-cycle rituals, as we celebrate the truth that divinity is present at every moment in our lives and we can celebrate that through blessings and ceremonies that honor the Torah of our lives as well as the Torah of tradition. It began with the creation of rituals for women: rituals for menarche, rituals for menopause, rituals for entering our daughters into the covenant, rituals for weaning, rituals for miscarriage and abortion. And it continues now as we notice a new life stage—between midlife and frail old age. The baby boomer generation is entering this new stage now, and with it comes an interest in rituals to mark new transitions: retirement, moving out of a family home, becoming a grandparent, removing a wedding ring after the death of a spouse, significant birthdays, or finding a way to move on even as one cares for a beloved spouse with dementia. Our male colleagues have joined in this liturgical creativity. Once these rituals were only photocopied and circulated among friends; now they are not only shared online but also published in rabbis' manuals and other volumes.

Reform rabbis in Los Angeles used to use the ocean as a mikveh for conversion because all the local ritual baths were Orthodox. When the University of Judaism (now American Jewish University) built its mikveh in 1981, I began to bring women there for healing rituals—an adult survivor of childhood incest, a college student after an abortion, a woman whose doctor declared her free of cancer. Now I bring men as well to the mikveh—a community leader celebrating his sixtieth birthday, a man ready to move forward after divorce. Mikveh is a powerful experience that often opens a door to a deeper spirituality. It is no wonder that the Reform Movement is celebrating a return to ritual and tradition; much of the impetus for it is the outgrowth of Jewish feminism and the leadership of women rabbis. Women rabbis have not only changed Judaism for other women; we have changed the face of Judaism for all Jews.

What began in the early 1970s as a movement focused on women's equality has also led to the transformation of Jewish theology and prayer. Once it became clear that women could be counted in a minyan, the next question was, how do women pray? Are tallit and *t'fillin* prayer garb of all Jews who pray, or just of Jewish men? This question continues to animate the struggle at the Kotel, where women have been, until recently, forbidden to pray in ritual garb. And when we take prayer seriously, the next question is: Who is the God we want to speak toward, and how do we find a language in prayer that reflects the complexity of how Jews experience God? Perhaps the resurgence of interest in Jewish mysticism is connected in part to the changes created by women rabbis over the past forty years.

The legacy of the past forty years of women in the rabbinate is that feminism is no longer on the margins of Judaism; it has transformed Judaism. Women are part of the story. Gender has become a lens to view all of Jewish experience. The explosion of Jewish feminist scholarship over the past forty years is breathtaking, nurtured in part by the dialogue between women rabbis and women scholars. Dr. (now Rabbi) Rachel Adler's book *Engendering Judaism* won the National Jewish Book Award—not in Jewish feminism, but in Jewish theology.

The Open Door,[10] edited by Rabbi Sue Elwell and illustrated by Ruth Weisberg, doesn't use the word "feminist." It doesn't have to. It is the Hagaddah of a movement that has been transformed by feminism. It is an inclusive Hagaddah, with writings of women and men, of Jews of all different backgrounds and sexual orientations. Feminism's focus on the marginality of women allowed us to notice which other groups have also been marginalized: gay and lesbian Jews, Jews of color, interfaith families, just to name a few. The contemporary notion of a "big Jewish tent" is in part the result of this consciousness. The Reform Movement's prayer book *Mishkan T'filah* was shepherded to publication by Rabbi Elyse Frishman; the new *machzor Mishkan HaNefesh* had as one of its editors Rabbi Janet Marder. Women are shaping the way we think about prayer and the way we pray. Women of Reform Judaism and URJ Press have published the *The Torah: A Women's Commentary*,[11] edited by Dr. (now Rabbi) Tamara Ezkenazi and Rabbi Andrea Weiss. It is used in our synagogues, alongside *The Torah: A Modern Commentary*, edited by Rabbi Gunther Plaut;[12] it asks questions about the experience of women that Rabbi Plaut never imagined.

Forty years…exactly how long it took us to reach the Promised Land. Are we there yet? Is the journey over? We asked the same question after twenty years. Then there were still significant differences between the careers of men and women rabbis. Women tended to serve in positions as assistants rabbis, campus and hospital chaplains, and educators, and no women served as senior rabbis of major metropolitan congregations. Some colleagues argued that women were choosing different career paths because they were looking for balance, intimacy, and empowerment in their rabbinates; others believed there was a stained-glass ceiling. I felt that both explanations were true and that until we paid attention to the real issues of discrimination against women that still existed, there would never be full equality. Those issues included the significant salary discrepancy between women and men rabbis, the difficulty of counting on adequate maternity leaves, and the reality of sexual harassment and boundary violations.

In the intervening years, the Reform Movement has confronted the issue of sexual boundary violation. The CCAR created a Code of Ethics that set tough standards and sanctions, enabling victims to feel safe about reporting rabbis who have transgressed boundaries. Some of those victims have been women rabbis. The old message that our institutions just look the other way has been replaced by the mandate to train rabbis about the devastation caused by sexual harassment and the establishment of a procedure to investigate complaints and monitor disciplinary action.

But some things haven't changed. Salary inequity remains an issue. So does the very real difficulty of balancing family life against the demands of a career in the rabbinate. Women's career paths still look different from men's. There is still a relatively small number of women serving as senior rabbis of large congregations, though as of this writing five women have newly stepped into senior positions. In the larger Jewish world, women are significantly underrepresented as executive directors and senior managers. Of the top forty-seven Jewish Federations across the country, only one is headed by a woman. None of the top twenty highest paid Jewish professionals are women. Women's salaries in Jewish organizations are considerably less than those of their male counterparts.[13] Women are still underrepresented on many of boards of Jewish organizations, including our own Reform Movement. But we have progressed enough that Advancing Women Professionals, the catalytic organization that has kept these issues front and center in the Jewish community, is handing off the ongoing work of challenging the status quo, empowering women and creating a new generation of women leaders to a myriad of new organizations, each doing a piece of that important work.[14]

One of those fears articulated in the 1980 was that female rabbis would give the same sermon on feminism over and over again. I confess: I have been giving this same sermon for all these years. The Torah portion might be different but the *nechemta*[15] is the same: when women's voices are around the page and women are at the table, the entire Jewish conversation is richer, more inclusive, more meaningful, more accessible, and more real. We may not have reached the Promised Land, but we are on our way.

NOTES

1. Pamela Susan Nadell, *Women Who Would Be Rabbis: A History of Women's Ordination 1889–1985* (Boston: Beacon Press, 1999).

2. Betty Friedan, *The Feminine Mystique* (New York: Norton, 1963).

3. Rachel Adler, "The Jew Who Wasn't There: Halakha and the Jewish Woman," *Davka* (Winter 1971), reprinted in *On Being a Jewish Feminist*, ed. Susannah Heschel (New York: Schocken Press, 1982), and in *Contemporary Jewish Ethics*, ed. Menachem Mark Kellner (New York: Sanhedrin Press,1978).

4. Rachel Adler, *Engendering Judaism: An Inclusive Theology and Ethics* (Philadelphia: Jewish Publication Society, 1998), 62.

5. Phyllis Trible, *Texts of Terror: Literary-Feminist Readings of Biblical Narratives*, Overtures to Biblical Theology 13 (Philadelphia: Fortress Press, 1984).

6. Chaim Stern, ed., *Gates of Prayer: The New Union Prayerbook* (New York: CCAR Press, 1975), xii.

7. CCAR Annual "Caucus of Women Rabbis of the CCAR," volume 89, 1979 (New York: Central Conference of American Rabbis, 1979), 179–87.

8. Carole Balin, "From Periphery to Center: A History of the Women's Rabbinic Network," *CCAR Journal* 44 no. 3 (Summer 1997): 7.

9. The first Episcopal priests were ordained "irregularly" in 1972.

10. Sue Levi Elwell, ed., *The Open Door: A Passover Haggadah* (New York: CCAR Press, 2002).

11. Tamara Cohn Eskenazi and Andrea L. Weiss, eds., *The Torah: A Women's Commentary* (New York: URJ Press, 2008).

12. W. Gunther Plaut, ed., *The Torah: A Modern Commentary* (New York: UAHC Press, 1981).

13. Maia Efrem and Jane Eisner, "Women Leaders of Jewish Non-Profits Remain Scarce Even as Pay Gap Narrows," *Jewish Daily Forward*, December 15, 2013, http://forward.com/articles/189200/ women-leaders-of-jewish-non-profits-remain-scarce/?p=all.

14. Shifra Bronznick and Barbara Dobkin, "Advancing Women Professionals: From Catalytic Intervention to Network of Catalysts," *eJewish Philanthropy*, October 14, 2013, http://ejewishphilanthropy.com/advancing-women-professionals-from-catalytic-intervention-to-network-of-catalysts/?utm_source=Mon+Oct+14&utm_campaign=Mon+Oct+14&utm_medium=email.

15. *Nechemta*: a comforting conclusion.

23

"I FIND BY EXPERIENCE"

Feminist Praxis of Theology and Knowledge

RABBI OSHRAT MORAG

The feminist study of religion stresses that because men have historically dominated theological discussions and religious institutions, the
knowledge and data we value today are those generated by men. This
was the case at a convention of the Reform Movement, where I was a
presenter on a panel entitled "Tradition and Modernity: Challenges of
Jews of Our Time." My two esteemed male rabbinic colleagues on the
panel drew heavily from rabbis of the Talmud, Maimonides, and Abraham Joshua Heschel, as well as from other Jewish male figures. I, too,
presented my views with great depth and knowledge of historical and
religious developments along with theological explanations. However,
when it was my turn to speak, I opened with an appeal: "Trust me," I
said. "I also know Talmud, Maimonides, and Heschel. But I would like
to introduce some less familiar names of scholars who have contributed
significantly to Jewish thought." My speech focused on feminism in
Judaism, and I named and quoted such luminaries of Jewish feminism
as Rachel Adler, Judith Plaskow, Tamar Ross, Blu Greenberg, Dalia
Marx, and others. The participants' faces, which had been painted with
curiosity and interest, melted into looks of uncertainty. Suddenly they
seemed unsure that I was a real rabbi with real Torah to teach. Finally,
I brought in Merle Feld's poem "We All Stood Together," as a way to

both discuss its content and demonstrate poetry as a legitimate source of knowledge. In the poem, she writes about a woman standing with her brother at Sinai. While he wrote down all that he saw and heard, the woman's obligation of child rearing kept her from recording her experiences. All that remains are her feelings:

> But feelings are just sounds
> The vowel barking of a mute
> my brother is so sure of what he heard
> after all he's got a record of it
> consonant after consonant after consonant
> If we remembered it together
> we could recreate holy time
> sparks flying[1]

At that point I could see that I had lost their support. While a few women smiled sympathetically at me, the majority of the audience was no longer listening to my words.

This incident is not unique. Women's contributions to Jewish knowledge are all too often ignored. And when they do receive attention, they are often considered less "authoritative" than traditional, male-authored texts. This results in a disproportionate absence of women's voices at the table during serious Jewish academic and religious conversations.

In the words of Rita Gross, "It is a judgment and a choice, rather than an objective datum, to conclude that these subjects [that are considered important today] are what one should study in the history of religion."[2] Gross's analysis challenges us to ask ourselves what kind of information we are focusing on in the Jewish community and what the origins of that information are—including its applications in language, symbols, and practice.

The realization that theology is the projection of human experiences and that those experiences are different for men and for women provoked feminist theologians—Jewish and non-Jewish—to see the need for new theologies. In their groundbreaking book *WomanSpirit Rising*, Judith Plaskow and Carol Christ ask, "What would it mean for women's experience to shape theology and religion in the future?"[3] While feminist theologians suggest different responses to this question, most of them agree that "the word 'experience' becomes a key term for creating new religious forms."[4] Generating these "new religious forms" is critical to feminist theology, for feminist theologians have insisted that their work is not theoretical but rather an essential agent of change.

In her teaching, Rachel Adler uses the term "praxis," explaining that "[a] theology requires a method that can connect what we believe with what we do."[5] While Adler uses the term "praxis" to reflect her understanding of halachah, I would like to suggest the use of the term "feminist praxis" to denote the practices that Jewish feminism has generated.

Theology and Praxis

Jewish feminist theology has influenced the way Jewish communities celebrate life-cycle rituals, experience prayer in community, and speak about God and religious matters. Women's language and experience lead to actions that form the bridge between "what we believe" and "what we do."

Feminist theology, built on women's language and experiences, has transformed Jewish rituals and life-cycle ceremonies. Feminists have drawn from the work of twentieth-century anthropologists Clifford Geertz and Victor Turner, whose theories of the roles of rituals and symbols as social expressions for the experience of the holy provided a way of understanding the interaction between sex roles and religious symbols. According to their research, patriarchal theology presents a worldview in which there are always two levels: the superior and the inferior. Classically, God is the highest figure in the hierarchy, and this provides a model for male domination in the human sphere as well. Women's inferiority in most cultures means that rituals often reassert the hierarchy and women are excluded as people who experience or can speak authoritatively about God. Mary Douglas maintains that this explains the religious rituals of some cultures in which women's subordination is publicly illustrated, reasserting their inferior position.[6] Women's voices provide a needed corrective to these rituals.

The understanding that symbols, techniques, and social expressions are practical means of transforming life, of giving new purpose, has led to new feminist praxis. For example, Jewish feminists have sought to liberate menstruation from its androcentric perspective of disorder, danger, and impurity (and hence a basis for women's exclusion), recasting it instead as a symbol of godly blessing and calling for celebration and thanksgiving. Elyse M. Goldstein wrote in 1986 of her response to the majority of Jewish women who refrained from ritual immersion in a mikveh: "[There was] a great deal of resentment toward the mikvah among modern women....I was going to take back the water.... As Miriam's well gave water to the Israelites, so too will the mikvah give strength back to Jewish women."[7] Additionally, Jewish feminists have created brand-new symbols to sanctify their experiences. Nearly forty years ago, Blu Greenberg wrote, "The most creative event in a woman's life is the act of giving birth. Yet it is striking that we have as yet neither ceremony, blessing or ritual to mark this holy event in a religious context."[8] Taking up this calling, Jewish feminists have created throughout the years new Jewish knowledge in the form of life-cycle ceremonies, blessings, and rituals. Such inspiring examples may be found in Vanessa Ochs's *Inventing Jewish Ritual*, the website Ritualwell (ritualwell.org), and the book *Parashat Hamayim*, on women and immersion, edited by Maya Leibovich, Dalia Marx, Tamar Duvdevani, and Alona Lisitsa.

The list of changes in our religious lives that link "what we believe" with "what we do" is thankfully long. In addition to changing our ritual practices, listening to women's voices is changing the very nature of what we consider authentic God talk. Women in our community, along with female academics and rabbis, contribute scholarship and insight. Though there is still a perceived gap in authority between men's and women's voices, we can help to show that women, too, have "authentic" knowledge. We need to listen to those voices. Many of us have at least a passing familiarity with some women scholars; we must remind ourselves constantly to include them in our sermons, *divrei Torah*, and academic discussions. A sampling of works that highlight these women's voices can be found in the references cited here. As women are quoted publicly in religious and academic settings, their voices will become established as an authentic part of our tradition and reduce the perceived gap in authority between men's and women's voices.

With this growing canon of women's voices comes also the charge to continue the efforts to improve women's status in our religious realm. Although women rabbis are in a much better place than they were forty years ago, they continue to press against the "stained glass ceiling" or the "glass *m'chitzah*." Female rabbis are still offered lower salaries than are male rabbis for similar positions, and still most senior rabbis of large congregations are men. Some of our congregants still prefer having a male rabbi officiating at their ceremonies and at services, and the preference for male voices of authority pervades our very understanding of Jewish knowledge.

Authority[9]

The impact of feminist theology and awareness on liturgy, rituals, and God language is significant in today's Jewish community. However, feminism still remains disproportionately absent from the more intellectual aspects of our Jewish communal life. Women's voices are not yet accorded equal respect in rabbinic seminars, Jewish academic conventions, and *d'rashot* from our pulpits. In these environments, as both a congregant and participant, I have repeatedly experienced multiple references to the same sources. Hillel, Ramban, and Mordecai Kaplan almost always beat out Sue Levi Elwell's view of poetry as Torah, Ruchama Weiss's interpretation on Beruriah, and the feminist work of Susannah Heschel. While it is true that every classical rabbi is a man and that the Talmud features many more men than women, we need not limit ourselves to ancient and medieval sources of knowledge. Just as we regularly include women's voices in ritual and liturgy, we should also include them in academic learning. Every time a rabbi or scholar quotes a man to support a point, he or she perpetuates the notion that men's voices are authoritative. Of course, some men's voices *are* authoritative; the challenge is that we must *also* demonstrate that women's voices are just as powerful and just as worthy of our respect. If we are interested in women's voices and knowledge, we have to be ready to look outside the traditional canon and accept that significant knowledge can come in non-traditional forms. Shulamit Magnus suggests, "To uncover women's reality we must look at pervasive and powerful expressions of Jewish identity as expressed in ritual observance, child rearing and healing practices, and in official and unofficial community service. From these behaviors we may be able to make deductions about the attitudes and beliefs of women."[10] By turning to the practices and experiences of women in our community and by relying on the scholarship and insights of female academics and rabbis, we may reduce the perceived gap in authority between men's and women's voices as representing "authentic" knowledge.

Tikkun

In reconstructing Jewish knowledge to include women's voices, feminist scholars have taken two practical paths: integrating women's voices into traditional texts, and creating new forms of knowledge. Following these practical paths, here are suggestions for *tikkun*:

1. Inviting women's voices into our public discourse: Judith Fetterley explains in the introduction to her book *The Resisting Reader: A Feminist Approach to American Fiction*, why she quotes many female thinkers: "The extensive quoting [of women] serves not simply to

establish points or to share important perceptions but to express the degree of my indebtedness to the work of other women."[11] We can follow Fetterley's example by including women's voices in our sermons, *divrei Torah*, and academic discussions. Many of us have at least a passing familiarity with some women scholars; we must remind ourselves constantly to add their words to our own. A sampling of works that highlight these women's voices can be found at the end of this chapter. It is critical to quote women publicly and often to establish women's place as generators of knowledge.

2. Suggesting a new style of expression: If we are interested in women's voices as knowledge, we have to be ready to look outside the traditional canon and accept that significant knowledge can come in non-traditional forms. Too often, we privilege written texts as the form of authentic Jewish expression. However, Mark B. Tappan reminds us that expression is "the move from lived experience to the symbolic representation of that experience. An expression can be a story, a poem, a painting, a film, a dance."[12] The authentic voice of Jewish expression has historically been textual; including other forms of expression from Tappan's list can serve to invite more women's voices into the conversation. These modes of expression are often associated with women: Miriam danced and sang to God,[13] Hannah prayed in her own unique way,[14] Gluckel of Hameln wrote a diary,[15] and many other women wrote poems—to mention only a few examples. Those representations of experiences were not considered valuable knowledge for most of Jewish history and often still are not. *The Torah: A Women's Commentary* includes a treasury of women's poetry, which we should regularly include in our congregational and communal Torah study classes and public *divrei Torah*. We must overcome the bias that warns against using poetry as a serious mode of learning, bringing to light the too-often silenced voices of Jewish women.

Experience as Knowledge

Poetry brought into the context of Torah study is, as David Bleich teaches, "a poetry that revises the sacred texts; a poetry that includes reference to the experiences of daily life; it is the poetry that is tied to established accounts of history and to the ability to change and add to those accounts."[16] With regard to the interrelations of poetry and theology, Jacob Petuchowski argues, "If poetry is the medium through which 'normative' theology... best expresses itself, then poetry becomes a still more fitting medium for the expression of theological views."[17] But beyond these theoretical constructs is the main reason I prefer to use poetry as knowledge: poetry is a window to an authentic and genuine expression of experiences, sincere and often more raw. Poetry is essential to Judaism; we use it all the time in synagogue, when we read or sing the psalms, when we chant *piyutim*, even when we declaim the Torah. This kind of poetry seems natural to us; it is spiritual and elevating. We appreciate it and are committed to it. I would like to suggest a shift in the way we think of knowledge by considering poetry as fitting also to the more academic part of our roles. More specifically, to advance our praxis, connecting "what we believe" with "what we do," we must include poetry written by women. Rachel Adler explains, "Female poets steal the language of tradition, extract it from masculine theology...and place it in physical, sensual and gender experiences."[18]

In the following poem, Lily Montagu writes about her religious experience:

I Find by Experience

I find by experience, not by reasoning,
but by my own discovery that God is near me,
and I can be near God at all times.
I cannot explain it, but I am sure of my experience

as I am of the fact that I live and love.
I cannot explain how I have come to live and love,
but I know I do.
In the same way, I know I am in contact with God.[19]

This poem expresses a sense of surety, though she feels the need to apologize for not being able to explain her experience in the traditional academic sense. The poet does not use reasoning—perhaps because she is a representation of women who were excluded from using the classical means of reasoning through canonical texts throughout Jewish history or perhaps because she simply does not need it, as the religious encounter is as natural to her as are love and living. The experience here is in itself the data, teaching us something about the poet's connection to God, her spirituality, and her Jewishness.

Some voices in our community have expressed concern at the increasing "feminization" of Reform communities and congregations. I believe that this discomfort is natural, as complex shifts in power structures and social patterns work slowly to transition our society from being dominantly patriarchal to being more egalitarian. Of course, there are many other voices that agitate that we are not making this transition fast enough; the days of perfect equality lie ever ahead of us.

Women may not have emerged from Sinai with authoritative speech about God, but it is now emerging. While the content and form of that speech may be different from that of male rabbis and academics, it deserves to be valued as authentic religious speech. Because of the hard work of women Jewish professionals and pioneer feminist rabbis and scholars, there have been significant changes in our religious lives that link what we believe with what we do in ways authentic to women's experience. Women will keep speaking the truth of their experiences using their own language for God. Let the community hear those voices and value them for the sparks of holiness they represent.

Until we create the ideal egalitarian society, the efforts of Jewish feminist scholarship continues daily to demonstrate the degree to which women contribute to authentic, significant knowledge. As we move forward, progressing toward a more harmonious conversation, I hope that the days of shock at hearing women scholars cited as authoritative knowledge at the academic table will fade into distant memory.

Works that Highlight Women's Voices

Adler, Rachel. *Engendering Judaism: An Inclusive Theology and Ethics*. Boston: Beacon Press, 1999.

Bleich, David. "Learning, Learning, Learning: Jewish Poetry in America." In *Jewish American Poetry: Poems, Commentary, and Reflections*, edited by Jonathan N. Barron and Eric Murphy Selinger. Hanover, NH: Brandeis University Press / University Press of New England, 2000.

Christ, Carol P., and Judith Plaskow, eds. *Womanspirit Rising*. San Francisco: Harper & Row, 1979.

Daly, Mary. "After the Death of God the Father." In *Womanspirit Rising*, edited by Carol P. Christ and Judith Plaskow. New York: Harper & Row, 1979.

Douglas, Mary. *Purity and Danger: An Analysis of the Concepts of Pollution and Taboo*. London: Routledge Classics, 2002.

Fetterley, Judith. *The Resisting Reader: A Feminist Approach to American Fiction*. Bloomington: Indiana University Press, 1978.

Glückel of Hameln. *The Memoirs of Glückel of Hameln*. Translated by Marvin Lowenthal. New York: Schocken Books, 1977.

Goldstein, Elyse M. "Take Back the Waters: A Feminist Re-Appropriation of Mikvah." *Lilith* 15 (Summer 1986): 15–16.

Greenberg, Blu. "Women's Liberation & Jewish Law." *Lilith* 1 (Fall 1976).

Gross, Rita. *Feminism and Religion*. Boston: Beacon Press, 1996.

Kedar, Karyn. "Metaphors of God." In *New Jewish Feminism*, edited by Elyse Goldstein. Woodstock, VT: Jewish Lights, 2009.

Lisitsa, Alona, Dalia Marx, Maya Leibovich, and Tamar Duvdevani, eds. *Parashat HaMayim: Immersion in Water as an Opportunity for Renewal and Spritual Growth*. Tel Aviv: Hakibbutz Hameuchad, 2011.

Magnus, Shulamit. "Out of the Ghetto: Integrating the Study of Jewish Women into the Study of 'The Jews.'" *Judaism* 39, no. 1 (Winter 1990): 28–36.

Montagu, Lilian H. *Lily Montagu: Sermons, Addresses, Letters, and Prayers, Studies in Women and Religion*. Edited by Ellen M. Umansky. New York: E. Mellen Press, 1985.

Ochs, Vanessa. *Inventing Jewish Riual*. Philadelphia, PA: Jewish Publication Society, 2007.

Petuchowski, Jakob J. *Theology and Poetry*. Cincinnati: HUC Press, 1978.

Tappan, Mark B. "Interpretive Psychology: Stories, Circles, and Understanding Lived Experience." In *From Subjects to Subjectivities: A Handbook of Interpretive and Participatory Methods*, edited by Deborah L. Tolman and Mary Brydon-Miller. New York: New York University Press, 2001.

NOTES

1. Merle Feld, *A Spiritual Life: Exploring the Heart and Jewish Tradition*, rev. ed. (New York: State University of New York Press, 2007), 245.

2. Rita Gross, *Feminism and Religion* (Boston: Beacon Press, 1996), 68.

3. Carol P. Christ and Judith Plaskow, eds., *Womanspirit Rising* (San Francisco: Harper & Row, 1979), 5.

4. Ibid.

5. Rachel Adler, *Engendering Judaism: An Inclusive Theology and Ethics* (Boston: Beacon Press, 1999), xxii.

6. Mary Douglas, *Purity and Danger: An Analysis of the Concepts of Pollution and Taboo* (London: Routledge Classics, 2002).

7. Elyse M. Goldstein, "Take Back the Waters: A Feminist Re-Appropriation of Mikvah," *Lilith* 15 (Summer 1986): 16.

8. Blu Greenberg, "Women's Liberation & Jewish Law," *Lilith* 1 (Fall 1976): 19.

9. The term "authority" is used here not to claim hierarchal structure or traditional demand of the text on its readers, but rather to suggest readers' appreciation of and commitment to the text.

10 Shulamit Magnus, "Out of the Ghetto: Integrating the Study of Jewish Women into the Study of 'The Jews,'" *Judaism* 39, no. 1 (Winter 1990): 31.

11. Judith Fetterley, *The Resisting Reader: A Feminist Approach to American Fiction* (Bloomington: Indiana University Press, 1978), x.

12. Mark B. Tappan, "Interpretive Psychology: Stories, Circles, and Understanding Lived Experience," in *From Subjects to Subjectivities: A Handbook of Interpretive and Participatory Methods*, ed. Deborah L. Tolman and Mary Brydon-Miller (New York: New York University Press, 2001), 47.

13. Exodus 15:20.

14. I Samuel 1:13.

15. Glückel of Hameln, *The Memoirs of Glückel of Hameln*, trans. Marvin Lowenthal (New York: Schocken Books, 1977).

16. David Bleich, "Learning, Learning, Learning: Jewish Poetry in America," in *Jewish American Poetry: Poems, Commentary, and Reflections*, ed. Jonathan N. Barron and Eric Murphy Selinger (Hanover, NH: Brandeis University Press / University Press of New England, 2000), 190.

17. Jakob J. Petuchowski, *Theology and Poetry* (Cincinnati: HUC Press, 1978).

18. Adler, *Engendering Judaism*, 148.

19. Lilian H. Montagu, *Lily Montagu: Sermons, Addresses, Letters, and Prayers, Studies in Women and Religion*, ed. Ellen M. Umansky (New York: E. Mellen Press, 1985), 90.

24

SHIFTING THE FOCUS
WOMEN RABBIS AND DEVELOPMENTS
IN FEMINIST THEOLOGY

RABBI KARI HOFMAISTER TULING, PhD

Theology is the narrative we use to explain our worldview: why we are here, who or what created us, what is demanded of us, and what is the meaning of our history. When it is done well, theology enables us to make sense of our world even in the face of change, to assert moral coherence even in the wake of tragedy, and to acknowledge the precarious nature of living even in the midst of celebration.

A relatively new area of theological inquiry, however, is gender and leadership. In light of recent scholarship in the area of contemporary gender studies, we are prompted to ask whether and to what extent we should acknowledge gender as essential, how we might embrace fluidity in gender, and what value there might be in transcending gender altogether.

What does it mean, for example, when a female rabbi stands before the ark as the leader of the congregation and intones, *"Avinu Malkeinu"* (our Father, our King), as part of the Yom Kippur liturgy? Does it matter in this situation that God is portrayed as a male whereas the leader of the congregation is a female? More importantly, *should* it matter?

Gender as It Relates to God

Many of the traditional images of God are that of a male—a warrior, a king, a father—and they valorize the male and reaffirm the male's prominence in the hierarchy. "Even the nouns in the liturgy are masculine," Tikva Frymer-Kensky writes, "in content as well as form: our father, our king, our mighty hero."[1] We will consider two possibilities here: either (1) masculine language reinforces patriarchy and therefore should be balanced, corrected, or replaced; or (2) the masculine language is a by-product of patriarchy and will evolve as patriarchal systems give way to egalitarian ones; our language will naturally evolve in response to deeper societal changes.

With regard to the first possibility, some have argued that it is necessary to actively oppose masculine images with alternate visions: to regularly or intermittently use "She" in place of "He" when referring to God, or to substitute invocations such as "Goddess, Creator of all" in place of "God, King of the universe." The difficulty occurs, however, in defining what it means to be "male" or "female." Is it simply an issue of pronouns, or are deeper changes needed?

Some feminists, such as Savina Teubal, have sought to revive Jewish goddess-language.[2] But in response, an objection may be raised: Would it not be true that using such language would be a step backward to an earlier time? After all, is it not true that Jeremiah warns of God's displeasure of the worship of the "Queen of heaven"?[3] Are we not concerned about the whiff of idolatry that might accompany this shift in language?

Furthermore, it could be argued that resurrecting the language of the "Queen of heaven" after her defeat by the "King of the universe" only reinforces the dominance of a masculine understanding of might. The "stronger" image has "won." Championing the "weaker" option only calls attention to the imbalance of power and does so without supplanting it with a new paradigm. Rather than hoping to "win" in the power struggle of King versus Queen, we might be better off rejecting the struggle altogether.

Emphasizing the priority of God's power and might distracts our attention away from other divine attributes that might be invoked—attributes that might be more desirable in a feminist and egalitarian theology. As Judith Plaskow writes:

> God is not male. God is not a lord and king. God is not a being outside us, over against us, who manipulates and controls us and raises some people over others. God is not the dualistic Other who authorizes all other dualisms. God is the source and wellspring of life in its infinite diversity.[4]

That is to say: there is more than terminology at stake here. According to Plaskow, a genuinely feminist God-concept would require moving past constricting masculine metaphors of conquest and domination to affirm a relational theology that emphasizes interdependence and connection over independence and control.

This critique has far-reaching implications: for one thing, not just Jewish theology but also Jewish philosophy would need to accommodate this shift in focus. As Hava Tirosh-Rothschild writes, a "feminist philosophy" would be one that "highlights interdependence and cooperation as human ideals at the expense of the autonomy and self-sufficiency emphasized by traditional philosophy."[5]

Similarly, this shift also might affect how we understand the Holocaust. Melissa Raphael convincingly argues that Holocaust theology ought to be reconsidered. In place of theodicies that provide excuses for an all-powerful God who either "lets" the Holocaust happen or that suggest God lacks the power to prevent it, post-Holocaust theology ought to focus on the relationships that endure.[6]

The second possibility is that changing the pronouns we use for God puts the cart before the horse. The use of masculine language is not what brings the patriarchy into being, but rather it is the persistence of patriarchal power that creates the demand for masculine language. In this view, it is not that speaking of God in the masculine leads us to think that men are more important than women. Rather, it is the reverse: the use of male imagery is a by-product of our assumption that men are more important or that stereotypically male attributes are more desirable. When we stop thinking of the male as being most powerful, most important, and most relevant, then our use of male imagery will naturally recede. And as our understanding of what is "male" changes, so will our understanding of the "male" imagery that persists.

Thus, it may be that terms such as "king" or "master" will become gender-neutral, and we will lose the feminine forms entirely—or the less-gendered word "sovereign" will take over completely. In the meantime, it is not productive to speak of a set of specifically "masculine" or "feminine" attributes as they relate to God; to do so only reinforces the idea that the feminine is weaker or inferior. In this view, it is better to concentrate on tangible gains (such as creating a favorable workplace for the ever-increasing number of female rabbis) rather than seeking to correct the language that we use—that is, make the changes first, and the language will follow.

Gender as It Relates to the Rabbi

Again, we have two possibilities here: (1) the rabbi's gender matters, for a woman's lived experiences will be fundamentally different from those of her male counterparts, as will her relationship to the congregation; (2) the rabbi's gender does not matter, and we should move past gender and focus on capabilities; talking in terms of gender only reinforces the false notion of a fundamental difference between the genders.

In the first case, even if essentialist positions are rejected—that is, if one assumes that gender is a social construct rather than a biological mandate—the fact that someone has grown and matured in a society that is stubbornly gendered will affect that person in a myriad of ways. Therefore, it is reasonable to conclude, a woman's spirituality will be fundamentally different from a man's spirituality. In fact, her experience offers an important alternative perspective that ought to be heard.

If that is the case, then it is reasonable to conclude that the exclusion of women up to this point has negatively affected the development of Jewish ritual, liturgy, and philosophy. As Cynthia Ozick explains, "This isolation, this confinement, this shunting off, is one of the cruelest events in Jewish history. It has excised an army of poets, thinkers, juridical figures; it has cut them off and erased them."[7] How much richer Judaism would be, she suggests, if the talents of the other half of the population had been recognized and encouraged.

When women were first ordained as rabbis, there was indeed a sense of difference for many of their congregants. In 1983, Rabbi Laura Geller wrote about her own experiences: she found that "people don't attribute to women the power and prestige that they often attribute to men." And from that observation, she derived the following conclusions: "When women become rabbis or priests, there is often less social distance between the congregant and the clergy." As a result, "the lessening of social distance and the reduction of the attribution of power and status leads to the breakdown of hierarchy within a religious institution." Thus, she argues, female participation had the effect (and, presumably, continues to have the effect) of redefining congregational life in more democratic and egalitarian terms.[8]

At the very least, ordaining women has meant that the life experiences that are uniquely female have become part of the congregation's discourse. For example, the rabbi might recount some of her own experiences in a discussion of the narratives of pregnancy and barrenness in the Torah. When the conversation is conducted solely among men, key aspects of the women's stories might be missed or dismissed.

The second possibility is that the rabbi's gender does not (or should not) matter, for the role of leadership in prayer is not dependent upon gender. That is to say, personal characteristics associated with either gender (such as "men are strong" or "women are gentle") are learned skills rather than innate traits, which means that women can learn to be strong and men can learn to be gentle, for biology is not destiny. In that sense, men and women are indeed interchangeable. What matters most is the level of skill, intelligence, and empathy that the rabbi might offer in the service of the congregation.

The Central Conference of American Rabbis (CCAR) endorses this position in its hiring process: congregations are asked to affirm that they will not discriminate on the basis of gender in their hiring decisions. In theory, therefore, it should not matter whatsoever whether the person hired is male or female. In practice, however, gender has made a difference: the 2013 salary survey of CCAR rabbis showed a gap in male and female salaries in nearly every category, even when taking into account issues of seniority and rank. Even when this specific commitment has been made in writing that gender will not influence hiring decisions, a subtle discrimination can occur as a result of hidden and unspoken assumptions regarding the candidates' relative worth.

In moving forward, it should be noted that *both* positions face inherent difficulties:

1. On the one hand, embracing the unique role of the woman reinforces the basic dichotomy of male and female and can lead to essentialist thinking. If so, female rabbis will continue to be hindered by hidden assumptions and stereotypes. They might not be offered a more demanding position out of a patriarchal sense of concern that she would not be able to (or want to) seek a balance between her work and home life.

2. Yet, on the other hand, rejecting this dichotomy—arguing that she is in fact interchangeable with her male counterpart—might serve to reinforce the understanding that what is universal is in fact male, and she is a defective approximation of that universal ideal. Her unique needs (time and space for nursing, for example) might be rendered invisible, for when they are visible, they might be used against her. The risk is that she will be considered valuable so long as she is able to conform to the expectations of what a male could do in her place.

In other words, both options can be used (and indeed are used) to reinforce the power of the patriarchy.

Gender as It Relates to *Avinu Malkeinu*

Avinu Malkeinu, a hallmark of the High Holy Day liturgy, seems to be an affirmation of the masculinity of God in its proclamation that God is "our Father, our King." In order to rewrite it in more egalitarian terms, *Gates of Repentance*, the Reform *machzor* published by the CCAR in 1978 and revised in 1996, includes a feminine alternative to *Avinu Malkeinu*. God's title in this prayer, *Shechinah M'kor Chayeinu*, is translated literally as "Holy Presence, Source of our lives," as well as figuratively: Motherly Presence, Gentle Presence, Compassionate Presence. But these revisions have not been popular: the gender-neutral versions seem to lack the same force as the traditional version. This unpopularity may be largely because of humans' attraction to the familiar; we want to hear the same moving music year after year regardless of what the words "say." That is, liturgy has a performative aspect, in that a prayer's meaning extends well beyond the words that are said; it includes the sounds and affects that are associated with those words.

But it should also be noted that there may be a more theological justification for adhering to the original version. What is interesting about this prayer is that the congregation is not identifying with the powerful one in this dynamic; rather, the congregation is identifying with the powerless subjects and dependents of this God–father–king. The worshipers are expected to feel—especially after fasting all day—as if they were at the mercy of this awesome power and are begging for their very lives.

In other words, this prayer is asking that all of the members of the congregation—including the leadership—understand in a most visceral way what it means to be utterly powerless.

Is this not a most radical inversion of power?

Too often, we as a community have not heeded *Avinu Malkeinu*'s insistence that all human beings are equally powerless before God. We ignore the basic message to know our own station and to empathize with others, recognizing that righteousness is in upholding the principles established by God. We are not justified on our own; only with God's help can any of us achieve wholeness and peace. *Avinu Malkeinu* urges us to acknowledge the power of God, and our own meekness in face of this reality. Our reluctance to know and empathize with those who are disenfranchised is merely testament to our unwillingness to fully absorb the demand for righteousness inherent in our tradition. No need to change things, we reason; we go home and enjoy our meal.

Perhaps, then, we ought to take more seriously the implications of this liturgy. And perhaps there are other masculine liturgies and other narratives that might be inverted in this manner. Could we not read our tradition in such a way as to reimagine and reinforce this demand for radical empathy? Dalia Marx's recent work *Tractates Tamid, Middot and Qinnim: A Feminist Commentary*[8] is an excellent example of this approach, and further similar explorations of the meaning of gendered language in Jewish tradition may help us reclaim the value of often alienating words. We ought to encourage more work in this vein.

On the other hand, it is possible that this act of debasing ourselves before a great power might be used to legitimate a similar power imbalance in the human realm. We may well be asked to identify with the powerless subjects, but we find that we want to identify with the powerful king instead.

What matters most, however, is the exegesis of this prayer and the context in which it is used. We have a need to affirm, as part of the High Holy Day liturgy, that God is fully in charge, so that there might be a way to confess our sins and ask for mercy. We should read this prayer, therefore, as a form of reassurance: it asserts that there is moral coherence in our relationship to God. But this single metaphorical image should not dominate our view of our relationship to God.

That is to say: our theological narratives certainly ought to emphasize our divine responsibility to empathize with and care for one another. But these grand affirmations of God's sovereignty (such as are found in the High Holy Day liturgy) also have an important function. Both are needed.

Davar Acheir: Another Interpretation

So, we might want to stop at this point and rethink the role and purpose of theology. Why, exactly, do we need to define God? What, precisely, is gained in this practice?

As I noted in the introduction, theology is the narrative we use to explain our worldview: why we are here, who or what created us, what is demanded of us, and what is the meaning of our history.

We are in need of a theology, therefore, that acknowledges that gender is not an eternal ideal, but rather a specific set of roles that are defined by our culture. Furthermore, it should be one that demands equality of us, one that does not express preference for one gender identity over another.

But what would such a theology look like?

First, I think that we must assume that there is chaos inherent in the structure of the world. This is both a theological and scientific statement: when we look at the substructure of the world around us, we find a surprising amount of flux. This kind of uncertainty is what allows for new, creative growth: something new and surprising and novel may at any time arise because the world is not rigidly deterministic. Not every outcome is predetermined; in fact, most are not. In this context we are affirming the creative aspect of God as the Source of all, as *Avinu*, our Father.

Though there may indeed be chaos, the system is not totally random. It has meaning, and the actions we take have consequences. There is coherence, particularly in the moral realm. In this context we are affirming the sovereign aspect of God, as the transcendent one who rules and judges. Thus, we say that God is *Malkeinu*, our King.

But these two aspects of God do not exhaust the full range of what might be said of God. Consider also, for example, the testimony of the mystics. Many of us have the awareness that there is something inherent and vibrantly real, deep within us and yet all around us. It is unseen yet powerful, possessed of a different kind of energy from those we can normally detect with our senses. It is that energy that convinced the ancients that God was an overflow of goodness or intellect. In this context, God is *Shechinah*, the One who dwells within.

Regardless of the pronouns or metaphors we use, however, we face great difficulty in addressing the Divine. Our understanding of the world is grounded in our lived experiences. Metaphors require a referent in our daily world in order to be meaningful; applying them to what is transcendent and eternal is a profound challenge. In this regard, we might want to take our cues from Maimonides: it might be more honest to refrain from asserting positive statements about God, and limit ourselves to speaking of what God is not.

Nonetheless, as Ozick rightfully points out, when men are the only source of those metaphors, our language becomes impoverished. The presence of women in the rabbinate, therefore, has enriched—and will continue to enrich—our understanding of God. The presence of women gives lie to the assumption that the only way to speak about power is to use male terminology; their presence affirms that women's life experiences are appropriate referents for God metaphors; and (most importantly) their presence points to the potential for the fundamental transformation of our present reality.

NOTES

1. Tikvah Frymer-Kensky, "On Feminine God-Talk," in *Studies in Bible and Feminist Criticism* (Philadelphia: Jewish Publication Society, 2006), 393.

2. Savina Teubal, *Sarah the Priestess* (Columbus, OH: Swallow Press, 1984).

2. Jeremiah 7:18, 44:17–19, 44:25.

3. Judith Plaskow, "Jewish Theology in Feminist Perspective," in *Feminist Perspectives on Jewish Studies*, ed. Lynn Davidman and Shelly Tenebaum (New Haven, CT: Yale University Press, 1994), 76.

4. Hava Tirosh-Rothschild, "'Dare to Know': Feminism and the Discipline of Jewish Philosophy," in Davidman and Tenebaum, *Feminist Perspectives on Jewish Studies*, 93.

5. See Melissa Raphael, *The Female Face of God in Auschwitz: A Jewish Feminist Theology of the Holocaust* (London: Routledge, 2003).

6. Cynthia Ozick, "Notes toward Finding the Right Question," in *On Being a Jewish Feminist: A Reader*, ed. Susannah Heschel (New York: Schocken Books, 1983), 137.

7. Laura Geller, "Reactions to a Woman Rabbi," in Heschel, *On Being a Jewish Feminist*, 211.

8. See Dalia Marx, *Tractates Tamid, Middot and Qinnim: A Feminist Commentary* (Tübingen: Mohr Siebeck, 2013).

25

REAL MEN MARRY RABBIS

A History of the Jewish Feminist Movement

Rabbi Rebecca W. Sirbu

After the Holy One created the first human being, Adam, God said, "It is not good for Adam to be alone." God created a woman, also from the earth, and called her Lilith.

They quarreled immediately. She said, "I will not lie below you but above you." He said, "I will not lie below you, but above you. For you are fit to be below me and I above you."

She responded, "We are both equal because we both come from the earth."

Neither listened to the other. When Lilith realized what was happening, she pronounced the Ineffable Name of God and flew off into the air.

Adam rose in prayer before the Creator saying, "The woman you gave me has fled from me." Immediately the Holy One sent three angels after her.

The Holy One said to Adam, "If she wants to return, all the better. If not, she will have to accept that one hundred of her children will die every day."

The angels went after her, finally locating her in the sea, in the powerful waters in which the Egyptians were destined to perish.

They told her what God had said, and she did not want to return.

—*Alphabet of Ben Sira 23a–b*

In the 1970s, American Jewish feminist women adopted Lilith, the mythical first wife of Adam who fought for her equality, as their mascot, a symbol that God created men and women as equal partners. The Jewish feminist movement grew out of the surge of Jewish pride generated by the Six-Day War, the Jewish student movement, and the women's liberation movement. These three events led Jewish women to examine their religious lives and to recognize that they were not treated as equals within the Jewish community. Women began organizing to change their status; numerous women's groups and conferences were established providing women with the opportunity to express their frustrations and desires. The impact of the Jewish feminist movement led to an increased role for women in all aspects of Jewish life, including the ordination of women as rabbis.

Historically, women did not have leadership roles in Jewish life as either lay or spiritual leaders. Jewish law, halachah, literally meaning "the way," lays out 613 commandments, which govern every aspect of life. Women were exempted from "positive time-bound commandments," which state that something should be done at a particular time of day. For example, this class of laws exempted women from the thrice daily command to pray, because the prayers had to take place at certain times of day: *Shacharit* (morning), *Minchah* (afternoons), and *Maariv* (evening). Because women were exempted from the obligation of prayer, they could not count in the traditional minyan, a quorum of ten men needed to say the prayers. Nor were they able to serve as the prayer leader or don the traditional prayer garb of tallit and *t'fillin* (phylacteries—black leather straps with boxes containing prayers that are wrapped around the forehead and arm during prayer).

The original reasoning behind women's exemptions is not known; however, many theories have been put forth. The most widely accepted theory is the belief that women had a separate but equal role in Judaism. A woman's role was to take care of her husband and children, while the man concentrated on study and prayer. Women's exemption from Torah study kept them from other leadership roles because they did not have the learning to serve as witnesses or judges in a court of law. Another theory for the exemptions, put forth by Dr. Saul Berman, a noted Jewish scholar, argues that women were exempted from serving in a minyan and from appearing in a court of law in order to keep them out of the public eye, for Jewish tradition asserts that women should be modest. Dr. Berman argues that the Rabbis wanted to respect women's modesty and thus exempted them from all public obligations. Whatever the original reasoning was, the practical effect was to set up a system whereby women were disadvantaged. A woman might have had profound power within her home but was not able to play a public leadership role.[1]

The early 1970s was a time of both great social upheaval and a high point in Jewish pride. Israel's resounding victory in the Six-Day War caused many American Jews to embrace their Jewish identity with newfound strength. Young people in particular began to explore their Jewish roots and proudly claim their ethnic identity, just as the black student movement was encouraging African American young people to do. These forces combined with the growing secular women's movement, causing Jewish women to apply their newfound feminist consciousness to their religious lives.

Jewish feminists discovered that they could not fully embrace Judaism knowing that they were excluded from positions of religious power and from completely expressing their religious identities. Dr. Judith Hauptman, the first woman to teach Talmud at the Jewish Theological Seminary of America, asserted, "In Jewish law, if you are not obligated, you are in an inferior position to those who are obligated."[2]

Feminist women could no longer accept this inferior status. In 1976, Judith Plaskow, a woman at the forefront of the Jewish feminist movement, said, "Every time I let myself be lulled into thinking that I as a whole person am a member of this community, some event lets me know in no uncertain terms that I am wrong."[3]

By "some event," Plaskow meant those times when she was excluded from participation in religious life because she was a woman. She and other women did not want Judaism to define the role of women as second-class citizens.[4] They wanted to be able to participate fully in religious expression along with men. The traditional Jewish argument that women had a separate but equal role was an "ideal difficult to realize" for many women because the separate but equal doctrine no longer held true in their everyday lives.[5] As part of the professional workforce, women worked in the same jobs as men. The majority of women no longer attended only to the separate sphere of housework and raising children. Feminist author Susan Weidman Schneider asserted that "women's exclusion [from fulfilling the Jewish laws] has been tantamount to prohibiting her from defining herself as a Jew."[6]

Despite Jewish women's complaints about their position, most Jewish feminists did not want to do away with all of Jewish tradition. They wanted Jewish and feminist identities that did not conflict. As Conservative activist and scholar Dr. Paula Hyman asserted in the 1980s, "Jewish feminists have not rejected Judaism; we are struggling with it in our desire to fulfill ourselves as Jews and as women."[7] Women wanted Judaism to accept them as full equals in the community. They wanted to feel that their religious development was a concern to the community, and they wanted to study Scripture—just as men could— so that they too could have a full understanding of Judaism.[8]

In 1972, the Reform Movement broke ground by ordaining Sally Priesand as the first female rabbi. The Reconstructionist Movement followed quickly, ordaining Sandy Eisenberg Sasso in 1974. Both of these movements took liberal approaches to Jewish law and were not shackled by its proscribed roles for women. In addition, both movements professed egalitarian values and had already begun incorporating women's participation in services and lay leadership. While ordaining women was a watershed moment in both movements, the decision itself was not mired in the controversy that erupted in the more traditionalist Conservative Movement.

The first challenge to the Conservative Movement's non-egalitarian policies came from a student group called Ezrat Nashim, meaning "the help of women," formed on the Columbia University campus in 1971. Ezrat Nashim was the first women's group to demand that the Conservative Movement change its treatment of women. The group was made up of women between the ages of nineteen and twenty-four who had been raised in the Conservative Movement. In 1972, the group placed a list of demands before the Conservative Rabbinical Assembly (RA), the rabbinical branch of Conservative Judaism. They insisted that Jewish tradition "has now fallen disgracefully behind in failing to come to terms with developments in the past century" regarding women.[9] Ezrat Nashim demanded, among other things, that women be counted in the minyan, be recognized as witnesses before Jewish law, be permitted and encouraged to attend rabbinical and cantorial schools, and be permitted to perform rabbinical and cantorial functions in synagogues. Most importantly, they requested that women be considered as bound to fulfill all commandments equally with men.[10]

When Ezrat Nashim expressed its demands for equality, the United Synagogue, the lay branch of Conservative Judaism, recognized that the Conservative Movement would have to make changes in order to keep feminist women involved in Conservative Judaism. At its annual meeting in 1973, one year after Ezrat Nashim presented its demands, the United Synagogue asserted that women should be included in the minyan, given *aliyot* (being called up to the Torah), and encouraged to assume leadership positions "in all phases of congregational activity."[11] The United Synagogue even went so far as to say that it "looks with favor on the admission of qualified women to the Rabbinical School of the Jewish Theological Seminary." In 1973, the Committee on Jewish Law and Standards of the Conservative Rabbinical Assembly, the group that ruled on all issues regarding Jewish law, ruled that women could be counted in a minyan as long as the local rabbi consented, and it disseminated a 1955 minority decision that allowed women to be called up to the Torah. This led to a rapid increase in the number of congregations willing to call women to the Torah.

However, the Movement was still far from deciding to ordain women as rabbis. Caught between wanting to adhere to Jewish law as it is traditionally interpreted and wanting to be relevant in the changing times, the Conservative Movement decided in 1977 to establish a national commission to investigate the sentiment of Conservative

Jews on the issue of ordaining women. Holding meetings throughout the country, the commission members heard the testimony of women who felt ignored in public Jewish life, as well as statements of men offering their support. Although it took note of the arguments against ordination, in its report submitted early in 1979, the commission recommended the ordination of women. However, the faculty of the Jewish Theological Seminary, the educational arm of the Conservative Movement charged with ordaining rabbis, was deeply divided on the issue and decided to table it.

While this was taking place, encouraged by the actions of Ezrat Nashim, the Jewish student movement organized the First National Jewish Women's Conference in 1973, which was attended by women of all denominations. Held in New York, the conference was the first ever to deal with problems faced by feminist Jewish women. Sessions dealt with women and spiritual Judaism, growing up Jewish, women in Israel, women and halachah, women in Jewish communal life, women in politics, and women in education. Five hundred women attended the conference, which called for gradual change within the system. At the conference, many projects were launched, among them consciousness raising and study groups; a Jewish women's speaker bureau; a newsletter, *Lilith's Rib*, to keep women up to date on Jewish women's activities; planning for another conference in the Midwest; and planning for a "literary, scholarly, intellectual journal," which evolved into *Lilith* magazine.[12]

In 1974, the Second National Jewish Women's Conference was held at Camp Harand in Wisconsin. The theme of the second conference was "Changing Sex Roles: Implications for the Future of Jewish Life."[13] Speakers represented diverse points of view, from Orthodox to Reconstructionist Judaism. The second conference's main achievement was the founding of the Jewish Feminist Organization (JFO).

The JFO filled the growing need for a permanent, national, feminist, Jewish women's organization. The purpose of the organization was to "seek nothing less than the full, direct and equal participation of woman at all levels of Jewish life—communal, religious, educational, and political."[14] Except for one professional coordinator, the organization was run on a volunteer basis. The JFO created a series of social action committees on Jewish education for women, law, communal life, day care, publicity, and fundraising. In addition, the organization appointed a liaison to the general women's movement and other Jewish organizations. The liaison protected the needs of Jewish women in other organizations, both Jewish and non-Jewish. For example, the JFO liaison attended the International Women's Conference in Mexico in 1975 and issued a statement condemning the conference for supporting the UN General Assembly's "Zionism is racism" resolution. Jewish women were made aware of the issues affecting them through the speakers bureau and newsletter. The JFO was successful in arranging the publication of Aviva Cantor's *Bibliography on Jewish Women*, which later became *The Jewish Woman 1900–1985 Bibliography*,[15] and in organizing the Third National Jewish Women's Conference in 1975.

The overwhelming amount of mail received by the organization demonstrated the need for a national Jewish women's headquarters. However, in 1976, the JFO disbanded due to lack of financial resources. The organization had been supported by membership fees, fundraising, and individual contributions, but these were not enough to support the overwhelming workload that the organization took upon itself.[16]

Spurred by the changing times, the Conservative Movement decided to address the issue of ordaining women as rabbis again in 1983. By this time, all arms of the Movement—the United Synagogue, the Rabbinical Assembly, and even the seminary chancellor Gerson Cohen—had come out in support of ordaining women. Though still divided, the faculty of JTS voted in October of 1983 to accept women into rabbinical school. Several women had already been studying at JTS's graduate school and quickly shifted into the rabbinical program. Amy Eilberg was the first woman to be ordained, in 1985.

The impact of women's leadership on Judaism began to be clearly felt in the 1980s and 1990s. Women were at the forefront of creating new rituals and reinterpreting old ones. A flourishing of new rituals emerged. Women's Rosh Chodesh groups, monthly gatherings of women modeled on an ancient women's holiday—celebrated, according to one tradition, because women did not give up their jewelry to make the Golden Calf—became increasingly popular. The nature of the groups ranged from serious text study to playful crafting of new rituals and art. In addition, women flocked to women's seders, Passover seders focused on retelling the Exodus narrative from a woman's point of view and highlighting the women who play a crucial role in the story—the midwives Shiphrah and Puah, and Miriam. Debbie Friedman, a renowned songwriter, composed many songs highlighting women's leadership, which were incorporated into some seder rituals. Women looked at how to use the mikveh, a ritual bath, in new ways. In traditional Jewish practice, a woman is required to immerse in the bath after her menstrual cycle finished each month. Some women reclaimed this ancient practice as a celebration of their bodies' natural functioning. Others shunned its traditional purpose but found great spiritual fulfillment by creating new mikveh practices. Rituals using an immersion in the mikveh were written for women recovering from cancer, finalizing a divorce, or marking menopause, among other things. Being renewed and reborn after an immersion was a powerful theme.

Simchat bat, a baby-naming ceremony for girls, also came into vogue during this time. Women felt that the birth of a girl should be celebrated just as the traditional bris ceremony celebrates the birth of a boy and welcomes him into the Jewish covenant. Today, new parents can select from a vast array of *simchat bat* rituals, choosing what is right for their family.

As these new rituals were created, women also sought to bring more egalitarian language into the traditional liturgy used in the synagogue. Not surprisingly, the more liberal Reform and Reconstructionist Movements again led the way, changing the language in the prayer books to be inclusive, referring to God in gender-neutral tones and adding the names of the Matriarchs—Sarah, Rebecca, Rachel, and Leah—to the prayers where the names of the Patriarchs—Abraham, Isaac, and Jacob—are traditionally recited.

Today, women are in all levels of leadership in Jewish communal life, yet issues still remain. The vision of the short-lived Jewish

Feminist Organization to "seek nothing less than the full, direct and equal participation of woman at all levels of Jewish life—communal, religious, educational, and political" has yet to be fully realized. The modern Orthodox Movement in the United States has made great strides in giving girls and women strong Jewish educations and encouraging women to take on leadership roles. Yet, they have stopped short of ordaining women as rabbis. Yeshivat Maharat prepares women with the same learning as men to be Orthodox religious leaders, yet they have chosen to ordain women as "maharats," a Hebrew acronym for *Manhigah Hilchatit, Ruchanit, Toranit*, one who is teacher of Jewish law and spirituality.[17] Ordaining an Orthodox woman as a "rabbi" remains highly controversial. Many women in the Orthodox world are struggling with the same issues that Conservative Movement women struggled with a generation ago in their quest to become full participants in Jewish life and rabbis.

While the number of women rabbis continues to grow in the liberal movements, women still face discrimination. Surveys of women rabbis in both the Reform and Conservative Movements show that women earn significantly less than do male rabbis with the same level of experience, that more women work part-time than do men, and that women have a harder time securing jobs in large congregations than do their male counterparts.[18] Women who work as leaders in the Jewish communal sector at Federations, Jewish community centers, and Jewish family service agencies earn "about 66 cents for every dollar earned by men" and still do not rise to the executive level in these organizations as men do.[19]

Since existing structures still discriminate against women, women rabbis have had to be particularly creative in finding work for themselves. Women rabbis are at the leading edge of the entrepreneurial rabbinate. In an age where synagogue attendance is declining and jobs are scarce, many women are striking out on their own, inventing new kinds of spiritual communities, worship services, and rituals. It is not surprising that 40 percent of the participants in Clal's Rabbis Without Borders Fellowship are women. The fellowship trains and supports entrepreneurial rabbis, pushing them to think outside the box and create new ways of sharing Jewish wisdom and traditions. Women apply and are accepted into the selective fellowship at a rate much higher than their representation in the rabbinate as a whole. Already adept at pushing the envelope, these women bring their creative skills to serve the larger Jewish population in new and exciting ways.

Thus Jewish women, those who are rabbis together with those who are lay leaders, will continue to push the Jewish world forward. Fifty years ago no one could imagine that women would be rabbis, create new rituals, and found new, alternative communities. Unlike the mystical figure of Lilith, Jewish women did not flee from the Jewish community; rather, they stayed and fought for the community to change. Just imagine what Jewish women leaders will do in the next fifty years!

NOTES

1. Blu Greenberg, *On Women and Judaism* (Philadelphia: Jewish Publication Society, 1981), 83–84.

2. "Interview: After a Decade of Jewish Feminism the Jewry Is Still Out," *Lilith* 11 (Fall/Winter 1983): 21.

3. Judith Plaskow, "The Jewish Feminist: Conflict in Identity," in *The Jewish Woman*, ed. Elizabeth Kuton (New York: Schocken Books, 1976), 4.

4. Ibid., 3.

5. Paula E. Hyman, "The Other Half: Woman in the Jewish Tradition, " in *The American Jewish Woman: A Documentary History*, ed. Jacob R. Marcus (New York: Ktav, 1981), 909.

6. Susan Weidman Schneider, *Jewish and Female* (New York: Simon & Schuster, 1984), 34–35.

7. Hyman, "The Other Half," 909.

8. Saul Berman, "The Status of Women in Halachic Judaism," in Kuton, *The Jewish Woman*, 122–24.

9. Ezrat Nashim, "Jewish Women Call for Change," in Marcus, *The American Jewish Woman*, 895.

10. Ibid., 896.

11. "The United Synagogue Accords Women Religious Equality," in Marcus, *The American Jewish Woman*, 919–20.

12. Reena Sigman Friedman, "The Jewish Feminist Movement," in *Jewish American Voluntary Organizations*, ed. Michael N. Dobkowski (New York: Greenwood Press, 1986), 582.

13. Ibid., 586.

14. Jewish Feminist Organization, "Statement of Purpose," adopted April, 28, 1974, at the National Jewish Woman's Conference on Women and Men.

15. Aviva Cantor, *The Jewish Woman 1900–1985 Bibliography* (New York: Biblio Press, 1987).

16. Friedman, "The Jewish Feminist Movement," 584–87.

17. Yeshivat Maharat website, http://yeshivatmaharat.org/.

18. "Survey: Women Earn Far Less Than Male Reform Rabbis," *Jewish Week*, June 20, 2012, http://www.thejewishweek.com/news/breaking-news/survey-women-earn-far-less-men-reform-rabbis.

19. Maia Efrem and Jane Eisner, "Women Still Lag Behind," *Jewish Daily Forward*, December 10, 2012.

26

BETTY FRIEDAN'S "SPIRITUAL DAUGHTERS,"
THE ERA, AND THE CCAR

Rabbi Carole B. Balin, PhD

The year 1972 was a milestone for American women in more ways than one. Besides the groundbreaking rabbinical ordination of Sally Priesand, Ms. magazine—co-founded and edited by Gloria Steinem and Letty Cottin Pogrebin, among other Jews—hit the presses for the first time, and the Senate passed the Equal Rights Amendment. In twenty-four words, it plainly states: "Equality of rights under the law shall not be denied or abridged by the United States or by any State on account of sex." In more specific terms, the amendment was expected to invalidate laws that imposed restrictions on women in business, favored women in child-custody and alimony cases, and denied compensation to pregnant women able to work. At the same time, it was to strike down differing standards for boys and girls in public school programs.[1] As students of American politics know, for passage, the amendment needed to be ratified by three-quarters of the states within a seven-year period.

Over the course of the long road toward ratification, the number of women in the rabbinate grew exponentially. By 1977, the number had tripled (to three!); and a year later, it more than doubled when four additional women received ordination.[2] In the fall of 1978, these pioneering women—whose ranks were still less than a minyan—found themselves at the center of a political maelstrom, which had erupted earlier that summer in Toronto at the annual meeting of the Central Conference of American Rabbis (CCAR). On the floor in Toronto, the membership of the CCAR had debated rescinding a contract with the Hyatt Regency Hotel in Phoenix, Arizona, the site of its meeting the following March, because of the state legislature's refusal to ratify the Equal Rights Amendment. The battle would test the fiber of a long-standing tradition of Reform Judaism: its commitment to equality between the sexes in religious life.

*   *   *

When feminism burst onto the American scene in the final decades of the last century, Jewish women were able to ride that second wave all the way to the bimah. However, not long after Rabbi Priesand's historic ordination, the leadership of North American Reform Jewry began to fret about the "significant number of women" who would be flowing into the rabbinate. Ordaining women was one thing, integrating them into the Movement was quite another.

Apprehensive about the "theatrical and circus-like atmosphere" that might result in congregations if and when female clergy walked through the temple doors, the leaders of the three official bodies of Reform Jewry (i.e., the Union of American Hebrew Congregations [UAHC], the CCAR, and the Hebrew Union College–Jewish Institute of Religion [HUC-JIR]) sent representatives to a strategy meeting in September 1976 to devise ways to stave off such scenes.[3] As a result of the meeting, two task forces were established to acquaint Reform laity and clergy with female rabbinical students, lest the latter be regarded as "something strange and unique."[4] Meanwhile, well aware of the extraordinary nature of their professional futures, female rabbinical students at the New York campus of HUC-JIR had already linked up with their counterparts at the Reconstructionist Rabbinical College in Philadelphia to address shared concerns. The fifteen women in attendance at a meeting on February 8, 1976, organized themselves into the "Women's Rabbinical Alliance" and invited their peers in Cincinnati and Los Angeles to join them.[5] Cincinnati students declined the offer, having already established the "Rabbinical Students' Organization for Women," which welcomed male students into its ranks. Neither group would want for members—by 1978, 62 of the 209 students enrolled at HUC-JIR's Rabbinical School were female.[6]

While it would obviously take the CCAR, with its membership at that time of over twelve hundred rabbis, many decades to catch up to HUC-JIR's 3:1 gender ratio, its support of women seemed unequivocal at the time. At its eighty-sixth annual convention in 1975, for instance, it passed a resolution in favor of the proposed Twenty-Seventh Amendment to the U.S. Constitution, stating in no uncertain times:

> WHEREAS we are heirs of a prophetic tradition which ever sought to repair the damaged world [emphasis added], and
> WHEREAS in our efforts to restore the world to sanity we affirm the following position which we take knowing full well the complexity of such an issue but knowing also that we cannot be silent, BE IT THEREFORE RESOLVED that we urge the speedy ratification of the Equal Rights Amendment and pledge our efforts in the various states to work for its ratification, recognizing that it is an important step toward insuring equal rights for women and men.[7]

Like millions of women and men across the country, Reform rabbis had been anticipating ratification of the Equal Rights Amendment since 1972. By law, three-quarters of the states—or thirty-eight states—would need to ratify the amendment by 1979 for it to become an amendment to the Constitution. While thirty states ratified it within the first year, the process slowed as anti-ERA forces mobilized with the intent of instilling fear that its passage would deprive women of privileges, such as exemption from the military draft and the ability to be supported by their husbands. Others, including the Reform rabbinate, dismissed such claims, which in 1976 reiterated its support of the amendment, adding, "We deplore the slowness with which our country has moved in approving the ERA and we again urge its speedy ratification by the States."[8]

As the 1979 deadline for ratification drew near, supporters of the amendment beefed up their efforts in non-ratifying states. Among CCAR members, there was talk of relocating their 1979 convention scheduled for Arizona, a non-ratifying state, to one that favored the ERA. In June of 1978, the CCAR Executive Board met for its usual pre-convention meeting. Regarding the issue of Arizona, the Executive Board voted ten to six in favor of "issu[ing] a carefully worded statement expressing the sentiments of the Executive Vice President [Joseph Glaser] concerning our unwillingness to rescind our former commitment to hold our 1979 convention in Phoenix, AZ, regarding such areas as business ethics and Constitutional problems." The board further instructed that the statement contain a reaffirmation of "our support" of the ERA and that the "CCAR go on record not to make further contractual arrangements in any state that had not adopted the ERA so long as the ERA remains a viable issue." Later in the same meeting, a motion was adopted to reconsider the issue, but it lost in a vote of eight to twelve.[9]

When the 1978 convention formally opened with 441 registered members, including four newly ordained female rabbis, the site of the next convention weighed on the participants' conscience. At a plenary business session, the membership voted 117 to 44 to overturn the executive board's decision to confirm Phoenix as the site of the 1979 convention. It was further moved to direct the officers "to make the best available arrangement for a site for the 1979 convention in a state on record as approving the ERA."[10] The motion carried by a vote of 132 to 85.

But the matter was not over. During the summer, the executive board found that the discussion and motions relating to rescinding the commitment in Phoenix "were not in accord with standard parliamentary procedure, by which the Conference is bound by its Constitution." Therefore, on advice of legal counsel (i.e., Weil, Gotshal, and Manges), the board deemed the "entire discussion…null and void."[11]

Rabbi Deborah Prinz did not mince words in her response to this decision. She sent a letter to CCAR president Ely Pilchik asserting that "the moral imperative of constitutional protection for equal rights for women must be pursued forcefully by boycotting non-ratified states."[12] A mere three months after being ordained as the fourth female Reform rabbi and attending her first CCAR convention, and only weeks after assuming the post of assistant rabbi at Central Synagogue in New York, Prinz put forward her argument for relocating the March 1979 meeting.[13] First of all, she reminded the president, the CCAR had already indicated its support for the proposed Twenty-Seventh Amendment in no uncertain terms in a resolution adopted in 1975. She additionally pointed out that the CCAR's fellow Reform organizations, the National Association of Temple Educators (NATE) and the UAHC, had elected to hold their conventions only in ratifying states and, in one case, had "even altered plans in the midst of contractual negotiations with [a] hotel."[14] Moreover, Prinz maintained, the CCAR's 1973 boycott of table grapes and head lettuce in support of the United Farm Workers (UFW) Union had created a precedent for exerting "financial pressure" as a protest strategy. She then examined and dismissed the possibility of legal action against the CCAR ("It is unlikely that a religious organization would be sued [for breach of contract] on what is clearly an ethical/moral issue") and of financial loss ("some members... offered monetary support...and...lay members of the Reform Jewish community would also be supportive"), and closed with the ringing exhortation, "In order to maintain its *tradition* of advocacy for equality for women, I urge the CCAR Executive Board to make alternate [*sic*] convention arrangements and not go to Phoenix" (emphasis added).

In historical terms, Prinz's invocation of the word "tradition" to describe Reform Judaism's aspiration to secure religious equality between the sexes is apt. The march toward gender equality among reform-minded Jews began in continental Europe at a private school in Berlin in 1814 when the first confirmation of Jewish girls took place.[15] In no time, the ceremony expanded to include boys and spread in Prussia and beyond, to Denmark and France. Confirmation's egalitarian ethos and doctrinal essence appealed to those seeking to adapt Judaism for the modern age. Three decades later, a cluster of liberal-leaning rabbis who met in Breslau in 1846 raised the general question of women's status in Judaism. In their words, "the female sex" was the "religious equal of the male" with regard to "obligations and rights."[16] To that end, they proposed expunging the prejudicial benediction "*shelo asani ishah*" ("who has not made me a woman") from the liturgy, obligating women like men to religious instruction and public worship, and raising the age demarcating girls' religious maturation from the Talmudically established twelve to thirteen, so as to match that deemed appropriate for boys.[17] In the same year, reformer Max Lilienthal imported the egalitarian spirit to America when he inaugurated confirmation at New York's Congregation Anshe Chesed. Others immediately followed suit, including Isaac M. Wise at his temple in Cincinnati.[18]

Like his German predecessors, Wise assigned women a strategic position in the project of Jewish reform. Coeducational confirmation was one of several activities—along with "allowing girls to read the Torah on that occasion," "admit[ing] females to the choir," and "introduc[ing] family pews into the temple"—that Wise believed would hasten the progress of reform. As he argued in 1876, "With the admission of mothers and daughters to a recognizable place in public worship, came order and decorum....But we cannot stop here." In addition, women needed a "voice and a vote." Enfranchisement would allow their uniquely female "heart[s] and piety" to hold sway over congregational meetings and their maternal "influences" to benefit the Sabbath-schools. Wise insisted that "the principle of justice, and the law of God inherent in every human being, demands that woman be admitted to membership in the congregation, and be given equal rights with man" so that "her religious feelings be allowed scope for the sacred case of Israel."[19]

Wise was under no illusion that men and women were created equal. His worldview was bifurcated along gender lines: he regarded women as "priestesses of the home," whose virtues were considered essential for the moral upbuilding of the family as well as the synagogue. Women's contributions to congregational life would lead to a purer, more moral, more "reformed" Judaism for all.

Wise's campaign to give women the congregational vote developed against the backdrop of the suffragette movement, which retrospectively became known in American history as first-wave feminism, to distinguish it from the next wave in the following century. Elizabeth Cady Stanton and Lucretia Mott convened the first conference on women's rights in Seneca Falls, New York, in 1848—approximately two hundred miles from Wise's home at the time, in Albany. As circumstances would have it, Wise and Mott met face-to-face in Boston in 1867 at the founding meeting of the Free Religious Association, an interfaith organization of liberal religious leaders attempting to shake free of the orthodoxies of their respective denominations.[20] While the degree to which the suffragettes directly influenced Wise can only be conjectured, the pages of his two newspapers, *The American Israelite* and its German supplement *Die Deborah* (intended for a female audience), demonstrate unabashed support of women's rights.[21]

Although Wise did not live to see women gain the vote, his colleagues raised the issue at several conventions. At its 1912 convention, the CCAR membership debated the matter of women's suffrage and concluded that it was "inadvisable for the Conference, as a body, to take action thereon." The shillyshallying persisted for half a decade, until 1917, when the CCAR went on record in support of granting women the vote:

> We feel it is our solemn duty as ethical leaders and as preachers of a religion which [sic] has stood throughout the centuries for justice and righteousness to assert our belief in the justice and righteousness of the enfranchisement of the women of our country.[22]

For some, the passage of the Nineteenth Amendment in 1920 aroused an expectation that all barriers to women's equality in American society would subsequently fall. For the CCAR, it meant opening a discussion on women's ordination.[23]

Such a discussion transpired at the 1922 CCAR Convention, but only after HUC professor Jacob Lauterbach, a member of the organization's Responsa Committee, presented what he called "the attitude of traditional Judaism on this point." The weight of his evidence pointed toward "debarring women from the rabbinate," a view he regarded as "strictly adhered to by all Jewry all over the world throughout all generations even unto this day."[24] As to the question of whether Reform Judaism ought to follow tradition in this regard, Lauterbach stated:

> We [Reform rabbis] are still carrying on the activity of the rab-
> bis of old who traced their authority through a chain of tradition
> [*shalshelet hakabalah*] to Moses and the elders…, even though in
> many points we interpret our Judaism in a manner quite different
> from theirs. We are justified in considering ourselves the latest link
> in that long chain of authoritative teachers who carried on their
> activity of teaching, preserving and developing Judaism, and for
> our time we have the same standing as they had.[25]…We should,
> therefore, not jeopardize the hitherto indisputable authoritative
> character of our ordination. We should not make our ordination
> entirely different in character from the traditional ordination, and
> thereby give the larger group of Jewry, following traditional Juda-
> ism, good reason to question our authority and to doubt whether
> we are rabbis in the sense in which this honored title was always
> understood.

In other words, Lauterbach feared that the authority of all Reform rabbis would be questioned, and perhaps diminished, were they to al-low women to enter their profession.

The lively discussion that ensued focused on the fact that, while Lauterbach had opined on the so-called traditional Jewish view on the subject, he had failed to express the Reform perspective. As Louis Witt (Temple Shaare Emeth, St. Louis, Missouri) contended:

> It is not a matter of *tradition* at all. I must confess that I was not
> the least interested in Rabbi Lauterbach's presentation.…I honor
> [him] for the learning contained therein but the point he pres-
> ents is not the point at issue.…I cannot believe that a religion…so
> splendidly…forward-looking as our[s] will stand in the way of [the
> women's] movement. [emphasis added][26]

Similarly, Joseph Rauch (Congregation Adath Israel, Louisville, Kentucky) reminded his colleagues that "in every line of endeavor in our temples, we have proceeded on the theory that woman is the equal of man."[27] Others maintained that Lauterbach's fear of creating a schism in Israel had never informed CCAR decisions. Had that been the case, according to Henry Englander (registrar and professor of biblical exegesis and biblical history at HUC), "we would not have taken stands on many subjects." He continued, "Years ago this Conference put itself on record favoring absolute religious equality of women with men. Are we going back on our action?"[28] Paradoxically, it would seem, the discussion participants had transformed their non-traditional approach to Jewish tradition into a hallowed Reform tradition. Like bygone generations of Reformers who had handed it down to them, they, too, hoped to transmit it to future generations.

Meanwhile the discussion continued, and the CCAR membership voted and approved that "the courtesy of the floor be extended to the wives of rabbis" in order to gain a female perspective on the subject.[29] Of the three women who participated, all favored women's ordination. Mrs. Ephraim Frisch explained how she initially opposed the notion on account of the practical concern of "how a woman could attend to the duties which devolve upon a rabbi and at the same time be a true home-maker." But she changed her view after listening to the arguments, adding, "I love the work of the rabbinate so much that could I have prevailed upon myself to forget the joys that come with wife-making, I should have become a rabbi." To most at the meeting, the idea that a woman could fulfill her roles as wife and mother while leading a congregation seemed unlikely. Though Joseph Leiser (Congregation Beth El, Helena, Arkansas) disagreed, saying, "[The] thesis that the rabbinical profession...involves the totality of life to the preclusion of...motherhood is not valid and is no more applicable to the Jewish woman as rabbi than...[as] lawyer, doctor, dentist, newspaper writer, musician, business woman or teacher."[30] In the end, with a nod to its own tradition, the CCAR's resolution affirming the ordination of women carried the day in a vote of 56 to 11.

Of course, it would take a half-century for that promise to be ful-filled—and even then, as Deborah Prinz's letter makes clear, the deci-sion to ordain women and accept them into the ranks of the CCAR did not necessarily mean that egalitarianism was at hand. In response to her objections to the convention being scheduled for Phoenix, she received a three-page, single-spaced letter in which the executive vice president painstakingly refuted each of her points. To her argument that the boycott of produce on behalf of the UFW had set a precedent in this instance, he retorted:

> You cannot in truth say that the CCAR has established a prec-edent for this when it urged the boycott of table grapes and head lettuce….You are calling here for something else—a secondary boycott: illegal based on its immorality. Your statement that "this is not a boycott against Hyatt Hotels, but rather support for the states which have ratified ERA" bears examination. First of all, pull-ing out of Hyatt really hurts only Hyatt. The State of Arizona will absorb the loss. The ranchers and miners against ERA don't give a hang. Then, too, it doesn't ring true about support for the other states. This whole operation is to punish Arizona, and everybody in it, in what I am afraid is a spiteful approach, an intervention of non-violent violence, which will lead to horrendous repercus-sions, into the constitutional, deliberative process of American democracy. Every pressure group in existence—anti-abortion, anti-homosexual, anti-anything and everything, will take its lead and turn our country upside-down.[31]

After weighing the issue, "thoroughly and deliberately" on four dif-ferent occasions, he explained, the CCAR Executive Board "has come down on the side of business ethics…of not punishing the guiltless and the powerless."[32] In closing, he urged Prinz to "go into the lion's den" and attend the convention in Arizona "instead of sulking off some-where else, unnoticed." At the same time, he expressed his fear that staging "an alternate simultaneous convention" would militate against the integration of women rabbis. This "would create a *havdalah* [ritual of separation between the Sabbath and the rest of the days of the week] in the minds of many—indeed, maybe even a *mechitzah* [separation between women and men during worship]—and neither of us want [*sic*] that." Tone notwithstanding, Glaser apparently conveyed Prinz's sentiments, along with those of other protesters, to the Executive Board, which reopened the matter at its fall meeting.[33]

In a last-ditch effort to settle the affair once and for all, the board sent a letter to its membership on October 19, indicating that as a result of direct negotiations with the management of the Hyatt Regency Hotel in Phoenix, there had been an offer to release the CCAR from its contract upon payment of $20,000.[34] The board was requesting an immediate response regarding this proposition from every one of its 1,262 members, as each would be "levied a general assessment to cover the $20,000 penalty" should the CCAR withdraw from its Phoenix contract. The letter contained arguments on both sides of the issue, along with a brief note that the U.S. Congress had recently extended the deadline for passage of the ERA to 1982.[35] In the end, the membership did not put its money where its mouth was, so to speak, and the contract remained intact. Consequently, planning continued apace for the convention in Phoenix, including the scheduling of additional activities designed to educate about and express support for women's rights.[36]

In the wake of the decision, the six female members of the CCAR were torn between the desire to boycott the convention as a pro-ERA gesture, on the one hand, and the need to be involved in the CCAR by participating in its convention, on the other.[37] They turned to an improbable but judicious source for guidance. As luck would have it, the brother of Laura Geller (the third woman to be ordained a Reform rabbi) maintained a friendship with a childhood friend by the name of Jonathan Friedan. Geller called his mother, Betty, for advice on the issue.[38] Betty Friedan suggested that the women attend the convention and also hold a rump convention where she would speak. And so they did.

Hundreds of rabbis crammed into a small room at the Hyatt Regency Hotel in Phoenix, Arizona, to hear Friedan speak. The room was the only space made available by the convention and hotel, and even that was rented with monies donated by a male colleague rather than CCAR funds.[39] Although this was not the first time Friedan had addressed a Jewish group in support of the ERA, it was the first time on record that she explicitly mentioned her Jewish roots as being dispositive in her own actions on behalf of women.[40] She opened with an explanation of how she came to write *The Feminine Mystique* (1963), which is often credited with launching second-wave feminism in America:

> What made me do it? Probably the simplest answer is that my whole life made me do it, or that I grew up as a Jewish girl in Peoria, Illinois. I grew up isolated and feeling the injustice, the burning injustice of the subtle and not so subtle anti-Semitism that was the experience of my generation....Then, too, I grew up in an era when Jews, if they could, would try to pass....When I went to Smith some wealthy girls from Cincinnati would talk in whispery voices and hold their hands behind their backs so they wouldn't talk with their hands. And when there was a resolution to open the College to any of the victims of Nazism and to ask President Roosevelt to undo the quotas that kept the Jewish refugees from coming here, the Jewish girls from Cincinnati didn't vote for that resolution. I, who was a freshman from Peoria, Illinois, with hayseed in my hair, was horrified. I had this burning feeling, all that I am I will not deny. It's the core of me. I had this feeling as a Jew first. First as a Jew before I had it as a woman. All that I am I will not deny.[41]

With this affirmation of her Jewish roots, Friedan went on to describe how Jewish self-awareness led her to question injustice against others in American society, especially women. And in an effort to make democratic principles like human freedom, dignity, and equal opportunity gender-blind, she started the women's movement. The mother of second-wave feminism publicly thanked her "spiritual daughters (some of whom are in the room)" for teaching her that it's "profoundly Jewish" to "take actions, not words, to break through barriers that keep us from participating."[42]

Friedan's actions on that afternoon in Phoenix did not go unnoticed. Two weeks after the convention, she received a letter of thanks addressed to "*Ms.* Friedan" from the Office of the Executive Vice

President of the CCAR. Glaser wrote with regret for not having had "an opportunity to provide the appropriate setting" for her presentation. Not only that. He explained that he was enclosing a check from the "Treasury of the CCAR" for $600 to cover her expenses, "inasmuch as [her] appearance did become part of the *official* program of the Conference"[43] (emphasis added). With this sleight of hand, Glaser was sweeping months—indeed decades—of rancorous debate over the Reform "tradition" of religious egalitarianism under a revisionist rug. A transcript of Friedan's speech even appears in the *CCAR Yearbook* (1979) alongside all the other proceedings of the convention in Phoenix as if it, too, had been part of the original, and approved, program.

*   *   *

What, a historian might ask, do thirty-five years and the unearthing of documents related to this incident come to teach us? The answer is heard in the words of Rabbi Laura Geller: "When women's voices are heard, traditions change."[44]

NOTES

1. *New York Times*, as reported on March 23, 1973.

2. They include Sally Priesand (1972), Michal S. Bernstein (1975; who subsequently left the rabbinate), Laura Geller (1976), Karen Fox (1978), Rosalind Gold (1978), Deborah Prinz (1978), and Myra Soifer (1978). Ben Gallob, "Special to the JTA Record Total of 75 Women to Study for Reform, Reconstructionist Rabbinate in 1978," *Jewish Telegraphic Agency*, August 24, 1978.

3. Eugene Mihaly, Minutes, "Meeting of representatives of the CCAR, UAHC and HUC-JIR on the significant number of women rabbis who will be ordained beginning with June of 1978," September 22, 1976, p. 1, American Jewish Archives, MS-677.

4. Ibid., pp. 1–2. In due time, the two merged into a single "Task Force on Women in the Rabbinate," which Sally Priesand initially chaired.

5. In 1980, both groups gave way to form the Women's Rabbinic Network (WRN), which functions today as an auxiliary of the CCAR. See Carole Balin, "From Periphery to Center: A History of the Women's Rabbinic Network," *CCAR Journal*, Summer 1997, reprinted here on pp. 137–52.

6. Ben Gallob, "Special to the *JTA*." In 1975, women constituted 2 percent of all ministers in the United States, while female enrollment in some seminaries jumped to more than 30 percent. *American Jewish Year Book*, 1977, 68.

7. http://www.ccarnet.org/rabbis-speak/resolutions/1975/equal-rights-amendment-1975/.

8. Resolution on the Equal Rights Amendment adopted by the CCAR at its 87th Annual Convention, 1976.

9. "Minutes of the Executive Board," *CCAR Yearbook*, 1978, 12. (Inexplicably, the tally for the second vote is greater than that for the first.)

10. *CCAR Yearbook*, 1978, 193.

11. Ibid.

12. Rabbi Deborah Prinz of Central Synagogue, New York, to Rabbi Ely Pilchik of B'nai Jeshurun, Short Hills, NJ, September 18, 1978, p. 2, SC-1692, AJA. Note that on February 21, 1979, Judge Hunter of the District Court for the Western District of Missouri, Central Division, held that action against non-ratified states is a form of free speech and is not subject to restraint under the anti-trust laws. In an ironic twist, Prinz currently serves as the director of program and member services and director of the Joint Commission on Rabbinic Mentoring at the CCAR.

13. The proposed ERA would have amended the Constitution to read: "Equality of rights under the law shall not be denied or abridged by the United States or by any state on account of sex."

14. The UAHC annulled its contract with a Chicago-based hotel for a Biennial Assembly meeting and held it in another state, largely due to pressure exerted by the National Federation of Temple Sisterhoods, according to Glaser. See Joseph B. Glaser to Deborah R. Prinz, September 20, 1978, SC-1692, AJA.

15. Michael A. Meyer, "Women in the Thought and Practice of the European Jewish Reform Movement," in *Gender and Jewish History*, ed. Marion A. Kaplan and Deborah Dash Moore (Bloomington: Indiana University Press, 2010), 141.

16. W. Gunther Plaut, *The Rise of Reform Judaism* (New York: World Union for Progessive Judaism, 1963), 253–55.

17. Riv-Ellen Prell has convincingly argued that Jewish reformers transformed the *legal* status of women but failed to challenge the gendered *cultural* practices in which men still dominated. See Riv-Ellen Prell, "The Dilemma of Women's Equality in Reform Judaism," *Judaism* 30 (Fall 1981): 418–26 and, in a similar vein, Karla Goldman, "Women in Reform Judaism: Rhetoric and Reality," in *Women Remaking American Judaism*, ed. Riv-Ellen Prell (Detroit: Wayne State University Press, 2007), 109–33.

18. Bruce L. Ruben, *Max Lilienthal: The Makings of the American Rabbinate* (Detroit: Wayne State University Press, 2011), 69, 85–86.

19. Isaac M. Wise, "Women as Members of Congregations (1876)," in *Selected Writings of Isaac M. Wise with a Biography*, ed. David Philipson and Louis Grossman (Cincinnati: Robert Clarke, 1900), 398–99.

20. Wise and Mott were among the thirty-seven founding members of the Free Religious Association, which included Ralph Waldo Emerson as well. Richard A. Kellaway, "The Free Religious Association" (Collegium Conference Paper, 2010), 5. Notably, the ERA was originally known as the Lucretia Mott Amendment, as drafted

by the women's rights leader Alice Paul in 1923. Variations of the amendment were presented to every session of Congress between 1923 and 1970, mostly remaining in committee. See *New York Times*, March 23, 1972.

21. Benjamin Maria Baader, *Gender, Judaism, and Bourgeois Culture in Germany, 1800–1870* (Bloomington: Indiana University Press, 2006).

22. The CCAR actually affirmed the non-decision three years later. See *CCAR Yearbook* 25 (1915): 133, and for the decision *CCAR Yearbook* 27 (1917): 175.

23. The ratification of the Nineteenth Amendment only indirectly sparked discussion on women's ordination. The direct issue at hand was the request of Martha Neumark, a seventeen-year-old student at HUC in Cincinnati, to be assigned, like her male rabbinical school classmates, to a High Holy Day student pulpit. Her request raised the possibility that Neumark, daughter of an HUC faculty member, might ultimately present herself as a candidate for ordination. Consequently, the HUC Board of Governors asked the Responsa Committee of the CCAR to answer the question: Shall women be ordained as rabbis? See *CCAR Yearbook* 32 (1922): 156–77; and Pamela Nadell, *Women Who Would Be Rabbis: A History of Women's Ordination 1889–1985* (Boston: Beacon Press, 1998), 62–66.

24. *CCAR Yearbook* 32 (1922): 160.

25. Lauterbach validates the Reform rabbi's authority on the basis of the dictum that every group of three that has acted as a *beit din* [court] over Israel is on a level with the *beit din* of Moses (Babylonian Talmud, *Rosh HaShanah* 25a).

26. Witt had argued in favor of women's rights before the Arkansas legislature in 1917 when he served Congregation B'nai Israel in Little Rock.

27. *CCAR Yearbook* 32 (1922): 166.

28. Ibid. Englander referenced the CCAR's anti-Zionist stance as one illustration.

29. Ibid., 51.

30. For both Frisch's and Leiser's comments, see ibid., 172.

31. Joseph Glaser to Deborah Prinz, September 20, 1978, p. 1, SC-1692, AJA.

32. Ibid., p. 3.

33. In his response to Prinz, Glaser referred to other letters that had been sent to the board in protest. See Elliot Stevens (CCAR administrative secretary) to Balfour Brickner, September 19, 1978, pp. 1–3, SC-1692, AJA.

34. Ely Pilchik to CCAR Membership, October 19, 1978, pp. 1–2, SC-1692, AJA.

35. Only thirty-five states ratified the ERA by the 1979 deadline. Even by 1982, no additional states ratified the amendment. Arguments in favor of paying for release of the contract and seeking an alternative site: (1) the CCAR plenum voted in Toronto not to hold the convention in Phoenix; (2) the most effective support for ERA is to refuse to hold the convention in a non-ERA state; (3) for the sake of movement unity, the CCAR should follow the lead of the UAHC, which refused to hold its next Biennial in a non-ratifying state. Arguments in favor of retaining the contract and holding the convention in Phoenix: (1) the most effective advocacy of the ERA is to bear witness in Phoenix in the convention itself, through plenum sessions, classes, etc., as well as in visits to the Arizona legislature, public statement, and demonstration; (2) rejection of the notion of secondary boycotts in attempts to secure state ratification; (3) the sole beneficiaries of the payment would be the (local) Hyatt;

(4) the UAHC was able to negotiate a release from its Chicago contract because it had eighteen months' lead time.

36. Activities would include, among other events, an optional visit to the state legislature, where an ecumenical worship service would be led outside the state capitol, and an invitation to hear Lea Goodman, the Arizona coordinator of the National Organization for Women (NOW). See Conference Program, *CCAR Yearbook*, 1979.

37. Letter of Karen Fox, Laura Geller, Rosalind Gold, Sally Priesand, Deborah Prinz, and Myra Soifer to CCAR Colleagues, March 26, 1979, pp. 1–2, SC-1692, AJA.

38. Phone conversation between author and Laura Geller, October 12, 2012.

39. Male colleagues helped the women arrange for Friedan's speech, including securing the room and putting up the funds for its rental. One rabbi told me privately that he became *persona non grata* at the CCAR as a result of his assistance. According to Judea Miller, a group of men who were longtime members of the CCAR decided to boycott the 1979 convention in support of the ERA. See Miller's letter in the *New York Times Magazine*, December 2, 1984.

40. Friedan appeared before 350 delegates of the National Jewish Community Relations. See "Friedan Says ERA Is a Jewish Concern," *Jewish Telegraphic Agency*, July 2, 1976.

41. For Friedan's full address, see *CCAR Yearbook* 89 (1979): 180–87. This excerpt appears on p. 180.

42. Ibid., 182.

43. Joseph Glaser to Betty Friedan, April 10, 1979, SC-1692, AJA.

44. As quoted in Dana Evan Kaplan, *American Reform Judaism: An Introduction* (New Brunswick, NJ: Rutgers University Press, 2003), 197n25.

I wish to thank Rabbis Deborah Prinz and Laura Geller, as well as Kevin Proffitt of the American Jewish Archives, HUC-JIR, Cincinnati.

PERSONAL REFLECTION

Finding a Seat at the Right Table
Gender at HUC-JIR

RABBI DANIEL KIRZANE

As a student at the Hebrew Union College–Jewish Institute of Religion's New York campus, you learn to appreciate your time in the elevator. Professors and students alike make their way up to the classrooms and back down to the library, and from time to time, you might catch a few moments with a distinguished guest heading to the administrative offices on the fourth floor. We all stand together in our ups and our downs.

The elevator is also the place to catch up on the school's special events, and that is where, during my second or third year of rabbinical school, I noticed a flyer for an upcoming conversation sponsored by the Women's Rabbinic Network (WRN). "That's an important organization," I thought to myself, "and I don't know very much about it. I'll make sure to drop by so that I can learn more about how I might support its work."

The following Tuesday, I made it to the conference room early to make sure I was able to get lunch before the program began. More and more of my classmates arrived, and Rabbi Jacqueline Ellenson, executive director of the WRN, began the conversation with words of welcome. She introduced the primary goal of the Women's Rabbinic

Network, to which many of my classmates would belong: "to promote the personal and professional growth of female rabbis and rabbinic students within the Reform Movement." And then she turned to me and remarked that it was appropriate that a male colleague had come to this event to show his support. Only then did I notice that I was the only man in the room, and Rabbi Ellenson, I believed, was making an extra effort to acknowledge and affirm my presence.

I was taken aback: Why did my presence deserve particular comment? I had simply assumed that, like every other program advertised in the elevator, all students had equal opportunity for investment. Why the special dispensation? I followed up with a friend after the program who assured me, "It's okay that you were there because you're *you*; no one would question your intention to be anything but entirely supportive. But if it had been another male student, I think it really could have made some people uncomfortable." And who knows: perhaps my presence *did* make some of my classmates uneasy. I never asked. The following year, however, I did notice the WRN elevator flyer suggested that only women students should attend.

This experience served as a wake-up call that there was a significant conversation at HUC-JIR of which I was not part and at which, indeed, I may not be welcome. To this day, I'm not certain what the details of that conversation are: How do my women classmates feel about their job prospects compared to the men in our class? What professional concerns do they hold on account of their gender? How does being a woman influence the messages they choose to preach, their emotional response in support of a congregant in need, or the job descriptions they negotiate? I suspect that these conversations happen among colleagues and classmates, but I have not found a seat at that table.

Of course, I respect the privacy and sensitivity of my classmates, honoring their experiences, and those of other women I've known, that single-gender spaces can be very meaningful and important. I wonder aloud, then: What is the best way for me to ally myself with colleagues whose gender differs from mine? And how will I come to uncover some answers to that question?

Even as HUC-JIR embraces and celebrates egalitarianism, gender dynamics are far from invisible. Consider: approximately half of the rabbinical students at the New York City campus during my years there (2009–2014) have been women, as have been the vast majority of cantorial and education students. Most of the school's administration are women, almost every member of the support staff is a woman, and every member of the maintenance staff is a man. Almost every faculty member "of a certain age" is a man, though our younger faculty includes a more comparable mixture of women and men. One thing is clear: there are definitely more women than men in the building.

Most of the time, it is unclear how, or even whether, this gender configuration impacts our education. Does it affect our instruction to learn biblical prose from a man and biblical poetry from a woman? Was my experience in the School of Education distinct because I learned primarily from women teachers and alongside primarily women students? Was the pastoral care in New York, directed by a woman, different from that in Los Angeles, where it was directed by a man? I don't know if it's possible to answer to these questions, and, at the same time, I don't recall ever having tried to formulate some responses. Perhaps— as a man not fully attuned to the sensitivities of gender dynamics—I simply do not see what is before my own eyes.

Certainly the presence of women and the influence of feminism have impacted the HUC-JIR curriculum. My Jewish literature classes included thoughtful attention to authors such as Devorah Baron and Chava Shapiro; my Jewish food class was guided by personal accounts of MFK Fisher and Elizabeth Erlich; and, in addition to being commemorated by the entire school on its one-hundredth anniversary, the Triangle Shirtwaist Factory fire featured prominently in my history class. The presence of women at the seminary and the academic openness to perspectives and experiences of women have brought a broader education to all HUC-JIR students.

Nevertheless, I have encountered some dissatisfaction about gender dynamics at HUC-JIR. For example, our professional development and social responsibility courses, designed and conducted by men, introduced us to a variety of congregational rabbis; to my memory, all of the full-time senior congregational rabbis were men, and every part-time or multiple-job rabbi was a woman. This fact did not escape notice or comment of students in these classes, especially women looking for congregational role models; however, the topic was never broached in class. Even though this factor was mentioned to school officials, the makeup of the class—to my knowledge—has not changed significantly during my tenure.

As well, I was eager to learn from Dr. Judith Plaskow, who taught a course on sexual ethics as a visiting professor. I was one of the few men in the class, and I heard the lament more than once, "Those students who need to study this material the most are those least likely to sign up for the class." The implication here was clear: some members of our community were uncomfortable with their classmates' unawareness or insensitivity about gender. I hesitated to ask—but was fairly sure of the answer—whether "those students" were all men.

Of course, for better or for worse, I, too, was a male student at HUC-JIR. I've often been asked what it's like studying at a seminary with mostly women. It's hard to answer because I don't know anything different. I can only reply that I feel fully comfortable and embraced as a student, and I sense that, for the most part, all my classmates felt the same.

Nevertheless, I have struggled with the sense of privilege I have felt in some roles. A few members of my first student pulpit told me they were glad to have a male student after a long run of women; I have had far fewer conversations about my professional, personal, and ritual wardrobes than have my women colleagues; and I knew that during congregational placement, interview committees won't know that I am expecting a child unless I volunteer that information. Processing and responding to this privilege has not been part of my seminary train-ing, and I am left with many questions about it. Still, I am grateful for the sensitivity and thoughtfulness I have developed at HUC-JIR to be aware of the gender dynamic implicit in all areas of my burgeoning rabbinate.

With generations of women now serving the Jewish people as rabbis and cantors, the face of Jewish leadership has changed dramatically from its historical roots. As a feminist man in this new paradigm, I commit myself to giving helpful and appropriate support to all my colleagues while also striving to understand and interpret the impact of my gender on my own career. My time at HUC-JIR has taught me that some conversations are best reserved "for women only," though the project of considering and reconsidering the place of gender in the Jewish community is incumbent upon us all. In the end, regardless of where I'm sitting, I'm eager to come to the table for the important conversation about women and the rabbinate.

PERSONAL REFLECTION

Becoming a Woman of the Wall

Rabbi Susan Silverman

When I became a Woman of the Wall, I became more fully Jewish.

I had been a rabbi for almost twenty years the day I was detained, with nine other women—including my seventeen-year-old daughter—by police for wearing a tallis and praying out loud at the Kotel. We were singing the psalms of *Hallel* when a young police officer waved for me to follow her out of the women's section. I shook my head. She approached me, her hand outstretched. I reached for my daughter, who is named for the prayers we sang—Hallel—and together we sat down. The police officer squatted in front of me and asked me to come with her.

I shook my head. I'm sorry, I said to her. I don't want to cause you trouble. But I'm not going. I looked directly at her. She must have been a new officer—fresh from the army. Dark hair pulled into a sleek ponytail. Black eyeliner under her brown almond eyes. Serious countenance under a layer of foundation, lipstick, and blush. What was the Kotel to her? What in our tradition did she own, create anew, love? Or was religion, like our country's army and police forces, designed by a few who commanded our actions, our rituals, and our dress code?

Arrest it would be. That was not a frightening thing. Israel is not Yemen or Russia or China. It would be a long day, some hassle, but no real personal risk.

The existential threat was to Sinai. And to democracy. And the inherent commonality in both.

We all stood at Sinai, we all saw the fire and heard the thunder. We all shook as God's words pierced us, a spiritual alchemy that transformed individuals—varied, colorful, damaged, hopeful, open-hearted, narrow-minded, good, cruel, passionate, listless—into a community in covenant with the Holy Blessed One. Monotheism means that nothing else is "mono." Only God is whole.

Some fear colorful variations—what if we step over the borders of God's will?

But I fear narrowness. I fear the few defining the many. Because that is idolatry—seeing a fraction as the whole. The centuries of missing women's voices created a skewed Judaism—like a tree that had been deprived the right balance of sustenance.

In Israel, public and private Jewish practices were more and more the jurisdiction of *Haredi* Jews. Mitzvot are seen by the ultra-Orthodox as ends in themselves—a kosher cheese borekas had to have a certain shape versus a potato borekas in order to maintain a perfect separation of milk and meat. This obsession in a country with rising poverty and suffering refugees? In a world with tens of millions of orphans at risk for starvation, disease, and trafficking?

I believe mitzvot are building blocks for a just and compassionate society—a land in in which the prophets could rejoice. And the Kotel just might be the cornerstone in that transformation. Judaism is at stake for women and men. For all our children. For the Jewish future. With Women of the Wall, I realized that my feminist, progressive fight was for the deepest purposes of our nation—for when a narrow, idolatrous view of God and covenant are codified in civil law, democracy ceases. And so does Sinai.

The prayer service ended. Women hugged each other, *Chodesh Tov, Chodesh Tov*. The police receded. I surveyed the near distance for that young woman officer. I wondered if our songs of praise reached her heart. If she remembered Sinai. We filed out of the women's section and were met by police. The eyes-traced-with-kohl met mine as her hand took hold of my arm. Hallel, my Hallel, and I were herded into the police van along with eight other women—two of whom were American rabbis who had just come from Ukraine, where they had prayed freely and publicly—and off we went to the station for questioning. *Do you know that your prayer is offensive to others? Do you know that it is illegal to wear a tallit? Do you know that singing loudly in the women's section is not allowed?*

As I answered the interrogation questions of this Jewish Israeli policewoman, I longed to say, *I am so sorry you have to enforce the religious laws that rob you of the very gift you are obligated to "protect."* I wanted to be her rabbi and raise the curtain of black and white hats to expose tradition's colors, layers, complexities, and growth—a Jewish world in which secular policewomen stood at Sinai, and received the Torah, with everyone else.

· Part Five ·

Jewish Life

Throughout Jewish history, women have enriched Jewish life with the home rituals. While the men were occupied with text study, women, who were tasked with establishing a Jewish home, were quietly (and not so quietly) transmitting Jewish values, stories, spirituality, and culture.

Once women had access to the entire annals of text and were functioning as rabbinic leaders, many combined their knowledge and communal standing to make significant contributions to a wide variety of aspects of Jewish life. Rabbi Debra Reed Blank ("Making Up for Lost Time: Female Rabbis and Ritual Change") uncovers the immediate impact women rabbis had on all areas of ritual life once no longer held back by the old models. Traditionally, ever since the destruction of the Temple, regular mikveh use has resided mainly with women. While mikveh was long rejected by the Reform Movement as an archaic relic, Rabbi Sara Luria and Shaina Herring ("The Mikveh as a Well of Creativity") explore the myriad ways women rabbis have encouraged the reintroduction of ritual immersion into contemporary Jewish life.

For centuries, the siddur and other liturgical tools reflected their male authorship. Rabbi Michele Lenke ("Offering a New Look:

Women Rabbis and Jewish Spirituality") suggests that the leadership of women rabbis on the pulpit and in community settings inspired new approaches to prayer, including in sanctuary worship, healing rituals, and Passover seders. Rabbi Eric Weiss ("El Nah R'fah Na Lah, Heal Us Now: How the Jewish Healing Movement, Led by Women Rabbis, Has Altered the Jewish Landscape") looks specifically at the seminal contributions made by women rabbis to a burgeoning Jewish healing movement.

Given the long road to the ordination of women, as well as a long history of societal marginalization, women in the rabbinate were well positioned to take up a variety of social causes. Rabbi Patricia Karlin-Neumann ("Kindling Change: Women Rabbis and Social Action") explores the critical role women have played to push the social action agenda to the forefront of the Reform Movement.

The absence of the female voice throughout biblical and Rabbinic literature has been alienating to many. Rabbi Sandy Sasso ("How Jewish Women Have Come to Read the Bible: The Creating of Midrash") and Rabbi Elizabeth W. Goldstein, PhD ("140 Faces of Torah and Counting: Communal Transformation, Theological Evolution, and the Authority of Interpretation") unravel the interpretive innovations that were born the moment that women became not just the receivers of the tradition but a new generation of its authors.

This section concludes with personal reflections from Rabbi Julie Wolkoff ("A Rabbi Goes to Mikveh"), Rabbi Sarah Schechter ("A Rabbi in the Military"), and Rabbi Elena Rubinstein ("Born in the USSR"), all of which illustrate how varied Jewish ritual can be.

27

MAKING UP FOR LOST TIME

Female Rabbis and Ritual Change

RABBI DEBRA REED BLANK, PhD

> How did so many of the [ritual] innovations pioneered by Jew-
> ish feminists…become mainstream so quickly in American Jew-
> ish life? One answer lies with the women who became rabbis.[1]

The Power of Print

The Title Is the Point: Access and Authority

The first publications of the first two female rabbis in the United States
dealt with ritual—one audacious and subversive, the other understated
yet direct. While still a student at the Reconstructionist Rabbinical
College in 1973, Sandy Sasso wrote an article critiquing the absence
of a covenantal ritual for a girl and proposing one that appropriated
the Jewish circumcision ritual's occasion, language, and theology for
a girl.[2] In her 1975 book, Reform rabbi Sally Priesand addressed the
absence of ritual opportunities for the female, writing pointedly, "It is
not unusual that so many women feel alienated from the Jewish community.…For thousands of years, ritual has been a man's privilege."[3]
These two publications were not isolated phenomena. Men (rabbis
and not) and non-rabbinical women were also writing baby-girl rituals

and feminist critiques of Jewish ritual in the early 1970s. What was significant is that two women were writing as rabbis. The title is everything when it comes to speaking about Jewish ritual, a point made most recently and poignantly by a woman studying for the Orthodox rabbinate.[4] I decided to explore the extent women have used their title to influence Jewish ritual, as evidenced by their written words, easily accessible and measurable, as opposed to their less measurable teaching, modeling, and leading of ritual. (Space and time limitations prohibited me from looking at the Internet, a fathomless, protean resource for Jewish ritual, with a couple of salient exceptions. Nor did I look at film and video resources.) I looked at women's roles in denominational publications, as well as their independent publications, both books and articles. To my surprise, I discovered that they have written about little else.

Female rabbis have played a leading role in the dramatic changes in the ritual landscape that have occurred in North America since the 1970s, and this is because they hold two keys to the door opening onto ritual change: access to people, and the religious authority and expertise to guide those people to and through ritual change. That authority is pragmatic and immediate, hands-on.[5] Unlike an academic or journalist, a rabbi's thoughts on ritual are not limited to the theoretical realm, but are directly applied to real-life situations. Rabbis occupy pulpits, whether literal or figurative, from which they speak as spiritual guide, teacher, counselor, community spokesperson—and pulpits can be "bully" on matters of ritual.

A female rabbi often has access to women and girls that a male rabbi lacks. (Male rabbis have long had the same kind of access to lay men and boys. My use of binary-gender specificity reflects social assumptions and behavior that still often hold in the rabbinical world.) Women are more likely to approach a female rabbi when they are looking for rituals that address their physical experience. One female rabbi and a laywoman together composed a ritual to mark the latter's grief after rape, a coordinated venture that likely would not have happened had the victim's rabbi been male.[6] A female rabbi also serves as a role

model for the ritual involvement of girls and women, whether traditional (leading worship, wearing tallit and *t'fillin*, using the mikveh) or
womanist and novel (Rosh Chodesh celebration, menopause marking).
The effects of rabbinic gender modeling are most recently argued by
an Orthodox woman: "Female spiritual leaders will model full participation…thereby normalizing and encouraging female congregants to
participate."[7] Girls and women model themselves on female rabbis, and
if female rabbis take an innovative approach toward ritual, laywomen
will follow, particularly in the non-Orthodox world, where the rabbi
is often the ritual leader. An early collection of women's rituals written and compiled by laywomen offers telling evidence. The book is
dedicated "To Rabbi Lynn Gottlieb, our teacher and friend," and one
prayer includes the note, "E. Etigson acknowledges the help of Rabbi
Lynn Gottlieb in preparing her ceremony."[8]

Several years ago I began studying ceremonies for baby-girl initiation, and many rabbis graciously opened their files to me. The twenty
ephemeral, unique rituals that one Conservative colleague crafted for
congregants beginning in 1980 amazed me. In the first place, baby-girl
rituals were still unusual in 1980. Secondly, most of the ceremonies involved ersatz-mikveh immersion.[9] One can only imagine the extent to
which this one rabbi's ritual leadership influenced countless laypeople's
thinking about ritual for Jewish females.

While I believe that female rabbis have played the leading role
in creating and disseminating new Jewish ritual and reinterpreting
the old, I also recognize that this is a simplified, even unfair, picture.
Non-clerical women—academics, educators, activists, writers, jour-
nalists—were necessarily the earliest Jewish feminist voices and were
thinking and writing about ritual innovation before women entered the
rabbinate. Female rabbinical students hit the ritual ground running,
thanks to the intellectual foundation for creative ritual already laid.
Secondly, men (rabbis and not) were also among the early voices calling
for ritual change, and women (rabbis and not) drew upon their work.
The same antecedent social and cultural factors that enabled women's
entry into the rabbinate also fostered people's interest in creative ritual.

Secular feminists attacked the mind-body, culture-nature dualism that denigrated women, and Christian feminists unveiled the male orientation of religion and ritual. A "hermeneutic of suspicion" already surrounded Jewish ritual before women entered rabbinical school. Moreover, North America's sophisticated and well-organized liberal-Judaism complex, alongside the relaxed and creative religious environment of the summer camps, supplementary schools, and *chavurah* culture, had educated Jewish women in ritual practice. Thus, the male and female feminists who fought for women's absorption into Jewish religious culture, including the rabbinate, were by definition interested in ritual. I do not mean to overlook these forerunners and co-runners. But the tremendous amount of written material suggests that female rabbis have taken the lead in advancing ritual change. (Despite their visibility, female cantors have not written much about ritual.[10])

Why look specifically at ritual?[11] Whether customary or creative, ritual is important in all religious practice, and many of Jewish feminism's early concerns dealt with women's equal access to and participation in ritual. Ritual involves physical engagement—one's experience of the spiritual world is necessarily filtered through physical perception—and many of women's ritual innovations have focused on the female body. Women felt, correctly so, that their life cycle had been ritually ignored—excepting the laws of *nidah* and mikveh, which are irrelevant for a non-menstruant or an unmarried menstruant. One woman explains, "Ritual seeks to provide a spiritual context for one's experience of the world."[12] If an experience perceived through the female body is ritually unmarked, then the experience has no opportunity for spiritual interpretation.

What follows is a chronicle that suggests how female rabbis have used print to influence change in Jewish ritual in the United States over the past half century.[13] I am not free from my biases—as a Jewish woman who was an adult when Sasso and Priesand were ordained, as one who received ordination, and as an academic with analytical interest in ritual. There are undoubtedly oversights. I have tried to offer a representative picture that treats denominational affiliations equally and reflects the many women who have written on this topic. Unless noted otherwise, I reference only material written by female rabbis. Ultimately I intend this overview to pay tribute to these women's creativity, leadership, and fearlessness that has resulted in tremendous religious and cultural transformation, all because of a determination to make up for lost time.

Which Female Rabbis? A Taxonomy

Women were first admitted to rabbinical training in the United States, where Jewish feminism was felt early and dramatically, and ritual experimentation first occurred in the United States. So my examples come largely from there. I began by focusing on the 1970s, when women began to speak about ritual qua rabbis. The earliest female-rabbinic voices regarding ritual were necessarily from the liberal Jewish world, and as coincidence would have it, the first woman ordained by the Reconstructionist Movement, Sasso, had (and has) a pronounced interest in ritual, setting a precedent with her 1973 article about baby-girl rituals. Her classmate Rebecca Alpert shared that interest and co-authored the earliest version of that ritual. But the evidence was more nuanced than I first assumed. The earliest rabbinical students, in the right place at the right time, were grappling with ritual alongside another group of women—those who were not yet ordained, either because they were already professionally involved, or too young, or identified with denominations not yet ordaining women. The precious few issues of the *Jewish Women's Resource Center Newsletter* (1979–81) provide illuminating evidence. The staff included (variously) three women who soon after entered rabbinical school: Nina Beth Cardin, Carol Glass, and Susan Grossman.[14] Recurring names within the issues include Margaret (Maggie) Moers Wenig, the undergraduate co-author of the 1976 feminist *Siddur Nashim*,[15] Lynn Gottlieb, and Sue Levi Elwell, all of whom would go on to rabbinical studies, becoming rabbinic spokeswomen for ritual change.[16] The contents of this newsletter, such as "Blessings for Menstruation" and critiques of and alternatives for the wedding and divorce rituals, testify to these women's already developed activist posture toward ritual.[17]

Education was the avenue to the ritual authority these women would ultimately wield as rabbis. One *JWRC Newsletter* includes a report on a 1979 pre-CAJE (Coalition for Alternatives in Jewish Education) meeting of twenty-five women that included rabbis and rabbinical students. The meeting included a Rosh Chodesh celebration led by a not-yet ordained woman and a discussion of the need for "creating rituals that begin to serve the spiritual needs of Jewish women."[18] The Jewish Women's Resource Center was an educational resource, freely offering source materials and serving as a site for hosting new ritual and classes on leading ritual.[19]

The tone of the *JWRC Newsletter* articles is assertive, yet loyally oppositional. While composing new ritual and critiquing the old, the writers all remained firmly rooted in the tradition, regardless of denominational affiliation (and all are represented, including Orthodoxy). Read in the present, the *JWRC Newsletter* seems to foretell the ritual change that would flourish in the next four decades. I use its demise in 1981 to roughly mark the end of the first stage of female-rabbinic voices around ritual creativity—a stage that necessarily includes some not-yet rabbis.

The women who entered rabbinical school in the 1980s represent the next stage, distinguished by those admitted into the Conservative Movement's Jewish Theological Seminary (JTS) in 1984, as well as by women too young to attend the other schools in the 1970s and others making a career change. The 1990s represent what I imprecisely designate the third stage, in which female rabbis of all the non-Orthodox denominations wrote extensively about ritual. The aforementioned names are still prominent, but there are many new and younger women who inherited an activist attitude toward ritual from their first- and second-stage colleagues. Two distinguishing features of the 1990s are the lesbian voices and the noticeable number of women's names affixed to same-sex wedding ceremonies, suggesting that female rabbis, already acculturated to the idea of changing ritual, found it easy to move into a new area of ritual concern. The fourth stage, gathering steam in the past few years, is marked by the entry of Orthodox women into the conversation and by female rabbis starting to speak out on issues beyond ritual.

Rabbinical School as Ritual Incubator

Many women have written about ritual while still students, suggesting rabbinical school is an important factor in cultivating rabbis who challenge traditional ritual practice.[20] Why is rabbinical school a ritual laboratory? In the first place, students are in close quarters for a lengthy time with peers with shared interests and concerns in an environment of intellectual and creative ferment. Even when the first women arrived in the schools, they were able to draw upon the efforts and support of like-minded men. (The 1973 Sasso-Alpert baby-girl ritual was written with two male classmates.) Secondly, in the schools the women encountered teachers (including the occasional female) who fostered student interest in shaping a ritually inclusive Judaism. Thirdly, part of rabbinical training is devoted to the leading and teaching of ritual. Even if a new student arrives with no particular interest in ritual per se, she or he is compelled to think about it. It isn't a big step to begin thinking about ritual change and then to begin experimenting with it. Thus the school context is one in which feminist ritual creativity was (and is) destined to occur, whether encouraged—as we might assume happened at RRC and HUC—or tolerated—as in the JTS case.

So what ritual creativity is apparent among female students? The Sasso-Alpert baby-girl ritual again comes to the fore, since all four authors were students. And the *JWRC Newsletter* proves that among those who entered HUC in the 1970s and '80s and JTS in 1984 were some already experienced in ritual creativity; once in rabbinical school, these women continued experimenting with ritual and fueling their classmates' interest. The student output has been prolific. Among the many examples from JTS students are a divorce ritual and the original versions of responsa on stillbirth and infant death.[21] In the past decade, students wrote two of the most innovative baby-girl rituals of the past twenty years.[22] The consequence is that women graduate to the pulpit, organization, school, and chaplaincy already adept at critiquing and expanding the ritual system.

The New Generation Meets the Old

Once in the professional world, women continue to incline toward ritual matters, and their colleagues accommodate their interest in ritual, indicated by their positions on editorial committees and their names on Movement publications. New siddurim and *machzorim* offer the opportunity to introduce different worship language and imagery. The new text, held in people's hands, influences ritual practice and prods clergy and laity alike into change.

The Reconstructionist Movement's 1989 siddur, *Kol HaNeshamah*, lists four female rabbis on the Prayerbook Commission (two ex officio) and two others on the Editorial Committee (both bodies also including non-rabbinical women).[23] The later Reform and Conservative siddur and *machzor* revisions were issued when women occupied senior positions in Movement publications offices. Although these roles are behind the scenes, these positions are influential in determining publication priorities and choosing editorial committees and contributors. A woman edited the 2007 Reform siddur, and female rabbis (and cantors and non-clergy) were well represented on the three participating committees, including the chair of the Committee on Liturgy and Practices.[24] Women's names are similarly prominent in the Reform Movement's new *machzor*, *Mishkan HaNefesh* (2015), and new life cycle manual (rabbi's manual), *L'Chol Z'man v'Eit* (2015).

The Conservative Rabbinical Assembly's female director of special projects, Rabbi Jan Caryl Kaufman, HUC-JIR '79, (since 1994 and recently retired) is listed as a member of the Joint Prayerbook Commission in that movement's 1998 siddur and as an ex-officio member of the Editorial Committee for the 2010 *machzor*.[25] However influential this position might be, the total female representation is somewhat other than the Reconstructionist and Reform examples: the 1998 Joint Prayerbook Commission included only one other woman (a non-rabbi) among fourteen men, and twelve years later, the ten-member *machzor* committee included only one female rabbi, suggesting that Conservative women have been integrated into these positions that heavily influence ritual practice at a slower pace than in the two more liberal movements. (It bears noting, however, that four out of eight members of the committee for the new Conservative prayerbook are women).

As women entered the Reform rabbinate in the 1970s, presumably editors and committees had new awareness of women's spiritual lives, but the early evidence is contradictory. The 1977 *Gates of the House* exhibits sensitivity to the range of lifetime experiences that includes females, such as prayers for the birth and adoption of children, including a covenantal ceremony for a baby girl.[26] The 1979 *Guide to the Jewish Life Cycle* ignores the female life cycle, except for the baby-girl covenantal ceremony.[27] The 1988 *Rabbi's Manual* included one woman on the committee, and the endnotes claim attention to ritual inclusion and egalitarian treatment, yet there are no female life-cycle rituals, the exception being the baby-girl covenantal ceremony.[28]

The 1994 *On the Doorposts of Your House* represents a significant transition, probably reflecting the increasing numbers of women in the rabbinate and their growing ritual presence. Its four editors included one woman, and there is attention to female biological experience with sections like "On Learning of a Pregnancy," "Menstruation," and "Upon Terminating a Pregnancy." The revised 2010 edition suggests the increasing visibility of female rabbis. Several are credited as helping "to move this project forward," including a female CCAR president. Most tellingly perhaps is the female rabbi's signature on the introduction to this revised version.[29]

Because women entered a professional world dominated and controlled by men, especially in the first couple of decades, it is not always possible to ascertain whether the women chose to pursue their school-fostered interest in ritual, and ritual for females in particular, or whether this was the niche given to them. Clearly women have played a role in Movement publications from the 1980s and especially the '90s, but committee lists offer no way to identify the nature of that role. Women's voices are better detected when their names are affixed to selections, and we have two examples. The Conservative and Reconstructionist Movements published rabbis' manuals within a year of each other, and in both, women participated as editors and contributors in numbers and ratios that suggest they were welcomed. But the two volumes reveal a striking imbalance in how women contributed. The 1998 Conservative manual's contributors included eleven women (plus one non-rabbi) alongside seventeen men.[30] But these women served as the authors or contributors only for life-cycle events, usually for parenting and fertility topics. As contrasting examples, women did not contribute the prayers for marriage, Thanksgiving, conversion, memorial-plaque dedication, shivah-candle lighting, divorce, establishing a household, or study. One could get the impression that a committee of men drew up the sections, identified those that are "female" (miscarriage, baby-girl initiation, grieving a terminated pregnancy, neonatal death), and said, "Let's put the women here." Or more cynically, a committee of men prepared a manual without these sections, women got wind of it and demanded the new material, and the men said, "Go ahead and write it."

The 1997 Reconstructionist manual offers a stark contrast. For each life-cycle event, "Personal Prayers and Supplementary Readings" are included, and these numerous selections appear to have male authors as often as female.[31] The female experience is reflected in passages like prayers for nursing for the first time, but that Movement's strong egalitarian commitment comes through in the companion pieces for a male parent.

The topical ghettoization of women in the Conservative manual contrasts with that Movement's recent responsa, suggesting that women's voices are being heard in a wider range of fields; even when looking at ritual matters, the authors are no longer focused only on women's unique, biologically based, experiences. Perhaps sheer numbers and generational variety result in expanded interests and perspectives among the women, no longer expected or wanting to conform to an essentialist niche. Nevertheless, the responsa show that women's interest in ritual has not abated with time. Considering that the first large group of Conservative women was ordained in 1988, it is striking that female-authored responsa began appearing already in 1989, suggesting a commitment to effecting change through institutional channels, out of proportion to their relatively few numbers. Most of the *t'shuvot* written by women relate to ritual, with topics ranging from the profound (women as religious witnesses) to the prosaic (can the chant marking the completion of a book of Torah be done if part of a triennial cycle).[32] More often than not, the topics suggest a woman's concerns, such as the matter of a non-fasting *sh'liach tzibur* on Yom Kippur (such as during pregnancy), mikveh use, and family purity laws.[33] But the ritual-related topics go beyond exclusively women's concerns, such as name options for converts and the ritual status of a deaf person and sign language.[34] To contextualize my claim that women write most frequently about ritual matters, their names are sparse in areas relating to kashrut, jurisprudence, or finances.[35]

Influencing Others: Editors, Authors, and Autobiographers

Women in the rabbinate influence ritual practice not only through their access to laypeople, activity in professional publications, and presence on legislative bodies, but also with their copious articles and books. Their edited volumes feature only or mostly female contributors, often their rabbinic colleagues. These articles and books frequently address ritual, and even when otherwise, the topic at hand often has ritual implications, such as feminism. Unsurprisingly women have embraced the Internet to disseminate their ideas about ritual. Ritualwell.org, for example, owes its formation to two women, one a rabbi.[36] The project editor and researcher for Keshetonline.org's LBGTQ-marriage resources were both women. A casual browse in these two sites suggests that women contribute in numbers that belie their actual proportion of the total non-Orthodox rabbinate.

Female rabbis across the denominational spectrum have taken to the genre of autobiography, perhaps explained by one's statement: "I have come to believe that all theology is autobiography, that to be a Jew means to tell my story within the Jewish story."[37] These writings are often of the Augustinian sort, typically rehashing the author's conversion to religious life; the spiritual quest involves exploration of expanded ritual practice, which leads in turn to searching for a new interpretation of traditional ritual or creating new ritual.[38] One woman wrote, "But as I slowly became more observant, I started to develop an increasingly strong awareness of nature's, and my body's, role in my spiritual life."[39] The pattern is this: a personal event reveals the need for ritualization, often concerning the female body, and then the author explores how to appropriate traditional language, actions, and symbols for this new ritual need. Women compose rituals for their own divorce and pregnancy loss, and they usually introduce their innovations with their personal story. An example is one woman's musing on her approach to and time in rabbinical school, when she grappled with liturgy and ritual; a key awakening was a teacher's remark that there is no event for which Judaism lacks a *b'rachah*, which caused her to remember her first period.[40] Women writing about homosexuality's challenges to Jewish ritual also adopt the autobiographical approach.[41] Sometimes the autobiographical element comes from pastoral experience. For example, the previously mentioned post-rape ritual is introduced by the personal perspectives of the two co-authors, one a rabbi, who describes her point of view as a spiritual resource. One rabbi writes about how she was compelled to create a healing ritual for a congregant who suffered a rape.[42] The pastoral concern can be traced back to the 1973 Sasso-Alpert baby-girl ritual, written for a classmate whose wife was expecting.[43] The pattern persists. A 2001 proposal for re-envisioning mikveh immersion is introduced by the author's description of the connection between her spiritual growth and her physical self, in this case menstruation, chronicling how her attitude toward mikveh and menstruation changed, and a 2007 book on mikveh is also flavored with autobiographical experience.[44]

The Upshot

Thus far, women's rabbinical activity in North America has been distinguished by a pronounced interest in matters ritual, even to the exclusion of other interests. Moreover, women have exhibited interest in ritual even before they enter rabbinical school, which has then fostered it. They have come to this interest largely from personal experiences that left them feeling religiously excluded, and they draw upon those experiences to craft new rituals, as well as tweak and reinterpret the old. The printed evidence alone testifies to the leading role female rabbis have taken in shaping Jewish ritual practice, whether through denominational publications or independent publications. Their efforts will leave a deep impression on Judaism, as other clergy and laypeople use the siddurim, *machzorim*, Haggadot, and prayer texts that these women have written and edited, as well as the individual rituals they have composed and published. This print activity is given visibility and authority by their clerical title, giving them entry into positions of ritual power with wide-ranging influence. The abundant publications, which have helped Jewish women make up their lost ritual time, foreground personal stories, illustrating another feature of the female rabbinate: informed by the personal and intimate. This is explored further in the next section.

The Individual Touch upon Jewish Ritual

Traditional Ritual Is Made Personal

Rabbinical women are necessarily thrust into negotiating the tension between feminism and Judaism, but they also appear to seek it out, motivated in great part by their personal experiences of exclusion, which shape their attitudes toward and expectations of ritual. Despite these experiences of exclusion, their abundant writing on ritual exhibits the pronounced preference for remaining within traditional, recognizable Jewish practice. For example, non-mainstream objects do not appear to have caught on.[45] Miriam joins Elijah at the seder, and she too has a cup; her tambourine hasn't widely caught on.[46] Nor have incantation bowls. Even when women's ritual changes are radical, they remain based within recognizable ritual culture. Novel *b'rachot* often use the traditional *b'rachah* formula (*Baruch atah Adonai*), despite its masculine language.[47] Worship directed to the Goddess hasn't taken root.[48] A woman still receives the *get*, but she augments that ceremony in which she is passively silent with another in which she is active and vocal.

On the other hand, women reinterpret and recontextualize traditional objects, imagery, language, and actions, and the new interpretations and contexts usually arise from or exhibit a personal focus. This spiritual valuation of personal experience stems in part from how many female rabbis see themselves: as independently expert in the making of ritual and free to create rituals that meet individual needs. The subtitle of one rabbi's edited volume is revealing: *Jewish Women on Life Passages and **Personal** Milestones* (emphasis added).[49] Nearly all the contributors (and many are rabbis) introduce their rituals with personal narrative that justifies the new ritual expression, explaining how it benefits the author's personal spiritual life. The pattern is for a ritualist to tell a personal story that resulted in her critique and/or innovation of ritual. Often a therapeutic benefit is attributed to ritual, used as spiritual balm that can transform personal experience, sometimes painful, into spiritual growth. The therapeutic expectation necessitates the autobiographical explanation, without which the ritual is less comprehensible. In explaining why she composed two healing rituals, one after an abortion, the other from sexual abuse, a writer forthrightly explains that ritual can salve people's deep-felt physical, emotional, and spiritual pain.[50]

The sections ahead survey examples of the kinds of changes in Jewish ritual that have occurred in the past fifty years in the United States, led in great part by female rabbis. I show how the traditional, the recognizable, remains constant, but placed alongside new emphasis on personal experience.

Altering Traditional Ritual: Marriage and Divorce

Marriage and divorce are two areas where women have refashioned traditional ritual with an eye toward more egalitarian involvement. Personal experience, often painful, with the traditional divorce ritual explains the many efforts to correct a woman's usual passive role: "I needed a ritual in which I was the actor, not the one acted upon—a ritual through which I could release myself."[51] But the happy occasion of marriage has also received much attention, starting already in 1979 and 1980, when two issues of the *Jewish Women's Resource Center Newsletter* published an egalitarian *ketubah*, a *ketubah* for an unmarried couple, and a new composition to "balance" the *Sheva B'rachot*.[52] In the 1990s attention to the wedding ritual swelled, with numerous proposed alternatives.[53] The urge to alter this ceremony persists. A 2012 article describing the innovation created by a female rabbi and her rabbinical-student husband-to-be (for themselves) has a revealing subtitle: "One Couple's Attempt to Create an Egalitarian Jewish Wedding Ceremony within the Traditional Framework of *Kiddushin*." The authors explain why and how they embarked on their project to revise *Birkat Eirusin* by consulting rabbinical literature. Their halachic concerns led them to consult other rabbis (including women). The "Attempt" of the title is explained in a coda, "Continuing the Process of Innovation," which acknowledges the imperfection of their result and critiques it from the perspectives of halachah and same-sex concerns.[54] Orthodox voices have also joined the discussion, suggesting changes for both the marriage and divorce rituals that respect halachah yet honor egalitarian principles.[55]

Female rabbis have taken an out-of-proportion leadership role in creating same-sex wedding rituals, traceable to lesbian voices and straight women's sensitivity to those voices. A 1994 volume included a commitment ritual for lesbians, a 1997 book on lesbian challenges to Judaism also offered proposals, and the Reconstructionist rabbi's manual of the same year included a ceremony for same-sex marriage.[56] Women were and are heavily represented as contributors to Keshetonline.org's wedding ceremonies for LBGTQ couples.

The fact that revision of the marriage and divorce ceremonies persists into the current decade suggests that the egalitarian-driven need to alter traditional ritual apparent in the *JWRC Newsletter* has not been satisfied. So perhaps it is not surprising that lately there is less emphasis on proposing "one" alternative and a move to offering choices and options. The author of a 2009 life-cycle guide titles her sections on wedding and divorce as "Jewish Weddings of Almost Every Kind," and "Rituals and Practices for When Relationships End."[57] Thus, ritual is tailored to the individual's needs, but the ritual moments remain defined by traditional categories like marriage and divorce.

Reinterpretation of Traditional Women's Culture: Mikveh and Housecleaning

Female rabbis have also reinterpreted traditional women's practices, especially in their advocacy of mikveh. In this case, the reinterpretation has completely inverted prior understandings, by connecting it to a forthright celebration of female sexuality.[58] Traditionally associated with a wife's return to sexual intimacy with her husband after menstruation, mikveh was either condemned or ignored by early egalitarian feminists, but subsequently redeemed as part of women's culture: "Mikveh links us to our community, to Jewish womanhood, and to the chain of tradition."[59] The necessary interpretive inversion drew its strength in part from mikveh's transformative powers associated with conversion—it has the power to transform essence. The advantage of immersion is its full involvement of the body, which can then be presented as restored, cleansed, or transformed by the ritual. The joining of water symbolism with essentialist interpretation is best seen in a 1986 pre-wedding ritual, wherein the two rabbinical-student authors explained that the objective was "to feel a spiritual cleansing from our former lives and loves. In *mikveh* we sought a tradition from our fore-mothers that would distinguish us as *kallot*."[60]

Those within the halachic camp, with Conservative rabbinical women leading the charge, have newly celebrated the *nidah* associa-tion of mikveh. As women, they have been able to put *nidah* back on the ritual radar and into the vocabulary of their male colleagues, who can no longer be accused of misogyny when speaking of it. Recent Rabbinical Assembly responsa testify to a newfound zeal for this practice.[61] We have yet to see how one Conservative woman's "user-friendly compendium" (edited by a male colleague) on mikveh will influence lay observance of *nidah*-based mikveh use, not to mention its creative-ritual use.[62]

An early female Orthodox rabbi remarkably critiqued usual *nidah* practice, introducing suggestions for a more reasonable approach, based on her personal experience.[63] Surely hers will not remain the lone voice on this topic. Referring to *nidah*, an Orthodox student, daring to speak in terms of a "Halachic and cultural evolution," writes, "I think about how women engaged in the Halachic system can be active part-ners instead of just swallowing the texts and bottling up frustration." She envisions "reviv[ing] the practice of the monthly ritual immersion" among the laity and teaching pre-wedding classes "to couples that are sex-positive and body-positive."[64]

The reevaluation of mikveh extends beyond essentialist physicality. A Conservative woman writes that *nidah*-based mikveh use supports a woman's "dignity, privacy and autonomy."[65] This goes together with her overall presentation of mikveh as personal religious experience rather than as halachic conformity. Another Conservative woman re-considers mikveh from a perspective of transgender theory, propos-ing different ways it might be used by someone not born a woman: "If people…can decide for themselves if the ritual fits the body it cir-cumscribes, then the ritual no longer forces certain bodies into certain boxes; our definitions of who must, who can and who might be exempt would be utterly transformed."[66]

Championing mikveh has gone beyond marriage and menstruation. Mikveh's symbolic advantages and ritual use of the body fit well with viewing illness through a spiritual lens. Healing rituals use mikveh, drawing upon its association with physical-spiritual transformation and also on water's association with cleansing and slaked thirst.[67] In another case, mikveh immersion enables healing and closure in the wake of sexual violence.[68]

Two writers from different denominations and time periods present a second example of the reinterpretation of traditional women's culture—in this case, female as housecleaner. The treatments are similar, but different in their feminist perspective. A 1982 prayerful supplement to *b'dikat chameitz* likens the process of pre-Pesach cleaning to "new life inside us / *Shechinah* / prepares for her birth," and the author describes how the cleaning unites women with "our ancient mothers." She also reaches for egalitarian involvement: "So we labor all women / cleaning and washing / now with our brothers / now with our sons."[69] Twenty years later, an Orthodox woman looks anew at her mother's cleaning practices, chagrined by feminist condemnation of this role she correctly labels a ritual. Giving it a theological spin via mystical literature, she imparts her personal custom as spiritual model: she makes a list of her personal *chameitz*, "the things that keep me enslaved to my evil inclination," which she burns along with the actual *chameitz*. Moving beyond this private ceremony, she explains what constitutes *chameitz* and compares the overdoing of Pesach cleaning to idol worship, thus using her rabbinic training to impart practical guidance about the ritual of cleaning. Despite the fact that she ends up valorizing woman's role of cleaner and rehashing a spiritualization of women and domesticity, her authoritative advice about sensible cleaning practice in the interest of fuller participation in the seder (if you're exhausted, you can't participate) speaks to a spirituality grounded in reality.[70]

One final, small example of how female rabbis participate in reinterpreting traditional women's culture is an article that offers a "feminist endorsement" of *Eishet Chayil*, the biblical passage a man sings in praise of his wife. The author doesn't reject the practice but suggests that the woman respond with similar biblical praise. Such an attempt at retention-with-balance is not new, but she takes a step further: she envisions the passage sung by a lesbian couple, among single women, and for single, divorced, and widowed women. She also imagines it taken out of the domestic context and put into any public setting that honors a woman's accomplishments.[71]

Recovery of Prayer Practice: *Tkhines*

No gender has a special claim on spirituality. Men penned the classical mystical literature, ancient Rabbinic discussions reveal a concern with the spiritual life, and contemporary men embrace spiritual inquiry and exploration. But female rabbis have taken a leading role in expanding religious practice with prayer (as opposed to liturgy, which is more standardized and formulaic). This interest can be traced to their discovery of *tkhines* (Yiddish prayers intended for women), and one of the earliest collections published in English grew out of a woman's 1984 rabbinical thesis.[72] This literary genre was celebrated as a remnant of traditional Jewish women's culture and bolstered essentialist claims of intrinsic female spirituality. *Tkhines* contextualize personal and domestic issues spiritually, addressing familial, bodily, and life-cycle concerns, especially those that might be considered as particular to women, such as fertility, candle lighting, and children. Female rabbis addressed these same topics in their own prayer compositions that began appearing in the late 1980s.[73] Like the *tkhines* they mimic, contemporary prayer compositions use the language and imagery of biblical and rabbinic literature.

This enthusiasm for *tkhines*-like personal prayer has recently moved beyond women's and life-cycle concerns, and even beyond specifically Jewish topics. A woman's 2002 collection exhibits a broader address (prayers for peace, overcoming competitiveness, job interviews), yet the contents suggest a persisting inclination toward what is perceived as women's experience: there is a section devoted to breast cancer, but not (for example) prostate cancer.[74]

Underlying *tkhines* is a theology of divine immanence, which complements the newer personalized prayer compositions and accords with feminism's rejection of hierarchical theology. The Hebrew and Jewish deity is classically portrayed as both immanent and transcendent, but rather than vacillating between these two poles as the traditional liturgy does (in order to capture the inexplicable ineffable), the new prayer compositions emphasize a deity of accessibility, one that dwells internally and is perceived through the experiences of the physical self. This theology and personal focus also characterize healing rituals, a religious development in which female rabbis have had a leading role. (Two women go so far as to credit their female colleagues with redefining the rabbinic role to include spiritual care—an overstatement for sure, but considering the prevalence of women in this field, their perception is understandable.)[75] Healing rituals draw upon the assumption of the personal prayer's therapeutic value. It isn't clear whether these rituals fostered the therapeutic quality of personal prayer, or whether personal prayer's therapeutic quality encouraged the formation of healing rituals. What is clear is that each element complements the others: the new prayers modeled on *tkhines*, the theology of immanence, personal focus, and therapeutic objectives. The selections in the 2013 Reform *Mishkan R'fuah: Where Healing Resides* (co-edited by a woman) exhibit this contemporary twist on *tkhines*.[76]

The supplementary prayers in the 1997 Reconstructionist rabbi's manual are *tkhines*-like, suggesting that the genre has moved, and will continue to move, into mainstream religious practice.[77] As rabbis continue to compose these prayers for themselves and their congregants (and publish them) and continue to use them in worship, laypeople will begin expecting this religious practice from their rabbis, whom they regard as speaking authoritatively about prayer. The author of a 2002 prayer collection writes that her rabbinic position leads people to ask her to pray "for them." And perhaps it is lay deference to the rabbi that leads her to intuit what the immanent deity wants and thinks: "God already knows us…God doesn't care…God listens…God is with us, God has filled us…God is praying for us. God is hoping…"[78] People perceive a rabbi as having unique insight into the Divine, so a rabbi can write (and pray) as if she does.

New Rituals for Women: Essentialism

Discussing female rabbis and ritual change usually brings to mind new rituals around the female experience, particularly the life cycle, and indeed, the evidence is plentiful. In a 1992 essay, one Conservative woman asked, "Do we, as women, have something from our own experience to offer?...What about ceremonies to mark the onset of menstruation, the onset of menopause, the adoption of a child, the loss of a child or a miscarriage?"[79] A 1994 edited volume is devoted exclusively to the female life cycle, and the chapters are arranged from birth to death with expansions that reflect a woman's experience—prayers for pregnancy (and its losses), childbirth, and infertility; rituals for weaning, midlife, menopause, and lesbian weddings.[80] Even rituals that initially appear to be non-gendered, as those proposed in the early 1990s for rabbinical ordination, are woman-centered: "affirming the continuity of friendship, of sisterhood, and of Jewish leadership," supporting each other "in a patriarchal rabbinical seminary," and celebrating admission into the rabbinate, and asking, "What would it mean for Jewish feminists to create our own ordination process, independent of the major rabbinical institutions and personalities? That is an idea whose time may have come."[81]

Despite the pronounced essentialism of the new rituals, authors continue to use traditional ritual language, texts, and symbols, for example, in the aforementioned ordination rituals, with the use of *Havdalah* timing, text study, and actions like anointing and *s'michah*. The combination of the new with the old was already apparent in the 1973 Sasso-Alpert baby-girl ritual, which radically co-opted the covenantal *b'rachah* of the circumcision, *l'hachniso bivrito shel Avraham avinu*, changing it to *l'hachnis et biteinu bivrito Am Yisrael*. A 1986 pre-wedding ritual for a woman includes a prayer comprising biblical verses and citations and two standard *b'rachot*, including that of mikveh immersion.[82] A 1987 pregnancy ritual includes a prayer that invokes the merit of the foremothers, the Exodus, and wishes for the child to have a life of Torah and good deeds.[83] A weaning ritual from the early 1990s comprises traditional language of intention and *b'rachah*, innovative *b'rachot* constructed from biblical language, and a rewording of the circumcision's naming prayer.[84]

Women's ritual activity has focused on the female body, and far less on the traditional calendar, but the two exceptions readily offer themselves for essentialist interpretation. Rosh Chodesh is easy to work with, because Rabbinic texts describe it as a women's holiday, and the moon's cycle serves as a metaphor for that of the menstruating females (and vice versa). Thus the rituals display a strong essentialist flavor, valorizing female biology, birth, and the round shapes of the moon and the female.[85] Groups and ceremonies began forming in the early 1970s, and female rabbis (and rabbis-to-be) quickly took to them, reminiscent of second-wave-feminist consciousness-raising groups. A 1981 issue of the *JWRC Newsletter* announces the formation of a group at the center (led by a woman who would go on to rabbinical school),[86] the editor of one of the earliest collections of Rosh Chodesh rituals includes three female rabbis in her acknowledgments,[87] and a 1993 analysis of these rituals describes one group that included a number of female rabbis.[88] These celebrations were introduced to synagogues and federations and sometimes superimposed upon a preexisting women's group.

The second temporal event that lends itself to feminist appropriation, given its theme of liberation and new identity, is the Passover seder. Again, a twist on an old ritual has been easily transferred to the public when female rabbis lead community seders (whether on the mandated night or not), help congregants plan their seders, and teach Passover-preparation classes. In 1981 the soon-to-be-rabbi editors of the *JWRC Newsletter* published a list of thirteen feminist Haggadot.[89] The names of female rabbis are on the earliest feminist Haggadot, and the acknowledgments in the 1986 *San Diego Women's Haggadah* include a female rabbi.[90] The original Ma'yan Haggadah was edited by a team that included a female rabbi, who wrote the Haggadah that served as the basis for this better known one; a subsequent revision acknowledges the input of three female rabbis (and two male) and at least one woman who later received ordination.[91]

The Upshot

Women's ritual activity, at least evidenced by the print they have produced, foregrounds personal stories, but also remains rooted in the recognizable tradition. Women write new rituals for previously unmarked occasions, retaining language and action from the past but imbuing it with wholly new interpretation, for ends that are informed by personal experience and narrative. Across the board, female rabbis exhibit a readiness to alter ritual practice to meet personal needs, both their own and that of their congregants. At the same time, they observe recognizably Jewish boundaries, even when crafting completely new ritual. This is the case even when the ceremonies are womanist, such as female life-cycle ceremonies, or deeply personal, including *tkhines*-like prayers that emerge from individual experience. However, this generalization is starting to be challenged by two factors, relatively new on the Jewish ritual scene: the growing concern with gender neutrality and the advent of female Orthodox rabbis (generally known as maharats), whose attitudes toward ritual and liturgy are at odds with those of their more liberal colleagues, including those of the Conservative Movement. I address these challenges, which are apt to color the future of female rabbinical influence on Jewish ritual, in the next section.

The Denominationally Divided Future

Moving Beyond Essentialism

The essentialist and physical flavor of the new rituals is usually attributed to the goal of reversing the perception of women's biology—that same biology that excluded them from synagogue ritual—by raising it to the status of sacred, a means of access to the Divine, stemming from feminism's valuation of spirit-body unity.[92] On the other hand, the essentialist physicality in the new rituals inevitably raised the question of the biological reductionism, in which critics detected anti-feminist values, as well as the risk of perpetuating women's ritual separation. A 1997 author captured the tension that exists between ritual innovation that grows out of egalitarian feminism with that which arises out of essentialism: she contrasted "imitative" rituals, which make women into "honorary men," with "inventive" rituals that are "uniquely female" but risk reducing women to their biology.[93] Resistance to essentialism was also raised by the early lesbian voices, critical of straight women's preoccupation with pregnancy and childbirth and of their ritual appropriations that used heteronormative assumptions, such as including chuppah in the circumcision-ritual triad with Torah and maasim tovim in their baby-girl ceremonies. Women who did not or could not have children also felt uncomfortable with the biological emphasis.[94]

Non-essentialist creativity grew out of this resistance, finding footing amid a growing concern with gender-neutral equal access to ritual life: "As we listen to the no longer silent voices of women we are reminded that there are others in our community who have been excluded and who we need to welcome back."[95] The first lesbian voices in the 1990s were influential in this shift, especially because gay men, who shared their concerns, could use their ritual proposals that were often gender-neutral.[96] Thinking about the distinction between sex characteristics and gendered behavior has led to more exploration with gender-free ritual, and recent innovations exhibit a desire to downplay gender specification, such as infant rituals that focus on the naming alone (separating the circumcision ritual from the public, celebratory context) and gender-neutral wedding rituals. Women's prominence in both these trends suggests how underlying concerns have shifted slightly, moving toward a purely egalitarian perspective that aims for equal ritual inclusion for all gender identities. For example, a recent proposal for renewing mikveh practice is based on the rejection of a binary understanding of gender, and unlike most recent writing about immersion ritual, the author doesn't romanticize the mikveh in a way that objectifies the female body.[97] My impression is that the move away from essentialism began around 1990. I note the striking absence of essentialist content in a 1989 mikveh ceremony for healing in the aftermath of sexual violence, which could be used by anyone who has been similarly victimized.[98] Men could use one woman's 1990 friends-parting ritual, based on Talmudic text and archaeological evidence, equally well.[99] Ditto a gender-neutral deathbed confession written in 1994.[100]

A recent volume suggests that women are beginning to look at the entire calendar and see it anew from an egalitarian, non-essentialist perspective. The author, coming out of the Reconstructionist and Renewal worlds, describes the ways that holidays and special dates present opportunities for personal spiritual expression. Rosh Chodesh is maintained as a woman's holiday, but is balanced with *Kiddush L'vanah* as a man's, both as opportunities for gender-specific group support or consciousness-raising (even though the author offers interpretations for both occasions that reflect a growing concern with gender-neutral access).[101] A final piece of evidence in this shift is that every calendar event is well represented on Ritualwell.org, with the content tending less toward gender-driven, alternative rituals for the holidays, and more toward the augmentation of traditional observance with gender-neutral meditations and prayers.

The question is whether the people in the pews are similarly evolving. Do they still expect a Rosh Chodesh group from their female rabbi? Are the women trained from the 1970s through the 90s reading the recent literature about gender, revisiting their own understanding of ritual and educating their congregants? Complicating matters is the introduction of women into the Orthodox rabbinate. If they are relegated to answering women's questions about *nidah*, a gendered expectation of female rabbis will be reinforced and validated. There are promising signs that Orthodox women's interests will transcend exclusively female concerns—for example, Rabba Sara Hurwitz's recent article arguing halachically for women's full inclusion in death rituals, including officiating.[102]

Female rabbis have begun to reconsider feminist nostalgia for traditional women's culture, such as one woman's analysis of the medieval

Central European *Hollekreisch* as an "authentic" baby-girl ritual. As her study proves, it was neither a necessarily Jewish practice, nor performed exclusively for girls.[103] One hopes that this author's sober revisionism will catch the eye of her pulpit colleagues who compose and conduct rituals for baby-girl initiation. Perhaps this critique represents a new hermeneutic of suspicion and augurs a growing hesitation about celebrating traditional women's culture just because it belonged to women.

In a 2003 volume devoted to circumcision, three articles by rabbis (two female and one male) discuss this essentialist, gendered ritual. The women question it, and the man defends it. All three write from a personal perspective, the latter with poignant regret at not having circumcised his infant son and then having to do it belatedly. Comparing circumcision to the "spiritual bonding power of blood every month" shared between mothers and daughters, he describes it as a "bonding ritual that I believe leads to higher levels of consciousness for both fathers and sons." This "most incredible father/son bonding experience" should not be seen as "a means of 'reproducing patriarchy, male privilege and entitlement.' On the contrary, it seems to be a means of reproducing male love and compassion."[104]

One woman also reflects on her son's circumcision, but she describes her ambivalence, even anger, and how she "was implicated in my own misery because I wanted to have our son circumcised—or at least I did not want to *not* circumcise him." She accuses the growing practice of separating the physical ritual from the public naming as deceptive, denying the "problem," which is that circumcision effects the "marginalization of Jewish women."[105] The other woman argues that rabbis must ritually accommodate people who choose not to circumcise their sons. Defending choice and inclusion, she lobbies for creating "spiritual opportunities" for people who are attuned to considering all the possibilities regarding religious life. She points out that feminism is about giving women choices, but boys and men have the same right to choices about their bodies.[106]

These articles unwittingly reveal how a person's own gender identity inevitably influences his or her attitude toward an essentialist ritual.

When the discussion concerns a male ritual, a man occupies the privileged, insider position and can argue in support of ancient tradition. A woman has an outsider status that both excludes her and enables her to question it from an egalitarian perspective. The inclination toward questioning will continue, and continue homing in on circumcision, as the discomfort with binary-gendered separation grows, at least among the non-Orthodox. Within Orthodoxy, allegiance to gender conformity and gender-determined ritual practice is enforced by allegiance to halachah. In such a setting, one cannot imagine circumcision—and its glorification, to the relative detriment of newborn females—to be questioned, even by female rabbis.

Denominations

The aforementioned three articles about circumcision also testify to the persistent factor of denomination in ritual change—the authors are all Reconstructionist, which positions them advantageously when questioning a traditional ritual. As one of the women writes, "Reconstructionists assert that 'the past has a vote, but not a veto.'…It was only a matter of time before *brit milah*…also became the focus of contemporary questioning."[107] Following those articles is an epilogue comprising fragments from a discussion among women about circumcision that eloquently falls along expected denominational lines.[108] The Orthodox speaker defends the practice—but significantly she joined the discussion (which I assume occurred around 2001). Once again, just like in the late-1970s *JWRC Newsletter* and a trans-denominational co-edited 1992 book,[109] Orthodox women were in conversation with non-Orthodox. Three Orthodox women were ordained in 2014, albeit with a title other than "rabbi." Their female dean was ordained in 2009. The first female Reform rabbi was in the audience, and she was publicly acknowledged, a telltale admission of the event's indebtedness to liberal Jewish influences.[110] How Orthodox female clergy will alter the ritual scene is impossible to predict, but they will, and the chain of influence will extend back to the liberal movements, which were first influenced by the secular feminist world.

One current Orthodox student in an article entitled "Can We Speak for Ourselves?" describes the questions and perspectives that she and her classmates bring to the texts they study, and she lets slip a sign of coming change when she refers to the inevitable "Halachic and cultural evolution" and challenges, "Are we taking rituals crafted by men and making them uniquely our own?"[111] Already women in the Orthodox rabbinate have begun modeling and teaching about ritual and are interpreting their ritual actions.[112] If Orthodox women have their say, change is not too far in the future regarding both marriage and divorce documents, particularly with respect to the *agunah* problem, where at least one writer thinks the male establishment has dragged its feet. She poignantly writes, "What is the point of all my studying if I am only going to perpetuate the status quo?"[113]

On the other hand, when historian Pamela Nadell wrote, "Feminism trumps the denominational divide" for female rabbis, she surely oversimplified the case.[114] There is no single definition of feminism, let alone what it means in a Jewish context. In fact, denominational patterns were strongly apparent from the outset, even more so now that women have moved into the leadership of their respective movements, and increasingly so since women have begun moving into the Orthodox rabbinate. Denomination expresses itself noticeably in attitudes toward traditional ritual—whether one is conciliatory toward it or willing to make a break. An Orthodox woman will not reject mikveh and *nidah*, even if she makes learned allowances in specific situations or establishes guidelines that reflect modern, shared child care. Not only are Orthodox women bound by halachic interpretation; they function with concerns about splitting their community.[115] Nevertheless, their writing indicates that they, too, intend to alter ritual practice, particularly in the areas of marriage, divorce, and *nidah*.

Conservative women, bound by halachic limitations, albeit of a liberal bent, struggle with equitable practice in rituals that have legal ramifications, such as marriage, divorce, and testimony. From the outset, they took their concerns to their movement's Law Committee, quickly made their mark there, and now are represented on that body.

Presumably they will continue to use this legal body to advance their ritual goals even as they continue to freely compose rituals for situations not governed by halachah.

Reform and Reconstructionist women were never encumbered by halachah, so they were free to ignore customary limits on women's practice. They also felt free to exploit traditional women's practice, such as mikveh, in order to explore avenues for new ritual expression. Reconstructionism has had from its birth a commitment to ritual and theological honesty alongside a willingness to change, and early ritual changes stemming from feminism were relatively easy to absorb. Because women were admitted to its school from the outset, its clergy has not had to struggle with integrating feminism to the same degree as in other movements.[116] A Reconstructionist colleague who has long had an active role in ritual innovation objected to my thesis that female rabbis have been more involved than men in new-ritual creation; she argued that women's inherent integration into the school has resulted in equitable cross-fertilization among that movement's male and female colleagues, in school and in the field, around *all* issues, including ritual. Because Reform and Conservative women entered school acutely aware of their historical secondary status, there was a tendency to self-segregate and explore ritual without their male colleagues.

Overall the evidence suggests that ritual innovation tends to come first from the Reconstructionist camp, moving along the ideological spectrum to Reform, Conservativism, and then to Orthodoxy. Recent examples are the earliest advocacy for lesbian ritual and ordination of gays and lesbians. The creeping of ritual (and other) change from left to right proves that denominational boundaries are not impermeable. A 1979–80 issue of the *Jewish Women's Resource Center Newsletter* announces the meetings of an Orthodox women's minyan and offers JWRC's assistance in organizing other such groups,[117] suggesting how non-Orthodox women were supporting changes in Orthodox ritual practice already in the late '70s. A 1992 book offers further evidence of change creeping into the Orthodox world from the liberal world. This book, dedicated to the idea that "women should more fully participate in all aspects of synagogue life and ritual" was co-edited by an Orthodox woman and a female Conservative rabbi, and the contributors span the denominational world. In one essay, two sisters reflect on becoming bat mitzvah in an Orthodox women's davening group, and another essay describes the first organized women's worship at the Temple Wall in Jerusalem, a trans-denominational feminist demonstration led by and involving both Orthodox women and non-Orthodox female rabbis.[118] Ritual innovation clearly interests Orthodox women, and liberal female rabbis are influencing them. It just depends on how one defines ritual innovation: for one person it is an egalitarian *ketubah*; for another it is a women's minyan.

In sum, attitudes toward ritual innovation are highly influenced by attitude toward halachah. On one side, women observe praxis boundaries and subject proposed changes to a halachic litmus test, be it their own or that of an authoritative body. On the other side, boundaries and tests are a non-binding consideration at most. The reality is that ritual change often occurs haphazardly—even in the halachic world—usually beginning at the less-controlled periphery, moving inward toward the larger community, and only later upward through and into the authoritative bodies. Examples of this messy process are the Conservative Movement's addition of the foremothers' names to the *Amidah*'s first *b'rachah* and Orthodox women's davening groups. As more Orthodox female rabbis join the discussion, they will add their perspectives to this evolving religious scene. Most likely the ritual practice of Jewish women in the United States will become even more differentiated along denominational lines.

Effects of the Personal

A distinctive tone in female rabbinical writing on ritual is personal autonomy; authors seem to assume that readers will consult what they're writing and then go on to compose their own ritual that will meet individual needs. A result of the emphasis on the individual, both as ritual composer and as ritual practitioner, is that no "one" ritual has emerged (nor is it likely to in the foreseeable future) for, say, baby-girl initiation, miscarriage, egalitarian marriage and divorce, or healing, and both the Reconstructionist and Conservative Movement rabbi's manuals (published in 1997 and 1998, respectively), which present optional readings for each life-cycle event, perpetuate a culture of individuality. In this vein, the Reconstructionist Haggadah published in 2000 offers four seder texts from which to choose.[119] The author of a recent life-cycle guide covers all the "usual" events but enlarges those categories with alternatives and options from which the reader can choose and adapt.[120] Perhaps more time is required for a uniformity to settle upon the tremendous variety. Or perhaps the celebration of individuality and the preference for ritual options are intrinsic to and emerge from feminism and reflect a new approach to religious practice. The individual is the new face of feminist-informed religion and replaces the earlier feminist program of women gaining control. Control has been gotten, and individuals who want to worship and pray *as individuals* have taken it, at least in the non-Orthodox camps.

Female-rabbinic guides to writing of one's own ritual began appearing in the 1990s, probably reflecting the abundant material available by then. One of the earliest examples is a step-by-step guide to assessing ritual need, finding resources, and ensuring Jewish content and meaning; significantly this guide includes a description of common pitfalls and a checklist for ritual critique.[121] This interest in providing guidance has not abated—the influential Internet sites Ritualwell.org and Keshetonline.org devote links to such guidance, suggesting that site editors assume their readers are not simply copying available ritual options.

Emphasis on individualized ritual experience and encouragement of personally meaningful prayer are defensible improvements in religious culture. On the other hand, such emphasis on the personal encourages an ephemerality that fails to support communal memory and continuity. One rabbi anticipated this problem when she mused about how much material is shared or recited only once and never again: "Does Rosh Hodesh, then, provide a vehicle only for the *temporary* reclamation of women's voices, while in fact perpetuating their ephemerality?"[122]

Personal focus also neglects a social purpose of ritual—to define and unify the *community*—and eclipses aspects of the Divine other than healer, listener, or empathizer, with an individual's *bakashah* overshadowing the community's *shevach*. One theological purpose of Jewish liturgy and ritual is to minimize the individual, placing him or her within the overall Grand Scheme, progress toward a messianic goal. That Grand Scheme framework is often absent from the new rituals, largely because of the focus on the individual's experience in the present. Rather than magnifying the Deity by minimizing the human (a non-feminist hierarchical schematic), individuality is magnified, with any praise of the Divine serving as a magnifying glass through which to view human experience—ironically, another kind of hierarchy.

The Upshot

With their goals of equal access increasingly achieved, female rabbis are beginning to advocate for others with personal experiences of ritual exclusion. Now that *women's* lost time has been made up, attention can shift to other examples of lost time. Consequently, they will continue to put the "big and hard discussions" about ritual practice onto the agenda, such as circumcision, led by those least hindered by halachah. However, the concerns will be less and less women's equitable access and more and more gender-neutral access. This in turn will open up discussions about the nature and purpose of ritual—for whom it exists, and what purpose it serves; whom it includes, and whom it excludes.

As their intra-denominational numbers increase, and as they find themselves surrounded by more and more like-minded male colleagues, female rabbis will have less need "to rise above denominational politics to talk to each other."[123] Women loyal to halachah have little in common with women not similarly constrained, and the latter are free to challenge and experiment without pausing to consider the formers' ideology. Denominational expectations of rabbis, and of women in general, will divide female rabbis, just as those expectations divide male rabbis. A woman will no longer be a "female rabbi" but a "female [denomination] rabbi" (etc.). This will become increasingly the case as women enter the Orthodox rabbinate in larger numbers.

Aside from equal access and gendered ceremonies for females, women's greatest influence on Jewish ritual has been the infusion of personal theology into ritual. How this will play out in the future, especially if membership in liberal congregations continues to decline, remains to be seen. Increasing numbers of female rabbis beholden to traditional ritual and liturgy could counteract this trend, at least to the extent that it can be associated with female rabbis.

Previously I mentioned how feminist ritual interest has been more devoted to the life cycle than to the calendar, a result of the intense focus on personal spiritual experience. Focus on the life cycle is also due to the nature of U.S. Judaism, in which life-cycle ritual is central—and the synagogue is the venue for these ceremonies.[124] Thus the interest of female rabbis on the female life cycle might simply have to do with how American Jewish identity is bound up with synagogue ritual. This also helps explain why female rabbis' writing exhibits so little interest in non-ritual areas in which women have traditionally played large roles, such as kashrut and Pesach. (Coincidentally, the centrality of the synagogue in American Jewish life explains why female rabbis have had an influential role in changing ritual.) A few Conservative responsa suggest that women's interests are expanding beyond life-cycle ritual, and female rabbis across the spectrum are proving to be prominent spokespeople concerning social and ethical matters.[125] The resistance against gender differentiation will begin to mute the limited, essentialist perspective that has hobbled feminism thus far. As equal-access values and gender-identity sensitivity are increasingly assumed in the discussions of more and more Jews, those who occupy a ritual world of choices and options will be separated from those whose ritual world is definitively without choices and options.

NOTES

1. Pamela S. Nadell, "Bridges to 'A Judaism Transformed by Women's Wisdom': The First Generation of Women Rabbis," in *Women Remaking American Judaism*, ed. Riv-Ellen Prell (Detroit: Wayne State University Press, 2007), 211–28; here 211.

2. Sandy Sasso, "B'rit B'not Israel: Observations on Women and Reconstructionism," *Response* 18 (Summer 1973): 101–5.

3. Sally Priesand, *Judaism and the New Woman* (New York: Behrman House, 1975), 55–67; here 55.

4. Sara Hurwitz, "Orthodox Women in Rabbinic Roles," in *New Jewish Feminism*, ed. Elyse Goldstein (Woodstock, VT: Jewish Lights, 2009), 144–54, esp. 150–53. See also Amy Stone, "Orthodox Women Rabbis by Any Other Name," *Lilith Blog*, June 21, 2013. Regarding the connection between authority and new ritual, see Lori Lefkovitz and Rona Shapiro, "The Politics and Aesthetics of Jewish Women's Spirituality," in Goldstein, *New Jewish Feminism*, 77–78. See also *Religious Institutions and Women's Leadership*, ed. Catherine Wessinger (Columbia, SC: University of South Carolina Press, 1996), 9–10; and Nadell, "Bridges to 'A Judaism Transformed by Women's Wisdom,'" esp. 212–14, 223.

5. Laura Geller, "From Equality to Transformation," in *Women Rabbis: Exploration and Celebration*, ed. Gary Zola (Cincinnati: HUC-JIR Rabbinic Alumni Press, 1996), 69–80; here 72.

6. Laura Levitt and Sue Ann Wasserman, "Mikvah Ceremony for Laura (1989)," in *Four Centuries of Jewish Women's Spirituality*," ed. Ellen Umansky and Dianne Ashton (Boston: Beacon Press, 1992), 321–26.

7. Sara Hurwitz, "Summon the *Mekonenot* (Dirge-Singers) and They Will Come," *JOFA Journal* 11 no 1 (Spring 2013): 5–7.

8. Irene Fine, *Midlife: A Rite of Passage, and The Wise Woman; A Celebration* (San Diego: Woman's Institute for Continuing Jewish Education, 1987), part 1, ii, and part 2, 22. Gottlieb was closely connected to the Institute (1977–2004), which published eight books relating to women and ritual. A similar example can be found in Umansky and Ashton, *Four Centuries of Jewish Women's Spirituality*, 259.

9. She modeled these on Sharon and Michael Strassfeld, "Ceremonial Welcoming for a Newborn Jewish Daughter: Brit Mikvah," *Lilith* 1, no. 1 (Fall 1976): 22–23.

10. Two rare exceptions are Judith Bender, "Jewish Divorce," in *A Ceremonies Sampler: New Rites, Celebrations, and Observances of Jewish Women*, ed. Elizabeth Resnick Levine (San Diego: Woman's Institute for Continuing Jewish Education, 1991), 67–69; and Barbara Ostfeld, "The Ascent of the Woman Cantor," in Goldstein, *New Jewish Feminism*, 133–43.

11. I use "ritual" loosely, beholden to Julie Greenberg's definition: "religious activity as opposed to religious thought." Julie Greenberg, "Reconstructing Jewish Women's Ritual," in *Worlds of Jewish Prayer*, ed. Shohama Harris Wiener (Northvale, NJ: Jason Aronson, 1993), 257.

12. Sue Levi Elwell, "Reclaiming Jewish Women's Oral Tradition? An Analysis of Rosh Hodesh," in *Women at Worship*, ed. Marjorie Procter-Smith and Janet Walton (Louisville, KY: Westminster/John Knox, 1993), 121.

13. My interest here is not liturgical language, the obvious examples being gender-free metaphors for the Divinity and alternatives to the usual *b'rachah* formula.

14. *Jewish Women's Resource Center* 1, no. 2 (Summer 1979): 2; 1, no. 3 (Fall 1979): B [*sic*]. Cardin and Glass were co-founders of the center.

15. Naomi Janowitz and Margaret Wenig, *Siddur Nashim* (Providence, RI: privately published, 1976). See also Naomi Janowitz and Margaret Wenig, "Sabbath Prayers for Women," in *Womanspirit Rising*, ed. Carol Christ and Judith Plaskow (San Francisco: Harper Collins, 1992), 174–78.

16. *Jewish Women's Resource Center Newsletter* 1, no. 4 (Winter 1979–80): 12, describes a university women's studies course that included a seder taught by Elwell. Gottlieb was privately ordained in either 1980 or 1981. See Pamela Nadell, *Women Who Would Be Rabbis* (Boston: Beacon Press, 1998), 280 n. 149.

17. *Jewish Women's Resource Center Newsletter* 1, no. 2 (Summer 1979): 3–4; 1, no. 3 (Fall 1979): 3–5.

18. *Jewish Women's Resource Center Newsletter* 1, no. 4 (Winter 1979–80): 13. The report's authors were Elwell and Linda Holtzman (newly ordained). The Rosh Chodesh celebration was led by Gottlieb.

19. *Jewish Women's Resource Center Newsletter* 1, no. 3 (Fall 1979): B [*sic*]; 1, no. 4 (Winter 1979–80): 14.

20. Thanks to Barbara Penzner for a helpful conversation on this point.

21. Stephanie Dickstein, "What Should Be Jewish Practice following the Death of an Infant Who Lives Less Than Thirty One Days?," 1992; Stephanie Dickstein, "What Should Jewish Practice Be Following a Stillbirth?," 1996; Diane Cohen, "The Divorced Woman: Toward a New Ritual," *Conservative Judaism* 44, no. 4 (Summer 1992): 62–68.

22. Debra Ruth Kolodny, "Mystery of the Covenant: A New Ceremony of *Simchat Brit*," *Kerem* (2007–8): 1–14; and Alana Suskin, "*Brit Melach*: Recalling the Covenant with Salt," in *Celebrating Your New Jewish Daughter*, ed. Debra Nussbaum Cohen (Woodstock, VT: Jewish Lights, 2001), 145–49.

23. *Kol Haneshamah: Shabbat Eve* (Wyncote, PA: Reconstructionist Press, 1989), vi. *Kol Haneshamah: Shabat Vehagim*, 2nd ed. (Wyncote, PA: Reconstructionist Press, 1994), iv, is very similar. See also the list of commentators, x.

24. *Mishkan T'filah*, ed. Elyse Frishman (New York: CCAR Press, 2007), xii. The 1975 *Gates of Prayer* lists no women on the Liturgy Committee. *Gates of Prayer for Weekdays and At a House of Mourning: A Gender Sensitive Prayerbook*, ed. Chaim Stern (New York: CCAR Press, 1992), does not have a list of contributors.

25. *Siddur Sim Shalom for Shabbat and Festivals* (New York: Rabbinical Assembly/United Synagogue of Conservative Judaism, 1998); *Mahzor Lev Shalem* (New York: Rabbinical Assembly, 2010). The RA's 1985 *Siddur Sim Shalom* lists a liturgy committee without any female members.

26. *Gates of the House*, ed. Chaim Stern (New York: CCAR, 1977); no woman is listed as contributor; the members of the CCAR's Liturgy Committee did not include a woman [297].

27. *Guide to the Jewish Life Cycle*, ed. Simeon Maslin (New York: CCAR, 1979); no woman is listed as contributor. There is attention to larger social reality with selections like "The Single Person, the Single Parent Family and Mitzvot."

28. *Maaglei Tsedek: Rabbi's Manual*, ed. David Polish (New York: CCAR, 1988).

29. *On the Doorposts of Your House*, ed. Chaim Stern (New York: CCAR, 1994).

30. *Rabbi's Manual*, vol. 2 (New York: Rabbinical Assembly, 1998), 64–67. The preceding manual was published in 1965: *A Rabbi's Manual*, ed. Jules Harlow (New York: Rabbinical Assembly, 1965).

31. *Rabbi's Manual*, ed. Seth Daniel Riemer et al. (Wyncote, PA: Reconstructionist Rabbinical Association, 1997). Editors comprised two women and three men, with a female editorial assistant. Additionally the preface acknowledges a pre-editorial committee (two women among three men) that had two chairs, one a women. Other contributors and participants include four women and ten men.

32. Amy Eilberg, "The Use of a Remote Audio/Video Monitor on Shabbat and Yom Tov: A Dissenting Opinion," 1989 in *Proceedings of the Committee on Jewish Law and Standards/1986–1990* (New York: Rabbinical Assembly, 1990): 297–98); Debra Reed Blank, "Response to Miscarriage," 1991 in *Responsa of the CJLS 1991–2000* (New York: Rabbinical Assembly, 2002): 357–63; Amy Eilberg, "Response to Miscarriage: An Alternate View," 1991 in *Responsa of the CJLS 1991–2000* (New York: Rabbinical Assembly, 2002): 364–466; Stephanie Dickstein, "What Should Jewish Practice Be Following a Stillbirth?," 1996 in *Responsa of the CJLS 1991–2000* (New York: Rabbinical Assembly, 2002): 367–76; Stephanie Dickstein, "What Should Be Jewish Practice following the Death of an Infant Who Lives Less Than Thirty One Days?," 1992; Nechama D. Goldberg, "Hazak, Hazak v'Nithazak," 2000 in *Responsa of the CJLS 1991–2000* (New York: Rabbinical Assembly, 2002): 43–49; Susan Grossman, "Edut Nashim k'Edut Anashim: The Testimony of Women Is as the Testimony of Men," Committee on Jewish Law and Standards of the Rabbinical Assembly, (New York: Rabbinical Assembly, 2001).

33. Gail Labovitz, "The Non-Fasting Shaliah Tzibbur on Yom Kippur," 2012; Miriam Berkowitz, Susan Grossman, and Avram Reisner, "Mikveh and the Sanctity of Family Relations," 2006; Susan Grossman, "Mikveh and the Sanctity of Being Created Human," 2006; Miriam Berkowitz, "Reshaping the Laws of Family Purity for the Modern World," 2006.

34. Miriam Berkowitz, "May a Convert Use a Name other than 'Ploni ben/bat Avraham Avinu'? A Dissenting Opinion," 2010; Gail Labovitz, "May a Convert Use a Name other than 'Ploni ben/bat Avraham Avinu'? A Concurring Opinion," 2010; Pamela Barmash, "Status of the *Heresh* and of Sign Language," 2011; Pamela Barmash, "Reading Torah in Sign Language," 2011.

35. A wider range of legal interests is apparent in the collection by Monique Susskind Goldberg and Diana Villa, *Ask the Rabbi: Women Rabbis Respond to Modern Halakhic Questions* (Jerusalem: Schechter Institute of Jewish Studies, 2010).

36. The other woman was a Reconstructionist Rabbinical College faculty member (the original material coming from a collection at that institution). See Lori Lefkovitz and Rona Shapiro, "The Politics and Aesthetics of Jewish Women's Spirituality," in Goldstein, *New Jewish Feminism*, 66–80.

37. Laura Geller, "Encountering the Divine Presence (1986)," in Umansky and Ashton, *Four Centuries of Jewish Women's Spirituality*," 242–47; quote on 245.

38. Two examples from opposing denominational poles are Lynn Gottlieb, *She Who Dwells Within: A Feminist Vision of a Renewed Judaism* (San Francisco: HarperSanFrancisco, 1995), and Haviva Ner-David, *Life on the Fringes* (Needham, MA: JFL Books, 2000). Both weave together autobiography, ritual, and theology.

39. Danya Ruttenberg, "Blood Simple: Transgender Theory Hits the Mikveh," in *Yentl's Revenge: The Next Wave of Jewish Feminism*, ed. Danya Ruttenberg (Seattle: Seal Press, 2001), 77–87; here 78.

40. Laura Geller, "Encountering the Divine Presence (1986)," in Umansky and Ashton, *Four Centuries of Jewish Women's Spirituality*, 242–47. See also many examples in Debra Orenstein, ed., *Lifecycles*, vol. 1, *Jewish Women on Life Passages and Personal Milestones* (Woodstock, VT: Jewish Lights, 1994), 45–51, 201–10.

41. Rebecca Alpert, *Like Bread on the Seder Plate: Jewish Lesbians and the Transformation of Tradition* (New York: Columbia University Press, 1997); Rebecca T. Alpert, Sue Levi Elwell, and Shirley Idelson, eds., *Lesbian Rabbis: The First Generation* (New Brunswick, NJ: Rutgers University Press, 2001).

42. Levitt and Wasserman, "Mikvah Ceremony for Laura (1989)," 321–26.

43. Bonnie Dalzell, "I Perceive Differently," [Philadelphia?] *Times Chronicle*, May 1974.

44. Ruttenberg, "Blood Simple: Transgender Theory Hits the Mikveh," 77–87; Miriam Berkowitz, *Taking the Plunge: A Practice and Spiritual Guide to the Mikveh*, ed. David Golinkin (Jerusalem: Schechter Institute for Jewish Studies, 2007), ix–xii.

45. Cf. Julie Greenberg, "Reconstructing Jewish Women's Ritual," esp. 267–68.

46. E.g., *A Night of Questions: A Passover Haggadah*, ed. Joy Levitt and Michael Strassfeld (Wyncote, PA: Reconstructionist Press, 2000), 13. Cf. Vanessa Ochs, *Inventing Jewish Ritual* (Philadelphia: Jewish Publication Society, 2007), 167–86.

47. For example, the recontextualizing of the covenantal *b'rachah* of the circumcision for a girl retains the traditional formula; e.g., Sandy Sasso, "B'rit B'not Israel: Observations on Woman and Reconstructionism," *Response* 18 (Summer 1973): 101–55; and this remains nearly universally constant in the myriad examples of baby-girl ceremonies up to the present. Cf. Lynn Gottlieb, "Speaking Into the Silence," *Response* 13, nos. 1–2 (Fall–Winter 1982): 27.

48. Barbara Penzner, "Women and the Reconstructionist Movement," in Goldstein, *New Jewish Feminism*, 338; Rebecca Alpert, "Our Lives Are the Text: Exploring Jewish Women's Rituals," *Bridges* 2, no. 1 (Spring 1991): 70.

49. Debra Orenstein, ed., *Lifecycles*, vol. 1, *Jewish Women on Life Passages and Personal Milestones* (Woodstock, VT: Jewish Lights, 1994).

50. Leila Gal Berner, "Our Silent Seasons," in Orenstein, *Lifecycles*, vol. 1, 121–36.

51. Laura Geller, "Mourning a Marriage," *Reform Judaism*, Spring 2000, 54–57; here 56. See also Jane Litman, "*Hafradah*: A Jewish Separation Ceremony," in Levine, *A Ceremonies Sampler*, 70–76; Diane Cohen, "The Divorced Woman: Toward a New Ritual," *Conservative Judaism* 44, no. 4 (Summer 1992): 62–68; Vicki Hollander, "Weathering the Passage: Jewish Divorce," in Orenstein, *Lifecycles*, vol. 1, 201–5; Nina Beth Cardin, "A Ritual Acknowledging Separation," in Orenstein, *Lifecycles*, vol. 1, 206–10; Lisa Greene and Laura Milsk, "*Tekes Ishur V'shleimut*: A Ritual of Affirmation and Wholeness after Divorce," *CCAR Journal* 44, no. 3 (Summer 1997): 114–19.

52. *Jewish Women's Resource Center Newsletter* 1, no. 4 (Winter 1979–80): 3–4, 9; 2, no. 2 (Fall 1980).

53. E.g., Einat Ramon, "A Wedding in Israel as an Act of *Tikkun Olam*," in Orenstein, *Lifecycles*, vol. 1, 161–72; and Renni Altman, "The Sheva Brachot Reconsidered," *CCAR Journal* 47, no. 2 (Summer 1997): 136–38.

54. Jill Jacobs and Guy Izhak Austrian, "The Choices of Marriage: One Couple's Attempt to Create an Egalitarian Jewish Wedding Ceremony within the Traditional Framework of Kiddushin," *Conservative Judaism* 63, no. 3 (Spring 2012): 32–41.

55. Ner-David, *Life on the Fringes*, 131–49.

56. Leila Gal Berner and Renee Gal Primack, "Uncharted Territory: Lesbian Commitment Ceremonies," in Orenstein, *Lifecycles*, vol. 1, 173–78; Alpert, *Like Bread on the Seder Plate*.

57. Goldie Milgram, *Living Jewish Life Cycle: How to Create Meaningful Jewish Rites of Passage at Every Stage of Life* (Woodstock, VT: Jewish Lights, 2009).

58. Among many examples are Rachel Adler, "'In Your Blood, Live': Re-Visions of a Theology of Purity," in *Lifecycles*, vol. 2, *Jewish Women on Biblical Themes in Contemporary Life*, ed. Debra Orenstein and Jane Rachel Litman (Woodstock, VT: Jewish Lights, 1997), 197–206; Berkowitz, *Taking the Plunge*.

59. Barbara Penzner and Amy Zweiback-Levenson, "Spiritual Cleansing: A Mikveh Ritual for Brides," *Reconstructionist* 52, no. 1 (September 1986): 25–29.

60. Ibid.

61. Berkowitz, Grossman, and Reisner, "Mikveh and the Sanctity of Family Relations," 2006; Grossman, "Mikveh and the Sanctity of Being Created Human," 2006; Berkowitz, "Reshaping the Laws of Family Purity for the Modern World," 2006.

62. Berkowitz, *Taking the Plunge*, xiv.

63. Ner-David, *Life on the Fringes*, 150–76.

64. Dasi Fruchter, "Can We Speak for Ourselves?," *Lilith Blog*, July 9, 2013.

65. Berkowitz, *Taking the Plunge*, 8.

66. Ruttenberg, "Blood Simple: Transgender Theory Hits the Mikveh," 77–87; quotes 81, 86. Creative use of mikveh by liberal Jews is only realistic where there is easy access to a liberal mikveh or one that tolerates unsupervised liberal use, and the emphasis on mikveh-based rituals in print thus perhaps misrepresents the reality of the situation. Berkowitz, *Taking the Plunge*, 140n234, lists Conservative, Reform, and pluralistic *mikvaot*. A study of the use of these is a desideratum.

67. E.g., Valerie Joseph and Alana Suskin, "Servants before the King," in Goldstein, *New Jewish Feminism*, 395.

68. Levitt and Wasserman, "Mikvah Ceremony for Laura (1989)," 321–26.

69. Lynn Gottlieb, "Spring Cleaning Ritual on the Eve of Full Moon Nisan," in Lynn Gottlieb, "Speaking Into the Silence," *Response* 13, nos. 1–2 (Fall–Winter 1982): 29–31; also in *On Being a Jewish Feminist*, ed. Susannah Heschel (New York: Schocken Books, 1983), 278–80.

70. Haviva Ner-David, "Thoughts on Cleaning for Pesach," in *The Women's Passover Companion*, ed. Sharon Cohen Anisfeld, Tara Mohr, and Catherine Spector (Woodstock, VT: Jewish Lights, 2003), 49–53.

71. Amy Bardack, "Praising the Work of Valiant Women: A Feminist Endorsement of *Eshet Hayil*," in Orenstein, *Lifecycles*, vol. 1, 136–40. Cf. Susan Grossman's version of *Eishet Chayil* for a woman to read to her husband, in *JWRC Newsletter* 2, no. 2 (Fall 1980).

72. *The Merit of Our Mothers: A Bilingual Anthology of Jewish Women's Prayers*, compiled and introduced by Tracy Guren Klirs, trans. Klirs et al. (Cincinnati:

Hebrew Union College Press, 1992). I know no collection in English that predates Klirs' thesis.

73. E.g., *tkhine* for pregnancy by Judy Shanks in Anita Diamant, *The Jewish Baby Book* (New York: Summit Books, 1988), 31; Sandy Sasso, "Personal Prayers," in *A Ceremonies Sampler: New Rites, Celebrations, and Observances of Jewish Women*, ed. Elizabeth Resnick Levine (San Diego: Woman's Institute for Continuing Jewish Education, 1991), 43–46; Nina Beth Cardin, *Tears of Sorrow, Seeds of Hope: A Jewish Spiritual Companion for Infertility and Pregnancy Loss* (Woodstock, VT: Jewish Lights, 1999). Also *Out of the Depths I Call to You: A Book of Prayers for the Married Jewish Woman*, ed. Nina Beth Cardin (Northvale, NJ: Jason Aronson, 1992), a translation of an eighteenth-century *tkhines* book.

74. Naomi Levy, *Talking to God: Personal Prayers for Times of Joy, Sadness, Struggle, and Celebration* (New York: Knopf, 2002), 128–29.

75. Joseph and Suskin, "Servants before the King," 382–96.

76. *Mishkan R'fuah: Where Healing Resides*, ed. Eric Weiss with Shira Stern (New York: CCAR Press, 2013).

77. *Rabbi's Manual*, ed. Seth Daniel Riemer et al. (Wyncote, PA: Reconstructionist Rabbinical Association, 1997).

78. Levy, *Talking to God*, 4, 263.

79. Elana Zaiman, "Grappling With 'Tradition and Change,'" *Masoret* 2, no. 1 (Fall 1992): 8.

80. Orenstein, *Lifecycles*, vol. 1.

81. Julie Greenberg, "Celebrating Rabbinic Ordination," in Levine, *A Ceremonies Sampler*, 101–5.

82. Penzner and Zweiback-Levenson, "Spiritual Cleansing: A Mikveh Ritual for Brides," 25–29.

83. Jane Litman, "*M'ugelet*: A Pregnancy Ritual," in Levine, *A Ceremonies Sampler*, 5–7.

84. Debra Newman Kamin, "A Jewish Weaning Ritual," in Orenstein, *Lifecycles*, vol. 1, 272–75.

85. E.g., Vicki Hollander, "A Rosh Hodesh Ceremony (1990)," in Umansky and Ashton, *Four Centuries of Jewish Women's Spirituality*, 314–21.

86. Carol Glass, "Festival of Joy," *JWRC Newsletter*, Winter–Spring 1981.

87. Penina Adelman, *Miriam's Well*, 2nd ed. (New York: Biblio Press, 1986).

88. Elwell, "Reclaiming Jewish Women's Oral Tradition?" in Procter-Smith and Walton, *Women at Worship*, 111–26.

89. *JWRC Newsletter*, Winter–Spring 1981, 1–2.

90. *San Diego Women's Haggadah*, 2nd ed. (San Diego: Woman's Institute for Continuing Jewish Education, 1986).

91. *The Journey Continues: Ma'yan Passover Haggadah*, ed. Tamara Cohen, Sue Levi Elwell, Debbie Freidman, and Ronnie Horn (New York: Ma'yan, the Jewish Women's Project, 1999), 49; based on *And We Were All There: A Feminist Passover Haggadah*, ed. Sue Levi Elwell (Los Angeles: American Jewish Congress Feminist Center in LA, 1994). A woman co-edited *A Night of Questions: A Passover Haggadah*, ed. Joy Levitt and Michael Strassfeld (Wyncote, PA: Reconstructionist Press, 2000); its commentators include five female rabbis (among other women and seven men,

some of whom are rabbis). The Prayerbook Commission lists one female rabbi (among other women and men, rabbis and not).

92. Alpert, "Our Lives Are the Text," 67; Lefkovitz and Shapiro, "The Politics and Aesthetics of Jewish Women's Spirituality," 69.

93. Elyse Goldstein, "Jewish Feminism and 'New' Jewish Rituals: Imitative or Inventive?" *CCAR Journal*, 44, no. 3 (Summer 1997): 105–10; revised as "The Pink Tallit: Women's Rituals as Imitative or Inventive?," in Goldstein, *New Jewish Feminism*, 81–89.

94. Alpert, "Our Lives Are the Text: Exploring Jewish Women's Rituals," 76.

95. Laura Geller and Sue Levi Elwell, "On the Jewish Feminist Frontier: A Report," *Sh'ma* 23, no. 441 (November, 13 1992), 1.

96. Alpert, *Like Bread on the Seder Plate*, 62–67, 78–88, 94–96; Rebecca Alpert, "Coming Out in the Jewish Community," in Orenstein, *Lifecycles*, vol. 1, 144–53.

97. Ruttenberg, "Blood Simple: Transgender Theory Hits the Mikveh," 77–87.

98. Levitt and Wasserman, "Mikvah Ceremony for Laura (1989)," 321–326.

99. Jane Litman, "Saying Goodbye to Friends," *Lilith* 15, no. 1 (Winter 1990): 31.

100. Vicki Hollander, "A Modern Version of the Confessional before Dying," in Orenstein, *Lifecycles*, vol. 1, 355.

101. Goldie Milgram, *Reclaiming Judaism as a Spiritual Practice: Holy Days and Shabbat* (Woodstock, VT: Jewish Lights, 2004),153–60.

102. Sara Hurwitz, "Summon the *Mekonenot* (Dirge-Singers) and They Will Come," *JOFA Journal*, 11 no. 1 (Spring 2013): 5–7.

103. Jill Hammer, "Holle's Cry: Unearthing a Birth Goddess in a German Jewish Naming Ceremony," *Nashim* (2005): 62–87.

104. David Zaslow, "A Covenant above Reason," in *The Covenant of Circumcision*, ed. Elizabeth Wyner Mark (Waltham, MA: Brandeis University Press, 2003), 194–96; quotes from 196.

105. Deborah Glanzberg-Krainin, "Noam's Bris," in Mark, *The Covenant of Circumcision*, 197–200; quotes from 197 and 199.

106. Elyse Wechterman, "A Plea for Inclusion," in Mark, *The Covenant of Circumcision*, 188–93; quote from 190.

107. Ibid., 189.

108. Mark, *The Covenant of Circumcision*, 188–203.

109. Susan Grossman and Rivka Haut, eds., *Daughters of the King: Women and the Synagogue* (Philadelphia: Jewish Publication Society, 1992).

110. Stone, "Orthodox Women Rabbis by Any Other Name."

111. Fruchter, "Can We Speak for Ourselves?"

112. For example, Sara Hurwitz, "Prayer: Serving a Purpose," *Sh'ma* 41, no. 675 (December 2010): 6.

113. Ner-David, *Life on the Fringes*, 142, 161.

114. Nadell, "Bridges to 'A Judaism Transformed by Women's Wisdom,'" 211–12, 222. Similarly Goldstein, *New Jewish Feminism*, xxiii–xxiv.

115. Sara Hurwitz, "Orthodox Women in Rabbinic Roles," in Goldstein, *New Jewish Feminism*, 144–54, esp. 150–52.

116. On Reconstructionism's openness to feminist-ritual change, see Barbara Penzner, "Women and the Reconstructionist Movement," in Goldstein, *New Jewish Feminism*, 334–43.

117. *Jewish Women's Resource Center Newsletter* 1, no. 4 (Winter 1979–1980): 14.

118. Grossman and Haut, *Daughters of the King*, xxvi, also 8–9; Yael, Talya, and Yonina Penkower, "Bat Mitzvah: Coming of Age in Brooklyn," in ibid., 265–70; Rivka Haut, "The Presence of Women," in ibid., 274–78.

119. Levitt and Strassfeld, *A Night of Questions: A Passover Haggadah*, 12.

120. Milgram, *Living Jewish Life Cycle: How to Create Meaningful Jewish Rites of Passage at Every Stage of Life*.

121. Debra Orenstein, "Afterword: How to Create a Ritual," in Orenstein, *Lifecycles*, vol. 1, 359–73. Similarly Berkowitz, *Taking the Plunge*, 145–46. Also Gottlieb, *She Who Dwells Within*, 119.

122. Elwell, "Reclaiming Jewish Women's Oral Tradition?" in Procter-Smith and Walton, *Women at Worship*, 111–26; here 122.

123. Goldstein, *New Jewish Feminism*, xxiii.

124. Rela Geffen Monson, "The Impact of the Jewish Women's Movement on the American Synagogue: 1972–1985," in Grossman and Haut, *Daughters of the King*, 227–36; here 229.

125. For example, Goldstein, *New Jewish Feminism*, part 7; Gottlieb, *She Who Dwells Within*. Pamela Barmash, "Veal Calves," YD 24.2007a; Jill Jacobs, "Work, Workers and the Jewish Owner," HM 331:1.2008a; Amy Eilberg, "On Halakhic Approaches to Medical Care for the Terminally Ill: A Response," YD 339:1.1990d.

Five rabbis shared their wisdom and insight with me while I was writing this article: Dianne Cohler-Esses, Carol Glass, Barbara Penzner, Hara Person, and Elaine Zecher. Women of valor, indeed.

28

THE MIKVEH AS A WELL OF CREATIVITY

Rabbi Sara Luria and Shaina Herring

We gathered—as women and classmates on the cusp of rabbinic ordination—in the lobby of the mikveh building. After we each paid the mikveh
lady, she asked us if we needed anything else, and we responded that we
would take it from there. Weeks later, we laughed as many of us noticed
the charge from the mikveh on our bank statements entitled "Jewish
Women's Club." We certainly had joined a Jewish Women's Club, but
perhaps not exactly how it is most often intended at the mikveh.

Each of us prepared for immersion separately, showering off the
layers of our student selves, looking in the wall-to-wall mirrors at our
naked bodies, realizing, each in our own ways, in our own minds, that
this is the body of a rabbi.

We met in the pool area in our robes and read a reflection from a
ceremony created for a joyous life transition:

I immerse today in celebration of ordination.
May this immersion help me move from what has been
and may my heart be open to what is yet to come.

When I emerge from these *mayim chayim*, these living waters,
may I be filled with renewed energy

and a sense of direction for my life's journey.

May God grant me strength, courage, and peace. Amen.[1]

Then, we turned around, our backs to the pool, and one-by-one, each of us entered the living waters, immersed our bodies and our hearts, and emerged fresh and new. We sang to each other during our immersions; water mixed with tears mixed with the sound of women's prayers.

The last woman emerged and read:

> To take the first step
> To sing a new song—
> Is to close one's eyes
> and dive
> into unknown waters.
> For a moment knowing nothing risking all
> But then to discover
> The waters are friendly
> The ground is firm.
> And the song—
> the song rises again.[2]

Before our immersion, we were bound together by our shared experiences in classrooms and lunch dates. After our immersion, we were bound together by an unforgettable sacred ritual that marked a transition for all of us, from what was to what will be, from student to rabbi, from past to present, and then to our shared future as women rabbis in the twenty-first century.

Ours is a story that began many years earlier with the ordination of the first female rabbi, Sally Priesand, in 1972. She not only broke the sacred glass ceiling; she opened the floodgates for women in positions of Jewish leadership to begin reclaiming the ancient ritual of mikveh immersion as a tool for creative ceremonies and religious expression.

This chapter explores how women rabbis have helped reimagine and renew the mikveh and its rituals.

Ordination of Women and the Need for New Jewish Rituals

In her compilation *New Jewish Feminism*, Rabbi Elyse Goldstein explains that with the ordination of women, "women's rituals proliferated and we began to create what was missing from the index of lifecycle events: rituals that spoke to the unique biological realities of being women."[3] With this new reality came the creation of new rituals to mark women's life-cycle events like childbirth, infertility, and menopause—topics that previously had been considered taboo. Women are, naturally, more attuned to these issues, and in their new leadership roles, women rabbis created ritual that began to open the conversation on how ritual could relate to uniquely female experiences. Yet, as we know, women rabbis do not exclusively serve women; as Lori Hope Lefkovitz, PhD, and Rabbi Rona Shapiro note in their article "The Politics and Aesthetics of Jewish Women's Spirituality," women's ordination raised awareness about the absence of rituals for life transitions for both men and women.[4]

Rituals provide "a framework of meaning around normal events [by making sacred] moments that at first glance appear to be mundane because they are in fact so universal, so predictable, and so cyclical."[5] Rituals insert holy space into our routines; Shabbat marks the passing of each week, Rosh Chodesh the passing of each month, and holidays such as Sukkot are tied to the seasons. In addition, many of us create our own personal or family rituals—a certain special food every year on a holiday, personal ways to remember our loved ones each year on their *yahrzeit* (anniversary of a person's death), or singing *Hashkiveinu*, a prayer of protection, each night with our children before putting them to bed.

When writing about the need for new rituals in her book *Taking the Plunge*, Rabbi Miriam Berkowitz clearly states, "The existence of a ritual indicates that the event is important and worthy of attention."[6] Yet, there are many private moments for which there are no Jewish rituals, including miscarriage, the onset of a girl's period, coming out, or divorce. There are also times for which there are public nonreligious rituals—graduation or a milestone birthday, for example—for which the traditional Jewish canon offers no ritual or space for personal reflection.

Mikveh Rituals Honoring Our Experiences and Transitions

Prior to the ordination of women, the mikveh was primarily used for conversions and women's monthly immersions (*nidah*). For some communities, this may still be the case today. Yet, as female rabbis began thinking and writing about broadening Jewish rituals, they simultaneously began to transform and expand the possibilities for what a mikveh immersion could be for everyone—simply and profoundly a ritual experience to mark life's transitions.

Some feminists may view mikveh as a misogynist practice, yet there are female rabbis who have begun to understand the power of mikveh in a feminist context. Rabbi Danya Ruttenberg explains:

> As feminists, we aren't obligated to accept everything handed to us by our patriarchal tradition. But as Jews, it behooves us to turn our traditions around a few times....We have the ability to transform many aspects of our tradition into vehicles that can help us seek the holy, and to serve God by learning how to better relate to others in caring and connection.[7]

The reclamation of mikveh reinvigorates an ancient Jewish space where transitions can be ritualized and marked; mikveh rituals help cultivate a Jewish practice that is relevant to our lived experience.

For example, in 1989, Rabbi Sue Ann Wasserman and Laura Levitt created a ceremony to mark Levitt's recovery from being raped. In reflecting on the ritual, Levitt explained:

> [The] mikveh offered me a place to acknowledge both that violation [of being raped] and my desire to heal. My need for ritual was very real. I needed to do something concrete to express my psychic and physical pain as a Jewish woman.[8]

The physical and embodied ritual of mikveh immersion contributed to Levitt's healing process—physically, emotionally, and spiritually. Rabbi Wasserman explained why she chose the mikveh for the ritual:

> (1) It was predominantly our foremothers' ritual. (2) It requires the whole body. (3) Its waters flow in and out—representing continuity and process. (4) Its waters symbolically flow from Eden, a place of wholeness. (5) The natural waters remind us of the constant intermingling presence of the Creator in our own lives. (6) Finally, water itself is cleansing, supportive, and life sustaining.[9]

These six reasons illustrate why the mikveh, in general, is such a powerful tool for transitional moments—it is an ancient and embodied ritual that engages the supporting and sustaining power of water. Rabbi Wasserman first explored mikveh as a ritual that spoke to her as a woman; as a rabbi, she used a mikveh ritual as a tool when working with her congregants. Rabbi Wasserman and Laura have published their ritual, allowing for others to use it and benefit from their work.

In addition to ceremonies created on a case-by-case basis by a rabbi and the person immersing, the Ritual Creation Team at Mayyim Hayyim Living Waters Community Mikveh, the country's flagship community mikveh, has published over forty-five immersion rituals for life-cycle transitions, including for the parents of the bride or groom, weaning, a challenging life transition, following the end of a relationship, and marking a sixtieth birthday.

In addition to new mikveh rituals, women rabbis have also written blessings and *kavanot* (meditative intentions) that can be said prior to immersing or while in the mikveh waters. For example, Rabbi Nina Beth Cardin wrote a prayer that can be said before entering the mikveh, expressing a woman's desire to become pregnant.[10] Rabbi Debbie Young-Somers wrote a prayer for women who are receiving infertility treatments.[11] In addition, the essential element of mikveh—water—can help to facilitate powerful rituals, even without full-body immersion. Diane Cohen describes a woman's hand-washing ritual after receiving the *get*, in which the woman washes her hands in the presence of a minyan in order to signify her transformation from married to not married.

These blessings, *kavanot*, and ceremonies "serve to create experience in the participant," as Rabbi Elyse Goldstein puts it, "by moving her from the realm of 'spectator' to the realm of 'actor.'"[12] As women rabbis and other female Jewish leaders engage with mikveh, they create opportunities for more Jewish people to become actively engaged with our tradition.

Currently, across the country, women rabbis and female Jewish leaders are creating community *mikvaot*, spaces where innovative Jewish ritual for women and men can take place. Rabbi Sara Brandes is working to build the Neshama Center for Spirituality and Wellness in Los Angeles; Naomi Malka directs the Adas Israel Community Mikvah in Washington, DC; Rabbi Jennifer Solomon directs the community mikveh Libi Eir, in Raleigh, North Carolina; Rabbi Sara (this chapter's co-author) recently founded ImmerseNYC, a project to bring a community mikveh to New York City; and of course, Anita Diamant and Aliza Kline began it all with their vision for Mayyim Hayyim Living Waters Community Mikveh, which opened in 2004 in Newton, Massachusetts. In this chapter, we have attempted to articulate the transformative potential of mikveh immersions; yet, we recognize that there is still mystery in why a water ritual can be so powerful. We conclude with our reflection about why we believe mikveh has, and will continue, to shape our Jewish community.

A mikveh is not just a pool, although it is one.

A mikveh is not just a place to mark transitions, although it is one.

A mikveh, a community mikveh project, is about the whole of lived
  experience, about reaching out and drawing in:
  Jews of color,
  Jews who don't otherwise participate in Jewish life,
  Orthodox women who have been immersing quietly,
  Queer Jews,
  Reform Jews who rarely experience embodied ritual.

Our mikveh will be a place where rebirth can happen even if the
  cancer has returned.
Our mikveh will be a place where gay men can immerse for their
  wedding anniversary.
Our mikveh will be a place where a girl becoming a bat mitzvah can
  reflect on this transformative moment in her life.
Our mikveh will be a safe, beautiful, light-filled, calm, warm, and
  welcoming Jewish place.

A mikveh, a community mikveh project, is about the whole of lived
experience, and our mikveh's waters will reflect the Jewish world we
envision for our children.

NOTES

1. "Kavannah for the Ceremony for a Joyous Life Transition," created by Matia Rania Angelou, Deborah Issokson, and Judith D. Kummer for Mayyim Hayyim Living Waters Community Mikveh.

2. "Reflection for the Second Immersion for the Ceremony for a Joyous Life Transition," ibid.

3. Elyse Goldstein, *New Jewish Feminism: Probing the Past, Forging the Future* (Woodstock, VT: Jewish Lights, 2009), xxiii.

4. Lori Hope Lefkovitz and Rona Shapiro, "The Politics and Aesthetics of Jewish Women's Spirituality," in Goldstein, *New Jewish Feminism*, 71–73.

5. Elyse Goldstein, "The Pink Tallit," in Goldstein, *New Jewish Feminism*, 82.

6. Miriam Berkowitz, *Taking the Plunge: A Practical and Spiritual Guide to the Mikveh* (Jerusalem: Schechter Institute of Jewish Studies, 2009), 144.

7. Danya Ruttenberg, "The Hermeneutics of Curiosity," in Goldstein, *New Jewish Feminism*, 62, 65.

8. Laura Levitt and Sue Ann Wasserman, "Mikveh Ceremony for Laura," Ritualwell, http://www.ritualwell.org/ritual/mikveh-ceremony-laura.

9. Ibid.

10. Nina Beth Cardin, "A Prayer for a Child: To Be Recited Before Entering the Mikveh," Ritualwell, http://www.ritualwell.org/ritual/prayer-child-be-recited-entering-mikveh.

11. Debbie Young-Somers, "A Meditation—Using the Mikveh When Dealing with Infertility," Ritualwell, http://www.ritualwell.org/ritual/meditation-using-mikveh-when-dealing-infertility.

12. Goldstein, "The Pink Tallit," 83.

29

OFFERING A NEW LOOK

Women Rabbis and Jewish Spirituality

RABBI MICHELE LENKE

The ordination of Rabbi Sally Priesand by the Hebrew Union College–Jewish Institute of Religion in 1972 served as catalyst for significant change within the Jewish community. The women's movement of the 1970s, '80s, and '90s gave birth to the renaissance of the Jewish spirituality movement that is so vibrant today. From 1972 to 1995, there were nearly 250 women ordained in the Reform Movement; yet, the liturgy used at that time did not reflect that rising number. With women rabbis on the bimah, and for many of their congregants, there grew an ever-greater dissonance within congregations. As more women were ordained, there was the awakening of the possibility that God could be understood not only through the exclusively male pronouns and God-language in the siddur, but also through exploration of the female and feminine aspects of God. In retrospect, these shifts seem subtle, and yet at the time they were seismic.

The shift from the *Union Prayerbook* to *Gates of Prayer* in 1975 introduced the first change in the English translations and prayer interpretations. It was not until the 1994 publication of *Gates of Prayer for Shabbat and Weekdays* that the Reform Movement had a prayer book that could be called "gender-sensitive" or "gender-inclusive."[1] This was accomplished by including the *Imahot* (Matriarchs) in the printed text, obviating the need to relegate them to a glued-in insert in the back inside cover. This change forced a close reexamination of the language used for God and led to the use of more suitable and inclusive terminology. This change was intensified with the publication in 2007 of *Mishkan T'filah*, the first Reform siddur edited by a woman, Rabbi Elyse Frishman. *Mishkan T'filah* provided congregations with a siddur using inclusive language and imagery, multi-vocal theologies, and opportunities for self-directed prayer.

The evolution of our siddurim was very important, but prayer is the not the exclusive expression of spirituality. At the same time that new siddurim were being created, there was an explosion of creativity in many modalities; in many cases, women rabbis were there to influence, support, and foster the creative process. One only needs to look in the opening pages of Rachel Adler's *Engendering Judaism* and Judith Plaskow's *Standing Again at Sinai* to see the tremendous influence of women rabbis on their work. In the acknowledgments of *Engendering Judaism*, Adler offers gratitude to the women in her Women's Hevra Shas, her weekly Talmud study group, including Rabbi Laura Geller, Rabbi Bridget Wynne, Rabbi Sue Levi Elwell, and Rabbi Jacqueline Koch Ellenson.[2] Plaskow gives great credit to the women of her Jewish feminist spirituality collective called B'not Esh (daughters of fire), as collectively they inspired her to write her theology of community.[3] The women who were members of B'not Esh at that time have since become some of the leading Jewish scholars and rabbis today. Among the B'not Esh members was poet Marcia Falk, who took a risk at rewriting *t'filot* using a variety of metaphors and images for the Divine as a way to be inclusive of all creation.[4] In her *Book of Blessings*, Falk introduced a major change from the traditional blessing opening (*Baruch*, or "Blessed are You") to *N'varech* (let us bless). This change extends the invitation to prayer to everyone, regardless of gender, as it is inclusive and active. It should be noted that changes to our liturgy have happened throughout the history of our people and will continue in the future. Our prayers need to speak to those who offer them to the Holy One, and thus we compose new prayers or new settings to prayers that suit our contemporary spirituality.

An expert in this realm was Debbie Friedman, *z"l*. Her music was popular not only in Jewish summer camps but in congregations as well. Friedman took beloved texts and made them accessible to young and old alike. Among her most significant contributions was the setting of *Mi Shebeirach* for healing.[5] It revolutionized the way that healing was perceived, and as a result a new prayer had suddenly made its way into the Reform Jewish liturgical canon.

The Friedman *Mi Shebeirach* inspired the creation of healing services in our congregations. These services were filled with creative readings and writings, both modern and traditional. Healing services gave participants freedom to express their feelings, permission to enable tears to flow, and the opportunity for shared experiences in which to offer others empathy and support. We began talking about the real pain and suffering in our lives and our desire to respond in both a Jewish and spiritual manner.

The impact of the Jewish healing movement is due in large part to the dedication of Rabbi Rachel Cowan, Rabbi Nancy Flam, Rabbi Susan Freeman, and Rabbi Amy Eilberg. According to Rabbi Cowan, "The healing movement, though not directed at issues unique to women, models the impact of women rabbis on Jewish life. I believe that it took a group of women—including rabbis—to break through the Jewish cultural barrier that saw medical treatment as the only response to illness."[6] Over the years, women rabbis have broken many cultural norms and know well what it means to be the "first" in almost any given rabbinic situation. From its earliest days, the Jewish healing movement introduced healing services, rituals, educational programs, support groups, and opportunities for people to seek relief from their suffering. Spiritual healing may not cure a cancer, but it is often able to get to the heart of an individual's suffering, and it enables one to be seen as a whole person rather than as just a diagnosis or disease. The Jewish healing movement's emphasis on wholeness led to Judaism's more recent embrace of the spiritual practice known as spiritual direction. It was perhaps a natural progression that as Rabbis Rachel Cowan and Nancy Flam moved on to create the Institute for Jewish Spirituality, Rabbi Amy Eilberg became the founding co-director of the Yedidya Center for Jewish Spiritual Direction.

In 1990, under the auspices of the American Jewish Congress, the Los Angeles Jewish Feminist Center was started by Rabbi Sue Levi Elwell and Rabbi Laura Geller. While not reflected in the name of the organization, this was a spiritual oasis for many women seeking a relationship with the Divine and provided a setting in which to engage in sacred study. Women from a multitude of backgrounds and religious experiences would join together for monthly Rosh Chodesh celebrations. In addition to the classes, lectures, and guidance offered, the LA Jewish Feminist Center created a women's seder that filled a tremendous void in the community. Year after year, women of all ages came together to tell the rest of the Exodus story.

The success of the LA Jewish Feminist Center inspired the creation of Ma'yan in New York in 1993. Its widely successful annual women's seder between 1994 and 2005 brought together hundreds of women of different generations. Their Haggadah, *The Journey Continues: The Ma'yan Haggadah*, continues to provide a feminist Passover ritual for people around the world.[7] By 2006, however, Ma'yan refocused its efforts on feminist-based education for girls, their parents, and youth professionals.

In more recent years, Moving Traditions, a Jewish nonprofit that runs educational programs for teens, has built upon its flagship program, *Rosh Hodesh: It's a Girl Thing!*, originally developed by Kolot in Philadelphia, as a way of reaching middle school and high school aged girls and engaging them in what it means to be a young Jewish woman today, creating a younger sisterhood cohort. Ritualwell.org, created collaboratively by both Ma'yan and Kolot and housed at the Reconstructionist Rabbinical College in Philadelphia, has been led over the years by women rabbis, such as Rabbi Rona Shapiro, Ritualwell's founding editor, as well Rabbi Roni Handler, Ritualwell's current editor, and its executive editor, Rabbi Deborah Glanzberg-Kranin.

Women rabbis have been instrumental in transforming how Jews engage with Jewish tradition.

Inspired by the success of the seders developed by the LA Jewish Feminist Center and Ma'yan, countless congregations now offer their own women's seder as an annual event. In fact, once known solely for organizing the *Oneg Shabbat* after Shabbat services or running the temple gift shop, Temple Sisterhoods now engage in political advocacy, women's leadership development, and spirituality, as evidenced by the organization's name change from the National Federation of Temple Sisterhoods to Women of Reform Judaism (WRJ) in 1993. This shift is no better exemplified than by their publications of women's prayers in the WRJ Covenant Series, most recently *The Covenant of the Generations*, celebrating the one-hundredth anniversary of Women of Reform Judaism. As the WRJ website states, "Written by women for women, these collections of poems, prayers, and meditations are among WRJ's most proud and prominent accomplishments, elevating the voice of women in religious and spiritual realms and speaking to the joys, struggles, special moments, and sacred journeys of women throughout the generations."[8] While WRJ has been well-known for their support of students at Hebrew Union College–Jewish Institute of Religion (HUC-JIR) over the years, it is worth remembering that it was the National Federation of Temple Sisterhoods that in 1963 called for the ordination of women as rabbis.[9] In 2011, NFTS Honorary President Norma U. Levitt said, "I am very proud of the stance that we take on issues and we go from issue to issue whether it starts with women rabbis and it ends with same-sex marriage.... I'm proud of the issues we take hold of."[10] The success of women in the rabbinate strengthens the WRJ, which today is led by its first rabbinic executive, Rabbi Marla Feldman, as its executive director, just as the women of WRJ strengthen women in the rabbinate.

Without women in the rabbinate, serving as leaders and sharing our understanding of Judaism's most sacred texts, much of the creativity in the area of Jewish spirituality would not have happened. The Women of Reform Judaism, in collaboration with URJ Press, published *The Torah: A Women's Commentary* in 2007. Brilliantly guided by Rabbi Tamara Eskenazi, PhD, and Rabbi Andrea Weiss, PhD, seen through to publication by another woman rabbi, Rabbi Hara Person, and including the work of several hundred women rabbis, scholars, and poets, this volume is a groundbreaking achievement that reflects the scholarship, creativity, and spirituality that women's voices, experiences, and souls bring to the sacred study of Torah.

In 2004, liberal Judaism in New England and beyond reclaimed the spiritual custom of using the mikveh to mark important moments and transitions in Jewish life, thanks to the dream of Mayyim Hayyim's founding president, Anita Diamant. When asked about the role that women rabbis played in the creation and formation of Mayyim Hayyim, Diamant said:

> Women rabbis were among the most important sounding boards while I mused about the possibility of a new kind of mikveh, among them Rabbi Liza Stern and, especially, Rabbi Barbara Penzner. Rabbi Penzner was a key participant in the creation of Mayyim Hayyim. A founding board member, she wrote the Seven Principles, which remain at the core of our mission. She was an emissary to the rabbinic community and an ambassador locally and nationally, especially within the Reconstructionist Movement. Rabbi Emily Lipof was a public supporter in a most personal way. Recently widowed, she came to the first Mayyim Hayyim "parlor meeting" where we started explaining the need for such an institution and seeking support. It was her first public appearance—an honor in itself. And then she told us that when—sometime in the future— when she was ready to consider a new relationship in her life, she wanted a mikveh where she could ritualize the act of taking off her wedding band. I remember her holding up her hand. Not a dry eye in the house, and more importantly, everyone understood *why* we needed Mayyim Hayyim. Since then, women rabbis have served on the board, on the rabbinic advisory committee, volunteered as mikveh guides, taught at Mayyim Hayyim and at our conferences.[11]

Today, Mayyim Hayyim serves the entire Jewish community, making the ritual of immersion possible for anyone who would like to participate in this mitzvah able to do so.

In her essay "From Equality to Transformation," Rabbi Laura Geller poses the following question: "What would Jewish institutions look like if they were shaped in response to the values that seem to be shared by so many women—balance, intimacy, and empowerment?"[12] At the turn of the twenty-first century, it became apparent that the rabbinate was in the process of changing in unprecedented ways. These changes were, in part, due to the tremendous influence of technology. A new reality was emerging: a tension between increased connection due to devices and nonstop technological connectivity, while simultaneously feeling the drain of constant availability. In response to these new realities, an idea emerged about finding a way to reach out to rabbis and encourage colleagues to meet *panim el panim*, "face to face." The need for colleagues to convene in person for spiritual sustenance was understood to be pressing; lay leaders were encouraged that they too would benefit from engagement within the world of spiritual practice. Out of this transitional moment emerged the Institute for Jewish Spirituality, in many ways the embodiment of the challenge put forward by Rabbi Geller.

The Institute for Jewish Spirituality was created for Jewish professionals, as well as lay leaders, to make more accessible the Jewish spiritual inheritance that belongs to each of us. This retreat-based model of intentional Jewish living began in January 2000. Though the leadership of the Institute for Jewish Spirituality (IJS) isn't exclusively female, the structure of its leadership is noticeably collaborative and inclusive. With women rabbis such as Rachel Cowan, Nancy Flam, Sheila Peltz Weinberg, Myriam Klotz, and Lisa Goldstein as its founders, teachers, and spiritual guides, the gifts of IJS have been and—continue to be—profound and sacred.

At any given retreat, participants from across the Jewish spectrum engage in the spiritual practices of prayer, yoga, meditation, study of sacred texts, eating, listening, and silence. With this variety of spiritual disciplines, there is bound to be at least one that borders on the uncomfortable upon first encounter. Among rabbis, it is likely that the spiritual practice of prayer is probably most familiar, and yet the prayer experience at IJS is anything but perfunctory performance. Davening with colleagues from a variety of movements and traditions ensures there is always something new to learn: a *niggun*, a melody, a teaching, an insight.

The influence of IJS and of Jewish spirituality in general is now seen and experienced in our seminaries and synagogues. At HUC-JIR in New York, Dean Shirley Idelson, a member of the sixth rabbinic cohort of IJS, introduced a spirituality initiative to the Reform seminary in 2011. Directed by Rabbi Myriam Klotz, this initiative has brought the spiritual practices of yoga, mindfulness, and spiritual direction and contemplation to the students, staff, and faculty of HUC-JIR and is now seen as an integral part of the HUC-JIR experience. It is hoped that through exposure and experimentation with these spiritual practices and learning opportunities participants will cultivate greater authenticity and create the space needed to let Torah live through them as well.[13]

Over the years, the Women's Rabbinic Network (WRN) has been a constant source of spiritual collaboration. Conferences are often filled with innovative prayer and spiritual experiences and modalities, from drum circles to praying in sign language to praying in solidarity with Women of the Wall. In addition to the academic papers offered at the 1993 WRN Conference to mark twenty years of women in the rabbinate, a re-ordination or pre-ordination ritual was debuted. With the guidance of renowned artist/educator Nancy Katz, we created the WRN tallit, which has been worn by WRN co-presidents ever since and, in 1997, graced the cover of a special edition of the *CCAR Journal*.[14]

It is no coincidence that Nancy and other Judaic artists' work experienced an explosion just as more women were entering the rabbinate. Rabbi Priesand's ordination forced people to take a new look at Judaism and Jewish expression. Katz rode the wave of excitement and creativity that women have brought to Judaism through the rabbinate, and she offers innovative ways to wrap ourselves in the fringes of the tallit. With women in the rabbinate she said, "Jewish feminism was no longer a conflict."[15] For most of Jewish history, Judaism was essentially black and white with just a hint of blue revealed in the stripes of the tallit. As women rabbis entered the picture, Judaism entered a technicolor world, and it is far more beautiful because of it.

NOTES

1. Chaim Stern, ed., *Gates of Prayer for Shabbat and Weekdays: A Gender Sensitive Prayerbook* (New York: Central Conference of American Rabbis, 1994), iv.

2. Rachel Adler, *Engendering Judaism: An Inclusive Theology and Ethics* (Philadelphia: Jewish Publication Society, 1998).

3. Judith Plaskow, *Standing Again at Sinai: Judaism from a Feminist Perspective* (New York: HarperSanFrancisco, 1990), 212.

4. Marcia Falk, *The Book of Blessings: New Jewish Prayers for Daily Life, the Sabbath, and the New Moon Festival* (San Francisco: HarperSanFrancisco, 1996); Ellen Umansky, ed., *Four Centuries of Jewish Women's Spirituality: A Sourcebook* (Boston: Beacon Press, 1992), 241.

5. "Healing," The Life and Legacy of Debbie Friedman, http://debbiefriedman.com/healing.

6. "Rachel Cowan," Jewish Women's Archive, http://jwa.org/feminism/cowan-rachel.

7. "History," Ma'yan, http://mayan.org/about/history.

8. Women of Reform Judaism, http://www.wrj.org/signature-products/covenant-book-series.

9. Ordination of Women Rabbis—Resolutions and Statements: 1963 http://www.wrj.org/node/113586.

10. Carole B. Balin, Dana Herman, Jonathan D. Sarna, and Gary P. Zola, ed. *Sisterhood: A Centennial History of Women of Reform Judaism* (Cincinnati: HUC Press, 2013), 102.

11. Interview, Anita Diamant, November 20, 2014.

12. Laura Geller, "From Equality to Transformation: The Challenge of Women's Rabbinic Leadership," in *Women Rabbis: Exploration & Celebration*, ed. Gary P. Zola (Cincinnati: HUC Press, 1996), 69–80.

13. "The Spirituality Initiative," Hebrew Union College–Jewish Institute of Religion, http://huc.edu/campus-life/new-york/spirituality-initiative.

14. Women's Rabbinic Network, http://womensrabbinicnetwork.org.

15. Personal interview with Nancy Katz, November 2014.

30

EL NA, R'FAH NA LAH,
HEAL US NOW

RABBI ERIC WEISS

WITH HILLY HABER

There is often a delicate dance woven into the relationship between a belief system and its practitioners. As Reform Jews, we are well acquainted with this. At times, we follow the rhythm and hum of tradition, submitting to thousands of years of practice and belief. Other times, however, we take the lead, introducing nuance and complexity to ostensibly set ways of thinking. Reform Judaism and its adherents revel in this dance—together, we bend, jive, and flow with history and nuance, ancient callings and everyday longings. Conceived of to meet people where they are and committed to offering a nourishing Jewish practice, Reform Judaism offers a Movement based on creativity, egalitarianism, and relevance.

In a world that is constantly changing, however, it can be difficult for a belief system to keep up with the ever-evolving needs of its adherents. True reform, then, relies on people, its clergy and lay leaders, to infuse tradition with new meaning—to allow thousands of years of tradition to speak with urgency and meaning in the twenty-first century.

Successfully taking on and modeling this process is no easy task, but it is possible. In the early 1990s, a group of female Reform rabbis fundamentally transformed the North American Jewish world. Revitalizing and reconstructing Jewish notions of the self, community, and care, these women birthed, out of their own life experiences, a movement centered on cultivating communal and individual Jewish practices and cultures of healing. Informed by personal narratives of illness, their rabbinic training, and Jewish notions of care, these women translated a liturgical call for healing into a spiritual practice previously missing from mainstream Reform Judaism. Their story, and the development of what has come to be known as the Jewish healing movement, speak to the power of individuals within the Jewish community to create new paradigms of practice and belief out of moments when tradition and liturgy fail to bring comfort in the face of trauma.

An understanding of this perceived failure requires an explanation of the Jewish healing liturgy and practices that then existed. Jewish tradition has long recognized a distinction between the physical experience of illness and recovery and the spiritual and emotional aspects of healing. Embedded in Jewish liturgy, this distinction speaks to the importance of caring not just for our physical health, but also for our mental and spiritual well-being. One example of a liturgical call for healing is the *Mi Shebeirach* prayer. The recitation of this prayer for healing enjoys a place at the core of our Reform liturgical experience. Indeed, the *Mi Shebeirach* and the unique rituals that accompany its recitation have long been fixtures of Reform worship and practice—rabbinic students learn the choreography of saying names aloud, cantors lead the congregation with the sacred notes of our musical tradition, and synagogue offices even have protocols on how to list names for their newsletters and Shabbat programs. All of this is a reflection of the prominent and powerful role the prayer for healing plays in daily practice today.

The dynamic nature of the *Mi Shebeirach* speaks more broadly to the multifaceted and diverse function of liturgy. Liturgy seeks to attach words to feelings or thoughts we cannot quite articulate on our own—offering insights into universal questions that we may not have previously considered; providing a sense of belonging and inclusion in a wider community; giving communities a common set of assumptions about the world; and offering us a relationship to God that is both communal and personal. Prayer, therefore, works not as a monologue or in a vacuum, but as a dialogue between the worshiper's innermost longings and the liturgical text. In this spirit, Reform tradition recognizes an element of malleability in prayer—empowering its leaders and laypeople to edit, resurrect, enhance, and expand liturgy, allowing our prayers to speak to those who recite them. The central presence of the *Mi Shebeirach* within the Reform canon is an example of how liturgical standards shift to reflect the spiritual yearnings of a people.

Further, prayer has the power to set the stage for conversation between a synagogue and its members. In many synagogues, members understand the inclusion of the *Mi Shebeirach* within the service as an indication of the synagogue's capacity to care. In reading aloud the names of those in need of healing, for example, we bring private struggle into the communal sphere. The public listing of names here implicitly functions as a spiritual and communal contract: we vow to take notice of and care for one another. The *Mi Shebeirach* also embodies a public declaration of individual vulnerability that is then acknowledged by the community and initially responded to through formal prayer. As an articulation of a communal, spiritual contract, the *Mi Shebeirach* allows us to express our highest hopes and dreams for our community—we seek to be a community of carers. In this context Reform Judaism is attractive to those who yearn for a place they feel cared for in the midst of a culture that otherwise can alienate the individual from the community.

The power of the *Mi Shebeirach* to create and inform a practice of care within our communities speaks to the power of liturgy to shape and inform communal notions of care and healing. Liturgy, however, can only take us so far in cultivating communal and individual practices of care. Today, the Reform Jewish conversation around healing that has developed beyond the recitation of the *Mi Shebeirach* owes its progress to the Jewish healing movement.

Coined by Rabbi Nancy Flam, the term "Jewish healing movement" was initially written with a lowercase "m" to acknowledge that while not a formal, structured movement, it represented a significant effort to bring personal pain and suffering into the collective consciousness of our people. Soon after its inception, the Jewish healing movement began to fundamentally shift the ways in which Reform communities spoke about illness. From smaller, more intimate conversations to formal gatherings of larger audiences, dialogues surrounding healing were launched, in an attempt to create communal spaces in which to engage issues of healing and curing, pursuits of wholeness, and structures of spiritual care. These conversations began happening across the country—most notably through liturgical changes, the establishment of synagogue caring communities, and the building of healing centers.

The Jewish healing movement came about through a confluence of factors, beginning in the late 1980s out of Rabbi Rachel Cowan's personal experience with her husband Paul's illness, and moving from there to a series of conversations and then formal efforts to construct a foundation to articulate Jewish resources to the service of the community during times of illness, grief, and dying. Other cultural factors in the movement included the then-nascent pandemic of AIDS within our communities, as well as other scourges like breast cancer, while reflecting the unique Jewish-American dual values of individuality and community. The movement also represented a significant shift away from Holocaust-centered Jewish communal identities, tapping into grassroots spiritual care movements popping up across the United States, influenced by, for example, 12-step programs.

The success of the Jewish healing movement in the western United States, in bringing the suffering of the individual to the communal sphere, may indicate a shift in the American Jewish landscape from the East to the West in terms of innovation and creativity within Jewish communities.

As a uniquely American creation, it can be suggested that the Jewish healing movement uses the American value of individuality to inform its construction of and relationship to God, Torah, and Israel. While many Jewish organizations hold on to rigid understandings of these concepts, the Jewish healing movement allows for the creation of flexible constellations and relationships among these three concepts in the context of individual and collective healing and spirituality. It is this freedom and fluidity that allows the Jewish healing movement to bring the personal into the communal in conversation with God, Torah, and Israel. In this way, the Jewish healing movement offers a new Jewish identity paradigm that melds personal experience to both the individual and communal Jewish spiritual experience.

Rabbi Rachel Cowen's own story of loss and trauma speaks to the ability of personal experience to inform and shape Jewish spirituality. In the early 1980s Rabbi Cowan's husband Paul was diagnosed with leukemia. His diagnosis coincided with the diagnostic rise of AIDS in the United States. The world of treatment they entered was marked by two things: a rise in the broader level of spiritual care for patients and a lack of specifically Jewish practices and conversations around illness. Rachel reflects that during her husband's many hospitalizations the only chaplains sent to her husband's room were Christian, and therefore, they were unable to speak to the spiritual longings of a Jewish couple. Further research revealed an overall lack of Jewish vocabulary and conversation around how we experience illness, how to approach the end of life, how to understand differences between curative efforts, and other efforts to buoy the spirit, assuage spiritual anxiety, and help to frame a response to questions about life beyond a physical reality.

In response to her experiences at her husband's bedside, Rabbi Cowen used her rabbinic thesis to both illuminate the Psalms as a tool for building a spiritual response to illness, and to begin a broader conversation with other Jewish professionals to challenge the status quo in Jewish response to illness.

Rabbi Cowen understood her identity as a woman to be central to her work at this time. She reflects, "From my experience as a woman and as a parent I have an understanding of what it means to nurture and so in leadership positions I prefer collaborative ways of problem solving and helping people come together. I am good at gathering people together to identify ways to solve a problem."[1]

Rabbi Nancy Flam, co-founder and pioneer of the Jewish healing movement, also highlights the role of her female identity in her work: "I have always felt most alive as a human being through the world of emotions....I am certain that part of the license I have experienced in deeply inhabiting the world of emotions comes from my being female in this culture....I view those who bear witness to deep emotion to be more warrior-like than anything."[2]

Together with Rabbi Nancy Flam, Rabbi Rachel Cowan, Rabbi Susan Freeman and others revolutionized Jewish notions of care and spiritual healing in America. One primary contribution these rabbis brought to the landscape of Jewish life is the singular healing service. Before their vision, the Jewish community did not have a viable vocabulary or liturgical framework to articulate spiritual yearnings for wholeness. At the time, the Jewish approach to illness was focused primarily on the medical and legal narratives. For example, Jewish life tended to focus on understanding the process of a disease and knowing the best physician for a referral. Efforts were made to ensure that estate plans were in place. While these are vitally important, the Jewish landscape did not attend to the one feature that a faith community is capable of providing: reflection on the spiritual narrative of one's life in the face of illness. The development of a Jewish healing service provided a foundation of vocabulary, theological frames, and personal experience to speak to deeper explorations such as: How do I live with illness? What happens to me after I die? What spiritual supports do I need as I adjust to a different lifestyle?[3]

While it is reductive and overly simplistic to assign specific gender qualities to how a culture shifts, Rabbi Susan Freeman reflects that "expressing the maternal instinct is a hands-on, very embodied experience. My sense is that a key impetus behind creating Jewish healing centers was a perceived need to create opportunities for support and connection in ways that may be in sync with the kind of intimacy associated with maternal instinct."[4] Certainly, the notions of Jewish healing have brought a direct relational aspect to the wider Jewish landscape as a legitimate frame for Jewish identity development.

These women cultivated a soil in the Jewish landscape that encouraged the growth of new vocabulary, new liturgical frameworks, and new relational models for Jewish identity development. Much remains still unexplored in regard to their efforts and the impact they have had on the American Jewish scene. Their work intersects with broader issues that call out for deeper exploration in the areas of gender identity, the elements necessary for cultural change, and how one articulates a communal vision. Ultimately, however, these women have shown us how we change a canon to keep our Jewish life vibrant—how as good dance partners we must demand support and relevance from Jewish tradition.

NOTES

1. E-mail correspondence with the author, August 26, 2015.
2. E-mail correspondence with the author, March 11, 2015.
3. The history of the Jewish healing service has yet to be fully written; however, an important historical foundation is the healing service developed under the auspices of Rabbi Yoel Kahn while serving Congregation Shaar Zahav and his collaboration with Rabbi Nancy Flam at the first Jewish Healing Center, in San Francisco, California.
4. E-mail correspondence with the author, April 2, 2015.

31

KINDLING CHANGE

Women Rabbis and Social Action

RABBI PATRICIA KARLIN-NEUMANN

His is the iconic image of a rabbi engaged in social justice in America. Leading black and white citizens of goodwill from Selma to Montgomery in the aftermath of Bloody Sunday, Rabbi Abraham Joshua Heschel marched beside the Rev. Dr. Martin Luther King Jr. with dignity and grace. With his white hair and beard, Rabbi Heschel personified the biblical prophets he wrote about. Of a dozen people whose faces can be seen in a photo of the march, all but one is male. While Jewish women were engaged in the movement for civil rights,[1] none were rabbis—not yet. Ten years later when I applied to rabbinical school, never having set eyes on the two women who had recently been ordained, for me a rabbi looked like Heschel—not like me.

But if in 1965 the opportunity to see an ordained Jewish woman fighting for justice still belonged to the future, Jewish texts from the past provided portrayals of female courage and conviction. In the Exodus story that inspired the civil rights movement, another iconic image emerges. Shiphrah and Puah, midwives of Egypt, defied the decree of the Pharaoh to kill all Israelite boys on the birthstool (Exodus 1:15–22). What might have been a private rebellion against unjust authority and for posterity by two lone women had public and enduring consequences—it set the stage for our biblical forebears to be redeemed and become the Jewish people. That Shiphrah and Puah are named and given a divine reward reflects the magnitude of their social action.[2]

How have Jewish women, who have added to their own name the illustrious title "rabbi," been engaged in social justice? What might be the next iconic images, as we look back on the past forty years of women in the rabbinate and look ahead to generations of Jews who have always known that women could be rabbis?

Our ancestors spent forty years in the wilderness, creating a marker for a time of transition, of pilgrimage, of improvisation. What have women who are rabbis during these past forty years learned about social action, about *tikkun olam* (public acts of repair)? How have the first generations of female rabbis engaged with the public square, with their communities, with other justice makers?[3]

Our nomenclature has changed. The "social action" of forty years ago is now variously framed as social justice or civic involvement, or politics or community engagement, and more broadly, even within the interfaith and secular world, as *tikkun olam.*[4] The issues on our agenda have proliferated, as have styles of leadership, in tackling those issues. What factors might encourage or discourage rabbis from providing public direction on those issues? What role did social justice play in the decision of women colleagues to become rabbis? How has gender affected the engagement of colleagues in the work of *tikkun olam*?

In order to attain an anecdotal sense of how women rabbinic colleagues think about these questions, I invited colleagues through the Women's Rabbinic Network and the Brickner Rabbinic Fellows Facebook groups to fill out a short survey in the fall of 2013. Twenty-four female colleagues graciously responded, in some cases offering comments or stories. I will refer to this as the "Women Rabbis' Survey," or WRS. All unattributed quotes in this essay come from the responses to the survey. Additionally, I interviewed six women, with at least one representative of each decade in which women have been ordained. (I found the book *Women with a Mission: Religion, Gender, and the Politics of*

Women Clergy, by Laura Olson, Sue Crawford, and Melissa Deckman, helpful in framing questions and providing national data.)

It may not be often that Jews use the language of "calling" to describe why we entered the rabbinate. And yet, sometimes it is precisely that language, suggestive of sanctity and certainty, that conveys the appropriateness of this choice.

A 2006 Hebrew Union College–Jewish Institute of Religion (HUC-JIR) New York ordinee wrote, "I feel utterly called to do this work, and having grown up in the Reform Movement, I've always understood Judaism to be inextricably linked with our charge to repair our broken world; for me, it is impossible to be fully embracing of Judaism without justice, compassion, and action as part of the equation."

This young rabbi is in good company—85 percent of Protestant and Jewish congregational clergy in four cities[5] interviewed by the authors of *Women with a Mission* discerned a calling to speak out on political issues. When asked in the WRS, "Did social justice play a role in your decision to enter the rabbinate?" 46 percent conveyed that social action was central to their decision to become a rabbi. Interestingly, the centrality of social action declines over the decades, from 80 percent of rabbis ordained in the 1970s and 1980s, to 50 percent among those ordained in the 1990s, to 20 percent among those ordained in 2000 and beyond. Fifty percent of the respondents communicated that social justice was one of many factors in their decision to become a rabbi.

For most of the rabbis, the Reform Movement's strong and unequivocal commitment to social responsibility played a significant role in affirming their own convictions. Ninety-two percent felt that the Reform Movement in effect said, "You go, girl!" when it came to work on behalf of social justice. The other 8 percent felt the Movement was "okay with" their involvement. A 1998 HUC-JIR Cincinnati ordinee who grew up in the Conservative Movement chose instead to become a Reform rabbi, expressing that the commitment to social justice is what allows her to be comfortably at home in her adopted Movement. In *Women with a Mission*, a Reform rabbi asserted that the Movement's commitment "to social justice issues and trying to follow the words of the prophets" is a "guiding principle for all rabbis."[6] A somewhat smaller, but still robust 81 percent of the clergy women interviewed for *Women with a Mission* in 1998 cited their denomination or religious tradition as influencing their political priorities, action, or strategies. They found encouragement in their tradition's history of social engagement, their denominational group that organizes around social issues, and the information provided by their Washington, DC, lobbying office.[7]

For 79 percent of the women in the WRS, their reading of Jewish texts and traditions strongly shapes their activism and sense of social responsibility. The other 21 percent find texts and traditions helpful and affirming. This is more universal than is reflected in the Cooperative Clergy Project (2000), a national study cited in *Women with a Mission*, in which 77 percent of women clergy in Jewish[8] and Protestant mainline denominations indicate that theological principles either greatly encourage or encourage them to engage in activities designed to mend the secular world.[9]

With Jewish sources and a Movement affirming their involvement in *tikkun olam*, what difficulties have rabbis articulated about being involved in social action?

While the information spans fifteen years, in both the published account of religion, gender, and the politics of women clergy[10] and the interviews and surveys of women rabbis, several themes present themselves. Women are concerned with the scarcity of time, with alienating congregants and the financial implications of doing so, and with maintaining their legitimacy as clergy.

For clergy who have families, the balance of being responsible at work and at home on "the second shift"[11] makes involvement in social justice both more difficult and more imperative. Women describe the tension between what it takes to be a good mother and a good clergyperson but "on the other hand, I am very aware of what kind of world that I want my son to grow up in and therefore I do feel that it is important that I speak out on certain issues."[12]

A valuable opportunity to foster a commitment to social justice in the Reform Movement is involvement with the Brickner Rabbinic

Seminar and Fellowship of the Religious Action Center (RAC), a program designed to provide the foundation and skills to enable rabbis to become more effective social justice advocates through text study and practical skills. In each of the three cohorts since 2008, about one-third of the participants have been women. Upon reflecting on the applications, the Brickner Fellows program coordinator, Rabbi Rosalind Gold (HUC-JIR '78), speculates that attending the five-day community building and study seminar deters many women. "Women with young children are more careful with what they do with their nonessential time—taking five days away from family may make it difficult to add this to their other responsibilities."

All rabbis grapple with the multiple roles they are asked to balance professionally. But women are often evaluated more critically than their male counterparts, which may put their civic or political involvement under greater scrutiny.

A newly minted rabbi, noting that her congregation has many political conservatives, weighs her words and deeds carefully. Her concerns about job security and a desire to be "professionally strategic" accounts for a disparity between what she and other colleagues would say or do privately or on their own time in contrast to what they are willing to say or do in public. She juggles the competing values of social justice and wanting to feel like she belongs. "When I look at my allocation of time and what is important and what I enjoy doing, social justice gets a high percentage and is rewarding for me, but it is not rewarded in the short term in the congregation."

A 2008 HUC-JIR Los Angeles ordinee wrote, "I have been told by the senior rabbi that I don't have time to engage in anything beyond my congregational work." Nonetheless, she identifies herself as engaged in social justice, civic or community activities, in a wide range of settings.

For Rabbi Mona Alfi (HUC-JIR '98), all the incentives align—her congregation, her reading of Jewish tradition, the Reform Movement, colleagues, rituals, and family all cheer her on:

Being at a congregation that has a history of seeing the connection between social justice, Judaism, and politics has made it easy for me. Both the men and the women in my family were engaged in social action, so I've never seen it as a gender thing. There is pride in our congregation that dating back more than one hundred years, both men and women in our synagogue have been involved in the political and social justice work of Sacramento.

I have the pleasure of working in a congregation that includes elected officials and state workers. Almost every senior rabbi in my congregation since World War II has served as the chaplain for the California Senate or Assembly. Being engaged in social justice is an unwritten item in my job description....Congregants on both ends of the political spectrum like that our congregation is engaged in and educated in social justice as a Jewish value. It is something that attracts people to our congregation. For many of my congregants, they know that the work they do (in politics, education, medicine, social work) is an expression of their Judaism. They are proud that both their rabbi and their congregation are outspoken on social justice issues.

In the WRS, 67 percent of the women wrote that their congregation, organization, or agency encouraged them to be involved in social justice. For 21 percent, their communities did not mind, and for 12.5 percent, their communities conveyed directly or indirectly, "If you must..." Ten percent had a supervisor or board who communicated, "Don't even think about it!" when it came to social justice work. But, in *Women with a Mission*, the authors note that more than the conservatism, political diversity within a congregation or community may actually may be a more powerful deterrent.[13]

Rabbi Laura Geller, one of the first women to be ordained by HUC-JIR in 1976 and throughout her rabbinate a strong and clear voice for social justice, whether in Hillel, in national organizations, or congregational contexts, has faced this dynamic in her present setting. "The congregation wants me to be a leader in the community but is ambivalent about social justice issues because congregants are on different sides of many issues."

While it is difficult to know whether female rabbis feel this more readily than male colleagues, there is an inherent tension between the prophetic and pastoral, between living out one's values of social responsibility and nurturing every member of the congregation, regardless of their political perspectives.[14]

If women are often thought to be more nurturing, how might women experience the relationship between their gender and their professional lives? In the four-city survey conducted by the authors of *Women with a Mission* of clergywomen's views on gender and politics, one in three women suggested that their gender itself is an impediment to active involvement.[15] Their findings were slightly higher than in the Cooperative Clergy Project, the 2000 national survey of clergywomen's views on gender and politics, in which 28 percent asserted that being female makes it difficult to be involved in community politics, 38 percent disagreed, and 34 percent were unsure.[16] The experience of women rabbis seems quite different. Eighty-two percent of women rabbinic respondents in the WRS disagreed or strongly disagreed with the statement "My gender makes it more difficult to be involved in social action." Only 9 percent agreed. (Fifty percent also disagreed or strongly disagreed with the statement "Because of my gender, I have easier opportunities to get involved in social action." Eighteen percent agreed with the assertion.)

A 2011 HUC-JIR New York ordinee commented, "I find [the claim that my gender creates difficulty] particularly true in interdenominational and interfaith settings." If women who are ministers find gender more of an impediment than do rabbis, perhaps it is not surprising that interfaith settings may be more challenging for women rabbis.

This young rabbi's experience is balanced by the comment of a colleague ordained in 2009 who wrote, "I work very actively with my local interfaith clergy group on community organizing issues and agendas. I find that as a strong, confident, passionate Jewish woman, I am encouraged to step in the spotlight and represent us regularly to influential partners in the government." Indeed, there were multiple descriptions of ways that their gender was an asset in social justice work.

A 1990 HUC-JIR Cincinnati ordinee wrote, "My gender has helped me draw more attention to the issues about which I am passionate. It has also been a boon in helping me connect with other female clergy."

Rabbi Lynne Landsberg (HUC-JIR '81) was previously the associate director of the Religious Action Center. Following her recovery from a traumatic brain injury sustained in a devastating automobile accident, she became the RAC's senior advisor on disability issues. She writes that throughout her career, in addition to building alliances with other female activists when she worked on women's issues, "in other issues, my gender helped progressive groups become more diverse."

Rabbi Landsberg's expertise and national influence reflect several of the qualities that women have identified as beneficial in community engagement: a collaborative style, credibility on topics such as abortion and domestic violence, the ability to raise issues in a nonthreatening way, and the invocation of personal experiences to inform policy.[17]

Women rabbis are passionate about a wide range of problems faced by our country. In the WRS, two-thirds of the respondents identified these as poverty/hunger/homelessness, abortion, civil rights/racism/discrimination, LGBTQ rights, and gun violence. About half of the rabbis identified feminism, women's equality in Judaism, health care, Israel, and education. Just below this list were the death penalty, immigration, climate change, family and children's issues, and church/state concerns. Compared to the priorities reflected in the national survey of women clergy, rabbis shared their concern for poverty, income inequality, and violence, but rabbis were far more passionate than the national clergywomen about abortion and all forms of discrimination, and were *significantly more* concerned with LGBTQ rights.

Several rabbis expressed surprise at encountering anti-Semitism and ignorance in their communities, thinking that in a pluralistic America, that battle was in the past. Their educational and diplomatic responses led them naturally to fight discrimination when others faced it as well. "Working against white supremacists created an alliance with the black church and the Muslim community. It helped me to develop real friendships with other clergy," one rabbi offered.

Rabbi Rosalind Gold (HUC-JIR '78) reflected: "Our experience as women is like our experience as Jews; they both make us sensitive to things. It is inherent in our way of looking at the world—we don't even think about why that is."

At the 1993 Women's Rabbinic Network conference, Rabbi Stacey Offner (HUC-JIR '84) gave a stirring talk to her colleagues about the discrimination she faced as a lesbian rabbi. She ended by telling a story about a minister friend who was asked at her own ordination, "Would you vote to ordain homosexuals once you yourself are admitted to the ministry?" Offner recounted, "In the context of her church, this minister knew this one answer could cost her her entire ministry. After a long pause, she finally responded, 'I am a woman struggling to be ordained. As part of an oppressed group of people, I could not possibly vote against another group of oppressed people struggling for their place and rights as well.'"[18]

Rabbi Mira Wasserman (HUC-JIR '98) identified a similar resistance to discrimination. She entered HUC-JIR in Cincinnati with a profound sense of indebtedness to the pioneering women who made it possible for her to become a rabbi. But for her gay classmates, she knew there was much injustice to confront. She arrived at her pulpit in rural Indiana when lawmakers were trying to amend the state constitution to ensure that marriage would remain only between a man and a woman. She had gay congregants. She recognized that because clergy sanctify marriage, this was an issue where being a clergyperson affirming same-sex marriage really mattered. She became a familiar figure in the state capital on behalf of the LGBTQ community.

The researchers for *Women with a Mission* discovered that "women's advocacy activities are overwhelmingly focused upon controversial rights-related issues. Clearly the women do not shy away from front-line controversy; instead they are vocal advocates for the rights of people of color, gays and lesbians, and women—despite facing some organizational pressures to eschew such issues. The stereotypical image of women clergy as fearful of acting on controversial issues because they feel their positions and status are vulnerable is simply not supported by our analysis."[19]

Perhaps it is not surprising that another book on women of faith and social change is titled *God's Troublemakers*.[20] For clergy concerned with social justice, some typical strategies for leadership include preaching and teaching on controversial issues, what researchers call "cuegiving";[21] direct action, such as facilitating soup kitchens, food banks, clothing drives, and local shelters; and advocacy, such as writing opinion pieces, contacting public officials, protesting, circulating petitions, engaging in boycotts, and working with neighborhood organizations. In *Women with a Mission*, the researchers note that of these strategies for engaging in *tikkun olam*, women clergy were more likely to engage in advocacy than in direct action and using the power of the pulpit.

In the WRS, 92 percent of the rabbis reported preaching and teaching in their communities on issues they were passionate about, and 71 percent reported being a leader in their local community. For some rabbis, direct action became a beeline to advocacy. This was the experience of Rabbi Stephanie Kolin (HUC-JIR '06), now co-director of Just Congregations, the community organizing strategy of the Union for Reform Judaism. As the coordinator for the HUC-JIR Soup Kitchen, she stumbled upon community organizing, where she warmed to ideas of building relational power. She was instrumental in creating "Leadership in Public Life"—an HUC-JIR course in the art of community organizing, providing tools for rabbinical students to engage in relational advocacy. "I've never needed a deep and booming voice from the bimah. If you believe in relational power, everyone's more powerful when you carry shared responsibility. Relational power has leveled the playing field."

For other women colleagues, advocacy led to scholarship on social justice. Rabbi Rachel Sabath Beit-Halachmi (HUC-JIR '95) recently joined the HUC-JIR administration to develop community engagement opportunities for rabbinical students. Her long-standing scholarship in Jewish texts on leadership and social justice will benefit the next generation of rabbis. Rabbi Mira Wasserman (HUC-JIR '98) will soon be teaching Talmud at the Reconstructionist Rabbinical College. Challenging the monopoly of the Orthodox on how to read Talmud, she finds in Rabbinic stories rich guidance for social justice. She notes that the "great instinct that the Rabbis had about ethics and politics is that justice begins in interpersonal relationships where the particular matters. [Through attention to] the particulars of the case, they are interested in the most just and compassionate outcomes."

After forty years, our image of a rabbi acting for social justice is no longer solely Rabbi Heschel's prophetic mien marching against injustice. Women delivering a future are no longer operating only in the hidden recesses of the community. The voices of women rabbis are heard in the halls of statehouses from Concord, New Hampshire, to Sacramento, California, as well as in the corridors of Congress. Women colleagues are helping to create Just Congregations; they are Rabbis Organizing Rabbis. They are preaching prophetic sermons from the pulpits of venerable congregations. They are teaching the Torah of tradition and the Torah of tomorrow. There is room for many styles and strategies of *tikkun olam*.

Rabbi Carla Fenves (HUC-JIR '11) describes herself as drawn to power that doesn't call attention to itself. She is more inclined to light the way for others. On Chanukah, *chanukiyot* have many different appearances, but what is essential to each is the *shamash*, the candle that lights all the others each night. It is the *shamash* that enables us to bring more light into dark places, the *shamash* that seeks companions of the spirit, the *shamash* that kindles another and enables them to shine. As we enter the fifth decade of women rabbis kindling change, as we engage in *tikkun olam*, the charge in our prayer book calls to us still:

> We live in two worlds: the one that is and the one that might be.
> Nothing is ordained for us: neither delight nor defeat, neither peace
>   nor war.
> Life flows and we must freely choose.
> We can, if we will, change the world that is,
> into the world that may come to be.[22]

NOTES

1. For a fine history of Jewish women in the civil rights movement, see Debra L. Schultz, *Going South: Jewish Women in the Civil Rights Movement* (New York: New York University Press, 2001).

2. Even as the civil rights movement invoked the language of the Exodus, at the Brandeis University Hillel Foundation, Rabbi Al Alexrad created an annual Shifra and Pu'ah Memorial Award for peacefully resisting an oppressive regime and responding to a higher authority. See Albert S. Axelrad and Stephen J. Whitfield, *Meditations of a Maverick Rabbi: Selected Writings of Albert S. Axelrad; Published on the Occasion of His 20th Anniversary in the Rabbinate* (Chappaqua, NY: Rossel, 1984), 156–57.

3. Social change within the Jewish ritual world, such as the sustained and significant work of Women of the Wall, is beyond the scope of this chapter.

4. See Mario Cuomo's description of his understanding of justice in E. J. Dionne Jr., Jean Bethke Elshtain, and Kayla M. Drogosz, eds., *One Electorate under God: A Dialogue on Religion and American Politics* (Washington, DC: Brookings Institution, 2004), 1–38.

5. The authors interviewed fifty-four women clergy from six mainline Protestant denominations as well as Reform and Conservative rabbis in Milwaukee, Indianapolis, Omaha, and Washington, DC, during the summer of 1998. Eleven percent of the respondents in the four-city sample of women clergy were rabbis. See Laura R. Olson, Sue E. Crawford, and Melissa M. Deckman, *Women with a Mission: Religion, Gender, and the Politics of Women Clergy* (Tuscaloosa: University of Alabama, 2005), 16–17, 37.

6. Ibid., 45.

7. Ibid., 44.

8. Fifteen percent of the respondents in the national sample of women clergy were rabbis.

9. Cooperative Clergy Project 2000, cited in Olson, Crawford, and Deckman, *Women with a Mission*, 35.

10. Olson, Crawford, and Deckman, *Women with a Mission*, 41.

11. Arlie Russell Hochschild and Anne Machung, *The Second Shift: Working Parents and the Revolution at Home* (New York: Viking, 1989).

12. Olson, Crawford, and Deckman, *Women with a Mission*, 51.

13. Ibid., 141.

14. For a fascinating reflection on this dilemma, see Cesar Chavez's 1968 speech "The Mexican American and the Church," http://www. chavezfoundation.org/_cms.php?mode=view&b_code=001008000000000&b_no=14 &page=1&field=&key=&n=5.

15. Olson, Crawford, and Deckman, *Women with a Mission*, 49.

16. Cooperative Clergy Project 2000, cited in Olson, Crawford, and Deckman, *Women with a Mission*, 50.

17. Olson, Crawford, and Deckman, *Women with a Mission*, 53.

18. Rabbi Stacy Offner, "Homophobia and Heterosexism," in *Papers of the Women's Rabbinic Network Conference*, March 21–24, 1993, Oakland, California; story cited in Christine M. Smith, *Preaching as Weeping, Confession and Resistance* (Louisville, KY: Westminster/John Knox Press, 1992), 91.

19. Olson, Crawford, and Deckman, *Women with a Mission*, 122–23.

20. Katharine Rhodes Henderson, *God's Troublemakers: How Women of Faith Are Changing the World* (New York: Continuum, 2006).

21. Identified by James Guth and colleagues as those activities conducted within the congregation and designed to influence congregants' political attitudes and behaviors. Olson, Crawford, and Deckman, *Women with a Mission*, 100.

22. Rabbi Chaim Stern, ed., *Gates of Prayer: The New Union Prayer Book for Weekdays, Sabbaths and Festivals* (New York: CCAR Press, 1975), 216.

32

HOW JEWISH WOMEN
HAVE COME TO READ THE BIBLE

The Creating of Midrash

RABBI SANDY EISENBERG SASSO DMIN

Early during my first year at the Reconstructionist Rabbinical College in 1969, I was asked to speak at the Newman Club at Temple University in Philadelphia on a panel about the role of women in Judaism. After a Catholic and Protestant woman decried the lack of equality for women in their respective traditions, I gave my presentation. I sympathized with the problems my Christian sisters faced but said, "There really is no problem in Judaism."

It did not take me long to learn differently. After a few weeks at the seminary, I began to notice that there was a problem, a serious one. What struck me most was the absence of text, the lack of female voices, women's names, thoughts, and stories. I read of men's struggles with God: Abraham before the destruction of Sodom and on Moriah, Jacob's at Beth-El and on one side of the river Jabbok, Moses on Sinai. There was no mention of women's struggles. What I read either did not understand who I was as a woman or excluded me altogether. In 1972, the year *Ms.* magazine was first published, no one was answering my questions, not even the newly emerging feminist movement; in fact, no one was asking them.

My interest in Jewish texts had taken me on long journeys with Abraham, Moses, and Elijah up Mounts Moriah, Sinai, Nebo, and Carmel. There were steep climbs and dizzy descents. But mountains and ladders with angels coming up and down did not find a resting place in my woman's soul. I decided to listen to the voices of women and their silences. I wondered what a pilgrimage to Sarah's tent and Miriam's well might feel like, whether women's spirituality was different.

I had always imagined myself with Jacob, having sent all his wives, children, servants, and cattle across the river, struggling with God and receiving a blessing. That is where I always believed the religious life was, having rid myself of all life's distractions. But then I read an article that asked a question I had never considered before: what of Rachel and Leah, Bilhah and Zilpah on the other side of the river, in the midst of life's myriad responsibilities and distractions?[1] What of Sarah listening to Abraham's conversation with the angels telling him that he would have a son? What of Miriam being cast out of the community because she criticized Moses, while Aaron, her brother, did the same and was allowed to remain inside?

These were the places where I lived—in the midst of the clamor of daily routine that could not be pushed aside, eavesdropping on Rabbinic conversation, cast out by those who did not feel a woman belonged. I decided to reside awhile with the women on the other side of the river, in the tent. There I found a life of the spirit that had long been silent. I decided to wrestle with traditional texts and not let them go until they blessed me.

Some women were not willing to wrestle. If tradition had excluded them, then so be it. They would no longer be a part of the religious community. But I discovered other women were doing the same kind of wrestling that I was, women who were not willing to turn the meaning of Scripture over to men. As more and more women entered seminary and began to engage sacred texts in new ways, they began to raise questions of the biblical narrative that had never been asked.

What had begun as a desire to affirm the presence of Jewish women in ritual and leadership became an effort to confirm women's ways of understanding tradition and text as worthy and authentic, to let women's experience help elucidate the text and to tell the sacred story. Women rabbis, especially those in congregations where they regularly delivered *divrei Torah*, brought their questions and perspectives to the text. They created midrashim that gave them a voice.

The desire for women to confront the inadequacy of traditional narrative seemed altogether new. But both Eastern European and Sephardic folk legend demonstrated it was an old yearning. A Yiddish folktale (1931) tells of a time when women complained that everything in the world belonged to men, including Torah. They decided they would build a tower of women, one on top of the other, until one woman could pull herself into heaven. They choose Skotsl to be that woman. All went well until the woman at the bottom of the tower could no longer bear the weight of the others. The tower collapsed and Skotsl disappeared. There was no one to talk to God. According to custom, from that time on, whenever someone comes into a house, women call out, "*Skotsl kumt*—Here comes Skotsl," in hope that someday she will really come and change things.[2]

A similar Turkish folktale tells of how women asked King Solomon why men were allowed to marry more than one woman but women could only marry one man. Solomon did not know the answer, so he wrote the question on a piece of parchment and tied it to the leg of a bird. He told the women that the bird was a messenger to God and would return with the answer. Unfortunately, the bird did not return and women are still waiting. Whenever a bird stands at a window, it is customary for women to say, "*Haberes buenos*—Good news," in hope that they will finally have an answer.[3]

An ancient longing was finally given fulfillment as women rabbis became not only receivers of Torah but narrators of our ancient stories. They began to have a conversation with the sacred narrative, and they invited others to do the same. Refusing to accept their absence from text, they became interpreters of Torah—writing commentary, creating midrash. In the process they have given voices, names, and stories to women who had none. Like the Rabbis of old, they listened anew to the stories and filled in the blank spaces.

Amos Oz, the renowned Israeli author, has been quoted as saying, "Fundamentalists live life with an exclamation point. I prefer to live my life with a question mark." That is how women began to read biblical texts, as generations before them, with question marks. But the questions they asked were different from men's.

The creators of women's midrash focused on whose story was really being told. Who was excluded from the narrative? Who was the subject, who the other? Who was the woman before Eve, created equal to Adam? What was her name and what was her story? Who really was Eve?

Who was Lot's wife, the woman who had become the symbol of female fickleness and disobedience? Who was the wife of Noah, what was her name, and how did she survive the long days and nights on the ark? What really happened between Sarah and Hagar, and what did they feel and think? Having understood all these biblical women through the writings of men, what might it mean to see them through the perspective of women? Who was the daughter of Pharaoh, who saved Moses from the Nile and gave him his name, calling him "Moses, my son"? How were women rabbis going to tell these stories to their congregations? Through midrash they began to retell these narratives and answer those questions.

While women rabbis were more confident in their ability to reimagine the biblical text, other women were reluctant at first to write new midrash, since masculine views had been seen as normative. Women questioned the normality of their own feelings and judgment and often suppressed those feelings in deference to others. But things slowly began to change. In the first class of midrash I taught to women at my congregation, I invited the participants to add their story to the ancient narrative. One woman remarked, "I didn't know that I could do that." I responded, "You can." And she and the other women did. I recall Letty Cottin Pogrebin once talking about the Passover seder. She said that if tradition won't give us a seat at the table, then we will set our own table. She was describing the creation of women's seders. I responded: *That is not enough. What we are doing is not counterculture; it is Jewish culture, and women need to claim their rightful place at tradition's table.*

The path of creating new midrashim offered women a traditional way of reconstructing Judaism in light of their present reality. By listening to the silences in the Bible, they poured their souls into the ancient text and allowed the narrative to speak anew, with a fresh and compelling voice, and in the process they transformed Judaism. They held in creative tension the text, its classical interpretation, memory, and imagination.

Perhaps one of the first formal expressions of this new way of understanding Torah came in 1972 when feminist theologian Judith Plaskow, author of *Standing Again at Sinai*,[4] wrote an article entitled "The Coming of Lilith: Toward a Feminist Theology."[5] Plaskow wrote about women's midrash, "It gives us the inner life history cannot follow, building links between the stories of our foremothers and our own joy and pain."[6]

From that time on women became captivated by this eleventh-century legend that was contained in *The Alphabet of Ben Sira*. Attempting to reconcile the two accounts of Creation in Genesis, the ancient figure of Lilith was given a Jewish telling. She was the first woman created before Eve, equal to Adam, from the same dust of the earth. In this medieval retelling, Lilith became the disobedient night demon who threatened grown men and male children. But in the hands of many a feminist midrashist, she became a symbol of independence and hope.

Since the early 1970s, women's midrash has flourished, not only for adults but for children. There is barely a Jewish child who does not hear anew the story of Miriam at the Passover seder when someone at the table lifts her cup filled with water from her well. My grandsons and the children in my congregation's religious school, familiar with my book *The Story of Naamah* (1996) about Noah's unnamed wife, insist that Noah's wife's name is Naamah and that she collected two of every seed and after the Flood replanted the earth's garden.[7] Like the midrash of Abraham and his father's idols, they believe that story of Naamah and the plants to be long-standing stories of our tradition.

Stories have tremendous power, sacred stories even more so. The stories that are told about our past shape our present and future reality. When the new ways of telling sacred narrative become a part of a community's collective memory, they are tradition. Alternative ways of looking at the world begin with alternative stories. Women's midrash helped the Jewish community to see itself in a new way.

I remember once being asked to write a midrash on a biblical woman and to base my retelling on classical midrashim. I chose Lot's wife. There was very little that had been written about her in Rabbinic texts. Visiting the Dead Sea region of Israel, I had bought a postcard of one of the salt formations in the region. On the other side of the card was a written description of the picture on the front. It said, "Lot's Wife." There she was, an eternal symbol of women's disobedience and inability to listen.

Rabbinic text gave her a name and a part of a story. She was called Idit, from the Hebrew word meaning "witness." One commentator suggested that she turned out of compassion to see her daughters who were following her. That was all I needed to feed my imagination.

I wrote a new midrash about Idit, the only witness to the destruction of Sodom and Gomorrah. No one else looked back; no one saw with her eyes the holocaust taking place. Lot was up ahead. He never turned around. Then came Idit and following were her daughters. Hearing the cataclysm behind her, she could no longer follow Lot without question. She did what any mother would do: she turned to check on the safety of her children. Seeing the devastation of the cities she had once called home, she wept. The pillar of salt is her tears.[8]

Women's midrash has helped us to hear Sarah's outcry as she learned of Abraham's decision to take their son Isaac up a mountain to sacrifice him. It has enabled us to feel the loving arms of a stranger, Pharaoh's daughter, Bityah, "daughter of God," who defies her father's decrees and saves Moses from the Nile. It has introduced us to Serach, the daughter of Asher, who held the memory of our people in her stories. It has told of Zelophehad's daughters and their efforts and partial success in changing inheritance law in the Land of Israel. Women's midrash has enabled us to know women's names, to hear their voices and their stories, and in the process, women came to better understand themselves and Torah.[9]

The creation of midrash that envisions women as subjects, as actors in a sacred drama, continues the tradition of our ancestors. Through midrash, women were claiming: In the name of all those who came before us, and in the name of all those generations yet to come, we preserve and create. We marvel at how much remains the same in our cycles of time, what ancient words still move us, how different we are, what silences must still be broken. What really matters is not just that we are descendants, but that we are ancestors who bequeath our spiritual quest to the next generation.

Women's collections of midrash and women's Torah commentaries have proliferated over the last decades. From *Miriam's Well* by Drs. Alice Bach and J. Cheryl Exum in 1991, to *Biblical Women Unbound* by Norma Rosen and *The Five Books of Miriam* by Dr. Ellen Frankel in 1996, to *Sisters at Sinai* by Rabbi Jill Hammer in 2001, to *The Women's Torah Commentary: New Insights from Women Rabbis on the 54 Weekly Torah Portions* by Rabbi Elyse Goldstein in 2000, to *The Women's Haftarah Commentary: New Insights from Women Rabbis on the 54 Weekly Haftarah Portions, the 5 Megillot and Special Shabbatot* by Rabbi Elyse Goldstein in 2004, and to *The Torah: A Women's Commentary* edited by Dr. Tamara Eskenazi and Rabbi Andrea Weiss in 2008, women have reshaped the way we read Scripture.[10]

Those women (and now also men) who have participated in this creative process to fashion new stories recognize it as an awe-filled responsibility and approach it with deep sense of humility. After all, who are we, tied as we are to our own time and place, to fashion the sacred words and create the holy drama to carry us through the passages of our years? We accept this responsibility with a strong sense of duty. After all, who are we, bearers of the image of God, not to pour

our souls into the crucible of time, to affix our name to the holy narrative of our people?

When Judith Kaplan Eisenstein, *z"l*, marked the seventieth anniversary of her bat mitzvah, I wrote the following poem:

Must we always go up to some mountain
With Abraham, with Isaac to Moriah?
The air is so thin up there,
And it's hard to breathe.

Must we always go up to some mountain
With Moses to Sinai?
It's so far from the earth,
And what's below appears so small
You can forget it's real.

Must we always go up to some mountain
With Moses to Nebo?
Climbing—there's only one way
And loneliness.

Must we always go up to some mountain
With Elijah to Carmel?
The ascent is not hard.
It's the descending
Too easy to slip with no one to catch your fall.

I'm weary of mountains
Where we're always looking up
Or looking down and sacrificing
So our neck hurts
And we need glasses.

Our feet upon the mountains
Are blistered
And or shoes are always wrong—
Not enough "sole."

Can we sit with Sarah in a tent,
Next to Deborah under a palm tree,
Alongside Rebekkah by the well—
With Judith in the synagogue reading Torah,
to wash our feet,
to catch our breath
and our soul?[11]

When the people of Israel crossed the Sea of Reeds, Miriam took a timbrel and led the women in singing and rejoicing. With no map to guide her, Miriam stood at the front of a multitude of slaves and taught them to dance. Like Miriam, women rabbis often felt they had no map, no guide to provide the words and the story to make sense of their sacred journey. Like Miriam, they took a chance and danced, and they lead a generation of women to do the same

In the last four decades, Jewish women have read traditional stories through the lens of their experience. They have poured their souls into the ancient text and affixed their names to the holy narrative of our people. The way we as Jews read texts, the way we understand Scripture, has been transformed. What happened was nothing short of a revolution. And it has strengthened and renewed Judaism.

NOTES

1. Linda Clark, "A Sermon: Wrestling with Jacob's Angel," in *Image-Breaking/Image-Building*, ed. Linda Clark, Marian Ronan, and Eleanor Walker (New York: Pilgrim Press, 1981), 98–108.

2. Beatrice Weinreich, "Skotsl Kumt: Skotsl's Here," in *Yiddish Folktales*, ed. Beatrice Weinreich, trans. Leonard Wolf (New York: Pantheon Books, 1988), 246.

3. Naftali Haleva, "Haberes Buenos," in *Chosen Tales: Stories Told by Jewish Storytellers*, ed. Peninnah Schram (Northvale, NJ: Jason Aronson, 1995), 142–44.

4. Judith Plaskow, *Standing Again at Sinai: Judaism from a Feminist Perspective* (San Francisco: Harper and Row, 1990).

5. Judith Plaskow, "The Coming of Lilith: Toward a Feminist Theology," in *Womanspirit Rising*, ed. Carol Christ and Judith Plaskow (San Francisco: Harper

and Row, 1979), 198–209. Originally published in Church Women United packet "Women Exploring Theology at Grailville," 1972.

6. Judith Plaskow, *Standing Again at Sinai, Judaism from a Feminist Perspective* (New York: Harper Row, 1990), p. 59.

7. Sandy Eisenberg Sasso, *Noah's Wife: The Story of Naamah* (originally published as *A Prayer for the Earth* in 1996) (Woodstock, VT: Jewish Lights, 2002). See also Susan Campbell Bartoletti, *Naamah and the Ark at Night* (Somerville, MA: Candlewick Press, 2011).

8. Sandy Eisenberg Sasso, "Idit," *Reconstructionist: A Journal of Creative Jewish Thought* 56, no. 2 (Winter 1990–91): 20–22.

9. Sandy Eisenberg Sasso, *But God Remembered: Stories of Women from Creation to the Promised Land* (Woodstock, VT: Jewish Lights, 1995).

10. Alice Bach and J. Cheryl Exum, *Miriam's Well* (New York: Delacorte Press, 1991); Norma Rosen, *Biblical Women Unbound: Counter-Tales* (Philadelphia: Jewish Publication Society, 1996); Ellen Frankel, *The Five Books of Miriam: A Woman's Commentary on the Torah* (New York: G.P. Putnam's, 1996); Jill Hammer, *Sisters at Sinai: New Tales of Biblical Women* (Philadelphia: Jewish Publication Society, 2001); Elyse Goldstein, ed., *The Women's Torah Commentary: New Insights from Women Rabbis on the 54 Weekly Torah Portions* (Woodstock, VT: Jewish Lights, 2000); Elyse Goldstein, ed., *The Women's Haftarah Commentary: New Insights from Women Rabbis on the 54 Weekly Haftarah Portions, the 5 Megillot and Special Shabbatot* (Woodstock, VT: Jewish Lights, 2004); Tamara Eskenazi and Andrea Weiss, eds., *The Torah: A Women's Commentary* (New York: Women of Reform Judaism and URJ Press, 2008).

11. Sandy Eisenberg Sasso, "Introduction: Unwrapping the Gift," in *Women and Religious Ritual*, ed. by Lesley A. Northup (Washington, DC: Pastoral Press, 1993), ix–xvi.

33

140 FACES OF TORAH AND COUNTING

Communal Transformation, Theological Evolution, and the Authority of Interpretation

RABBI ELIZABETH W. GOLDSTEIN, PhD

Introduction: Seventy Faces of Torah

Sefer B'midbar, the Book of Numbers, describes the offering that each head of tribe presents at the Tabernacle, the portable, sacred shrine in the desert. The first offering comes from the tribe of Judah followed by the second from Issachar. The Torah says:

> On the second day, Nethanel son of Zuar, chieftain of Issachar, made his offering. He presented as his offering: one silver bowl weighing 130 shekels and *one* silver basin of *70* shekels by the sanctuary weight, both filled with choice flour with oil mixed in, for a meal offering. (Num. 7:18–19)

The midrash offers different explanations for the numbers found in these descriptions and gets quite creative, since the numbers of bowls and shekels are the same for each of the twelve tribes. I cite *Midrash Rabbah*'s comment on Issachar's offering because we find therein the origin of a familiar teaching: *shivim panim laTorah*, "seventy faces of Torah." The midrash says:

OF SEVENTY SHEKELS, AFTER THE SHEKEL OF THE SANCTUARY (*B'MIDBAR RABBAH* 13:15–16) Why? As the numerical value of *yayin* [wine] is seventy, so there are seventy modes of expounding the Torah. Why does it say ONE in connection with the dish? It symbolizes the Torah, which must be one; as you read, *One Torah and one ordinance shall be...for you* (Num. 15:16). Why does it say ONE in connection with the basin? Because the words of the Written Law and those of the Oral Law were all given by one Shepherd; one God communicated them all to Moses on Sinai."[1]

The expression "seventy faces of Torah" is fairly well known and cited in several other places in Rabbinic literature.[2] The concept is much the same as *Eilu va'eilu divrei Elohim chayim*, "These and these are both the words of the living God."[3] Jews who study Torah are familiar with multiplicity; we engage Torah with the help of five or more commentaries on a page. Because of this now old phenomenon, we allow many interpretations of Torah an authoritative place at the table, even as we circumscribe the many inside the boundary of one Torah given at Sinai. It is part and parcel of our Jewish heritage to live with this contradiction.

The midrash's comment on "one" is less well known. One basin represents not, as we would expect, all of the words of Torah, but rather the Oneness of the Shepherd who gave them to us. It is through God that our interpretations gather holiness and go forth to the next generation with both raging shouts and still small voices. The one basin juxtaposed with the seventy shekels is, from the midrash's perspective, the interconnection between God and the multiplicity of Torah's interpretations. While there can be no boundary around God, we place limits on what constitutes acceptable interpretations in every new generation. In this way we engage in the push-pull of God and Torah. We are Israel—we struggle with God—but we also struggle with Torah and its boundaries and with who gets an authoritative voice to speak through it.

Approaching the Question

As both a rabbi and a professor of biblical studies, my initial reaction to the question of how the study of Torah has been impacted by the result of women serving as rabbis is to reject the basic premise implied therein. By rejection I do not mean that it is an irrelevant question or, furthermore, that I might not be able to provide a meaningful answer. Rather, the question forces me to first examine the ways we delineate the differences between men and women.

Initially, I think about the scholarly contributions of women to Torah study. First and foremost, and perhaps because I was a contributor, *The Torah: A Women's Commentary* comes to mind.[4] Two female biblical scholars, one of whom was a rabbi, initiated this project.[5] Only female scholars were enlisted to contribute. Is this what made it a women's commentary? Or was it the nature of the comments themselves? One could look at the poetry sections of the commentary and suggest that women were more likely than men to think to enhance a biblical commentary with poems. Alternatively, one could look at the four different types of commentary on each *parashah* and judge the decision to include multiple perspectives on Torah to be a Jewish decision, rather than focus on the potential "femaleness" of the decision to include poetry. The point is, what makes the commentary a "women's" commentary is not obvious at all. And further, the extent to which the ordination of women can be considered a contributing factor to the existence of this commentary is also unclear.

In the same vein, because Rabbi Benay Lappe is a woman, one might look at the yeshivah that she founded in Chicago, Svara, and attribute this highly innovative Talmud-study experience to the ordination of women. Lappe's website explains:

> SVARA is a traditionally radical yeshiva dedicated to the serious study of Talmud and committed to the Queer experience. Our mission is to provide serious Talmud study as a spiritual practice to all who want to learn, in an environment that recognizes as crucial

the insights of transgender, intersex, queer, lesbian, bisexual and gay Jews.

But these wonderful contributions cannot be reduced to the "femaleness" of the rabbis who created them. Nor, however, can and should the "femaleness" of these rabbis be ignored. It does, however, stymie me when trying to pinpoint a specific answer to the question of how the study of Torah has changed as a result of women serving in the rabbinate.

This quagmire is larger than my own struggle in approaching this particular essay. It pertains to the question of essentialism. Essentialism is that thing Simone de Beauvior warned us about back in 1952. Women should not be reduced to their biological essence; their difference may be socially constructed.[6] "One is not born, but rather becomes a woman. No biological, psychological, or economic fate determines the figure that the human female presents in society; it is civilization as a whole that produces this creature, intermediate between male and eunuch, which is described as feminine."[7]

My wanting to dismiss the question comes from my own experience as an American, female, and lesbian Jew, and one who has lived in several denominational worlds. My doctoral work in biblical studies focuses primarily on purity and gender. Subsequently, in the theological arena as well, I have developed my own religious approach to holiness and purity over the years. I have found myself advocating that mikveh not be reserved as a solely female space. I believe this is a social justice issue. I also believe that *t'fillin* can be adopted to enhance the spiritual life of both women and men. If we open the cornucopia of Jewish ritual to both men and women, as we have done by ordaining women, then to ask how women in the rabbinate have shaped Torah study over the last forty years seems to be asking what aspects of Torah study can be quantified and relegated to the realm of the female. But the "feminine," as de Beauvoir has shown us, cannot and should not be reduced to an essential aspect. When we do, we limit both women and men. The dangers of drawing these boundaries outweigh the benefits.

While it is true that women have been central to the creation of these new modes of study, men have made significant contributions to Jewish progress as well. How can the success of *The Torah: A Women's Commentary* or Svara be measured against Hazon, founded by Nigel Savage, who envisioned experiences that "are multi-generational and give entry points for Jews of all backgrounds who are concerned about the environment and the world"?[8] And to what do we owe Rabbi Steve Greenberg's brave step as he revealed his gayness to the Orthodox world?[9] In other words, we have seen great changes in the Jewish community over the last forty years. We have seen Judaism and feminism birthed and rebirthed. We have fought for gay rights from the chuppah to the rabbinate, from the Reform Movement to Orthodox institutions. We have seen great yeshivas like Machon Pardes in Jerusalem, in which men and women study together in the presence of Orthodox teachers, and Svara, a school in which Talmud shines through a queer lens, change the lives of energetic and committed Jews. As a result of Hazon, we have seen secular Jews who ride bicycles and care about composting become immersed in the deepest spirit of religious Jewish communal experience. What part of all of this, or any of this, can be attributed to the ordination of women?

It is for all of these reasons that I want to hide from this question. I want to believe in progress for the sake of progress, for the sake of belief in a God who transforms and evolves through every one of us, man and woman, Jew and Christian and Muslim. I want to think about issues related to women, but I know that ultimately, issues related to women are also related to men. So to write an essay on how Torah study has been shaped by women in the rabbinate is perhaps to overlook a larger religious phenomenon: the evolution, progression, and process of God.

I can give an example from my own experience as a contributor to *The Torah: A Women's Commentary*. I was asked to write the primary commentary for *Parashat Matot* and I also collaborated on *Parashat Mas'ei*. These two portions are the last in *Sefer B'midbar* (Numbers). Of course, several things stood out with regard to women in these *parashiyot*: Moses's rebellion against the Midianites, including the women, for the heresy of Peor (Numbers 31; previously told in Numbers 25); the laws regarding vows and, specifically, vows made by women (Numbers 30); and the final word on the marriage arrangements of the daughters of Zelophehad (Numbers 27: 1–11) (the women who claimed, and were given, the right to inherit their father's estate since he had no sons). However, my examination of these episodes came from my unique perspective as a female biblical scholar and a rabbi. Might a man have come up with the same interpretations as I on these episodes? Likely he would not—perhaps because he is a man, but primarily because he is not I. He has not had my experience nor seen the world through my eyes. Neither, though, has any other woman.

We are different not because of our sex, but because each person in the world is unique. Gender is just a piece of that uniqueness that makes each one of us the singular individual created in the image of *Elohim*, the image of God. Genesis 1:27 utilizes the term *Elohim* and not the personal name of the god of the Israelites, *YHVH*. The name *YHVH*, when subjected to midrashic interpretation, could render a genderless deity. However, literally and most basically, *YHVH* is a male deity. He is a male deity who fiercely protects his people, who sweeps away the Egyptians, and who is worthy and demanding of our love, as stated in the *V'ahavta* (Deut. 6:5). *El* is also a male god, inherited from the Ugaritic pantheon by our ancient ancestors. (Ugarit was a prominent kingdom that existed from the fourteenth to the twelfth centuries BCE, located in modern Lebanon.)

The Torah utilizes *Elohim*, the strange plural construction, more often than *El*. It is strange because everyone agrees that the Torah intends *Elohim*, a plural, to be understood as a singular construction. By way of example, consider the following: "And *Elohim* said, 'Let there be light'" (Gen. 1:3). Midrashically, however, I would suggest that *Elohim*, more than *YHVH*, conveys the multiplicity of ways we reach for the Divine; God cannot be reduced to a singular entity.

Oneness does not necessarily mean singularity in human terms. God is greater than any one image, than any one teaching, than any one gender, than any one essence. God is an explosion of every energy, great and small, of every size, color, and shape; of every word, of every language, of every cell, and every combination therein.

Rabbinic Authority and the Fluidity of the Interpretation

Despite all of this, I must engage in the question posed by this volume because to hide behind the postmodern trappings of the accusation of essentialism ultimately seems cowardly. What does it mean, without bowing to essentialism, to consider the way that the study of Torah has changed as result of women serving in the rabbinate? The crux of the question must be the following: How does Judaism change when women are accepted as authoritative transmitters and interpreters of Torah?

The essence of who can transmit Torah is not a small matter. Feminism is a slippery slope, argue some Jews, Orthodox and otherwise. If women are given the authority to interpret Torah, who is to say that a non-Jew or a homosexual cannot interpret Torah? And, in fact, that is indeed what happens when we swing open a door. More and more non-Jews sit in synagogues all over America and participate in Torah study. More and more LGBT Jews and non-Jewish partners of Jews are finding the doors of the synagogue welcoming to them. Just as feminism was not just for women but has changed the way we view white men, women of color, and Third World Women, women in the rabbinate have changed what is acceptable in the Jewish community. Some may not like this comparison. Some may want the boundaries to stretch just a little but not break open fully.

To this day the battle continues in the Reform Movement among rabbis who will officiate at gay weddings but not interfaith weddings. Some still find it amazing that a rabbi could be so open to homosexual unions, a practice that seemingly violates a law in the Torah, but who simultaneously stands firmly against allowing *kiddushin* (Jewish marriage) for an interfaith couple, even when our first "rabbi," Moses, married a Midianite woman.

The question of drawing boundaries speaks directly to the question of who is a valid interpreter of the tradition. Women rabbis, no less than men, at least in my HUC-JIR class (New York, 2001), took an equally hard stand on interfaith marriage (that is, in the discussions we had before ordination; I would not speak for any of them now, nor do I know how many of them may have changed their opinions on this issue). However, many were openly in favor of gay weddings and would excitedly talk about developing ceremonies for them, but would not perform an interfaith marriage.

Drawing lines around what is authoritatively Jewish is not a new phenomenon, and women rabbis, no less than Reform Jews, no less than Zionists, have sought to solidify their authority by upholding a boundary between what is Jewish and what is not. I am not above or beyond this very understandable dynamic and have found myself, a white, lesbian, PhD rabbi working at a Catholic Jesuit institution, drawing these boundaries at different times and in different contexts. Just as the pendulum swings between God and Torah (where our evolving understanding of God changes the way we understand Torah and, as we engage more deeply in Torah, we glimpse more of the Divine), so swings another pendulum, simultaneously, that moves between communal boundaries and the authority of the interpreter. If and when these two pendulums intersect, we take notice of a shift in our religious and social structure; it is when transformation happens in the Jewish community.

Speaking Words of Torah: How We Respect or Accept Authority

To speak authoritatively about Torah for a rabbi is different than for a layperson, who, in Jewish tradition, has every right to offer a public interpretation of Scripture. Even Jewish biblical scholars who are not rabbis do not command the same authority as a rabbi—who may not be nearly as familiar with biblical scholarship. To be a rabbi and to speak words of Torah is something that continues to emerge as sacred. We, as listeners, pay attention to it. We know when a rabbi or a rabbinical student gets up to speak and it doesn't ring true or it doesn't feel well crafted. We begin to offer internal and sometimes external critiques. We feel disappointed, cheated, or even angry sometimes that the rabbi has not invested the time, the thought, or the intellectual effort in transmitting his or her relationship to Torah to us. We feel this more intensely than when a layperson gets up to deliver a *d'var Torah* and it falls short of our expectations. There has always been and there always will be something special about a rabbi. We know this is true because many fought so hard against women's ordination and, today, continue this fight in the modern Orthodox community. If it were no different to be rabbi than an educated layperson, there would not exist the battle over the title "rabbi" versus "maharat."[10]

What does it mean for a rabbi to teach Torah? To answer that question, we must define the nature of Torah study and determine how we relate to it. The nature of Torah study is to probe the Jewish tradition in a deeper way, to interpret sacred texts and find our connection to God (whether we understand God to be internal or external to us), to ourselves, and to others. Have women in the rabbinate changed the way we connect to ourselves and to others? Absolutely. Women have added a new face to Torah, and since Torah traditionally has had seventy faces, we now have added at least another seventy. Women have added 50 percent more faces or insights to Torah. Women in the rabbinate have opened seventy new windows for the souls of the Jewish community to commune with the Eternal One.

The New Idolatry

Two feminist theologians, one a Jew and one a Christian, have highlighted the limitations we, as a community, place on God when we imagine God as exclusively male. Both Judith Plaskow and Rosemary Radford Reuther have named this phenomenon "idolatrous."[11] Why is it idolatrous to imagine God as exclusively male? It is the same reason that the kabbalists would not let their followers contemplate any one *s'firah* exclusively? When we limit our human imagination to one picture, idea, or concept, the result, over time, is that the said picture, idea, or concept becomes interchangeable with the thing itself. When we imagine God as a King on a throne, a resurrected holy man, or Father in heaven, we minimize God. Pushing ourselves to imagine God as Mother, Queen, Whirlwind, Forest, or Ocean sets our human mind free to embrace both the multiplicity and the Oneness of the Divine Force. We embrace the expansiveness and evolution of God, and we reinvigorate our interpretation of Torah.

We commit idolatry when we only depict God as male, and we stagnate Torah when we restrict its interpreters to only men. Women in the rabbinate changed the atmosphere of Torah study because they have become authoritative and influential interpreters—in having a seat at the table in *chevruta*, in delivering sermons and *divrei Torah*, and in informal Torah studies. Female interpreters—and not just female rabbis—have examined and reexamined biblical women in new and diverse ways. But it is not just biblical women who have a renewed life through women's interpretation; all of Torah comes alive again in our generation because women have lent their own unique voices to it. This was the premise of *The Torah: A Women's Commentary*. The editors specifically instructed the writers that we not focus solely on the women of the Torah or even on laws that specifically relate to women. All of Torah, not just the parts that seem to pertain to women, can and should be seen anew through the scholarship and commentary of women in our generation. Of course, giving new voices to female biblical characters and laws relevant to women in each generation is also obligatory for us. As every dot and letter of Torah is essential, no less important are those directly and indirectly relevant to women. And like all of Torah, the female voices of forty years ago are not the voices of today. They must be renewed in every generation.

Have women rabbis changed the way we approach the study of Torah? Most certainly! We have allowed every man and every woman a chance to open themselves to the exquisite wrestling of Torah study in seventy more new and multifarious ways. At this moment and in every generation to come, the Jewish community can boast 140, female and male, faces of Torah and counting.

NOTES

1. Adapted from *Midrash Rabbah*, vol. 4, *Numbers II*, trans. Judah J. Slotki (London: Soncino Press, 1983), 534.

2. Allen S. Maller writes, "The earliest source for the term *Shivim panim la-Torah* is Numbers Rabbah 13:15–16, customarily dated to the twelfth century. The concept, though not the exact wording, also appears in another post-talmudic midrash, *Otiyyot de-Rabbi Akiva*, as *Torah nilmedah be-shivim panim*—'Torah is learned through 70 faces/facets.' The term was used by the rationalist Abraham Ibn Ezra (d. 1167) in the introduction to his Torah commentary, and a century later by the mystic Nahmanides (d. 1270) in his commentary on Genesis 8:4. It also appears several times in the Zohar. That this concept was used both by rationalist and mystical Torah exegetes indicates how fundamental it is to understanding the meaning of Divine revelation. The figure 70 is used in rabbinic literature to indicate a large number, e.g., seventy nations or seventy languages, and here too it reflects the idea that there are many different ways to interpret a biblical verse." *Jewish Bible Quarterly* 41, no. 1 (2013): 28–31, jbq.jewishbible.org/assets/Uploads/411/jbq411shivimpanim.pdf.

3. Babylonian Talmud, *Eiruvin* 13b.

4. Tamara Cohn Eskenazi and Andrea L. Weiss, eds., *The Torah: A Women's Commentary* (New York: URJ Press and Women of Reform Judaism, 2008).

5. Since the time of publication, Dr. Tamara Eskenazi has also become a rabbi.

6. Simone de Beauvoir, *The Second Sex* (New York: Vintage Books, 1989; first published in English by Knopf, 1952).

7. Ibid., 267.

8. Hazon, www.hazon.org.

9. Steve Greenberg, *Wrestling with God and Men: Homosexuality in the Jewish Tradition* (Madison: University of Wisconsin Press, 2004). See also Greenberg's anonymous piece: Yaakov Levado, "Family Values: A Response to Reuven Kimmelman," *Tikkun* 9 (1994): 57–60.

10. Batya Ungar-Sargon, "Orthodox Yeshiva Set to Ordain Three Women: Just Don't Call Them Rabbi," *Tablet*, June 10, 2013, http://www.tabletmag.com/jewish-life-and-religion/134369/orthodox-women-ordained.

11. Judith Plaskow, *Standing Again at Sinai: Judaism from a Feminist Perspective* (San Francisco: HarperSanFrancisco, 1990), 151–52; Rosemary Radford Reuther, *Sexism and God-Talk: Toward a Feminist Theology*, 10th anniversary ed. (Boston: Beacon Press, 1993), 66–67.

PERSONAL REFLECTION

A Rabbi Goes to the Mikveh

Rabbi Julie Wolkoff, DMin, CT

I used to love listening to my grandfather, of blessed memory, tell stories about his family. He would tell me about his maternal grandfather, a man so pious that before my great-grandparents got married he checked to make sure that my great-grandfather was observant enough to marry into the family. One day he stopped eating in his daughter's kosher home. What changed? Why did he now bring his own knife and a piece of fruit when he visited his daughter? My great-grandparents had gotten indoor plumbing, and my great-grandmother stopped going to the mikveh. "How did her father know?" I asked my grandfather. "The mikveh lady told," he replied. "She was no longer getting her five-cent tip."

For my great-grandmother, immersing in a mikveh was an act that had no meaning. It held no ritual or spiritual power for her. It was little more than a communal bath, which she easily gave up once she no longer needed it. Her experience was the experience of many Jews as they threw off rituals that no longer fit their lives. I grew up without knowing about mikveh and only learned about it later. Since then, my experience with mikveh has been very different from that of my great-grandmother.

My initial forays into the mikveh were not as a user. Instead, as the female Reform rabbi in my community, I was constantly asked to serve on *batei din* for conversions. Most of those converting were women, and I was able to be both part of the rabbinic panel and the witness to their immersion. While making sure they fully immersed, I also witnessed their happiness and joy, their relief when they made it through the new prayers, and the smiles and family hugs once they dressed and returned to the lobby. Through them, I was privileged to see mikveh as a powerful act of spiritual transformation.

Eight years ago, when I took a job as a hospice chaplain, I also became a volunteer mikveh guide at Mayyim Hayyim, in Newton, Massachusetts. For me, the mikveh is a calm, peaceful, deeply spiritual place. I volunteer in the evenings, and the stillness of the building quiets my soul. The living waters of the mikveh help me maintain my spiritual equilibrium as I spend my days immersed in death and dying. One of my most powerful experiences as a mikveh guide came the evening that a group of women came to prepare for Rosh HaShanah. I had begun that day reciting the *Vidui* at a patient's deathbed. I ended it surrounded with music as the women sang their way into the New Year.

I am the guide who signs up to be at the mikveh when Rosh HaShanah ends and after *N'ilah* on Yom Kippur. Although I no longer have a High Holy Day pulpit, my body still remembers the intensity of being a rabbi on those days. On these nights, after long days in the synagogue, the mikveh feels even more sacred. The quiet allows me to reflect on the prayers and the rituals and helps me move into the New Year.

Since becoming a mikveh guide, I have also become an occasional mikveh user. Mayyim Hayyim has special times for clergy to immerse before holidays and special pre-holiday immersion ceremonies, and like many of my colleagues, I set aside that time to immerse. I have also immersed for life-cycle events, personal transitions, and healing. Through my immersions, I have learned that it is not just the living water that makes the ritual so powerful. The preparation, using preliminary *kavanot*, walking slowly and deliberately down the steps into the water, opening the *bor* cap and feeling the waters "kiss," all combine to create potent spiritual moments. The time I spend alone in the mikveh allows me to reflect and connect. I feel God's presence, and I open my heart in prayer.

Being a mikveh guide reminds me that tears can be sacred. I have guided women who walk into the water and find that their tears flow as the water surrounds them. Some tell me that they don't know why they are crying. Some don't mention it or they ask for time alone in the mikveh. For me and for many others, the mikveh is a safe place to cry. Hot tears join the living waters and they mix together, just as opening the *bor* allows the outside waters and the inner pool to "mix," making the mikveh kosher. I believe that the tears we add to the mikveh increase its sanctity. They connect us—our hopes, our dreams, and our pain—to the living waters, the waters that bring healing. As a guide, it is not my task to try to "fix" whatever brings someone to tears, but to be present, to be their witness, to create a safe space that allows for their emotions.

PERSONAL REFLECTION

A Rabbi in the Military

RABBI SARAH SCHECHTER
CHAPLAIN (MAJOR), UNITED STATES AIR FORCE ACADEMY

Ten years ago, I entered the United States Air Force, committed to serving my country yet uncertain of what this world would bring me. *K'lal Yisrael* and *K'lal* America are what come to mind as I reflect on my first ten years and on the momentous fortieth anniversary of women in the rabbinate.

I joined the Air Force chaplaincy because of 9/11. On that day, within seconds of hearing that our country was under attack, I knew I wanted to show our military that rabbis were standing with them, shoulder to shoulder. The next morning I called the recruiter.

Six months later, I took the oath of office before the American flag. I can only liken this ritual to a wedding, a commitment ceremony between my country and me. I held my hand up before the flag and swore to "support and defend the Constitution of the United States against all enemies, foreign and domestic....So help me God." The flag was our chuppah. Witnesses signed the document, our *ketubah*. The chaplain's badge I received upon ordination was my ring.

Wherever I have been stationed, as well as in my deployments, I have found a world quite different from that of most Americans and a rabbinate very different from most. Rather than a congregation or organization, I serve military personnel, and I serve the United States. These are the poles of my daily life.

K'lal Yisrael

We live in a world where, tragically, there is much strife among Jews. For the last ten years, however, I have been blessed to work in an environment where the top military rabbis, including the Orthodox, have firmly stated that women rabbis are to be respected as equal professionals in the field. Naturally we have our differences, sometimes ideological and sometimes theological. Yet we rise above them and work together toward the common goal of keeping Judaism and Torah alive for our people.

Most rabbis serve as the sole Jewish chaplain in their settings. Of course, we respond to every serviceperson, regardless of denominational allegiances. We also communicate with each other. So, a new "rookie" Orthodox chaplain may approach me at a conference and ask advice about his new position. I may need a contact at another base and find myself sharing information with a Conservative colleague. This phenomenon is due, in no small measure, to the existence of the Jewish Welfare Board (JWB).

Every military chaplain must be approved by an endorsing agency. There are three such bodies for rabbis, but only the JWB endorses rabbis from all movements. The JWB is a unifying group within the world of diversity. The CCAR has a place at the JWB table along with the Rabbinical Assembly (Conservative) and the Rabbinical Council of America (Orthodox); together these leaders enable the collegiality of all military rabbis. I am a woman rabbi, and the JWB is the one organization that allows for and honors the plurality and diversity of Jews across the religious spectrum. Reform, Reconstructionist, Conservative, and Orthodox working together! It is a taste of heaven. It is truly K'lal Yisrael.

K'lal America

I had no idea into what a relationship, what a community I was entering. Countless times I've been stopped by strangers who thanked me for my service or shared personal stories: "Hi, Captain! I was a Navy captain once a long time ago. Sure wore a lot of mud in those days in Vietnam." I thank them all for their support and their service. When I walk out of customs on my return from a deployment and am met by a crowd of cheering people I have never met before, the feeling is overwhelming.

These brief exchanges with people, young and old, retired, civilian, and many others, felt awfully familiar, and then one day I realized—it felt just like *K'lal Yisrael*. When I wear the uniform, strangers are no longer strangers. We become *K'lal* America. What gets vocalized is not criticism for being a woman or a rabbi. Rather, people are grateful, and what gets expressed is reverence and thankfulness, or in our language, *nachas*.

One day, while deployed to Iraq, I was approached by an American Muslim sergeant. He said to me, "Rabbi, I see that you keep kosher. Can you help me keep halal?" The uniqueness of this moment was not lost on me. I am a woman rabbi in an Arab country approached by a Muslim soldier for help in being more observant. This was a "God Bless America" moment. This is truly *K'lal* America.

Women Clergy in the Military

This year we also celebrate the fortieth anniversary of women in the military chaplaincy; we have much to be thankful for. As an airman, not only do I receive equal pay as my male counterparts, but as a chaplain, I am blessed to work daily in an interfaith environment where Catholic, Orthodox, Muslim, Mormon, and a range of Protestant leaders collaborate to ensure the religious freedom and expression of all military and their families.

I'm able to play this role because being a woman in this position has become much less of an issue than it once was. Of course, some people have their preference of a male rabbi over a female. That's a personal opinion that is valid. But my experience in the U.S. military has been that when quality work and a positive attitude are there, the doors have been wide open to me.

PERSONAL REFLECTION

Born in the USSR

RABBI ELENA RUBINSTEIN

Less than a year after my family immigrated from Russia to Israel, I found myself one May evening in 1993 at Beit Shmuel, the center of Reform Judaism in Jerusalem. A Muscovite and a research expert on the War of 1812 between Russia and Napoleonic France, I had most recently been a sales executive in a jewelry store. I could not imagine that this visit would be my first step toward the calling of becoming a rabbi. On that evening, I was accepted into the training course for community workers Movement for Progressive Judaism.

My career in the Reform Movement began as a new immigrant coordinator at the center, first in Beer Sheva and then in Tel Aviv. Though we lived in the south, my studies extended from Ben-Gurion University (Beer Sheva) to Hebrew Union College–Jewish Institute of Religion (Jerusalem), while my work was in Tel Aviv. Traversing the country by bus, I would get up at five every morning and return home late at night.

Looking back, I wonder how I had the strength. I was over forty, and my Hebrew was still very far from perfect. For my Hebrew-speaking classmates, the lesson of the Talmud said, "We do not understand what is written." I, however, was "dying" from despair. If they only

545

knew how much I did not understand of their Hebrew and the level of apprehension I had!

And yet…the support from my colleagues, friends, and family was overwhelming. In no small measure, it is because of their love and encouragement throughout those twelve years that I am proud to say, "I was the first Russian-speaking woman to become an ordained rabbi. I, an immigrant from the former USSR, was consecrated as a rabbi in the Land of Israel."

After ordination, I headed the department that works with new immigrants as well as the conversion program of the Reform in Israel. Five years ago, I was invited to become a rabbi in the Reform community Shaarei Shalom in St. Petersburg, Russia, where I continue to work to the present day.

Upon reflection, I see that the rabbinate is my professional destiny. I served as a rabbi in Israel and now serve as a rabbi in Russia. With all the complexities of Reform Judaism in Israel, despite all the difficulties of its development in the challenging conditions of a near-monopoly of the religion by the *Haredim*, it remains easier to be a female rabbi in Israel than in Russia.

The vast majority of Russians believe that women cannot, or rather should not, become a rabbi or read the Torah in the synagogue. It is unthinkable to them that men and women may pray in the same room, that a woman may perform religious ceremonies, and that men and woman can be seen on an equal footing with one another. Though devoid of their own Orthodoxy or ritual practice for so long, the majority of Russian Jewry quickly adopted a shallow and one-sided view of Judaism. They erroneously understood this monolithic approach as *Torah mi-Sinai*, and as such, they appear extremely reluctant and completely closed off to the concept that different ideas about our religion actually exist.

I have been given a unique opportunity to expose the Jews in Russia to a liberal approach to Judaism. Here we have been able to build a truly progressive community where people can draw their own conclusions and build their own Jewish way of life, one based upon a deep learning, a personal knowledge, and genuine free choice.

Our community consists mainly of young people and young families who want to gain knowledge *by* themselves and *for* themselves and are interested in understanding what it means to be a Jew in the modern world. Here they learn how to combine the ancient Jewish traditions with our modern lifestyle in the twenty-first century.

I believe in a bright future for Reform Judaism in Russia. I believe that the high intellectual and spiritual level of our community will prove in time to be a great asset, a seed in the fertile soil of the development of Judaism; that such a process serves to evolve all who come into contact with it; and that it puts forward new questions and simultaneously seeks its very own new answers.

And I am happy to have been given an opportunity to play my part, to truly be part of this amazing and vibrant process.

· Part Six ·

Congregational Culture
and Community Life

Though rabbis serve God and the people Israel in a variety of settings, the overwhelming majority of them are called to the congregational pulpit. And it is on the pulpit and in congregational life where we see some of the most radical changes effected by women rabbis. Rabbi Judith Schindler and Cantor Mary Thomas ("Weaving Webs of Sacred Connection: Women Rabbis and Congregational Culture") examine the myriad ways women rabbis have redefined the understanding of a successful pulpit rabbi.

More and more studies indicate that women have leadership styles that diverge greatly from conventional ones established by men. Riffing on this, Rabbi Amy M. Schwartzman ("Forty Years—What Moses Might Have Learned [from His Women Colleagues]") imagines how Moses might have approached the Israelites differently if he had been given the opportunity to learn from women rabbinic models. Necessity is, as the saying goes, the mother of invention. So, it seems, is finding creative solutions. This is exactly what Rabbis Linda Motzkin and Jonathan Rubenstein ("Creating a New Model: From Rabbi and Rebbetzin to Co-Rabbis") did when creating rabbinates that met the needs of their growing family.

While male rabbis and women rabbis are supposed be to regarded equally and receive comparable pay and benefits, the essays by Michael J. Gan and Joshua Scharff ("Women Rabbis and the Gender Pay Gap: Lessons from the CCAR's 2012 Landmark Study and a Call to Action") and Rabbi Alysa Mendelson Graf ("Getting to the Gold Standard in Maternity Leave Clauses") reflect the disappointing reality of the disparity between the genders.

In prior generations, the rabbi was not the primary parent; it was the rebbetzin who was responsible for home and hearth, kith, and kin. With women entering the rabbinate, however, traditional roles needed to be redefined. Rabbi Rebecca Einstein Schorr ("Figuring It All Out: The Parenting Balancing Act") explores the different choices women rabbis have made to achieve some type of work/family balance.

Part 6 draws to a close with five distinct voices, sharing five very different accounts of their rabbinates: Rabbi Alysa Mendelson Graf ("Why I Almost Did Not Become a Rabbi") on how the pressure of congregational judgment nearly dissuaded her from being a rabbi; Rabbi Rebecca Gutterman ("Being a Public Person, Suffering a Private Loss") on how her congregation helped her through the stillbirth of her daughter; Rabbi Sara Yellen Sapadin ("The 'Part-Time' Rabbinate"), Rabbi Ruth A. Zlotnick ("Journeying to the Edge of the Known and Comprehended World—Becoming a Senior Rabbi"), and Rabbi Hara E. Person ("Leaning In, Leaning Out, and Just Managing to Stand Up: Notes from a Rabbinic Working Mother") on the deliberate career choices they made.

34

WEAVING WEBS OF SACRED CONNECTION

Women Rabbis and Congregational Culture

RABBI JUDITH SCHINDLER AND CANTOR MARY THOMAS

Baruch atah, Adonai Eloheinu, Melech haolam shelo asani ishah.
Blessed are You, *Adonai* our God, Sovereign of the universe, for not
having made me a woman.

Much feminist ink has been spilled lamenting, dissecting, or reclaiming this startling blessing from the traditional *Nisim B'chol Yom*, where
we acknowledge God's miracles evident in our daily lives. It is easy to
imagine that before Rabbi Sally Priesand received ordination in 1972,
our best and brightest Reform Jewish women could have looked at
that sentence and felt the weight of centuries of clearly defined men's
and women's spheres, spheres in which there was no room for women
rabbis or cantors. Clergy, before Priesand's time, were as masculine as
the God-language that filled our prayer books and the theology that
filled our seminaries. Rabbi Priesand, and those women who followed,
stepped into a world of traditional male leadership and through fortitude and presence began a slow process of institutional change that
would ultimately transform the synagogue.

While Rabbi Sally Priesand holds the watershed designation of the
first woman ordained by the Reform Movement in 1972, it is Rabbi

Laura Geller who shattered the stained-glass ceiling in 1995. It took over two decades of continuous female clergy leadership in synagogues before one would rise to head one of the largest congregations, a synagogue of more than one thousand families. Since that time, twelve other women have assumed the helm of the fifty largest synagogues in the Reform Movement. The members of this first group of barrier breakers were each the first in their regions: in Southern California, in the Midwest, in Northern California, in the mid-Atlantic, and in the South. With such a distance between them and such heavy demands upon them, connecting with one another for support, to compare leadership styles, organizational structures, worship team approaches, visioning, contract negotiations, and how each created values-driven places of work was simply impractical. Yet, echoes of their successes and dynamic choices were heard across the continent. Slowly, men and women rethought the models of high-level leadership and inspired entire cities to hear the voices of women as they, with the authority vested in them by their prominent roles, commented on the crises they saw and crafted community efforts of change.

Women ascending to the role of the senior rabbi since then did not grow up with same-gender models for the work they are doing, yet they did have the Jewish feminist theological and liturgical voices to guide them. Women clergy leading synagogues today studied and internalized Judith Plaskow's groundbreaking text *Standing Again at Sinai*. The incompleteness of the patriarchal texts of Written and Oral Torah were unveiled as we struggled to hear the whispered voices of the women who stood with our people at Sinai and always. We were given permission not only to rewrite ourselves through midrash into the past, but to rewrite our roles as rabbis and cantors in the present. Strong women's voices emerged in the academy as they did within the seminary: Rachel Adler, Ellen M. Umansky, Paula E. Hyman, Hasia Diner, and Anita Diamant among many others helped to excavate the Jewish woman's story from the corners of our history, from behind the shadows of the letters of sacred text.

Marcia Falk's liturgical thought, turning dominant images of God on their head, no doubt resonated in the hearts and minds of women clergy as they shaped their institutions. Falk's liturgy affirms God's immanence, rather than further elevating hierarchical and transcendent images of God. As Falk noted in the commentary to her prayer book, "The conception of God as transcendent Other is based on a hierarchical construct of God and world that can be highly problematic for modeling relationships, especially from a feminist perspective, since it provides theological underpinning for the hierarchical dualisms—including the foundational dualistic construct of female and male—that characterize and plague Western culture."[1] If one envisions and prays to a notion of the Divine who is above and beyond, the worshiper may well strive to be like this image of a transcendent God who reigns and rules, rather than dwells among us.

If we follow this line of reasoning, how might it impact leadership? Today's women clergy largely reject a hierarchical model of leadership—a transcendent presence on the bimah and sequestered CEO behind layers of institutional protection. Rather, we long to connect deeply and personally with our collaborators, coworkers, and congregants so that we may all dwell as partners in the creation of our world and experience together the Divine Presence in our lives. As women clergy have embodied Falk's liturgy, they have chosen to break down models of hierarchical leadership, valuing partnership over dominance. They have crafted models of leadership teams based on collective decision-making and structures for congregational visioning where large teams share their voices and varied perspectives on re-imagining congregational life, from membership structures to facilitating warm, welcoming, and inclusive congregations.

Baruch atah, Adonai Eloheinu, Melech haolam, she-asani ishah/ish.
Blessed are You, *Adonai* our God, Sovereign of the universe, who has made me a woman/man.
Proverbs 31 describes the traditional woman of strength, the *eishet chayil*. She, who is worth far more than rubies, headed her house as

she supported her husband in his endeavors, creating an environment where all could feel secure, supported, and content. This text, traditionally recited or sung by a husband to his wife on Shabbat evening at the dinner table, came under sharp criticism as Jewish women made their way from the private sphere to the public, from head of the home to head of the boardroom. While we have much evidence that women were always the backbone of Reform synagogue life, through Sisterhoods, in the religious school classroom, and through lay leadership, women had yet to step forward and similarly share our voice from the center of the bimah, in the boardroom, and on our temples' letterhead. Just as women were called to "reenvision the Jewish past"[2] and "reshape Jewish memory"[3] by Judith Plaskow in her groundbreaking book of feminist Jewish theology, so too were women called to innovate what the ideal *eishet chayil* might look like. The woman of strength could now head her congregational home, exerting influence in both the private and the public sphere, in her home and at work, acting as a model in speech and in action toward which younger women could aspire.

As women have come into positions of considerable influence and prominence, they have experienced challenges unique to their gender identity and assumed gender roles. In a January 2013 *Harvard Business Review* blog,[4] three female authors examine several remaining challenges of women's leadership in business. First is the "double-bind paradox," where a woman can only be perceived as either "aggressive" (read: masculine) or likable (read: feminine), never both. Women in synagogue leadership are certainly subject to pressure to project an air of masculinity, stepping solidly into corporate and hierarchical structures that demand senior clergy assert themselves as CEOs of the synagogue. This type of leadership expectation perpetuates organizational structures that do not necessarily best serve the needs of the congregation; this is our transcendent image of the God who is too far for mere mortals to reach. Furthermore, the CEO model does not give the clergy permission to care for congregants in a way that might be perceived as overly feminine, when that is in fact what is best for the congregation. Yet, for those rabbis and cantors who lean too far to the "likable" or "feminine" side of this paradox, assuming the role of "boss" and chief decision maker can be challenging.

A second, critical issue is the "careful-what-you-wish-for paradox," the pressure so many women feel to "have it all." Anne-Marie Slaughter's article in the Atlantic, "Why Women Still Can't Have It All," garnered much social and mainstream media attention. In her treatise, Slaughter explains why she "hurried home" as fast as she could when her two-year public service leave from Princeton University ended.[5] She examines the "myth" of work/life balance prescribed to high-achieving women, exploring the cultural assumptions that if women are only "committed enough," "marry the right person," or "sequence it right," they can surely rise to the highest levels of their field and raise a happy and healthy family. For women in high-level synagogue leadership, these ideas continue to be perpetuated. Surely if we are the best, brightest, and most driven of our generation, we can, through sheer will, head major Jewish organizations while also living out the values of *Eishet Chayil*.

Commitment is paramount for any senior clergy to succeed, male or female. Yet for women seeking the helm, rather than relying on the perfect partner or the ideal timing, they need to structure their lives in such a way that home and work are deeply integrated and there are adequate support structures in both realms. The drive as clergy, both male and female, to model both excellence and strong family life (in whatever form the twenty-first-century family takes) is precisely the reason that more women are needed to take on the roles of senior clergy, for women clergy have led the way in transforming congregational cultures into both empowering and collaborative environments.

The synagogue and clergy for our contemporary society require innovative approaches to time management. Consider how many hours a week a dynamic and innovative synagogue might be in operation: opening early in the morning to handle routine business, staying open late into the nighttime hours so that the needs of working congregants can be met as well, not to mention Shabbat and weekend religious school and family programming. It is easy for clergy to fall into the trap of trying to be present for all these myriad events, packing calendars with synagogue business from morning until night.

Yet, women clergy have demonstrated that these long hours can be an advantage rather than a burden. By working with their partners in the synagogue and at home, clergy can arrange to be present where and when they need to be, sharing responsibilities with a collaborative team. By carefully planning around family schedules and the rhythm of the most significant hours of synagogue life, clergy can work in partnership with their work partners and life partners to be present where they are most needed throughout the day, be that at the middle school carpool or the religious school carpool. Women clergy work no fewer hours than their male counterparts but have led the charge to allocate those hours differently, to meet the needs of both work and home.

Another suggestion Slaughter poses and that women clergy can embrace is redefining the "arc of a successful career," meaning that we should inherently change the assumption that a career should peak between ages forty-five and fifty-five, where it is possible, given good health, to work for another twenty years. She points out that it has become de rigueur for many highly successful individuals to take on "encore" careers after retirement in their early sixties. This is very true of clergy who take on institutional leadership, speaking engagements, writing and publishing, and even chaplaincy after leaving the pulpit. For some women, these posts will crown their careers, but others will not be able to attain such positions unless they manage to fight their way to a coveted senior position at a major synagogue before that point. Slaughter explains that if we understand women to have a long working life, spanning a potential fifty years, we can begin to appreciate that the rise to top leadership may not be linear. Perhaps a woman starts in a prominent assistantship, only to take off a number of years to have children, and then resumes work as an associate with somewhat less responsibility while children are school-aged, delaying entry into the solo pulpit or senior position until much later in their career. "Peaking in your late 50s and early 60s rather than your late 40s and early

50s," she writes, "makes particular sense for women, who live longer than men."[6]

Ultimately, the clergy that lead and serve our contemporary synagogues must not be divided along gender lines. When leaders are evaluated and compensated using gender as a factor, it is highly problematic. It should be that men and women spiritual leaders are afforded the opportunity to reap all of the benefits that both sexes have won: leadership that allows for partnership, shared responsibility, personal fulfillment, and compensation that is commensurate with our high level of education, expertise, and experience and with the enormity of the responsibilities we shoulder.[7] Women need to have the courage to "lean in," to use Sheryl Sandberg's terminology, and seek to make significant contributions as they choose to assume the highest levels of leadership.[8]

When women embrace their potential by pursuing paths of high-level leadership in our Jewish world, the Jewish people will reap the full benefits that women in the rabbinate have to offer. When both male and female clergy use their powerful voices of leadership to fight the injustices of our society, the needs of the community will truly be served. When male and female clergy are both articulating a strong vision for our Jewish future as they inspire the creation of programmatic, organizational, and financial support structures to get there, our potential for success will be expanded. When *kol ishah* and *kol ish*, women's and men's voices of Jewish wisdom, are loudly heard, then the fabric of our faith and future will be ensured.

> *Baruch atah, Adonai Eloheinu, Melech haolam, she-asani b'tzelem Elohim.*
> Blessed are You, *Adonai* our God, Sovereign of the universe, who has made me in God's image.

In recent years there has emerged a new model of leadership in organizations led by both men and women—not the hierarchical model of old but one with circular webs of connections with the leader at the center. This alternative model of leadership was first noted in women leading businesses and not-for-profits. Sally Helgesen, in her 1990s study of women's leadership, noted that "women, when describing their roles in their organizations, usually referred to themselves as being in the middle of things. Not at the top, but in the center; not reaching down but reaching out."[9] We, as women clergy, largely did the same. Rather than seeing ourselves as the inheritors of an evolving and formerly masculine hierarchical leadership tradition and maintaining that status quo, we turned our organizational structures on their sides and began to understand them as the rich tapestries of relationships, roles, and responsibilities that they really are. The partnership of women and men in religious leadership roles has inspired new models of Jewish communal leadership, focusing on collaboration rather than hierarchy, relationships rather than programming.

In embracing the traditional *eishet chayil* who once wove the linens on her Shabbat table, women rabbis embraced the role of being weavers of communities, congregants, and lay and professional leadership. Beth Kantor and Allison H. Fine's work *The Networked Non-Profit* describes a world in which nonprofits are transparent organizations with low barriers to participation, uniting people based on their shared interests through relationship building. The nonprofit that they describe is inherently non-hierarchical: the organization's finances are clear and accessible on the website, appropriate staffers throughout the organization are empowered to use their own social capital to engage in conversation over social media, participants—congregants—are regularly engaged in conversation and the grassroots shaping of their organization, and the rabbis and cantors are as accessible as their administrative assistants. The networked nonprofit understands that it is in the business of connecting people, deeply and meaningfully, one to the next. As Dr. Larry Hoffman has noted, at each watershed moment in Jewish history there has been a significant technological advancement. Perhaps the gift of the Internet is the flattening of the hierarchy, now a series of strong, interconnected webs of sacred connection.

What happens to synagogue leadership when women and men alike recognize that the greatest gift they can give their congregants is profoundly meaningful relationships? Ron Wolfson asks this important question in his 2013 publication *Relational Judaism*. For generations, synagogue goals have been participation (in the forms of attendance and membership) and positive experience (with the hopes of strong identity formation), but what if the articulated goal was simply creating sacred connections between people? If the forward-thinking synagogue was to change the mission from numbers in the door and member units on the roster to lives profoundly touched and souls profoundly connected one to the next, how much more meaningful and deeply Jewish could lives become? Ultimately, from these sacred connections, between people longing to come into close and personal contact with those around them, could emerge spaces conducive to sacred Jewish learning, living and ritual, social action and justice, and covenantal giving. The clergy as weavers of webs need not have the sole voice in the community; rather their creative task is to work seamlessly to facilitate their congregants' entering into sacred relationship with one another. Web-weaving clergy need only to be prepared to care for a community of tightly bound souls, not individuals so single-mindedly immersed in the day-to-day.

Women at the highest levels of leadership have embraced shared leadership models as co-rabbis and with associate rabbis and cantors, educators and executive directors, each as skilled individuals who have their own sacred threads to weave into the fabric of the community. For the relationship-weaving leader, others' successes are not threats to power but credits to the strength of precious community. Shared leadership has enabled clergy to step down from the bimah routinely on Shabbat. As clergy partners assume programmatic and ritual leadership, they can then model appropriate work/life balance and alternative ways of observing Shabbat, whether that be at home with one's family, with friends, or caring for oneself.

Like the uniqueness of each human being created in God's image, so too does each clergyperson, male or female, create their own senior role, crafting organizations and a lay and professional leadership structure that reflects and accommodates their own individual values and leadership style. Being in the image of God means developing leadership styles that are best suited to the millennial congregation—qualities that are neither masculine nor feminine but reflect the Jewish values upon which our synagogue community will most successfully be built.

For Judaism to thrive we need to support all our rabbis who are gifted visionaries and weavers of sacred Jewish community. In the words of Rabbi Jacqueline Ellenson, Director Emerita of the Women's Rabbinic Network, "We have arrived at a third stage of feminism, which accepts distinction without difference. Our goal now is to create a world that is less sharply gendered but more just. If we discuss the impact of gender, and see our choices as a reflection of our society and our culture, we come closer to understanding gender and affirming the available range of choices."[10] Those congregations who embrace senior leaders who are skilled in weaving sacred communities will weather well the storms and challenges that come to each generation, and they will emerge with greater strength and beauty. Over the past four decades, women senior leaders have bequeathed to the rabbinate a vision for weaving sacred communities of connection where the leader is at the center but all share in the strength of building the organization. We continue to heed Jethro's profound advice to Moses even today: high-level leadership must be shared so that no one person carries the burden alone. The fabric women clergy have woven with *chochmah*, *binah*, *v'daat*—wisdom, understanding, and knowledge—has indeed enabled God to continue to dwell in our midst, as God has from the times of Sinai until today.

NOTES

1. Marcia Falk, *The Book of Blessings* (Boston: Beacon Press, 1996), 420.

2. Judith Plaskow, *Standing Again at Sinai* (San Francisco: Harper & Row, 1990), 28.

3. Ibid., 52.

4. Jill Flynn, Kathryn Heath, and Mary Davis Holt, "Six Paradoxes Women Leaders Face in 2013," *Harvard Business Review*, January 3, 2013, http://blogs.hbr.org/cs/2013/01/six_paradoxes_women_leaders_fa.html#disqus_thread.

5. Anne-Marie Slaughter, "Why Women Still Can't Have It All," *Atlantic*, June 13, 2012, http://www.theatlantic.com/magazine/archive/2012/07/why-women-still-cant-have-it-all/309020/.

6. This paradigm shift is particularly challenging in the cantorate, where the pressure to have what is new, innovative, and cutting edge is so great. There is even more pressure to organically provide "current" music, and there are natural vocal changes that occur with even the healthiest voices as they age.

7. According to the CCAR's 2012 salary survey, women in senior positions of large-size synagogues (over 1,000 family units) are receiving 89 percent of men's earnings, and that distinction grows greater in solo pulpits of slightly smaller size (600–800 family units).

8. There are large congregations seeking to replace their senior rabbi, and anecdotally, hardly any women are applying. It seems that the women rabbis of today cannot envision themselves in these jobs that are often perceived as corporate and rigid rather than dynamic and flexible.

9. Sally Helgeson, *The Female Advantage: Women's Ways of Leadership* (New York: Doubleday, 1995), 45–56.

10. Phone interview, February 21, 2013.

35

FORTY YEARS—
WHAT MOSES MIGHT HAVE LEARNED
(FROM HIS WOMEN COLLEAGUES)

RABBI AMY M. SCHWARTZMAN

Looking back on the last forty years of Reform Judaism, one sees that the arc of change is broad and expansive; it's colorful and rich with texture. Much of this change can be attributed to the hundreds of women who have joined the rabbinate and left a lasting mark on the communities in which they have served. New visions, new interpretations, and new rituals have brought welcomed transformations to the landscape of our contemporary Judaism. Perhaps among the most significant of these shifts have been new models of leadership.

To begin a conversation about change in leadership patterns, we might consider contrasting the short forty years since women were ordained as rabbis with the seemingly longer forty years of Moses's leadership as the Israelites wandered in the desert. Both are filled with stories of challenge and change. Each one presents different models from which we might learn a great deal.

Imagine if the forty years of women in the rabbinate had coincided with the forty years of Israelite wandering. While the hundreds of women rabbis of today would seem to be an insignificant addition to the reported hundreds of thousands of fleeing Israelites (Exodus 38:26), their influence would have surely compensated for their relatively small numbers. Perhaps they would have brought the women out from the back of the pack; maybe they would have created new models of community engagement that would have helped the Israelites through the difficult moments. How might Moses's leadership have been different had he sat down with Sally Priesand (the first woman ordained by the Hebrew Union College–Jewish Institute of Religion) over coffee and manna? What might have changed in the Book of Exodus had he walked from Hazerot to the desert of Paran with Janet Marder (the first woman president of the Central Conference of American Rabbis), chatting, comparing stories, and exchanging ideas along the way?

It's likely that the impact of women rabbis in Moses's world would have been profound and the outcome would have had a lasting effect not only on our journey to Israel but also on the history of our people. Perhaps the Israelites would have arrived in Israel in less than forty years. Maybe they would have established a democracy instead of a monarchy. It might even be possible that the nation would have interacted differently with its neighbors and the course of the Jewish people would have taken an entirely alternative trajectory.

Considering different leadership models and styles, both those of Moses and those of rabbis today, provides insight on issues of change, management, and organizational success. By reflecting on the change that women leaders have brought to contemporary Judaism through their choices in leadership, we can appreciate the progressive evolution our communities have experienced in recent decades. As well, our study of the issues of leadership and the diverse techniques that rabbis employ can continue to bear fruit in our own communal contexts and future enterprises.

Command-Control: A One-Man Show

For a significant portion of his forty years in the desert, Moses's leadership was one of a single-leader system. While there were a number of times when he shared his authority and power with others, Moses more frequently embraced the "command-control" model of leadership. This autocratic style is one in which one person at the head makes the most important decisions and closely supervises and controls others. It is entirely possible, of course, that Moses did not have the freedom to embrace any other leadership style, since God usually told him precisely what to do. Regardless of Moses's intentions, the Israelites' experience was largely that of one person in charge, one person who was the supreme holder of wisdom, experience, and vision.

There were certainly moments of shared leadership, such as the time when Moses took his father-in-law Jethro's advice and empowered the seventy elders to manage disputes among the people (Exodus 18:13–26). There were times when Moses probably consulted with his brother Aaron for advice. But events at the Sea of Reeds, Sinai, and Rephidim all present a solo leader, one person emboldened to determine a singular path that only he knew.

At times, this type of leadership can be efficient and expedient. In emergencies especially it can be the best option. In our Torah, it might have been God's preferred model. But the command-control prototype also presents many challenges. Often, when only one person owns the map that outlines the path to the goal, the movement of the group may be very slow (forty years!). When an entire community needs to embrace a paradigm shift—a change in the way members see themselves, their purpose, and their place in the world—diverse approaches are helpful in achieving a successful and timely transformation. More than that, the end goal should never be the only item on the agenda. Our very being with one another in community should always be part of the goal. Unlike a command-control approach, a leader whose style is inclusive not only helps everyone get to their destination but also strengthens and enriches the group by empowering and engaging others along the way.

Nonetheless, for centuries and even today, those who embrace the command-control model are often hailed as "charismatic" and as people who "get the job done." This approach is prevalent among so many of our institutions. But a worthy question is how well this style serves those organizations: Might it lead to a tension between the quantitative goal of getting things done and the qualitative goal of spiritual development and community growth? Moses did employ other techniques of leadership throughout his forty years at the head of the Israelite people, but the rabbis who called him "Moshe Rabbeinu" were clearly drawn to this single-leader model. This might very well be a reflection of the authority and control that they themselves sought. Perhaps in elevating Moses's moments of command-control, they gave themselves permission to do the same.

As a people, we are deeply respectful of Moshe Rabbeinu, Moses our great teacher. It is difficult to consider questioning his leadership style; but given the chance to be reflective, Moses himself may have been willing to make some changes. Consider the well-known midrash about Moses traveling forward through time to the classroom of the famous scholar Rabbi Akiva. While listening to Akiva's insights, Moses learns that his laws and teachings were only the beginning of an expansive understanding of Jewish tradition. Imagine if Moses had been transported into the classrooms, board meetings, or sanctuaries of some of today's rabbis (both women and men). There he might have realized that his leadership was also only one approach to moving the Jewish people from one "place" to another. There he might have been inspired to embrace new ways to set the direction for the Jewish people.

Distributed Leadership: Inviting Many to Step Up

Had Moses the chance to sit in a classroom today he might have observed a highly effective rabbi or teacher inviting her students to stretch themselves into leadership roles in order to enable the entire group to grow and learn and advance in a subject. Distributed leadership, an approach developed within the education world, is just what one might imagine it to be: the creation of an environment that enables many to step into leadership roles.[1] While utilized most often in the classroom setting, this model can be applied to any group situation.

Standing in front of a committee, a board, a class, or even a tribe, leaders resort to the command-control style, in which they simply put forth their plan, take questions, and hope that all present will nod their heads and commit to the new direction or vision. But imagine how the system changes when everyone in the room or tent is asked to take responsibility for some facet of the project or is invited to be engaged in one or more dimensions of formalizing the goal and determining the path toward that end. The capacity of an organization grows when leadership is distributed to capable participants who can share in the decision making—often bringing their own expertise into the conversation. The end result brings a broad base of individuals into leadership roles. It widens the circle of those who share a common set of values. It increases the number of people who feel a personal ownership for the success of the group. Distributed leadership gives many people experience at a high level of engagement, thereby priming them for future leadership roles. Further, it makes an organization much more resilient in the face of anticipated or unanticipated change.

Is it possible that the story of Korach, Datan, and Aviram might have had an entirely different outcome had Moses approached their challenge from an alternative angle? Perhaps he might have stepped back from this perceived rebellion to see that these men were both eager to and even capable of sharing leadership roles. In the scenario that the Book of Numbers describes (chapters 16–18), there is little space for distributing power, and the only possible outcome appears to be that of one winner and everyone else a loser. Imagine if these men had been invited into some higher level of leadership. Their loyalty to the mission of Israel and even to Moses as the "senior leader" might have grown. Perhaps more people would have been invested in the long-term goal, and our forty years in the desert might have been reduced to thirty.

Distributed leadership requires a shift in the governance of the group. It calls for a change from valuing one or two individuals to valuing the unique contributions of many. Women rabbis did not invent this philosophy, but many embrace a collaborative approach in their relationships with their colleagues, congregants, and the communities that they lead. As our institutions develop in size or complexity, this becomes even more important. With growth or expansion comes the natural tendency to put more controls in place and institute more confining structures. But a strong leader must resist the desire to grab onto more power and more control. Constant attention must be given to creating an environment that allows untapped leaders to emerge.

Getting to this new model takes courage. It means changing the furniture around so that the rabbi may not be sitting at the head of the table; alternatively, it may mean taking away the table itself! It takes an ongoing commitment to revisit the values that reinforce the institution and put the goals of the group ahead of one leader's individual gain. Moses and the Israelites did experience this type of leadership at times. Perhaps Bezalel used it as he drew upon the creativity of the people to build the *Mishkan*. Jethro certainly used it as he helped Moses to step back from being the only person available to resolve conflicts. He invited others into leadership roles, not only freeing up Moses to work in other realms, but also empowering a larger group of people to take responsibility for the well-being of the community.

Stewardship: Helping Others Succeed

Once opportunities for leadership are shared, what is the role of the senior leader in supporting others as they carry out their accepted tasks? Do senior leaders, professional or lay, have a responsibility to ensure that others succeed? And if so, how do they do that best?

Stewardship is an approach to leadership in which the senior leader is committed to serving others and the greater goal, as opposed to controlling others as well as controlling the greater goal. She not only makes room for other leaders, but also nurtures their talents and helps them maximize their potential. Business consultant Peter Block articulates stewardship as "the willingness to be held accountable for the well-being of the larger organization by operating in service, rather than in control, of those around us."[2]

Most congregations, other than the smallest, are led by staff teams made up of clergy, education and program specialists, and business managers. All congregations are blessed with gifted lay leaders who can also serve in a stewardship role for both their peers and professionals. The senior leader, often the rabbi, increases the potential for congregational success when she or he ensures that all members of the team are operating at their full potential. If the rabbi is thriving and is given the chance to experiment and expand into new dimensions while the other staff members do not feel supported or encouraged to grow professionally, the organization will likely fail. The rabbi or senior leader must be committed to ensuring that all members of a team are nurtured (even if she herself does not provide that nurturance directly to each individual), because leadership is an activity of a system and cannot be held by one individual at the expense of others.

Leading through stewardship takes a great deal of time, thoughtfulness, and intentionality. Stewardship begins with the establishment of a relationship of trust between the parties involved. The rabbi and the cantor, the educator and youth director, the preschool director and the administrator operate in a partnership based on the assumption that they share the ultimate goal of serving their congregation. They expect loyalty and acknowledge their interdependence to achieve many shared objectives.

Achieving such a relationship takes time and patience. The steward-leader invests many hours in listening, conversation, visioning, and reflection with others. One of the major tasks of the steward-leader is to help others identify their own aspirations and to help them clarify an effective path to those ambitions. This requires spending less time talking and more time asking questions then answering them. It means suppressing the urge to jump in with a solution or resolution to a problem or challenge. It also requires the steward-leader to be in constant touch with her or his motivations within a discussion. She or he must keep a watchful eye on her or his own feelings and keep self-interest in check.

In Jewish terms, a steward needs to exercise *tzimtzum*—the act of contracting or shrinking oneself to make room for others to grow. Both in distributed leadership and in stewardship, the senior leader must practice restraint in order for others to emerge and discover their own unique gifts and leadership style. In 1974, Rabbi Eugene Borowitz wrote an essay entitled "*Tzimtzum*: A Mystic Model for Contemporary Leadership."[3] There he criticized leaders who are focused on growing their own base of power and who are driven by the "accomplishment of plans" instead of being concerned with "the humanizing effect on the people they lead."

What would it have been like to be the fly on the wall of the Tabernacle when Moses and Aaron were talking before the Israelites were allowed to enter? Do you think Moses stepped back and waited for Aaron to make some new suggestions about how the sacrificial system could become more meaningful to the people? When they were sitting together in their tent at night, did Moses ask Aaron about his dreams as High Priest? Perhaps he did. Perhaps Aaron became the beloved leader he was because Moses invited him to grow in his relationship with the community and empowered him to take on that role. In Exodus 40:12–16, Moses not only anoints Aaron and his sons into the priesthood; he washes them and clothes them, humbly lifting them up into their roles as leaders. Here Moses steps away from his usual place at the head and steps into the role of steward, shepherding others' success.

Another moment when we see stewardship at its best is in the relationship between Deborah and Barak (Judges 4). Deborah was a prophetess, influential among and esteemed by the Israelite people. When the Israelites where called by God to engage in war with the Canaanites, she supported Barak in his role as leader of the Israelite forces. She went along with him and encouraged him, but neither devised the plan nor took the glory. Deborah's ability to empower others is a model for all of us.

The Balancing Act: Style, Personal Voice, Method, and Technique

There is no question that Moses was a powerful and dynamic leader. Whether depicted in the stories in the Torah or Talmud or in midrash or movies, we see him as a compelling figure who not only engaged with the Divine "face to face" (Deuteronomy 34:10), but also inspired the people. Many would call him a charismatic leader, a man with all the traits necessary to direct his people to their Promised Land. But can a leader depend solely on his or her charisma to become successful? Is it possible that Moses himself leaned too heavily on his unique characteristics to secure his place at the head of the tribes?

Today's leaders may be aware that success comes through a balancing act that integrates personal style and gifts with learned methodology and techniques. There is no question that leadership is personal and that there is no one way to lead. But relying too much on individual voice or style will rarely get leaders to the end goal. Effective leadership is a combination of that which is special to each one of us and the many systems and methods that we acquire from teachers and experiences.

MIT professor Deborah Ancona, in a research brief entitled "Leadership in an Age of Uncertainty," suggests that a good leader thoughtfully combines core skills of leadership with something she calls our "change signature."[4] A change signature is a leader's unique way of making change happen. Methods and capacity focus on what a leader does, while change signature is about who the leader is. Personalities, values, and beliefs all contribute to our change signature. Moses had a very clear change signature. We saw it at the Sea of Reeds, at Sinai, and many other times in the desert—a large presence, a strong voice invoking God's commands, and clear vision of right and wrong.

Forty years ago, many rabbis may have aspired to embrace a leadership model similar to that most often depicted of Moses—one that was defined a great deal by personal style and charisma. Today many understand the value of the broader view that stresses the balance between individual traits and widespread tried-and-true techniques. To be a leader in a congregation, Hillel, Federation, hospital, or summer camp means being able to lead in numerous settings, each of which may require a different approach. In the staff meeting, the rabbi may use her skills to bring about collaboration. In the parking lot, she may need to stand in as the moral compass for a group who has continued a disagreement that began inside the building. At the annual meeting, there may be a "Sinai" moment where the rabbi needs to stand as Moses did before the people and draw upon divine inspiration. Leadership is a balancing act as well as a twenty-four-hour job. Leaders are called upon all of the time, in small and large settings, during intimate moments and very public events. Leaders can only sustain this type of ongoing demand by using a variety of skills along with their voice, their unique style, or their personal change signature.

Summing Up: Forty Years of Lessons in Leadership

It is impossible for us to reflect on the full spectrum of change in rabbinic leadership over the last forty years or more. It is certain that the single-leader model that the rabbis of old loved to highlight in Moses's leadership moments no longer dominates the rabbinic stage. New methods are utilized, and the expectation that a rabbi will employ many different leadership techniques is the norm. This path of change has come about as a result of a multitude of resources, pressures, opportunities, and trends in society. Women rabbis have certainly played a role in facilitating these new approaches to leadership. There is no question that the profile of the rabbi for both men and women continues to be dynamic, and in the dimension of leadership, a rabbi's role continues to change and grow.

It's amusing to imagine how Moses might have been influenced by today's rabbis and in particular today's women rabbis. It is equally interesting to consider how generations of rabbinic leadership might have been different if Moses's many leadership skills had been highlighted with equal value to his moments when he stood before the people as the solo commander. While sometimes hidden in the text, Moses does teach us about sharing leadership, mentoring, and using a variety of techniques to help the people make their way to their Promised Land. Many rabbis today, both women and men, draw upon a spectrum of leadership qualities to help their communities not only reach their end goals, but reach them with greater strength and clarity. Forty years is a long time to be a leader, but it is only a short time to see how a new group of leaders might influence a community. The journey has just begun.

NOTES

1. "What Is Distributed Leadership?," http://emedia.rmit.edu.au/distributedleadership.

2. Peter Block, *Stewardship: Choosing Service over Self-Interest* (San Francisco: Barrett-Koehler, 1996), 16.

3. Eugene Borowitz, "*Tzimtzum*: A Mystic Model for Contemporary Leadership," *Religious Education* 69, no. 6 (November–December, 1974).

4. Deborah Ancona, "Leadership in an Age of Uncertainty" (research brief for the MIT Research Center, Cambridge, MA, 2005).

36

CREATING A NEW MODEL

From Rabbi and Rebbetzin to Co-Rabbis

RABBI LINDA MOTZKIN AND
RABBI JONATHAN RUBENSTEIN

We were ordained in 1986, riding the wave of American Jewish feminism that developed in this country in the 1960s and '70s. Our generation of Reform rabbis was self-consciously challenging the paradigm of Jewish leadership that preceded us; we were breaking open the bonds that had limited the roles of both women and men, or so we thought. We were concerned with gender equality, with equal access to leadership roles, with demonstrating that women could do everything that men could do, that they could be successful Jewish leaders, synagogue presidents, and rabbis, while still having babies, being good mothers, and ensuring the next generation of liberated Jewish women and men.

The two of us were classmates, having met in our first year of rabbinical school in Jerusalem. As we approached placement and ordination in our final year at HUC, there were few models available to us of how to balance our rabbinical careers as husband and wife. The majority of couples ordained before us had opted either to search for separate "his and her" congregations in close geographical proximity to one another or to pursue different types of rabbinical work. This entailed either avoiding the congregational rabbinate entirely or deciding that one partner accept a full-time congregational position, while the other (generally, but not always, the female rabbi) followed her or his spouse to their new community, seeking part-time congregational work, or embarking on a rabbinic career in Jewish education, academia, chaplaincy, or institutional work.

We were, at that time, the parents of an infant, born during the summer before our senior year at HUC, and planning to have more children. We had been fortunate to have access to affordable quality child care (JELC—the Jewish Early Learning Cooperative) on the Cincinnati campus, a cooperative day care center established primarily for the offspring of HUC students, faculty, and staff. JELC involved both fathers and mothers in the care of their children and enabled both mothers and fathers to pursue their careers and further their education. Neither of us had taken a leave from school after the birth of our firstborn; thanks to JELC, we both finished our coursework and wrote rabbinic theses during the first year of our daughter's life. So, for us, these questions were not theoretical: How to craft a rabbinate that would provide equal leadership status for both of us, without subsuming the career of one under the other? How to create a balance between career and family that would enable both of us to be actively involved in parenting our children?

We were privileged to have parents who had wrestled with some of these questions and had modeled different ways of balancing family and career. Linda was the child of two physicians; her mother, Dr. Evelyn Herszkorn Motzkin, was a woman ahead of her time, who had been one of very few females in her medical school class when the profession was overwhelmingly dominated by men. In many ways, Linda's choice of a career in the rabbinate in the early 1980s paralleled her mother's choice of a career in medicine in the 1950s, in breaking new ground for women. Linda's mother, however, did not embark on her medical career during a wave of American Jewish feminism; the overwhelming expectation for a Jewish woman of Evelyn's era was that she devote herself to raising children and caring for her family. Though both of Linda's parents were physicians, Linda's father, Dr. Donald Motzkin, was always the family's primary breadwinner, maintaining a full-time medical practice while Evelyn's part-time practice was confined to the hours that her children were in school. In considering our own child-care needs, we found appealing this model of having a parent available before and after school and evenings. The gender liberation notions of our era, however, challenged the assumption that the at-home parent should be the mother.

Jonathan's parents provided a different sort of model for a rabbinic couple. Jonathan's father, Byron Thomas (BT) Rubenstein, was a Reform rabbi, ordained in 1942. His mother, Suzanne Lieblich Rubenstein, was the quintessential *rebbetzin*. The two of them represented the "rabbinic couple" of their generation: the male rabbi and his unpaid wife, who, while never formally acknowledged as part of the synagogue staff, nonetheless played a key role in welcoming and providing for the needs of members of the community. A warm and gracious *rebbetzin* like Sue was more than incidental to her husband's career; her ability to fulfill the expectations of her role was often essential to the success or failure of her husband's rabbinate. Suzanne served as the community's role model of Jewish mothering, as counselor and sympathetic ear to those in need, as teacher, baker, hostess, instant database of key names and details whispered into her husband's ear, and a multitude of other equally indispensable tasks. The two of them were a team, known as "Rabbi and Sue" to their congregants, equally beloved and respected. But their roles were clearly distinct: he was the one with the professional title, identity, and salary; she was his wife.

It was clear that neither of us wanted to be the *rebbetzin* of the other's synagogue. Our generation was the one in which it became improper for congregations to inquire about the rabbi's spouse during the job interview, when it became a point of pride for rabbis (whether male or female, but especially male) to assert that the congregation was not hiring their spouse, that the spouse had a separate life and career of his or her own (but especially "her"), and that this spouse should not be expected to chair committees or bake cookies or fulfill congregational obligations. While never explicitly saying so, there was a subtle denigration of the traditional role of the *rebbetzin*, completely understandable and perhaps inevitable as the first generation of women rabbis strove for acceptance and equality within the overwhelmingly male rabbinate. It was an important part of the feminist aspirations of our generation for women to establish their own professional titles and identities, and not be dependent on those of their husbands.

In considering our options as a rabbinic couple, we rejected the possibility of seeking separate "his and her" congregations, though we appreciated the commitment to gender equality that it represented. Perhaps because we had already become parents, we did not want to consider a rabbinate that would require our family to be separated on Shabbat and Jewish holidays, never able to be together in synagogue. Our vision of the congregational rabbinate was one in which the rabbis' personal family life was embedded within the life of the community. In this regard, we were certainly influenced by the type of family life that Jonathan's parents had modeled in their rabbinate. We did not want to have a separation between the synagogue in which we worked and the Jewish community in which our family would be involved and actively participating.

We didn't rule out the possibility of a future career for one of us in academia or Jewish institutional life. But, after five years of rabbinic training mostly directed toward the congregational rabbinate, we realized that it was important to both of us to at least try out that role, even if the destiny of one of us might ultimately lie elsewhere. At that time, we were aware of only two other rabbinic couples who had chosen to work as rabbis in the same congregation. Rabbis Susan Talve and James Goodman had shared an assistant rabbi position, working under a senior rabbi in a congregation in St. Louis. Rabbis Sandy Eisenberg Sasso and Dennis Sasso occupied two separate, not shared, positions at Congregation Beth-El Zedeck in Indianapolis. We were not interested in attempting to negotiate the complex triangle of relationships involved in working together under a senior rabbi, and there were no congregations at the time looking to hire two rabbis.

So we became the first rabbinic couple to job-share a solo congregational position in a small synagogue. The members of Temple Sinai of Saratoga Springs, in upstate New York, were willing to embark on this experiment with us for an initial two-year contract. That was over thirty years ago; Temple Sinai has been the only pulpit of our career (aside from our student pulpits during rabbinical school). Essential to the success of this job-sharing rabbinate was the fact that there were additional part-time chaplaincy positions available in the local community, which the synagogue had helped to arrange: a Jewish chaplaincy at Skidmore College, which Linda filled, and a pastoral position at just-opened Four Winds Psychiatric Hospital, which became Jonathan's job. These additional hours of work provided the necessary supplement to our income, for it would have been difficult for our family to manage with just the single salary provided by a small congregation. The part-time chaplaincies also gave us an arena in which to work independently of one another, with separate constituencies outside of our shared congregation.

Job-sharing enabled us to fulfill the feminist aspiration of working as equal partners with equal titles, professional responsibilities and obligations, commanding the same degree of community acknowledgment and respect. It also reinforced the notion that the domestic sphere of our life, our household chores, and child care were our mutual responsibility no less than the shared synagogue tasks. It was an important principle of gender liberation that both partners in a marriage participate in cooking meals, changing diapers, doing dishes and laundry, and all the other household tasks formerly belittled as "women's work." As job-sharing co-rabbis, it was clear that whether one of us was attending a committee meeting or bathing our children, we were fulfilling part of the overall work that our family and professional lives required.

The generation before ours had entrusted most of the daily tasks of child rearing to women; our generation put a priority on enabling fathers to be actively involved in the day-to-day parenting of children. Drawing on the model of Linda's mother, we deliberately enrolled our baby (and each of her two siblings after they were born) in day care only half-time, during approximately the same hours that they would later attend school. This was partly to serve as a check on our rabbinic availability, to ensure that it would not be possible for us to work full-time as "two rabbis for the price of one," and partly to enable each of us to be part-time homemaker and child-care provider. Sometimes it was tricky for us to schedule our appointments, as we had to take care not to double-book ourselves, to make sure that one of us would always be home with our children in the morning before day care or school began and in the afternoons and evenings. But having this degree of parenting time with our children was a benefit of job-sharing that we most appreciated, aware that it was a luxury generally not afforded to rabbis serving full-time solo congregational pulpits.

When we were first ordained, the phenomenon of women rabbis was still new enough that Linda would occasionally hear, "You are the first woman rabbi I've ever met." The model of Jonathan's parents, with the rabbinic couple consisting of a male rabbi and his *rebbetzin*, was still far more familiar to many people than the idea of husband and wife rabbis, and we were conscious of the need to communicate both implicitly and explicitly that we were co-rabbis, not rabbi and *rebbetzin*. Even small details, such as the first order of new synagogue stationery with our names on the letterhead, took on added significance. We decided that Linda's name had to appear on the letterhead over Jonathan's, because the senior rabbi always appeared on top, and at that time there were no senior female rabbis with male assistants or associates. Were Jonathan to appear on top, it would imply that he was the more important or more senior rabbi. With Linda's name on top, it would suggest that we were equal partners. (One notable change in the intervening decades is that today such a letterhead does, in fact, communicate that the female is the senior rabbi.) For many years, despite communicating our status as co-rabbis to our Reform Movement organizations and affiliates, only Linda's name appeared on letters or mailings that were intended for senior or solo rabbis, but not assistants or associates.

In our division of professional tasks, we tried not to be rigid, while at the same time making sure that it was clear to everyone that we were both "the rabbis," and both empowered and capable of fulfilling every rabbinic task and function within the congregation. We divided up the leading of services, *divrei Torah*, and attendance at committee and board meetings. We alternated teaching adult education class sessions. The group of bar/bat mitzvah students each year was divided between us, each of us working individually with half of them. We regarded it as a sign of the success of our job-sharing endeavor when we would receive phone calls from congregants or members of the greater Saratoga community asking to speak with "either one of the rabbis."

Despite our pointed efforts at avoiding the casting of either of us (especially Linda) in the role of *rebbetzin*, it became clear to us that many of the tasks traditionally undertaken by the *rebbetzin*, not just in the home but also in the community, still needed to be filled in some fashion or another. We joked early in our career that we needed a *rebbetzin* to prepare Shabbat and holiday meals for us and our guests; lacking one, we nonetheless invited friends and members of the community to such meals in our home, sharing the cooking and cleanup that, in Jonathan's childhood, had been the responsibility of his mother. Because we had chosen to become rabbis in a small community, many of our congregants were also our personal friends; their children were our children's friends. In a small community, the members look out for one another and take care of each other. In practical terms, this meant that if a congregant was sick, it was no longer the *rebbetzin* but one of the rabbis who would cook and drop off a meal (or organize a cadre of congregants to cook and drop off multiple meals). If there was a community function that required baked desserts, it would most likely be Rabbi Jonathan who would be in the kitchen making chocolate chip cookies. As co-rabbis we both wound up filling many of the traditional roles of the *rebbetzin*, re-creating much of the rabbinic leadership team of Jonathan's parents, with the key difference that either one of us could and did fill both of their "rabbi" and "*rebbetzin*" roles.

We embarked on our careers with the sense that we were forging new ground, part of a wave of feminism breaking open the bonds limiting the roles of both women and men. And, in many respects, we did just that, for we modeled through our job-sharing a novel way of balancing family and professional concerns and of creating gender equality in personal and professional lives. But one could also say that the congregational rabbinate we created was actually, in some respects, a fairly traditional one and perhaps not so very different from the rabbinate of Jonathan's father and mother. In our case, the synagogue's one rabbi existed in two bodies, one male and one female, together earning one salary, sharing one title—but we also filled together the roles that the previous generation might have seen filled by their rabbi and *rebbetzin*, who also earned one salary. The key difference is that our model transformed the role of the female member of the rabbinic couple, making her not just an adjunct to her husband, dependent on his status and salary, but a co-equal partner.

Our generation of feminists was very much concerned with questions of equal access and with challenging notions of gender limitation. The career we fashioned was a product of those concerns. The generations to come will face their own unique concerns and their own unique challenges and possibilities. Developments such as the use of distance technology, social media, and changes in congregational membership patterns may result in transformations of the shape of the congregational rabbinate, for both male and female rabbis, in ways we cannot imagine.

37

WOMEN RABBIS AND
THE GENDER PAY GAP

Lessons from the CCAR's 2012 Landmark Study
and a Call to Action

MICHAEL J. GAN AND JOSHUA SCHARFF

For more than forty years, women have been ordained as Reform rabbis, and today they are a fixture in congregational life across North America. While there may be stylistic differences between some men rabbis and some women rabbis, those differences also exist within homogenous groups of male and female rabbis. There should be no disagreement, however, that the "work" of a rabbi is the same irrespective of gender.

Over the decades, many observers close to rabbinic employment and compensation trends, including both male and female rabbis, have discerned, if only anecdotally, differences in the compensation between male and female rabbis doing the same work. To address the perceived discrepancies in rabbinic compensation, the Central Conference of American Rabbis (CCAR) commissioned a study that would for the first time confirm the existence of a pay gap between male and female rabbis. In June 2012, the CCAR released its landmark *Study of Rabbinic Compensation by Gender* (Gender Pay Study)[1], which documents a quantifiable gender pay gap in the Reform rabbinate. The Gender Pay Study has prompted important conversations about the Reform

Movement's commitment to the principles of gender equality and how that commitment translates into action for the affected women rabbis. These conversations necessarily require an explication of the Gender Pay Study results as well as an inquiry into how the rabbinic pay gap may have developed. Perhaps most importantly, the Gender Pay Study helps the Reform Movement to squarely confront and hopefully eliminate the inequalities. Success will require collective action by all of the stakeholders in the Movement.

The Study of Rabbinic Compensation by Gender

The CCAR specifically designed the June 2012 Gender Pay Study to control for gender as a variable in rabbinic compensation. It relied on data from the *2010–2011 Study of Rabbinic Compensation* (2010–11 Salary Study), a partnership project of the CCAR and Union for Reform Judaism conducted by Buck Consulting, LLC, a Xerox Company. Mayeri Research/The Internet Poll was retained to compute and analyze the study data.

Prior to June 2012, the Reform Movement's rabbinic compensation surveys and studies did not control for gender. Moreover, most of the previous efforts to study compensation depended on voluntary, self-reported data. However, both the 2010–11 Salary Study and the 2012 Gender Pay Study relied on Reform Pension Board (RPB) data, not individual, voluntary reporting from rabbis. Therefore, the data underlying the 2010–11 Salary Study and the Gender Pay Study do not suffer the same criticisms associated with previous efforts, as the 2010–11 data set is complete and inclusive of all congregational rabbis who participate in the RPB.

One unique advantage of the Gender Pay Study as compared to other secular analyses of gender differences in compensation is that it disaggregates the Reform rabbi gender pay gap by job title and congregation size.[2] The Gender Pay Study organizes the data for three different rabbinic positions: senior or solo rabbis, associate rabbis, and assistant rabbis. It then breaks down that information into CCAR/ URJ/HUC Joint Rabbinical Placement Commission Categories: the "A" category (up to 300 family units), "B" category (301–599 family units), "C" category (600–999 family units), and "D" category (1,000+ family units). The study also looks at the data in smaller segments based on congregation size (ranging from 150 to 200 family unit increments), which rabbis and congregations frequently use as a basis for comparison during rabbinic contract negotiations. Where the sample size is too small, the Gender Pay Study combines smaller categories to reach statistically significant conclusions. The gender pay gap for each category is then calculated by dividing the mean (average) female rabbi salary within a certain grouping by the mean male rabbi salary in that same grouping and then converting the result into a simple percentage. For example, senior or solo female rabbis in congregations of 401–600 family units make an average annual salary of $134,033, while senior or solo male rabbis in that same category make an average annual salary of $155,371, a difference of $21,338; $134,033 divided by $155,371 equals a gender pay gap of 86%, meaning that female rabbis' wages in this category are only 86% of male rabbis' wages in the same category.[3]

The findings of the Gender Pay Study are summarized in the tables on the next page.

These results reveal a few key points regarding rabbinic compensation. First, and perhaps most importantly, the discrepancy in base compensation between male and female senior/solo rabbis increases as congregational size increases, with women making less than men on average. This fact is particularly significant, as senior/solo rabbis in larger congregations are the most highly compensated rabbis. The Gender Pay Study also highlights the fact that female assistant rabbis make less on average than male assistant rabbis. Although female assistant rabbis in congregations of 1,001–1,200 family units make more on average than their male counterparts, the Gender Pay Study reveals that the aggregate gender pay gap for assistant rabbis in all congregations of over 1,000 family units (CCAR/URJ/HUC "D" category) is 91%. The data also show that, for reasons explored later in this chapter, female associate rabbis make slightly more on average than male associate rabbis.

Senior or Solo Rabbis	
Size of Congregation	**Gender Pay Gap**
Up to 150 family units	93%
151–250 family units	97%
251–400 family units	93%
401–600 family units	86%
600+ family units	80%

Associate Rabbis	
Size of Congregation	**Gender Pay Gap**
401–600 family units	111%
601–800 family units	90%
801–1,000 family units	122%
1,001–1,200 family units	90%
1,201–1,800 family units	107%
1,801+ family units	118%

Assistant Rabbis	
Size of Congregation	**Gender Pay Gap**
1,001–1,200 family units	106%
1,201–1,800 family units	97%
1,801+ family units	81%[4]

According to the American Association of University Women (AAUW), in 2011, the gender pay gap in American society in was 77%.[5] It is encouraging that the gender pay gap in the Reform rabbinate—even at its widest (80% among senior/solo rabbis in congregations of 600 or more members)—remains narrower than the national gender pay gap. However, this is not cause for celebration or even complacency. The Reform Movement's goal should not be to minimize the gender pay gap, but rather to eliminate it in its entirety.

How the Gender Pay Gap Developed
in the Reform Rabbinate

Identifying the primary causes of the gender pay gap in the Reform rabbinate is not a simple task. If one looks to secular society for clues, many reports and studies examine a range of variables that are thought to impact the gender pay gap in American society as a whole. For example, data from the AAUW suggest that education levels do not affect the gender pay gap. The gender pay gap among individuals who have less than a high school education and the gender pay gap among individuals with doctoral degrees are both 80%. Similarly, the gender pay gap for individuals who have high school degrees and no further education is 76%, while the gender pay gap for those who have obtained a master's degree is also 76%.[6] On the other hand, data suggest that age has at least some correlation to the size of the gender pay gap. The gender pay disparity is narrower among younger workers (93% for individuals twenty to twenty-four years old) and widens among middle-aged and older workers (79% for individuals thirty-five to forty-four years old and 81% for individuals sixty-five years old and up).[7]

It is too simplistic, however, to conclude that age alone is a primary cause of the wage disparity. Rather, experts and observers have hypothesized a variety of factors—many anecdotal in nature—that may also contribute to the gender pay gap. One such factor is personal choice, including choice of college majors and occupations, the number of hours spent working, and decisions to leave the workforce. According to the AAUW, women tend to work fewer hours than do men and are more likely to leave the workforce or work part-time when they have young children. Yet this "motherhood penalty" affects the gender pay gap beyond a woman's personal choice to reduce her hours in the workforce. An example of this is easily found in the Reform rabbinate.

Because the United States is one of the few industrialized nations that does not mandate paid maternity leave, female rabbis must negotiate it into their employment agreements.[8] Of course, to get something in negotiations often means to give something else up, and many times this sacrifice involves salary dollars.

In addition to the "motherhood penalty," another factor that may be driving the gender pay gap is the (increasingly false) perception that women are less mobile than men because they are not the primary wage earners in their families. This perception may embolden employers to discriminate against women by offering them less money or taking a harder line in salary negotiations. In the congregational setting, there are a finite number of rabbinic job opportunities within a community (in some areas, there may only be one rabbinic position). Thus, the lack of comparable job opportunities within a community only exacerbates this problem for female rabbis who are unable move to find a higher-paying rabbinic position. While these factors may explain some of the gender pay disparity, they are not the only variables driving it.

Finally, researchers have found that negotiation outcomes are directly correlated to an employee's tolerance for conflict. Some have argued that women are more conflict averse in negotiations, tend to anticipate lower salaries, and undervalue their economic value to their employers. A series of studies conducted by Dr. Linda C. Babcock, an economist at Carnegie Mellon University, demonstrates this point. Dr. Babcock invited 74 volunteers to play the word game Boggle and informed them they would be paid between three and ten dollars for their participation. Each participant was paid three dollars at the end of the game and asked if this amount was acceptable. The male participants asked for more money at a rate of eight times more than the female participants. Dr. Babcock then repeated the experiment with a different twist. Dr. Babcock informed a new group of 153 volunteers that they would be paid between three and ten dollars to play Boggle but explicitly stated that this sum was negotiable. While 83% of the male participants asked for more money, only 53% of female participants did so.[9] In a 2003 book entitled *Women Don't Ask: Negotiation and the Gender Divide*, Dr. Babcock and Sara Laschever take a deeper look at the reluctance of women to negotiate and find that it is partially based on the strange phenomenon that women tend to be more satisfied with their earnings than are men despite making less money than their male counterparts. The authors delve into this concept and show that women are more satisfied with their earnings because they have lower expectations regarding their economic value. This perception partially stems from a "historical predisposition against recognizing the economic value of what society deems to be women's work" and mistakenly limiting comparisons of their economic value to other women. As a result, Babcock and Laschever conclude that women are less likely to negotiate for higher salaries because they are simply not sure that they deserve more money.[10]

A series of additional studies conducted by Dr. Babcock and Drs. Hannah Riley Bowles and Lei Lai revealed that a woman's reluctance to negotiate is also partially based on an entirely reasonable and accurate perception that they would be penalized for doing so. In one study, 119 random volunteers were provided descriptions of qualified candidates for a hypothetical job and informed whether each candidate attempted to negotiate a higher salary. These volunteers were then asked if they would hire these candidates. The study found that these 119 volunteers rejected female applicants who attempted to negotiate a higher salary at twice the rate than they rejected male applicants who did the same. In another study, 285 volunteers were shown videos of men and women either accepting an offered salary or asking for more pay. These volunteers were then asked if they would be willing to work with these individuals. While the female volunteers tended to penalize both the men and women who attempted to negotiate, the male volunteers were much more likely to penalize the women who attempted to negotiate than the men who did the same.[11] Thus, entrenched societal norms and the pressure to conform to gender expectations can lead to an impossible catch-22 for women in salary negotiations. In *Women Don't Ask: Negotiation and the Gender Divide*, Babcock and Laschever observe that in our society, "men are thought to be assertive, dominant, decisive, ambitious, and self-oriented, whereas women are thought to be warm, expressive, nurturing, emotional, and friendly."[12] When a woman breaks from these gender stereotypes in negotiations simply by being assertive and asking for more, she may become less "likeable" and face social sanctions that hurt her job prospects and opportunities for advancement. The authors explain, "Unfortunately, research has revealed that assertive women are less well-liked than those who are not assertive. This means that an assertive woman, no matter how well she presents her arguments in a negotiation, risks decreasing her likeability and therefore her ability to influence the other side to agree with her point of view."[13] As a result of this double standard, many women who have experienced or are aware of the social sanctions that may come with being assertive are reluctant to ask for more in negotiations, to avoid hurting their likeability. Employers, of course, are highly unlikely to increase an offer of salary and benefits without a request to do so.

All of these factors may indeed contribute to the gender pay gap in both secular society and in the Reform rabbinate. Yet the Gender Pay Study data beg a simple question that, on the surface, seems to run contrary to traditional gender pay disparity theories. Why are female associate rabbis paid slightly more, on average, than their male counterparts? The answer may be unpacked from the data underlying the Gender Pay Study. The RPB data used in the Gender Pay Study reveal that of all the male Reform rabbis, 81% are senior/solo rabbis, 14% are associates, and 5% are assistants. On the other hand, only 60% of female Reform rabbis are senior/solo rabbis, 29% are associates, and 11% are assistants. Thus, there is a significantly larger proportion—over twice the percentage—of female associate rabbis to male associate rabbis. One possible explanation for this anomaly is that female rabbis tend to remain in associate rabbi positions longer than do their male counterparts—perhaps because they have less opportunity for advancement or make personal choices not to assume a senior/solo pulpit. While a longer tenure within the associate rabbi position may mean higher salaries for women (as compared to lower salaries for their shorter-tenured male counterparts), women are either not being offered or are not pursuing the higher-paid senior/solo rabbi positions. In the largest congregations, the contrast is particularly stark. Male rabbis predominate in senior/solo congregations of 801 family units and larger (70 male rabbis to 10 female rabbis, or 87.5 to 12.5 percent). By comparison, in the smallest congregations, the numbers shift substantially. In congregations of 250 or fewer family units, there are 117 male senior/solo rabbis and 46 female rabbis, or 72 to 28 percent. These numbers suggest that further inquiry is needed to determine whether a glass ceiling exists for women seeking senior rabbi positions in the largest congregations.

How to Close the Gender Pay Gap in the Reform Rabbinate

Secular American society has made progress in narrowing the gender pay gap, although it has not yet achieved equality—not even close. From 1979 to 1989, the gender pay gap in the United States narrowed from 59.7 to 68.7 percent. From 1989 to 1999, the gender pay gap continued to narrow, albeit at a slower rate, from 68.7 to 72.2 percent. In 2011, it was roughly 77%. According to the AAUW, at the current rate of improvement, it will take over sixty years to entirely eliminate the gender pay gap in the United States. The Reform Movement can learn lessons from the collective American experience in working to narrow the gender pay gap, although certain unique challenges exist within the Reform rabbinate.

Over the last sixty years, the federal government has taken well-publicized steps to narrow the gender pay gap in the United States. In 1963, President John F. Kennedy signed the Equal Pay Act into law, when the gender pay disparity was roughly 59%. Most recently, President Barack Obama signed the Lily Ledbetter Fair Pay Act of 2009, which ultimately allowed individuals a longer time period to bring pay discrimination lawsuits. Two additional pieces of anti-wage discrimination legislation are currently pending in Congress as of this writing—the Paycheck Fairness Act and the Fair Pay Act—although the prospect for their speedy passage is not particularly strong. While legislation has served a role in narrowing the gender pay gap, government action is certainly not the only or even the most important factor.

Francine D. Blau and Lawrence M. Kahn, two Cornell University professors of labor economics who have written extensively about the gender pay gap, have identified four categories of improvements in gender-specific factors that have narrowed the gender wage gap in the United States: (1) a narrowing gender disparity of full-time work experience, which serves to improve women's relative level of measured (and perhaps unmeasured) skills; (2) an increase in the proportion of women holding professional and managerial positions and a decrease in proportion of women in clerical and service jobs; (3) a national declining rate of unionization in the workforce that affects men more than women and leads to a reduction in male wages; and (4) a decrease in the "unexplained gender gap" that "reflects either an upgrading of women's unmeasured labor market skills, a decline in labor market discrimination, or a combination of the two."[14]

With regard to the Reform rabbinate, both collective and individual action is required to eliminate the gender pay gap. Although some of the forces that narrowed the gender pay gap in American society are inapplicable to the Reform rabbinate, other lessons from the experience of secular society may provide guidance. For example, although the Reform Movement cannot pass binding legislation in the same manner as Congress, the Reform Movement can and should institute policies and pass resolutions committing the Movement to the elimination of the gender pay gap in the rabbinate. Furthermore, the Movement must also focus on policies that support the advancement of female rabbis to senior pulpits and take concrete steps to level the playing field for such professional development. The Movement may look to adopt a version of the "sponsorship" model that is growing in popularity in corporate America, where successful, established leaders work to clear obstacles, network, and ultimately position female protégés into roles where they can advance professionally. The "sponsorship" model goes one step further than the traditional, advice-centered "mentorship" model, which has been less successful in promoting female advancement.[15] As Blau and Kahn have noted, and the data from the Gender Pay Study suggest, female professional advancement into previously male-dominated positions is related to the narrowing of the gender pay gap. The Reform Movement must also continue to regularly study the size of the gender pay gap among Reform rabbis and track its trajectory.

It is one thing to draft policy statements and regularly monitor the size of the gender pay gap, but what is paramount is that Movement stakeholders are educated at every reasonable opportunity about the gender pay gap in the Reform rabbinate. The CCAR has taken the lead in these efforts, but in every corner and among every constituency in the Movement, rabbis and lay leaders must work together to preach and teach about the social costs of ignoring the gender pay gap in the Reform rabbinate. This is an in-house, homegrown social justice issue that must be confronted. On the congregational side, every Reform synagogue lay leader must understand that intentional pay discrimination is not only illegal, but it is contrary to the moral compass of the Reform Movement. Moreover, congregational leadership must also be advised to avoid unintentional pay discrimination, in which they approach negotiations with female clergy in a different manner than they would approach negotiations with male clergy. Finally, it is necessary to impress upon these lay leaders that decreasing the salaries of its male rabbis is not the appropriate way to eliminate the gender pay gap; rather, female rabbi salaries should be increased to levels on par with their male counterparts (serving similarly sized congregations) in order to reflect the true value of their work.

Individual rabbis—both female and male rabbis—can have an immediate and substantial effect on closing the gender pay gap. Female rabbis must be proactive in negotiations with their congregations. They must not hesitate to use the Movement's salary and gender pay studies as important reference points in making the case for increased compensation and benefits. Such increases are unlikely to be offered without being requested and justified. Therefore, it is entirely appropriate for female rabbis to bring issues of pay inequality into contract negotiations. Indeed, if gender pay equality is truly a shared principle of the Reform Movement and an issue of social justice, there is no better or more practical place to discuss this principle than in contract negotiations with lay leaders. Male rabbis can also play an important role in eliminating the gender pay gap in the Reform rabbinate. They should not hesitate to vocalize their support for eliminating the gender pay gap and advocating for pay equality both within and outside of their own congregations. Indeed, a full chorus of voices is necessary to achieve gender pay equality.

Conclusion

The Gender Pay Study is the first major step taken in the Reform Movement to acknowledge—and hopefully eliminate—pay inequalities among its rabbis. The Movement, however, still has much work to do. In order for the Reform Jewish community to be successful in eliminating the gender pay gap among its rabbis, all stakeholders must take an active role in effecting change. The Movement must make a continuing, well-publicized commitment to working to eliminate the salary inequities between male and female rabbis. Reform rabbis and other clergy, Movement leadership, congregational lay leadership, and Reform Jews generally must all be educated on the existence of the gender pay gap and how each stakeholder can be part of the solution. Education efforts have little value unless they can also be transformative. They must result in tangible, practical measures taken to narrow and ultimately eliminate the gender pay gap among rabbis in the Reform Movement. It is time to collectively roll up our sleeves, just like the iconic picture of Rosie the Riveter, and get to work.

NOTES

1. See http://ccarnet.org/rabbis-communities/professional-resources/compensation/.

2. Neither the Gender Pay Study nor the Study of Rabbinic Compensation breaks down the data by age or years of experience within the rabbinate or at a particular congregation. The effect of such data on compensation and the gender pay gap is therefore unknown. That said, previous salary surveys (2008–2009 and earlier) identified size of congregation as the primary factor in determining compensation. The *2008–09 Joint Survey of Rabbinic Compensation* notes, "While one might expect compensation to increase with longevity in one position, in fact, sometimes larger increases result because of a move to another position" (p. 1).

3. Compensation differences are magnified when one includes a pension component, as pension deposits to the RPB are based on a percentage of the rabbi's salary.

4. The number of female assistant rabbis in the 1,801+ family units category did not meet the Gender Pay Study's minimum number for disclosure, but was provided for "informational purposes only."

5. The American Association of University Women (AAUW), "The Simple Truth about the Gender Pay Gap," PowerPoint presentation, 2013 ed., slide 3.

6. Ibid., slide 8.

7. Ibid., slide 7.

8. The URJ-CCAR *Guidelines for Rabbinical-Congregational Relationships* (last reprinted in 2002) includes the following statement regarding maternity leave:

> Given Judaism's traditional commitment to the family, Congregations should gladly support the decision of women Rabbis to bear children. Fathers, as well as mothers, should be afforded every opportunity to devote themselves to parenting. For women Rabbis, Congregations shall grant at least a two-month maternity leave at full pay. If additional leave is indicated, the Rabbi may borrow against future vacation time. The Congregation will compensate substitute Rabbis, if their services become necessary during the Rabbi's maternity leave. The Rabbinical Placement Commission, the URJ Regional Director, colleagues in the Central Conference of American Rabbis, and the Rabbi herself will endeavor to assist the Congregation in finding substitute Rabbis as required. Well in advance of her taking maternity leave, the Rabbi should plan for the continued functioning of the Congregation's programs during her absence.

9. Shankar Vedantam, "Salary, Gender, and the Social Cost of Haggling," *Washington Post*, July 30, 2007.

10. Linda Babcock and Sara Laschever, *Women Don't Ask: Negotiation and the Gender Divide* (Princeton, NJ: Princeton University Press, 2003), 41–54.

11. Vedantam, "Salary, Gender, and the Social Cost of Haggling."

12. Babcock and Laschever, *Women Don't Ask*, 62.

13. Ibid., 87.

14. See Francine D. Blau and Lawrence M. Kahn, "Gender Differences in Pay," *Journal of Economic Perspectives* 14, no. 4 (Autumn 2000); Francine D. Blau

and Lawrence M. Kahn, "The US Gender Pay Gap in the 1990s: Slowing Convergence," *IZA Discussion Papers* 2176 (2006).

15. See Brigid Schulte, "Major National Companies Try 'Sponsorship' as New Hammer to Break Glass Ceiling," *Washington Post*, November 14, 2013.

38

GETTING TO THE GOLD STANDARD
IN MATERNITY LEAVE CLAUSES

Rabbi Alysa Mendelson Graf

For women rabbis who are intent on raising families, negotiating a maternity leave is often the first of many challenges that come with parenting. It also may be their first dose of reality with respect to the difficulties that women still face in the rabbinate. Women rabbis may expect that their congregations will support their goals, both professionally and personally. And yet, at the very beginning of a woman rabbi's relationship with her new congregation, she may discover during contract talks that the synagogue leadership or even her senior rabbi does not support her having a paid family leave that will meet her needs or, even, any paid leave at all.

The Law

In his 2015 State of the Union address, President Obama recognized that that United States "is the only advanced country on earth that doesn't guarantee paid sick leave or paid maternity leave to our workers." Current federal law guarantees new parents twelve weeks off, but only at companies with fifty or more employees. This law, called the Family and Medical Leave Act of 1993 (FMLA), entitles eligible employees to take "unpaid, job-protected leave for specified family and medical reasons," which include the birth or adoption of a child or the placement of a foster child with the employee. Unpaid leave under the FMLA is gender neutral; women and men are both entitled to it. In addition, "employers are usually permitted to distinguish between maternity leave, which recognizes a woman's need to recover following childbirth, and parental leave, which recognizes the necessity of a parent—female or male—to care for a new baby." Consequently, under the current law, birth mothers may be eligible for more leave than fathers, partners, or adoptive parents. Some states have expanded the FMLA's unpaid leave benefits by including more acceptable reasons for taking leave, expanding the definition of family, or applying the law to smaller businesses. In addition, three states—California,[1] New Jersey,[2] and Rhode Island[3]—have passed paid family leave insurance laws. These state laws provide for employees to receive a portion of their wages while they are on parental leave. During 2014 and 2015, to encourage other states to enact their own laws on paid family leave, the Department of Labor awarded a total of $1,500,500 in grants to individual states to study the feasibility and implementation of paid family leave programs.[4] However, at this time no other states offer paid leave. The other legal option some rabbis and their congregations have turned to is temporary disability insurance, which provides for wage replacement when an employee takes disability leave. This option is not available in all states and only provides relief for biological mothers.

In the hopes of ensuring a national paid family and medical leave insurance program that would benefit workers, businesses, and their families, the Family and Medical Insurance Leave Act (the Family Act) was introduced to Congress in March of 2015. The bill would provide up to twelve weeks of partial income (66 percent) when employees take time off for their own serious health condition, including pregnancy or recovery from childbirth, as well as the adoption of a child. The bill would cover employees in all workplaces, regardless of size. Synagogues typically are not large enough to be governed by the FMLA, which entitles only eligible employees[5] of covered employers,[6] and even when they are, as religious institutions they cannot be required to comply with the law's requirements.

However, there are some congregations who look to the law for guidance. Indeed, some take their leave policies directly from the federal statute. That is why when it comes to maternity leave clauses for women rabbis, it is important to point out that the FMLA is *inadequate* because it is still *unpaid leave*. It simply does not take into account the need for women on maternity leave to continue to collect an income in order to support their family. Practically speaking, disability insurance can provide a portion of missed income. However, that is often not enough for a family to cover its expenses during this critical time of life. Unless a woman has financial resources outside of her paycheck, such as savings or a second income in the family, she may not be able to take advantage of unpaid time off. Certainly, the Family Act, if passed, will be an improvement on the FMLA. It is a step in the right direction, but it does not do enough. In all likelihood, it will not be a guarantee of the economic security needed by families during their childbearing years.

In addition to federal law, Reform rabbis and congregations can turn to the *Guidelines for Rabbinical-Congregational Relationships* (the *Guidelines*), known as the "Gold Book" (because its cover was once gold-colored), which includes a section that sets forth certain guidelines for the terms of agreement between congregations and their rabbis. These guidelines were adopted in 1984 by the URJ (then UAHC) Board of Trustees and the CCAR, and include salary, pension and disability insurance, leisure time, and sick leave. In 1984, the maternity leave section of the guidelines was seen as advanced.

With respect to maternity leave, the *Guidelines* state:

> Given Judaism's traditional commitment to family, Congregations should gladly support the decision of women Rabbis to bear children. Fathers, as well as mothers, should be afforded every opportunity to parenting. For women rabbis, Congregations shall grant at least a two month maternity leave at full pay. If additional leave is indicated, the Rabbi may borrow against future vacation time. The Congregation will compensate substitute Rabbis, if their services become necessary during the Rabbi's maternity leave. The

Rabbinical Placement Commission, the URJ Regional Director, colleagues in the Central Conference of Rabbis, and the Rabbi herself will endeavor to assist the Congregation in finding substitute Rabbis as requires. Well in advance of her taking maternity leave, the Rabbi should plan for the continued functioning of the Congregation's programs during her absence.

Although the *Guidelines* propose a paid leave of "at least" two months, it does not require it. Indeed, in its preamble, the *Guidelines* state, "The adoption of these *Guidelines* by the URJ Board of Trustees and the CCAR Executive Board does not automatically make them a part of the agreement between a Congregation and its Rabbi." A survey of women rabbis about maternity leave confirmed that this is, in fact, the case that agreements do not automatically have fair and reasonable terms for maternity leave, whether those proposed by the Guidelines or alternate terms proposed by a rabbi or her counsel.

The Challenges Women Rabbis Face

Over the last forty years, the pipeline for women in the rabbinate has certainly widened. In 2015, over 50 percent of rabbis ordained were women. In addition, women have made inroads into senior positions in congregations, large and small, and in major Jewish organizations. In just the last few years, women have been appointed to senior rabbi positions in congregations with over one thousand family units in New York City, Chicago, Seattle, San Antonio, and Miami. These are not the first large congregations at which women have been at the helm; however, the large number of women recently hired in such a short period of time has been both notable and exciting. Women rabbis are also at the helm of organizations like the Wexner Foundation, the Institute for Jewish Spirituality, and Rabbis Without Borders. And yet, as author Peggy Orenstein writes, women are advancing in a "half-changed world," which means that they do so while continuing to deal with the same challenges to balancing their jobs and responsibilities at home.[7] For women rabbis who choose to have children and remain in the workforce, family leave policies are critical to their ability to succeed.

Despite the growing number of women in senior leadership positions in Jewish organizational life, there are still "fewer women at the high echelons in the Jewish communal arena than in comparable organizations in academia, philanthropy, and the secular non-profit sector."[8] This challenge in the Jewish world is one that Advancing Women Professionals (AWP), a national nonprofit organization, has been addressing in its work since 2001. AWP's mission is "to advance women into leadership in Jewish life; stimulate Jewish organizations to become productive, equitable, and vibrant environments; and promote policies that support work-life integration and new models of leadership."[9] As part of its work, AWP published *Leveling the Playing Field*, authored by AWP founder and president Shifra Bronznick, Didi Goldenhar, and Marty Linsky. In *Leveling the Playing Field*, the authors maintain that one of the eight "cultural attitudes" that have contributed to this gap is the misguided belief that "women won't put their professional lives ahead of their families" to meet the "24/7 or 24/6" demands of a senior leadership position.[10]

At the heart of any rabbinic career is the relational aspect of the work. With each position we begin, we enter into a covenant that we hope reflects the mutual obligations we have to one another. Most especially, our congregations want us to be there for them in their major life moments, beginning with the arrival of a child, and continuing through every milestone—bar and bat mitzvah, chuppah, and death. And so, when a woman rabbi reaches this sacred moment in her own life, she wants nothing more than to feel that her congregation, its leadership, and, if she has one, her senior rabbi are just as invested in her well-being after the birth of her children. And yet, some women rabbis are still reporting that their leadership and the senior rabbis with whom they work "are reluctant to consider that their own sacrifices, which they accepted as the price of leadership, will not be embraced by the next generation."[11]

The Survey

In an effort to understand women rabbis' experience with maternity leave, I sent out a survey to all 695 women members of the CCAR. Of the 123 respondents, there were certainly women rabbis who have been blessed to settle in congregations, organizations, and institutions that gave them no challenges whatsoever in negotiating and, later, implementing leave. For example, one respondent shared, "I suggested and created the policy and they eagerly followed it here." Another reported:

> My laity and senior have always been mensches and flexible. While my contract says three months, for both children I came back for the holidays, *b'nei mitzvah*, and the occasional funeral, but didn't put the baby in day care for six months. The key element was flexibility on both sides. I was happy to get my feet wet and help with things where I knew I was needed. In the same way, the rest of the staff and leadership were more than happy to have my baby along for certain meetings and know that I wouldn't be full speed for programming for a few months.

Indeed, some women received gold-standard leave clauses of three months in the first contracts that they were offered. Others only had to ask and were given maternity leave clauses that addressed their needs. At least one rabbi reported receiving additional time while taking her leave when she realized that she needed it. However, an overwhelming majority of respondents encountered difficulties when negotiating and implementing this aspect of their employment contract.

Some faced challenges from their leadership, as this rabbi shared:

> I had to negotiate hard for them to raise the maternity leave from eight weeks to ten weeks. The president of the temple at the time, with whom I was negotiating, was very unforgiving. She, who had her only child in the late 1970s, received no family leave and did not see a need to change.

Others had to overcome a lack of support from their senior rabbis, as another rabbi shared: "I had a big argument from my senior rabbi.

He did not understand." Another respondent reported that while she negotiated for two months of leave, the wording in her contract was "up to two months," and "my senior wanted me to take one month and one month vacation. I really had to lobby for the full two months, and even then it was very contentious." In the early days, some even encountered a lack of support from the CCAR itself, as one colleague shared:

> [My congregation] never had a female rabbi before and did not consider the importance of paternity leave.[12] It was difficult for them to add this to the contract. The CCAR encouraged me to leave it out of my first contract, to negotiate it later on. I'm glad I didn't listen.

Today, CCAR chief executive Rabbi Steven A. Fox advocates for twelve to sixteen weeks of paid family leave and refers rabbis to lawyers who will work with them on this and other contractual issues. In looking back thirty years ago, long before he was at the CCAR, when he began representing rabbis in contract negotiations as an attorney, he recalls the early women rabbis struggling to lay a foundation that included a combination of advocacy and education around the issue of maternity leave. This foundation benefited not only the rabbis, but also women in their congregations who were fighting for the same rights in their work environments.

On the one hand, no one (rabbi or otherwise) negotiating a contract should simply decide to settle and accept whatever offer she receives. However, unless she is willing to walk away from a negotiation, and possibly her job, every contract talk has its limits. Consequently, if she has a strong interest in obtaining or keeping a position, she may be limited in how many aspects of an offer are open to modification in a counteroffer. It should come as no surprise, then, that women have reported having to choose between pushing for a fair maternity leave and receiving an equitable salary. For example, one rabbi reported that while she stood her ground in negotiating for leave of three months and received it instead of the two months she was being offered, she received a much smaller salary than she wanted. While that does not mean that receiving a longer maternity leave necessarily means receiving a lower salary, when negotiating those two elements of a rabbinic contract as if they have parity, something may have to give. We see this in another anecdote in which the respondent shared that her congregation increased her leave from eight to ten weeks as a "gift" when contract negotiations took a negative turn and they were not increasing anything else, including her salary. One rabbi, ordained during the last decade, illustrated the limited choices and financial consequences some women have when it comes to the offer of a short leave and the choice to extend it with unpaid time:

> Ultimately, what I have is okay even though it was a significant financial hardship for my family when we had the last month unpaid since, at the time, I was the only income earner, and there was no way I would have been ready to go back to work just two months after having my son.

Some women report being advised to wait for their second contract, ostensibly to give her new congregation time to get to know, love, and trust her, before pushing for a better maternity leave. When women feel as though their congregations "won't budge," what are their choices?

Of the rabbis ordained in the early 1980s, and thus some of the "first" to negotiate leave, maternity leave was uncharted territory for their congregations. One rabbi reported that her congregation gave her one month of paid maternity leave, which she was then allowed to combine with vacation time. Then, she reported, "we had major debates about who would pay for coverage in my absence. In the end, of course, I had colleagues who filled in for free. Ten days after giving birth, I conducted the confirmation service and officiated at funerals too."

Another reported that her leave was based on the then-current business model, six weeks of paid leave with the option to take vacation time adjacent. Today, negotiating maternity leave is not an act of first impression. In addition to the *Guidelines* and guidance from current and proposed federal law, there are many women rabbis who have gone down this path and have been willing and able to share their experiences and their maternity leave clauses to help new colleagues with their negotiations. In addition, many rabbis, both female and male, now hire attorneys with an expertise in rabbinic contracts to help them.

What We Get

Despite all the resources available to women rabbis today, a gold standard for maternity leave still does not exist for women. Such a standard would be most helpful to women rabbis. Although women no longer need to navigate the path toward a fair and equitable maternity leave clause on their own, each still must "make her own Shabbes" when it comes to how much time off she receives for maternity leave. One rabbi explained that her congregation used the language from a Conservative colleague's contract, and while she is happy with her maternity leave clause, if her leadership "had not had a benchmark from which to start, [her leave] would not have been this generous." Another respondent complained, "I wanted three months paid, they went off the *Guidelines* 'suggestion' of two months paid."

Of the 123 respondents to the family leave survey, 67 provided the terms of their current maternity leave clauses. Only three women had the maternity leave clause (eight weeks paid leave) suggested by the *Guidelines*. The good news is that the trend is for longer maternity leave clauses. Here are the results:

3 months	29
10 weeks + 4 weeks paid vacation	2
10 weeks	4
2 months + 4 weeks paid vacation	2
2 months + 4 weeks unpaid	6
2 months	12
8 weeks (per *Guidelines*)	3

6 weeks	2
4 weeks	1
3 weeks + 9 weeks unpaid	1
Nothing in contract	5

Below is contractual language shared by some of our colleagues.

Three Months (Plus Additional Time)

- Family Leave: The Rabbi is entitled to up to three months of paid family leave and up to three additional months of unpaid family leave, for the purposes of childbirth, adoption, or serious medical care for members of her immediate household. The Rabbi may request other unpaid family leave, such as for purposes of caring for members not in her immediate household, but such requests are subject to approval by the President, as representative of the Board.

- Maternity/Parental Leave: Given Judaism's traditional commitment to the family, the Rabbi shall be entitled to paid maternity/parental leave for three months in the event Rabbi gives birth to or adopts a child during the term of her employment hereunder. The scheduling of the Rabbi's leave under this paragraph shall be in consultation with the Senior Rabbi. The Rabbi shall plan for the continued functioning of the education programs of the Congregation during her absence for maternity/parental leave.

- The congregation will provide Rabbi three months maternity leave at full pay, to be taken immediately preceding and/or following the birth or adoption of a child or children. Rabbi has the option to take eight weeks at full pay, and in addition, the congregation will provide Rabbi an additional eight weeks of half-time maternity leave at full pay following the expiration of her full maternity leave instead of the full three-month period. This option will be determined three months prior to the expected start of her leave. During the half-time leave, Rabbi will work no more than twenty hours per week, the schedule to be agreed upon by Rabbi, the Senior Rabbi, and the congregation's vice-president of administration.

- Rabbi will be granted twelve weeks of paid maternity leave. Unused vacation time may be added to the end of the twelve weeks with prior permission from the President of the Congregation. If Rabbi's physician deems it necessary for more than the twelve weeks of leave, a letter from the physician will be required stating the amount of additional time needed and such additional time will be granted by the Board of Directors. Such additional time will be unpaid leave; however, the Rabbi may use any unused paid vacation time concurrently with the period of any additional unpaid leave time granted beyond the twelve weeks.

- Rabbi shall be entitled to twelve weeks of paid maternity leave in total in the rolling twelve-month period measured backwards from the date such leave is used. Paid maternity leave shall be counted as time used under the Family Medical Leave Act and may be taken by Rabbi if medically necessary due to pregnancy, childbirth or related medical condition and/or to care for her newborn baby. Any such leave must be concluded within one year of the birth of the child. To the extent possible, Rabbi agrees that she shall coordinate her time off under this section with the Senior Rabbi and Temple President.

Two Months to Ten Weeks plus Vacation Time

- In the event the rabbi needs Maternity Leave, she can take two months at full pay. If additional time is needed, she may use current or borrow against future vacation time.

- If it should become necessary, the congregation shall grant up to ten weeks maternity leave with full pay. If additional leave is necessary, the Rabbi may borrow against the current year vacation time. Well in advance of her taking maternity leave she will plan for the continued functioning of the congregation's programs during her absence.

- Maternity Leave: Rabbi will be entitled to two months paid maternity leave should she be blessed with a child during this contract period. Additional time up to four weeks may be arranged based on the needs of the Congregation and at the discretion of the Clergy and the President. If there were not sufficient vacation time available, the additional leave would be unpaid. Vacation benefits will not accrue while Rabbi is on maternity leave.

- Maternity Leave: In the event that the Associate Rabbi has a child during the Term of this Agreement, she shall be entitled to take up to two months of maternity leave. During any such leave, the Associate Rabbi will receive full compensation and continue to receive all benefits to which she is entitled under Agreement. The Associate Rabbi will be entitled to a third month of unpaid leave if requested. The Associate Rabbi may also utilize, for additional maternity leave, any days of paid vacation during that year of the Term that have accrued but not been used. If additional time is desired, the request must be made to the Executive Committee for consideration in its sole discretion. The Associate Rabbi shall give the Temple notice of her intent to take maternity leave at least sixty days before the anticipated need for such leave and shall not be entitled to more than one paid maternity leave during the Term of this Agreement.

- In the event that she becomes pregnant, Rabbi will be entitled to up to eight weeks of maternity leave at full pay. If Rabbi delivers a baby by Caesarean Section, then an additional two weeks will be added to this total. In either case, if additional leave is desired, the Rabbi may: (i) use unused vacation time from the present fiscal year; (ii) borrow against future vacation time available under this Agreement or any renewal hereof; and/or (iii) discuss with the Executive Board extending the maternity leave on an unpaid basis. Well in advance of taking maternity leave, Rabbi will assist in planning for the continued functioning of the Congregation's programs during her absence.

- Maternity Leave: The Congregation shall provide paid maternity leave for two months.
- Rabbi will be entitled to two months paid maternity leave or coverage under the then current congregational policy, whichever Rabbi chooses, in connection with the birth of any child during the Employment Period.
- Two months paid maternity leave (delivery or adoption) at the regular rate of pay. Rabbi shall be responsible for arranging for rabbinic coverage for life cycle events during maternity leave, such as baby-naming and brit, bar/bat mitzvah, weddings, funerals, and conversions. Shabbat and holiday arrangements will be made by the Congregation with the Rabbi's input. This leave is in addition to regular vacation and weeks away as noted above.

Four Weeks

- Employees that have worked for Temple for a minimum of twelve months will be eligible for four weeks paid Maternity/Paternity leave for the birth or adoption of a child. Any remaining PTO must be utilized before using unpaid leave. FMLA leave will run concurrently with this paid leave.

FMLA (Unpaid Leave)

- The Rabbi may take up to twelve weeks off each year as Family Care Leave consistent with the principles and definitions of the Family Medical Leave Act. This time shall be unpaid, but the Rabbi shall be permitted to use any sick and/or vacation time available at the start of the leave.

Notably, many of these clauses take into account the need to smooth the transitions out of work and back to work, both for the sake of the new parent and her colleagues who will be covering for her while she is away. This includes giving notice "well in advance" of a likely departure date, creating a plan of action for "the continued function of the congregation's programs" during her absence, and whether she is responsible for arranging coverage while she is on leave.[13] Some provide the option of extending leave without pay. Others extend leave (usually by two weeks) if the birth was via caesarean section. Some, though not all, directly stipulate that the rabbi must consult with her senior rabbi, administration, and/or leadership (often the temple president) with respect to scheduling leave.

The Gold Standard: Three Months of Maternity Leave

While the trend in maternity leave clauses for women rabbis is toward three months, we have not arrived at the Promised Land just yet. Too many women rabbis still endure tense negotiations or accept abbreviated maternity leaves or lower pay in order to do the holy work to which they have committed their professional and personal lives. Three months should be the "gold standard" for all maternity leave clauses for women rabbis. This is supported by Advancing Women Professionals, which recommends that Jewish organizations formalize and expand their parental leave policies to three months of paid maternity leave.[14] Such leave, the AWP argues, "protects an organization's investment in its workforce. Paid leave, accompanied by flexible scheduling, increases the probability of the parent returning to the organization as a productive professional and making a long-term commitment."[15]

Moreover, there are profound "organizational benefits of generous parental leave policy," as set forth in a report by the Boston College Center for Work & Family, which underscored the following:

- Reduced recruitment and training costs;
- Improved staff productivity and morale;
- Increased number of employees returning to work; and
- Organizational effectiveness, resulting from longer tenure, e.g., institutional memory, industry knowledge and robust networks.[16]

Recently, some high-tech companies have been making the news with their unlimited or lengthy maternity leave policies.[17] They argue that offering longer maternity leave can help companies attract and retain female employees. When it comes to maternity leave policies, it is critical that we be expansive in our thinking about how to address the needs of women rabbis and the congregations they serve.

When a rabbi has a child, as one respondent wrote, "it is a wonderful opportunity to lift up the values we teach, to celebrate as a community the birth of a new life, and to show how we support and build family in our community." There are already many positive examples of rabbis and congregations who have had wonderful experiences (on both ends) of a woman rabbi's maternity; there need to be even more. Women rabbis should not have to choose between whether to grow their family or whether to ensure the economic stability of their families. I believe that congregations want to be able to retain their current rabbis rather than retrain new rabbis, and to do this they must find a way to financially support their rabbis' decisions with respect to growing their families. The three-month maternity leave will result in even greater job satisfaction in the women rabbis of the Reform Movement, thereby better enabling them to serve their communities. The CCAR and the URJ should work together to educate congregational leaders that adopting the three-month maternity leave standard is a way to meaningfully promote and support women's rabbinic leadership in our Movement.

NOTES

1. Cal. Unemp. Ins. Code §§ 3300–3306 (six weeks of paid leave).
2. N.J. Stat. § 43:21–25 et seq. (six weeks of paid leave).
3. R.I. Gen. Laws § 28–41–34 et seq. (four weeks of paid leave).
4. *Investing in Our Families: The Case for Paid Family Leave in New York and the Nation* (New York: A Better Balance: The Work and Family Legal Center, May 2015), http://www.abetterbalance.org/web/images/stories/Documents/familyleave/PFL2015.pdf.
5. 29 U.S. Code Chapter 28, Family and Medical Leave, subchapter I, § 2611(2) (A): "The term 'eligible employee' means an employee who has been employed—(i) for at least 12 months by the employer with respect to whom leave is requested...;

and (ii) for at least 1,250 hours of service with such employer during the previous 12-month period."

6. 29 U.S. Code Chapter 28, Family and Medical Leave, subchaper I, § 2611 (4): "The term 'employer'—(i) means any person engaged in commerce or in any industry or activity affecting commerce who employs 50 or more employees for each working day during each of 20 or more calendar workweeks in the current or preceding calendar year."

7. Peggy Orenstein, *Flux: Women on Sex, Work, Love, Kids and Life in a Half-Changed World* (New York: Doubleday/Anchor, 2000).

8. Steven M. Cohen, Shifra Bronznick, Didi Goldenhar, Sherry Israel, and Shaul Kelner, *Creating Gender Equity and Organizational Effectiveness in the Jewish Federation System: A Research-and-Action Project* (New York: Advancing Women Professionals and the Jewish Community and United Jewish Communities, 2004), 2–3.

9. The rest of AWP's mission statement declares: "AWP seeks to leverage the talents of women on behalf of the Jewish community and to act as a catalyst for change. AWP has found that identifying the systemic barriers that prevent women from advancing leads to discovering the challenges that exist for everyone in the workplace—women and men, professionals and volunteers. Through research, pilot projects, advocacy, and publications, AWP is removing barriers and helping Jewish organizations establish policies and practices that expand opportunities for everyone" (www.advancingwomen.org).

10. Shifra Bronznick, Didi Goldenhar, and Marty Linsky, *Leveling the Playing Field: Advancing Women in Jewish Organizational Life* (Advancing Women Professionals and the Jewish Community, and Cambridge Leadership Associates, 2008), 28–31.

11. Ibid., 31.

12. This colleague's congregation had never considered any kind of family leave in the past. Specifically, when it had only male rabbis, the congregation had not discussed any kind of contractual family leave, which would be paternity leave in the case of male rabbis. Thus, when this female colleague asked for maternity leave, it was an issue entirely of first impression for her congregation.

13. The call for giving notice and creating a departure plan presents a challenge to women going through the adoption process, who may not have much lead time around which to plan. Similarly, for women who experience unexpected complications during pregnancy, their time to "plan ahead" may be cut short by an emergency hospital stay or a premature delivery.

14. Didi Goldenhar, Shifra Bronznick, and Rachel Ellison, *Better Work, Better Life: Practices and Policies in Jewish Organizations*, rev. ed. (New York: AWP, 2010), 4, http://advancingwomen.org/wp-content/uploads/2013/09/Better-Work-Better-Life-Practices-and-Policies-in-Jewish-Organizations-Report1.pdf.

15 Ibid., 12.

16. Ibid., citing Fred Van Deusen, Jamie Ladge, Jaqueline James, and Brad Harrington. *Building the Business Case for Work-Life Programs* (Chestnut Hill, MA: Boston College Center for Work-Life, 2008), https://www.bc.edu/content/dam/files/centers/cwf/research/pdf/BCCWF_Business_Case_EBS.pdf.

17. Rebecca J. Rosen, "Netflix's New Parental-Leave Policy: 'Just About Ideal,'" *Atlantic*, August 5, 2015, http://www.theatlantic.com/business/archive/2015/08/netflix-parental-leave/400541/.

39

FIGURING IT ALL OUT

The Parenting Balancing Act

RABBI REBECCA EINSTEIN SCHORR

When I was in rabbinical school, I thought I had it all figured out: husband, kids, pulpit. I envisioned a home life that included a Shabbos dinner with bright-shining faces beaming up at me from around the table. After *z'miros* and *bentching*, I would kiss each one in turn before heading to shul for services. I would return home to a quiet house, a clean kitchen, and my husband waiting up for me in the flickering candlelight. It would be, in many ways, a replica of my childhood home.

Except for one significant difference: the husband was the rabbi in my childhood home. And it was my mother, the *rebbetzin*, who provided the type of home life that enabled my father to be present at the shul at all times.

Over the past four decades, the notion that there is only one rabbinic model has been repeatedly challenged. Unlike our male predecessors, women rabbis have forced a reexamination of how to approach the rabbinate. Not satisfied with the outmoded hierarchical leadership approach, women rabbis have forged new paths that have redefined the modern rabbinate as well as radically changed how success is measured.

Being professionally ambitious has been the typical model of men in the workplace. Women have challenged the definition of success. They have disputed the idea that bigger is better and that what makes a successful rabbinic career is the size or location of the synagogue. In fact, women rabbis have often promoted a different model entirely, that one need not be in a synagogue setting whatsoever to have a fulfilling and successful rabbinate.

But it didn't start out that way. The first woman rabbi, Sally Priesand (HUC-JIR '71), has said that she always intended to get married and have a family.[1] Ultimately, Priesand determined that balancing a family life with her rabbinate was not something she was capable of doing, and she felt forced to choose one over the other. How different things might have been if there had been others to show her how to strike that balance.

The importance of having role models and mentors is undeniable. These individuals can inspire and motivate as well as act as critical sounding boards for those new in a field. For the first generation of women rabbis, finding a female rabbinic role model was impossible; there weren't any. Those women (students and the newly ordained) seeking role models for career choices and balance had to look to women in other professions or male rabbis, because the rabbinate was still a male-dominated field; there were not yet any female rabbis with children.

Though Hebrew Union College–Jewish Institute of Religion (HUC-JIR) had made the decision to admit women in 1968, it seems as though nothing was put into place to support female students who decided to become pregnant while in school. Nor did it prevent faculty members, at that time all male, from voicing their disapproval. One rabbi ordained in the 1980s recalls being told, "Don't bother becoming a rabbi; just make babies."[2] For decades, there was a great deal of inflexibility on the part of the faculty and staff, and no guidelines existed for either students or their supervisors at their internships. Pregnant students were often made to feel uncomfortable or less valuable. This did not stop women from having babies or from pursuing their studies and careers in the rabbinate, but it did create, at times, a less-than-supportive environment in which to do so.

Being a woman also affected the job interviews. It was not uncommon for students preparing for placement to be informed by the search committee of the appropriate time to get pregnant. Mona Alfi (HUC-JIR '98) recalls being told as a fifth-year student that "women of child-bearing age would be seen with hesitation by congregations while we were in placement and that women who were pregnant [during place-ment] would be at a disadvantage."[3] Though Keara Stein (HUC-JIR '14) says that the faculty was extremely supportive about childbearing in the fifth year, she was given similar advice from mentors as she was preparing for the search process. Additionally, Stein remembers, "in terms of placement I was written off a lot by my classmates; it can be so competitive and my pregnancy was seen as a handicap." Though the Rabbinical Placement Commission cautions congregational search committees against asking "questions of a personal nature (i.e., re-garding one's spouse, future family plans, etc.),"[4] citing them as "in-appropriate to an interview setting and an invasion of an applicant's privacy,"[5] many women admit to being asked about future children. And quite a few believe that they were passed over for a job because of their desire to have children in the immediate future. Stephanie Alexander (HUC-JIR '03) recalls being asked in every interview how she thought that potential children would affect her ability to serve a congregation. "Note," she wryly added, "my husband, who is also a rabbi, has never been asked that question."

Sarah Hronsky (HUC-JIR '03) has had a completely different ex-perience. She was pregnant with her first child when hired by the synagogue where she would eventually succeed to the senior position some years later. Though she had three children at that time, she did feel as though she needed to wait until she was some years into the senior position before having her fourth child.

It has taken some time for HUC-JIR to incorporate discussions about family/career balance into its curriculum, either formal or in-formal. Though it appears that for the first several classes of women the topic was not yet on HUC's radar, discussions about the challenges of a rabbinate and family have become far more common. One recent ordinee was encouraged by the advice of a rabbinic mentor who had a baby the summer after ordination. "[She] said it helped her be a better rabbi, making it easier to relate to parents in the Early Childhood Center."

Open conversations, even the negative ones, are useful in helping both men and women rabbis craft rabbinates that reflect their personal as well as professional goals. Nearly every rabbi interviewed had at least one example of a conversation that helped her conclude what she wanted in her rabbinate. Even the awful conversations yielded something positive. A rabbi ordained in the 2000s recollects a visit from a rabbi in the field during her fifth year at HUC-JIR. He advised them that "any meal we ate alone was wasted time. He was in a huge congregation in a major city and claimed to always have breakfast, lunch, and dinner with either congregants or family. But the impression was that breakfast and lunch, in particular, were far more with congregants than with family. I was disgusted then, and remain disgusted now, but the assertion went unchallenged." This encounter confirmed that this was not what this rabbinical student wanted as her rabbinate.

One thing that nearly all women rabbis mentioned is the need for a supportive partner. In fact, as Leah Lewis (HUC-JIR '02) says, "in a congregation, it's only doable with good help and a giving partner." Heidi Cohen (HUC-JIR '98) would concur. From the very beginning of her relationship with her husband, Matt, they agreed that they would go wherever her job was. Matt's job as a webmaster allowed for flexibility in his work and the ability to be the full-time parent. "I'm very lucky and know that I could not be a successful rabbi without him. It's an awesome partnership!"[6] Vered Harris (HUC-JIR '00) and her husband, Benji, have a similar arrangement; he is the primary hands-on parent, allowing Vered's career to determine where they live.

It gets more complicated, of course, when both spouses are rabbis. In the case of Phyllis Sommer (HUC-JIR '03), it was "a purely economic decision."[7] Since Michael was still in school at the time of her ordination, she "went into placement with an eye on a city that would allow Michael to commute on a weekly basis to Cincinnati.... After his ordination, it was clear that we weren't quite ready for a two-full-time-rabbi home. I'm not sure that Michael would say that he always *loved* being the primary at-home parent, but he saw the value in it for our children and our family.... When the opportunity arose for him to take on a full-time position, we were ready.... Our roles have always been a little bit fluid and unconventional, but so far it's worked for us."[8] Joanna Tract (HUC-JIR '99) and her husband, Tony Fratello, started out as full-time pulpit rabbis. Once they had children, however, Tract yearned for more balance. "I wanted to enjoy motherhood. I wanted to be there for the kids and not miss baby/school stuff, but I also wanted to feel fulfilled as a rabbi."[9] For her, that meant leaving the pulpit and doing part-time chaplaincy work. Tract says that this arrangement works for their family; she feels very fulfilled, and Tony is also happy in his congregation. Tract sums it up best: "Job satisfaction and maternal/paternal needs are different for each person at different times."[10]

In discussions about gender equality in the rabbinate, the dearth of women serving in senior positions of large synagogues has long been used as the litmus test to prove that there is, in fact, a lack of equality. That statistic, however, fails to account for the deliberate choices women rabbis have made in order to strike the right work/family balance for themselves. This is reminiscent of the question asked by Lisa Belkin in her well-known 2003 article "The Opt-Out Revolution." Belkin, reflecting on the decision of several women to leave high-powered positions in order to return home, posited, "Why don't women run the world? Maybe it's because they don't want to."[11]

Ellen Weinberg Dreyfus (HUC-JIR '79) recalls the negative reaction she received when she made the unprecedented decision to pursue a part-time pulpit. "The notion of a part time rabbi was simply unheard of, but I couldn't do it all. I turned in my cape, I was not superwoman, I couldn't do everything."[12]

Dreyfus was not alone in her desire to carve out a position that would allow her to dedicate time to her congregation while devoting herself to her family. Subsequent women colleagues have rejected the all-or-nothing approach, recognizing that innovation would be required in order to reinvent the definition of a successful rabbinate. Keara Stein (HUC-JIR '14) says that she "specifically chose a job that is extremely open to my family and flexible to allow me to work from home and from the park with my kids."[13] In fact, as director of Inter-faithFamily/Los Angeles, she admits that having a family and being involved with her kids is considered an asset for her current job, though she is the first to admit that she had to seek out such a position, to "go completely outside the mold to find it."[14]

Women rabbis were ahead of the trend, however. For many years, the CCAR Placement office gave less attention to those women rabbis who declined to pursue a full-time rabbinate; more than one colleague ordained in the 1980s who sought only part-time positions report unreturned phone calls during the placement process. Those women perceived a bias against those who were not prepared to make a full-time rabbinate their primary focus to the exclusion to all else.

For decades, success in the rabbinate was defined by climbing the ladder of succession. The preferred trajectory was to begin in a large congregation as an assistant, progress to associate in another large congregation, and ultimately work as a senior rabbi in an even larger congregation. It was also possible to attain the highly desirable senior position by serving as solo rabbi in a smaller congregation early on in one's career. This accomplishment paralleled making partner in a law firm or accounting firm, having your own practice as a doctor, or becoming a tenured and respected professor.

Wendi Geffen is one such rabbi. After thirteen years as an assistant and then associate rabbi, she assumed the senior position of that same synagogue in 2015 with a clear vision of what she wanted her rabbinate to look like. "I really don't like the term 'work/life balance'—I think it was set up to be just one more 'standard' to which we are supposed to be beholden."[15] Geffen has a much more realistic approach. She simply tries to be present in whatever situation she finds herself. Geffen is not alone; she is one of a handful of women who are now at the helm of large pulpits.

More than a few women rabbis, however, have intentionally chosen not to "advance" to the senior position. They want to have more availability for their family, and they see the senior position as being incompatible with that priority. One 1990s ordinee, whose first child was born during her fifth year of school, had three more children while she was in a part-time congregational position. At different times, she has looked for other positions, sometimes withdrawing because of impact on her family. "It's hard to say if I sacrificed career advancement because of my children or because of the holistic family picture (my husband's job, work/life balance, etc.)."

Another colleague, after serving as associate rabbi at a large congregation, was approached by the leadership to discuss successorship when her senior rabbi announced his retirement. "I told the leadership that I was not interested in the position at least in part because I have young children (but that I was also not willing to be told what to do by a senior who felt the need to direct me). I was given a partnership role in choosing the new senior, and for the last six years, we have worked beautifully as colleagues. In his position, I would make more than double my current salary, but the money and prestige are not reason enough for me to want his job.... I don't see this as a sacrifice."

A 1980s ordinee made the very deliberate decision to prioritize her children once she realized that she couldn't "'have it all' the way I conceived of 'all.'" Several others have shied away from congregational work because of work/life balance issues. A 2014 ordinee has created a rabbinate quite different from the one she originally envisioned. "I decided that I will be a rabbi forever but will only have this time to spend with my infants, and I want to cherish it."

Once in a position, trying to achieve a balance between pulpit and family life has been challenging for all and extremely difficult for some. Synagogues, understandably, want their rabbis to be part of the community. But only up to a point. And there do seem to be gender differences. While a male rabbi wearing his baby in a baby carrier is met with approving comments, his female counterpart is often perceived as having difficulty maintaining proper boundaries. One woman colleague from the 1990s recalls, with some amount of irony, being told by her male senior rabbi that bringing her young son to the synagogue's family weekend would be a distraction, while a 1970s colleague was given a performance review that commented on her failure to control her children during the family service while she was on the bimah and they were sitting with their father.

When asked, an overwhelming majority of women interviewed responded that the most challenging aspect of balancing parenthood and the rabbinate is having enough time for one's children. This is a concern shared by women across all industries; the reality that having it all does not mean having it all at the same time. A 2012 article by Anne-Marie Slaughter set off a maelstrom when the author suggested that the notion of a perfect work/life balance is flawed. Looking at the career trajectories of dozens of successful women and some men, Slaughter draws out a complex set of criteria meant to help contemporary women determine how to manage work and family.[16]

Women rabbis have long been at the forefront of re-envisioning a life that includes a passionate calling as well as the rearing of children. Their efforts have opened the door for their male colleagues to insist on a healthier work/life balance. Advances in this area positively affect all rabbis, regardless of gender, their families, and ultimately their congregations and communities. It is a worthy struggle. As Keara Stein (HUC-JIR '14) reflects, "Family is such an essential value to Judaism, and I hope that we can be encouraging our rabbis to start families rather than discouraging it."[18]

I managed to find a balance for twelve years. Ironically, that very same *rebbetzin*, my mother, was still the one getting the Shabbos meal on the table. I would kiss each one of my children in turn before leaving my parents' home and, with my father, head to shul for services. After services, I would go to my own home, a clean kitchen, and my husband waiting up for me in the flickering candlelight. It was, in certain ways, a replica of my childhood home. Until it didn't work for us anymore. With one of our children on the autism spectrum and his needs becoming more pronounced with every passing year, I eventually turned down the opportunity to succeed my senior rabbi and left the pulpit entirely. It is a classic case of opting out. However, like most decisions, it is not set it stone. While my rabbinate looks nothing like that which

I had originally planned, I know that it will continue to evolve as the needs of my family change. And I have the generations of women rabbis who paved the way to thank.

NOTES

1. Paul Zakrzewski, "Pioneering Rabbi Who Softly Made Her Way," *New York Times*, May 20, 2006.

2. Anonymous comment made to author, August 27, 2014.

3. Correspondence with Rabbi Mona Alfi, August 27, 2014.

4. *The Placement of Newly-Ordained Rabbis: A Handbook of Procedures*, Rabbinical Placement Commission, Hebrew Union College–Jewish Institute of Religion, and Class of 2015/5775, p. 12, http://ccarnet.org/media/filer_public/2014/09/16/huc-jir_placement_handbook_2015_10_22_13.pdf.

5. Ibid.

6. Conversation with Rabbi Heidi Cohen, August 2015.

7. Conversation with the Rabbi Phyllis Sommer, August 2015.

8. Ibid.

9. Conversation with Rabbi Joanna Tract, August 2015.

10. Ibid.

11. Lisa Belkin, "The Opt-Out Revolution," *New York Times*, October 26, 2003.

12. Correspondence with Rabbi Ellen Weinberg Dreyfus, September 2, 2014.

13. Conversations with Rabbi Keara Stein, November 2014 and July 2015.

14. Conversation with Rabbi Keara Stein, July 2015.

15. Conversation with Rabbi Wendi Geffen, August 2015.

16. Anne-Marie Slaughter, "Why Women Can't Have It All," *The Atlantic*, July/August 2012.

17. Conversation with Rabbi Keara Stein, July 2015.

PERSONAL REFLECTION

Why I Almost Did Not Become a Rabbi

Rabbi Alysa Mendelson Graf

When I was ten years old, a decade after Sally Priesand was ordained, my congregation hired its first woman rabbi. Our new "woman rabbi" was young and pretty, smart and strong, had a beautiful voice and a tremendous presence on and off the bimah. My parents took to her immediately. They were proud of our congregation's choice of assistant rabbi, not just because she was a woman, but because they felt she was an outstanding rabbi. And so, during my formative and most impressionable years, I watched my rabbi navigate her role as the first woman rabbi in our large Reform congregation in suburban New York.

When the senior rabbi of my congregation was scheduled to be out of town on the weekend I became a bat mitzvah, my parents received a letter with an apology for the conflict and, from what I understand, the implied option to switch weekends if they wanted. I don't think that the option was offered because the assistant rabbi was a woman; I am sure it was made with the assumption that we would prefer the senior rabbi, who had known us longer. However, for my parents, switching was not an option. Yes, the date had been on my family's calendar for over a year (think deposits and travel plans). More importantly, they were thrilled that as I became an adult in the eyes of the Jewish people, it would be with a dynamic female rabbi standing by my side. As the parents of two daughters, my mom and dad were raising my sister and me to believe that we could be anything we wanted to be and could do anything we wanted to do. What better expression of these feminist values could there be than a woman breaking through the stained glass ceiling and becoming an ordained leader of our people?

My parents' commitment and dedication to Jewish life, coupled with their service to and love for the Jewish people, embedded in me a deep commitment, dedication, and love of Judaism. But it was being taught by a woman rabbi how to stand proudly on the bimah, how to project my voice and my truth all the way to the back of the sanctuary, and how to teach the meaning of my bat mitzvah *parashah* with passion that sparked my interest in pursuing the rabbinate. I knew that this was something I could spend a lifetime doing. And yet, despite knowing in the deepest recesses of my soul that serving the Jewish people as a rabbi was what I wanted to do with my life, I almost did not become a rabbi.

I was probably too young to appreciate all the nuances of the challenges that our rabbi had to face, but I knew it was not easy for her. I watched well-meaning members of my congregation react to our rabbi and to the different choices she made and paths she took. There was great love and affection for her and a deep appreciation for the Torah she brought to our temple. And yet, there were myriad discussions about how she dressed, the makeup she did (or did not) wear, her pregnancy, her parenting. She was complimented, but she was also questioned in ways that I knew our congregation's male rabbis had never been. She was living in a fishbowl. When thinking about what I wanted my future to be like, I felt certain that I did not want it to include a congregation's worth of commentary on my looks, my parenting, or any other part of my personal life. Consequently, I put the dream of becoming a rabbi away. I told myself that I didn't want to live in that kind of fishbowl, and instead I became a lawyer.

As a lawyer, I felt intellectually stimulated but spiritually stunted. I had an active Jewish life, but it was never enough. And so, eighteen years after my childhood synagogue made its momentous decision, I made one of my own. I would brave life in the fishbowl, so that I could serve the Jewish people. The choice to go to rabbinical school remains one of the best decisions I have ever made.

It is not always easy. Congregants have often commented on my haircuts, my makeup, and my clothing, but that mostly does not bother me. I have discovered that there are much more complicated things about which to be concerned. When I was interviewing for my first job, a congregational president (a woman) asked me to wait at least a year before I had my first child. Some of my struggles are the same as those of many women in the workforce. As the mother of three young children, I simply cannot be in all places at all times, and yet I try. There are still too many times when a male colleague will repeat the exact same thing I have just said as if it were the first time the idea were being offered. I once thought success in the rabbinate meant being the senior rabbi of a large congregation; I now know that for me success is measured not by how many, but how meaningful the relationships are that I develop with those I serve.

I am now the rabbi at a very small congregation in the suburbs of New York. Remarkably, since my congregation began hiring full-time rabbis over three decades ago, they have only hired women rabbis! Though there will always be challenges, I know that my life as a rabbi gives my spirit a chance to soar each day in ways it never would have had I remained an attorney. And I pray that as I continue to navigate the path of my rabbinate, I will inspire others to pursue a path through Judaism that gives them as much satisfaction and joy as mine has given me.

PERSONAL REFLECTION

Being a Public Person, Suffering a Private Loss

Rabbi Rebecca Gutterman

This month, a new documentary called *All of the Above: Single, Clergy, Mother* was released. I look forward to seeing it. And I look back, waiting for something else to be released that hasn't been yet. Bewilderment? Regret? Grief, again? A short time ago I wouldn't have been watching this film. Chances are good I would have been in it.

In July of 2010 I was a congregational rabbi, newly pregnant, on my own, and excited to distraction. Granted, my congregation didn't know yet. And there was the occasional mention of that pesky little phrase "advanced maternal age," which didn't feel especially true at thirty-nine, but I reasoned *was* true...more or less. Mostly I felt like I was in the process of getting—no, of creating—everything I had ever wanted, if not in the order I had expected. How, at my advanced maternal age, had I gotten so lucky?

It's tempting from where I sit now to rewrite that part of my story, but of course a child wasn't everything I had ever wanted. I had hoped to find someone to marry too. My journey to single motherhood followed all the conventional benchmarks of an unconventional choice. There were my roaring twenties, followed by rabbinical school and settling into my congregation, many bad dates and some okay relationships. In the background, always, was my feeling that whatever happened, life without a child felt impossible. I promised myself the winter I turned thirty-seven that if the makings of plan A didn't materialize in one year, I would start to assemble plan B. Once I got pregnant, plan B became plan A, morphing into the rest of my life… our lives now. Me and this baby, conceived with an anonymous donor somewhere between instantly and arduously. My little star.

The next two months were a blur of disclosures and plans. Mostly I was flooded with joy and astonishment as the realization hit home that there was going to be another human being in the world because of something I had done. Not for nothing are the words "fear" and "awe" so bound up together! When I finally shared the news with my synagogue, I found that they were almost as elated at the prospect of their rabbi becoming a mother as I was. On Rosh HaShanah, I spoke about listening as a sacred obligation, all the while listening for the tiny fluttering kicks that had begun a week or so before. My pregnancy was already going wrong, but those kicks felt like champagne bubbles. Congregants who hadn't already known my news congratulated me. The stage had never been set more beautifully. Or so I thought.

The following Monday, at my twenty-three-week checkup, my doctor wanted more extensive lab work, as my blood pressure was up and I was down to one pair of sandals that still fit, straps stretched to the breaking point. The next day I was sent to the hospital for evaluation. That hospital was the last building I would walk into pregnant.

They took my blood pressure again. This time it was off the charts. Was I having headaches or vision changes, the doctors asked, each looking more concerned than the one before. No, I told them…I felt fine. *What was happening to my baby and me?* It wasn't long before I knew. The diagnosis was severe preeclampsia—a pregnancy related condition that induces hypertension. I remembered *What to Expect When You're Expecting* mentioning it in the final chapters detailing the things that can go awry out of nowhere with disastrous results, but probably won't happen to you. "So what do we do?" I asked. My voice sounded small, because the doctors' expressions told me the answer would be the slamming of doors, not a series of next steps. As my condition declined, they broke the news that in order to protect my health and possibly my life, the baby would have to be delivered now. "It's too early!" I protested, looking pleadingly from one doctor to the other. Both understood exactly what was at stake. The first one was visibly pregnant herself and had to look away, but I saw her tears. The second one held my gaze. "Yes," she said solemnly. "It's too early." My labor had begun.

My family arrived the next morning. The head of the NICU came to speak to us, even though we knew there would be no NICU for us. A hospital social worker asked if I wanted to talk to clergy or to plan a service. "I am clergy," I thought. I pictured us gathered around a casket the size of a breadbox, and I swallowed hard and shook my head. I had no idea how to say hello and good-bye at the same time, but we would say ours here.

My daughter was born just before midnight, weighing thirteen ounces. Of course there was no crying. The nurse who had attended to all of us spectacularly through the day, who later told me she had lost a baby too, said she still had a very slow heartbeat and asked if I wanted to hold her. "Yes I do," I managed, through my daze of exhaustion. She came right away and put her in my hands.

My girl, I marveled. I touched her tiny face, her lips. No baby fat at this stage; she was just perfectly formed and very, very little. How could I have thought this would be the worst part? I held her feet, no bigger than my fingertips, and told her I remembered her kicks. She left this world as peacefully as she'd come into it. It wasn't until the next morning that I broke down, because it was the first of every morning I would now face without her.

I don't remember much about the weeks that followed my discharge from the hospital, arms and belly empty. Friends and relatives rallied around. Members of the congregation brought meals and sent cards. Fellow parents told me their stories of lost children and said they hoped I would regain my balance in time. I both loved and hated the attention and insulation that came with being a public person surviving a private loss. For every misstep or story about IVF or adoption I wasn't ready to hear—and there weren't many—there was also a palpable longing on their part to be there for someone who had long been there for them. As much as anything could, this proved a great comfort.

In early November, I sat in a wine bar with a good friend who said there was someone she wanted me to meet when he was in town next. The idea felt a million miles away, but I nodded offhandedly.

His name was Michael. We had dinner the night before Thanksgiving. He was steady and funny and calm. We talked about his theater background, about what rabbis do when they're not leading services, about what the restaurant's hostess might have meant when she said she'd seat us in the slow section. We both knew the name of an obscure folk band that no one would have any reason to know. Over the next two months, we visited each other's cities and talked more—about his choice to convert to Judaism a few years before, and a little bit about my baby girl. I was coming to realize that she had stripped me of whatever pretenses I had carried into relationships before. Now there was no reason not to talk right away about kids and timing and what we both wanted. Michael made me laugh when I had thought I never would again. He looked at me like we had all the time in the world. It didn't take us long to realize that what we wanted was each other.

One year after staring fixedly at a positive pregnancy test, I find myself planning a wedding. I will never be the subject of the story or the documentary that I might have been. And yet. The life we are beginning together is already filled with happiness. Michael and I have every plan for a family, even as we know anything can happen. That's the bad news, but I'm beginning to believe again that it's the good news too.

How do you say hello and good-bye at the same time? I still don't know. I look at the sky and pray my own little star is up there somewhere. I remember the months and then the minutes I was someone's mother, and in my heart of hearts I still am. I look at the hands she rested in, the hands that fit so beautifully into Michael's now. My blessing, my pain. Hello and good-bye. I wonder if a day will come that I won't always find myself saying both.

PERSONAL REFLECTION

The "Part-Time" Rabbinate

RABBI SARA YELLEN SAPADIN

My first son Ezra was born three weeks before I was ordained by Hebrew Union College–Jewish Institute of Religion. I have distinct memories of leaving my ordination ceremony to go to the bathroom so I could pump milk for my infant son. There I was in that tiny stall, trying to maneuver this relic of a hand pump under my ridiculously large robe. I ended up missing the keynote speaker because I spent so long trying to coax milk with that dinosaur pump! Two and half years later, my second son arrived into this world, and now, two years following, I am expecting my third.

Indeed, as I have become a rabbi, so too I have become a mother. Just as both roles are challenging, so too are they incredibly gratifying. Since the inception of my career, I have tried to forge a path that accommodates both motherhood and the rabbinate, a path that, theoretically, allows me to be the kind of mother I want to be and the kind of rabbi I'd like to be. And for me, these worlds are inextricably linked, not seamlessly by any means, but in some kind of patchwork fashion.

I knew that I did not want to pursue a full-time rabbinate and that I would need to carve out a career that was part-time, whatever that meant, whatever that means. Four and a half years into my part-time career, I am still unsure how to define it. "Part-time" is one of those amorphous terms, so fluid and changeable at any given moment. Especially in the rabbinate, a career defined by spontaneity and circumstance, by unpredictability and uncertainty, the notion of part-time becomes harder and harder to pinpoint. I don't know many people who are pursuing the rabbinate part-time, perhaps because we as a body have yet to really formalize these kinds of positions or maybe because the idea of part-time differs so dramatically from place to place and person to person. Indeed, how can one serve a congregation "part-time"? How can a rabbi establish boundaries if he or she is supposed to be available and accessible to everyone? How does "part-time" account for pastoral urgencies, family emergencies, and life-cycle events that happen outside the strictures of a nine-to-five day? The part-time rabbinate is a riddle, one that I have yet to adequately solve.

I have two children now, ages two and four, and the questions I most often field are, "Are you *really* part-time?" "How much time do you *really* spend at synagogue?" "Do you know how many hours a week you work?" And I've never quite mastered the art of answering these questions—usually I just laugh and divert the conversation—probably because I have yet to really answer them myself. I don't know if my job would be considered "part-time" outside the rabbinate. Frankly, I don't even know if it would be considered "part-time" by certain folks *within* the rabbinate. Every week, my hours shift. Sometimes I work more and sometime I work less. Should I count the Shabbat I attended services but didn't preside? Should I mention the hours I spent catching up on work while waiting for my son to finish school? Should I include the time I dedicate to work after the children go to bed?

Being a rabbi, whether part-time or full-time, is an intense job, and it can sometimes feel all-consuming. Even if I don't work a certain day or days of the week, programs still need to be planned, classes need to be prepared, sermons need to be written. Even with boundaries in place, many congregational matters transcend those limits, and certainly there is very little room to argue in matters of life and death. And now, in this technological age of e-mails, smartphones, and social media, there is no tolerance for responses returned days later, questions left unanswered, or matters left unattended just because they were presented on a day or weekend off. In this day and age, we expect a certain level of responsiveness every minute of every hour, working day or not.

And herein lies the rub: even with boundaries in place, even with constrictions, even with two (and soon-to-be three) small children demanding so much time and energy, the rabbinate is part and parcel of my every day. It is what I live and breathe, what I eat and drink. It is part of my days and my nights; it is there whether I am in the synagogue or away from it. It is the text I get while sitting in my son's music class and the apologetic phone calls I receive on my days off. It is the pile of e-mails that await my checking after but one hour and the work that continues to build up regardless of whether I am home or at work. Indeed, a rabbi's work, for better or worse, is never done. There is always more to do, and there are always better ways to do it. There are always more people to connect with, more congregants to reach out to, and there are always more questions to ask and more avenues to investigate. There is always more to think about, dream about, envision for the future. And indeed, this is both deepest challenge and the greatest blessing of this sacred work.

Last year, I wrote a sermon about this life of constant interplay between work and home, between the outside world and our internal one, between our public personas and our personal. In the sermon, I looked at *hineini*, the idea of being present for those you love. I concluded with the following words:

> In order to say "Hineini" to someone else, we must first be able to own the word for ourselves. We can't honestly say "Here I am" if we cannot answer the question "Who am I?" And perhaps this is the heart of the matter; in the frenzy and fury of life, we sometimes lose sight of ourselves.

As a female rabbi and as a mother, I ask myself daily, "Who am I?" How will I merge these two roles today? How will I merge them tomorrow? And beyond? Is there a calculation for such a process; is there an equation that guarantees success and satisfaction? How much of my life should be defined by work and how much by family? At the end of the day, I am the only one who can guide this relationship between mother and rabbi; I am the only one who can paint this picture. It is me who must decide how I mix or separate the two identities, how one does or does not influence the other. And it is I who must forge this path, I who must determine my future. No one else can articulate what it means for me to be a mother; no one else can express what it means for me to be a rabbi.

That sermon reflected my struggle, in my fourth year of the rabbinate, to define my boundaries both at work and at home. It is an ongoing struggle, this bifurcated life. But as trying as this life may be, I know it is worthwhile. For in the moments when I am able to extend my hand to another, to embrace someone in need, or to offer words of comfort, I am grounded and I am sated. And when I seize the opportunity to say "*Hineini*" to my children, to my husband, to the congregants I serve, I know why I do what I do. In these moments, God abides. And I see: I am a rabbi. I am a mother. I am a work in progress. And life is a blessing.

PERSONAL REFLECTION:

Journeying to the Edge of the Known and Comprehended World—Becoming a Senior Rabbi

RABBI RUTH A. ZLOTNICK

I received the request to write this reflection just before an eighteen-wheeler pulled out of the driveway of my house in northern New Jersey and hauled the contents of my life to what Annie Dillard has called "the edge of the known and comprehended world,"[1] the Pacific Northwest. As my life was being turned topsy-turvy, I was asked to write about the path that led to my becoming a senior rabbi of a large congregation, because this is a career choice that is somewhat unusual for women.

Now, as I write this from our home on a garden-filled street in the north end of Seattle, I also wonder how I got to this point. I left my small, intimate congregation in the New York area—the only region I've ever called home—to become senior rabbi at Temple Beth Am, a synagogue of close to nine hundred families in what feels to me like the farthest reaches of the continent.

This journey has been somewhat surprising to me. It has been a journey of discovery, of shedding preconceived notions of what leadership is—especially as a female leader—and of learning from missteps and challenges I've experienced along the way.

Early in my career, as an assistant rabbi at a huge urban congregation, I was certain I wouldn't remain in the pulpit rabbinate. I couldn't envision myself as a solo rabbi. I suspect that despite my female rabbinic role models and my feminist consciousness, I had a (false) preconception of a successful pulpit rabbi as a forceful man who inspired others through charismatic persuasion. In thrall to this misconception, I simply assumed that I could not fit the pulpit rabbi mold.

I came to realize that I am not the only one with these false notions. Throughout my career, in many different settings, I have encountered obstacles based on my gender, sometimes because I was the first woman rabbi in the community. I have been critiqued in ways that I suspect reveal an underlying discomfort or lack of familiarity with female leaders. I have been told that my voice is too loud and too soft; my manner is too nice (read: weak) and too professional (read: strong); my clothes are too frumpy and too elegant. At times, I have been hindered by these contradictory voices, not sure how to express my personal leadership style.

Despite these obstacles, however, something always draws me deeper into the congregational world. Although it is sometimes fear inducing, I find synagogue life stretches me in ways I never dreamed possible. For example, while still in my assistantship, I realized that I wanted the challenge of testing my rabbinic skills and surprised myself with a desire to find a pulpit of my own. I focused on small or mid-sized congregations because I felt safer exerting my authority on a smaller stage. Unfortunately, I began my solo career in suburban New Jersey in 2008 during the economic collapse. My community, like so many others, faced devastating fiscal and membership crises.

Being a pulpit rabbi was exhilarating. I was humbled to be brought into people's lives at special moments; I was grateful for the opportunity to teach and preach; I learned from every difficult interaction; I was inspired by so many quietly heroic congregants. Yet I also contended with the lack of resources, the changing demographics, the challenges based on my gender, and the demands of being a working parent. I grew weary, and when my contract came up for renewal, I again questioned my desire to remain on the pulpit.

I raised the issue of leaving congregational life with Rich, my husband, who is a stay-at-home parent, which frees me up to serve a synagogue full-time. No one knew better than he how much stress I was under. His response changed the course of our lives. After a long silence, he said quietly, "I think there is still more for you to discover as a rabbi. I don't think you're done yet." Meanwhile, Rich had hit a milestone birthday that cracked open in him a willingness and desire to explore something new before it was too late, even if it meant that he, a lifelong New Yorker, would have to move away from home.

So the search began. We were fortunate because we were content in our current situation and didn't feel compelled to leave. However, we'd always said that if we were going to leave the New York area, we would seek a place that reflected our values. I also sought a well-resourced, vibrant congregation devoted to egalitarianism. In addition, I was committed to being as authentic as possible during the search process, throwing out any preconceived ideas about what the search committee might be looking for.

I had noticed an application from Temple Beth Am that stood out from the others for me. They wrote that they were not looking for "the best" candidate; instead, they were looking for the best candidate for *them*, they were seeking their *bashert* rabbi. I sensed that this was a congregation who knew who they were and what they stood for. They did not necessarily need to follow the conventional wisdom of what a senior rabbi should be. Instead, they needed to find the right match, someone who also believed in their commitment to full participation, social justice, and innovation.

The rabbinic search process is much like dating—the phone and Skype interviews are first dates when you get to know each other; the in-person interviews bring the relationship to a different level. All the while each party is wondering: can I marry the other? From the very beginning, the search committee and I were in step with each other. I presented a leadership vision focused on collaborative partnerships, consensus building, and Jewish values. In this congregation, because of its culture, its ethos, and its history, my vision was one that was easily accepted and shared.

It has only been a month, and we are still in our "honeymoon" period. Even so, despite the increased responsibilities, my experience at Temple Beth Am has been off to a wonderful, positive beginning. The lay leaders, the staff, and I are all aligned with our shared vision; it has been energizing to roll out that vision with the larger congregation. It helps that I am a more seasoned professional and my husband and daughter are also excited to begin anew in Seattle.

What went into my decision to become a senior rabbi of a large congregation, bucking the conventional path for women rabbis? It was certainly not any goal-oriented plan or desire to achieve a certain status. Instead, it was an unfolding relationship-based process: having a supportive life partner who challenges me to grow spiritually; finding a congregation that shares my sensibilities and values; letting myself experience the uncertainty and risks of a faith journey.

It has been a long path from there to here, the edge of the known and comprehended world. And I am ready. Ready to explore this new horizon and ready to embrace the experience of being a senior rabbi.

NOTE

1. Annie Dillard, *Holy the Firm* (New York: HarperCollins e-books, 2009), loc. 96.

PERSONAL REFLECTION

Leaning In, Leaning Out, and Just Managing to Stand Up
Notes from a Rabbinic Working Mother

Rabbi Hara E. Person

My youngest child has just turned twenty, which means that I am no longer the mother of teenagers. A major life phase is over. I know full well that I'll still be doing plenty of parenting for many years. But symbolically, it feels like the end of something and the start of something new.

These kinds of transitional moments are always opportunities for looking back, and as it happens, a recent encounter provided a further push down reflection road. At a presentation about the choices I made in creating my rabbinic career, I was asked to address my decision to first "lean out" and then "lean in."

The question caught me off guard. When I was first making choices about my career, Sheryl Sandberg had yet to write *Lean In*, nor did that expression exist. But we did talk back then about the "mommy track," and I spent a lot of time in my last year of rabbinical school stressing about the idea that in making a choice based on my children's needs, I was somehow making a choice that was "less than." To my great embarrassment, I remember breaking down in tears to both my rabbinic mentor and my work supervisor because I couldn't figure out how I was going to make it all work. Choosing to not go into congregational work felt like being all dressed up and nowhere to go—like I was wasting my education and letting down the system created to train rabbis.

I had children before I ever had a career. I entered rabbinical school (placing out of the first year in Jerusalem and starting as a second year stateside) with a one-year-old and became pregnant with my second child in my second semester. So all of my rabbinic career decisions have centered around the basic fact of being a parent.

When my classmates in rabbinical school were heading out at the end of the school day to internships, I was heading to the babysitter to pick up my kids. My summers in school weren't spent doing valuable residency internships or CPE training—I was taking care of toddlers who were too young for day camp.

From the moment I had children, I was a working mother. When my first baby was born I was a temple educator; my first separation from her happened when I went in to work ten days after giving birth to run teacher orientation. It was a tough balancing act from the start.

I chose non-congregational work when I was ordained because my children were, at that time, very young. I didn't want a job that would keep me away from them on weekends and evenings and where every phone call could be a possible funeral or congregational crisis. But I never chose to not work.

I never chose to not work partly because I always *wanted* to work—I wanted to contribute to the world, and I wanted to use my skills and education in interesting and stimulating ways. I recognize that a lot of stay-at-home moms feel that they do that by raising their children, but I knew that that would not be true for me. Moreover, I wanted to share the responsibility of supporting my family financially. I did not want to be financially dependent on a man. And I couldn't afford not to work. When I was ordained, my husband was just starting graduate school himself. Realistically, there was no way I couldn't work.

Yes, I was often jealous of the stay-at-home moms who could socialize with each other during afternoon playdates. I worried that I didn't go to enough mommy-and-me classes with my children and that I wasn't around to go to the park. But I found the best balance I could—working two days a week at home for the first few years, being willing to work often crazy hours, and taking on an increasingly taxing travel schedule at some times so that I could be present for school plays and teacher meetings and basketball games at other times.

Early on, I formulated a personal give-and-take policy about work, not one for which I sought approval, but one that helped me make it all work. As the job that I initially accepted because I thought it would provide a good work/life balance began to expand and become huge and insatiably demanding, I made a decision that I would give it my all, but that I would also take when needed. That is, if I was required to be away for travel or expected to get back on the computer at night once my kids were in bed, that was okay; however, when I had a sick child at home or needed to be present for a visit to the orthodontist or a class presentation, I would not apologize for taking the time I needed for my children. Once they were old enough, I also occasionally took them with me to conferences; if I was required to be away from my family over a weekend or over a school break, which was often the case, then they could come. They got to ride a mechanical bull at a CCAR conference in Houston during a spring break, they got to throw themselves against a Velcro wall at a NATE conference in Kansas City during a winter break, and they helped set up book displays at many CAJE conferences during summer breaks.

The dichotomy between leaning in and leaning out is not a helpful or accurate way to describe the reality of balancing parenting and career. It was never a matter of choosing one option over the other. What I did do, in those early years, was find a way to just simply stand up and not collapse. That is, my need and desire to work were in conflict with my need and desire to be a good parent. I found the best imperfect solution possible, one that allowed the insanity of being a working parent to whirl forward.

There was no one magical moment where I suddenly switched from "leaning out" to "leaning in." My job grew and grew, and then I eventually took a different job that continues to grow, and I continue to love what I do and feel challenged and fulfilled by it. And at the same time, my children grew and grew, and their needs and schedules continued to change. Of course there were challenges along the way. Of course there were moments of guilt and worry. Of course there were moments of realizing the balance was way off, and then recalibrating. Of course there were compromises, some satisfying and some utterly not so, and attendant feelings of frustration or inadequacy. It was never a perfect balance, but it worked. All the various pieces in the constellation of my life somehow held up.

From the start of my career, I jumped in with both feet. I was fully committed to my job and its overall mission, even as I was committed to my children. It was never a matter of leaning in or leaning out. Making a career choice based on being a parent is not about leaning out; it's about finding a workable solution. It doesn't mean not being fully committed to one's job or not being ambitious or driven. It's about trying to find a healthy—and feasible—balance.

Along the way, the landscape shifted. Two years ago, my youngest left for college, and my oldest is now a college graduate out in the world, living and working in a different city. As someone who is transitioning out of the "working mother" phase of my life and my rabbinate, I suggest that we talk about the real underlying issues about women and work, like child care, equal opportunities, and equal pay. The false polarity between "leaning out" and "leaning in" is one more way that our society expresses its ambivalence about working mothers. It's one more way that we judge each other. It's one more way that we hold women to a different standard than men. I just did what I had to do to make it all keep spinning.

Part Seven

Image

For decades, the word "rabbi" conjured up a certain stereotypical image. Most pictures or sculptures depict the rabbi as an old man with a long white beard, garbed in Chasidic clothing, and either poring over sacred texts or dancing. This final chapter challenges old images and expectations of what a rabbi looks like and the important ways women have changed perceptions of what a rabbi is and can be.

The ideal rabbi, according to Rabbi Jack H. Bloom's oft-quoted book *The Rabbi as Symbolic Exemplar*, is one who, among other things, stays at a distance from his congregants and is called to put his rabbinic duties ahead of personal ones. Rabbi Sara Mason-Barkin ("The Rabbi as Symbolic Exemplar: A Feminist Critique") argues that Bloom's ideal is a "masculine paradigm" and does not reflect the impact of feminist thought or the ways in which women have challenged the older model. Old models informed how Rabbi Mindy Avra Portnoy ("From Imagination to Reality: *Ima on the Bima*") portrayed the woman rabbi protagonist in her iconic children's book *Ima on the Bima*. Now, thirty years later, she reflects back on the writing of that book and how different—and the same—things look today for women rabbis.

People's outmoded perceptions informed their ideas of what women rabbis ought to be and what they should and should not do. Rabbi Ellen Jay Lewis ("'Funny, You Don't Look Like a Rabbi': Transference and the Female Rabbi") illustrates how the first generation of women rabbis needed to push beyond the conceptions of others in order to define themselves. Rabbi Wendy Spears ("The Public Image of the Woman Rabbi") describes how people expect women rabbis to look and act a certain way and why that needs to change, while Rabbi Leah Rachel Berkowitz ("A Mirror, a Prism, and a Telescope: Reimagining Role Models") reconciles prior standards by recasting them through the prism of biblical women.

Fictional women rabbis, in print and on screen, both reflect and impact how Jews and non-Jews perceive women rabbis. Dr. Wendy Zierler ("Portraits of the Rabbi as a Young Woman") and Rabbi David J. Zucker ("Searching for the Fictional Woman Rabbi on the Small and Large Screen") illustrate the myriad ways the publishing world and Hollywood have portrayed the female rabbi and their implications.

This section concludes with personal reflections from Dasi Fruchter ("Rabbis in Red Lipstick"), Rabbi Jordie Gerson ("Letter to Hollywood—I Don't Have a Beard or Side Curls and I Look Just Like You: American Judaism's Image Problem"), and Rabbi Elizabeth S. Wood ("Dropping the 'R-Bomb'") of how others' perceptions of what a female rabbi should look like or how a female rabbi should behave have directly impacted their lives.

40

THE RABBI AS SYMBOLIC EXEMPLAR

A Feminist Critique

RABBI SARA MASON-BARKIN

There was one afternoon in rabbinical school that left many of my thoughtful and articulate classmates speechless. While examining the complexity of dual relationships, we were assigned reading from Rabbi Jack H. Bloom's *The Rabbi as Symbolic Exemplar*.[1] Bloom warns his readers that congregants will peek into their rabbis' shopping carts at the store and gossip about the rabbi's children. As Bloom explains, "The rabbi's family never really belongs." My peers left class that day wondering about the career they'd chosen and how it would impact their families and themselves. They now understood that their spouses and children would never live normal lives again because they chose to enter into this "fishbowl" life. They were overwhelmed by Bloom's designation of the rabbi as a symbol for God on earth.

Having lived a version of Bloom's story as the child of a rabbi, I left class frustrated. In *The Rabbi as Symbolic Exemplar*, Bloom advocates for strictly drawn boundaries and hierarchies, placing the rabbi on a different level from the laity he serves. Bloom writes that the rabbi will always symbolize a God on high, always separate from the people. This was not the life I'd known as a rabbi's daughter, and it was not the life that I intended to live after my own ordination.

Rabbi Jack H. Bloom was ordained in 1959 by the Jewish Theological Seminary. He developed the concept of the "rabbi as symbolic exemplar" as his doctoral dissertation in 1972. (As a result, the book exists in a context in which all rabbis were men.) Bloom's proposed model emerges as a distinctly masculine paradigm of what it means to be a rabbi, simply by virtue of the fact that it does not, and could not in its time, take into account the effects of feminist thought on rabbinic practice or the ways in which women themselves—directly and indirectly—have changed the role of the rabbi. In 1991, Rabbi Janet Marder noted that nineteen years of women in the rabbinate had led to noticeable changes in what had previously been an exclusively male profession.[2] Marder noticed trends related to the ways that women set boundaries differently than did their male colleagues, the kinds of congregational jobs that women prefer, and the ways that women build relationships with co-workers and congregants.[3]

Since Marder's article was published more than twenty years ago, the presence of women rabbis has become normative. When I entered Hebrew Union College–Jewish Institute of Religion (HUC-JIR) as a rabbinical student in 2004, my rabbinical class was made up of fifty-four students, only sixteen of them men. As of 2012, nearly one-third of Reform rabbis were female.[4] In 2006, HUC-JIR ordained the first openly transgender rabbi,[5] adding further complication to the supposed male-female gender binary and expanding our understanding of what it means to identify as either male or female in the rabbinate. The complexity with which we now understand gender roles—sets of expectations and behaviors that were assumed and taken for granted in previous generations—brings new sophistication to how we understand the role of "rabbi." While Bloom does not intentionally present a gendered model of the rabbinate, his model is androcentric simply because he was unable to imagine a rabbinate that would be so deeply influenced by feminism or simply by the presence of women. Evidence suggests that a new rabbi has emerged in the present day, a role that blends, in myriad ways, those voices that we might once have labeled "male" and "female." This is, without a doubt, a positive development. In addition to having a more holistic tool set with which to serve congregants and constituents in varied rabbinic roles, today's rabbi is better able to be accepted as his or her authentic self without building the walls, boundaries, or limitations of separation that Bloom insists are the hallmark of the rabbinic life. Thankfully, the yoke of symbolic exemplarhood is not one that today's rabbis must bear—at least not by necessity.

The world and the rabbinate have changed since the publication of *The Rabbi as Symbolic Exemplar*. Feminism has given us new language to describe and participate in relationships where power differentials exist, changing—if not eliminating—the need for Bloom's concrete boundaries. In her book *In a Different Voice*, groundbreaking ethicist and psychologist Carol Gilligan emphasized relationship rather than hierarchy.[6] Published in 1982, ten years after the publication of *The Rabbi as Symbolic Exemplar*, *In a Different Voice* documents different and distinct ways in which males and females arrive at moral decisions. For males, Gilligan describes hierarchical systems of justice. For females, she describes a web of interconnected relationships.[7] According to Gilligan, this is a result of a difference during childhood: boys identify themselves as "separate from" their typically female caretakers, whereas females grow up "in relation to" their typically female caretakers.

According to Bloom, a primary role of the rabbi as symbolic exemplar is to be a model of moral Jewish living for his "flock." But if men and women approach moral decision making from different perspectives, then male and female rabbis are likely to approach their moral exemplarhood from these separate perspectives as well. Bloom's description of the rabbi as a moral exemplar aligns with Gilligan's description of a typically male system of hierarchy. Bloom explains that the rabbi is expected to be above and beyond the ordinary expectations of morality at all times and in all situations.[8] This obsessive attention to separation appears throughout *The Rabbi as Symbolic Exemplar*, and it is the primary reason the work demands reexamination since the ordination of women has become mainstream.

Bloom describes "rules," or boundaries, that a rabbi must draw between himself and his congregants. Because "the rabbi's family never really belongs," the rabbi cannot establish true friendships. Within Bloom's conception of the rabbinic role, the rabbi, who practices a Judaism that is ancient, fragile, and untouchable, symbolizes both God as well as the ideal Jew. To adhere strictly to Bloom's model and accept the role of symbolic exemplar results in a rabbinic life absent of relationship (aside from those with other rabbis) amid unreasonable pressure to meet impossible expectations. A symbolic exemplar lives a life mired in the deepest loneliness: the kind one feels while always surrounded by people.

For those who have always known the rabbinate to be egalitarian and who are the product of a Reform Movement that was deeply influenced by feminism and feminist thought, I propose a new model for the rabbinic role—one rooted in Gilligan's language of relationship rather than Bloom's language of hierarchy. It is possible to define the role of rabbi as part of an interconnected web of true, albeit complicated, relationships. The rabbi may decide for herself when to build a wall and how porous it will be, and when to build a bridge of connection. This paradigm of a rabbinate of relationship rather than hierarchy is favorable not only because it may feel more authentic to rabbis born after 1972, but also because it offers a potential for all rabbis to expand their ability to realistically, and honestly, touch the lives of the people with whom they interact.

The Hierarchical Rabbinate versus the Relational Rabbinate

Feminist therapy introduces a nonhierarchical understanding of the therapist-client relationship, offering a model that is adaptable to the rabbinate. In feminist therapy, patient and therapist work together to address the challenges the client is facing.

> Feminist therapy has…re-examined the role of the therapist and the nature of the therapeutic relationship. It has questioned the notions of professionalism which many of us have inherited from our traditional training. We have seen this to be an eminently

masculine model of therapy in which the therapist is yet another patriarchal figure, the Expert whose superior knowledge cures the passive, powerless and unknowing patient. In feminist therapy, the ideal of an all-powerful, distant, patriarchal expert has given way to an ideal of two women working together in a much more egalitarian, empathic, and responsive way.[9]

In a hierarchical model of therapy, the patient puts his complete trust in the therapist to do the healing. This is parallel to symbolic exemplarhood, where the rabbi is expected to facilitate Jewish life on behalf of his congregants as well as provide for their pastoral needs. In contrast, the feminist therapist works *with* the patient to facilitate solutions, rather than directing the patient in the way that that feminist critics see in "traditional" therapy. An onlooker of feminist therapy might see two women sitting side by side: one with a problem and one who is an expert assigned to help solve it. While boundaries between client and therapist exist, they are not hierarchical. Rather, they are defined individually and organically by those involved in the relationship.

In a hierarchical rabbinate, it may be shocking for the congregant to see the rabbi engaging in ordinary tasks about town. In this model, when the congregant sees the mysterious and ethereal rabbi doing the ordinary things that humans do, it confuses the relationship. Proponents of feminist therapy address similar, though not identical, scenarios and suggest ways to transfer a relational perspective to the clergy.[10] The author suggests that the feminist therapist may find herself in a similar multiple-role situation as the rabbi, particularly if the therapist practices in a small community. The therapist, too, may encounter the moment when she runs into a client at the grocery store and has to transition from a personal mentality to one that is professional. Feminist therapy offers a view on these scenarios, whereby the transition from professional to personal is downplayed by the relational nature of their association.

Katherine M. Clarke, professor and chair of applied psychology at Antioch University writes, "Feminist therapists have adopted a conceptual framework in which boundary maintenance and the therapist's self-care are synergistic rather than competing principles of ethical action."[11] By beginning from a basis of one-to-one relationship, rather than a power differential, feminist therapy encourages both the patient and the therapist to enter the relationship from a human level from the very beginning, so that when the two women encounter one another outside the context of therapy, there is synergy rather than conflict. This does not assume an automatic mutual closeness, nor does it automatically mean that therapist and client are friends. There is a power difference that exists because one is the client paying for a therapeutic service, and the other is the expert who is entrusted with the client's vulnerability. What it *does* do is allow for the two people in question to determine the boundaries as they deem appropriate within the boundaries of established professional ethics—rather than boundaries that are assumed by the power differential. When the two see one another in public, there does not have to be excessive sharing, but there can be a warm hello and smile—or even conversation, if it is comfortable and the situation allows, without detriment to the therapeutic relationship. In this case, the interaction is guided by the relationship, rather than the relationship guided by hierarchical boundaries.

Martin E. Marty, religious scholar and Lutheran pastor, writes about the importance of relationships for clergy, explaining that "friends say to people who acquire power and position—and even the pastor of the humblest parish has some of that—'Watch it, buddy,' or 'we knew you when....'"[12] When the rabbi embraces the charge to be completely "separate from" his congregation, true human relationship is lost. While the rabbi is filling symbolic functions for congregants, everyone forgets the rabbi's true status as human being. Bloom argues that congregants do not *want* to hear that their rabbis are just like them: "For if the congregations were to treat the rabbi as simply human, as the rabbi might sometimes like them to, there would be no need to have a rabbi."[13] However, Marty teaches that if clergy are constantly operating among the pressures of symbolic exemplarhood, they will be ineffective in their roles. In a relational model of the rabbinate, rabbis need to teach their congregants how to care for themselves and their families.

The relational model of the rabbi begins with authenticity. The rabbi does not need to argue the ways in which she is "ordinary"; rather, as a fellow human being and not a symbol, she must let people into the ways in which she understands Judaism and God. This requires the rabbi to be honest and vocal about the ways that she finds meaning in text, brings *simchah* (joy) to Jewish ritual even in busy times, and notices the *kodesh* (sacred) in the everyday. The rabbi can do this by telling personal stories, when appropriate, from the bimah, meeting in coffee shops and community gatherings for conversations, and sharing the ways she reconciles theology with modern life.

Consequences for the Rabbinate

It is difficult, if not impossible, to change others' expectations of who the rabbi ought to be; it is possible, however, for the rabbi to be intentional in the way that she fulfills social expectations. Instead of seeing herself as separate from the people, living a holy life in a fishbowl on display, the rabbi can enter into relationship with congregants, teaching and preaching from an authentic perspective as one who dwells among them.

In a feminist re-visioning, where the whole community is simply striving for authenticity rather than perfection, the rabbi's spouse and the rabbi's children can come down from the pedestals upon which they have been placed alongside their rabbinic family member. When the rabbi is just a Jew on the path to realizing her own potential, the rabbi's family can be Jews on the path as well. Though it seems simple, the move away from symbolic exemplarhood is more drastic than it sounds. Perhaps this is because it requires a reeducation for the congregation about who and what the rabbi really is. It requires the rabbi to open up in a way that she has likely been taught not to do. It requires the rabbi to be a little bit vulnerable and a little bit exposed. It requires the seminaries to rethink the ways that they teach rabbinical students to understand their role—for all rabbinical students are, at first, observers of rabbis. Some rabbinical students might enter rabbinical school thinking of themselves as "separate from," expecting to undergo a transitional moment in their education when they become a symbol. Rabbinical students might feel that they deserve a position "on high." The goal of seminaries ought not be to raise up rabbinical students to this falsely elevated position, but rather to bring rabbinical students to understand their roles as teachers and as guides on the ground and in relationship with laypeople.

Lastly, this vision for the rabbinate requires some sacrifice on the part of the rabbi. While Bloom's depiction of the symbolic exemplar is ultimately lonely and unfulfilled in day-to-day life, some of that emptiness may be filled by the power and prestige that the rabbi gains as a symbol for God. When a rabbi is "separate from" the community, he may find he is regarded with an element of celebrity. When he stands in for God, he will be revered and honored. Symbolic exemplarhood is seductive. To be a symbol, however, is as dangerous as it is attractive. In order to be fulfilled by this feminist "re-visioning" of the rabbinate, the rabbi must relinquish any desire that he might have to be seen as a symbol on high.

Balancing Relational and Hierarchical

It should be noted that Gilligan's ideas are not without significant critique.[14] It is possible that a purely relational model (in Gilligan's terms, operating exclusively in an "ethic of care" rather than an "ethic of justice") is not achievable or even desirable for the rabbi who is personally or professionally committed to maintaining systems of rules and regulations. Indeed, this is often an issue of personal style more than one of ideology. Similarly, the rabbi who is unfailing and unequivocal in her empathy will burn out as quickly as the rabbi who is stringent in her adherence to logic and problem solving. In other words, all rabbis must exhibit a balance of both *chesed* (compassion) and *din* (judgment) in daily interactions and be able to decipher which is appropriate at which time. There may be times when a "relational" rabbi needs to work from an "ethic of justice." (For example, consider the beloved administrative assistant who must be dismissed and reported to authorities after being found to have stolen funds from the synagogue.) Similarly, there may be times when a rabbi chooses to violate her own personal boundaries—for example, choosing to miss a usually prioritized dinner at home because a congregant has suffered a personal tragedy. Such balance makes sense for us as Reform Jews; Torah gives a clear set of guiding principles, and as autonomous individuals, we can use Torah to guide our empathetic hearts.

Critics of the relational rabbinate argue that because of the multiple roles that a rabbi must occupy, it is impossible to enter into an authentically intimate relationship with congregants. They argue that because the rabbi is in the position to counsel and advise congregants, and also to schmooze at an *oneg* with them or negotiate a contract with them, it is in the rabbi's best interest to protect the way that she is separate from them. In other words, the rabbi has an "on" persona, whether it is on the bimah or at the supermarket, and an "off" persona that is seen only in the home or with other rabbinic colleagues. Bloom's model asserts that the rabbi needs to maintain strict boundaries in order to protect the mystique and the authority of the position. If the rabbi is to enter into *true* relationship—not a hierarchical relationship, but one where rabbi and congregant can sit face to face and truly see one another as people—the rabbi would be needlessly exposed as human, and she would lose the *kavod* that is demanded by the position.

In Conclusion

In order to find satisfaction in a relational rabbinate, one must gently and thoughtfully introduce this new framework in which respect for the rabbinic position is enhanced by the way that the rabbi approaches her position with humanity and authenticity.

In the relational rabbinate, the rabbi is expected to be a guide and a role model—not a symbol. The relational rabbi can enable other Jews to be comfortable with their own Jewish lives as well. When rabbis are no longer pretending to be symbols of God and the ideal Jew, congregants can realize that they, like their rabbis, are able to realistically live authentic Jewish lives. Such authenticity allows the whole community to see that the ideal Jew does not have to be like God; the ideal Jew simply has to be oneself, already made in God's image, striving for meaning in a thoughtful and purposeful way.

NOTES

1. Jack H. Bloom, *Rabbi as Symbolic Exemplar* (NY: Routledge, 2012).

2. Janet Marder, "How Women Are Changing the Rabbinate," *Reform Judaism*, Summer 1991, 1–8, 41.

3. Ibid.

4. "Survey: Women Earn Far Less Than Men as Reform Rabbis," *Jewish Week*, June 20, 2012, http://www.thejewishweek.com/news/breaking-news/survey-women-earn-far-less-men-reform-rabbis.

5. Rebecca Spence, "Transgender Jews Now Out of Closet, Seeking Communal Recognition," *Jewish Daily Forward*, December 31, 2008, http://www.forward.com/articles/14854/.

6. Carol Gilligan, *In a Different Voice: Psychological Theory and Women's Development* (Cambridge, MA: Harvard University Press, 1982).

7. Ibid., 29.

8. Bloom, *Rabbi as Symbolic Exemplar*, 149.

9. Miriam Greenspan, "Should Therapists Be Personal? Self Disclosure and Therapeutic Distance in Feminist Therapy," in *Dynamic of Feminist Therapy*, ed. Doris Howard (New York: Hayworth Press, 1986), 6.

10. Katherine M. Clarke, "Lessons from Feminist Therapy for Ministerial Ethics," *Journal of Pastoral Care* 48, no. 3 (September 1994), 233–43.

11. Ibid., 240.

12. Martin E. Marty, "What Friends Are For," *Christian Century* 109 (November 1992): 988.

13. Bloom, *Rabbi as Symbolic Exemplar*, 136.

14. In addition to the critiques mentioned here, other critiques of Gilligan's work include questions about the methodology she used in her research (whether they upheld commonly practiced research standards). See Christina Hoff Sommers, *The War against Boys: How Misguided Feminism Is Harming Our Young Men* (New York: Simon and Schuster, 2000), 107.

Feminist scholars also critique the theory of "difference feminism," born out of Gilligan's work. Scholars question whether difference, the idea that men and women are inherently different from one another, has created an impasse for feminist thought by claiming that the differences are essential, and not related to culture. See Diana Fuss, "The 'Risk' of Essence," in *Feminist Theory: A Reader*, ed. Frances Bartkowsky and Wendy Kolmar (Mountain View, CA: Mayfield Publishing, 2000), 423–32.

41

FROM IMAGINATION TO REALITY

Ima on the Bima

RABBI MINDY AVRA PORTNOY

I was thirty-five years old, married, and the mother of an infant and a two-and-a-half-year-old when my children's book (ultimately, the first of five) *Ima on the Bima (My Mommy Is a Rabbi)* was published in 1986.[1] I had been ordained a rabbi in 1980 at Hebrew Union College–Jewish Institute of Religion (HUC-JIR, New York campus) and had spent five years serving as a Hillel director at the American University in Washington, DC. I had just begun working part-time at a Reform congregation (Temple Sinai) and knew little about the life of a congregational rabbi, and only a little more about raising children. The book evolved more from my imagination than from reality and experience. *Ima on the Bima* was more reflective of the person I thought I would become than the person I already was.

I had conceived of the title first: *Ima on the Bima*. Such a "cute" title; surely one of my colleagues would write it. Why not me? I still had a lot to prove, as did all of us who were women rabbis by 1986 (about one hundred). Until that date, I was "just" a Hillel rabbi; what would happen when I entered a "real" congregation?

Ima on the Bima would become a template for me, as it would for many women who came after me. In its early days, the book became the perfect baby gift for women rabbis who became mothers; twenty-seven years later, young women rabbis tell me at conventions of the Women's Rabbinic Network (WRN, the association of Reform women rabbis) that their parents read them the book when they were young. For some of them, it sparked the desire to become rabbis themselves.

The life I created in this simple children's book turned out differently for every woman in the rabbinate. Every woman's personal situation, background, aspirations, geographical location, sexual orientation, and family structure were unique. Astonishingly enough, not all women rabbis looked alike, although early on we were often mistaken for one another (how often I was thanked for speeches I had not delivered!).

And yet, the experience of being a woman in the rabbinate bonded us all together back then in a tight sisterhood, and even now there is a personal connection that transcends even our profound differences and particularities. After forty years of women in the rabbinate, there is no single reality that fully represents the totality of who we are. We are a myriad of realities, able to look to others as role models, teachers, mentors.

But in the beginning there was only the imagination…

And Sally went first. When Sally J. Priesand entered the joint University of Cincinnati and HUC-JIR program in 1964, "few people paid that much attention, thinking I came to marry a rabbi rather than be one."[2] In the spring of 1972, my mother sent me the article about Sally in the *New York Times*, titled "Her Ambition Is to Become a Rabbi— and a Housewife."[3] I ignored the rather deprecating headline and focused instead on the accompanying picture showing soon-to-be Rabbi Priesand clad in typical 1970s mini-skirted garb, perusing a text in the library, someone just like me. The evidence was in my hands: Sally Priesand's imagination had transcended the experience of thousands of years of women in Judaism.

As Rabbi Karen Fox wrote, "For five thousand years women were involved in the private domain of Jewish life while men controlled the public arenas. A few women were prophets—Devorah, Miriam, Huldah, and Noadia, a few were military leaders—Yael and Devorah…a few women (were) scholars—Ima Shalom and Bruriah. But until very recent times women did not count in a Minyan...could not be witnesses.... Within the structure of Jewish law and, therefore, within the reality of Jewish life, women were obligated only to house-bound, family-centered Mitzvot."[4] Women rabbis, beginning with Rabbi Priesand, would not only transcend the past but transform the present and the future for all Jewish women.

Fourteen years after Rabbi Priesand's ordination, the cover of *Ima on the Bima* still seemed like a pictorial oxymoron. A young woman with dark curly hair was depicted at a podium, wearing a tallit and leading a service (the *kippah* would not visibly appear until the inside pages). It was provocative enough that certain Jewish bookstores would not stock it or would keep it hidden "behind the counter." The concept of a woman as *sh'lichat tzibur* (representative of the congregation, i.e., prayer leader), now commonplace in all but Orthodox synagogues, was still unusual enough in 1986 to elicit frequent comments, most often "I've never met/seen a woman rabbi before." That would often be followed by "How many women rabbis are there?" and then, as the years passed, the replacement and/or additional question, "Do you know _____ [insert name of another woman rabbi]?" For at least a decade, we usually did. And even now, more than six hundred Reform women rabbis later, our WRN meetings, conventions, and dinners often seem in part like family reunions, as we aging women rabbis marvel at our growing numbers and the fact that we don't know everyone's first names (and personal life histories) anymore!

The Ima in the book was of course a rabbi serving a congregation. At the beginning, aspiring to any other rabbinic role felt like a compromise. And in fact, the Reform rabbinical seminary, HUC-JIR, encouraged that thinking. Although many rabbinical students (both male and female) would serve as educators, hospital chaplains, organizational assistants, and social activists as part of our training, the ultimate internship goal was the "bi-weekly," which meant serving as a rabbi in a small, underserved congregation or (even better) as an assistant to a rabbi in a large congregation. This would hopefully lead to a plum offer in one's last year of school for a full-time job in a congregation following ordination.

In order for Ima to serve as a role model in 1986, she had to be depicted as a rabbi in a congregation. That would be the ultimate test, so we thought, of the success or failure of women in the rabbinate. Even now, as jobs in congregations have become more scarce for all rabbis and as we have expanded the concept of success (at least, to some degree) to include rabbis in non-congregational settings, notions of "senior rabbis," particularly in large, urban congregations, still serve as a benchmark for many (not to mention offering the highest salary levels).

Ima had a male cantorial colleague. In 1986, it would have seemed unrealistic to show two women professionals on the bimah together, at a time when concerns had already begun to be expressed about the potential "feminization" of the synagogue.

Ima dressed for services in traditional Jewish male ritual garb, tallit and *kippah*. Her choice of ritual vestments had as much to do with the era as with her gender. By the 1980s, many Reform rabbis, unlike their earlier counterparts, were becoming accustomed to leading services in tallit and *kippah* over their regular clothing or clerical robe. No woman wore pants on the bimah at the time; the only time Ima wore pants in the book was when she was at home with her daughter, a clear representation of the work/home divide. However, many women rabbis did wear robes, as did the male cantor in the book, so that comments on choice of dress (length of skirt, style of suit, color of blouse, choice of jewelry) would wait until *oneg*-time evaluation.

Other women (as Ima), like some of their male colleagues, were eschewing the "robe" model as too formal and not particularly Jewish in origin. But a tallit and a *kippah* made a major feminist statement, particularly in congregations where most women and even many men did not wear them. In a paradoxical way, women rabbis in traditionally male ritual garb were viewed as both "more traditional" and a "total break with tradition." No one quite knew what to make of us, and we ourselves struggled to piece together the sartorial puzzle. In the late

1970s, at an early WRN meeting, Rabbi Carole Meyers (z"l) led a discussion about clothing as symbol; one of the pertinent questions was how to dress for an evening wedding ceremony when one is both the officiant and a guest. In most places, the "pants" issue has long been resolved, with the advent of pantsuits, but even today, at our WRN conventions and on our women rabbi's listserv, women occasionally ask for advice and offer suggestions about appropriate dress and share inappropriate comments they hear about their fashion style, their hair, their weight, their nail polish color, their shoes, and so on (much of this is shared by female clergy of other denominations, as well as women professionals in general).[5] In 2013, however, the issue is seen as far more trivial, and we have discovered that our male colleagues receive their share of such comments as well. Today, we are much more likely to dress to individual taste even on the bimah, rather than in a monochromatic manner.

Ima on the Bima was really a book about what all congregational rabbis do, including but not limited to women, but only young children with no preconceptions of who should do what or children in congregations with women rabbis saw it that way. In an article I wrote about Ima in 1988, I remarked, "Nowhere in the book does the five-year-old daughter of the rabbi comment on the fact that it is strange or peculiar for mommy to be rabbi, rather than daddy."[6] Everyone else saw the woman before the rabbi.

And just by the nature of the gender transformation, the book was subversive. The very first thing Ima does professionally is escort a man out of her office who has presumably been seeing her for some kind of counseling. What have they been talking about? Who knows? The shock is softened by the rabbi's daughter innocently sitting outside the office waiting for the meeting to be over. "Part of Ima's job is to make people happier, and I try to help Ima do her job."[7] In those early days, when laypeople thought about pastoral counseling at all, it was most often suggested that women rabbis might be especially adept at counseling other women, who would be more "comfortable" speaking to a female clergyperson, especially about "women's issues." In a sense, a woman rabbi could be an effective marketing tool for a synagogue with multiple clergy perhaps.

Did it work that way? The statistics are hard to gauge. There is no question that many more women came to see the rabbinate as more accessible and that the increase of women in leadership roles in the synagogue more generally can be attributed in part to female rabbinic leadership, but the man emerging from Ima's office was no aberration. Men, too, would change their evaluation of the rabbinate in light of female rabbinic leadership and the changing roles of women everywhere in society; the idea of seeing a woman pastoral counselor/rabbi would seem less and less idiosyncratic. And in my temple, for example, with two full-time rabbis (one male, one female) for many years, I was the one who knew far more about sports!

Ima of course officiates at life-cycle ceremonies; due to the brevity of the book, I chose the "safe" one, a wedding. In retrospect, I regret that I did not include the one I came to see as central to the spirit of the times, the naming ceremony for a baby girl. By 1986, there was an explosion of interest in this redefined ritual, and often parents looked to women rabbis (known personally to them or referred by others) to officiate. Similarly, women rabbis would more and more often receive phone calls from individual unknown to them looking for a "woman rabbi" to officiate at their wedding ceremony. (As my esteemed colleague Rabbi Rosalind Gold would say with an ironic smile on her face, when someone who doesn't know you personally calls you looking for a "woman rabbi," make sure you tell them you charge extra for your uterus!).

We all officiated at hundreds of these naming ceremonies, using creative readings, texts that mimicked the *b'rit milah* ceremony (minus the circumcision): a few substituting new rituals, such as ear-piercing or foot washing, others invoking the Matriarchs and other heroines of Jewish history, some taking place on the eighth day after birth, others when it was more convenient for the family. Eventually, these baby-naming ceremonies (*b'rit banot*, "covenant for daughters," or *simchat bat*, "rejoicing in a daughter," the most commonly used titles) became standard operating procedure for most non-Orthodox Jews, just as the bat mitzvah (later in the book) had already become *de rigueur* in synagogues. Without women in the rabbinate, this reconceived and elaborated rite of passage would not have flourished. It was part of a new package of gender-equal Judaism, a tide that might flow in gentler or stronger ways in different communities but could not be turned back.

The wedding in the book was a little bit of a compromise. Ima officiates at the wedding, but there is no mention of an egalitarian *ketubah*, female witnesses, two rings, perhaps both bride and groom breaking the glass. And Ima even throws in her daughter as the flower girl (at no extra cost?). But in 1986 the wedding page showed that women rabbis, at the very minimum, could be in charge of life-cycle ceremonies.

In reality, it was more often the idea of women officiating at funerals that gave congregants pause. Even though the rabbi as *m'sadeir/m'saderet kiddushin* (organizer of the wedding ceremony) is much more critical than his/her role at a funeral, at which any individual can officiate, the question of tradition and "what looks right" took hold more strongly for the latter. In an article in 1985, Rabbi Joy Levitt quoted the words of a congregant who asked her not to officiate at the funeral of his mother "because, well, it's not that I don't like you, but people just wouldn't feel comfortable with a woman."[8] Should a new edition of *Ima on the Bima* appear today, there would be no life-cycle ceremony, at least within the Reform Movement, that would appear out-of-bounds for female rabbinic officiation. Familiarity with women clergy officiating has bred—well—familiarity.

Another missing piece in *Ima* is liturgical language. In retrospect, it may have seemed a dangerous topic at the time. If women were to be rabbis, they would have to be "replacement males," doing the same work in the same way with the same language as their male counterparts. Even though liturgical language for God (and certainly inclusion of the Matriarchs) had begun to change, and a significant number of male rabbis supported and contributed to this linguistic revolution, *Ima* was shocking enough without toppling any basic traditions. When an article appeared in an Israeli newspaper about women rabbis, the Hebrew descriptive term was *Rav Isha* (essentially, a "male rabbi who is a woman").[9] And that's what Ima would be, at least for a while: a male rabbi in female guise. After all, male rabbis too had small children, although Rebecca's ubiquity in the book was notable. But Ima in 1986 could not be publicly pregnant, even though a number of women rabbis already had been. We were still on the cusp of widespread acceptance, and to acknowledge pregnancy in a children's book would have doomed the book's success, perhaps even its publication. But Rebecca never disappears, and she is ultimately the fulcrum of the story, and the inevitable ostensible obstacle to Ima's role on the bimah.

Throughout the book, Rebecca shows up, at work and at home. She is old enough to be somewhat independent (no need for Ima to deal with a clinging infant), but not old enough to rebel at having to be at the temple so often. She is well-behaved, affable, an only child, at least so far. A moment of possible tension arises when she acknowledges the work/life problematic of any rabbi: "Sometimes, Ima's job just doesn't make sense. Jewish people aren't supposed to work on Shabbat and the Jewish holidays, but rabbis have to." Clearly, this young daughter is beginning to realize that the rabbinate is a demanding profession, which takes the parent away from family at precisely the moments when Jewish families are intended to be together. The "problem" is temporarily resolved by Ima's apparently working in a congregation where she doesn't have to officiate at every Erev Shabbat service. A neat literary trick, but it was (and is) no doubt an anomaly for most female rabbis (male ones, too), who in all likelihood must be present on the bimah every Friday night.

Ima also seems to work at home. In fact, Ima apparently operates on a seven-day work schedule. At home, she writes and talks on the telephone (in the days before e-mail) "too much." People call her to ask questions and invite her to meetings. Sometimes I hear her say, "No, I'm sorry I can't come. Rebecca (that's me!) and I are busy that day." That makes me smile. Although Rebecca is smiling in the accompanying illustration, there exists an edgy competition between professional and personal life throughout the text. Today we call it "work/life" balance, and we still struggle with all its implications. In 1986, the goal was to project a woman who could do it all, with perfect equanimity, a supportive husband in the background, and a very helpful child.

The reality of a rabbi who was also a single mom, for example, would have seemed beyond the imagination, and yet of course they too existed. As Rabbi Vicki Hollander writes, "Once when my daughter was in preschool (I was a single mom), in the car she announced she wanted to be a rabbi in the morning and a tightrope walker in the afternoon. The perfect image of rabbinic work."[10]

Perhaps most importantly, Ima was a role model, and not only for her daughter. In the book, Rachel becomes a bat mitzvah, standing next to her female rabbi. Rabbi Ellen Jay Lewis's story about an experience in 1977 encapsulates the image best. She was serving a congregation outside Pittsburgh as a part-time student rabbi when she met a young girl who was soon to become a bat mitzvah. Rabbi Lewis wrote, "As the time grew closer, we began to rehearse in the sanctuary. One day as we were standing on the bima working out the final details of the ceremony, Beth looked up at me. 'Rabbi Lewis,' she began hesitantly, 'for my Bat Mitzvah, do you think we could wear matching dresses?'"[11] Rabbi Lewis perceptively noted that the entrance of women would broaden the rabbinate and expand possibilities for the next generation. If you were a thirteen-year-old girl and your rabbi was a female rabbi, then you could be a rabbi too.

Ima as a role model would herself embody limitations. It would turn out as the years passed that some women rabbis might be older (mid-career); lesbian; single; single mom. Ima would open the door not only for herself and other mothers and other women, but also for men who did not fit the traditional model of "married heterosexual with two children." And as the first generation of women rabbis enters retirement, we will create new models for that stage as well.

Other women had earlier made the attempt to be ordained before Sally Priesand but had been denied the opportunity. When Sally sought ordination, she had the support of many in the institutional

Reform Movement, and the climate of late-1960s second-stage feminism provided fortuitous timing as well. And yet even with that support and that timing, all of this began in the imagination of one woman, one individual. Forty years later, that imagination has been so fully realized that it is possible now for some of us simply to be rabbis who happen to be women, others of us to choose to focus on issues of particular concern to women, some of us to identify most strongly with our female colleagues, others with all colleagues, most of us with both.

We know there is still work ahead of us as women rabbis, even in the Reform Movement, particularly on issues such as pay equity, senior rabbinical placement, and leadership in the Movement, not to mention, of course, in the larger Jewish world.

But Ima accomplished her task, which was simply to make women rabbis look normal, fulfilled, capable, and in charge. Twenty-seven years later, I think I should have made Ima look a little tired, but in 1986, there was no time to rest. Realism still needed to look optimistic, hopeful, energetic.

Perhaps only in retirement do rabbis learn to rest on Shabbat. Women rabbis included.

NOTES

1. Mindy Avra Portnoy, *Ima on the Bima* (Rockville, MD: Kar-Ben Copies, 1986).

2. Sally J. Priesand, "Reflections of a Retired Rabbi (Almost)," *WRN News*, June 2006.

3. George Vecsey, "Her Ambition Is to Become a Rabbi—And a Housewife," *New York Times*, April 13, 1971.

4. Karen L. Fox, "Whither Women Rabbis?" *Religious Education* 76, no. 4 (July–August, 1981): 361.

5. Elizabeth Hayt, "Women of Which Cloth? Tweed? Cashmere?" *New York Times*, March 28, 1999.

6. Mindy Portnoy, "A Mommy, a Rabbi: The Jewish Juggling Act," *Washington Jewish Week*, May 5, 1988.

7. Portnoy, *Ima* (unpaginated).

8. Joy Levitt, "Woman Rabbis: A Pyrrhic Victory?" *Reconstructionist*, January–February 1985.

9. Yoram Lehman, "Kawl Isha Yechola" ("Every Woman Can"), *Koteret Rashit*, March 3, 1984.

10. Rabbi Vicki Hollander, personal correspondence, November 20, 2012.

11. Rabbi Ellen Jay Lewis, "The Priorities of a Woman Rabbi," *Sh'ma* 13, no. 250 (March 18, 1983): 75–76.

42

"FUNNY, YOU DON'T LOOK LIKE A RABBI"

Transference and the Female Rabbi

RABBI ELLEN JAY LEWIS, LP, NCPsyA

Looking back over the last forty years, it is not hard to see how the decade of the seventies provided fertile ground for the ordination of the first American woman rabbi. The late sixties had been a time of turmoil. Political upheaval and social rebellion had filled the air and spilled over into the streets. How unlikely it would have been, had the American Jewish community remained exempt from this revolutionary zeal and promise, particularly given the Jewish commitment to justice as a core value. Given how political radicalism spawned modern secular feminism, the rise of Jewish feminism appears now as having been inevitable. Initially, Jewish women strove for inclusion in ritual and professional arenas—to be counted in a minyan, to recite *Kaddish*, to have an *aliyah*, to read Torah, to become president of the congregation, and to become rabbis. The goal was not to make radical changes but to participate fully in the existing institutions of American Jewish life.

If you had walked the halls of Hebrew Union College–Jewish Institute of Religion (HUC-JIR) academe in the mid- to late 1970s, you would likely have heard some of the following statements:

- "People won't want female rabbis to officiate at sad events, only happy occasions."
- "Sisterhood women are going to be your worst enemies."
- "Female rabbis don't talk loudly enough."
- "Female rabbis don't know how to carry the Torah."
- "We can't promise you anyone will hire you once you are ordained."

The speakers of these words included male faculty, administrators, staff, and rabbis, none of whom intended conscious ill will. Because fewer than a handful of women had been ordained at the time, however, these statements could not have reflected the actual situation of women in the rabbinate. Rather, these comments reflected the fantasies of faculty and staff about how they and others might respond to women in the rabbinate. Fantasies, by definition, come from the unconscious area of the brain.[1] The very lack of conscious awareness leads people to believe that their deepest longings represent fact rather than feeling. That is why people behave as if their fantasies represent reality, and these faculty members and administrators were no exception.

As it happens, none of these particular fantasies came true. Laypeople adapted much more quickly than predicted and accepted women rabbis in all areas of Jewish life. The National Federation of Temple Sisterhoods (now Women of Reform Judaism) was among the earliest and staunchest supporters of women in the rabbinate, offering scholarships to female rabbinical students and inviting female rabbis to speak at their regional and national conventions. The women ordained early on were not always hired as quickly as their male classmates, but with minimal difficulty, most women who wanted an entry level rabbinic position found one. And no one seemed to complain about how the women carried the Torah.

While the predicted problems did not come to be, however, other more subtle challenges presented themselves. People said things to female rabbis they did not dream of saying to male rabbis, but that was seen as a time-limited state. Once there was a critical mass of women ordained, the thinking went, those comments would stop. In those first years of women in the rabbinate, most women thought that once the novelty wore off, people would relate similarly to male and female rabbis. It has turned out that they do and yet they don't. Among all the fantasies entertained about female rabbis, no one foresaw the enduring power of unconscious psychological attitudes toward female rabbis. Even after forty years of women in the rabbinate, female rabbis continue to evoke gender-specific responses.

Of course, it isn't just female rabbis who elicit unconscious responses in those with whom they interact. Both male and female rabbis spark an intrapsychic reaction in which people transfer[2] onto the rabbi their deepest and most archaic feelings. The rabbi becomes the object of the fantasies and feelings of each and every congregant, client, patient, or other constituent. For some, the rabbi is the parent they never had; for others, the rabbi is the parent with whom they still struggle for resolution. As people unknowingly play out their old personal patterns, they alternately idealize and vilify the rabbi. These transferences might or might not lead to pathological behaviors. While the phenomenon of transference is merely human and operates all of the time (between spouses, with colleagues, toward authority figures, between parent and child), it frequently appears in response to religious leaders. The very role of rabbi provokes strong transferences.

While transference impacts all rabbis, unconscious fantasies about women have particular import for the female rabbi. In the unconscious primitive mind, the Mother Rabbi is enshrined as the source of unconditional love in a way that the Father Rabbi is not. The Father Rabbi may elicit a desire to feel protected and guided, but when you cry— and sometimes before you cry—it is the Mother Rabbi you turn to for comfort and sustenance. The only problem is that no one ever has the perfect mother. Some are lucky and have a mother who is "good enough" (the idea that the mother only needs to be "good enough" to raise a healthy child is a concept offered by the British pediatrician and psychoanalyst Donald Winnicott[3]). Real mothers come too late or too early and offer too much or not enough. So real children necessarily feel deprived, and by extension, so do adult congregants who unknowingly respond to those emotional triggers. Running into the Father Rabbi in the supermarket might make you feel safe and cared for, while encountering the Mother Rabbi on the soccer field sparks your old feelings of deprivation as you imagine her putting her family's needs ahead of yours. While all rabbis trigger unconscious responses in their parishioners, women rabbis evoke particular responses associated with their gender.

Now that the Reform Movement has ordained women for over forty years, there is no need to speculate about what might be the reaction to ordaining women. The sheer numbers of women ordained have created a track record. Women rabbis have not only entered the sanctum; they have transformed it. Seeing a woman draped in a tallit on the bimah is no longer a surprise. Female rabbis have created new rituals that give voice not just to the missing female experience but also to the deep human need to acknowledge previously neglected life-cycle moments. The language of the newest prayer books reflects a feminist sensibility. Yet people's responses to female rabbis are not necessarily any more grounded in reality now than before women were ordained. Psychological transference remains a complex powerful phenomenon, as evidenced by what people have said and continue to say to female rabbis over these forty years.

Some remarks reflect a positive transference. There is the teen who shyly confesses to her female rabbi, "Rabbi, when I was little, I thought you were God." There is the hopeful groom whose feminist girlfriend objects to the patriarchal nature of Judaism and so refuses to get married: "I think if a female rabbi would marry us, she might change her mind and agree to marry me." There is the bat mitzvah girl whose identification with her female rabbi leads to the spontaneous plea, "For my bat mitzvah, do you think we could wear matching dresses?" These expressions reveal a positive identification with the female rabbi, an experience of being accepted and welcomed, and even a transcendent connection with the Divine. For some people, the presence of women rabbis unlocks a feeling that resolves an unconscious conflict. People who have felt marginalized in the Jewish world—because they were women of a certain generation, because they were gay or lesbian or transgender, because they were single parents, because they were divorced, because they were not married, because they were otherwise not considered part of mainstream Jewish life—experience the possibility of being included in a new way. The subtext of their words reflects the deeper meaning: "If there is room for you, a woman, to be a rabbi, maybe there is room for me after all."

Some comments reveal a more negative transference. People for whom it would be ego-dystonic (i.e., not in accordance with their usual sense of self) to say something socially inappropriate do not hesitate to utter words that would offend in a different social context. "Wow, I never saw a rabbi dance like that before." "Those shoes you wear on the pulpit are so ugly." "Do you not wear makeup as a feminist statement?" "Our other rabbi was so warm; why are you so cold?" "I know where you can go for a good haircut." The responses are one-sided and unconcerned with the rabbi's feelings, as if only the speaker is participating in the conversation. Often the rabbi wonders if she is even there. In these puzzling comments, one can find traces of the individual's early emotional development. Just as the crying infant only cares about relieving its discomfort and satisfying its hunger, so the "crying" adult is aware only of his or her needs in that moment. The infant that continues to live in the adult psyche experiences a reawakening in the presence of the female rabbi. Even the most mature-seeming people are capable of reverting to narcissistic infancy. "I sat outside your office and watched people go in and out. Why do you have time for everyone but me?" "Why do you talk to everyone else at the *oneg* but me?" "I sent you an e-mail last night; why didn't you e-mail me back?" Infants at times feel merged with their mothers in that early bliss of unconditional love and do not know—or want to know—that there is anyone else in mother's world. Traces of those old preverbal fears of abandonment, engulfment, envy, impulsivity, anxiety, and separation live on in varying degrees in every adult brain. They remain alive in the fantasy world of the adult.

Such old fears help to explain the observer's awareness of and at times discomfort with the rabbi's sexuality. "I can't believe my rabbi can wear a dress like that; you must work out." "I can hire a female rabbi, but I can't hire a female rabbi who doesn't wear a robe." "I've never kissed such a pretty rabbi before." Sometimes the trigger is auditory, particularly when it comes to female cantors, not all of whom are sopranos: "I can't sing with female cantors." Appearance and voice call up amorphous sexual feelings. Two male rabbis or cantors on the bimah look normal; two women clergy on the bimah create a sense of discordance and unease. It is still not unusual in a congregation with a female rabbi for a ritual committee to debate whether hiring a female cantor would make the bimah look "too female." The rabbi's pregnancy might seem to make her femaleness hard to hide, but there are those people whose emotional relationship to the rabbi prevents them from noticing her burgeoning belly. Pregnancy itself stimulates all kinds of transferential responses, from identification and love to jealousy and hatred. The rabbi's pregnancy might make one person want to have a baby and another want to be the (rabbi's) baby. One young woman who became pregnant immediately after her wedding said only somewhat jokingly, "See what happens when you get married by a pregnant rabbi?"

One early and enduring question asks how a female rabbi should be addressed. The first generation of female rabbis all nod in recognition at the question "What do you call a female rabbi?" In Hebrew, a language that distinguishes gender, that question indicated a functional problem. There was no obvious word for a woman rabbi in Hebrew unless people reclaimed the word *rabbanit* from its present-day title of the rabbi's wife. Israeli-ordained women have since chosen the title *rabba*. In English, a language that knows no gender, calling a female rabbi by the title "rabbi" would seem to be the obvious answer. And yet native English speakers did not find that answer obvious. In their unconscious minds, rabbis were men, even when an actual female rabbi stood before them. When Rabbi Sally Priesand was ordained, the newspapers dubbed her "Rabbi Sally." Perhaps saying Rabbi Priesand felt too formal and not sufficiently intimate for addressing a woman. Even after forty years of ordaining women as *rav b'Yisrael* (rabbi in Israel), there are congregants and constituents who have difficulty calling a female rabbi by her last name and choose to compromise by using the title "rabbi" along with her first name. Some female rabbis, as if sensing the discomfort, resolve the conflict before it occurs by introducing themselves as "Rabbi First Name," especially if they are young when they are ordained.

Some attitudes toward women rabbis reflect the long tradition of male rabbis and have become embedded in people's psyches. "You don't look like a rabbi" is a common refrain from people whose rabbis never were old men with beards but who have internalized that archetype. While the age of the rabbi plays a role here, one has to assume that this reaction has more to do with gender than with age. After all, these mythic old rabbis with beards presumably were young once. And what is the subliminal message of a Reform congregation's decorating its walls with paintings of dancing Chasidic men? What people see right in front of them cannot always overcome the images enshrined in their unconscious, particularly when those images continue to be reinforced. At the bat mitzvah of the young girl who asked to wear matching dresses with the rabbi, two women were overheard talking afterward in the women's bathroom: "It was a lovely bat mitzvah," they said, "but who was that other girl up on the pulpit?"

There are other influences at play when it comes to how people relate to women rabbis. As people get to know an individual female rabbi, for example, they might adjust their transference in response to her personality and style. They no longer say, "I've never kissed such a pretty rabbi before," when they are talking about the rabbi they know and love. If the rabbi is particularly nurturing, people will respond in whatever way they usually respond to a nurturing personality. Congregational personality also frames people's attitudes. A congregation that is emotionally secure and stable might rejoice in the pregnancy of its female rabbi; a congregation that has a more depriving character might express more resentment.

Culture and history also have bearing on how people relate to women rabbis. Some congregations in those early days hired women rabbis to run schools on the cultural assumption, often mistaken, that all women know something about education. A culture in which many women are teachers may be more likely to accept a woman rabbi in the role of teacher. A culture in which women are paid seventy cents on the dollar will likely pay its female rabbi less than a male rabbi. While this can be a deliberate action (years ago, one male senior rabbi was heard to ask a colleague, "How much do you pay your female rabbi?"), it is usually a more complicated mix of cultural assumptions and unconscious fantasy (e.g., does paying a female rabbi feel like paying your mother to love you?). Women rabbis, in turn, who have been raised within that same culture, fear that being a tough negotiator might have negative impact on their relationship with the congregation. They just might not be wrong.

So much has changed since 1972 when the first woman was ordained. The Reform Movement has since ordained over six hundred women. Women have led both large and small congregations and have broadened the base and definition of rabbinic work. Women participate fully in the CCAR and have achieved its presidency. Women teach on the faculty of HUC-JIR. The presence of women rabbis has led to the creation of new prayer books, innovative rituals, and expanded theologies. And yet these deeper responses to the woman rabbi persist. Unconscious attitudes do not change in a generation or even two. The question "What do you call a woman rabbi?" has been answered. The question of whether people will ever relate the same way to a woman rabbi as to a male rabbi remains one for the ages.

NOTES

1. Sigmund Freud, "The Unconscious," in *Standard Edition* (London: Hogarth Press, 1915), 14:175. The idea of the unconscious was not original with Freud, although he expanded the concept. It has become part of accepted social parlance. The

unconscious mind contains thoughts, feelings, motivations, memories, and ideas that are not available to the conscious mind.

2. "In [Freud's] metaphor, transferences are 'new editions or facsimiles' of old emotional experiences, and 'they replace some earlier person by the person of the physician'" (S. Freud, "Fragment of an Analysis of a Case of Hysteria," in *Standard Edition* [London: Hogarth Press, 1905], 7:3–122, quoted in Benjamin Margolis, "Narcissistic Transference: The Product of Overlapping Self and Object Fields," *Modern Psychoanalysis* 4, no. 2 [1983], p. 131–140). Also, "the experience of feelings to a person which do not befit that person and which actually apply to another. Essentially, a person in the present is reacted to as though he were a person in the past" (R. Greenson, *The Technique of Practice of Psychoanalysis* [New York: International Universities Press, 1967], p. 131, quoted in Margolis, "Narcissistic Transference").

3. D. W. Winnicott, "Transitional Objects and Transitional Phenomena: A Study of the First Not-Me," *International Journal of Psycho-Analysis* 34 (1953): 89–97. "The good enough 'mother' (not necessarily the infant's own mother) is one who makes active adaptation to the infant's needs, an active adaptation that gradually lessens, according to the infant's growing ability to account for failure of adaptation and to tolerate the results of frustration...in fact, success in infant-care depends on the fact of devotion, not on cleverness or intellectual enlightenment. The good enough mother, as I have stated, starts off with an almost complete adaptation to her infant's needs, and as time proceeds she adapts less and less completely, gradually, according to the infant's growing ability to deal with her failure."

43

THE PUBLIC IMAGE
OF THE WOMAN RABBI

Rabbi Wendy Spears

Mark Twain famously said, "Clothes make the man; naked people have
little or no influence on society." Although Twain lived in the nineteenth century, his assertion could not be more true for rabbis in the
twenty-first century, especially female rabbis. The appearance of community leaders has been of interest throughout history, as described in
literature and depicted in artistic work. In traditional Jewish texts, this
is most evident in the biblical books of Exodus and Esther. As leaders
of the Jewish community as well as "symbolic exemplars" of God's
presence, what the rabbi wears makes a statement about the rabbi's role
as well as being a reflection of individual personal style. The rabbi's
attire has been cause for even more intense debate and speculation
since women were first ordained as rabbis in 1972. During much of the
twentieth century, rabbis, like their Christian counterparts, dressed the
part, typically by wearing a pulpit robe. There was a certain amount of
respect accorded to the rabbi because of that unique look. As there has
been a shift away from particularistic and formal rabbinic clothing and
a preference for more casual clothing in general, this has had an effect
on the public perception of the rabbi and the rabbinate. Historically,
the rabbi was perceived as the expert authority on Judaism and even a

representative of God. *Kavod harav*—respect and honor for the rabbi—in private, professional, and spiritual matters is connected to the rabbi's personal presentation. Once the formal attire, such as the pulpit robe, was removed, rabbis were perceived less formally as well—as parent, nurturer, companion, and comforter. The medium is the message; the rabbi herself represents God and Judaism.

The role of the rabbi parallels the role of the biblical priest. From biblical times to the present, it is widely believed both consciously and subconsciously that rabbis are representatives of God in the world, whether or not this perception by Jews is comfortable for the individual rabbi. While it can be argued that the biblical priests weren't necessarily God's representatives—that role fell to Moses—their involvement in the rituals of the Tabernacle greatly influenced the people's experience of these rituals and God's presence among them. So important was the priests' clothing in the biblical period that the entirety of chapter 28 of Exodus, as well as most of chapter 39, is devoted to its description. In Exodus 28:2, God instructs Moses to make sacred vestments for the priests to convey dignity and adornment. Priests were attired differently from laypeople in order to highlight their role and its importance to the community, specifically when they were involved in the Tabernacle rituals. Exodus 28 and 39 can serve as a detailed style guide for dressing for the rabbinic role. In studying the Exodus passages for advice in redeveloping the image of the female rabbi, it becomes clear that color, fabrication, design, and jewelry contribute to the sacred persona. The description of the priestly vestments is quite detailed: pants, turbans, fringed tunics, headdresses, robes, sashes, shoulder pieces, all made of a fine twisted linen in a figured pattern. They were gorgeous to see, colored crimson, blue, and purple, finely embroidered, decorated with sculpted pomegranates and golden bells that chimed whenever the priest moved. There was also a finely wrought golden breastplate, bejeweled in a rainbow of colored stones. Seeing such a majestically attired person contributed to the perception that the priest was a holy personage rather than an ordinary Israelite.

This attention to personal detail is also depicted in the Book of Esther. In a "Women in the Bible" teleconference sponsored by the Women's Rabbinic Network on October 21, 2013, Rabbi Tamara Cohn Eskenazi, PhD, taught that Esther "puts on her queenship" (Esther 2:17) in addition to Ahasuerus putting the crown on her head. As Esther prepared for her queenship, cosmetics are mentioned three different times in chapter 2, certainly a sign of their importance (2:3, 2:9, 2:12). Just as Esther went through a transformation, so too does an individual undergo an internal change at the moment of *s'michah* (ordination), transforming her personal identity as well as being publicly identified by the community as one of its religious and educational leaders. In the Bible, for both the Aaronide priests and Queen Esther, the garments and the cosmetics supported their roles. So, too, rabbinic clothing today supports the rabbinic role, but exactly how one's clothes should look in supporting that role has become unclear. For that matter, it seems that rabbis question that they should dress for their role in the first place, especially with the nearly universal abandonment of the pulpit robe in the late 1990s.

Rabbis, like the biblical priests, are engaged in sacred theater. The Tabernacle ritual was a grand spectacle that engaged all the senses. There was the singing and talking of the crowd among the lowing and bleating of animals awaiting sacrifice. People touched the textured hides of the animals they led to the altar. The Tabernacle was adorned with gold furnishings and burnished wood, just as the priests were grandly arrayed. The burning altars and roasting meats filled nostrils with fragrance, while the flavorfully cooked meats apportioned after the sacrifices satisfied both palate and stomach. In American synagogues today, sacred theater is still performed, with the rabbis as the primary actors. The bimah is often decorated with tapestries and stained glass, furnished with candelabras, flags, and the ark in which the Torah scrolls are kept— a stage set for a grand drama. Candles, the Torah scrolls dressed in velvet mantles and silver, and a variety of musical instruments are the props. With everything arrayed, it is appropriate for rabbis to be costumed beautifully for the important role of facilitator of God's presence in the sanctuary among the people.

Even when stepping away from the bimah and out of the synagogue, a rabbi should still adorn herself in keeping with the dignity and spirituality of her role as symbolic exemplar. Rabbi and psychologist Jack Bloom, PhD, coined the phrase "symbolic exemplar" to indicate the role that rabbis play in modern Judaism and the general community. In his book *The Rabbi as Symbolic Exemplar: By the Power Vested in Me*, he proposes that rabbis are walking, talking, living examples of the very best qualities of humanity. This is the feature of the rabbinate that underlies rabbinic authority and authenticity. It spills over into the rabbi's personal life from the professional life. Whether on the pulpit or during her leisure time, the rabbi is *always* the representative of God, Judaism, and right behavior. Rabbi Bloom notes that no matter how hard rabbis try to dissociate themselves from this responsibility, it clings to them like a second skin.

Rabbis are the public face of Judaism, but most are woefully unprepared for this public aspect. It has caused heartache and burnout in numerous rabbinic careers, as well as providing some of the most meaningful moments. As Bloom indicates, a rabbi's role as symbolic exemplar is subject as much to the perceptions of others as it is to the rabbi. While a rabbi may look in the mirror and see herself as she was before she became a rabbi—as a friend, daughter, parent, spouse, woman—most others see "rabbi" first, before the other descriptors. This image is clear in a wedding announcement in the *New York Times* on February 17, 2013: a man marrying a rabbi said that when he met his bride he thought, "She's adorable. I had to 'unrabbi' her. I think of [rabbis as] standing on a stage looking down at people below. They're this holy figure, but [my] bride-to-be is [also] a human being."

It is tremendously challenging for the rabbi to always be concerned about other people's expectations for her behavior and appearance, but in many respects she has little choice in this matter. The reverence accorded to her, *kavod harav*, comes primarily from being a symbolic exemplar. Jews assume that the rabbi can make God a part of each congregant's personal reality by embodying sacred qualities of compassion, kindness, mindfulness, and wisdom. The rabbi represents Jewish learning and values, by standing up for what is right and making the world a better place in the public sphere and private home. Rabbis embody the metaphor that God is in the world. They must, therefore, take this challenge seriously and act and dress accordingly to the best of their abilities.

It is rare for anyone to comment on what a man wears unless he is particularly flamboyant or neglected. This is not to say that men don't care about their appearance. In his 1975 book *Dress for Success*, John T. Molloy showed men that their choice of suit, accessories, and hairstyle in the workplace could affect their career possibilities and advancement. Dressing well was correlated with career success. While the issues discussed in that volume apply to male rabbis, they are particularly crucial for female rabbis. Women's appearance and clothing seem to be fair game for discussion privately, publicly, and in the media. Both men and women are invested in how women look; there are just as many, if not more, male fashion designers of women's clothing as female designers. Molloy followed up on the popularity of his 1975 book with one for women in 1978. "Power dressing," the phrase he coined, is a timeless concept. Power dressing guided men to wear conservative, dark suits with lighter-colored neutral shirts if they wanted to become influential power brokers. A pop of color could be added with a tie or pocket square. Hair should be cut to a medium length, and nails cut short. Professional women were guided to dress similarly in dark suits, lighter blouses, and a loose, fluffy bow at the neck in place of a man's tie. Minimal makeup and conservative nail polish were encouraged, along with low-heeled pumps for a woman to achieve the career success she desired. Power dressing was adopted by both male and female rabbis during the 1970s.

When women entered the rabbinate in 1972, the image of what a rabbi looked like drastically changed. Many of the early conventions of the Women's Rabbinic Network from the 1980s onward included discussions of what look female rabbis should strive to achieve, since power dressing seemed to be too restrictive for the variety of roles the women were expected to fulfill beyond being the scholar or CEO of the synagogue. Congregants routinely made comments about their female rabbis' hairstyles, makeup (or lack thereof), nail polish, shoes, accessories, and overall clothing choices. It was, and continues to be, common for female rabbis to receive unsolicited style advice from congregants and male colleagues, often due to a perceived lack of a "proper" style in the opinion of the person offering the advice. The protective boundary that had previously shielded male rabbis from this type of advice and criticism became permeable as women became rabbis. There was a principled response to this among female rabbis: it shouldn't matter what a rabbi wears; it should only matter the message that a rabbi speaks. Sadly, this is not the reality. For example, in a Facebook discussion from October 24, 2013, involving rabbis and other professional women, one rabbi shared that a congregant criticized her lipstick color by saying it was too dark and would have been more appropriate in the 1940s rather than in 2013. The smallest aspect of the female rabbi's appearance is scrutinized. It is, therefore, extremely important for female rabbis to show extreme care and concern in their appearance.

With the new informality of our times, including the more casual style of attire that is currently in vogue, there is an overfamiliarity that people feel with their clergy that allows them to confront female rabbis in ways they would not consider approaching male rabbis. For the first twenty years or so of women in the rabbinate, there was a dress code for worship and life-cycle officiation: the rabbi wore a pulpit robe. The approachability, or rather inapproachability, of a rabbi may have had something to do with the image this "uniform" created. A uniform accords the wearer a certain amount of respect and recognition, defining and declaring professional roles. The pulpit robe is not unlike the formal black robe worn by judges on the bench; a defendant wouldn't really consider hugging a judge, even if the court case came out in her favor. The neutral robe serves as a separation or barrier between the rabbi and the congregant, much as the white lab coat separates the doctor from the patient or the judicial robe separates the face of the law from the rest of the court. Judges' robes and doctors' lab coats denote the office of the professional and add gravitas to the person wearing them.

In the absence of the pulpit robe, many rabbis (and many liberal Christian clergy) seem to be at a loss as to how to present themselves through their clothing and grooming. Since there is currently no particular advice offered to rabbis on this topic at the seminary nor at professional conventions, it has fallen to the blogosphere to fill this vacuum. Reverend Victoria Weinstein, a Unitarian-Universalist minister, writes a daily blog pointing out the fashion faux pas and successes of fellow clergy. The header of her blog "Beauty Tips for Ministers" reads: "Because you're in the public eye, and God knows you need to look good." Reverend Weinstein gives advice on garments, hair styles, makeup choices, and beard grooming. She is very specific on what works and what doesn't. While some may see this as a frivolous ministry, it is vitally necessary to protect and define what it means to be a member of the clergy in concrete, physical ways.

While female rabbis may have similar struggles with their appearance and attire as do many female professionals, they have the added responsibility of being symbolic exemplars. The more rabbis dress the part, the more respect is accorded to them. In the Facebook discussion previously referenced, nearly one hundred professional women and rabbis discussed their use or nonuse of cosmetics on a daily basis. Most of the participants felt that wearing makeup helped a woman look and feel more polished and professional; it enhanced their self-esteem in addition to their appearance. Some women don't use any cosmetics because they are allergic to them or don't like the way they feel. But by far, the most frequent reason given for not wearing makeup was the lack of knowledge on how to use it. An October 13, 2011, article in the *New York Times* titled "Up the Career Ladder, Lipstick in Hand" affirmed that women who use makeup tend to be paid at a higher rate because they are seen as more competent and trustworthy than those who don't. Makeup should enhance a woman's natural beauty but not look overdone or like a costume. Both women themselves and men and women who observe them confirmed that cosmetics boost a woman's attractiveness. There were women quoted in the article who objected to the amount of time spent applying cosmetics, and as women rabbis have said, the quality of women's job performance should not be based on competence with cosmetics. However, like the women in the Facebook discussion, women in the article's study felt more confident wearing makeup. Their confidence translated into their ability to project an aura of capability, reliability, and amiability. Cosmetics can be strategically chosen, depending on the situation; as boardroom attire differs from entertaining attire, so can makeup go from professional to glamorous as necessary to project the appropriate impression. Also, there has been a cultural shift in American society in women using adornment and cosmetics to please themselves, rather than being concerned about pleasing men. Cosmetics and clothing are tools that are completely within women's control in enhancing (or choosing not to enhance) their appearance. Appearance plays a major part in how a woman feels, and thus how she is able to present the truth of herself to the world. Certainly it would be a fairer world if beauty were not rewarded any more than those who are more ordinary in appearance, but that is not yet a world that currently exists.

As Mark Twain said, how we dress creates an impression. Dressing too casually invites congregants and clients to behave in an overly familiar way with the rabbi. Even without the pulpit robe, there was a type of uniform for the first wave of female rabbis, including suits and dress shoes—much like the male rabbis. The first and second generations of female rabbis generally preferred short haircuts and minimal use of cosmetics, again seemingly in imitation of male attire and grooming. As more women have entered the rabbinate, more diversity in dress and grooming styles has emerged. If, as Reverend Weinstein suggests, rabbis are representatives of God, they need to present themselves as serious and as polished as possible, while reflecting their personalities and the spirituality of their vocational calling.

For the female rabbi, developing and maintaining a rabbinic style is a synthesis of her professional and private roles, between the sacred and the ordinary. With no outside guidelines, it falls to each individual rabbi to define her personal rabbinic style. This requires an examination of her inner self, since how she perceives herself should be reflected in what she wears. She needs to define what type of rabbi she is off the bimah: a still and reflective scholar; an exuberant and creative teacher full of new ideas; an enthusiastic marketer of Jewish ways of doing and being; a nurturing comforter at the bedsides of the sick and dying. Each rabbi must find her true inner self and present that self in what she wears, as well as in how she lives her life and practices her rabbinate. This is in addition to her performance attire during worship and at life-cycle ceremonies. Especially in this age of constant social media access, the ways in which a rabbi presents herself at any time necessitates her energies and attention. The ubiquity of the mobile phone camera makes it likely that a rabbi could be photographed and that photo published at any time. Social media also is relatively eternal, in that once an image is publicly available, it will most always remain available.

Christian ministers often own a variety of seasonal vestments that they wear for leading worship, in colors that complement the minister and the event. Perhaps rabbis might attire themselves with a pulpit robe or other garment acting as the canvas for color and accessories. Pulpit robes now come in both festive and somber colors, as well as the popular (but often funereal) black. The pulpit robe, though, is not nearly decorative enough on its own. Just as the biblical priests wore a fine array of vestments, so too might rabbis consider an array of colorfully designed tallitot and *kippot* or other head coverings. Modern *kippot*, already available in a variety of colors and materials, are becoming more like jeweled adornments. Female rabbis could easily add substantial jewelry to this combination, reminiscent of the priestly breastplate. And like Esther putting on her queenhood, female rabbis can enhance their image with cosmetics as needed. This all takes practice, especially for rabbis accustomed to dressing more casually without many accessories or cosmetics, but it is worth the time and effort to perfect. There is the added benefit of building the rabbi's self-confidence as she presents her most beautiful self in reflecting on the outside the true beauty that can hide on the inside.

If a rabbi wants her rabbinate to be perceived with gravitas and respect, she must dress the part. Thinking about the image she wants to project should inform what she wears, since communicating her role visually is as important as her auditory communication. What she looks like has an impact before she even opens her mouth. She should spend time and consideration creating her outfits and complementary accessories, just as she devotes thought and effort to writing a sermon. Far from being frivolous, this is holy work, part of creating and maintaining a sense of the sacred, of celebrating God's presence in her own life and being as well as in the lives of the Jewish people she serves.

44

A MIRROR, A PRISM, AND A TELESCOPE

Reimagining Role Models

Rabbi Leah Rachel Berkowitz

No one ever told me that I couldn't be a rabbi because of my gender. That was one of the gifts of growing up in a Reform synagogue in the 1980s. Although our congregation's senior rabbi adhered to one of the classic male clergy stereotypes—a tall, well-groomed, be-robed figure with four children, and a wife who sang in the choir and taught Hebrew school—I saw many women serving as cantors and assistant rabbis, both in my home congregation and at my Jewish summer camp. One Shabbat, just a few months before my bat mitzvah, I looked at our rabbi and said to myself, definitively, "I can do that." I felt this revelation in my entire body, as though a switch had been flipped and the light had come on.

I didn't think of my choice as "feminist," nor did I see myself as wanting to be a "woman rabbi." This was simply what I wanted to be when I grew up—a rabbi. Young girls of my generation expected to find the doors to every possible career open to us. We were told to "reach for the stars." We believed that we would be able to simultaneously pursue exciting professions, loving partnerships, and a fulfilling family life, without any difficulty. The only person who showed any hesitation was my grandmother, who considered religion a "dirty business" for either a man or a woman.

As an undergraduate student at Brandeis University, I began to understand some of the challenges I would face as a woman in this field. During my first conversation with an Orthodox Jew, I asked what he thought of women rabbis and he said, "No such thing." I realized that in this world beyond my Reform synagogue, I was going to have to fight to prove my authenticity: as a student of Judaism, as a community leader, as a Reform Jew, and as a woman.

Ironically, this fight only intensified when I began my rabbinical studies in Jerusalem. While questions of pluralism and authenticity were aired in the open at Brandeis, some members of the faculty at HUC-JIR in Jerusalem warned us against engaging Israelis about the nature of our studies. Because many Israelis I met felt disdain toward women rabbis and suspicion of Reform Jews in general, I was unable to share my experience outside the walls of HUC-JIR. I returned to the United States feeling as if I had spent a year living underwater.

When I began teaching Torah to children and adults, the challenge of proving my own authenticity in the context of the Jewish tradition gave way to the challenge of proving the relevance of our sacred stories in the context of modernity and feminism. If my goal was to convince my students—many of whom were young women—that the Bible was pertinent to their lives, I was going to have to help them find characters to whom they could relate and heroines they could admire.

This was not an easy task, and one incident sticks out in my mind. One morning after religious school *t'filah*, a feisty twelve-year-old girl approached me with a question—or rather, a comment—about our prayer service: "Why do we bother to include the names of the Matriarchs in the *Amidah*?" she exclaimed. "I don't *want* to be like Sarah, Rebecca, Rachel, and Leah. They're just the Patriarchs' *wives*. They didn't *do* anything."

This student's words helped me to realize that I couldn't escape from the challenges of being labeled a "woman rabbi." While I had once shied away from a gendered study of Judaism, I now faced opposition both from those who thought I should not be a rabbi and those who, like my student, thought that Judaism was inherently patriarchal.

This opposition inspired me to look to Jewish literature for models of powerful women. The stories I found—particularly in the Bible—turned what I thought I knew about biblical women on its head. Scattered among the narratives in which women were portrayed "only" as wives and mothers—or, worse, as concubines and prostitutes—were scenes in which women showed agency and effected change, both through their words and through their actions.

When I teach Bible and midrash, I tell my students that we can view the Torah as a mirror, a prism, and a telescope: a mirror in which we can see ourselves, a prism through which we can look at the world, and a telescope that we can point heavenward in our search for God.

Looking back on the stories that inspired me at various phases of my own learning, I realized that I was not only seeking out these stories for my students. I needed to find them for myself. I, too, was looking for the mirror, the prism, and the telescope in our sacred stories, and the women I studied reflected where I was in my own journey, how I saw the world I lived in, and the woman, and the rabbi, that I hoped to become.

Having It All: The Woman of Valor

I first encountered *Eishet Chayil* ("The Woman of Valor," Prov. 31:10–31) during my four years of attending Shabbat dinners at Brandeis University Hillel. The only thing I knew about the poem was that the Orthodox students would drone its melody as my egalitarian peers and I conspicuously left the table to wash our hands. Because I associated the hymn with Orthodox men—who continued their singing while the rest of us cleared the table after the meal—I assumed that it was archaic, misogynist, and best ignored. My perception changed at my mother's fiftieth birthday celebration, when a friend recited the poem in her honor. It was the first time I had heard the words in English, recited about a woman I loved and admired. In the mirror of this text, I saw reflected not only my mother, but many of the strong, vibrant, multitasking women who had been instrumental in my upbringing. I was intrigued.

The following year I chose *Eishet Chayil* as the subject of my first-year liturgy paper at HUC-JIR. When I began to study the biblical poem in depth, what I discovered did not mesh with my assumptions. *Eishet Chayil* celebrated the woman as a wife and mother, but also as head of household, seamstress, vintner, businesswoman, and philanthropist. If anything, the modern difficulty with the poem emerges from the impossible standard it sets for women today, both in the public and the domestic spheres.

Like many biblical texts that show women in a positive light, there have been attempts by the Rabbis to detach this poem from the woman it praises. Perhaps suggesting that no ordinary woman could be worthy of such praise, one midrash attributes each verse of the hymn to a different biblical matriarch, from Noah's wife to Queen Esther.[1] Some traditional sources claim that the poem is not about a human woman at all, but rather describes any number of religious symbols that are feminine in gender: the Torah, the Sabbath, Wisdom, the soul, or the *Shechinah*, the feminine understanding of God.[2]

While I appreciated these alternative explanations, I was drawn to the notion of praising real women and the ways in which this ritual could be expanded to celebrate the contributions of each person at the table. I discovered that some households with both a mother and a father balance the ritual by reciting both *Eishet Chayil* and Psalm 112:1–9, *Ashrei Ish*. Others use *Shir Yedidot*, a new poem constructed of biblical and Rabbinic verses about love and family that can be sung to the traditional tune.[3] I learned that a colleague's spouse composed an alphabetical song of praise to sing to her at the Shabbat table, following the acrostic structure of *Eishet Chayil*. Still others scrapped the original text altogether and used the model of *Eishet Chayil* to offer extemporaneous praise to every member of the household.[4]

With this in mind, I chose to endorse the ritual of singing *Eishet Chayil*, or some modern interpretation, as a way of celebrating the members of one's family. My conclusions were challenged by the first-generation woman rabbi who read my paper and urged me to remember that my opportunities were handed to me on the backs of generations of feminists who had rejected this poem. I now recognize that there are more challenges to the poem than I was prepared to acknowledge during my first year of rabbinical school. For instance, what do we do for those in our community whose gender identity or family structure does not fit into one of the categories provided by our tradition? How do we create rituals that celebrate those who are single or childless, by choice or by circumstance? In short, what do we do for those in our community who cannot find themselves reflected in the mirror of this text?

Amy Bardack writes:

> Eshet Hayil becomes more powerful when it is not sung exclusively by a husband to his wife....More women should feel free to sing it to themselves and one another. As lesbian partners, unmarried heterosexual couples, and single women adopt Eshet Hayil, it becomes a celebration of all women, not just wives.[5]

However, I also came to believe that it was necessary to provide alternatives to the traditional text. In my liturgy paper, I offered my own interpretive translation of the hymn, where, for example, "She rises while it is yet night / And supplies provisions for her household" (Prov. 31:15) is "translated" as follows:

> She wakes up early in the morning, to make certain that everyone is nourished, physically and spiritually: be it breakfast with her family, feeding her dog, coffee with a friend she hasn't had time to visit, or picking up muffins for people at work.

In the spirit of informed choice, I took it upon myself to introduce the women of liberal communities to the poem and its associated rituals by teaching a class I call "The Woman of Valor: Who Is She and What Is She Doing at My Shabbat Dinner Table?" When I teach this class, we analyze the various versions of this poem and its alternatives, then work together to craft a poem offering praise to the women they admire and aspire to be in modern times. That way, instead of measuring ourselves against the impossible standards of the original hymn, we can use the biblical text as a framework for praising modern women.

The women at my home synagogue, Temple Sholom in Broomall, wrote this modern-day interpretation of *Eishet Chayil*:

> She is not afraid to make choices, and stands by her convictions.
> She believes in and trusts herself.
> Patient and resilient, she copes well with change.
> Even in a crisis, she has control over her emotions.
> She knows how to stay strong, until she has time to fall apart.
> Her household is fragrant, but she is not a martyr or a doormat.
> She is able to live her life while raising her family.
> She is mindful of the decisions she has made with her life, as is her
>   husband:
> He takes pleasure in his family, and she is faithful to him.
> She teaches her children what their choices are in life.
> Likening her family to a team, she gives them pride in what they
>   can do.
> She recognizes that who she is more important than what she does.
> She is aware that one woman cannot do everything.
> Just like the scholars of our time, she deserves a Sabbatical.
> Even while caring for others, she takes time for herself:
> She cares for herself by reading, by being present, by being HERE.
> Knowing that she needs other women, she makes herself a gatherer
>   of friends.
> A woman of valor we have found…she sits at every place at our
>   table.[6]

Striking Out on One's Own: Shiphrah and Puah

While studying *Eishet Chayil* gave me an incredible tool to praise the role models I had grown up with—women who had prioritized raising families and still sometimes managed to work and lead outside the home—this text fell short for me in significant ways. I had to recognize that the prism through which our biblical authors saw the world and the women who lived in it was drastically different from my own worldview.

Although I came to understand that there are many different definitions of family life and career success for both men and women, my own ideas about career and family life were evolving: I no longer planned to leave the workforce in order to raise a family, as my own mother had done. I bristled when people referred to me as the *rebbetzin* and when my grandmother suggested that if I *had* to be a rabbi, I should at least take an education job that would allow me to raise my still nonexistent children. (I later discovered that rabbi-educators face similar challenges carving out time for their families, so this is not the solution to the work/life balance problem in any case.) I needed to know—both for myself and for my students—that there were women in our sacred story who had made a name for themselves, not just for their husbands or sons.

One challenge of introducing young students to compelling biblical narratives about women is that supplementary religious education tends to focus mostly on the stories of Genesis, where women appear primarily as wives and mothers or—in the stories we don't teach—as rape victims, concubines, or prostitutes. Women in these narratives often conform to our stereotypes: wives of prominent male characters known for their reproductive woes, infighting, and trickery. In our rush to meet Moses in Exodus 2—and, perhaps, the three women who conspire to save his life: Yocheved, Miriam, and the Pharaoh's daughter—we often skip over Exodus 1, where we find the midwives to the Hebrew women, a courageous pair who defy the orders of the Pharaoh himself.

Alarmed by the Hebrew birthrate in Egypt, the Pharaoh summons the Hebrew midwives, Shiphrah and Puah, and commands them, "When you deliver the Hebrew women, look at the birthstool: if it is a boy, kill him; if it is a girl, let her live" (Exod. 1:16). The midwives, fearing God, do not obey the Pharaoh. When called to account for their actions, they cover up their disobedience with a well-crafted lie, saying, "Because the Hebrew women are not like the Egyptian women: they are vigorous. Before the midwife can come to them, they have given birth" (Exod. 1:19).

Unlike the sister-wife and wife-concubine rivalries of Genesis, this text shows women acting in cooperation with each other, rather than competition, as they engage in civil disobedience and "radical acts of compassion."[7] These women attained a position of prestige, due to both their profession as midwives and their defiance of the Pharaoh. The midwives display altruism and courage, but also quick thinking. According to Renita J. Weems:

> [The midwives' cover story] cleverly arrogates the Pharaoh's assumption about Hebrew difference to their own advantage. That is, since the Egyptians believe that the Hebrews are different from Egyptians anyway, they are sure to believe that even in labor, a common female drama, Hebrews are different: Hebrew women deliver before the midwife comes to them.[8]

As with *Eishet Chayil*, there have been attempts by Rabbinic sources to weaken this powerful story of female heroism. Rashi suggests that Shiphrah and Puah are actually code names for Miriam and Yocheved, consolidating the number of heroic females in the Exodus story and diminishing the significance of two named female characters whose husbands and male children are not mentioned.[9] In contrast, Carol Meyers points out the significance of the number of heroines in the early chapters of Exodus: five women in Exodus 1 and 2—Shiphrah, Puah, Miriam, Yocheved, and the daughter of Pharaoh—added to the seven daughters of Yitro gives us twelve heroic women who bring about the Exodus from Egypt, one for each of the twelve tribes.[10]

This story became one of the chapters of my master's thesis. However, when it came to the midwives, I was not satisfied with mere study. I wanted to celebrate the midwives at my Passover seder. I decided to represent them at the seder table with a cup of strong tea or coffee. Hot water has an association with childbirth, while coffee and tea are substances that transform their environment. This ritual also brings to mind the famous quote, attributed to Eleanor Roosevelt, "A woman is like a teabag; you never know how strong she is until she's in hot water."

The midwives also feature prominently in a lesson I teach about the Hebrew word *ivri*, the origin of the word "Hebrew," often used in the Bible as a (derogatory) ethnic designation: Potiphar's wife uses it when she accuses Joseph of rape (Gen. 39:14, 39:17); Joseph uses it to explain why he, still disguised as an Egyptian, cannot dine with his brothers (Gen. 43:32). First used to describe Abraham in Genesis 14:13, the word *ivri* captured the imagination of the Rabbis in *B'reishit Rabbah* 42:8. While some felt that the term signified Abraham's lineage (descendant of Eber) or geography (across [*mei-eiver*] the river), Rabbi Y'hudah claimed that the name *ivri* signified that "the whole world was on one side [*eiver*] while he was on the other side," referring to Abraham's then unique position that there was only one God.[11]

Although *ivri*—and *ivriyot*, the feminine plural version used in Exodus 1—often has a negative connotation when used by non-Hebrews, we can also use it to understand ourselves: as Jews, as women, and as rabbis. While we identify ourselves by our lineage and where we came from, our lives are also defined by the stands we take and the boundaries we cross.

There is a legend that during World War II, an itinerant preacher known as "Fritz the Wanderer" stood on the pulpit of a Calvinist church in Holland, read the story of the midwives, and gave the following sermon:

> Who is Pharaoh today? The Nazis! Who are the babies that have to be hidden? The Jews! Who are the midwives today? We are! It is our job to outsmart the Pharaohs, to have the courage of the midwives and to protect the Jews and all those being persecuted.

The legend continues that inspired by the Wanderer's words, several families in this community sheltered their Jewish neighbors from the Nazis.[12]

While in this story, the churchgoers are presented as *ivriyot* and the Jewish community is portrayed as the Hebrew babies, I often present this story as an example of how *ivri* can be understood as a symbol of our people's commitment to social justice. As *ivrim* or *ivriyot*, we, too, must see the world through the prism of justice and compassion. We must be ever on the lookout for today's Pharaohs, in order to assume the role of the *ivriyot* midwives and save today's Hebrew babies.

Standing Up, Speaking Out:
The Daughters of Zelophehad

"When I decided to study for the rabbinate, I never thought much about being a pioneer, nor was it my intention to champion the rights of women. I just wanted to be a rabbi."[13] This statement—made by Rabbi Sally Priesand to the Jewish Women's Archive—could have been my own. Entering the rabbinate more than thirty years after Priesand, in a class that was made up of 50 percent women, I didn't expect that there would be any walls left for me to break down.

Even in the twenty-first century, however, there are still stereotypes to confront and inequities to challenge. In many communities in which I've worked, I've been the first woman rabbi. My gender, age, sexuality, marital status, and appearance have all been considered alongside my experience and skill in the placement process. Certain benefits that I thought were a given in the congregational rabbinate, or any major profession, have been repeatedly denied.

Moreover, I continue to watch women all over the world who are still treated as second-class citizens, whether they are working women seeking pay equity and positions of leadership in the United States, young girls pursuing an education in the Middle East and Asia, or Israeli women fighting for the right to pray at the Western Wall in Jerusalem. I grew frustrated by stories about religious and political leaders who refuse to acknowledge that their traditions can evolve and change over time.

I once expected that, like the midwives, I could accomplish my personal and professional goals simply by doing what I had been trained to do. I didn't anticipate that advocacy would be a part of my rabbinate. As I began to work in the field, I realized that it wasn't enough to do my work. I needed to find my voice.

At this juncture, I was drawn to the story of the daughters of Zelophehad, five unmarried women who appear in Numbers 27 and 36, demanding to inherit their father's tribal landholding. Their father had no male children, and because up to that point Torah law had dictated that Zelophehad's land would go to the nearest male kinsman, his daughters would be left with nothing.

That women did not typically inherit land is not the primary issue in the biblical discussion. What concerns the women—and Moses, to whom the women address their concerns—is that if Zelophehad's inheritance were to go to his male kinsmen, instead of his own children, his "name would be lost" when the landholding is absorbed by another kinsman (Num. 27:4). After discussing the matter with God, Moses responds that women could inherit land in limited circumstances: provided there were no sons, and as long as the women married within their tribe, so that the land would not pass to another tribe in the event of their marriages.

This resolution is imperfect when read through the prism of a modern feminist sensibility. The women become placeholders, not equal candidates for inheritance. This is one of many instances in the Bible where the well-being of women is considered only insomuch as it affects the lives of men. This decree places limitations on their marriage prospects and continues to exclude women from inheritance in cases where they have male siblings. It is clearly a compromise, though one that was progressive for its own time.

What is remarkable about this story is not the result of the women's protest, but rather the process by which this new law came about. The daughters of Zelophehad—Machlah, Noah, Choglah, Milcah, and Tirzah—come before Moses and an assembly of chieftains and demand a "holding among our father's kinsmen" (Num. 27:4). They are not ignored or dismissed. Rather, their case is brought by Moses directly before God, who decides in their favor. Masha Turner writes:

> The Torah could have preserved only the final laws, without the narratives that describe their emergence. But it seems that the Torah intentionally highlights a principle of dialogue between human groups and divine legislation. The purpose of the laws is "one shall live by them" (Lev. 18:5), meaning that the laws of the Torah must fit life. Such a goal is achieved by an openness to change, albeit with God's explicit consent and command.[14]

This story shows us not only that women were able to effect change through mere speech, but also that the Torah evolves and adapts to new situations. Through the telescope of this text, we can see a vision of God that is different from the rigid and immutable Giver of law that we find in other places in the Bible. Here, even God recognizes that the law is not always infallible. As we challenge those who seek to define Jewish practice—or secular law—according to "tradition" or "Scripture," this story gives us an example of how even God's law can change when it causes harm to a particular subgroup. It also provides a model of women who were not afraid to advocate for themselves and who were treated with dignity and respect when they do so.

A Mirror, A Prism, and a Telescope

Throughout my life, as a woman and as a rabbi, the Torah has provided me and my students with a mirror, a prism, and a telescope through which to see ourselves, our world, and our God. But just as it is with any of these actual reflective or refractive objects, we don't always like what we see.

In the stories of the Matriarchs and in the case of Hannah and Peninnah (I Sam. 1:1–2:11), we bear witness to the rivalry that besets women who would otherwise share the common goal of building and raising a family. We also note the tension between a woman who has children but nothing else and a woman who has everything except a child. In the stories where women act as prostitutes—whether permanently or temporarily—we see women who use their bodies as currency because they are taught they have nothing else of value to give. In the story of Zipporah, Moses's wife, we find a non-Israelite struggling to find her place in her husband's Israelite world and a woman whose knowledge and actions in a time of crisis earn her banishment instead of praise (Exod. 4:24–26, 18:1–7). Even in the stories where women act as heroines, we might be troubled by the limitations their society placed on them.

We may wrestle with the texts themselves: What exactly did they mean? How does the historical context change our understanding of them? Why did our ancestors tell them? Why did the Rabbis respond to them in the way they did? In many ways, however, the stories of the Bible remain relevant precisely because of their imperfections. In these stories, we see women who, imperfect themselves, worked to achieve their goals in an imperfect system. What could be more relevant to today's women—and women rabbis—than that?

When we read these with the mirror in mind, we can still see ourselves, even in the stories of women whose lives were not like ours at all. We see ourselves in stories of rivalry, jealousy, and acts of desperation. We see ourselves, and the world in which we live, in the struggle for recognition and fairness and in the difficulty of doing the right thing, even when it means taking a risk. And in those miraculous stories where women speak and act to effect change in their male-dominated worlds, we might find images of the women, and the rabbis, we hope to become.

NOTES

1. Burton L. Visotzky, *"Midrash Eishet Hayil,"* in *Conservative Judaism* 38, no. 3 (Spring 1986): 21–25.

2. *The Complete Artscroll Siddur* (New York: Mesorah Publications, 1984), 359.

3. Sharon Bromberg, *Shir Yedidot*, http://www.ktav.com/index.php/mizmor-shir-bencher.html.

4. Jules Harlow, *Pray Tell: A Hadassah Guide to Jewish Prayer* (Woodstock, VT: Jewish Lights, 2003), 136.

5. Amy Bardack, "Praising the Work of Valiant Women: A Feminist Endorsement of *Eshet Hayil*," in *A Shabbat Reader: Universe of Cosmic Joy*, by Dov Peretz Elkins (New York: URJ Press, 1998), 48.

6. Written by the Temple Sholom Women's Spirituality Group, Temple Sholom in Broomall, PA, January 5, 2005.

7. "Book Chronicles Warsaw Zoo as Refuge in WWII," interview with Diane Ackerman by Ira Flatow, *Talk of the Nation: Science Friday*, National Public Radio, Jan. 18, 2008, http://www.npr.org/templates/transcript/transcript.php?storyId=18222827.

8. Renita J. Weems, "The Hebrew Women Are Not Like the Egyptian Women: The Ideology of Race, Gender, and Sexual Reproduction in Exodus 1," *Semeia* 59 (1992): 29.

9. As quoted in Moshe Greenberg, *Understanding Exodus*, Heritage of Biblical Israel 2 (New York: Behrman House, 1969), 26.

10. Carol Meyers, *Women in Scripture* (Grand Rapids, MI: William B. Eerdmans, 2000), 187.

11. *B'reishit Rabbah* 42:8.

12. David Dishon and Noam Zion, *A Different Night: The Leader's Guide to the Family Participation Haggadah* (Jerusalem: Shalom Hartman Institute, 1997), 49.

13. "Sally Priesand," Jewish Women's Archive, http://jwa.org/feminism/_html/JWA059.htm.

14. *The Torah: A Women's Commentary*, ed. Andrea L. Weiss and Tamara Cohn Eskenazi (New York: Women of Reform Judaism and URJ Press, 2008), 1030.

45

PORTRAITS OF THE RABBI
AS A YOUNG WOMAN

Wendy Zierler, PhD

In 1889, journalist Mary M. Cohen published a story called "A Problem for Purim" in the Philadelphia *Jewish Exponent*, marking the beginning of the literary representation of the American woman rabbi. In the story, a female superintendent of a sewing school named Dora Ullman conjectures out loud about the possibility of Jewish women "ministers."[1] The context of the story is a Purim Eve get-together organized by Lionel Martinez, a young Jewish (Sephardic) man himself "preparing for the ministry."[2] There is little to the discussion or the story that calls to mind contemporary observances of Purim—no chanting of the *M'gilah*, no drinking or masquerading. Dora Ullman gives voice, however, to a proto-feminism that finds precedence in the biblical Book of Esther. Like the biblical Esther, Dora is lodged in a traditional female sphere, and yet her ideas push the boundaries of gender roles. Over the course of the Purim Eve discussion, Dora adduces the biblical leadership examples of Miriam, Deborah, Hannah, and Huldah as proof of women's capacity for leadership; she quotes Margaret Fuller (who encouraged "conversations" as a way for women to gain knowledge otherwise denied them by a lack of higher education) and provocatively suggests that "there are trials in the lives of men and women that men do not and cannot understand. About these our sex could probably preach and teach better than men could."[3] The story concludes with a reference to Purim as "the Festival of Queen Esther," underscoring the notion of female leadership as well the Purim motif of *v'nahafoch hu*—the overturning of previously established norms. If the Book of Esther begins with an indulgent, patriarchal king endeavoring to show his power by objectifying his queen, all gets turned over when the new queen successfully influences—indeed, determines—the king's agenda. And if Lionel Martinez initially hesitates to invite women to his to Purim Eve get-together because "some of the fellows will dislike it,"[4] his eventual invitation of Dora Ullman and her unconventional portrait of women as potential clergy members constitutes a Book-of-Esther-esque *v'nahafoch hu* moment.

Almost a century separates this literary representation of the *idea* of the woman rabbi from the first literary portraits of actual American women rabbis. Sally Priesand is ordained in 1972, but it is not until the 1980s and, really, the 1990s that fiction writers begin to populate their fiction with women rabbis.

In 1983, Rhonda Shapiro-Wieser publishes a novel called *A Place of Light*, the last chapters of which depict a Reform woman rabbi, who manages, despite the opposition of the ailing senior rabbi and the bitter resentment of his jealous wife, to gain the position of senior rabbi. Four years later, Joseph Teluskhin's *The Unorthodox Murder of Rabbi Wahl* (1987) kills off the woman assistant rabbi before she can get that far. The title character of Telushkin's mystery novel is Rabbi Myra Wahl, a strident and angry feminist who is despised not only by Rabbi Winter, the male rabbi protagonist of the novel, but also by her own congregants, who want to fire her. Telushkin decides to have Rabbi Wahl murdered early on in the novel, a plot detail that bespeaks a certain anxiety about women in the rabbinate, to say the least. Alex J. Goldman's *The Lady Is a Rabbi*, published the same year, offers a more supportive, albeit implausible, picture of the widow of a Conservative rabbi, who without being ordained or trained in any way, is permanently appointed to her departed husband's pulpit.[5]

Next comes Erich Segal's *Acts of Faith* (1992), which tells the story of the son and daughter of the Silczer Rebbe, both of whom become rabbis. The son, Danny Luria, initially turns his back on the Chasidic world of his father, while the daughter, Deborah Luria, goes the even more errant way of Colleen McCollough's *The Thornbirds*: she falls in love with a Catholic boy named Timothy, who becomes a priest, and she escapes to a secular kibbutz in Israel, during which time she sees Timothy again and becomes pregnant with his son. Possessed by a desire to study Torah, she then leaves kibbutz and Israel to become a Reform rabbi but ultimately abandons the pulpit as well, on the grounds that it doesn't afford a good lifestyle for a (single) mother. The narrative line of Danny's story runs from his early rejection of the Chasidic rabbinate to his later acceptance of his destiny to marry his *basherte* and become the Silczer Rebbe after all. Deborah's rabbinate, initially an expression of feminist defiance, is literally and figuratively brushed aside by the narrative sweep of Danny's story. Danny finds love and divine vocation by the novel's end; for Deborah, her love of Timothy becomes enough.[6]

In large part, these novels are of middling literary quality, lacking believable characters and credible incident. Perhaps the most interesting representation of a woman rabbi to surface during this period is a quirky, Malamudesque story by Eileen Pollack entitled "The Rabbi in the Attic," the title of which evokes Sandra M. Gilbert and Susan Gubar's now-classic feminist study of nineteenth-century women's poetry and fiction.[7] Even here, however, Pollack's cartoon depictions of a crackpot Old-World-style male rabbi (dubbed "Rabbi Or Else") and his hyperbolically leftist female successor, a Reform rabbi whose "voice sounds like fishbones,"[8] bring little glory to the rabbinate either in masculine or feminine guise.

The next major turning point in the literary representation of the American rabbinate (and the role of women therein) occurs in 2004, with the publication of three novels that deal either with woman rabbis or rabbis-in-training: Amy Sohn's *My Old Man*, Julius Lester's

The Autobiography of God, and Jonathan Rosen's novel *Joy Comes in the Morning*.

Amy Sohn's *My Old Man* opens as Rachel Block, a fledgling female rabbinical student at the Rabbinical College of Reform Judaism (RCRJ, an obvious stand-in for Hebrew Union College–Jewish Institute of Religion) and a pastoral intern at Memorial (Sloan Kettering) Hospital, is confronted with some tough questions by a thirty-nine-year-old terminal leukemia patient named Neil Roth. The patient wants to know why all this is happening to him and if he is being punished. "Why," for starters, "would a just God let a decent person die?"[9] Rachel, the first-person narrator of the novel, attempts to draw on her limited training and education to answer essentially unanswerable questions. She quotes Harold Kushner, Abraham Joshua Heschel, and others, and offers to say a *Mi Shebeirach* for him, but Neil remains unconvinced and uncomforted by any of her attempts to counsel. Rachel begins to feel "lost, like a total fraud."[10] As a result she decides to "level with him," to admit that her "own God-vision isn't all that strong."[11] More than that: she agrees with him that it makes no sense to put a positive face on his situation: "You'll never get to see your daughter grow up. It totally sucks!"[12] In response to this pastoral about-face, Neil becomes even more desperate and pained: "You are the worst...rabbi...I ever... met,"[13] and seconds later, he dies right before Rachel's eyes. As a consequence of this encounter, Rachel decides she is neither leadership nor pastoral material, drops out of rabbinical school, and becomes a bartender in a Brooklyn bar. Soon thereafter, she begins a torrid and self-abasing affair with a famous gentile writer/filmmaker named Hank Powell, whom she meets through an actor friend. Essentially unable to muster the faith or acumen to serve in the traditionally masculine profession of the rabbinate, she opts instead to become "arm candy"[14] for an old man—to worship and be sexually dominated by a male cultural icon. While all this is happening, Rachel's father (her other "old man") loses his job, starts working out, and begins having an affair with Rachel's upstairs neighbor and nymphomaniac friend, Liz. The title of the novel thus reflects a multilayered preoccupation with older men/

father figures, with their potency and genius as well as their impudence and impotence.

Amy Sohn spent many years as a sex columnist, and so this novel reads more like a series of racy episodes from *Sex in the City* than as a serious literary or theological exploration of the rabbinic vocation for women. The novel derives much of its energy from Rachel Block's scandalous sexual adventures with Powell. How could sexy, artsy, mouthy Rachel Block have ever even thought of being a rabbi? Indeed, from the outset the novel betrays an anxiety and titillation over the idea of female rabbinic sex appeal. In the aftermath of her dropping out of rabbinical school, Rachel recalls how ecstatic her father was when she was initially accepted: "he got a custom-made T-shirt that said 'BLESS ME—I'M A RABBI'S DAD' on the front and 'SHE AIN'T BAD-LOOKING, EITHER' on the back, in big, felt block letters."[15] Similarly, when she first meets Powell and tells him that she had been in rabbinical school, he says with a smirk, "I didn't know rabbis came like this."[16] Powell repeatedly tells her that her interest in being a rabbi is the result of her excessively strong (Jungian) anima or masculine side. Her affair with him thus represents a quest to subdue her anima and better inhabit the feminine role. She fantasizes about going to the theater with Powell and being introduced to others as "his little rabbi."[17] In the end, Rachel has the good sense to dump Powell and all this nonsense; and as the novel closes, she frankly embraces the alternative pastoral/counseling function of bartending. The novel, however, does not leave the rabbinate at that. After his marital infidelity comes to light and Rachel's mother refuses to reconcile, Rachel's hapless father decides that what he wants to do most is apply to rabbinical school himself, an announcement that Rachel somehow greets with joy. He plans to write his admissions essays on *t'shuvah*. Will Rachel help him with the application?

Needless to say, this novel does not offer a very flattering portrait of the Reform rabbinical college or the students it attracts. That said, there are a number of elements to this novel that make it somewhat noteworthy. First, it reckons frankly if disturbingly with the issues surrounding the sexual lives of young clergy-in-training. Second, it portrays and reflects the biases that govern these sexual lives, showing that in the minds of most people, men can still get away with sexual misbehavior; these same men can even become rabbis. Rachel's philandering father is ultimately presented as a more credible candidate for the rabbinate than Rachel ever was. Sohn's novel thus raises some salient issues but falls back on entrenched, essentialist views of gender, sexuality, and the rabbinate, even as it trumpets a kind of unabashed spirit of female sexual exploration.

In *The Autobiography of God*, Julius Lester, a former black civil rights activist and convert to Judaism, whose own identity represents a form of postmodern multiplicity, plays midrashically with the idea of revelation and truth and offers a (post)modern challenge to the traditional theology. The counter-traditional image of the woman rabbi helps support and advance this challenge to the authority of and truth of Scripture. On one level, Lester's novel, which takes place in a college in the Northeast and includes a murder-mystery element, can be seen as an outgrowth of the rabbi-mystery-novel genre created by Harry Kemelman.[18] Like Rabbi Small in the Kemelman novels, Rebecca Nachman, the protagonist of Lester's books, has an uncompromising streak and tendency toward traditional ritual practice. In contrast to Rabbi Small, however, who endures each and every crisis in his synagogue despite constant opposition, Rebecca Nachman resigns her rabbinic post in frustration after five years on the job and instead seeks employment as a college psychologist. It is in this post-rabbinic phase of her career that we meet our protagonist; over the course of the novel, one of her patients at the college is brutally murdered, and by the end, she possesses the knowledge of the murderer's identity. Unlike Rabbi Small, Rebecca does not herself solve the murder mystery. The murderer (a former colleague and admirer) *reveals* himself to her in the form of a confessional letter, which Rebecca dutifully hands over to the police.

The concept of revelation (as opposed to logical deduction) is crucial to this novel, for in addition to the mystery murder plot, the novel includes an even more important revelatory strain, including

surrealistic/humorous elements evocative of the tales of Rabbi Nachman (as hinted by the name Rebecca Nachman) and the short stories
of Bernard Malamud, particularly "The Jewbird" and "Angel Levine."
Halfway through the book, Rebecca, the daughter of Holocaust survivors, is visited by the angelic spirit of her dead Aunt Devorah (a victim
of the Holocaust), who brings with her (at the request of a black angel
named Hymie Brown) a text entitled "The Autobiography of God,"
purportedly written by God Himself.[19] A beautiful and provocative
work of modern midrash, the text-within-the text is a boldly irreverent
attempt to rewrite the Genesis Creation story as well as other chapters in Judeo-Christian theology in light of the persistence of evil, as
epitomized by the Holocaust. Lester's *The Autobiography of God* thus
becomes not only one of the first books to present an admiring portrait
of the rabbi as woman, but also one of the first works of postbiblical
Jewish literature to imagine a woman as the recipient of revelation.

A descendant of other truth-seeking women, Rebecca receives this
revelation in her dual role as a student of religious texts and as a therapist, who must listen with empathy and without judgment to all sorts
of personal revelations in order to help a person heal. In His autobiography, Lester's God writes of His attempt to take on flesh to promote
goodness and His distress that in response, humans begin to separate
love/good and evil into different spheres of operation, with a much
greater interest, all around, in evil. In the hope of redressing this imbalance, God takes on flesh as Evil, but in the process gets stuck in the
role of evil incarnate. God's "Autobiography," as written to Rebecca,
is a call for "someone to retrieve me from evil."[20] Rebe(cca) Nachman
thus becomes rabbi/therapist not only for her students/congregants
but for God Himself.

In comparison to Lester's novelistic combination of detective novel
and Rabbi Nachman tale, Jonathan Rosen's *Joy Comes in the Morning*
insists that rabbis have access neither to coercive immovable authority
nor to revelatory truth. More than that, Rosen's novel makes the postmodern argument that being a rabbi is an identity that is constructed
rather than received, that is performed and imitated. The rabbinic

performances of identity in *Joy Comes in the Morning* seem authentically linked with the Jewish past, even as they depict a rabbinate that is very much part of a changing, postmodern Jewish reality. Rosen's rabbi protagonist is Deborah Green, a name that calls to mind the biblical judge/prophet Deborah in Judges 4–5 and also points to the newness or "greenness" of the very idea of a woman rabbi:

SOMEONE WAS DYING.

Deborah felt it in her chest. She felt it along her spine. She felt it, though she could not have explained it, in her womb. The feeling stirred her out of half sleep. She opened her eyes. The shades were drawn but a blue light had begun to seep in around the edges. It was 6 a.m.

Now would be a good time to hear a voice. She would like to have been called. *Deborah! Deborah!* But it no longer happened that way, if it ever had.[21]

Here too, as in the case of Amy Sohn's Rachel Block, we have a portrait of a woman rabbi as chaplain, but Rosen's Deborah Green is far better and more natural at her job. She is still single and not yet a biological mother, and yet she is one who looks after her congregants physically, emotionally, and spiritually, feeling their pain as if in her womb. Like the biblical prophet Deborah, Deborah Green is a Mother-in-Israel who is not limited by the womb, who rises up rather than disappears through her feminine role.

Note, however, that if Deborah Green's role recalls the biblical Deborah, the concluding lines of the quoted passage make clear the distance between Deborah then and now: "She would like to have been called. *Deborah! Deborah!* But it no longer happened that way, if it ever had." Though the womb imagery suggests an innate, biologically ordained kind of leadership, Deborah Green avers that leaders aren't born, or chosen by God, but made. To be a rabbi is to construct and perform a rabbinic identity, even in the face of the sort of doubts that compel Rachel Block to abandon the whole project, even before it has really begun.

An acceptance of the unsettled, endlessly constructed nature of rabbinic identity pervades Rosen's novel. In part this proceeds from the particular kind of liberal rabbinate exemplified by Deborah Green, itself a recent construction or iteration of an ever-changing Reform Judaism. As Deborah reflects, "she resented terms like *Orthodox* and *Reform*—they seemed a substitute for the inner state."[22] This is a woman rabbi who defies easy categorization, who keeps kosher and tries to observe minor fasts, who prays daily in tallit and/or *t'fillin*, who once dated an Orthodox man (Reuben)[23] and now is living with another boyfriend (Lev), whom she met while visiting his father (who had a stroke after trying to commit suicide) in the hospital. When Lev first sees Deborah bending over his father in his hospital room, her lips moving but inaudibly (recalling Hannah in I Sam. 1:13), he mistakes her for a nun or minister administering last rites. By past definitions of Reform Judaism, or any Judaism for that matter, Deborah's rabbinate is an unexpected, even queer thing.

The ghost of Isaac Bashevis Singer's famous 1962 story "Yentl the Yeshiva Boy" hovers over this novel, further "queering" the idea of rabbinic identity. Unlike Yentl, Deborah need not masquerade as a man to study Talmud with Lev and fall in love. And yet, she remains anxiously cognizant about the way in which her rabbinate and Jewish practice constitute a kind of cross-dressing, what theorist Marjorie Garber has termed a "crisis of categories."[24]

Early on in the novel, in a scene where Deborah is saying her morning prayers and wearing her grandfather's tallis, Deborah recalls indignantly that when Reuben (her Orthodox ex-boyfriend) "had seen her in her tallis for the first time he had called her a transvestite."[25] Later on in the novel, again when Deborah is praying in her tallis, Lev mistakes her for a "strange ghostly man."[26] Deborah is described as not wanting to "be one of those desexed rabbis who hung around the synagogue like neutered housecats. Or like so many of the women in her graduating class with their close-cropped Yentl-the-yeshiva-boy haircuts and frumpy clothes, you half expected their voices to begin cracking.

Deborah disliked being around them and hoped that this aversion was not because her sister, Rachel, was gay."[27]

Like Deborah, Lev Friedman has his own anxieties about the way in which his identity confounds categories. At the end of the chapter where Deborah and Lev first get together to study Talmud, a sexually charged scene, Deborah, puts "her hands up to his face" and tells him that in his face she sees "intelligence...gentleness. You have a great capacity for understanding. A kind of old-world quality. A real Jewish face."[28] Lev takes offense at Deborah's remarks about his Jewish face and abruptly leaves her apartment in embarrassment over his "throw-back face and [unmanly] old-world longings."[29]

The journey of development that both Deborah and Lev undergo in the novel thus involves learning how to accept rather than rail against the crisis of categories that their lives represent. Throughout the novel, we see characters assuming different identities and a persistent challenging of the notion of a fixed, coherent self. The most significant instance occurs when Deborah herself experiences a crisis of faith, both in God and in her relationship with Lev, compelling her to flee her own apartment (as Lev did early on in the novel) to seek refuge in her lesbian sister's home in New Jersey. While Deborah is away—Lev has no idea where she has gone—he takes a call at Deborah's apartment from a woman who is looking for a rabbi to perform her mother's funeral; somehow, over the course of this conversation, Lev decides to open up Deborah's *Gates of Mitzvah: A Guide to the Jewish Life Cycle* and quote from it to reassure the bereaved woman. "You must be a rabbi yourself," the woman says. Before long, Lev is acting the part of rabbi and arranging to perform the funeral. If Singer's "Yentl the Yeshiva Boy" is about a woman who poses as a man in order to study Torah, the scene in this novel in which Lev conducts a funeral puts a new spin on the Yentl plot, offering an instance of a man impersonating a (woman) rabbi.

It is worth noting that almost all of the recent fiction portraying women rabbis place great emphasis on their role as hospital chaplains. My survey of twenty-first-century portraits of the woman rabbi began with the failed chaplaincy of Rachel Block, and the most recent American literary depiction of a woman rabbi, Michael Chabon's story "Citizen Conn," once again features a female rabbinic chaplain who seems almost preternaturally good at her job, even as she is willing to admit the limits of understanding when it comes to the mysteries of both human relations and mortality. Myra Teplitz, the chaplain in an assisted-living facility called Zion Pointe, narrates the story, which focuses on a resident named Morton Feathers, the former co-creator with a man named Artie Conn of a series of comic books Teplitz's husband had adored as a child. Like Neil Roth in Sohn's book, Feathers is dying of cancer. Over the course of the story, Artie Conn attempts visits to Zion Pointe several times to make amends for wrongs he had previously done to Feathers, including negotiating a publishing deal without Feathers and behind his back. Teplitz witnesses Conn's failed attempts to reconcile, which include an abortive attempt to give Feathers a large check. When Feathers dies and leaves Conn his copy of their high school yearbook, Rabbi Teplitz intuits that Feathers had been a lonely boy and man, who felt Conn's betrayal so keenly and unremittingly not because he was cheated out of money, but because when they met as high schoolers, it was the first time in Feathers's outcast life that he did not feel alone. Ultimately, Teplitz's success as a chaplain inheres in her paradoxical ability to comprehend the fact of human cluelessness:

> I didn't know what to say, how to explain to him [Conn] that this—our everlasting human cluelessness—was his unforgivable sin. I went around to my desk, and hugged him goodbye. As he walked, limping, out of my office and my life—a month later he had a stroke and died, on his knees, beside his bed, while feeling around for a lost slipper—I said a prayer for him. I prayed that one day, here or in another place, Mr. Conn would find the forgiveness that he sought from the shade of the boy he once chatted with, for an hour, about life on other worlds, on what had been, though he was blind to it, the happiest day of his life."[30]

This chapter began with Mary Cohen's late nineteenth-century hunch that there were problems in the lives of women that men did not understand and about which women "ministers" might be able to teach, preach, and counsel. It fittingly culminates with a story by a twenty-first-century Pulitzer Prize–winning author, who takes for granted women's capacity for understanding not only the problems of women, but also of men. Cohen's Dora Ullman argued that the rabbinic "desk must reverberate the full heart of humanity, or its eloquence will become a vanishing sound."[31] Fittingly it is Myra Teplitz's eloquent voice and subtle understanding that frame Chabon's entire story. It is a voice quite unlike her predecessors, with little misgiving about the job she occupies and yet with few illusions about how easy any of it is ever going to be.

Some of the material in this chapter is adapted from my previously published article "A Dignitary in the Land? Literary Representations of the American Rabbi," *AJS Review* 30, no. 2 (November 2006): 255–75. Reprinted with permission from Cambridge University Press.

NOTES

1. Mary M. Cohen, "A Problem for Purim," *Jewish Exponent* 4, no. 23 (March 15, 1989): 1. For historical information about Mary M. Cohen and for an analysis of the story, see Pamela M. Nadell, *Women Who Would Be Rabbis: A History of Women's Ordination, 1889–1985* (Boston: Beacon Press, 1998), 1–7. See also Nadell, pages 31–43, this volume.

2. Cohen, "A Problem for Purim," 1.

3. Ibid.

4. Ibid.

5. Alex J. Goldman, *The Rabbi Is a Lady* (New York: Hippocrene Books, 1987). In 1987, Goldman's book was already a bit dated, given that the vote on whether to ordain women in the Conservative Movement had already taken place in 1983. In Pamela Nadell's path-breaking study of the history of women's ordination, she tells the story of a woman named Paula Ackerman, whose husband Rabbi William Ackerman, rabbi of a congregation in Meridian, Mississippi, died on November 30, 1950; a week later the synagogue's board asked Mrs. Ackerman "to carry on the ministry until they could get a rabbi" (see Nadell, *Women Who Would be Rabbis*, 120–26). It is possible, therefore, that Goldman based his novel on this real-life story. It is worth noting, however, that Goldman sets his story in suburban Long Island rather than in a place like Meridian, Mississippi. It is unlikely that a congregation located so near to the center of American Jewish life and to the Jewish Theological Seminary would feel the need to take this step of appointing the (untrained) *rebbetzin* as rabbi.

6. For another perspective on these novels as well as discussion of other works, see David J. Zucker, "Rebbetzins and Woman Rabbis: Portrayals in Contemporary American Jewish Fiction," *CCAR Journal* 42, no. 1 (Winter–Spring 1995), 1–12. Also see his book *American Rabbis: Facts and Fiction* (Northvale, NJ: Jason Aronson, 1998). Of all the works I surveyed, Roger Herst's *Woman of the Cloth* (Rockville, MD: Shengold Books, 1998), which features both a male and a female rabbi, was the most problematic. The novel begins with the mysterious disappearance of the senior rabbi Seth Greer amid a string of sexual scandals. By the end of the novel, the sleuth-like junior rabbi Gabrielle Lewyn has managed to vindicate her former boss before the entire congregation, on the grounds that Rabbi Greer's various sexual encounters with women congregants were undertaken not for reasons of lust but for the "kabbalistic" purpose of helping these depressed, postmenopausal women achieve an encounter with the Divine. That anyone on earth would buy that argument, let alone a supposedly brilliant, independent-minded woman rabbi, is nothing short of incredible. Both Seth Greer and his assistant Rabbi Gabby occupy an oversexed presence in this novel. While the novel promotes the idea of women's place in the rabbinate, it seems in part to want to detach women rabbis from the feminist movement, placing Gabby and a strong woman lawyer in the position of defending an accused rapist against a female accuser named Elisheva Waller, dubbed in the novel as the "Queen of Feminism." This is a woman rabbi who is allowed her place because she drinks with men, sleeps with Jewish and non-Jewish men, fights like a man (in and out of the courtroom), and ultimately deals several major blows to the idea of (feminist) political correctness. For other recent novels in which women rabbis appear, see Anita Diamant, *Good Harbor: A Novel* (New York: Scribner, 2001), Athol Dickson, *They Shall See God: A Novel* (Wheaton, IL: Tyndale House, 2002), and Leora Freedman, *The Ivory Pomegranate: A Novel* (Hewlett, NY: Gefen, 2002). In Freedman's novel, as in Erich Segal's *Acts of Faith*, the woman rabbi is given the name Deborah/Devora.

7. See Sandra M. Gilbert, *The Madwoman in the Attic* (New Haven, CT: Yale University Press, 1977).

8. Eileen Pollack, *The Rabbi in the Attic and Other Stories* (Harrison, NY: Delphinium Books, 1991), 103.

9. Amy Sohn, *My Old Man* (New York: Simon & Schuster, 2004), 2.

10. Ibid., 5.

11. Ibid.

12. Ibid., 6.

13. Ibid.

14. Ibid., 64.

15. Ibid., 16.

16. Ibid., 37.

17. Ibid., 66.

18. Lester acknowledges reading the Kemelman novels in his memoir *Lovesong: Becoming a Jew* (New York: Henry Holt, 1988), 142.

19. Lester insists, in the name of his woman rabbi, that God must be male. "She never understood why some of the women she went to rabbinical school with had insisted that God was female.…Obviously God was male because who except a man would try to show how clever he was by coming up with something as ridiculous as vagina, clitoris, uterus, and stick them in the narrow space between a woman's legs

where they could not be seen, were hard to find, and then cover them all with hair."
See Julius Lester, *The Autobiography of God* (New York: St. Martin's Press, 2004),
131–32.

20. Ibid., 155.

21. Jonathan Rosen, *Joy Comes in the Morning* (New York: Farrar, Strauss, and
Giroux, 2004), 3.

22. Ibid., 5.

23. Considerable controversy has erupted in the press, both general and Jewish,
over Rosen's portrayal of Orthodox men. See Bezalel Stern, "Can You Fall in Love
with a Concept?," JBooks.com, http://www.jbooks.com/fiction/index/FI_Stern_
Rosen.htm. See also Wendy Shalit, "The Observant Reader," *New York Times Book
Review*, Sunday January 30, 2005, 16–17; and the various responses to Shalit's piece
including Sandee Brawarsky, "The Novel as Tzitzit Check," *Jewish Week*, February
4, 2005, as well as Sara Horowitz's essay, "Mediating Judaism: Mind, Body, Spirit,
and Contemporary North American Jewish Fiction," *AJS Review* 30, no. 2, (November 2006), 231-53.

24. Marjorie Garber, *Vested Interests: Cross-Dressing and Cultural Anxiety* (New
York: Routledge, 1992), 16.

25. Rosen, *Joy Comes in the Morning*, 5.

26. Ibid., 172.

27. Ibid., 39.

28. Ibid., 154.

29. Ibid., 156–57.

30. Michael Chabon, "Citizen Conn," *New Yorker*, February 13 & 20, 2012,
p. 101.

31. Cohen, "A Problem for Purim," 1.

46

SEARCHING FOR THE
FICTIONAL WOMAN RABBI
ON THE SMALL AND LARGE SCREEN

RABBI DAVID J. ZUCKER PHD

The lack of examples of women as rabbis in TV shows and in the cinema was recently lamented by Rabbi Jordie Gerson in a blog posting titled "Letter to Hollywood—I Don't Have a Beard or Side Curls and I Look Just Like You: American Judaism's Image Problem (see page 741)." She concludes with these words: "The problem is this: These images make our jobs harder. Especially for female rabbis.... The Jews we serve don't recognize us. I don't either. It's time for that to change."[1] Stated simply, compared to the relative ease with which it is possible to find women rabbis in fiction, it is nearly impossible to find women rabbis as characters in fictional television programs or in films produced in North America.

Rabbis have long appeared as fictional characters in novels and short stories, reaching a heyday in the three or four decades at the end of the twentieth century. This is the period that includes the groundbreaking rabbi as central character in such books as Harry Kemelman's "Weekday Rabbi" series, *Friday the Rabbi Slept Late* (1964), *Saturday the Rabbi Went Hungry* (1966), and on for a total of twelve novels up through *That Day the Rabbi Left Town* (1996). It is the time of Herbert Tarr's

The Conversion of Chaplain Cohen (1963) and *Heaven Help Us!* (1968); it includes Noah Gordon's novel *The Rabbi* (1965), Chaim Potok's *The Chosen* (1967), Jerome Weidman's *The Temple* (1975), Howard Fast's *The Outsider* (1984), and Morton Levine and Hal Kantor's *The Congregation* (1985). Rabbis were also featured in print as important, although not central characters in short stories by Philip Roth, "The Conversion of the Jews" (1959), and Bernard Malamud, "The Silver Crown" (1973), as well as in Sylvia Tennenbaum's novel *Rachel, the Rabbi's Wife* (1978).

When rabbis were just briefly presented in fiction, most often they were teaching classes, conducting services, or officiating at life-cycle events such as *b'nei mitzvah*, weddings, and funerals. These examples include Bernard Malamud's *The Assistant* (1957), Saul Bellow's *Herzog* (1964), Herb Gold's *Fathers* (1966), Mordecai Richler's *St. Urbain's Horseman* (1971), Alice Kahn's *Fun with Dirk and Bree* (1991), Philip Roth's *Sabbath's Theater* (1995), and Allegra Goodman's *Paradise Park* (2001).The rabbis in Pulitzer Prize–winning Michael Chabon's noir novel set in Alaska, *The Yiddish Policemen's Union* (2007), stand out, with their gangland ties.

As I explain in my book *American Rabbis: Facts and Fiction*, a reader needs to explore a variety of stories to get a feel for rabbinic life in North America.[2] It is not possible to read only a novel or two to obtain a realistic view of the American rabbinate. When, however, such works are read more widely, there does emerge a broad and accurate view of rabbinical life in our contemporary world.

Characters depicting male rabbis appear in various TV shows and numerous films, but it is rare that they have major roles. Often these rabbis are bearded and Orthodox, although exceptions exist. An example is Kemelman's Conservative rabbi David Small, who appears in a made-for-TV adaption in 1975, *Friday the Rabbi Slept Late* (with Art Carney as Chief Lanigan and Stuart Margolin as Rabbi Small). Later there is the film *Keeping the Faith* (2000) with Ben Stiller.

Like the ordination of women, the introduction of women rabbis as fictional characters in print is also more recent.[3] In nearly all cases, these women are less than central characters. Still, women rabbis do occasionally have a significant role in some novels and short stories,[4] in some cases even a lead character.[5]

Nonetheless, even though women now have a forty-year history in the rabbinate,[6] as fictional characters—with the rarest of exceptions—they do not appear in films or TV shows. To date, there are no examples of a fictional woman rabbi as the lead character in a film or TV production.[7] Indeed, having scoured the Internet sources and polled rabbinic listservs for ideas, the clear answer is that as noted at the beginning of this chapter, a woman rabbi portrayed in a fictional TV or film story in North America is nearly impossible to find.

In several cases, where a woman rabbi does appear, she makes only a cameo appearance. The earliest example of a woman rabbi character on TV is on the "soap" *One Life to Live* (1995). Actress Camryn Manheim is featured in three episodes as Rabbi Heller; in two episodes she has a speaking role when she co-officiates with a Christian minister at an interfaith wedding. The next year (1996), on the well-received comedy series *The Larry Sanders Show* (starring Garry Shandling), actress Amy Aquino has limited, but more substantial appearances as Rabbi Susan Klein in the episode "My Name Is Asher Kingsley." A few years would go by until the successful series *The Nanny*, starring Fran Drescher, would feature a woman rabbi. In the episode "Maggie's Wedding" (1999), Sue Goodman as an unnamed rabbi conducts an interfaith wedding with a Christian cleric, who co-officiates next to her.

The opening decade of the twenty-first century sees an increasing number of examples featuring women rabbis in the fictional media. The TV drama series *Six Feet Under* (2001–2005) is about the family dynamics of the Fisher family and the business of owning and running a mortuary. Created and produced by Alan Ball, it won numerous media-related awards (Emmy, Golden Globe, Screen Actors Guild, Peabody). Rabbi Ari Hoffman (played by Molly Parker) appears in the second season (2002) in two nonconsecutive episodes. As shall be discussed below, the figure of Rabbi Ari Hoffman was developed after one of the writers for the series, Jill Soloway, met with real-life rabbi Michelle Missaghieh, the associate rabbi at Temple Israel of Hollywood.

Rabbi Missaghieh herself agreed to appear in an episode of a different series, *Grey's Anatomy*, which aired in mid-2005. There, a real-life rabbi portrays an unnamed fictional rabbi brought in to offer support for a young, newly Orthodox woman who is about to undergo emergency heart surgery. Fully garbed in a medical gown, the rabbi chants the *Mi Shebeirach*, the prayer for healing, in the operating room.

A woman rabbi is featured in a few scenes in the Hallmark Channel's made-for-TV movie *Loving Leah*, which first ran in 2007. There Rabbi Gerry Schwartz (played by Rikki Lake) serves Temple Judah Reform Congregation in Georgetown/Washington, D.C.

On the TV series *Eli Stone* (2008–2009), which centers on a law practice, Rabbi Rebecca Green (Jayne Brook) is featured prominently in one episode (2008). Her businessman husband has cancer. He feels God has spoken to him and given him permission to stop treatment. Although Rabbi Green appears to have an ongoing loving relationship with her husband, she nonetheless petitions the secular courts to override his decision. She claims that this is a manifestation of his depression and that he should fight for his life, for his family's sake, for her sake, and for his own sake.

Finally, Rabbi Renannah Zimmerman (Maggie Siff) appears in the 2009 movie *Leaves of Grass*. Again, the woman as rabbi is a minor figure. In her limited appearances, Rabbi Zimmerman is depicted as serving a Conservative synagogue in Tulsa, Oklahoma. She is featured conducting Shabbat services, on another occasion briefly interviewed by a TV news team, and finally meeting in her office with the lead character.

While these women rabbis may be only guest characters in these shows, they play important roles when they appear. For example, the episode of *Eli Stone* featuring Rabbi Rebecca Green was significant in that it depicted a religious practitioner going to the secular courts to seek a decision concerning her husband's body. It was also significant in showing a woman making a decision about a man's (her husband's) body.

The character of Rabbi Ari Hoffman (Molly Parker, *Six Feet Under*) is substantial. She interacts with lead characters in several episodes, providing an ongoing thread related to the pastoral and ritual work of a rabbi. She first appears at a congregant's funeral and at the cemetery. Later she offers premarital counseling to two of the lead characters.

Sometimes the woman rabbi is a catalyst for important conversations. Rabbi Susan Klein (Amy Aquino, *The Larry Sanders Show*) initially is invited to visit the TV set backstage prior to a taping of the Larry Sanders Talk Show. She has a spirited conversation with the Jewish character, Hank Kingsley, who is working through what it means for him to be a *baal t'shuvah*. On a subsequent night she is featured again backstage. Rabbi Gerry Schwartz (Rikki Lake, *Loving Leah*) meets the lead male character presumably following a Shabbat service. The lead female character meets Rabbi Schwartz earlier on a weekday at the synagogue. Although this is not an extensive role for the rabbi, she does have meaningful conversations on both of these occasions, which help provide depth and background for the more major characters.

When considering the more prominent portrayals of women rabbis, to what extent are they realistic, and how positive are these presentations? What do they tell us?

Sometimes the rabbi is presented as an authority figure, who explains rules and customs. Rabbi Gerry Schwartz (*Loving Leah*), probably in her later thirties, chats with the lead character, Leah Lever, in the sanctuary of Schwartz's suburban synagogue. Leah is the young widow of a Chasidic rabbi in Brooklyn. She recently married his brother, Dr. Jake Lever, a thirty-year-old cardiologist living in Washington, D.C. Her new husband comes from a Reform background, but he appears to be non-practicing. Leah, who has never been in a Reform synagogue, has come into the building to see what one looks like. A sign in front of the synagogue says that the rabbi is Gerry Schwartz, but this could be a man or a woman. Leah is amazed to find out the rabbi is a *woman*. Given Leah's Chasidic background, this creates conflict in two ways: her experience dictates that women are not rabbis, but it is likely easier for Leah to speak to another woman. In that conversation, Rabbi Schwartz learns that Leah and Dr. Lever decided to wed as an alternative to his being required to "renounce" Leah at a Chasidic-organized *chalitzah* ceremony. Rabbi Schwartz says to Leah that she did not believe that the *chalitzah* ritual was still being practiced.

Later in the film, Dr. Lever briefly chats with Rabbi Schwartz following a synagogue service. By this point, he has fallen in love with Leah. He wants to "explain" this to his deceased brother. Rabbi Schwartz says that often the souls of the deceased are in a kind of holding pattern for a time after death. On one hand, while not commonly taught as Reform theology, this view is consonant with elements of Jewish tradition (cf. Babylonian Talmud, *Bava M'tzia* 85b; *Bava Batra* 58a). In this example, Rabbi Schwartz is depicted as warm, caring, and sympathetic in her pastoral encounters, as well as educated in Jewish tradition.

The depiction of the woman rabbi as religious authority figure is often intertwined with the idea of woman rabbi as a sexual figure in these screen depictions. Dressed in a red pantsuit with matching shoes, Rabbi Susan Klein initially appears backstage speaking with one of the lead characters, Hank Kingsley (Jeffrey Tambor), an indifferent, unaffiliated secular Jew (*The Larry Sanders Show*). Apparently, the two met at the previous week's Shabbat services at her synagogue. He invited her to come backstage for a tour prior to a taping of the TV show where he appears. Hank tells Rabbi Klein that he wants to join her synagogue, but she discourages him from doing so. She observes that such a decision "requires a deep, deep commitment." She questions if he possesses the necessary purity of intent to join the synagogue. He insists his intent is pure.

This kind of conversation is unrealistic; Jews join synagogues for a variety of reasons, and rabbis do not speak of a membership prerequisite concerning one's purity of intent. Also unrealistically, she is depicted as sending a mixed message. For some reason, she brings him a present of a white *kippah* and then actually places it on his head.

There is a strange sense that she is portrayed as acting in a priest-like manner, both blessing him and offering him atonement.

In her other appearance in the same episode, Rabbi Klein wears a dark suit with a white blouse. Some time has passed since she gave Hank the *kippah*. Hank has insisted on wearing it on air, causing discomfort to the show's staff and sponsors. Apparently Hank has been in touch with Klein and has asked her to come to offer pastoral support. In their private conversation backstage, Rabbi Klein offers wise counsel to Hank. She suggests that wearing a *kippah* is important, but it is only a symbolic gesture. What is essential is one's spirituality, which "comes from within." She concludes with a positive affirmation, noting that she looks forward to his future involvement at the temple. He then changes the subject and professes his attraction to her as a woman, not as a rabbi. Taking his cue, Rabbi Klein proposes that his newfound spiritual awakening is actually a manifestation of his sense of attraction for her. He persists that he wants to further this relationship, but she states unequivocally that while she is flattered, she is not interested in him. This awkward moment is handled both professionally and courteously on her part.

Women rabbis are also depicted as leaders of life-cycle rituals and involved in pastoral counseling. In those roles too, the woman rabbi's sexuality often plays a part in how other (particularly male) characters interact with her. Rabbi Ari Hoffman (*Six Feet Under*) appears in the show's second season, in the episodes "Back to the Garden" and "The Liar and the Whore." She is a young rabbi, unmarried, in her thirties. She is portrayed authentically and positively. At the funeral in the mortuary's chapel, she wears a dark suit with a *kippah* and tallit. Just prior to her beginning the eulogy for the deceased man, a woman cantor, also wearing a tallit, chants part of *El Malei Rachamim*. Rabbi Hoffman begins her remarks with a statement from the Talmud. She then says, "Better is one day in this life than all eternity in the world-to-come," a paraphrase of *Pirkei Avot* 4:17, "[Rabbi Yaakov] used to say, Better is one hour of repentance and good deeds [*maasim tovim*] in this world than the whole life of the world-to-come [*olam haba*]."

Following the funeral service itself, the lead male character, Nate Fisher (Peter Krause), approaches Rabbi Hoffman and explains that as a funeral director he has questions about the Jewish views of death. She offers him her card, but he presses that he would like to discuss this immediately. She explains that she needs to go to the cemetery and invites him to accompany her. At a later point she speaks about the mitzvah of accompanying the dead as a great kindness, as a godly act, because the dead cannot repay the gift (reflecting the teachings in Babylonian Talmud, *Sotah* 14a; *B'reishit Rabbah* 96:5; Rashi's comment on Gen. 47:29).

At the scene at the cemetery awaiting the hearse, Rabbi Hoffman stresses the virtue of living a meaningful life day-by-day. One should be moral and consonant with what God wants of us. She says that she is not speaking for all of Judaism but for herself, what she does as a moral person. During this conversation, Rabbi Hoffman refers to God as "him" and Nate comes back with "or her." Rabbi Hoffman replies simply, "Here he comes," referring, it turns out, to the body in the hearse.

Later at the shivah house, Nate overtly flirts with Rabbi Hoffman, even though he has already explained that he is engaged. He asks her if she would go out on a date. She hesitates but then flatly declines, citing the fact that he is not Jewish. He pushes her on this, but she stands her ground.

In the second episode featuring Rabbi Hoffman ("The Liar and the Whore"), she is in her office offering premarital counseling to Nate and his fiancée, Brenda Chenowith. Here the emphasis is on her counseling skills and ability to communicate. She tells them that this will be a six-session course. It is not stated but can be inferred that she will conduct an interfaith marriage, because while Brenda is Jewish, Nate is not. Brenda challenges Rabbi Hoffman, "Have you ever been married?" She replies that she has not but that she has successfully counseled many couples in her congregation. The counseling techniques used by Rabbi Hoffman are sound and appropriate. She stresses the importance of mutual honesty and models the importance of being sympathetic to the other person. Brenda and Nate accept her advice.

There is a further scene that is perhaps less credible. On a subsequent night, Rabbi Hoffman shows up at the funeral home dressed in slacks and a sweater. Her stated reason for being present is that she has the name of someone who wants to make funeral arrangements long before the actual need arises. She quickly admits that this was only an excuse to come over. She asks Nate for a drink, and he hands her a beer. She acknowledges that she has a messiah complex: she tries to save men. It is unclear whether by this she means people or just men, but it is probably the former. During this visit, she comments that Nate is not honest with women. He replies that he is honest with her. She then uses this as an opportunity to once again underscore that she would never date him because he is not Jewish. He appears to accept this. With his no longer seeing her as a possible sexual conquest, they conclude that he can be honest with her.

These Rabbi Ari Hoffman episodes portray a rabbi acting professionally, personally, compassionately, and with *seichel* (common sense). The scenes are authentic and believable, and the rabbi alludes to standard Jewish traditions and principles. Notably, in a series that prominently explores a gay character's relationships, these rabbi-centered episodes present a conservative view of hetero-normative relationships.

Rabbi Hoffman initially flirts with Nate Fisher, but then she makes it abundantly clear that she would never date him because he is not Jewish. She gently rebuffs his advances, just as Rabbi Klein (*The Larry Sanders Show*) rebuffs Hank Kingsley. In each of these cases there is a sense that in addition to her basic sexual appeal, the male character is also is attracted to a perceived "otherworldliness/mystique/exotic/godliness" of the woman rabbi. To successfully seduce not only a woman, but a woman rabbi, would be a "double victory."

With limited examples of rabbinic conversations on the screen (unlike the extended examples one finds in print fiction, especially with Kemelman's Rabbi Small series, Howard Fast's *The Outsider*, or Noah Gordon's *The Rabbi*),[8] it is difficult to generalize as to the authenticity of how women rabbis are presented. That caveat offered, where women rabbis do have more than cameo roles, generally they are presented in a reasonable and realistic, though sexualized, fashion. They are dressed professionally for the occasions where they appear. Rabbi Susan Klein, in the episode "My Name Is Asher Kingsley" (*The Larry Sanders Show*) is abrupt but credible when she observes that the apparently non-practicing, non-associating, non-synagogue-attending Jewish figure Hank Kingsley is not much of a Jew. She asks him if he observes Shabbat. He says no. She asks about the High Holy Days. He answers yes, "Yom Kippur and the Fourth of July." She asks if he keeps kosher. He does not. He laughs and then admits, "As a Jew, I'm not very good." Rabbi Klein responds with the quip, "As a Jew, you're almost a Methodist."

Considering the credibility of the scripting of the part of female rabbis, it is important to keep in mind the limitations of screenwriters. Jewish or non-Jewish, writers—like many Americans—may be insensitive or undereducated about matters such as Jewish holidays, expectations or requirements for joining a synagogue, kashrut, conversion, or the denominational politics of ordaining women. Actress Amy Aquino relates the following story:

> When I auditioned for this episode [The Larry Sanders Show], I went into the room and there were four or five of the writers there. Super nice, very enthusiastic. I started to ask some questions because in the script she's talking about keeping kosher and I said, "If she's referring to practices that are Orthodox, but she's a woman...I don't think she would be a rabbi if it's Orthodox." They all gave me these blank stares. I looked around and said, "I'm sorry. Is this the only writers' room in Hollywood where there is not a single Jewish person? Am I the most Jewish person here and I am not Jewish?"[9]

Another consideration is the scripting process itself, which includes numerous edits and cuts. Such seems to be the case with *Grey's Anatomy*:

> A producer on *Grey's Anatomy* asked [the associate rabbi of Temple Israel of Hollywood, Michelle] Missaghieh to consult and take a small role in an episode. "There were a lot of Jewish problems with the script, actually," [Rabbi Missaghieh] recalls. An

Orthodox teenage patient needed a heart-valve replacement. The doctors wanted to give her a pig valve, which the show's writers believed would pose a religious quandary in that it wouldn't be kosher. "They thought this was sort of sexy," Missaghieh explains. "I told them this was not an issue; you do almost anything to save a life." The writers also wanted the teenager's rabbi to be an Orthodox woman, a plot twist Missaghieh disputed as nearly impossible, because the Orthodox movement does not permit female rabbis.

But as any religious leader can tell you, the counsel of clerics isn't always followed. When she watched the show, Missaghieh discovered the producers had ignored her advice on both counts. "I was naive," she says.[10]

Rabbi Missaghieh relates another real-life situation. At one point around 2000, her congregant Jill Soloway, a scriptwriter for *Six Feet Under*," approached her. She wanted to meet with Rabbi Missaghieh to get a sense of what was/was not possible for a woman rabbi in a particular script. Soloway took Missaghieh to breakfast, where she explained that the script involved a single man and a single woman rabbi. Missaghieh asked Soloway if the man is Jewish? "No," Soloway responded and then asked, "Could they date?" "No," Missaghieh responded. Why not? Because a single woman rabbi would not date and then marry a non-Jew. Could there be a sexual interest? Missaghieh responded, "No." "What could there be? Flirtation?" Missaghieh responded, "Yes, flirtation."[11]

It was important to writer Jill Soloway to have a woman rabbi. As she explained in an interview, when working "on *Six Feet Under*, she modeled a potential love interest for Nate on Missaghieh. 'There are so few Jewish women on television that are positive and smart and sexy,' says Soloway. 'It's always been my secret wish to put more women like that on television for Jewish girls to relate to.'"[12] Soloway's wish is both significant and regretfully unfulfilled, certainly in terms of women rabbis portrayed in the popular media. Soloway herself, however is committed to her quest. She went on to create the series *Transparent*, starting Jeffery Tambor. She has both directed (12 episodes 2014-2015) and written scripts (credits for 31 episodes 2014-2016) for the award-winning TV show. In that series Rabbi Raquel Fein (Kathryn Hahn) is a important recurrent character. She often serves as a moral compass as well as a foil for the Pfefferman family's twists and turns, emphasizing their Jewish identity and bringing Jewish values and traditions to the fore, while standing for a progressive Judaism working hard to embrace the contemporary reality of what makes up a family. Her commitment to Judaism enables her to set boundaries that appear much more difficult for the other characters on the show.

There are insufficient examples to make sweeping statements about the portrayal of these women rabbis, the credibility of their actions, or even how mainstream their positions are on various issues. In terms of weddings, there are two examples of women rabbis conducting interfaith marriages, in both cases alongside Christian clergy. There certainly are some real women rabbis who follow this practice, as do some of their male colleagues, but it is not a widespread practice within the major North American Jewish denominations. The theological talk put into the mouths of these fictional women rabbis is generally limited, but overall what is scripted is well within mainstream thought and practice.

This survey of women rabbis in television and film does not seem to indicate that there is any one reason that some shows wind up with women rabbis as characters. The actresses themselves sometimes are Jewish; usually they are not. Some of the writers, or even lead writers, of shows in which women rabbis appear are Jewish, but this is not a universal phenomenon. That said, the large number of Jewish television and screen writers does not equate with the relative paucity of women rabbis on TV and in cinema.

Is it significant that these rabbis on the screen are women? Let me suggest three reasons that it is. First, presenting the rabbi as a woman destabilizes the presumption that rabbis can only ever be men. Second, these women rabbis are portrayed possessing stature, authority, and power in the community, and not as subsidiary to men or other characters. Third, women view the representation of other women in popular media positively.

In ritual officiation, as well as in offering counseling or pastoral support, a female rabbi's practice may or may not differ from a male rabbi's approach. Yet gender plays a significant role in moments where the script wants to address male/female attraction (to my knowledge there have not been any TV or cinematic examples of fictional rabbis—women or men—portrayed as gay men or lesbians).

Rabbinic life is of course much wider than what is portrayed in these examples above. Rabbis—female and male—regularly meet with committees, are involved with interfaith matters of social justice, minister to the aging, educate teenagers, and so on. They preach and teach about Judaism's traditions and values, and they lead trips to Israel. Rabbis also are chaplains in a variety of settings: hospitals, long-term care centers, hospice, and the military. There are—female and male—rabbi-educators and rabbi-administrators. In addition to their professional duties, they have internal religious and personal family lives. None of these professional or personal dimensions have yet to be explored in these TV and cinema productions.

Women have been an active part of the contemporary rabbinate for over forty years. To date, worldwide, there are about a thousand women rabbis. There are now generations of children who have grown up never having known any rabbi other than a rabbi who is a woman. It is surprising, therefore, that there have not been more instances of women as rabbinic figures on TV or film. Perhaps it will just take some more time before these real-life exemplars make their way to become fictional depictions on the small and large screens.[13]

NOTES

1. Jordie Gerson, "Letter to Hollywood—I Don't Have a Beard or Side Curls and I Look Just Like You: American Judaism's Image Problem," *Huffington Post*, November 8, 2013 or this volume, pp. 741–42.

2. David J. Zucker, *American Rabbis: Facts and Fiction* (Northvale, NJ: Jason Aronson; Lanham, MD: Rowman and Litttlefield, 1998).

3. See the chapter "Women Rabbis" in Zucker, *American Rabbis: Facts and Fiction*; David J. Zucker, "Women Rabbis: A Novel Idea," *Judaism* 55, nos. 1–2 (Summer/Fall 2006): 108–16; and David J. Zucker, "Women Rabbis (and Rebbitzins) in Contemporary Fiction," *CCAR Journal* 54, no. 3 (Summer 2007): 68–91. See also Pamela S. Nadell, *Women Who Would Be Rabbis: A History of Women's Ordination 1889–1985* (Boston: Beacon Press, 1998).

4. Rhonda Shapiro-Rieser's *A Place of Light* (1983, Lynda Klein); Joseph Telushkin's *The Unorthodox Murder of Rabbi Wahl* (1987, Myra Wahl); Erich Segal's *Acts of Faith* (1992, Deborah Luria); Anita Diamant's *Good Harbor* (2001, Michelle Hertz); and Athol Dickson's *They Shall See God* (2002, Ruth Gold).

5. Alex Goldman's *The Lady Is a Rabbi* (1987, Sara Weintraub); Eileen Pollack's "The Rabbi in the Attic" (1991, Marion Bloomgarten); Roger Herst's *Woman of the Cloth* (1998, Gabrielle Lewyn) and *A Kiss for Rabbi Gabrielle* (2011); Jonathan Rosen's *Joy Comes in the Morning* (2004, Deborah Green); and Ilene Schneider's mysteries, *Chanukah Guilt* (2007, Aviva Cohen) and *Unleavened Dead* (2012).

6. The first woman rabbi, Sally Priesand, was ordained in 1972.

7. Dana Evan Kaplan states that the controversy over the hiring of women rabbis has now largely become a nonissue because people have become accustomed to that idea, citing as evidence his observation of women rabbis acting in television shows. To my knowledge, however, Michelle Missaghieh is the only woman rabbi who has done this. Dana Evan Kaplan, *Contemporary American Judaism: Transformation and Renewal* (New York: Columbia University Press, 2009), 233.

8. See, e.g., Zucker, "God, Israel, and Tradition," in *American Rabbis*.

9. Edward Copeland, "Larry Sanders: Changing Television and Changing Lives," RogerEbert.com, September 14, 2012, http://www.rogerebert.com/demanders/larry-sanders-changing-television-and-changing-lives.

10. http://forward.com/news/israel/3416/tinseltown-rabbi-saves-a-prayer-for-prime-time-sho/. In a personal conversation with Rabbi Missaghieh (February 20, 2013), she confirmed this report.

11. Personal communication with Rabbi Michelle Missaghieh, February 20, 2013.

12. http://forward.com/news/israel/3416/tinseltown-rabbi-saves-a-prayer-for-prime-time-sho/In a personal conversation with Rabbi Missaghieh (February 20, 2013), she confirmed this report.

13. Special thanks to Rabbi Dr. Bonita E. Taylor, BCC, my friend, colleague, and *chevruta* partner, who read this in an earlier iteration and offered excellent stylistic suggestions. Thanks also to Ian M. Zucker, who provided important feminist and gender studies insights. I also offer my appreciation to the many colleagues across the streams of Judaism who replied to my request for suggestions for this subject via the various rabbinic electronic mailing lists. This is a work in progress. If you know of other examples, please do share them with me, the author, DavidJZucker@gmail.com.

PERSONAL REFLECTION

Rabbis in Red Lipstick

DASI FRUCHTER

There are many things that play an important part in my morning ritual—a nice hot drink, a shower, morning prayers. One of the most important elements of my morning routine, however, is putting on my red lipstick. There is something so satisfying about applying the final smear of the creamy red across my lips before I walk out of the door—I feel instantly like a brighter, better version of myself.

My red lips have been my trademark for the last several years, and though the shade has varied, it's always been red, red, and red. I've ventured from candy pink to seductive purples, and my personal favorite and general default, a true candy-apple red. In college, I spent hours defending my cosmetic habits to my feminist friends, who accused me of buying into patriarchal conceptions of beauty. I knew, however, that they didn't quite understand why the contents of that tiny red tube were so vital. It was about making an active choice about my own gender expression in a way that made me feel all at once powerful, beautiful, and uniquely feminine.

These days, as a person embarking on a lifelong journey of Jewish professional leadership—beginning my studies toward nonprofit management at New York University's Wagner School of Public Service—I continue try my hardest to bring my authentic self to the table as

735

often as I can. Be it at a fundraising dinner, a board meeting, or in the office, I attempt to be fully present, bringing the traits I know to be my strengths—my energy, my genuine desire to connect with others, and my drive to create inclusive community spaces—to my work. Oddly enough, the lipstick has become an essential part of making this happen. It is a final, dramatic touch—a flash of vibrant color—that urges me to truly turn up in the fullest way possible, wherever I am.

Alongside my graduate studies, however, I've also chosen recently to embark on another journey toward social change through spiritual leadership. I've enrolled and begun to learn at Yeshivat Maharat, a seminary seeking to confirm Orthodox women as halachic and spiritual leaders. I have always embraced and loved learning, and studying at Yeshivat Maharat is a perfect way for me to be involved in a profoundly change-making movement and also to engage in vibrant Torah leadership. The conversation about women occupying positions as clergy in Orthodox institutions is a certainly a contentious one, and also one of which I'm so excited to be a part.

The program is going well so far, days spent with my head buried in ancient Rabbinic texts, exploring and wrestling with the complex nuances of Jewish law. A few weeks ago, however, something happened that struck a particular nerve for me—something having to do with my struggles and questions regarding gender and sexuality in my new community and line of spiritual work. I was sitting and eating lunch with a colleague of mine in between classes, and we were having a discussion about what would be the appropriate attire when performing ritual duties. Considering the controversial space the yeshivah already occupies in a broader global Orthodox context, we agreed that though our clothing choices should not completely hide the fact that we are, in fact, sexual beings, that anything *too* provocative was inappropriate.

I paused for a moment and gestured toward my lips.

"What about my lipstick?" I asked nervously, almost unwilling to hear her response.

She paused.

"Maybe pick a different color," she said.

And thus entered a complication into my morning rituals. I found myself actively questioning whether or not calling attention to my lips by way of history's most notoriously seductive color would be wise as a newly emerging Orthodox female leader.

As I looked into the mirror one morning, my Sephora Lip Stain No. 1 open in my hands, I thought about the women who have preceded me and moved on to become spiritual leaders, activists, and strong voices in their communities. I meditated on the ancient Rabbinic texts I review every day, which often indicate a fear of female "otherness" and sexuality.

The truth is, I want to push back against centuries rife with the sentiment that men are unable to control themselves in the presence of beautiful women. I want to push back against the idea that there is anything deviant about a woman who is comfortable with her sexuality.

In a position that sometimes feels powerless, I don't want to disappear into the folds. The work before me is enormous—I seek to be among the Jewish leaders whose leadership lends itself to radical shifts in power structures and to creating more expansive and inclusive communal and ritual spaces. Given the enormity of this work and my passion for doing it well, I seek to bring the entire expression of myself—not a compromised or compartmentalized version of me—to all of my pursuits. The thought of ducking into the bathroom to wipe off the lipstick I wore to my nonprofit board meeting before I go to teach Jewish texts is troubling to me. We live in an era when Orthodox women are finally studying to be members of clergy, which, in and of itself, is wildly radical. It seems like this era should also be able to accommodate a broad diversity of women committed to this risky work—women who have loud voices and bright colors, women who are comfortable with who they are and what they bring.

I am certainly not the first woman to think about the question of attire and the rabbinate. Ever since Sally Priesand's ordination in 1972, women rabbis have been thinking about how expressions of their sexuality interact with their spiritual work. But due to the particularly strong emphasis on modesty and the accompanying specific restrictions in the Orthodox tradition, however, I am finding these questions harder to answer. I can't pretend that wearing red lipstick isn't provocative. But is that really a bad thing? I find the effort to deny the presence of sexuality usually only draws more attention and makes that presence even stronger. Being real about my sexuality and the ways I enjoy expressing it seems like a much better and more honest idea.

It's also about so much more than how the lipstick looks. Upon reflection, I also realize that when I think about what I now refer to as "the lipstick question," I think of the countless men in leadership who have questioned my own capacity as a leader. Without fail, this conversation isn't about my qualities as a leader or my skills as a student at all—most often, it's about whether someone who looks or dresses the way I do can possibly helm a Jewish community, drive an organization, or deliver an inspiring sermon.

Ultimately, I'm not sure where I stand on the lipstick question. Maybe my colleague was right. Maybe I should forgo the red for something a bit more muted—perhaps a subtle berry tone or even a nude pink. I'm already attempting a course of study that is considered controversial in the Orthodox world. I find myself pushing the envelope in my work and trying to make Orthodoxy a space that can accommodate different expressions of gender. But why exacerbate my already contentious journey by adding a layer of suggestive lipstick? I *could* switch shades—but red is my trademark. It's the color that announces my presence in a room. Red is the color that says I'm not ashamed to be doing what I'm doing.

My answer varies from day to day, but both on the morning in question and upon writing these words, I realize that I feel it vital for people whose goal is to be godly to do their best to be fully present in their devotion to spiritual community building. I'll take things slow and won't push social change when my community is not ready for it. But I'll still provide a burst of color to reassure to myself and others that I am indeed a change-maker. I thought of the women in the Talmudic era who wore *kochelet*, a type of blue eye makeup. I wondered that if in their effort for aesthetic beauty, they also made an implicit statement about their power.

As a scholar, professional, and spiritual leader, I will lead with words of Torah as my backdrop, using effective strategies and tactics to foster strong communities. I want to constantly grow and use innovative strategies: walking the crucial line of progressive social change and rooted tradition. So, sometimes I'll have to choose a different shade, but I'll keep the red lipstick in my pocket. When I feel it there, I'll look forward to feeling empowered as opposed to tolerated. To thinking about reclaiming the redness of lipstick and the legacies of Deborah, Eve, and Huldah. To adding the tone of women's voices to centuries of *p'sak*. Finally, I'll know that when I utter words of Torah, I'd love nothing more to envelop those words in a deep, rich red.

Note: This essay was originally published at the Lilith Blog, 2/20/13.

PERSONAL REFLECTION

Letter to Hollywood—I Don't Have a Beard or Side Curls and I Look Just Like You
American Judaism's Image Problem

RABBI JORDIE GERSON

Almost every time I see myself represented in American movies, television shows, or advertisements, I have a beard and a *kippah*. Often I'm wearing a black hat and side curls, and almost always a white button-down shirt and black jacket. I am almost never a woman. I am, according to American media, what a rabbi looks like.

Except, of course, that that's no longer what most of America's Jewish leadership looks like. We look like you, dear reader. We're young women, old women, clean-shaven young men, LGBTQ, and sometimes we're even blonde, or red-headed, or of Middle Eastern, Asian, or African descent. Some of us are even attractive. Personally, I'm five feet tall, blue-eyed, with long brown hair, and I rarely wear a *kippah* unless I'm officiating at life-cycle events or prayer. I couldn't grow a beard if I wanted to (I'm not complaining).

So then why does Hollywood think I look like something out of *Fiddler on the Roof*? Why does Hollywood (and the *New York Times*, and Comedy Central, and even American Apparel) insist on portraying me and my colleagues as bearded ultra-Orthodox rabbis or nebbishy older men? Why does Hollywood need us to look so distinctively "Jewish," so "other," so male and "different"?

I'd point to Daniel Boyarin's thesis in *Unheroic Conduct*, that the ideal image of Jewish masculinity was constructed in the yeshivot of Europe and idealized a bookish, pale, bearded, feminine male and hasn't evolved much since. But that's Jewish self-construction, just as early Zionism's creation of the macho, strapping new Jew/Israeli valorized traditional ideals of masculinity. That was also Jewish self-construction. Is this too? I honestly don't know. How many casting agents and writers in Hollywood or on Madison Avenue are Jewish? And if they are, why are they so set on portraying Jewish leadership so narrowly? Why do the entertainment and advertising industries need us to look like Chasids or caricatures of Jewishness? Why is the image of a female rabbi or a clean-shaven, young, attractive male rabbi with all his hair so rare? Why do they insist on "other-ing" us?

The problem is this: These images make our jobs harder. Especially for female rabbis. When we stand on the bimah to deliver a sermon, or officiate at a wedding or funeral, or comfort a family by a deathbed, or meet with students on university campuses, and the first reaction is that we don't "look" like rabbis, or that we're too young, or too feminine, our holy vocation is denigrated and belittled, and we're judged less fit for the job before we've even opened our mouths. That's because the Jews we serve don't recognize us. I don't either. It's time for that to change.

Note: This essay was originally published online at the Huffington Post, November 8, 2013.

PERSONAL REFLECTION

Dropping the "R-Bomb"

Rabbi Elizabeth S. Wood

"So...what do you do?" Silence. Even though the music was blaring and the glasses were clinking, I could barely hear what he said amid the din of a lively bar on a Saturday night. Suddenly all I could hear was stillness. The world muted. It felt like an eternity had passed since he spoke. I had dreaded this moment. From the minute we locked eyes and he had the courage to walk over and initiate witty banter, I feared this moment. The moment when I would have to reveal who I am, what I represent, and the enigma and weight of this title that I carry. All I wanted to do was have a fun night out, maybe meet someone interesting, create a memorable story or two. But, now I have to deal with this. All the questions. All the singular focus on what I do and not on learning about the facets of who I am. As if the two were somehow inseparable, even just for a night. I have to do it. He's been waiting patiently for my response. I weigh out the options of making up a little white lie or simply grabbing my purse and running for the door. Instead, I stand my ground. He seems interested in me; maybe he will find this whole side of my professional life somehow endearing. I have to drop the "R-bomb" on him. I swallow hard and prepare for the fallout. "I'm a rabbi," I yell out, a little more forcefully than necessary, just to make sure he heard it clearly. I feel the bomb explode, and I wait for the dust and ashes to settle.

What happens next is almost always the same. He usually follows up with something like "Cool" or "No way, that's so awesome," because that's the polite thing to say in a social situation with someone whom you've obviously made a connection. And then begins a little game I like to play with myself called "How many seconds, minutes, or hours does it take before they have realized that they've bitten off way more than they can chew?"

For a young female rabbi living in New York City, dating is a huge challenge. Let's face it, dating in general is already enough of a struggle. From navigating dating websites to trying to catch someone's eye in a group of people at a party or a cool venue or even on the streets of the city, it's hard to ever make a real and true connection. And let's say you do manage to find someone you like and with whom you have great interests in common, who really gets who you are as a person, and whom you also happen to find attractive. Add on top of that the ability to understand your professional life as a synagogue rabbi—the long hours, the working weekends (every weekend), the phone calls and e-mails at all hours of the day, vying for your attention. Being a female rabbi and trying to balance a family and children is exceedingly difficult—trying to sell it as an idea to a future husband, comical.

Now don't get me wrong, I'm a great sell. I am smart and articulate, well educated, successful, confident, and a lot of fun. In fact, I'm a great first date. Since my whole job is based around working with, understanding, and reading people, I have a tendency to want to schmooze my date. I show great amounts of interest and laugh at all the jokes. I spin everything toward the positive. I am overly empathetic when he is sharing heartfelt thoughts. I am an active listener and reflect back what he says to me. It's hard not to like me by the end of that date.

Except that's not real. A real relationship is built on much more than a first date. It's built on mutual trust and respect. It's built on shared experiences and adventures. It's built on growth and love. And it takes a genuine and mature person to know that and to be that kind of partner in a relationship, no matter what the occupational obstacles.

"Dropping the 'R-bomb'" is a term I've come up with over the last few years to create a kind of litmus test for potential suitors. For some people, it is explosive. Depending on the date and his particular Jewish upbringing or baggage, it can put an immediate end to the conversation and the date. They don't want to get to know anything about me because what my job represents to them is too much to bear. For some, it is a bizarre fascination and becomes a prized trophy to say, "I dated a female rabbi." They love to show me off at parties and play the game "Guess What She Does for a Living?" with their friends. For others, the ones I like to keep around longer, it's simply a part of who I am. It's one of the many pieces that make up the puzzle of me. It may be a cool or quirky thing, but they don't let it define me or our relationship. They find a way to see me, through my title and job, and understand that while being a rabbi is *what* I am, it doesn't entirely dictate *who* I am.

One of the things I love most about being a young Reform female rabbi in New York City is my anonymity. I can ride the subway, go to the movies, shop in the grocery store, and attend cool concerts without anyone knowing who I am or what I do. I look just like any other young professional who is trying simultaneously to live her life and figure "it" all out. But, I'm not. My job is big and, at times, very heavy. And when I get to know someone, beyond a first date or a casual meeting at a bar, and develop a meaningful relationship with him, he will have to learn the ways in which my job weaves in and out of my life—in complicated, messy, hilarious, sad, wonderful, and intense ways. I love what I do; I wouldn't trade it in for anything. It just makes dating a little harder than usual, sometimes. But it can also be a great test of the kind of person with whom I want to find myself in a relationship—one who can handle all the things that life throws at us. As the fictional Carrie Bradshaw, from *Sex & the City*, once said, "The most exciting, challenging, and significant relationship of all is the one you have with yourself. And if you can find someone to love the you that you love, well, that's just fabulous."

For Further Reading

Jewish History through a Feminist Lens

Balin, Carole B., Dana Herman, Jonathan D. Sarna, and Gary P. Zola, eds. *Sisterhood: A Centennial History of Women of Reform Judaism*. Cincinnati: Hebrew Union College Press, 2013.

Bar-Ilan, M. *Some Jewish Women in Antiquity*. Atlanta: Scholars Press, 1998.

Baskin, Judith. *Jewish Women in Historical Perspective*. Detroit: Wayne State University Press, 1998.

Bird, Phyllis A. *Missing Persons and Mistaken Identities: Women and Gender in Ancient Israel*. Philadelphia: Fortress Press, 1997.

Goldstein, Elyse. *Seek Her Out: A Textual Approach to the Study of Women and Judaism*. New York: URJ Press, 2003.

Henry, Sondra, and Emily Taitz. *Written Out of History: Our Jewish Foremothers*. Fresh Meadows, NY: Biblio Press, 1996.

Ilan, Tal. *Integrating Women into Second Temple History*. Peabody, MA: Hendrickson Publishers, 2001.

———. *Jewish Women in Greco-Roman Palestine*. Tübingen: J. C. B. Mohr, 1995.

Ingall, Carol K. *The Women Who Reconstructed American Jewish Education, 1910–1965*. Hanover, NH: University Press of New England / Brandeis University Press, 2010.

Meyers, Carol. *Rediscovering Eve: Ancient Israelite Women in Context*. New York: Oxford University Press, 1988.

Nadell, Pamela S., and Jonathan D. Sarna. *Women and American Judaism: Historical Perspectives*. Hanover, NH: University Press of New England / Brandeis University Press, 2001.

Prell, Riv-Ellen. *Fighting to Become Americans: Assimilation and the Trouble between Jewish Women and Jewish Men.* Boston: Beacon Press, 1999.

Prell, Riv-Ellen, and David Weinberg, eds. *Women Remaking American Judaism.* Detroit: Wayne State University Press, 2007.

Shepherd, Naomi. *A Price below Rubies: Jewish Women as Rebels and Radicals.* Cambridge, MA: Harvard University Press, 1993.

Jewish Feminist Theology

Adler, Rachel. *Engendering Judaism: An Inclusive Theology and Ethics.* Boston: Beacon Press, 1999.

Christ, Carol P., and Judith Plaskow, eds. *Womanspirit Rising: A Feminist Reader in Religion.* HarperCollins: San Francisco, 2004.

Firestone, Tirzah. *The Receiving: Reclaiming Jewish Women's Wisdom.* San Francisco: HarperCollins, 2003.

Goldman, Karla. *Beyond the Synagogue Gallery: Finding a Place for Women in American Judaism.* Cambridge, MA: Harvard University Press, 2000.

Goldstein, Elyse, ed. *New Jewish Feminism: Probing the Past, Forging the Future.* Woodstock, VT: Jewish Lights, 2009.

Grossman, Susan, and Rivka Haut, eds. *Daughters of the King: Women and the Synagogue.* Philadelphia: Jewish Publication Society, 1992.

Heschel, Susannah. *On Being a Jewish Feminist: A Reader.* New York: Schocken Books, 1995.

Plaskow, Judith. *The Coming of Lilith: Essays on Feminism, Judaism, and Sexual Ethics, 1972–2003.* Boston: Beacon Press, 2005.

———. *Standing Again at Sinai: Judaism from a Feminist Perspective.* New York: HarperCollins, 1991.

Plaskow, Judith, and Carol P. Christ. *Weaving the Visions: New Patterns in Feminist Spirituality.* San Francisco: Harper & Row, 1989.

Ruttenberg, Danya, ed. *Yentl's Revenge: The Next Wave of Jewish Feminism.* Seattle: Seal Press, 2001.

Biblical Interpretation through a Feminist Lens

Adelman, Penina, ed. *Praise Her Works: Conversations with Biblical Women.* Philadelphia: Jewish Publication Society, 1995.

Bach, Alice, ed. *Women in the Hebrew Bible: A Reader.* New York: Routledge, 1999.

Diamant, Anita. *The Red Tent.* New York: St. Martin's Press, 1997.

Eskenazi, Tamara Cohn, and Andrea L. Weiss. *The Torah: A Women's Commentary.* New York: Women of Reform Judaism / URJ Press, 2007.

Exum, J. Cheryl. *Fragmented Women: Feminist Subversions of Biblical Narratives.* Harrisburg, PA: Trinity Press International, 1993.

Frankel, Ellen. *The Five Books of Miriam: A Women's Commentary on the Torah*. New York: HarperCollins, 1998.

Frymer-Kensky, Tikva. *Reading the Women of the Bible: A New Interpretation of Their Stories*. New York: Schocken Books, 2002.

Goldstein, Elyse. *ReVisions: Seeing Torah through a Feminist Lens*. Woodstock, VT: Jewish Lights, 2001.

———, ed. *The Women's Haftarah Commentary: New Insights from Women Rabbis on the 54 Haftarah Portions, the 5 Megillot and Special Shabbatot*. Woodstock, VT: Jewish Lights, 2004.

———. *The Women's Torah Commentary: New Insights from Women Rabbis on the 54 Weekly Torah Portions*. Woodstock, VT: Jewish Lights, 2000.

Graetz, Naomi. *Unlocking the Garden: A Feminist Jewish Look at the Bible, Midrash, and God*. Piscataway, NJ: Gorgias Press, 1994.

Hammer, Jill. *Sisters at Sinai: The Tales of Biblical Women*. Philadelphia: Jewish Publication Society, 2001.

Hyman, Naomi M. *Biblical Women in the Midrash: A Sourcebook*. New York: Jason Aronson, 1997.

Kates, Judith A., and Gail Twersky Reimer. *Reading Ruth: Contemporary Women Reclaim a Sacred Story*. New York: Ballantine Books, 1994.

Koltuv, Barbara Black. *The Book of Lilith*. York Beach, ME: Nicolas-Hays, 1987.

Labowitz, Shoni. *God, Sex, and Women of the Bible: Discovering Our Sensual, Spiritual Selves*. New York: Simon and Schuster, 1998.

Pardes, Ilana. *Countertraditions in the Bible: A Feminist Approach*. Cambridge, MA: Harvard University Press, 1992.

Schussler Fiorenza, Elisabeth. *Bread Not Stone: The Challenge of Feminist Biblical Interpretation*. Boston: Beacon Press, 1995.

Trible, Phyllis. *Texts of Terror: Literary-Feminist Readings of Biblical Narratives*. Philadelphia: Fortress Press, 1984.

Women as Rabbis

Greenberg, Simon, ed. *The Ordination of Women as Rabbis: Studies and Responsa*. New York: Jewish Theological Seminary of America, 1988.

Klapheck, Elisa. *Fraulein Rabbiner Jonas: The Story of the First Woman Rabbi*. Translated by Toby Axelrod. San Francisco: Jossey-Bass, 2004.

Nadell, Pamela, S. *Women Who Would Be Rabbis: A History of Women's Ordination 1889–1985*. Boston: Beacon Press, 1998.

Ner-David, Haviva. *Life on the Fringes: A Feminist Journey towards Traditional Rabbinic Ordination*. Needham, MA: JFL Books, 2000.

Priesand, Sally. *Judaism and the New Woman*. Springfield, NJ: Behrman House, 1975.

Sheridan, Sybil. *Hear Our Voices: Women in the British Rabbinate*. Columbia, SC: University of South Carolina Press, 1998.

"Wisdom You Are My Sister: Twenty-Five Years of Women in the Rabbinate." Special issue, *CCAR Journal*, Summer 1997.

Zola, Gary P., ed. *Women Rabbis: Exploration and Celebration.* Cincinnati: HUC-JIR
Rabbinic Alumni Association Press, 1996.

Sexuality

Alpert, Rebecca T., Sue Levi Elwell, and Shirley Idelson, eds. *Lesbian Rabbis: The
First Generation.* Piscataway, NJ: Rutgers University Press, 2001.
Aviv, Caryn, and David Schneer. *Queer Jews.* New York: Routledge, 2002.
Beck, Evelyn Torton, ed. *Nice Jewish Girls: A Lesbian Anthology.* Boston: Beacon
Press, 1989.
Grushcow, Lisa J., ed. *The Sacred Encounter: Jewish Perspectives on Sexuality.* New
York: CCAR Press, 2014.

Jewish Law, Rabbinics, and the Female Voice

Abrams, Judith. *The Women of the Talmud.* Northvale, NJ: Jason Aronson, 1995.
Baskin, Judith. *Midrashic Women: Formations of the Feminine in Rabbinic Literature.* Ha-
nover, NH: University Press of New England / Brandeis University Press, 2002.
Biale, Rachel. *Women and Jewish Law: The Essential Texts, Their History, and Their
Relevance for Today.* New York: Schocken Books, 1995.
Calderon, Ruth. *A Bride for One Night: Talmud Tales.* Philadelphia: Jewish Publica-
tion Society, 2014.
Hauptman, Judith. *Rereading the Rabbis: A Woman's Voice.* Boulder, CO: Westview
Press, 1998.
Peskowitz, Miriam B. *Spinning Fantasies: Rabbis, Gender, and History.* Berkeley: Uni-
versity of California Press, 1997.
Suskin, Alana. "A Feminist Theory of Jewish Law." In *The Unfolding Tradition: Jewish
Law after Sinai,* edited by Elliot Dorff. New York: Aviv Press, 2005.
Wegner, Judith Romney. *Chattel or Person? The Status of Women in the Mishnah.*
London: Oxford University Press, 1988.

Ritual and Language

Anisfeld, Sharon Cohen, Tara Mohr, and Catherine Spector, eds. *The Women's
Passover Companion: Women's Reflections on the Festival of Freedom.* Woodstock,
VT: Jewish Lights, 2003.
———. *The Women's Seder Sourcebook: Rituals and Readings for use at the Passover Seder.*
Woodstock, VT: Jewish Lights, 2003.
Falk, Marcia. *The Book of Blessings: A New Prayer Book for the Weekdays, the Sabbath
and the New Moon Festival.* San Francisco: HarperSanFrancisco, 1991.

Frymer-Kensky, Tikva. *In the Wake of the Goddess: Woman, Culture and the Biblical Transformation of Pagan Myth.* New York: Macmillan, 1992.

Hammer, Jill. "An Alter of Earth: Reflections on Jews, Goddesses, and the Zohar." *Zeek*, Fall/Winter 2004, 7–20.

Hammer, Jill. *The Jewish Book of Days: A Companion for All Seasons.* Philadelphia: Jewish Publication Society, 2006.

Orenstein, Debra, ed. *Lifecycles.* Vol.1, *Jewish Women on Life Passages and Personal Milestones.* Woodstock, VT: Jewish Lights, 1994.

Orenstein, Debra, and Jane Rachel Litman, eds. *Lifecycles.* Vol. 2, *Jewish Women on Biblical Themes in Contemporary Life.* Woodstock, VT: Jewish Lights, 1997.

Sasso, Sandy Eisenberg. "Unwrapping the Gift." In *Women and Religious Ritual: An Interdisciplinary Investigation,* edited by Dr. Lesley A. Northrup. Washington, DC: Pastoral Press, 1993.

Other Torah Commentaries and Texts by Women

Hellner-Eshed, Melila. *A River Flows from Eden: The Language of Mystical Experience in the Zohar.* Stanford, CA: Stanford University Press, 2009.

Leibowitz, Nehama. *Studies in Bereshit, Shemot, Vayikra, Bamidbar, Devarim.* 6 vols. Jerusalem: World Zionist Organization, 1980.

Zakon, Miriam Stark, trans. *Tzenah U'Renah: The Classic Anthology of Torah Lore and Midrashic Comment.* Jerusalem: Mesorah, 1983.

Zornberg, Aviva. *Bewilderments: Reflections on the Book of Numbers.* New York: Schocken Books, 2015.

———. *Genesis: The Beginning of Desire.* Philadelphia: Jewish Publication Society, 1995.

———. *The Particulars of Rapture, Reflections on Exodus.* New York: Schocken Books, 2001.

Contributors

Rabbi Judith Z. Abrams, PhD, *z"l*, was the founder and director of Maqom (www.maqom.com), which was a pioneer in the area of online teaching of Talmud to adults. She authored over twenty books for adults and children, including *The Other Talmud*.

Rabbi Richard F. Address, DMin, is the founder/director of www. jewishsacredaging.com. He served for over three decades on the staff of the Union for Reform Judaism as a regional director and as founder/ director of the Department of Jewish Family Concerns. Most recently he completed tenure as senior rabbi of Congregation M'kor Shalom in Cherry Hill, New Jersey. He currently serves as adjunct faculty at Hebrew Union College–Jewish Institute of Religion in New York. He was ordained by HUC-JIR in Cincinnati in 1972.

Rabbi Carole B. Balin, PhD, is a professor of history at Hebrew Union College–Jewish Institute of Religion in New York. She is the narrator for the PBS special *The Jewish People: A Story of Survival* and a blogger for the *Huffington Post*, and she writes on topics ranging from the Maxwell House Haggadah to the history of bat mitzvah. Her most recent book, co-edited with Wendy Zierler, *"To Tread on New Ground": From the Hebrew Writings of Hava Shapiro*, contains the life story and writing of the first woman to keep a diary in Hebrew, to compose a feminist manifesto in Hebrew, and to contribute prolifically to the Hebrew press.

Rabbi Karen Bender was born and raised in Los Angeles in the home of Israeli parents, studied Political Science at UC Berkeley and was ordained by HUC-JIR in 1994, having interned at Central Synagogue in Manhattan. Rabbi Bender served as rabbi of Temple Beth-El of Great Neck, NY, for seven years, Temple Judea in Tarzana, CA, for thirteen years and is currently the Skirball Director of Spiritual Life and Campus Rabbi at the Los Angeles Jewish Home. Rabbi Bender has been active on social justice issues throughout her rabbinate, has published numerous sermons, articles, poems and original prayers and in 2015 received the Eisendrath Bearer of Light Award for outstanding civil rights work and the Distinguished Community Leader Award of the San Fernando Valley Council of Na'amat USA. She has served on the Board of the Central Conference of American Rabbis and currently on the Advisory Council of the Valley Interfaith Council. Rabbi Bender enjoys travel, the theater and adventure, especially with her three children, Josie, Joshua, and Shoshana.

Rabbi Leah Rachel Berkowitz was ordained in 2008 by Hebrew Union College–Jewish Institute of Religion in New York, where she also earned a Master of Arts in Religious Education. She recently became the rabbi at Vassar Temple in Poughkeepsie, NY, the first woman to hold this position in its 167-year history. Leah served as the associate rabbi of Judea Reform Congregation in Durham, NC for five years, and spent two years at Gann Academy, a pluralistic Jewish high school in Waltham, Massachusetts. Her writing has appeared in

Covenant of the Generations; *Spirituality 101: The Indispensable Guide to Keeping—or Finding—Your Spiritual Life on Campus*; *God? Jewish Choices for Struggling with the Ultimate*; and the *Reform Jewish Quarterly*. She blogs at thisiswhatarabbilookslike.wordpress.com.

Dr. Debra Reed Blank teaches the history and theology of Jewish liturgy at the School of Jewish Music of Hebrew College in Newton, Massachusetts. From 1998 to 2009 she was a faculty member of the Jewish Theological Seminary in New York City, teaching liturgy and Talmud. She has also taught at the Academy for Jewish Religion in New York and the Russian State University for the Humanities in Moscow. Her recent publications include "Reflections upon Creating Innovative, Jewish Life-Cycle Ritual" (keshetonline.org) and her edited volume *The Experience of Jewish Liturgy: Essays in Honor of Menahem Schmelzer*, which includes her article "The Curious Theological Grammar of *Ga'al Yisra'el*." Her most recent article, "Bossing God Around: Demand, Creed, and Covenant in Jewish Liturgy," is forthcoming in a volume edited by Evelyn Cohen. She received her PhD in liturgy and Rabbinics and ordination from the Jewish Theological Seminary.

Rabbi Ellen Weinberg Dreyfus is rabbi emerita of B'nai Yehuda Beth Sholom in Homewood, Illinois. She is past president of the Central Conference of American Rabbis, is a founder and past president of the Women's Rabbinic Network, and was the first woman to be elected president of the Chicago Board of Rabbis. She is a Senior Rabbinic Fellow of the Shalom Hartman Institute in Jerusalem. Ordained by Hebrew Union College–Jewish Institute of Religion in New York in 1979 (the first rabbi to be ordained pregnant), she spent most of her career serving small congregations and raising three children. She has taught and lectured nationally and internationally in Jewish and interfaith settings.

Rabbi Renee Edelman currently serves as Rabbi of Temple Sha'arey Shalom in Springfield, New Jersey. She received her ordination from Hebrew Union College–Jewish Institute of Religion in 1997.

Since then, she has served three congregations; been a community rabbi; written many essays, articles, and poems for publications including her own blog, *Chaffing the Wheat—Musings of a Woman Rabbi*; and has been featured in an article in *Glamour* magazine. Rabbi Edelman has a deep passion for connecting Jews to Judaism whatever their age or stage of life. Married to Shane Edelman, mother to Bailey, Jackson, and Sophie, she considers her greatest blessing to be her family and watching as her children develop some of their parents' interests: playing tennis, skiing, playing guitar, singing, mastering the inner workings of the computer, and watching football.

Rabbi Denise L. Eger is the founding rabbi of Congregation Kol Ami in West Hollywood, California. She was elected president of the Central Conference of American Rabbis in March 2015. She is a leading activist for LGBT equality, civil rights, and racial justice and has been acknowledged as one of the most influential rabbis in the *Forward* as a "Forward 50" and as one of the most influential women rabbis by the *Forward* "Sisterhood 50."

Rabbi Jacqueline Koch Ellenson is director emerita of the Women's Rabbinic Network, the international support and advocacy organization for women in the Reform rabbinate. She is an international vice-chair of Rabbis for Women of the Wall, has served on the boards of the Rodeph Sholom School, New York, and the Central Conference of American Rabbis, and the Yedidya Center for Jewish Spiritual Direction. She currently serves on the board of Friends of Kehillat Kol HaNeshamah. From 1992 to 2002 she was the Jewish chaplain at Harvard-Westlake School in Los Angeles and led a Rosh Hodesh: It's a Girl Thing! group for four years at Congregation Rodeph Sholom. She is a graduate of the Rabbinic Enrichment program of the Institute for Jewish Spirituality. Jackie is an active member of Congregation Rodeph Sholom in New York City, where she leads text study groups, and facilitates a "Wise Aging" group. Her community work focuses on adult spiritual formation and direction, in the general community and with students at HUC-JIR, as well as activism on behalf of religious pluralism and women's rights in Israel. She received her AB in psychology from Barnard College, Columbia University, in 1977 and was ordained by Hebrew Union College–Jewish Institute of Religion in 1983.

Rabbi Sue Levi Elwell, PhD served the Union for Reform Judaism for nearly two decades strengthening congregations by building strong partnerships between professional and lay leaders. The founding director of the Los Angeles Jewish Feminist Center and the first rabbinic director of Ma'yan, she has served congregations in California, New Jersey, Virginia, and Washington, DC. She co-edited *Chapters of the Heart: Jewish Women Sharing the Torah of Our Lives*, a finalist for the 2014 National Jewish Book Award. She also edited *The Open Door*, the CCAR Haggadah; served as the poetry editor and member of the editorial board of the award-winning *The Torah: A Women's Commentary*; and co-edited *Lesbian Rabbis: The First Generation*. She was ordained by Hebrew Union College–Jewish Institute of Religion in 1986, is the joyful mother of two adult daughters, is an ecstatic *savta*, and lives in Philadelphia with her wife, Nurit Levi Shein.

Rabbi Marla J. Feldman is the executive director of Women of Reform Judaism. Previously she was the director of development for the Union for Reform Judaism and the director of the Commission on Social Action of Reform Judaism. She served Jewish community relations councils in Detroit and Delaware and congregations in Orlando and Sarasota, Florida. She is a Reform rabbi, lawyer, and certified fundraiser. She is the author of numerous Reform Movement public policy manuals, and her articles and modern midrash have appeared in Jewish publications, newspapers, and blog sites throughout the United States.

Rabbi Michael S. Friedman was named senior rabbi at Temple Israel of Westport, Connecticut, in July 2104. He grew up in Great Neck, New York, where his family was proud to be dedicated members of Temple Beth-El. Michael holds a BA in history from Yale University and was ordained by Hebrew Union College–Jewish Institute of Religion in 2004. Prior to joining Temple Israel, he served as associate rabbi at Central Synagogue in New York City from 2008 to 2014 and as assistant rabbi at Congregation B'nai Jeshurun in Short Hills, New Jersey, from 2006 to 2008. In his free time he likes to play golf, hike, run marathons, and cook.

Hadas (Dasi) Fruchter was ordained by Yeshivat Maharat in June 2016. She thrives on spiritual leadership, vibrant Torah learning, and community building. Originally from the Washington, DC area, she recently completed an MPA in non-profit administration and an MA in Jewish studies from New York University's Wagner School of Public Service as a Wexner Graduate Fellow/Davidson Scholar and is the program director at ImmerseNYC, New York's only community mikveh project.

Michael J. Gan is a labor and employment law attorney and managing partner at Peer, Gan & Gisler LLP in Washington, DC, and has been representing labor unions and professionals in collective bargaining, litigation, and contract negotiations for more than twenty-five years. He also maintains a significant practice working with Reform rabbis and other Jewish professionals in a wide variety of employment matters. He is a graduate of the University of Michigan and Boston University School of Law.

Rabbi Laura Geller, senior rabbi of Temple Emanuel of Beverly Hills, California, was one of the first women to be selected to lead a major metropolitan synagogue. She was twice named one of *Newsweek*'s "50 Most Influential Rabbis in America" and was featured in the PBS documentary *Jewish Americans*. She is author of numerous articles in books and journals and was on the editorial board of *The Torah: A Women's Commentary*. She is a fellow of the Corporation of Brown University, from which she graduated in 1971. Ordained by Hebrew

Union College–Jewish Institute of Religion in 1976, she was the third woman in the Reform Movement to become a rabbi.

Rabbi Jordie Gerson currently serves as the assistant rabbi at Congregation Beth Israel in San Diego, California. Previously she served as the Senior Jewish Fellow and associate rabbi at the Slifka Center for Jewish Life at Yale University and as assistant director at University of Vermont Hillel. She is a frequent contributor to the *Huffington Post* and a graduate of Harvard Divinity School. She was thrilled with the portrayal of the female rabbi in the new Amazon show *Transparent* and thinks you should check it out.

Rabbi Elizabeth W. Goldstein, PhD, is a professor in the Department of Religious Studies at Gonzaga University and teaches Hebrew Bible, Judaism, and Hebrew. She completed her rabbinic studies at Hebrew Union College–Jewish Institute of Religion in New York in 2001. Her PhD in ancient Jewish history focuses on Hebrew Bible and particularly its intersection with gender studies. Goldstein completed her doctoral work in 2010 from the University of California at San Diego. She is the author of *Impurity and Gender in the Hebrew Bible* (Lexington, 2015) and has contributed to several volumes including *Jewish Blood: Reality and Metaphor in History, Religion, and Culture* (edited by Mitchell B. Hart) and *Embroidered Garments: Priests and Gender in Biblical Israel* (edited by Deborah W. Rooke) and *The Torah: A Woman's Commentary* (edited by Andrea Weiss and Tamara Eskenazi, URJ Press, 2007). She is the co-editor of *Music, Carrier of Intention in 49 Jewish Prayers* (with Kimberly Burnham, PhD, Creating Calm NPC, 2014). Her most recent articles are "To See or Not to See: A Call for Consciousness and Cognizance in Jewish, Progressive, and Public Readings of Esther," in the *Journal for Peace and Justice Studies* (2015) and "Women and the Purification Offering: What Jacob Milgrom Contributed to the Intersection of Women's Studies and Biblical Studies" in *Current Issues in Priestly and Related Literature: The Legacy* *of Jacob Milgrom and Beyond* (edited by Roy E. Gane and Ada Taggar-Cohen, 2015). In addition to her part-time rabbinic work in Spokane at Temple Beth Shalom and her role as rabbinic advisor to the Gonzaga Jewish student group, Goldstein serves the Jewish Community of the Palouse in Moscow, ID. Goldstein is the mother of two sets of twins: Coby and Aviel, Yair and Shaya.

Rabbi N. Samuel Gordon leads Sukkat Shalom of Wilmette, Illinois. He was ordained by Hebrew Union College–Jewish Institute of Religion in 1980 and later received an MBA degree from Northwestern University's Kellogg Graduate School of Management. In 2005 he was awarded the degree of doctor of divinity from HUC-JIR. He served as vice president of the Central Conference of American Rabbis and was a member of the Reform Pension Board. Rabbi Gordon is a member of the President's Advisory Council of the Hebrew Union College and a Senior Rabbinic Fellow of the Hartman Institute of Jerusalem. In 2013 President Barack Obama appointed Rabbi Gordon as a member of the United States Holocaust Memorial Council. In 2015 the *Forward* named him as one of "America's Most Inspiring Rabbis."

Rabbi Alysa Mendelson Graf received ordination from Hebrew Union College–Jewish Institute of Religion in New York in 2004. She has been the rabbi of Port Jewish Center, a small, haimish synagogue in Port Washington, New York, since July 2014. Prior to coming to PJC, she served Temple Israel in Westport, Connecticut, for almost a decade as its assistant, then associate, rabbi. She grew up in Scarsdale, New York, and has an undergraduate degree in history from the University of Pennsylvania and a law degree from Fordham University School of Law. She worked as a matrimonial attorney in Manhattan before deciding to pursue the rabbinate. Since her ordination, she has been an active member of the Central Conference of American Rabbis and of the Women's Rabbinic Network. She has served on the board of the WRN for ten years and is serving her last year on the board as its immediate past co-president. She is married to Adam Graf; they have three sons, Gideon, Solomon, and Rafi, and reside in Port Washington.

Rabbi Rebecca Fay Gutterman was ordained by Hebrew Union College–Jewish Institute of Religion in New York in 2004. During the time this essay was written she was the associate rabbi of Temple B'rith Kodesh in Rochester, New York. She and her husband, Michael, now live in Walnut Creek, California, where she is the rabbi of Congregation B'nai Tikvah.

Shaina Herring is a graduate of the dual degree program at New York University, where she studied health policy and management and Jewish studies. She worked at ImmerseNYC, a community mikveh project, to help educate the Jewish community about diverse and creative uses for mikveh. She is particularly interested in the intersection of women's health and Judaism and is currently studying to be a nurse-midwife at Columbia University.

Rabbi Kari Hofmaister Tuling, PhD, received her rabbinic ordination in 2004 and earned her PhD in Jewish Thought in 2013, both from the Hebrew Union College–Jewish Institute of Religion in Cincinnati. She currently serves as the rabbi of Temple Beth Israel in Plattsburgh, New York. Additionally, she teaches Jewish Studies courses at the State University of New York at Plattsburgh, and serves as their Jewish Chaplain and Hillel Co-advisor. Previously, she taught for five years at the University of Cincinnati, in their Judaic Studies Department.

Rabbi Patricia Karlin-Neumann is senior associate dean for religious life at Stanford University, the first chaplain in Stanford's history from a tradition other than Christianity. She was ordained by Hebrew Union College–Jewish Institute of Religion in 1982. Her work has appeared in the books *College and University Chaplaincy in the 21st Century*;

Encountering Disgrace: Reading and Teaching Coetzee's Novel; and *Reading Ruth: Contemporary Women Reclaim a Sacred Story* and in the *Journal of College and Character*. She enjoys swimming, learning, knitting, hiking, and sharing time with friends and family.

Rabbi Naamah Kelman is a descendant of ten generations of rabbis, becoming the first woman to be ordained in Israel by Hebrew Union College–Jewish Institute of Religion in 1992, where she currently serves as dean. Born and raised in New York City, she made *aliyah* in 1976. She lives in Jerusalem with her husband Elan Ezrachi. They have three children and three grandchildren.

Rabbi Daniel Kirzane was ordained by Hebrew Union College–Jewish Institute of Religion in New York in 2014 and serves as assistant rabbi at The Temple, Congregation B'nai Jehudah in Overland Park, Kansas. He is an alumnus of the Wexner Graduate Fellowship and the CLAL Rabbis Without Borders Fellowship and is on the rabbinic cabinets of T'ruah: The Rabbinic Call for Human Rights and J Street. He and his wife Jessica, a PhD candidate in Yiddish studies at Columbia University, live in Overland Park with their son, Jeremiah.

Rabbi Darren Kleinberg, PhD, was ordained in 2005 and completed his doctorate in 2014. The topic of his dissertation and the working title of his forthcomng book is *Hybrid Judaism: Irving Greenberg, Encounter, and the Changing Nature of American Jewish Identity*. He currently serves as Head of School at Kehillah Jewish High School in Palo Alto, California. Prior to arriving at Kehillah, he was the founding executive director of Valley Beit Midrash in Phoenix, Arizona.

Rabbi Neil Kominsky is a graduate of Harvard College and of Hebrew Union College–Jewish Institute of Religion, where he was ordained in 1970. During his rabbinic career, he served congregations in California, Connecticut, and Massachusetts and served on the staff of Harvard-Radcliffe Hillel. He is rabbi emeritus of Temple Emanuel of the Merrimack Valley in Lowell, Massachusetts, and Jewish chaplain emeritus of Phillips Academy in Andover, Massachusetts. He served on the Taskforce on Women in the Rabbinate from its inception and was chair from 1978 to 1984.

Rabbi Charles A. Kroloff, a past president of the Central Conference of American Rabbis, is rabbi emeritus of Temple Emanu-El, Westfield, New Jersey, which he served for thirty-six years. He is currently vice president for special projects at Hebrew Union College–Jewish Institute of Religion, where he teaches rabbinical students. A past president of ARZA, the Association of Reform Zionists of America, he is certified as a marital and family therapist. A graduate of Yale University, he is the author of *When Elijah Knocks: A Religious Response to Homelessness*; *54 Ways You Can Help the Homeless*; *Reform Judaism: A Jewish Way of Life*; and numerous essays and articles.

Rabbi Jeffrey Kurtz-Lendner is the Director of Jewish Learning, Engagement and Outreach at the David Posnack Jewish Community Center in Davie, Florida. Previously he served as the rabbi of Temple Solel in Hollywood, Florida and the rabbi of the Northshore Jewish Congregation in the New Orleans suburb of Mandeville, Louisiana. While in Mandeville he oversaw the congregation's recovery efforts during Hurricane Katrina. He is a member of the Central Conference of American Rabbis and the board of the southeast region of the CCAR (SEACCAR). He sits on the Faith-Based and Community-Based Advisory Council to Florida governor Rick Scott. Rabbi Kurtz-Lendner delivered an invocation at an event featuring First Lady Michelle Obama and another invocation at an event featuring President Barack Obama in Hollywood, Florida.

Rabbi Michele Lenke was ordained from the New York campus of the Hebrew Union College–Jewish Institute of Religion in 1996. She is past co-president of the Women's Rabbinic Network and has been involved with WRN ever since she was a rabbinical student. She is currently pursuing a doctor of ministry degree in the Interfaith Clinical Education for Pastoral Ministry Program at HUC-JIR and is a member of the first cohort of Bekhol Levavkha, training to become a Jewish spiritual director. This focus on spirituality and pastoral counseling are a natural outgrowth of Rabbi Lenke's rabbinate and sense of calling. She has been blessed to serve as a rabbi in the Greater Boston area for the past twenty years.

Rabbi Ellen Lewis has more than thirty-five years of experience as a rabbi and a therapist. Ordained at Hebrew Union College–Jewish Institute of Religion in 1980, she was a member of the first generation of women rabbis. Having served congregations in Dallas, Texas, Summit, New Jersey (named Rabbi Honorata), and Washington, New Jersey (named Rabbi Emerita), she recently retired from congregational work to practice full-time as a therapist, supervisor, pastoral counselor, and professional coach. Rabbi Lewis is a certified and licensed modern psychoanalyst in private practice in Bernardsville, New Jersey, and in New York City. While she works with people from all walks of life, she specializes in working with rabbis and cantors to develop the emotional resiliency and flexibility required for contemporary congregational and organizational work. She received her analytical training in New York at the Center for Modern Psychoanalytic Studies and has served on the faculty of the Academy of Clinical and Applied Psychoanalysis. She is a fellow in the American Association of Pastoral Counselors.

Rabbi Sara Luria is a trained community organizer, birth doula, and chaplain. She incorporates her passion for justice, belief in the centrality of relationships, and dedication to marking transformative, sacred experiences into her rabbinate. She recently founded ImmerseNYC, a community mikveh project, which works both to introduce individuals to the myriad ways that mikveh immersions can add meaning to their lives and to build and strengthen community through ritual.

She lives in her hometown of Brooklyn, New York, with her husband, Isaac, and their young children, Caleb, Eva, and Judah.

Rachel Marder is a third-year student at the Ziegler School of Rabbinic Studies in Los Angeles, where she is a Wexner Graduate Fellow. She has been an AIPAC Leffell Fellow, has taught in IKAR's Limudim program, and is currently studying to be a *schochetet*. She received her BA from Brandeis University, where she studied Islamic and Middle Eastern studies, and her MA in conflict research, management, and resolution from Hebrew University in Jerusalem. She has written for the *Jerusalem Post, Jewish News Service, j. the Jewish News Weekly of Northern California*, and other publications. She is spending the year studying in Jerusalem at the Conservative Yeshiva.

Rabbi Dalia Marx, PhD, is a professor of liturgy and midrash at the Jerusalem campus of Hebrew Union College–Jewish Institute of Religion and teaches in various academic institutions in Israel and Europe. She earned her doctorate at the Hebrew University in Jerusalem and her rabbinic ordination at HUC–JIR in Jerusalem and Cincinnati. She is involved in various research groups and is active in promoting liberal Judaism in Israel. She is the author and editor of a few books, among them a feminist commentary of three rabbinic tractates (Mohr-Siebeck, 2013). She lives with her husband and three children in Jerusalem.

Rabbi Sara Mason-Barkin is currently the associate rabbi/educator at Peninsula Temple Beth El in San Mateo, California. She began to examine a new perspective on the rabbi as a symbolic exemplar in her rabbinic thesis "The Rabbi as a Symbolic Exemplar: A Feminist Critique," advised by Dr. Rachel Adler. As the daughter of a rabbi and a Jewish educator, she was particularly interested in thinking about the way clergy families are a part of the communities in which they live and work. She was ordained by Hebrew Union College–Jewish Institute of Religion in Los Angeles in 2010.

Rabbi Oshrat Morag, born and raised in Haifa, Israel, was ordained by Hebrew Union College–Jewish Institute of Religion in Jerusalem in 2008. She is currently the rabbi of congregation Or Hadash in Haifa and a doctoral candidate in the field of feminist theology at the HUC-JIR Cincinnati campus. Her articles, modern midrashim, poems, prayers, and life-cycle ceremonies have been published in books and journals throughout Israel and the United States. She is the mother of four children.

Rabbi Linda Motzkin has served since 1986 as co-rabbi, with her husband, Jonathan Rubenstein, of Temple Sinai in Saratoga Springs, New York, and until December 2014 also served as Jewish chaplain at Skidmore College, where she continues to serve as the High Holy Day chaplain. She is the author of the Reform Movement's four-volume adult Hebrew-language curriculum: *Aleph Isn't Tough*, *Aleph Isn't Enough*, *Bet Is for B'reishit*, and *Tav Is for Torah*. She is also a Judaic artist and one of a handful of women in the world trained as a *soferet*, currently writing a Torah scroll. She and Rabbi Rubenstein founded the Bread and Torah Project, www.breadandtorah.org.

Professor Pamela S. Nadell holds the Patrick Clendenen Chair in Women's and Gender History at American University, where she chairs the Department of History. In 2007 she received AU's highest faculty award, the Scholar/Teacher of the Year. In 2010 the American Jewish Historical Society recognized her distinguished service to American Jewish history with its Lee Max Friedman Award. She is a member of the founding historians' team for the National Museum of American Jewish History and president of the Association for Jewish Studies. Her books include *Women Who Would Be Rabbis: A History of Women's Ordination, 1889–1985*.

Maharat Rori Picker Neiss serves as the Executive Director of the Jewish Community Relations Council of St Louis. Prior to that she was the Director of Programming, Education and Community Engagement at Bais Abraham Congregation, a Modern Orthodox Jewish synagogue in University City, MO. She is one of the first graduates of Yeshivat Maharat, a pioneering institution training Orthodox Jewish women to be spiritual leaders and halakhic (Jewish legal) authorities. She previously served as Acting Executive Director for Religions for Peace-USA, Program Coordinator for the Jewish Orthodox Feminist Alliance, Assistant Director of Interreligious Affairs for the American Jewish Committee, and Secretariat for the International Jewish Committee on Interreligious Consultations, the formal Jewish representative in international, interreligious dialogue. Rori is the co-chair of the North American Interfaith Youth Network of Religions for Peace, a CLAL Rabbis Without Borders fellow, and co-editor of "InterActive Faith: The Essential Interreligious Community-Building Handbook." Rori is married to Russel Neiss, a Software Engineer for Sefaria, and they have two daughters and a son: Daria, Susanna, and Shmaya.

Rabbi Hara E. Person is the Publisher of CCAR Press, and the CCAR Director of Strategic Communications. Rabbi Person was ordained in 1998 from HUC-JIR, after graduating from Amherst College (1986) and receiving an MA in Fine Arts from New York University and the International Center of Photography (1992). As publisher, she oversees the CCAR publication programming, and served as Executive Editor of *Mishkan HaNefesh*, the Reform Movement *machzor*. Before coming to the CCAR, Rabbi Person was the Editor in Chief of URJ Books and Music, where she was responsible for the revision of *The Torah: A Modern Commentary* (2005) and the publication of many significant projects, including *The Torah: A Women's Commentary*, named the National Jewish Book Award Book of the Year in 2008. Since 1998, Rabbi Person has been the High Holy Day rabbi of Congregation B'nai Olam, Fire Island Pines, NY. Rabbi Person lives in Brooklyn, NY, and is the mother of two young adults.

Rabbi Mindy Avra Portnoy is rabbi emerita of Temple Sinai in Washington, DC, and the author of five Jewish children's books, including the groundbreaking *Ima on the Bima* and the popular *Matzah Ball*. A graduate of Yale University, she is a well-known speaker, teacher, and life-cycle officiant and currently serves as adjunct rabbi at Congregation Beth El in Bethesda, Maryland. Her most recent children's book is *A Tale of Two Seders*, and she has written blogs for *Lilith*, *Ha'aretz*, *RavBlog*, the Religious Action Center, and the Women's Rabbinic Network. She is a former national co-coordinator of the WRN.

Rabbi Sally J. Priesand, America's first female rabbi, was ordained in June 1972 by Hebrew Union College–Jewish Institute of Religion in Cincinnati, Ohio. From 1981 to 2006 she served as rabbi of Monmouth Reform Temple in Tinton Falls, New Jersey, becoming rabbi emerita upon her retirement. In 2007 she invited her female rabbinic colleagues of all denominations to join her in donating their professional and personal papers to the American Jewish Archives in Cincinnati, Ohio, in order to document the history of women in the rabbinate.

Rabbi Elena Rubinstein was born in Moscow in the former Soviet Union in 1955. She graduated from the Faculty of History at the Pedagogic University in Moscow and worked for fourteen years as a scientific member of staff at the Borodino History Museum in the city. In 1992 she made *aliyah* together with her family. She has worked in a number of positions in the Israel Movement for Progressive Judaism (IMPJ) since 1994, including coordinator of the Legal Action Center for *Olim* in Beersheva and Tel Aviv and coordinator of programs for *olim* at Beit Daniel Congregation. In December 2002 she was appointed director of the *Olim* Department in the IMPJ headquarters. She began her studies at Hebrew Union College–Jewish Institute of Religion and at Ben-Gurion University of the Negev in 1997. She now holds an MA in Jewish history and has joined the growing list of women who have been ordained at HUC-JIR in Jerusalem, among whom she is the first immigrant from the

FSU. Since 2009 Rabbi Rubinstein has been a head of the the Sha'arei Shalom community, St. Petersburg, Russia. Elena is married to Semion, is the mother of Rabbi Julia Margolis in Johannesburg, South Africa and grandmother of Emily and Victoria.

Rabbi Jonathan Rubenstein has served since 1986 as co-rabbi, with his wife, Linda Motzkin, of Temple Sinai in Saratoga Springs, New York, as well as part-time pastoral care director of Four Winds–Saratoga, a private psychiatric hospital. He is also a bread maker and baking teacher and operates Slice of Heaven Breads, a not-for-profit, volunteer, charitable community bakery out of the temple's kitchen. He and Rabbi Motzkin founded the Bread and Torah Project, www. breadandtorah.org.

Rabbi Sara Yellen Sapadin is a rabbi, mother, and vigorous spiritual seeker. She graduated magna cum laude from Harvard College and received her ordination from Hebrew Union College–Jewish Institute of Religion, where she earned marks of distinction in Bible, liturgy, and homiletics. She most recently served Temple Israel of the City of New York, where she focused on issues of social justice, Israel engagement, and revitalizing Jewish living for young families. Rabbi Sapadin has never met a text study she didn't love or a song she wouldn't sing. She and her husband and their four children reside in New York City.

Rabbi Sandy Eisenberg Sasso, DMin, was the first woman to be ordained by the Reconstructionist Rabbinical College in 1974. She and her husband, Dennis Sasso, were the first practicing rabbinical couple in world Jewish history. She served Congregation Beth-El Zedeck in Indianapolis for thirty-six years before becoming rabbi emerita. She is presently the director of the Religion, Spirituality and Arts Initiative at Butler University and the author of many award-winning children's books and two books for adults, *Midrash: Reading the Bible with Question Marks* and *Jewish Stories of Love and Marriage*, co-authored with Peninnah Schram. Rabbis Sasso have two children and three grandchildren.

Joshua Scharff is an attorney at Peer, Gan & Gisler LLP and frequently represents rabbis, non-profit employees, and other professionals in negotiations concerning individual employment contracts, separation agreements, and other workplace disputes. He is a graduate of the George Washington University Law School, the Johns Hopkins University School of Advanced International Studies, and Rutgers University.

Chaplain, Major Sarah D. Schechter is the first woman rabbi in the United States Air Force. She has two master's degrees and ordination from Hebrew Union College–Jewish Institute of Religion in Los Angeles (2003). She was the Outstanding Company Grade Chaplain of the Year for the Air Education and Training Command in 2010 and for the Air Force District of Washington in 2012. She was chaplain to Air Force One 2011–13 and was awarded an honorary doctor of divinity by Washington and Jefferson College in 2014. Rabbi Schechter is a wife and a mother and is currently stationed at the United States Air Force Academy in Colorado Springs, Colorado.

Rabbi Judith Schindler has been senior rabbi of Temple Beth El, the largest synagogue in the Carolinas. She was named Charlotte's Woman of the Year in 2011 and is a past co-chair of the Women's Rabbinic Network. She is known for her activism and responsible for creating four educational and social justice documentaries on diversity, education, and affordable housing. She is a regular contributor of articles for publication and delivers lectures at religious and academic institutions across the South.

Rabbi Rebecca Einstein Schorr was ordained by the Hebrew Union College–Jewish Institute of Religion and was a CLAL Rabbis Without Borders fellow. Editor of the *CCAR Newsletter* and a contributor to *The Sacred Encounter: Jewish Perspectives on Sexuality*, Rabbi Schorr is a contributing author to Kveller.com and *The New Normal: Blogging Disability*, and her essays appear regularly on a variety of sites. She is a frequent speaker on disability and the Jewish imperative for inclusion, and her recent TED Talk chronicled her efforts to organize a global social media campaign to benefit pediatric cancer research. Writing at her blog, *This Messy Life*, Rabbi Schorr finds meaning in the sacred and not-yet-sacred intersections of daily life. Follow her on Twitter @rebeccaschorr.

Rabbi Amy Schwartzman is the senior rabbi of Temple Rodef Shalom in Falls Church, Virginia, where she has worked since her ordination from the Hebrew Union College–Jewish Institute of Religion in 1990. In addition to serving a dynamic congregation, she is involved in leadership roles for her community as well as the Reform Movement. She is especially active in housing issues, mental health initiatives, and supporting those on the fringes of our society. Within the Reform Movement she serves in a number of leadership roles for the Central Conference of American Rabbis as well as HUC-JIR. Rabbi Schwartzman and her husband, Kevin Moss, live in McLean, Virginia, with their two daughters.

Rabbi Susan Shankman is a rabbi at Washington Hebrew Congregation. In addition to officiating at services, life-cycle events, and pastoral care and counseling, she coordinates the confirmation program and focuses on programming for families with young children, Sisterhood and women's issues, social action, and outreach to interfaith families. She is immediate past president of the Washington Board of Rabbis and serves on the board of the Central Conference of American Rabbis, as well as Vice President of Organzational Relations of the Jewish Federation of Greater Washington. Rabbi Shankman is married to Rabbi Michael Namath, program director at the Religious Action Center of Reform Judaism, and they are the parents of Isabel, Jacob, and Evie.

Rabbi Kinneret Shiryon, DD, is the first woman to serve as a congregational rabbi in the history of the State of Israel. She established and is the spiritual leader of the YOZMA Jewish Community Educational, Spiritual and Cultural Center, which includes an early childhood educational center, the first public Reform Jewish elementary day school in Israel, an active synagogue prayer community, and a myriad of award-winning social justice programs serving the Modi'in area. She is married to Baruch and has four children and two granddaughters.

Rabbi Susan Silverman is a speaker, activist, educator, and author. Her latest book is *Casting Lots: Creating a Family in a Beautiful, Broken World*, (DaCapo Press). She promotes liberal Judaism and the rights of asylum seekers in Israel and is the founding director of JustAdopt. net. She and her spouse, Yosef Abramowitz, have five children and live in Jerusalem.

Rabbi Rebecca W. Sirbu, is the director of Rabbis Without Borders at CLAL—The National Jewish Center for Learning and Leadership. Rabbis Without Borders stimulates and supports innovation in the rabbinate. In 2013 Rabbi Sirbu was named as one of the most inspirational rabbis in America by the *Forward*. She speaks and writes about Jewish life, health, healing, and spirituality. A Phi Beta Kappa graduate of Vassar College, she holds a master's degree and ordination from the Jewish Theological Seminary of America.

Rabbi Wendy Spears was ordained by the Hebrew Union College–Jewish Institute of Religion in 1991. For twenty years she has been reaching and teaching unaffiliated Jews outside of synagogue walls to introduce them to the joys and resources of the Jewish community in Los Angeles. She learned sign language to aid in outreach to deaf Jews. Rabbi Spears is experienced in issues of food and health, spiritual enlightenment, grief, feminism, and LGBT equality, and how what we wear can reflect our inner truth. Her most challenging and rewarding work has been as a life partner to her husband and as a mother to her two sons. Her writing has been published in the *CCAR Journal*, *The Women's Haftarah Commentary*, and on *Kol Isha*, the blog of the Women's Rabbinic Network. Find her at www.rabbiwendy.com.

Cantor Mary Rebecca Thomas studied history and Jewish studies at Rutgers University before attending the Debbie Friedman School of Sacred Music of Hebrew Union College–Jewish Institute of Religion, from which she received ordination in 2011. At the College-Institute, Cantor Thomas received several prizes in worship and Jewish thought. She is Associate Cantor at Temple Beth El in Charlotte, North Carolina, where she is the founding managing professional of The Porch: Temple Beth El's Young Adult and Young Families Community, the synagogue's small group network, Jewish Living Groups, and other engagement initiatives. Cantor Thomas and her husband, Matthew, are privileged to raise Johannah and Ezra.

Rabbi Eric Weiss is CEO/president of the Bay Area Jewish Healing Center. He is formally trained in Jewish education, clinical chaplaincy, and spiritual direction. He lives with his husband, Dan, in San Francisco.

Julie Wiener is the manging editor of MyJewishLearning, the premier online resource for information about Judaism. For six years she wrote "In the Mix," a column and blog on interfaith relationships for the *New York Jewish Week*. In addition to writing extensively for Jewish publications, her work has been published in the *Wall Street Journal*, *New York Sun*, *The Associated Press*, *New York Family*, and the *Tribeca Trib*, and she has edited two books. She lives in Jackson Heights, Queens, with her husband and two daughters. Follow her on Twitter @Julie_Wiener.

Rabbi Julie Wolkoff, DMin, CT, is a hospice chaplain with Ascend Hospice in Massachusetts. Prior to that she was the director of Judaic Activities at Gann Academy—The New Jewish High School of Greater Boston. She served as a Jewish community chaplain and an AIDS Care Team coach for Eddy VNA, both in New York's Capital District. She is a volunteer mikveh guide at Mayyim Hayyim in Newton, Massachusetts.

Rabbi Elizabeth S. Wood was ordained by Hebrew Union College–Jewish Institute of Religion in Cincinnati in 2009 and served as the interim educator and soloist at Temple Beth El in Tacoma, Washington, before coming to The Reform Temple of Forest Hills, New York, as the associate rabbi educator in 2010. Rabbi Wood currently serves as the Director of Learning and Innovation for NFTY. She has served on the board of the Women's Rabbinic Network and on the executive board of Faith in New York, an interfaith community organizing group working to help those in need in New York City, as well as serving as summer faculty at the Union for Reform Judaism's Eisner and Crane Lake Camps. Rabbi Wood was also a contributor to *The Sacred Encounter: Jewish Perspectives on Sexuality*, writing about issues of sex and technology in Judaism. Since writing this reflection, Rabbi Wood dropped the "R-bomb" one last time and has found her *beshert*, David, with whom she plans to spend the rest of her life.

Rabbi Mary L. Zamore is the editor of and a contributing author to *The Sacred Table: Creating a Jewish Food Ethic* (CCAR Press, 2011), which was designated a finalist by the National Jewish Book Awards. She was ordained by Hebrew Union College–Jewish Institute of Religion in New York in 1997, graduated from Columbia College, and also studied at Yad Vashem and Machon Pardes. Rabbi Zamore currently serves as the Executive Director of the Women's Rabbinic Network. Rabbi Zamore is a frequent contributor to the *Huffington Post*.

Rabbi Deborah Zecher recently completed twenty-two years as rabbi and leader of music of Hevreh of Southern Berkshire, in Great Barrington, MA, and was named rabbi emerita of the congregation at the conclusion of her tenure. She loved being part of Hevreh's joyful and spirited community and was delighted to share this special congregation with the rabbinical students and rabbinical colleagues she was fortunate enough to mentor and work with. Rabbi Zecher is also an accomplished cabaret singer and hopes to focus her attention on this area of her life in the coming years. She is married to Rabbi Dennis Ross, and they are the parents of three now-grown children, Joshua, Adam, and Miriam.

Dr. Wendy Zierler is Sigmund Falk Professor of Modern Jewish Literature and Feminist Studies at Hebrew Union College–Jewish Institute of Religion in New York. Together with Carole Balin, she is editor of *Behikansi atah*, a collection of the Hebrew writings of Hava Shapiro. Their English volume of Shapiro's writings, featuring Dr. Zierler's translations of Shapiro's stories, diary, and letters, was published in 2014, and her book *Reel Theology* is forthcoming. Other publications include a feminist Haggadah commentary in *My People's Haggadah*, and *To Speak Her Heart*, an illustrated anthology of Jewish women's prayers and poems, to which she contributed the introduction, several translations, and an original poem. As a fiction writer, she was recently a finalist in the *Moment Magazine*–Karma Foundation fiction contest for her story "The One Lamb You Should Offer"; another story, entitled "The Great American Canadian Jewish Chinese Novel," was published in 2013 in Jewishfiction.net.

Rabbi Ruth A. Zlotnick is the Senior Rabbi at Temple Beth Am in Seattle, WA, a congregation that prides itself on social justice and engaged and joyous Jewish living. Previously, she served as Rabbi at Temple Beth Or in the Township of Washington, New Jersey, and as Associate Rabbi and Director of Lifelong Learning at New York's Central Synagogue. She began her rabbinic career as Associate Director of Programs at Synagogue 2000 (now 3000). As newcomers, she, her husband and their daughter are still in awe of Seattle's majestic natural beauty and are adjusting to the difficulty of finding an excellent New York-style bagel.

Dr. Gary Phillip Zola is the executive director of the Jacob Rader Marcus Center of the American Jewish Archives and professor of the American Jewish experience at Hebrew Union College–Jewish Institute of Religion in Cincinnati, Ohio. From 1982 to 1998, Dr. Zola served as HUC-JIR's national dean of admissions and student affairs.

Rabbi David J. Zucker, PhD, who was ordained by Hebrew Union College–Jewish Institute of Religion in Cincinnati in 1970, retired as rabbi/chaplain at Shalom Cares, a senior continuum of care center in Aurora, Colorado. In 2014–2016 he was recruited to serve as interim rabbi at North West Surrey Synagogue, Weybridge, England. His newest books are *The Bible's Prophets: An Introduction for Christians and Jews*, *The Bible's Writings: An Introduction for Christians and Jews*, and *The Matriarchs of Genesis: Seven Women, Five Views* (co-authored with Moshe Reiss). He publishes in a variety of areas. See his website, www. DavidJZucker.org.